Body & Soul

escapes

Caroline Sylge

❝ ❞

The present moment is all you ever have.

Eckhart Tolle

Contents

Northern & Central Europe

Africa & the Levant

Introduction

Southern Europe

India & the Himalaya

Indian Ocean

Asia

Australia, New Zealand & Pacific Islands

The Americas

Contents

Body and soul symbols

Each entry in this book is accompanied by a series of symbols. These are designed to give readers a quick summary of what each body and soul trip or retreat has to offer.

- Yoga.
- Chinese martial arts and treatments such as tai chi or acupuncture.
- Meditation.
- Creative self-expression through the arts, dance or writing.
- Nutritional advice, detox or cookery lessons.
- Any type of bodywork such as massage or pilates classes.
- Holistic therapies such as ayurveda or reiki.
- Any form of hydrotherapy such as watsu or thalassotherapy.
- Beauty treatments such as facials, wraps and pedicures.
- Treks or fitness activities organized by the venue or available nearby.
- Personal development through life coaching or group courses.
- Places suitable for the casual body and soul traveller, or where you can simply do nothing.
- Indicates location on map.

Map symbols

- Motorway
- Main road
- Secondary road
- Trips & retreats
- Various locations – not shown on map
- City/town extent
- Capital city
- City/town/village
- Mountain
- National park
- Archaeological site
- - - - - International border
- - - - Regional border

Introduction

Body & Soul escapes is a resource book of journeys and retreats aimed at anyone who needs a real break. You might be tired, bored, restless and in need of a challenge, stuck in the wrong career or relationship, or unfit and determined to change your lifestyle. You may be a yoga, tai chi or pilates enthusiast who wants to explore your practice on a deeper level, a sybarite in need of a good pampering, a spiritual warrior wanting to get back to basics, or a stress addict who has forgotten how to eat, sleep and breathe properly. You may well want different things at different times: practise yoga on an African safari, cycle alongside monks in Buddhist Laos, or learn to meditate on a hillside in Australia. You may want to enjoy solitude or reconnect with a friend, organize a DIY retreat at a family-run holistic haven in Europe, or lounge somewhere beautiful at a luscious island villa in the Indian Ocean and dip in and out of treatments. A body and soul escape can be as upmarket or as rustic, as light-hearted or as serious as you want it to be. Take a risk, try something new. The most nourishing experiences are sometimes found in unexpected places. So start exploring; find your own journey.

About this book

The journeys and retreats in Body & Soul escapes have been labelled to help the reader easily find what they want. Those with one main purpose have been labelled accordingly – choose a dance, tai chi, yoga, pilates, adventure or life coaching holiday, visit a retreat dedicated to ayurveda, health and fitness, creativity, detoxing or meditation, or get a quick fix at a hotel and spa. Holidays with an all-round approach to feeling good are labelled 'wellbeing holidays'. The rest of the book covers places to stay that offer too large a range of activities and treatments to pin down to any one label. For simplicity, these have been identified instead by their geographical location. Take your pick from retreats in a rural setting, on the coast, in the desert, up a mountain, by the water and so on. The symbols with each entry (see the key on the contents pages) will give you a quick summary of what each journey and retreat has to offer. If you're unfamiliar with any terms used, you should find most things explained in the glossary at the end of this section. The majority of body and soul escapes in this book have been experienced in person by the author, or by a hand-picked researcher. The rest have been strongly recommended by word of mouth, and followed up by phone and email. There is no charge for inclusion; each entry has been selected on its own merits.

Prices quoted are usually based on two people sharing a room in high season unless stated otherwise. For the sake of clarity, prices are in UK pounds sterling (£) in the Britain entries, euros (€) in Europe, and

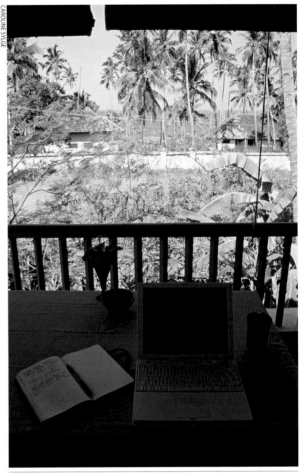

Photographic evidence that the author did take the occasional break while researching and writing this book.

US dollars (US$) everywhere else. As prices were converted into US dollars and euros at the correct exchange rate at the time of going to press, be sure to check current prices before booking, as well as up to date retreat programmes. Also note that places change, owners, therapists and teachers move on, properties close or are sold, and facilities improve or deteriorate. If you experience a journey or retreat in this book and find it has changed for the better or worse, or if you'd like to recommend a new place for the next edition, please go to www.footprintbooks.com and send in your comments.

About the author

Caroline Sylge is an experienced travel journalist who has written for books, magazines, newspapers and websites internationally. Born in London and brought up in Surrey, she first discovered yoga over 10 years ago in a chilly English village hall, and the power of meditation

Left: Be massaged in Mexico at the Maya Spa, near Tulum. **Above**: Practise yoga on the shores of the Ganga, at Haridwar, India, one of the seven holy cities of Hinduism.

in a Thai jungle five years after that. She lost her cynicism about alternative therapies when a hypnotherapist and reiki master helped her give up her smoking habit at Spa Samui in Thailand in her late twenties. Now 37, she is a dedicated yoga student whose daily practice is influenced by iyengar, yin and a touch of vinyasa flow. She regularly attends silent meditation retreats, and attempts (and often fails) to meditate daily. Her favourite treatment is a massage – especially deep tissue, watsu and Thai. She has a penchant for the good things in life, including organic wine, natural hot springs and lounging about in sassy hotels, and is passionately curious about everything to do with wellbeing, from life coaching to detoxing. Caroline has spent the last five years experimenting with such things on her travels all over the world, and Body & Soul escapes is the book she would like to have read before she set out. Writing it has been a major challenge, and has revealed to her once again the important things in life – don't spend too long at a computer, breathe deep, put honey on your tongue, eat your main meal at lunchtime, eat cake when you feel like it, and don't take life too seriously. Her poems have been published by Carcanet Press, and she has an MA in English from Sussex University. Caroline lives in Devon, and this is her first book.

Acknowledgements

I would like to say a big thank you to everyone who has contributed to this project. Especially to my colleagues Hana Borrowman, Jo Hegerty and Olivia Mackinder, for their fearless exploration and for being a dream to work with; Nicki Grihault, for having fabulous ideas and believing in the subject as passionately as I do; and Heloise Crowther, for her hard work and light-heartedness, and for contributing most of the Costa Rica section. I would also like to thank Swami Yogaratna Saraswati, for inspiring me more than she will ever know; yoga teachers Jane Craggs, for her gentleness and humour, Tuesday McNeill, for her knowledge and expertise, and Roger Ash Wheeler, for his calm and for The Barefoot Barn; homeopath Ivy Dieltiens, for setting me back on track in Sri Lanka; life coach Rosie Walford, for helping me learn to breathe from the belly; and agent Rob Shreeve, for believing in the project from the outset. Heartfelt thanks go to all the team at Footprint, but especially to my editor Alan Murphy, for his kindness, patience and wit. Thank you also to all the owners, managers and teachers out there who provide these uplifting body and soul escapes. With thanks also to fellow travel writers across the globe: Lexy Adams, David Atkinson, Cherine Badawi, Sarah Cameron, Louisa Carter, Annie Dare, Christabelle Dilks, Elain Evans, Lucy Greeves, Irvina Lew, Mari Nicholson, Jane Onstott, Lawrence Pettener, Adrian Phillips, Ruth Rosselson, Eleanor Seaman, Gail Simmons, Rosie Walford and Lizzie Williams. Also to Katie Brown, Samantha Coomber, Theresa Corbett, Kate Cracknell, Lucy Edge, Vita FitzSimons, Sophie Forte, Jane Foster, Kathy Fur, Mary-Ann Gallagher, Jemma Guthrie, Sara Harper, Sally Matthews, Katie Pisa, Jill Starley-Grainger, Tania Unsworth, Neil Wilson, Sarah Woods, Lydia Zabarsky and Linda Zanella. Thanks to body and soul travellers, researchers and enthusiasts Danielle Aubree, Jan Atkins, Melanie Bass, Tracey Benton, Harriet Bristow, Lucinda Carling, Caroline Cunnington-King, Cloe Clayton, Catharine Christof, Diana von Cranach, Phil Dane, Angela Dugdale, Lucy Fennings, James Fellows, Bill Foley, Maria Grima, Dan & Fiona Hiscocks, Puma Hammar, Louise Hindley, Rosie Inge, Carolyn Kohl, Juliet Leary, Leza Lowitz, Louise Marix Evans, Maureen McDonagh, Annie McGann, Kate Meere, June Mitchell, Catherine Moran, Lisa Nicholas, Julia Perowne, James Rhodes, Billee Saade, Bianca Schwengler, Catherine Somers, Jenny Wilson and Liz Wong, as well as to Luciana LoPresto of Yogatrips, Francesca Quaradeghini of Yogoloji, Judith Seelig of Yoga & Sound, Zoe Stebbing of Lotus Journeys, Sue Weston of Relaxing the Mind and Richard Williams of Chiva Som. I would like to pay tribute to my mother, Ann, who expertly filled the job of librarian, researcher and editorial assistant during the course of this project with intelligence, grace and love. To my dad, Herbie, for his constant kindness and smiles, and to my brothers Chris and Olly, for never taking me too seriously. Finally, to my fiancé Tom, for proposing to me in a chocolate jacuzzi, for being beautiful in both body and soul, for lifting my spirits, but mostly for carrying my bags.

CAROLINE SYLGE

VEENA AT SVC

Essentials

What is a body and soul escape?

A body and soul escape allows you to step out of your daily life and get back in touch with yourself. Ashrams, meditation retreats and some yoga retreats offer more traditional monastic-style surroundings for time out, but 'retreat' in this guide also refers to any place of sanctuary where you can rest, replenish, re-evaluate and renew. Pick a destination devoted to one purpose such as ayurveda, health and fitness, or creativity, or go for one of the broader-based retreats which are defined here by geographical location: these range from purpose-built venues offering a range of holistic courses to inspirational guesthouses, lodges and villas, where you 'do-it-yourself' by dipping in and out of treatments and activities. There are holidays dedicated to yoga, dance, tai chi, swimming, pilates, fitness, spirituality and general wellbeing, and life coaching trips for the chance to reconsider a career or a relationship. For quick fixes, there's a sprinkling of exceptional hotels and spas.

What to expect

Most of the trips and retreats in the book are open to people of any faith, age, background or sexual orientation. You can expect a fairly even split of men and women – except for yoga, dance and pilates holidays, many personal development courses, and at health and fitness retreats, where women predominate. Be prepared for an emotional time, confronting things in your life that you may have kept locked away for a while. Many of the retreats listed – even less intense ones – are designed to release mental and emotional energy blocks. You may also experience a physical low, as a lack of stimulants, a lighter diet and physical activity are naturally detoxing. After a few days, however, you'll feel your energy levels start to rise. You can also be more proactive by communicating your needs, be it for a stronger massage, a wheat-free breakfast or something altogether deeper.

The long and the short of it

If time is limited, take regular weekend and week-long breaks rather than saving up for a month's holiday and leaving it till you're mentally and physically exhausted. Travelling to short-haul destinations will minimize jet lag and give you a better chance of prolonging the benefits you've gained. If you choose a long-haul destination, go for at least two weeks to give yourself time to get over jet lag, adjust to the change of climate and culture and feel comfortable with those around you. Going for three weeks or more will give you the time to travel to some very special and remote places, and to go deeper into yourself. Check out any vaccinations you may need at least six weeks in advance (see www.netdoctor.co.uk), organize travel insurance, know your own blood group, visit your dentist and tell your hosts about any special dietary requirements.

Going green

The World Health Organization defines health as a state of 'complete physical, mental and social wellbeing'. Being in tune with the world outside of ourselves will make a body and soul escape an infinitely richer experience. However long you go for, consider the environment. Try to avoid jumping on a plane just for a weekend, and consider taking overland routes for short-haul destinations from the UK such as southern Europe and even Morocco; see the excellent **www.seat61.com** for comprehensive details of alternatives to flying. When you do fly long haul, give something back and offset carbon emissions with a legitimate company such as **Climate Care** (www.climatecare.org), and consider staying for longer and doing some voluntary work (see Soul Food boxes). Stay at eco-friendly hotels, try to encourage those that aren't to change, and bring your own water bottle to refill instead of buying plastic bottles.

Who to go with

Most retreats defined by geographical location in this book are safe havens for the lone traveller, and many are great places to go specifically to reconnect or chill out with a friend or partner. If there's a group of you, consider organizing a bespoke retreat (see Beyond Retreats, page 29, Peter Sommer Travels, page 151, Sarah Rosenfield Pilates, page 113, or a villa in Bali, page 258). Detoxing can be more fun with a trusted friend, but the process can make you extremely grumpy. If you have serious emotional stuff to sort out, it's best to go alone. Some of the more affordable holidays offer only shared rooms or a limited number of single rooms, so if you'd prefer not to share with a stranger, take a friend along. You'll find it more interesting and less lonely to have company at a hotel and spa or natural spa retreat. The same goes for dedicated health and fitness retreats – though most welcome single travellers, in reality many of them attract mainly pairs of friends or couples.

The rest of the body and soul escapes featured in this book are mainly group experiences which are designed specifically to help people break free from the limitations they impose on themselves, and they're a lot more effective if you attend them alone. You'll have more space to explore yourself, and the chance to meet like-minded people who often help you to grow in unexpected ways. A group becomes a tight, self-contained unit, and it's very rare that the people in it don't gel. You'll get a wonderful feeling of togetherness, which you might not enjoy as a couple or with friends.

Group dynamics

Putting yourself into a group environment can be a challenge for some, but it's actually a familiar experience to us all. When we're in a group, we replicate the place we have in our family, whether we're quiet and withdrawn, seeking attention or acting as the diplomat. As UK-based psychotherapist Malcolm Stern (www.malcolmstern.com) points out, a 'healthy' group will encompass all members of a family, with each person noticing what goes on and 'bringing in' people

LORNA MACKENZIE

Some retreats are great places to reconnect with a friend or partner.

everything from depression to degenerative diseases.

Most meditation retreats in this book are Buddhist venues offering courses in vipassana or Tibetan meditation (see glossary), and promote a way of living rather than a set of strict religious rules to be followed. They are open to everyone regardless of beliefs or background, and to beginners as well as experienced practitioners. They require a serious interest in meditation, a high degree of self-sufficiency and a stable emotional state. Most charge a small fee for food and accommodation, with teachers paid by donation. Accommodation is basic, the sexes are segregated, and stimulants such as alcohol, caffeine and tobacco are not allowed. A vipassana silent meditation retreat is especially beneficial: without daily chit-chat and petty concerns your mind is freer to learn to meditate (see page 282). Sociologists have measured the silences in conversations between English speakers and concluded that we cannot bear a pause of longer than four seconds. So why not give yourself a break?

where necessary. A good host will act like a wise mother or father, dealing with any issues that arise.

The group environment of a body and soul escape is an excellent space in which to break the patterns we've developed within our own families, by taking the chance to behave differently and, as Stern says, 'speak our truth'. "If you usually speak first in your family, try hanging back in a group situation. If you're usually the last person to speak or don't really get 'heard', try to speak out sooner." A good host will be sensitive to each member's needs, whether that's to have time out alone or to be encouraged to get more involved. Remember this is your trip, so take time out if you need it, and be sure you're getting what you need.

There's often one person in a group with a lot of personal baggage who demands too much attention. In this situation, Stern says, the person is needing to be fed. A good host will work with them and manage the situation healthily, but you can also have an effect. "Telling someone they are taking up a lot of space and that you are feeling resentful of it may help that person to grow," Stern says. But do it kindly: "Honesty is a gift, savaging someone is not, so slay your dragons with compassion."

Meditation retreats
Learning to meditate or deepening an existing practice at a retreat is one of the most replenishing things you can do. Meditation is designed to help us tame our 'monkey minds' by concentrating on a symbol, a mantra, or – more usually - our breathing for set periods of time. This recreates the central Buddhist philosophy that the past has left us, the future is (always) yet to come, and this moment is all there ever is. This process of 'letting go' also has a direct effect on our physical health: as UK-based meditation teacher Guy Burgs says, "The quality of your consciousness affects the biorhythms of your body". Meditation is increasingly used by health care practitioners to treat

Yoga holidays and retreats
Rather than physical beauty or contortionism, calming the mind is the main goal of yoga, and many people develop an interest in meditation through it. As Indian yoga guru TKV Desikachar says: "A lot of people can do a beautiful posture, but their life is a big headache." Effective yoga is measured, he says, by "how it enhances our relationships and promotes clarity and peace of mind". Going on a yoga holiday will tone up and energize the body, but it's also a brilliant way to release pent up stress and anxiety and reconnect with yourself. Don't be daunted by the somewhat confusing mix of styles around: whether you choose ashtanga vinyasa, iyengar, sivananda, satyananda, kundalini or something more contemporary, all good yoga has the same goal. If you're new to it, try a few classes before choosing a holiday, and be prepared to experiment with different styles as you progress.

Good yoga holidays will offer a mix of asanas, pranayama, relaxation, healthy food, fresh air, a rejuvenating location and an inspiring teacher. Many good teachers have been influenced by a range of styles, and will bring their own secret ingredient to a class, as well as a sound knowledge of anatomy to help prevent injuries. Feel at liberty to ask about training, but do bear in mind that this is not like training to become a fitness instructor – teachers will have to draw on their own experience and the depth of their practice. The yoga retreats in this book are usually set venues which remain open all year round. They tend to be more serious in nature than the yoga 'holidays', where fun, free time and sometimes even alcohol are key elements. Unless we specifically say otherwise, most 'holidays' are aimed at all levels.

Detox retreats
We consume toxins in the air we breathe, and through the pesticides, hormones, antibiotics and preservatives in the food we eat. Though the body detoxes naturally through the skin, liver and kidneys, a

To make the most of your body and soul escape, it's important to stay calm and relaxed during the journey to your destination and on the way back home.

build-up of toxins can lead to excess weight, stressed skin, exhaustion and digestive disorders. Stepping out of life to do a dedicated detox will not only help you lose weight, clear up skin and digestive problems and massively boost energy levels, but also allow you to process and let go of accumulated stress and negative mental patterns. As your physical body releases toxins, so all the negative energy that you've stored up on an emotional and mental level also starts to drain away. Don't undertake this challenging process lightly; expect to experience a real low in your energy levels and state of mind before you see any improvements. The ideal time for a detox is a week to 10 days, or in the case of ayurveda (see page 210), at least two weeks. Give up toxins such as caffeine, alcohol, wheat, red meat and (preferably) other animal proteins at least a week before you start, and once back home try to sustain good eating habits; overindulging too soon will set you back very quickly to the physical and mental state in which you started.

Hotels and spas are us

Traditionally referring to a healing place with a natural source of mineral water, the word spa has come to mean anything and everything to do with health and pampering, and gives unscrupulous hotels around the globe the chance to charge extortionate sums for gimmicky treatments with inexperienced, fresh-out-of-beauty-college therapists. In 2007, the Italian government banned establishments from calling themselves spas unless they had a natural water source. Elsewhere, a place can, technically, only use the word if it has a bona fide 'wet area' with a steam room, sauna and jacuzzi (or more). The 'natural spa retreats' in this book have their own natural water source and are far more eco-friendly than those that use fossil fuels to heat their water. A few places are leading the way – Daintree Eco Lodge in Australia (see page 307) uses its own natural supply of water and eco-friendly ways to heat it, as does England's Titanic Spa (see page 42). To get the most out of any spa experience, exercise and warm up

the muscles, open pores and de-stress in a sauna and/or a steamroom, and leave time for a rest before a treatment.

When it comes to spas, book time slots rather than specific treatments, and ask in advance for the best therapists. Experienced masseurs will ask you beforehand about any areas that need work and leave you in peace during the experience. If they don't, or if you want a deeper massage, or you're too hot or cold, or you want the music turned off, then speak up. During treatments that require waiting time, such as a facial or a wrap, make sure that the therapist gives you a scalp, foot or hand massage rather than leaving you alone like an abandoned child in a darkened room. In the right hands, a basic massage using rancid oil on a far-flung beach can be highly rejuvenating, but it goes without saying that the fresher and more natural the products used in your treatments the better. Ayurveda advocates that you shouldn't put on your skin what you wouldn't put into your mouth.

What to pack

Be ruthless and pack light – heavy bags and too many clothes are a strain on body and mind. Bring layers of clothing for daywear and exercise in breathable natural fibres, a warm fleece, trainers and worn-in walking boots. Other useful items include: travel blanket or shawl to wear during yoga and meditation retreats (blankets provided can be scratchy), yoga mat (those provided can be worn and tatty), travel candle and matches (for calm and comfort anywhere), water bottle, travel pillow, earplugs, sarong, swimsuit, flip-flops, sun hat, sunglasses, sun protection, universal washbasin plug, toiletries (including detoxing items such as a dry skin brush, Epsom salts and a good face mask), books, camera, travel paints, pens and a notebook, natural remedies and herbal tea bags.

Staying stress-free on the move

Attitude is everything – expect the journey to take longer than scheduled, keep a light heart, breathe deeply at regular intervals and maintain a sense of humour. Planning ahead helps. Leave plenty of time for your journey, arrange a pickup in advance at your destination or familiarize yourself with local taxi and public transport information. Book accommodation if you need to stay overnight en route – preferably calm, safe places which offer therapies. We have listed a selection throughout the book. And, when it's time to come home, take it easy on the return journey to help retain the benefits of your escape, and make time to incorporate any changes into your daily life.

What to drink on the move

Give alcohol and caffeine a wide berth; they will make you dehydrated, bloated and groggy, and irritate delicate stomachs. Drink plenty of water, and avoid fizzy drinks, which will leave you feeling gassy, though a small glass of tonic water can calm an unsettled stomach, as can peppermints (with natural peppermint oil), and fresh root or crystallized ginger. Take a selection of fruit and herbal tea bags:

ginger and peppermint help cure travel sickness, camomile encourages sleep, and nettle helps keep your liver healthy. Bring along your own citrus or fresh berry juices, which are high in Vitamin C and antioxidants to keep your immune system strong. Pomegranate juice contains more vitamin C than most, while cranberry juice helps ward off urinary tract infections. Sachets of miso soup that only need boiling water added are perfect for travelling (opt for the additive- and MSG-free versions).

What to eat on the move

Eat little and often. Keep foods light and simple and avoid stodgy, greasy or very rich foods including red meat, which will take a long time to digest and sit heavily in your stomach. Take your own snacks with you, as these will be fresher and healthier than those available en route. Take stress-busting and fibre-rich foods such as pecans, walnuts, almonds, brazil nuts (unsalted) and plain popcorn; gentle fruits such as melon, coconut, bananas and avocado, pumpkin, sunflower and sesame seeds, oatcakes and crispbreads. Whole grains and leafy greens are fibre-rich to keep your system moving, and full of vitamin B6 to help counter feelings of lethargy and water retention; eat a bowl of porridge or a stir-fry if it's available, or take your own brown rice or leafy green salads. Avoid too many pulses and beans, which can make you uncomfortably gassy.

The executive chef at Thailand's Chiva Som has devised hydrating and delicious meals for British Airways first-class flights, but for most of us, plane food is a singularly grim and unhealthy experience. You should choose the vegetarian option, or at least the chicken or fish dishes, but the wisest thing is not to eat any of it. Buy sushi, vegetarian wraps and noodles, couscous or rice salads, and green and fruit salads before you board. Better still, bring your own meals in tupperware boxes with a wedge of lemon for squeezing just before you eat.

The following are some suggestions: roast mediterranean vegetables with olive oil then mix through steamed couscous and tear in fresh herbs; roast root vegetables and squashes with olive oil, turmeric, cumin and coriander seeds then mix with pearl barley or quinoa; buy mini falafels and take with chopped fresh tomatoes, parsley and wholemeal flatbreads; mix finely chopped red pepper, courgette, spring onion and fresh herbs with quinoa, couscous or brown rice.

Flight survival

Flying is tiring, dehydrating and disorientating for the body and mind, leading to broken sleep and a weakened immune system. To give yourself the best chance of feeling comfortable, take lots of physical exercise the day before, and sneak in a massage if you can. Take your shoes off as soon as you board, moisturize well, and wear earplugs to minimize noise. Make eye contact and say hello to the person beside you to help create a tension-free atmosphere. If you're not one for small talk, wait for a lull and then get out your book, headphones or eye shades. If you feel harassed, the cabin crew may reseat you.

Walk up and down the aisles regularly, do seated exercises such as ankle rotations, shoulder stretches and knee raises, consciously breathe at regular intervals. The website www.yogi2go.com has an in-flight selection of downloadable yoga classes specially designed to ease anxiety, back pain and tiredness, or www.meditainment.com has downloadable guided meditations with stories, music and natural sounds. Change your watch to the time of your destination as soon as you board and try to sleep and eat at the right time for that country from then on. Once at your destination, keep to local time, and do gentle exercise before you go to sleep.

Staying healthy in hot climates

Drink lots of water, wear plenty of adequate sun protection at all times, and don't do strenuous exercise at the hottest part of the day. To avoid getting bitten by insects, wear clothing that covers arms and legs from dusk till dawn, and reapply repellent as often as possible, especially if you are sweating heavily. Citronella oil is a natural repellent, but apply it by the hour to make it effective. Rooms with air conditioning or fans help ward off mosquitoes, but try to sleep under a mosquito net. Avoid malarial areas (see www.malariahotspots.com), especially if you are on a detox. The chemoprophylactic antimalarial drugs that are recommended are very strong antibiotics which the body will find too toxic to deal with when the immune system is very clean. Paula Gilbert (BSc, SRD), a dietician at Grayshott in England, recommends Demal 200, an antimalarial homeopathic treatment; Paraclens, taken twice daily in tablet form; Clarkia 100, taken in drop form; and Higher Natures True Food B Complex, the smell of which mosquitoes don't like. You can find all these at online health shops such as www.nutricentre.com.

Natural remedies for the traveller

Melotonin is naturally produced by the body to help regulate sleep cycles, and as a supplement it's a natural alternative to the sleeping pill to ease jet lag. It's freely available throughout Asia and the US, but only on prescription in the UK. To help keep your gut healthy, take – before meals – Biocare's natural product TravelGuard, a mix of probiotics, garlic and antiseptic herbs to aid your digestive system. Supplements of the herb astragalus will help strengthen the immune system, which weakens during travel, especially flights. Rub tiger balm on pressure points to ease headaches and general pains. Try aloe vera gel for too much sun, and arnica cream for bruises. Plant-based essential oils are easy to take travelling to use in your bath, mixed with water as an elixir or with a base oil on your skin: lavender is a general cure-all, camomile is a relaxant, lemongrass is great for clearing your nose and your head, and tea tree oil is an all-round antiseptic. A homeopathic first aid travel kit is also easy to carry and a few remedies can address a wide range of complaints, from fear of flying and travel sickness to constipation and anxiety. The basic principle is to take a dose of the remedy every three to four hours and to stop once improvement occurs (see www.helios.co.uk).

spabreak
the spa travel experts

Too busy to shop around?
We help you choose the right venue for you
we make the booking and do the running around
all you have to do is choose, then relax and enjoy...

Only the best spa resorts are included in spabreak's
ultimate spa collection

With the pace of life today, it's often difficult to afford the time to recharge your batteries, you certainly don't want to waste time and get stressed out just finding somewhere to relax. With Spabreak you are just a click or a phone call away from the best spa hotels and health farms in Europe.

Spabreak offers a unique concierge service to clients, offering the best prices from the spas themselves. Spabreak do not take payment and only showcase the venues' own special offers and packages.

Whether you are looking for a day spa, or for a residential stay, Spabreak can ease your way through the booking and selection process and offer impartial advice. Spabreak can also arrange group and corporate bookings.

Simply call the number below to be connected to an expert advisor or visit our website where you can also book online.

As an extra special treat Spabreak offers gift vouchers and has regular special offers plus complimentary beauty products from companies including Decléor.

01883 724 843
www.spabreak.co.uk

spabreak
we do it for you

Resources

Books

Meditation and being in the now *The Power of Now* by **Eckhart Tolle** (Hodder & Stoughton) is an enlightened and heartening book about living in the moment. For an excellent guide to meditation, *Wherever You Go, There You Are* (Hyperion) is by **Jon Kabat-Zinn**, the down-to-earth director of a stress reduction clinic in the US. **Martine Batchelor**'s *Meditation for Life* (Frances Lincoln) is a clear and comforting book to have beside you, and for depth in an accessible form, try *The Sivananda Book of Meditation* by the **Sivananda Yoga Vedanta Centre** (Gaia Books).

Buddhism *The Tibetan Book of Living and Dying* by **Sogyal Rinpoche** (Rider Books) is inspirational, as is anything by **Stephen Batchelor**, especially *Buddhism without Beliefs* (Bloomsbury). *When Things Fall Apart: Heart Advice for Difficult Times* by the Tibetan Buddhist nun and former housewife **Pema Chodron** (Shambhala Classics) has been known to save lives. Also recommended is *The Art of Happiness* by **HH The Dalai Lama with Howard C Cutler** (Hodder & Stoughton), and *Peace Is Every Step* by Vietnamese Zen meditation master **Thich Nhat Hanh** (Rider Books).

Yoga *The New Book of Yoga* by **The Sivananda Yoga Centre** (Ebury Press) is easy to understand and has good information on yogic philosophy. For a mellow but supremely energising self practice, try *Yin Yoga* by **Paul Grilley** (White Cloud Press), while *Light on Life* by **BKS Iyengar** (Rodale) is an accessible read.

Living well For a spot of DIY life coaching, *How To Have Kick-ass Ideas* by **Chris Barez-Brown** (What If) is really about how to have a fresh, stimulating happy life. The charming *In Praise of Slow* by **Carl Honoré** (Orion) will inspire you to slow down in every aspect of your life. For the lowdown on mental, emotional and physical detoxing, try *Life Detox* by **Sandy Newbigging and Amanda Hamilton** (Piatkus). The *Shamanic Path Workbook* is a clear introduction to shamanism by the founder of Eagle's Wing, **Leo Rutherford** (Arima Publications). If you're looking for a spiritual retreat that isn't Buddhist in origin, *The Good Retreat Guide* by **Stafford Whiteaker** (Rider Books) has a large selection of Christian, Roman Catholic, Anglican and Quaker retreats in the UK and Europe as well as those that are non-denominational.

For the journey For an unexpected take on the art of searching, try *Siddhartha* by **Herman Hesse**. **Rainer-Maria Rilke**'s *Letters to a Young Poet* (Norton) is an inspiring read on how sensitive souls can flourish in a seemingly hostile world, while *A Million Little Pieces* by **James Frey** (John Murray) is a liberating story of transformation by a former drug addict. A life-altering accident is the subject of the absorbing *Where is the Mango Princess?* by **Cathy Crimmins** (Vintage), while travellers inspired by serendipity should get hold of the 1950s classic *Royal Challenge Accepted: Around the World on Five Pounds* by **Alistair Boyd** (Ocean Media). *Yoga School Drop Out* by **Lucy Edge** is

funny and forthright, or for an amusing first-hand account of personal development courses, try *The Battersea Park Road to Enlightenment* by **Isabel Losada** (Bloomsbury). **Anne Donovan**'s novel *BuddhaDa* (Canongate) is a down to earth absorbing read on how a Scottish working class family is affected when the dad discovers Buddhism.

Magazines US-based **Yoga Journal** (www.yogajournal.com) regularly covers yoga retreats worldwide, as does the UK's **Yoga Magazine** (www.yogamagazine.co.uk), while **Yoga & Health** (www.yogaandhealthmag.co.uk) focuses on wellbeing. **Psychologies** (www.psychologies.co.uk) runs articles on spirituality and wellbeing.

Organizations, websites and exhibitions

In the UK, the **Independent Yoga Network** (www.independent yoganetwork.org) has interesting articles, information about training courses and a sister site (www.theyogaregister.org) to help you find a teacher in your area; also visit **The British Wheel of Yoga** (www.bwy.org.uk) and the **Yoga Alliance** (www.yogaalliance.org). Check out the **Tai Chi Union of Great Britain** (www.taichiunion.com), the **Pilates Foundation** (www.pilatesfoundation.com) or the **Pilates Institute** (www.pilates-institute.com), the **Ayurveda Company of Great Britain** (www.ayurvedagb.com), and the **Thai Massage Organisation** (www.thai-massage.org.uk). For information on Buddhism, try www.buddhanet.net and www.fwbo.org.

Exhibitions can be a useful source of ideas. In the UK, the annual **One Life Live** offers life-changing inspiration (www.onelifelive.co.uk). The **Yoga Show** (www.theyogashow.co.uk) is also worth visiting.

Travel agents and tour operators

Lotus Journeys (www.lotusjourneys.com) is a small online travel company offering mid-range to upmarket holistic retreats and yoga holidays. **Wellbeing Escapes** (www.wellbeingescapes.co.uk) sells a range of wellbeing breaks and often has good deals to further-flung destinations . To find healthy stopovers as well as places to hole up, the excellently researched **i-escape.com** features hotels with character around the world. **Responsible Travel** (www.responsibletravel.com) offers body and soul options under its 'special interest' category, while **Wonderful World** (www.wonderfulworld.uk.com) has eco-chic and adventure experiences with a holistic twist. **Neal's Yard Agency** (www.nealsyardagency.com) specializes in affordable holistic breaks, as does **The Retreat Company**, which also offers an online shop (www.theretreatcompany.com). For more traditional spa breaks, **Erna Low Body & Soul Holidays** (www.bodyandsoulholidays.com) has been selling spa holidays since the 1960s, while **Thermalia Travel** (www.thermalia.co.uk) specializes in natural spa retreats. For pampering, try **Essential Escapes** (www.essentialescapes.com) and **La Joie de Vivre** (www.lajoiedevivre.co.uk). US-based **Spa Finder** (www.spafinder.com) is a good resource, while in the UK **Spabreak** (www.spabreak.co.uk) and **Eyespa** (www.eyespa.co.uk) both offer deals to mainly UK hotels and health and fitness retreats.

Everyone's favourite
yoga magazine

YOGA Magazine is the title that each month brings you hot yoga news, yoga features, celebrity interviews and everything that's new in the world of yoga. YOGA Magazine enjoys a reputation for dynamic, creative and editorial excellence. Our list of high-profile contributors and A-list teachers who are regularly featured inside the magazine reads like a Who's Who of the yoga and holistic lifestyle community. YOGA Magazine is available at all leading retail outlets.

www.yogamagazine.co.uk

Glossary

Aarti Also spelt arati, Sanskrit word from 'aa' (towards) and 'rati' (highest love for god), a Hindu ritual where lights made from wicks soaked in ghee are offered to deities. It also refers to the song sung during this ritual.

Abhyanga Ayurvedic oil massage where two therapists perform a gentle, rhythmic and synchronized massage with pressure suited to the client's dosha.

Acupressure A treatment which puts physical pressure on different points of the body to improve the flow of chi, release muscle tension and promote healing.

Acupuncture Ancient Chinese healing technique using needles to balance chi, following diagnoses by the tongue, pulse and personal history.

Aikido Japanese martial art techniques include spherical movements to turn the opponent's energy back on himself.

Alexander technique Devised by Australian actor Frederick Alexander, a simple, practical method that teaches how to recognize and overcome habits that cause unnecessary body tension, so improving movement, balance and body awareness.

Ama Sanskrit for toxins blocking the body.

Anusara yoga Founded by American yoga teacher John Friend in 1997, a hatha yoga system backed by an uplifting philosophy that looks for the good in all people and all things.

Applied kinesiology Alternative medicine that claims to be able to diagnose imbalances in the body by using tools such as gentle non-intrusive muscle tests. Massage, nutritional advice and counselling are then used to stimulate the body's own healing ability.

Aquawellness Deep relaxation using a form of shiatsu with the body supported in warm water.

Aromatherapy Ancient healing art using essential plant oils to aid circulatory and digestive problems, act as sedatives or stimulate the nervous system. Containing antibacterial and therapeutic qualities, the essences are used in massages, can be inhaled, or used as a relaxant in the bath.

Asana Literally 'seat' in Sanskrit, the word originally referred to the sitting position used for meditation. Yogis started to experiment with different body postures, and the term now refers to any physical posture used in yoga.

Ashram Place of solace where a community drawn by a common (usually spiritual) goal lives together.

Ashtanga (or Astanga) yoga The yogi's code of practice, ashtanga (Sanskrit for 'eight limbs') is the eight-limbed path set out by the Indian sage Patanjali in his Yoga Sutras. In theory any yoga taught according to these principles may be called ashtanga yoga, but it usually refers to the ashtanga vinyasa style of yoga taught by Sri K Pattabhi Jois in Mysore. This is a cleansing, moving meditation using a dynamic breathing technique with three progressively more difficult series of asanas (primary, second and advanced). The system was discovered in an ancient palm leaf manuscript in the 1930s by the grandfather of modern yoga Sri T Krishnamacharya, whose students were Sri K Pattabhi Jois and BKS Iyengar. To teach ashtanga vinyasa, a teacher must have trained with Sri K Pattabhi Jois in Mysore and have been given permission to teach by him.

Astral Body A subtle body corresponding to the physical body through which our vital energy, or prana, flows. It contains our emotional, mental and intellectual faculties. When we die, the astral and physical bodies separate.

Autobiographical work Self assessment process to identify issues or events in your life that have formed your needs, desires or behavioural patterns.

Ayurveda Indian holistic system of health dating back over 5000 years.

Bandhas Internal muscular locks used in yoga.

Bastis Oil enemas used for detoxing.

Belly dancing Ancient art of self-expression for women of all ages.

Bentonite clay Sedimentary, swelling clay composed of weathered volcanic ash that opens like a sponge when mixed with water. Often used during detoxing to help absorb and dislodge toxins.

Bhagavad Gita Ancient Sanskrit text revered as one of the most sacred by most Hindu traditions. Its teachings embrace all aspects of human actions searching to resolve the eternal struggle between the material and the spiritual.

Bikram yoga Created by Bikram Choudhury, this is 'hot' yoga, a series of 26 postures practised in a temperature of 37°C (108°F).

Bio dancing Style of dance which stimulates the mind and body with music, rhythm and emotion. It focuses on the 'five lines of the Vivencia' (living experience): vitality, sexuality, creativity, affectivity and transcendence. Has been used to treat depression and promote a fuller enjoyment of life.

Biodynamic food & wines Developed from the anthroposophical teachings of Rudolf Steiner where an ecological and sustainable farming system is based on ethical and spiritual as well as practical considerations.

Bio-resonance Also called bio-magnetic resonance, a therapy based on the idea that the body is made up of energy and has an electromagnetic field, or resonance. Electrodes attached to a specially designed machine measure vibrations emitted by the different meridians of the body to help diagnose and treat conditions such as skin and weight problems, asthma, allergies, viral infections and fibromyalgia.

Body composition Analysis of body mass index (BMI) to discover percentage body fat and help work out a nutrition or exercise programme.

Bodywork Therapy using massage or exercise for relaxation or to ease tension and pain. May involve correction of posture or movement, and some methods treat both mind and body.

Body wraps Used to detox the system, soothe aching muscles or hydrate skin, the body is smothered in mud, seaweed, fruit or herbs then wrapped in linen.

Bowen technique Holistic therapy devised by Australian self-taught osteopath Tom Bowen in the 1940s, involving application of gentle pressure on the fascia (connective tissue) to trigger energy release and rebalance the body.

Breathwork Method of continuous, circular breathing to produce a relaxed state and release deep emotions. Also see Pranayama.

Buddhism Practical philosophy of living and a non-theistic religion based on the teachings of the Buddha. A Buddhist aims to overcome the stress of existence and achieve nirvana (the end of suffering). Followers train and purify the mind by following the Four Noble Truths and the Noble Eightfold Path to understand the true nature of everything, and find peace and liberation.

Budokon Fusion of martial arts, meditation and vinyasa flow yoga.

Burpee Vigorous, fast exercise beginning in a squat position, kicking feet back to press up position, returning feet to squat position then leaping up as high as possible.

Capoeira Afro-Brazilian martial art.

Chakras From the Sanskrit meaning 'wheel' or 'circle'; each of seven energy centres in the body that are concerned with its psychic energy flow.

Chakra balancing Energy work using gentle touch to align the chakras.

Champissage see Indian head massage.

Chanting The repetition of a mantra, often used to prepare the mind for meditation. See Kirtan.

Chavutti thirumal In ayurveda, a massage done with the therapist's feet, while they hold onto a rope for balance, adjusting their weight to relax the muscles and work on marma points and nadis.

CHEK (Corrective Holistic Exercise Kinesiology) An approach to exercise devised by American Paul Chek.

Chi Also qi, Chinese word for the life force or vital energy of the body and the universe. Known as 'ki' in Japanese and 'prana' in Sanskrit, chi flows through channels called meridians in the body.

ChiBall Exercise using coloured, sometimes scented balls combined with graceful, flowing movements to achieve physical and mental wellbeing.

Chi Kung See Qigong.

Chi Nei Tsang Thai abdominal massage used to treat digestive problems and help release blocked energy and negative emotions.

Chinese five elements Wood, fire, earth, metal and water. Traditional Chinese medicine (TCM) is based on several different philosophical frameworks, one of which is the five elements.

Chinese medicine See traditional Chinese medicine.

Chiropractic From the Greek, meaning 'done by hand'. A chiropractor manipulates the spine to treat a whole range of symptoms from slipped discs to sciatica.

Colonic irrigation Also known as colonic hydrotherapy, an ancient if controversial treatment for detoxing the body by unblocking the large intestine of accumulated faecal matter, bacteria and toxins. It claims to increase overall wellness and help treat specific conditions such as irritable bowel, constipation, headaches, chronic fatigue and emotional stress. Often done in conjunction with a cleansing fast, it involves slowly pumping up to 20 gallons of body temperature filtered water through a tube deep into the colon and allowing it to flow back out. Water is sometimes infused with minerals or diuretic ingredients such as vinegar or coffee.

Colour therapy Also known as chromotherapy; alternative healing method using colour and light to balance physical, spiritual, emotional or mental energy in the body, often relating the seven spectrum colours to the seven chakras.

Core muscles Deep, stabilizing muscles around the spine, trunk and abdomen used in everyday movements.

Core stability Learning how to locate the core muscles and exercise them.

Craniosacral therapy Gentle, hands-on method of stimulating and restoring the function of the craniosacral system, the membranes and fluid that surround and protect the brain and spinal cord.

Crystal healing Gentle, intuitive therapy using the natural vibration of crystals to activate the electromagnetic field that surrounds the physical body, and balance problem areas. Crystals such as quartz, amethyst, malachite and tiger's eye correspond to the chakras and their colours, and are said to have different healing properties.

Dance therapy Also called dance movement therapy or choreotherapy, the use of rhythm (with or without music) and physical movement to liberate body and soul.

Daoism See Taoism.

Deep tissue massage Firm and deep therapeutic massage using specific techniques to release tensions and knots that have built up over a period of time, and relieve emotional tension.

Detox The removal of toxins from the body. The body does this naturally through the skin, liver and kidneys but many therapists believe the process can be helped by various treatments and activities from sweating in a sauna to undertaking a cleansing fast with or without colonic irrigation.

Dharma Right or wise way of living that leads to liberation, emphasized in the philosophical teachings of Buddhism, Hinduism, Jainism and Sikhism. In yoga philosophy, following your own dharma means acting responsibly and behaving in a manner appropriate to your level of spiritual awareness.

Do-in Acupressure with massage and physical exercise resembling yoga asanas to balance the flow of energy through the body.

Doshas The three bodily energies vata, pitta and kapha, which dictate our individual constitution.

Dru yoga From the Sanskrit 'dhruva', meaning still and unchanging, uses unique Energy Block Release Sequences to release tension and stress from the mind as well as the body, and focuses on increasing the powerful energy of the heart by using flowing movements between postures.

Dry flotation Version of flotation therapy; the body is cocooned and suspended above a water bed rather than in a tank of water.

Dynamic yoga Version of ashtanga vinyasa yoga. Teacher Godfri Dev teaches his own dynamic yoga training method based on the Eight Limbs of Yoga.

Ear candling Originally a folk medicine used to remove wax and 'toxins' from the ear, this therapy involves placing one end of a hollow candle into the ear and lighting the other end. It is thought to be effective in relieving headaches, tinnitus, sinus problems and stress.

EFT (emotional freedom technique) Psycho-therapeutic method based on the belief that there is a link between the body's energy system and our psychology, used to relieve depression, anxiety, stress, addictions, phobias and

more. The client focuses on a negative emotion or memory while a therapist taps the fingers on the meridians of the body to restore balance.

Eight Limbs of Yoga Series of steps to purify the body and mind and reach enlightenment written by the Indian sage Patanjali in the Yoga Sutras. They are the yamas, or abstentions such as non-violence and non-stealing; the niyamas, or observances such as purity and living with awareness; the asanas, or bodily postures; pranayama, or breath control; pratyahara, or drawing the senses inward; dharana, or concentration; dhyana, or meditation; all of which lead to samadhi, or superconsciousness.

Enema Procedure of introducing liquids into the rectum and colon to loosen and remove the toxic waste. See colonic irrigation.

Esalen massage First developed at the Esalen Institute, a massage using long strokes with other techniques such as shiatsu, acupressure, lymphatic drainage and reflexology to unblock energy and promote deep relaxation.

Essential oils Concentrated oils extracted from plants and flowers used in massage or aromatherapy for their relaxing and rejuvenating properties. There are over 100 types with different therapeutic and antibacterial qualities.

Fasting Abstaining from the intake of food for a period of time to detox the system, one of the oldest healing techniques in the world. A properly supervised cleansing fast may involve some light meals such as soups and broths, supplements such as probiotics, and lots of water and herbal teas.

Feldenkrais method Focuses on awareness through movement to improve posture, relieve tension and muscle pain, create greater relaxation and increase vitality.

Feng shui Literally 'wind' (feng) and 'water' (shui); the art of harmonious living, an ancient Chinese practice of arrangement of space to achieve harmony with the environment. Based on the idea that different things contain different energies which affect us physically, emotionally and spiritually.

Five/5 Rhythms Devised by Gabrielle Roth in the 1960s, improvised and expressive movement based on five musical rhythms; flowing, staccato, chaos, lyrical and stillness. Each has a different energy which enables participants to find their own musical expression and so free the mind, body and spirit.

Flotation therapy First used by NASA scientists to simulate a zero-gravity environment. You float in an enclosed tank full of salt and mineral water heated to body temperature. Being isolated from external stimuli in a weightless environment totally relaxes the muscles and joints, improves sensory awareness and brings about a deep feeling of wellbeing.

Flower remedies Homeopathic form of healing using dilutions of flower essences to treat emotional imbalances. Devised by Englishman Dr Edward Bach in the 1930s, other versions now exist such as Australian Bush Flower Essences.

Flow yoga See Vinyasa yoga.

Four Noble Truths Series of truths mapped out by the Buddha after he obtained Enlightenment, which now form the bedrock of Buddhist teachings. They are The Noble Truth of Suffering, The Noble Truth of the Origin of Suffering, The Noble Truth of the Cessation of Suffering, and The Noble Truth of the Way Leading to the Cessation of Suffering. The last one is the Noble Eightfold Path (see below).

Fusion yoga Melding of different styles of yoga with qigong to produce physical and emotional self-awareness.

Guru Spiritual guide or teacher who has attained complete insight. In Hinduism, Buddhism and Sikhism the guru is seen as a sacred path or way to self-realization.

Gyrotonic Exercise using rhythmic, sweeping movements derived from yoga, tai chi, swimming, dance and gymnastics. Based on spherical awareness, it addresses all seven elements of spinal movement, uses breathing techniques similar to those used in Pilates.

Hammam Turkish bath.

Hasya or laughter yoga Simulated laughter which, changing the breath, relaxes the mind, increases the blood flow and strengthens the immune system.

Hatha yoga Derived from ha (sun) and tha (moon), this style of yoga aims to balance and unite these masculine and feminine energies in the mind and body, and was developed by the ancient rishis (sages) of India for purification and spiritual evolution. It has become a generic term for the practice of yoga asanas, pranayama, mudras and bandhas, all of which seek to stabilize the mind and body and harness kundalini energy. Although 'hatha' is sometimes used to describe a more gentle yoga practice, ashtanga vinyasa, sivananda and iyengar yoga are all examples of hatha yoga.

Hawaiian temple bodywork Also known as lomi lomi (literally, taking everything apart from the heart), a ceremonial four-handed massage originally devised for Hawaiian royalty. Two therapists perform rhythmic movements while you focus on your breathing. As you relax, the massage becomes more vigorous and you are moved and cradled in any direction necessary to release bodily and emotional tensions.

Hellerwork Created by American Joseph Heller, who trained in rolfing; treatment based on the belief that the body stores the trauma we have experienced in our lives and keeps us stuck in the past. Given as a course of treatments, the often painful deep connective tissue work aims to release built-up stresses and tension. Discussion of feelings that come to the surface during treatment is a key part.

Herbal medicine Also known as herbalism or phytotherapy, an ancient practice using the healing powers of plants and plant extracts as teas, pills, elixirs, creams and oils to prevent and cure illness. Used in many types of complementary therapies including ayurveda, homeopathy, naturopathy and Chinese medicine.

Holistic From the Greek 'holos' meaning 'whole', a holistic approach to health and fitness seeks to harmonize your lifestyle by looking at your mental, physical, emotional and spiritual wellbeing, rather than just one element in isolation.

Homeopathy From the Greek 'homoios' (like) and 'pathos' (suffering), a holistic health care practice developed by German Dr Hahnemann in the 18th century and based on the concept of treating 'like with like'. The belief is that disease can be cured by giving patients minute doses of natural substances which, when given in undiluted form to healthy people, produce symptoms similar to the disease.

Hot-stone therapy Speciality massage using smooth, heated basalt stones on the chakras of the body.

Hydrotherapy Therapeutic use of water ('hydro' in Greek) which may involve exercise, immersion and massage in hot or cold water.

Hypnotherapy Treatment that uses hypnosis to help people understand the underlying causes of their addictions, phobias, insomnia, amnesia, stress, pain, inhibitions and more.

Indian head massage Also known as champissage, an ayurvedic massage of the head, neck, face and shoulders, which manipulates the body's energy channels to reduce muscular and nervous tension.

Infra-red sauna Small pod which produces heat from infra-red rays to help detox the body.

Insight meditation See vipassana meditation.

Integral yoga Holistic style of yoga originally taught by Indian Swami Satchidananda, incorporating pranayama, asanas, relaxation, visualisation, meditation, chanting, philosophy and spirituality.

Iyengar yoga Highly structured form of yoga devised by BKS Iyengar, who is based in Pune, India. As well as following The Eight Limbs of Yoga, the style uses props such as belts, blocks, ropes, bricks and chairs to assist in performing asanas, with a great attention to detail so that the body is correctly aligned. Iyengar was a student of the grandfather of modern yoga, Sri T Krishnamacharya.

Jamu Traditional Indonesian herbal medicine.

Janzu Warm water therapy similar to watsu; the body is manipulated to unblock physical, emotional and mental energy. Often seen as a rebirthing therapy, with the water representing the amniotic fluid of the womb.

Jnana yoga One of the four main paths of yoga, the path of self-knowledge or wisdom.

Kalari a specially built practice and worship area used for the Indian martial art kalarippayattu.

Kalarichikitsa Ancient Indian healing tradition combining ayurveda with marma therapy, which manipulates the energy points of the body to ease pain. Devised by Kalari warriors, who were healers as well as fighters.

Kalarippayattu Ancient martial art from Kerala in Southern India combining body movements with a strong spiritual focus.

Kapha Dosha made up of the elements earth and water.

Karma yoga One of the four main paths of yoga, the path of selfless action. In an ashram or on a retreat, it entails helping the community with practical tasks such as gardening and cleaning. The idea is that during the task you observe how your mind reacts.

Ki Japanese word for 'life force' or 'vital energy'. See Chi.

Kinesiology Scientific study of human movement and posture. Not to be confused with applied kinesiology, see above.

Kirtan Devotional chanting.

Kneipp therapy Founded by Bavarian priest Sebastian Kneipp in the 19th century, a hydrotherapy using herbal extracts in alternating hot and cold water treatments including wraps and baths.

Kripalu yoga Founded by Amrit Desai, kripalu yoga focuses on the potential for transformation and fulfilment through deep asana practices that emphasize inward focus, meditation and breathwork. Kripalu yoga teachers are trained at Kripalu in the USA.

Kriya From the Sanskrit for 'action' or 'deed', any technique or practice within a yoga discipline, often used to refer to yoga cleansing techniques such as jala neti (sinus irrigation) and kunjal (a system of stomach cleansing using salt and water).

Kriya Yoga A yoga with a strong spiritual element brought into public awareness by Indian yogi Paramahansa Yogananda through his book Autobiography of a Yogi.

Kundalini 'Kunda' is Sanskrit for 'to coil or spiral', and in tantra and yoga this is the energy or life force which lies like a coiled serpent at the base of our spine. It is seen as the link to a higher awareness which, once awakened, calms the mind and turns the body into a vehicle of bliss.

Kundalini yoga Devised in 1969 by Yogi Bhajan, a Sikh, this 'yoga of awareness' concentrates on releasing kundalini energy from the base of the spine. Working on opening up the chakras or energy centres of the body, it usually includes a series of fast repetitive movements as well as chanting, meditation, classical yoga postures and pranayama.

Laughter yoga See Hasyar yoga.

Life coaching Practice of working with people to determine and achieve personal goals. The coach will use various methods, tailored to the individual. Life coaching addresses every aspect of the their life; career, relationships, health, home and finances, as well as life purpose and the wider world.

Lingam From the Sanskrit for 'mark' or 'sign', used as a symbol for the worship of the Hindu god Shiva.

Live blood analysis Diagnostic test used by some health care practitioners to determine a course of treatment. A drop of blood is taken from the patient's fingertip and viewed through a microscope to ascertain their current state of health.

Lomi lomi See Hawaiian temple bodywork.

Macrobiotics From the Greek 'macro' (large, long) and 'bios' (life), an alternative health practice which connects diet and health to balance lifestyle. Macrobiotic diets focus on the energetic properties of food to create balance inside the body, and consider individual needs, the climate and environment lived in, and seasons of the year.

Mahayana Buddhism One of the major branches of Buddhism, meaning the 'great vehicle', practised in Tibet, China, Japan and elsewhere in northeast Asia. Building on the foundation of the Four Noble Truths, followers of the Mahayana focus on 'bodhicitta'; the intention to strive for an awakened mind for the benefit of all sentient beings. A continuation of the Mahayana, the Vajrayana (indestructible vehicle) emphasizes direct access to the nature of our mind, the state of enlightenment. Vajrayana Buddhism is mainly practised in Tibet.

Mandala From the Sanskrit for 'circle' or 'completion'; intricate geometric circular patterns of bright colours that represent the universe and its powers used in Dharmic religions such as Buddhism and Hinduism, especially for meditation.

Mantra From the Sanskrit 'man' (to think) and 'tra' (to protect from the world); powerful words chosen for their spiritual element which when reproduced clearly as sound or vibration clear the mind for meditation.

Marma massage Massage applying pressure to marma points to release physical and emotional blocks.

Marma points The hidden points on the body containing life force or vital energy. For the mind and body to be well, these need to be in balance.

Meditation In Buddhist and yogic philosophy, the practice of concentration (on the breath, a mantra, a mandala, a question or a visual symbol) and of enquiry (into the nature of ourselves and all things) to calm the mind, relax the body and achieve awareness of the inner self, and ultimately of the true nature of existence.

Meridian In the Chinese system of health, the channels in the body through which chi flows.

Metabolic typing Process to determine what foods are best for your body based on the concept of everyone having a unique metabolism; how well our bodies absorb nutrients from different foods depends on how quickly our bodies oxidize food and how the nervous and other systems react. Diet appropriate to one type could be detrimental to others.

Method Putkisto Exercise method to strengthen and lengthen the muscles and realign the body, developed by Marja Putkisto.

Metta In Buddhism, unconditional and unattached loving kindness. Buddhists believe that those who cultivate metta in their lives will develop compassion for themselves and others.

Mouna Buddhist concept meaning 'measurement', specifically the measurement of words. Practising mouna means not speaking unnecessary words, a process which eventually leads to more meaningful and powerful speech. Also see Noble Silence.

Mudra Ritual hand or body gestures.

Mysore-style yoga See Self practice.

Nadis Channels in the body through which the vital force, or prana, flows. There are 72,000 nadis in the astral body, which correspond to the nerves in the physical body.

Naturopathy Holistic approach to health that believes in the body's ability to heal itself. A naturopath will hand-pick a range of treatments tailored to a person's needs, from osteopathy and acupuncture to traditional Chinese medicine and nutritional advice.

Nia (neuromuscular integrative action) Aerobic exercise created in 1983 by Debbie and Carlos Rosas, Nia is a unique blend of nine movement forms: three dance arts (Isadora Duncan, jazz and modern), three martial arts (tai chi, tae kwon do and aikido) and three healing arts (yoga, feldenkrais method and Alexander technique).

NLP (neurolinguistic programming) Range of personal development techniques set up in the New Age era of the 1970s in California. NLP explores how a person's negative thought processes, often unconscious, may be preventing them achieving what they want in life. The therapist or coach listens to the client's language patterns and works with them to show how this can reveal self-limiting beliefs. The client can then understand they have the power to change and can 'reprogramme' their

brain and create more useful thought patterns.

Noble Eightfold Path The fourth of the Buddha's Four Noble Truths. In the Buddhist tradition these are practical ways of being that lead to the end of suffering and consist of eight elements: wisdom, right view, right intention, ethical conduct, right speech, right action, right livelihood, mental development, right effort, right mindfulness and right concentration.

Noble Silence Silence of body, speech and mind. A part of the daily schedule on most Buddhist retreats is given over to Noble Silence. See Mouna.

Om Sacrad symbol for absolute consciousness. It is referred to in the ancient scriptures, the Mandukya Upanishad, as "what was, what is and what shall be". It is a mantra, often chanted at the beginning or end of a yoga practice .

Osteopathy Established system of medicine involving manual treatment of the musculo-skeletal system. Osteopaths use their hands for a variety of gentle treatments including soft tissue massage, joint mobilization and thrust techniques. Particularly effective for back pain and postural problems.

Oxygen therapy Treatment where medical grade oxygen is given to provide relief from fatigue and to oxygenate the blood.

Panchakarma Ayurvedic detox.

pH Measure of the acidity or alkalinity of a solution. Before cleansing fasts the pH balance of your saliva or urine is tested to determine the present state of health, as it is believed that alkalizing the blood leads to healing.

Pilates Whole body conditioning system developed in the early 20th century by German boxer and self-defence teacher Joseph Pilates. Its emphasis is on building strength from the inside out by teaching awareness of correct breathing and body alignment, using the core muscles of the abdomen, lower back and buttocks as a 'power centre'. It can be taught as mat-work exercise or by using specially designed equipment.

Pitta One of the three doshas, made up of the fire element.

Power yoga More energetic and dynamic form of ashtanga vinyasa yoga asanas.

Prana From the Sanskrit for 'breath', this is the vital energy or life force in living beings. Known as chi in Chinese and ki in Japanese.

Pranayama Yogic breathwork using a range of breathing exercises to learn control ('yama' in Sanskrit) of the life force ('prana').

Probiotics Dietary supplements said to contain potentially beneficial 'friendly bacteria', often administered during cleansing fasts.

Puja Daily Hindu religious ritual.

Qi See Chi.

Qigong Also spelt chi kung, a Chinese exercise regime using breathing and movement to develop a strong chi. At its core is the art of wu wei: letting go of habitual striving through simple movements and standing postures.

Raja yoga One of the four main paths of yoga, the yoga of physical and mental control. Set out by Patanjali in his Yoga Sutras, it's the yoga that most people in the West intend to practise when they take up yoga, though many Western yoga classes purely focus on bodily control.

Raw food diet Uncooked, unprocessed and usually organic food. Proponents claim that by eating a diet of 80% raw and 20% steamed or flash fried food, the live enzymes that aid digestion are not lost, so boosting the immune system and raising energy levels.

Reflexology Use of fingertip pressure on the reflex zones of the feet, to ease pain and discomfort, relax the body and improve energy flow. The theory is that these reflex zones correspond to particular areas of the body, and the manipulation of the feet will bring corresponding relief to the relevant area or organ.

Regression therapy Hypnotherapy going back into a person's past in order to find reasons for behaviour patterns and help the person heal.

Reiki From the Japanese 'rei' (universal) and 'ki' (life force), a healing practice developed by Japanese Christian theologian Mikao Usui from ancient Tibetan teachings. The therapist places their hands over or on the body for a few minutes in 12 basic positions to open up the chakras and balance the body physically, mentally and emotionally. Reiki is passed from teacher to student by particular initiation rites; reiki masters follow a spiritual way of life as well as treat people.

Rinpoche Or Rimpoche, Tibetan word meaning 'the precious one', this is a Tibetan Buddhist honorific title used for incarnate lamas. It is also used as a term of respect for teachers and gurus.

Rolfing Named after Dr Ida Rolf (1896-1979), a biochemist who developed this system of soft tissue manipulation she called Structural Integration. In a course of treatments, the therapist works on the fascia (connective tissue) to improve posture by helping the body to relax in natural positions rather than fight gravity, so easing pain and stress, and improving everyday movement and activity.

Sangha From the Sanskrit for an assembly, used to refer to a group of ordained Buddhist monks responsible for maintaining and spreading the teachings of the Buddha.

Satsang Sanskrit for 'true company', a spiritual gathering where you chant, meditate and listen to a reading or a talk on an essential aspect of yogic philosophy.

Satvik energy therapy Form of healing that works on the electromagnetic field that surrounds the body. By facilitating the flow of this energy, it aims to boost physical, emotional and spiritual health.

Satyananda yoga Style of yoga devised by Paramahamsa Satyananda and taught at the Bihar School of Yoga in India, it combines an effective set of uncomplicated, stretching and meditative movements to exercise every joint and muscle in a methodical way, with practices such as yoga nidra, kirtan, mouna and karma yoga.

Scaravelli yoga Based on the style of yoga developed by Vanda Scaravelli (1908-1999), who was a student of BKS Iyengar and TKV Desikachar, and who emphasized the importance of the spine, the natural gravity of the body and awareness of the breath.

Self practice The way yoga was originally passed on from teacher to student, on a one-to-one basis, with the student working on the practice given by the teacher until they were ready for the next stage. Today it is used at the Ashtanga Yoga Research Institute in Mysore, India and in group ashtanga classes around the globe, with students working at their own pace and level within a class, and the teacher offering individual help when needed.

Seva Selfless service, especially in Sikhism, also in Hinduism. It specifically means serving others, where Karma Yoga is selfless service which is also done for your own spiritual growth.

Shadow yoga Energetic practice combining hatha, aspects of ayurveda and martial arts, designed by Shandor Remete to prepare Western students for the more difficult asanas.

Shala Sanskrit word meaning 'school'; refers to a room, pavilion or centre for yoga practice.

Shaman The mediator or interpreter for the 'universal field of consciousness' or spirit world of which, shamanism understands, we are all a part. It is often said that the shaman walks with one foot in the everyday world and one foot in the spirit world.

Shamanic healing Practices performed by a shaman or practitioner to help or heal another person. Methods, tools, symbology and medicines will vary across cultures, but primarily the healing is a three-way connection between the client, shaman and the universe or spirit.

Shamanism Ancient spiritual path based on the knowledge of a 'universal field of consciousness' or spirit world through which humans are connected with each other, the earth and all things. Shamanism aims to diagnose and cure human suffering by accessing and controlling the 'spirits' or fundamental energies through a series of practices such as the shamanic journey, the trance-dance, the vision quest and the purifying ceremony of the sweat lodge. Practitioners understand that all of us come from shamanistic cultures if we look back far enough in time. Similar to animism, which believes

everything to have soul or spirit.

Shiatsu Means 'finger pressure' in Japanese. Similar to acupressure, this is a massage technique that applies pressure to the various acupoints to improve the flow of chi and relax the body, and is good for treating musculoskeletal problems.

Shirodara Ayurvedic treatment where a continuous stream of warmed herbal oil is poured across the forehead for about 25 minutes. Calming and relaxing, it is often used to treat insomnia.

Sitting meditation Meditating in a sitting position, ideally with the knees below the hips by sitting cross-legged, raised on a cushion or a small meditation stool, or seated on a chair.

Sivananda yoga Style of yoga devised by Indian Swami Sivananda and brought to the West in 1957 by his disciple Swami Vishnu-devananda, promoting five easy to understand principles for healthy living, based on the balance achieved by combining the four main yogas, karma, bhakti, raja and jnana, with proper relaxation, exercise, breathing and diet, and positive thinking and meditation. The asana practice is based on 12 postures performed in a specific order with breathing and relaxation between each posture. Sivananda yoga teachers can qualify after just one month's training, though most who take this course are extremely devoted to their practice and to living a yogic life.

Somatic movement Healing exercise based on the link between our physical movement and nervous system. Becoming conscious of how we move and being able to express inner feelings through movement and dance is all part of the Somatic process.

Sophrology From the Greek 'sos' (harmony, serenity), 'phren' (consciousness) and 'logos' (science, study), meaning the study of the harmony of the human consciousness, created by Dr Alfonso Caycedo in the 1960s. It is a technique of simple, easy to learn exercises based on relaxation and concentration, which teach you to become more aware of how your body and mind function in harmony.

Sports massage Deep tissue massage aimed at the muscles used in physical activity, to prevent injury, enhance performance, restore muscle tone and relieve stress and muscle pain.

Sufi dance Whirling or spinning meditation practised by the dervishes in Turkey as a symbolic ritual to get rid of ego and desire and thus reach a higher state of being.

Swami Sanskrit word meaning 'owner of oneself'. It is used in Hindu as an honorary title meaning 'lord' or 'master' and denotes learning and knowledge of a particular religious or spiritual field.

Swedana Ayurvedic purifying steam and herbal baths.

Swedish massage Classic massage developed by Swedish fencing and gym teacher Pehr Henrik (1776-1839). Oils are applied to the body and the masseur uses long, flowing strokes to increase circulation, and relieve stress, muscle tension and pain.

Tai chi chuan, or tai chi Ancient non-competitive Chinese martial art, which combines gentle, graceful movements with meditation.

Temazcal Mexican version of the sweat lodge, practised by the indigenous people for hundreds of years.

Tantra Ancient tradition based on the original purity of the nature of mind, whose fruit is the realization of that nature. Tantra recognizes that everything in the universe is a concrete manifestation of the divine energy that creates and maintains the universe.

Taoism Also spelt daoism, a Chinese philosophical and religious tradition based on the sixth-century writings of Laoze, advocating humility in life and believing that harmony exists between the individual and the natural world, and within all natural things. Taoists founded the science of acupuncture, and described in detail the idea of chi and the meridians. Also see yin and yang.

Thai massage Traditional method from Thailand combining massage, acupressure and deep stretches.

Thalassotherapy Hydrotherapy treatments using mineral-rich seawater and seaweed, considered to have many therapeutic and curative purposes.

Theravada Buddhism From the Sanskrit meaning 'way of the elders', the form of Buddhism practised in Sri Lanka, Thailand and other parts of southern Asia. Its followers practise vipassana (or insight) meditation.

Tibetan Buddhism see Mahayana Buddhism.

Tibetan meditation Various methods that Tibetan Buddhists use to meditate, which include systematic reflection on death, reciting mantras, and visualizing mandalas.

Toxin Poison produced by a living micro-organism in the body which can cause diseases and disorders. Pesticides, hormones, antibiotics, artificial colourings, flavourings and preservatives in food produce toxins, as does indoor and outdoor pollution.

Traditional Chinese medicine (TCM) Ancient holistic system of care that treats the mind and body as a whole, based on the concept of chi or life force. Treatments include herbal medicines, exercises which combine the physical and mental such as tai chi and qigong and therapies such as acupuncture.

Trigger point therapy Stress relieving treatment similar to acupressure.

Tui na massage Also spelt tuina, an ancient style of Chinese massage that uses acupressure to stimulate the flow of chi and balance the body.

Ujjayi breathing A way of deep breathing in yoga using the back of the throat.

Vata One of the three doshas, made up of the space and air elements.

Vedanta Ancient Indian philosophy providing the bedrock of yoga. Vedanta bridges the gulf between the known universe and what Vedanta philosophers call the unknown reality, the consciousness which underlies the universe. Literally translated it means the culmination of knowledge: 'veda' means knowledge in Sanskrit, 'anta' means end.

Vedas Ancient Indian scriptures which form the main sacred texts in Hinduism. A section of the Vedas, the Upanishads, provides the main foundation of yoga teaching and the yogic philosophy, Vedanta.

Vedic chanting Chanting from the vedas.

Vinotherapie Term patented by wine-based skincare company Caudalie, in France, to mean skincare based on wine grape seeds.

Vinyasa Sanskrit meaning 'to place in a sequence', or 'flow'.

Vinyasa flow yoga Also known as vinyasa yoga, a dynamic, flowing style usually set to music to create a rhythmic sequence of postures linked with alignment, breath and deep intention. It follows the lineage of the grandfather of modern yoga, T Krishnamacharya, whose three students each added one thing: the idea of flow from Sri K Pattabhi Jois, the importance of alignment from Sri BKS Iyengar, and 'yoga of the heart' (otherwise known as vini yoga) from T Krishnamacharya's son, TKV Desikachar.

Vipassana meditation Also known as insight meditation (vipassana is the Pali word for insight), the style of meditation practised by Theravada Buddhists, it promotes staying in the present whatever arises, by sustained attention (to the breath) and mindfulness(of the self and others), which cultivates awareness, inner peace, kindness and compassion.

Vital ageing Literally, ageing with vitality; many high-profile destination spas have an on-site doctor who will analyse your diet and lifestyle to advise on how best to maximize your vitality well into old age.

Walking meditation Slow walking using the sensation of the feet on the ground to anchor your thoughts and slow the breath.

Watsu Shiatsu in water, developed by American Harold Dull, a kind of floating massage in warm water combining stretching with gentle acupressure massage to rebalance the body and mind.

Working meditation Meditating while carrying out everyday tasks. Ideal for people who do not think they have the time for sitting or walking meditation.

Yantra Symbolic representation of a sacred object, usually used as a meditation tool.

Yin and yang In Chinese Taoist philosophy, the primal opposing but complementary forces found in all natural things. Yin is dark, night, female, receptive; Yang is light, day, male, active.

Yin yoga Quiet and still but no less challenging form of yoga created by American yoga teacher Paul Grilley to balance the more 'yang' or muscular aspects of yoga in the West. Based on the Chinese system of the chi which flows through the meridians of the body, the postures stretch the body's deep connective tissue, particularly in the hips, pelvis and lower spine, and are held for about five minutes to increase flexibility, encourage physical and emotional release and prepare the body for sitting meditation.

Yoga The world's oldest system of personal development, which began in India over 5000 years ago.

Yoga diving Combination of classical yoga asanas and breathing with scuba diving. The yoga skills can help with the technique needed for diving, and participants discover that a physical experience such as a yoga posture or a dive can also become a spiritual experience.

Yogalates Founded by Louise Solomon, an exercise combining the flexibility and meditative elements of yoga with the muscle strengthening and toning of pilates.

Yoga nidra Practice of yogic sleep, or deep relaxation. A state between sleep and wakefulness, this psychic sleep is a powerful technique used to combat daily stress and tension, producing calm and mental clarity.

Zazen meditation Sitting meditation in Japan.

Zen meditation Zen Buddhism originated in China and spread to Japan and Korea. Zen Buddhists practise two kinds of meditation; in the Rinzai school, you sit and repeat to yourself a question, such as 'what is this?'. In the Soto school, you practice 'silent illumination', by sitting still and doing nothing but being (or attempting to be) present in the moment.

CAROLINE SYLGE

Lake Geneva, Switzerland.

Northern & Central Europe

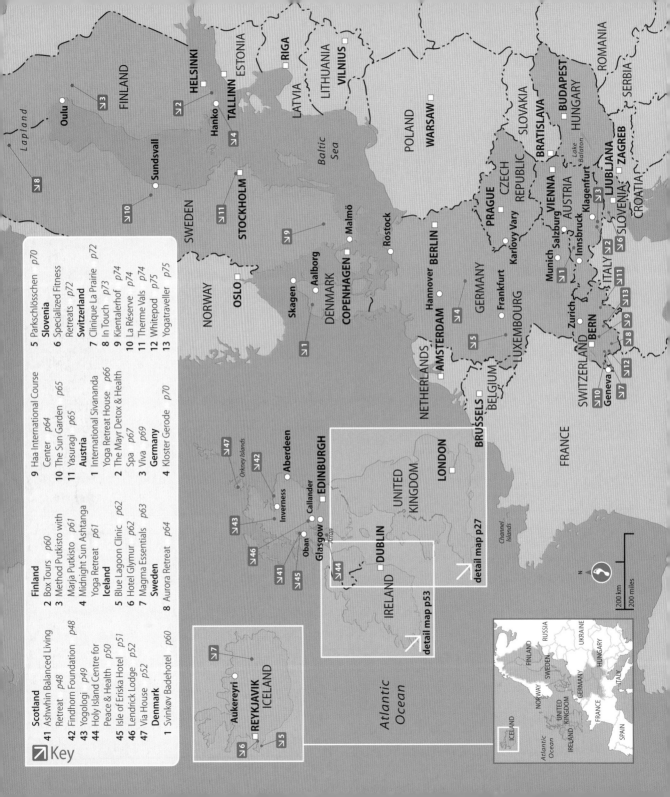

↗ Key

Scotland
41 Ashwhin Balanced Living Retreat *p48*
42 Findhom Foundation *p48*
43 Yogologi *p49*
44 Holy Island Centre for Peace & Health *p50*
45 Isle of Eriska Hotel *p51*
46 Lendrick Lodge *p52*
47 Via House *p52*
Denmark
1 Svinkøv Badehotel *p60*

Finland
2 Box Tours *p60*
3 Method Putkisto with Marja Putkisto *p61*
4 Midnight Sun Ashtanga Yoga Retreat *p61*
Iceland
5 Blue Lagoon Clinic *p62*
6 Hotel Glymur *p62*
7 Magma Essentials *p63*
Sweden
8 Aurora Retreat *p64*

9 Haa International Course Center *p64*
10 The Sun Garden *p65*
11 Yasuragi *p65*
Austria
1 International Sivananda Yoga Retreat House *p66*
2 The Mayr Detox & Health Spa *p67*
3 Viva *p69*
Germany
4 Kloster Gerode *p70*

5 Parkschlösschen *p70*
Slovenia
6 Specialized Fitness Retreats *p72*
Switzerland
7 Clinique La Prairie *p72*
8 In Touch *p73*
9 Kientalerhof *p74*
10 La Réserve *p74*
11 Therme Vals *p74*
12 Whitepod *p75*
13 Yogatraveller *p75*

Europe's colder climes are excellent for cosy retreating: take yourself off to an eco pod on a snowy Swiss hillside to reflect, do some head-clearing at a family-run retreat on Orkney in Scotland, or pitch up in Scandanavia, where you'll find a range of inspiring places to think and heal in some of the least polluted landscapes on the planet.

There are haven hotels for sophisticates who want to hole up with a friend or lover, or you can sample ayurveda without the cultural shock at an elegant art deco hotel in Germany. Those who relish a detox challenge can try it the Mayr way in Austria, while the more physically active should consider Specialized Fitness holidays in Slovenia, or go jogging along the English coast with The Running Inn. Yoga enthusiasts can do ashtanga vinyasa on a remote Finnish isle, sivananda in alpine Austria or have fun in Switzerland mixing skiing and snowboarding with yoga. For all round wellbeing, Yogoloji offers luxurious breaks on a remote Scottish wilderness reserve, while The Grange on the Isle of Wight recruits expert teachers for life-changing personal development and creative courses in a convivial atmosphere.

Alternatively, learn to meditate at one of many Buddhist sancturies. Especially inspirational is Dzogchen Beara, a Tibetan Buddhist centre on the Irish coast under the spiritual direction of Sogyal Rinpoche, author of *The Tibetan Book of Living and Dying*. Whoever you are, whatever your needs, you'll find something to help you recharge.

❝❞ *Today is the tomorrow you worried about yesterday, and all is well.*   Anon

Travel essentials

Britain

Getting there The easiest way to get to the UK from Europe is to fly. There are direct flights to London from all major European cities, and also to many provincial cities, including Birmingham, Manchester, Bristol, Glasgow and Edinburgh, as well as several smaller cities. The most carbon-efficient way, of course, is to take a ferry and train, though it's worth noting that mainland UK rail services are not up to the standards of continental Europe. From **North America**, there are direct flights to London from major cities. **Continental** flies non-stop from New York to Bristol and several charter airlines such as **Excel Airways** (www.xl.com) fly direct from Orlando to Newcastle.

Best time to visit Britain has a temperate, unpredictable climate. It is generally wetter in the west, the west coast of Scotland being the most notorious. July and August are the busiest months, so for a quieter time, travel in spring or autumn. The coldest months are usually January and February, with snowfalls most likely in the mountains in northern England, Wales and Scotland.

Ireland

Dublin, Belfast (for Donegal), Cork, Kerry, Knock and Shannon are served by many low-cost flights from London and regional airports in the UK. Travelling by sea from the UK, there are several ferry routes: Holyhead and Liverpool to Dublin, Fishguard and Pembroke to Rosslare, Swansea to Cork and Holyhead to Dun Laoghaire. **Aer Lingus** flies to Dublin and Shannon from New York, Boston, Baltimore, Chicago and Los Angeles. **Continental** and **Delta** also go to Shannon and Dublin. From Canada flights involve a stop in London. There are no direct flights from Australia or New Zealand.

Best time to visit Ireland has a similar climate to the west coast of Britain, though the west coast of Ireland is particualrly notorious for wet weather. Temperatures usually stay above 3°C in winter and it rarely snows.

Scandinavia

Getting there Numerous international carriers fly to Stockholm, including **Scandinavian Airlines** (www.sas.se) with non-stop flights to New York. For southern Sweden, **Ryanair** flies from the UK to Malmö. Alternatively, fly to Copenhagen in Denmark and continue overland by train or car. The Öresund bridge connects Copenhagen and Malmö, providing a link to mainland Europe's motorway network. From the UK, ferries sail from Newcastle to Gothenburg.

Helsinki airport is served by flights from major European cities. Non-stop flights operate from Boston and New York in the US. For travellers from Australia and New Zealand, there are flights to Helsinki via Bangkok and Hong Kong. Travelling by car from other European countries, take a Baltic Sea ferry from Stockholm and Kapellskär in Sweden and from Rostock in Germany. There are no direct ferries from the UK; travel via Sweden.

Many European carriers fly daily to Reykjavik. **Icelandair** flies direct from North America, out of Baltimore, Boston, Minneapolis, New York and Orlando. **Smyril Line** sails from Lerwick in Shetland to Iceland via the Faroe Islands (www.smyril-line.com), a journey of around 27 hours plus a 12-hour ferry from Aberdeen to Lerwick.

Best time to visit The warmest and sunniest months in **Sweden** are usually May to September. Except in the south, where temperatures are moderated by the ocean, much of the country is influenced by a continental climate, with great differences in temperature between summer and winter. Sweden's high-latitude location means that most of the country has long hours of daylight in summer and long hours of darkness in winter, more extreme the further north you travel. For round-the-clock daylight and midnight sun in Lapland, travel in the summer months. See the spectacular Northern Lights in mid-winter. Lapland's ski season runs from October to May. In **Finland** travellers can experience the midnight sun throughout the summer. In winter, the Northern Lights can be seen all over the country, although it's visible less frequently in the south. The southwest region has the country's mildest winters. Finnish winters are generally long and cold,

● Soul food

Get physical in the open air and help to build healthy and sustainable communities at the same time by joining **BTCV Green Gym** (T+44 (0)1302-572200, www.btcv.org/greengym), which offers opportunities across the UK for local gardening or practical environmental work. You go at your own pace, and get support and guidance from trained leaders – over 140,000 volunteers are placed annually in projects throughout the UK, and BTCV has bases in England, Wales, Scotland and Northern Ireland.

SIVANANDA YOGA RETREAT HOUSE

Sivananda Yoga Retreat in Austria, see page 66.

with most precipitation in winter falling as snow. In northern Finland, there is snow cover from October to April. In summer, this region often enjoys long hours of sunshine. **Iceland**'s climate is influenced by the Gulf Stream, so its climate is temperate with cool summers and mild winters. The weather is very changeable; autumn and winter are the wettest seasons. The busiest tourist season is summer, June to August, when travellers can see the midnight sun and experience 24-hour daylight in the north. In mid-winter, with only four hours of daylight, there's a good chance of seeing the Northern Lights.

Rest of Europe

Getting there   For the Austrian Tirol, fly to Innsbruck or Munich. From Dublin, **Ryanair** operates flights to Friedrichshafen in Germany, across the border from the Tirol. **Ryanair** flies from London Stansted to Salzburg and Graz, and to Klagenfurt in the southeast. Austria is well connected to European cities by rail. From the UK, take the Eurostar to Paris and then an overnight train to Vienna, or travel via Munich; see www.seat61.com. If travelling during the ski season, take the **Eurostar** to Brussels and then the overnight **Bergland Express** to Zell am See and Innsbruck (www.ttconline.nl). Geneva and Zurich airports are Switzerland's main international gateways, with numerous intercontinental flights including direct flights from New York and Los Angeles to Zurich. Travellers from Australia and New Zealand need to fly via Bangkok, Singapore and other Asian hubs. Switzerland is easily accessible by

66 99

It is never too late to become what you might have been.

George Eliot

daily rail services from many European cities; see www.seat61.com.

Best time to visit   Austria and **Switzerland** have a temperate climate, with variations according to terrain. Alpine regions are characterized by high precipitation and long winters. Due to extreme topographical differences – high peaks and deep valleys – weather conditions can be very localized. The busiest time is during the summer months of June, July and August. June and July are the best months to see Alpine wild flowers. Ski resorts are generally open from late November until April, although the highest peaks can have snowfalls all year round.

Eat me

While the cooler climes of these countries mean there are plenty of rich and calorie-laden dishes appearing on menus, there's also an abundance of light local dishes and some great produce to be enjoyed. Think local, eat seasonal and you'll automatically be fuelling your body in the way that mother nature intended.

In summer, Scotland produces some of the best soft berries you'll ever find thanks to its cool climate. Try the sweet strawberries and plump raspberries which are high in polyphenols (which research has shown may reduce the risk of cardiovascular disease and cancer), but also look out for cloudberries which are high in vitamin C and antioxidants. Eat them as they come or try them at breakfast with a bowl of organic muesli and yoghurt.

Make the most of the asparagus season between April and June. Asparagus encourages the growth of 'friendly' probiotic bacteria in the gut and is high in the B vitamin folate, making it especially good for expectant mothers. Try it in salads, mixed with other spring vegetables such as baby broad beans, or simply steamed or grilled with extra virgin olive oil.

Rhubarb's another detox-friendly ingredient as it's rich in vitamin C and dietary fibre so is great for stimulating the gut. Try it stewed, poached with other flavours such as elderberries, or whipped into a healthy yoghurt-based fool.

If you're following a dairy-free diet then seek out Wales' world-famous goats' cheese, milk and yoghurt – organic if you can. It's lower in lactose than cows' milk products, so can often be enjoyed by people who are mildly lactose intolerant.

In England, try bread made with spelt flour, which is enjoying a renaissance thanks to its health benefits. It has more protein, fat and fibre than wheat and contains mucopolysaccharides that help stimulate the immune system. In Austria, Germany and Switzerland try dark rye and pumpernickel breads which contain B vitamins, vitamin E, fibre and a wide range of minerals.

In Switzerland you should breakfast on Bircher muesli - the oats that form the bulk of this dish are soaked overnight in apple juice or milk then served with natural yoghurt, fruit or honey. Oats contain essential fatty acids, are high in fibre and are a great source of vitamins E, B1 and B2.

Britain

From the Scottish islands to England's southwest, you can cosy up in the countryside or explore yourself in a safe environment.

Fact file

- ➲ **Visa:** None required for citizens of EU countries, the US, Canada, Australia and New Zealand
- ❶ **IDD:** +44
- ❺ **Currency:** UK pound sterling (£)
- ❷ **Time zone:** GMT
- ❹ **Electricity:** 230v
- ❶ **Tourist board:** www.visitbritain.com

England

Arimathean Retreat

🌐 🍴 ⭕ 🔥 ⊙ ✵ ⚲ ⌖1

Glastonbury, Somerset
T +44 (0)1458-830230
www.arimatheanretreat.com
From £65 per person per night

A 15th-century family home in the hippy, happening town of Glastonbury, Arimathean Retreat is run by Lisehanne Webster, a supportive, down-to-earth and inspiring teacher with over 30 years' experience in yoga therapy and counselling. Open to everyone, the retreat offers healing, counselling, personal and spiritual development courses and detoxing as well as yoga.

On retreats you'll practise yoga and meditation each morning and relaxation techniques in the evenings. Therapy allows the individual to find their own answers through gentle coaching, regression and breathwork. Groups are small and sessions can be taken privately. Lisehanne teaches satyamvidya yoga, which she devised in 1987, based on what she terms 'The five layers of consciousness': body, breath, mind-emotions, soul and spirit. The method combines asanas for self-realization with meditation. You can also take courses with Lisehanne to become a yoga therapist,

❝ ❞

I like Lisehanne because she is so real and so grounded, as well as being wise and spiritual. I always feel happy and calm as soon as I enter her house, and I know that I will be amongst people who genuinely care about others and the world we live in, which is very nourishing, as you can sometimes feel isolated from your spiritual side when you are heading into the office everyday, quietly burning out.
Maria Grima

psycho-spiritual counsellor or healer.

The Georgian cottage is warm and welcoming. Incense burns in the doorway and there are fresh flowers in most rooms. Sessions take place in the group room, where the fireplace is adorned with crystals, candles, plants and a singing bowl to emphasize positive energy. Outside, there's a pretty walled garden and you can eat or study on the patio surrounded by baskets of flowers. Inside, a large inglenook fireplace is homely and guests gravitate to the kitchen to chat over tea and chocolate brownies.

Bedrooms have attractive wooden shutters and come with a meditation journal. You are invited to use candles, aroma burners, books and relaxing music. Choose a room overlooking the garden if you can; front rooms overlook the busy High Street. Bedrooms share a bathroom and shower.

Food is mostly organic, fish or vegetarian meals. Alcohol is not appropriate here, but you can smoke at the end of the garden. Mobile telephones must be confined to bedrooms. Beauty treatments can be arranged at the nearby Bluebird Sanctuary, and you can walk to Glastonbury Tor, or join Lisehanne on her daily dog walk. Glastonbury is renowned for its New Age crowd and has fantastic bookshops, cafés and a host of other alternative workshops on offer.

The retreat attracts men and women. A two-night minimum stay is required, three-week maximum. Weekend workshop retreats start from £275 including breakfast and supper. The nearest train station is Castle Cary (15 miles), which is on the main London–Plymouth line.

ARIMATHEAN RETREAT

Offshore treats

Enjoying stunning views of the hills and countryside, **Brightlife**, on the Isle of Man (T+44 (0)1624-880318, www.brightlife.com), offers an impressive range of personal development courses in a tranquil, well-run environment with luxurious bedrooms and delicious food. You'll find courses on offer to suit all tastes and temperaments, from drumming, pilates, yoga and chakra healing to nature walks, life coaching, past-life regression and animal communication. Daniel Stone of The Centre of the Conscious Dream in Mexico runs courses here (see page 351). There are just 12 bedrooms, eight of them en suite. Food, sourced locally and organic where available, is creative and delicious. Vegetarian and special diets are catered for, and alcohol is served. Retreats cost from £300 per weekend including flights from mainland UK.

On the edge of St Helier, capital of Jersey, is the **Hotel de France** (T+44 (0)1534-614172, www.defrance.co.uk), the first hotel with a spa in the UK or Channel Islands to dedicate itself to ayurveda. In early 2007 the hotel's 17,000-sq foot Ayush Wellness Spa started to offer residential ayurveda retreats of between two and 21 days. The two-day package is simply a taster, and the spa aims to be an education centre for this ancient Indian art. Ayurveda practitioner, Dr Prasanna Kerur, is just 33 but has 11 years experience and trained at Rajiv Gandhi University of Health Sciences near Bangalore, India. Two other Indian therapists work with him, together with Western therapists trained by Dr Kerur. A seven-day package costs £1142 per person, or 21 days cost £95 per night, with daily treatments extra. The Hotel de France is a short taxi ride from Jersey's port or airport.

Northern & Central Europe England

Key

1 Arimathean Retreat *p26*
2 AyurvedicYogi *p28*
3 Babington House *p28*
4 Beyond Retreats *p29*
5 Careys Manor Hotel & Spa *p30*
6 Cedar Falls Health Spa *p30*
7 Charlton House & Monty's Spa *p30*
8 Duncton Mill *p31*
9 Eagle's Wing Centre for Contemporary Shamanism *p31*
10 EarthSpirit *p32*
11 Florence House *p32*
12 The Grange *p33*
13 Gaia House *p34*
14 Grayshott *p34*
15 High Green Arts *p35*
16 Journeying *p35*
17 Martins Retreat *p36*
18 Middle Piccadilly *p37*
19 Monkton Wyld Court *p37*
20 The Orange Tree *p38*
21 Pennyhill Park *p38*
22 Qigong Southwest *p39*
23 Ragdale Hall Health Hydro *p39*
24 Relaxing The Mind *p40*
25 Revitalise Tai Chi *p40*
26 The Running Inn *p40*
27 Ruth White Yoga *p42*
28 Saol Retreats *p42*
29 Titanic Spa *p42*
30 Tregoddick Farm *p43*
31 The Vale Healing Centre *p43*
32 WildWise *p44*
33 Cae Mabon *p45*
34 Gaia Cooperative *p45*
35 Pen Pynfarch *p45*
36 Snowdon Lodge *p46*
37 Snowdonia Retreat *p46*
38 Vajraloka Buddhist Meditation Centre *p46*
39 West Usk Lighthouse *p47*
40 White Horses Retreat *p47*

YOGA & ACTIVITY HOLIDAY

AyurvedicYogi

Somerset and Dorset
T+44 (0)7753-678582
www.ayurvedicyogi.com
From £250 per person for a weekend

A young company founded by sivananda yoga teacher and ayurvedic therapist, Jo Johnston, AyurvedicYogi offers ayurveda and yoga weekends at private homes in Somerset and Dorset. Held every three months throughout the year, their focus is practical yoga and ayurvedic dietary and lifestyle advice to help you get back in balance within yourself and with the world.

Daily yoga sessions include pranayama, the 12 basic sivananda asanas and their variations, as well as relaxation and chanting. Ayurvedic or Indian head massages are given by Bristol-based practitioners. The weekends are aimed at anyone wanting a break from busy lives, and beginners to advanced yogis are catered for. Food is organic, vegetarian and as local as possible. The maximum group size is 10.

The price includes two nights in a shared room, four 90-minute yoga classes, advice on ayurvedic cooking for your body type and ayurvedic theory workshops. They also runs Snow Yogi trips to France, see page 95.

HOTEL & SPA

Babington House

Near Frome, Somerset
T+44 (0)1373-812266
www.babingtonhouse.co.uk
From £225 per room per night

There are country house hotels with spas all over the UK, some better than others, and only a few offering true respite for body-and-soul-weary weekenders or those with time out during the week. Babington House is an unusual contemporary haven set back along a long private lane where

freedom is key – you can eat where you want and when you want, hole up in your room the whole time, or have tea and cake (or something stronger) rubbing shoulders with film stars and media types in the spacious, wooden-floored, well-lit bar.

The Cowshed spa is unpretentious and boasts some good therapists – the facials, massages, wraps, scrubs and reflexology treatments use its own very delicious range of products. Go for the 'Pampered Cow', 'Pummelled Cow', 'Complete Cow' or 'Holy Cow', depending on your mood, though we recommend the 'Stoned Cow', a Native North American full body massage using smooth hot and cold volcanic stones. Treatments are in individual log cabins, which you have to go outside to reach, but there are huge umbrellas in case of rain, and tasting the English country

BABINGTON HOUSE

air en route is all part of the therapy. Aroma, steam and sauna pods, an indoor pool, and an outdoor pool for invigorating morning dips complete the picture.

Pilates, yoga and salsa classes run during the week for Cowshed members, and guests can join. Simon Low-trained, UK-based yoga teacher **Jane Kersel** (T+44 (0)20-7221 3272, www.homepractice.co.uk), who fuses iyengar and yin yoga into her teaching, runs midweek yoga retreats here in the spring and autumn.

The Grade II listed Georgian house has a lake and pretty church in its grounds, and the interiors are retro chic – think anglepoise lamps the size of small trees, giant handmade walnut and yew beds and 1960s hanging chairs. Rooms have decent white linens, huge baths, powerful walk-in showers and plenty of space. In the summer go for Room 6, which has a bath on its balcony.

It's a two-hour drive from London, where you'll find its sister day spa (see page 29), and 15 minutes from Frome train station.

Left: Babington House, in Somerset, is the height of rural chic. **Below:** Expect walks through lovely countryside on County Durham's Beyond Retreats weekends.

BEYOND RETREATS

London healthy stopovers

For privacy and pampering 10 minutes from central London, **K West Hotel & Spa** (T+44 (0)8700-274343, www.k-west.co.uk) is a stylish option. Its sumptuous treatments include ayurvedic massages and dry flotation. For affordable quiet, **The Coach House** (T+44 (0)20-8772 1939, www.coachhouse.chslondon. com), in Balham, serves organic suppers and is 15 minutes from a day spa. Elegance and romance comes at a price at the Mandarin Oriental (T+44 (0)20-7235 2000 www.mandarinoriental.com/london) whose spa offers expert holistic and beauty treatments in tranquil surroundings.

For Heathrow stopovers, try **Park Inn** (T+44 (0)20-8759 6611, www.parkinn.com), whose ugly exterior belies the contemporary rooms inside. Its Pulse Café offers healthy fusion dishes and there's a reasonable swimming pool, sauna and gym. While at Heathrow, visit members' club **Rejuve** (T+44 (0)845-222 2644, www.rejuve.info), Terminal 1 departures, which has great treatments for pre and post flying (£25/day).

Alternatively, **The Grove** (T+44 (0)1923-807807, www.thegrove.co.uk) is just 30 minutes from Heathrow. Enjoy its 'Jet Lag Recovery Ritual' and the eco-friendly saltwater swimming pool at the Sequoia Spa, or give up the treadmill for tree trunks with the Green Gym, where personal trainers will help you work out in the estate's 120 ha of park and woodland. Stay in the main house for character.

In London itself, Babington House's sister **The Cowshed** on Portland Road (T+44 (0)20-7078 1944, www.cowshedclarendoncross.com) is urban-trendy, uses home grown herbs and serves champagne, or try **Calmia** on Marylebone High Street (T+44 (0)845-009 2450, www.calmia.com). For Indian wellbeing, try herb oil massages, yoga and holistic treatments at **Shymala Ayurveda** (T+44 (0)20-7348 0018 www.shymalaayurveda.com) on Holland Park Avenue. The **Organic Pharmacy** on Kings Road (T+44 (0)20-7351 2232, www.theorganicpharmacy.com) sells homeopathic remedies, natural skin products and supplements that are free of parabens and other nasties.

For drop-in classes, **Triyoga** (T+44 (0)20-7483 3344, www.triyoga.co.uk) offers yoga and pilates classes from fully equipped studios in Primrose Hill, Covent Garden and Soho, and there's a good selection of professional therapies, yoga and pilates at **The Life Centre** on Edge Street (T+44 (0)20-7221 4602, www.thelifecentre.com). Find meditation drop-in sessions at the **London Buddhist Centre** on Roman Road (T+44 (0)845-4584716, www.lbc.org.uk).

You won't find it hard to eat healthily across the metropolis but, if you'd rather stay in, UK-based organic food company **My Little Earth** (T+44 (0)7834-988522, www.mylittleearth. co.uk) offer a 'jet setter' service and can deliver delicious raw and cooked foods specially designed to combat the effects of jet lag (from £50 per day).

Northern & Central Europe England

YOGA & ACTIVITY HOLIDAY

Beyond Retreats

Teesdale, County Durham
T+44 (0)20-7226 4044
www.beyondretreats.co.uk
From £575 per weekend

Beyond Retreats specializes in luxurious holidays, combining yoga with walking, climbing, skiing, cooking and nutrition, and bringing workshops to groups or families. It runs a regular Beyond Yoga & Walking retreat to Durham. Locations vary but include comfortable Middleton House, a Georgian mansion set in 80 ha of parkland with a tennis court and outside hot tub.

Expect easy walks, pre-dinner drinks and canapés, wine and meat served at dinner, for which guests usually dress up. Co-founder, Jacqui Sread, nurtures and pampers participants; Anni Fast's massages are excellent; food is sumptuous and perfectly cooked by chef Sera Irvine – vegetarian options are available. Beyond uses local markets and consults a nutritionist. Long food gaps are bridged by late-afternoon tea and freshly baked cakes.

Yoga teachers include iyengar specialist, Gerry Ross, who expertly provides for less flexible and advanced participants at the same time. There's 3½ hours of yoga per day, in two sessions. Walks are easy and chatty strolls of an hour or more, mostly on level ground, some with stunning views.

Participants are in their thirties to fifties, English and US middle-class professionals. Beyond breaks would suit those who can't face a strict retreat, are into sports, and, for bespoke retreats, birthday celebrants with rich friends. Beyond also runs a yoga and nutrition weekend in Durham with renowned nutritionist, Dr John Briffa, and yoga teacher Chris Swain, as well as similar trips to Italy (see page 123).

66 99

This is more a weekend for sybarites than an austere yogic retreat. I was the only vegetarian out of eight yoga retreat guests, and the wine flowed. If Sufis mix wine and spiritual practice, though, it's a good-enough mix for me. I realised Beyond has it right: westerners want to have it all, and preferably at once.
Lawrence Pettener

Careys Manor Hotel & Spa

Brockenhurst, New Forest, Hampshire
T+44 (0)1590-623551
www.careysmanor.co.uk
From £178 per room per night

Carey's Manor is in a pretty New Forest village and boasts the SensSpa, whose director, Lina Lotto, has used her experience of spa retreats in Australia and the Far East to offer a fusion of Eastern and Western philosophies, and is helped by 16 Thai therapists personally chosen and trained by her. Their calm and tranquillity envelops the whole place.

Come here for a few days respite – the hotel offers, one-, two- and three-night spa packages. Bedrooms and suites have been individually designed, and quiet public spaces and landscaped gardens complement the spa, which is connected to the 80-room hotel by a covered walkway. The signature treatment is Thai massage, carried out expertly by the therapists. Other body and beauty treatments use organic aloe vera with honey, ground lemongrass and brown rice, manuka oils and echinacea for their healing properties.

Facilities include a state-of-the-art

CEDAR FALLS

hydrotherapy pool, a crystal steam room, an ice room, herbal sauna, and two relaxation areas plus a laconicum and a tepidarium. A Thai chef (who used to work at Chiva Som, see page 273) is on hand to serve delicious spa lunches using local organic produce in the Zen Garden Restaurant, and the smoothie menu runs to two pages. Take mind and body classes in the Thai Temple Studio, or try Body Balance, a mixture of yoga, tai chi and pilates.

The New Forest offers excellent walking and cycling, or sailing from any of the nearby coastal villages. Nearest airport is Southampton, approximately half an hour's drive (transfers can be arranged). Rail and bus connections to Brockenhurst are frequent.

HEALTH & FITNESS RETREAT

Cedar Falls Health Spa

Bishops Lydeard, Taunton, Somerset
T+44 (0)1823-433233
www.cedarfalls.co.uk
From £125 per person per night

An 18th-century country house in 18 ha of mature landscaped grounds is the setting for this elegant but unpretentious health spa. The original interior – where the Boles family once entertained the likes of Winston Churchill at their famously lavish dinner parties – has been lovingly restored to accommodate 32 en suite bedrooms. Public rooms boast superb carved panelling and welcoming open fireplaces. The 'no children' policy helps to keep the atmosphere serene.

Facilities include 25 treatment rooms, indoor and outdoor pools, sauna and steam room, gym with class fitness timetable and personal training, tennis and badminton courts, croquet lawn, French boules and a nine-hole golf course. For walkers and wildlife enthusiasts, the Quantock Hills, coastal walks and Exmoor National Park are within easy driving distance. Cedar Falls does make an effort to appeal to male visitors, with a dedicated treatment menu, so although the majority of guests are women, it's a good couples' getaway too.

The budget rooms, though comfortable, are small, and soundproofing is imperfect, so consider upgrading for guaranteed peace and quiet. The day spa packages are good value (from £79 per person) – but take your own bathrobe to save a £4.50 hire charge!

Treatments run the gamut from reiki to sports massage, with a wide range of holistic options including meditation, hypnotherapy and one-to-one counselling – the reflexology treatment was particularly impressive. Cedar Falls' beauty therapists use Clarins, Elemis, Moor and Phytomer products, and alongside the expected range of body and face treatments, there is the 'aqua-jet' massage, cellulite-busting wraps and a dry flotation tank.

The restaurant uses local, seasonal products and willingly caters for special diets and healthy eating plans, although nothing is off limits so you can indulge yourself if you want. Informal after-dinner talks and demonstrations on health and wellbeing topics – from natural skincare to stress management – are an unusual and welcome extra. It's a three- to four-hour drive from London, and the nearest train station is Taunton.

HOTEL & SPA

Charlton House & Monty's Spa

Shepton Mallet, Somerset
T+44 (0)1749-342008
www.charltonhouse.com
From £180 per room per night

An ancient manor house converted by Roger and Monty Saul, the creators of Mulberry, Charlton House is a sassy hotel with pretty gardens, an intimate spa and just 25 rooms. Some are funky and split level with secret patio gardens and cinema screens, others have more of an elegant 1920s feel.

The Sauls live at nearby Sharpham Park, a 1000-year-old deer park which supplies organic meat to Charlton, as well as spelt germ; you can have a massage with spelt germ oil, a scrub with the chaff of the spelt, or enjoy delicious spelt bread and muesli at the

CHARLTON HOUSE

Bottom left: Relaxation at Cedar Falls. **Above**: The elegant Charlton House and Monty's Spa.

hotel. A midweek wheat-free pampering break includes a two-hour 'Ultimate Spelt Therapy' of your choice, a wheat-free afternoon tea and three-course dinner (from £590 per double room).

Also on offer midweek is a bespoke Free 2 Be package for jaded souls. With at least three weeks' notice, the hotel can put together a package of treatments: therapies include shiatsu, tui na, life coaching, hypnotherapy, naturopathy, counselling and acupuncture. If you want to be active, boxercise and aqua tone classes run midweek, or you can have personal training sessions in the small gym. Alternatively, join the weekenders and indulge in organic food and wine and the boudoir-style Monty's Spa: there's a crystal steam room, sauna and hydrotherapy pool, decent treatments, and a Moroccan-Indian café serving yummy spa cuisine.

RURAL RETREAT
Duncton Mill

Petworth, Sussex
T+44 (0)1798 342281
www.dunctonmill.co.uk
From £85 per person per night

There's a wide range of courses to be explored at this idyllic South Downs retreat centre, owned and run by craniosacral therapist Mike Boxhall and family. An hour's train journey from London Victoria and 10-minute taxi ride takes you to another world, where you can see the stars and hear yourself think. An old trout pond, now home to koi carp, lends a particular tranquillity to the extensive grounds, while a heated outdoor swimming pool and grassy yoga and tai chi areas help visitors make the most of the fresh air.

On any given week or weekend you might find yoga, personal development, dance or Boxhall's own courses for bodywork professionals. The owners are very hands-on and you can rely on a high standard whatever course you choose. The 18th-century farmhouse and outbuildings have been sympathetically converted into two workshop spaces and accommodation for 20. If group activities aren't your thing, three self-contained cottages are let separately on a self-catering basis when no course is running. Privacy comes at a premium on busier courses as there are only two single rooms. Food is vegetarian with an international flavour, taking in Thai, Middle Eastern, South American and Italian influences. Some courses feature vegan and raw food; check with the course leader for details. Menus are imaginatively planned and lovingly prepared, with lots of local seasonal produce.

SPIRITUAL RETREAT
Eagle's Wing Centre for Contemporary Shamanism

Various locations in the UK
T+44 (0)1435-810233
www.shamanism.co.uk
Weekend retreats from £140 per person

Founded in 1985 by leading shamanic practitioner, Leo Rutherford, the Eagle's Wing Centre brings the ancient practices of shamanism into a modern context. Their workshops and retreats offer paths into the traditional rituals and ceremonies, revealing ways to reconnect with the natural world and yourself, and live more freely, spiritually and healthily.

Eagle's Wing introductory weekends provide a solid starting point for those wishing to learn about these powerful methods of self-discovery, which can be very intense and emotionally disturbing if you don't understand them. Additional workshops offer the space and guidance to delve deeper. The groups gather in locations around the UK, such as Gaunts House and Monkton Wyld (see page 37), as well as further afield in the Amazon rainforest of Peru. They draw people from all backgrounds, men and women, mostly in their thirties and forties.

The first steps are taken with an introduction to the Shamanic Journey, a fundamental aspect of shamanism. This is a way of 'seeing' beyond the literal and physical to explore the psyche and access inner wisdom, as well as encountering your spirit guides. You will also learn about divination, energy work and the Medicine Wheel, an ancient template based around the points of the compass to explain the cosmos and our place and purpose in life.

The other Eagle's Wing workshops build on these foundations with, for example, sweat lodges, a purification ceremony to eliminate emotional, spiritual and physical toxins, and the Firebird Trance Dance – a combination of celebration, self-expression and 'letting go', to invite the healing process and free the mind.

RURAL RETREAT

EarthSpirit

🌐 🍃 🈂 ☀ 🐎 🔊 ⚽ ⬆ ⬆10

Dundon, Somerset
T+44 (0)1458-272161
www.earthspirit-centre.co.uk
From £235 for a weekend

Here is rural England at its most charming: beautifully restored 17th-century farm buildings nestled into a gentle landscape, the stillness broken only by the cry of buzzards or mewl of lambs. EarthSpirit hosts weekend workshops and week-long retreats run by a huge variety of leaders and teachers year round.

You have to book directly with the organizers of each retreat, so prices will vary (check the website for details). Offers include plenty of yoga, dance, voicework, meditation, silent retreats in the Buddhist tradition and spiritual practices ranging from tantra to shamanism. Yoga and sound teacher Judith Seelig, runs spiritual retreats here twice a year (from £395 for four days, www.yogaandsound.com, see also Morocco, page 171).

At the centre of the seven-acre site is a

52-ft barn with a soaring, reed-lined roof, underfloor heating and a sculpted dragon emerging from an interior wall denoting the earth's energy currents. Trees sacred to the Celts are planted in the meadow. Rare-breed sheep graze beyond the lawn and you can eat on the terrace with all this in view.

Accommodation is comfortable but basic. The dairy has been converted into single and twin rooms that share a bathroom. In the old cowsheds are twin-bedded rooms with en suite showers and loo. Secreted around the land are four caravans with double beds. By far the most beautiful bedroom is the seven-bed dormitory in the eaves of the great barn, with windows to the sky and roof struts that form a natural division between beds. The two newest twin-bedded Skylight rooms, beautifully fashioned from French oak, share a shower room and loo. Be prepared to share if the retreat is heavily booked.

All meals are vegetarian and the delicious soups memorable. Some groups drink wine. In a building beyond the herb and flower garden there's a cedarwood hot tub with views onto distant hills. The land is full of little private corners and there are plenty of country walks on hand. Bring towels and, in winter, outdoor gear for dashing between buildings. The nearest station is Castle Cary. EarthSpirit is 20 minutes' away by taxi.

Cosy interior at EarthSpirit.

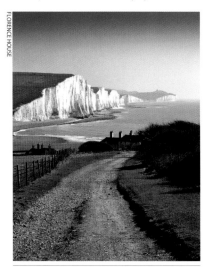

Energizing views at Florence House.

RURAL RETREAT

Florence House

🌐 🍃 🈂 ☀ 🐎 🔊 ⚽ ⬆ ⬆11

Seaford, Sussex
T+44 (0)1323-873700
www.florencehouse.co.uk
From £350 per person per retreat

Located in Seaford, a 20-minute drive from Brighton on the south coast, Florence House is a restored 1920s country retreat set in five acres of grounds. Holistic residential courses are hosted here throughout the year, including yoga, music, dance and personal development retreats.

The interior is beautifully refurbished with traditional touches such as oak panelling, antiques and open fires, but otherwise has a contemporary feel, with modern furniture. The dining room is regal; chefs here cook very healthy home-style cuisine and will cater for all dietary needs if they have advance notice. The meeting room is large and bright with French windows overlooking the gardens. Some 24 people can be accommodated in bedrooms for a variety of budgets; all are cosy, painted in warm colours with double-glazed windows and beautiful views of the gardens or sea.

Simon Low, co-founder of Primrose Hill's triyoga in London, and founder of **The Yoga Academy** (www.theyogaacademy.org), runs regular retreats and yoga teacher training courses here. Join one of Nikki Slade's (www.freetheinnervoice.com) courses and learn how to access your inner voice. The course shows how vibrations may be picked up through the body on a cellular level, stimulating emotional and mental responses. The **Hoffman Institute** (www.hoffmaninstitute.co.uk), which has attracted some publicity, runs regular retreats throughout the year. They focus on letting go of past issues as well as dealing with past and present relationships.

The house is set on the edge of the South Downs, accessible for coastal walks along the hauntingly beautiful white cliffs. It is popular with city workers looking for a rewarding

Island retreat

The Grange

An elegant 19th-century country house near the sea on the Isle of Wight, The Grange is a luxurious and welcoming retreat running a range of creative and personal development weeks and weekends. It was set up by Yannis Andricopoulos, co-founder of Skyros holistic holidays (see Greece, page 142), and is now run by him and the programme director, Christine Schulz.

Where you stay The Grange is set down a quiet lane in Shanklin's Old Village, with tea and cake shops and a long sandy beach a five-minute walk away. The Isle of Wight may be stuck in the 1950s, but a lot of it is a designated Area of Outstanding Natural Beauty, and it's a charming, safe and friendly place to be with lots of sunshine and good trails for walking and cycling.

The 17 elegant bedrooms are decked out in calming shades with splashes of colour, good linens and contemporary art. Communal areas are high-ceilinged and inspiring: the large sitting room has an open fire and wooden floors, funky modern art and shelves of books; everyone eats communally in a spacious well-lit dining room, and there's a small bar. Enjoy views out to sea, a large garden with mature trees, and a sauna.

What you do Like Skyros, The Grange offers a holistic approach to self, and uses trusted tutors who are experts in their field. An exciting

> 66 99
>
> My Grange weekend took me by surprise. I took part in very intense group workshops learning to 'live life passionately' with expert psychotherapist, Malcolm Stern, with an unexpectedly diverse group of people. It was a heart-warming experience, as was a singing course the same weekend taken by Abbie Laithe, who taught me that I could actually sing, and gave me the courage to stand up and do so solo in front of everyone, which made me feel very liberated. The Grange is for people who don't have lots of time, but who want to get back in touch with what makes them happy.
>
> *Caroline*

range of courses is on offer, covering life coaching, creative writing, health and wellbeing, art, music and dance, as well as walking and sailing. You can be as serious or as frivolous as you want to be: kick-start a whole new lifestyle, discover Hawaiian massage, learn about ayurveda, sing your heart out, write fiction. One-to-one tuition in most subjects, as well as yoga, qigong and tai chi, can be arranged in advance. Massages, holistic therapies and beauty treatments can be booked with local therapists.

What you eat and drink Tasty, healthy food is served buffet-style, and prepared with fresh, locally sourced and organic produce wherever possible. Meat and fish are served, but vegetarians and special diets are catered for. You can buy wine at the bar to have with your meal.

Who goes A whole host of people of all ages, many from London and the south of England. Some have been to Skyros, others have never been in a group setting before.

Essentials The Grange (T+44 (0)1983-867644 www.thegrangebythesea.com) is a casual place and you'll need only warm and comfortable clothing. It costs from £80 per person for two nights. The Isle of Wight is a 2½-hour train ride from London Waterloo to Portsmouth Harbour, then a 15-minute ferry crossing to Ryde. You can take a train from here to Shanklin, from where it's a short walk or taxi ride. If you have a car, go from Portsmouth to Fishbourne with Wightlink Ferries and drive to Shanklin. Parking is limited.

THE GRANGE

❝❞

Gaia House is where I go when I need true respite from the world. After each meditation retreat, I come away intensely happy, no matter how much I've struggled with meditating in their giant hall. I've weeded plants from the garden, done yoga in one of the upstairs rooms, cleaned their toilets, washed their floors, and eaten bread and honey in the library looking at their red geraniums; alongside many others who move in silence, yet at peace with one another.

Caroline

break, though your fellow guests could be from any part of the globe. Fly to London Gatwick and take a train to Seaford (about an hour); it's then a five-minute taxi journey from the station.

MEDITATION RETREAT

Gaia House

🌐 ⚠ ↘13

West Ogwell, Devon
T+44 (0)1626-333613
www.gaiahouse.co.uk
From £90 for a weekend

A converted convent surrounded by tranquil countryside by the village of West Ogwell, near Newton Abbot in Devon, Gaia House is a non-denominational Buddhist retreat centre which was founded by renowned Buddhist teachers, Christina Feldman and Christopher Titmuss. The house has a lovely organic herb and vegetable garden, a pond area with a bench and mosaics, spacious grounds with mature trees, and clean, well-decorated and comfortable rooms.

Gaia House runs an impressive range of weekend, week-long, 10-day and longer retreats all year round, led by expert teachers, from silent vipassana meditation retreats to those mixing meditation with yoga, qigong or a Buddhist theme such as compassion, joy or wisdom. Learn more about the philosophy of Buddhism with lecturer Dr John Peacock, or about Zen meditation with Martine Batchelor, who lived in Korea as a Zen nun for 10 years and is the author of some wonderful books – as is her husband Stephen, who also teaches at Gaia (see Essentials, page 14). Guided personal retreats of two weeks or more are also possible. The rate includes all meals and accommodation – teaching is by donation.

If you want to learn more about the philosophy of Buddhism, Gaia House runs a joint study programme with **Sharpham College** (www.sharpham-trust.org). Based in Ashprington near Totnes, Sharpham also runs **The Barn**, a rural retreat centre which offers

seven people at any one time the chance to retreat and integrate meditation and activities such as yoga and qigong with community living. Gaia House teachers offer meditation tuition on the annual Buddha Dharma Sangha camp on Dartmoor (see page 39).

HEALTH & FITNESS RETREAT

Grayshott

🌐 🌿 ❷ ⬢ ◯ 👥 ◉ ⬡ ✿ ✹ ❂ ↘14

Hindhead, Surrey
T+44 (0)1428-602000
www.grayshottspa.com
From £180 per person per night

An ancient manor house set in 19 ha and adjoining 160 ha of National Trust land, Grayshott is a highly civilized place to be, with an unpretentious holistic approach to health. You could turn up in any state and find what you needed, whether it's dealing with a bereavement, overhauling your lifestyle or enjoying a short break.

Grayshott's strength is its therapists, some of whom have been here for over 35 years. Elaine Williams is a particularly expert naturopath and osteopath specializing in craniosacral therapy and acupuncture. Treatments include food intolerance testing and stress management, hypnotherapy,

Below left: Gaia House. **Below:** Grayshott.

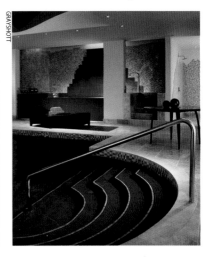

emotional freedom techniques, reflexology and hydrotherapy. The 'Oriental Wisdom' treatment combines tuina massage and shiatsu with Chinese herbs and essential oils to harmonize your chi. Beauty wraps, floats, facials and body polishes using delicious products complete the picture.

One-to-one coaching in fitness, yoga, tai chi, Alexander technique and pilates is available (from £40). Complimentary group classes include power walks and circuit training, but if you want group yoga, tai chi or pilates you need to pay extra (from £10 a session). There's a heated indoor and outdoor pool, steam room, whirlpool and tennis courts. Wonderful paintings of women by Caribbean artist Rosie Cameron Smith adorn the treatment areas.

Set up in 1965, Grayshott received a thorough revamp in 2005 and all the rooms are now inoffensively contemporary, with neutral shades set off with splashes of reds, purples and greens. Most are in a 1970s extension, which is ugly from the outside. If you want character, it's worth paying more to stay in the main manor house. The Tennyson Suite is the best room, named after the poet himself who rented the house in the 1860s. The pink and purple sitting room has a marble fireplace. There's a small cinema, and a bar serving low-calorie and organic champagne and wine in the evenings – though by 2100 most people are in bed.

The conservatory restaurant does organic meat and fish grill while, in the main dining

> **❝❞**
>
> *Despite a rather cold whirlpool and the unpretty extension, Grayshott was a calm and very comfortable place to be. Both my boyfriend and I really relaxed here, and every treatment we had was expertly delivered with kindness and love. We played badminton on the grass in bare feet, had a very interesting food intolerance test, and enjoyed organic champagne (alone) in the bar.*
>
> *Caroline*

room, food is served buffet-style for breakfast and lunch, and by waiters in the evening. You get colour-coded plates fired at their own pottery to portion control your protein, carbs and veggies. Food is simple modern British – think carrot and sweet potato soup, pan fried red mullet and aubergine, and goats' cheese cannelloni.

Fellow guests are mostly women in their forties and upwards, with a few couples, and some men alone. Grayshott attracts its regulars: in the past these have included many British actors such as Judi Dench, Roger Moore and Joan Plowright. One guest loved it so much she actually gave up her house in Surrey and lives here permanently.

Two-, three-, four- and seven-night packages are available, from £425 for a two-night de-stress. Grayshott is off the A3, an hour's drive from London. The nearest train station is Haslemere, and there are frequent trains from London Waterloo which take 55 minutes. It's an hour's drive from Heathrow and Gatwick airports.

CREATIVE RETREAT

High Green Arts

🧭 ☀ ◯ ⟳ ↘15

Northumberland National Park
T+44 (0)20-7602 1363
www.highgreen-arts.co.uk
From £100 per person per week

A Grade II listed manor house set on the open moorland of the Northumberland National Park, High Green Arts is the base of independent poetry publisher, Bloodaxe Books. Various courses on the visual arts, creative writing and yoga are held here by visiting teachers during the summer months, with guests sleeping in simple comfy rooms in the manor house.

Courses take place in the Dovecote, a converted stable and loft, which, deliciously, you can hire out for yourself during the winter months. Come here to write, paint, take photographs or just down tools for a while. Light and spacious, the Dovecote has an open-plan living area, small kitchen,

shower with toilet and a galleried sleeping area with great views out to the hills.

A long-weekend yoga course costs from £230 per person, a week-long writing course from £475. The nearest train stations are Newcastle (east) or Carlisle (west). There is a branch line to Hexham from both. The nearest airport is Newcastle.

SPIRITUAL HOLIDAY

Journeying

⛺ ☀ ◉ ◯ ⟳ ↘16

Wiltshire
T+44 (0)1225-866787
www.allaboutthejourney.co.uk
From £180 per person per weekend

Journeying runs weekend and week-long walking and singing trips through the peaceful hills, woods and valleys of Wiltshire. A lot more than just a walking or singing holiday, it's an opportunity to walk alone and reflect and assess where you are on your life's journey and to see what you have learnt so far.

Your guides are singing tutor, Candy Verney, and life coach, Sue Glanville – both expert at creating a safe and inspiring space for you to explore your surroundings and yourself. Candy leads four successful community choirs and though the trip attracts her students, it is open to anyone interested in reconnecting with themselves, including those who don't think they can sing a note. A willingness to engage with the journey is all that is required.

Your walks will take you through tranquil and wild countryside to prehistoric sites and

Journeying through the Wiltshire countryside.

Breathe deep – where to meditate in England

There are many meditation retreats across the UK which run superb courses – for beginners or for those who want to deepen their practice – based in inspiring houses with unpolluted and serene surroundings. See page 14 for more on meditation retreats.

Meditation teacher **Guy Burgs** (from £395 per person for eight days, www.justletgo.org) runs accessible and rewarding meditation courses at various locations in Devon, Shropshire and Herefordshire, including an eight-day Foundation in Healing meditation and qigong course three times a year, which combines six or seven daily vipassana meditation sessions with qigong and yoga classes. Most of the course is held in silence, and everyone is welcome, including beginners. Burgs also runs a detox retreat in Bali (see page 261).

The wonderful **Gaia House** in Devon is non-denominational (see page 34). For equally peaceful settings, **Amaravati** (www.amaravati.org), near Great Gaddesdon in Hertfordshire, is a monastery with a resident community of monks and nuns where you can also stay and take courses in meditation or just retreat from the world a while. Every evening there is a dharma talk, open to the public. **Manjushri Kadampa Meditation Centre** (T+44 (0)1229-584029, www.manjushri.org.uk, from £20 per person per night) based in Ulverston, in Cumbria, runs various meditation retreats; classes offer practical advice on how to apply Buddha's wisdom to our daily activities. Stay from one night or for a long retreat in winter.

The **Tara Buddhist Meditation Centre** (T+44 (0)1283-732338, www.taracentre.org.uk, from £68 for a weekend) is in Ashe Hall , an ancient manor house in 15 ha of woodland and lawns, six miles outside Derby. Established by meditation master Geshe Kelsang Gyatso (or Venerable Geshe-la, as he is known), it teaches Kadampa Buddhism, which focuses on using the Buddha's teachings as practical methods for transforming daily activities. There's a basic Buddhism weekend for beginners, a meditation workshop weekend, or various formal retreats for experienced practitioners throughout the year. Comfortable bedrooms, including some en suite singles, are available in Ashe Hall, or come as an individual and stay at the Barn in the grounds. You can rent one of its 18 pleasant rooms on a B&B basis for short or long periods (from £35 per person per night) and drop-in on classes at Ashe Hall.

Rivendell (T+44 (0)20-8688 8624, www.rivendellretreatcentre.com, from £90 for a three-day retreat) is a Buddhist retreat centre on the edge of Ashdown Forest in East Sussex, set in a lovely red brick house and offering a varied programme of meditation retreats throughout the year as well as yoga, walking and arts retreats. Meditation retreats for beginners look at the mindfulness of breathing and the metta bhavana, or 'development of universal loving kindness'.

monuments including Avebury and Silbury Hill. You'll have the opportunity to share life stories, sing together, and have a laugh. There's also the chance for group meditation, and to find quiet spaces in nature to be alone.

You stay in a mixture of hotels, retreat centres, tented camps and youth hostels. Walking distances are between five and 10 miles a day, and you need only carry a daysack. Journeying also runs a trip to India (see page 232).

RURAL RETREAT

Martins Retreat

🌐 ⓐ ☀ ○ ⓝ N17

Hursey, Dorset
T+44 (0)1308-868759
www.soulfriendretreats.com
From £35 per person per night

Nestled in the hills of west Dorset, seven miles from the sea, Martins Retreat is run by holistic therapist and yoga teacher, Geraldine Sherborne, whose undiluted attention you'll have virtually 24 hours a day. Come here to learn how to breathe and get back in touch with yourself, with daily gentle hatha yoga, meditation and qigong as well as therapies. You can also just stay here on a B&B basis.

Therapies on offer include the Bowen Technique, deep tissue and lymphatic drainage massage, reflexology and chakra balancing. Geraldine also offers nutritional advice and counselling. Try a dawn meditation by a hilltop fort to greet the day in all its beauty, or on the beach for a sundown contemplation, followed by supper by the sea and a late swim (if you're here in the summer).

Martins sleeps up to three people comfortably. The decor is simple, with fresh, light pastel colours, thick cream curtains, antique furniture and (good) paintings on the walls. The sitting room has deep sofas and lots of books on alternative subjects. You eat in the conservatory dining room, which is also used as a quiet room for writing. The country garden has a waterfall and small pond, and a little wooden house for writing or meditation. Geraldine is a trained chef and only uses fresh, local ingredients, organic wherever possible. It is a strictly non-smoking venue. There are no other rules, but as most people come to detox, alcohol often gives way to juices.

Martins attracts couples, friends and single travellers. Geraldine speaks good French and some German. Age is immaterial (quite a few youngsters come for guidance and to chill in a quiet haven from the rush of life). The venue is open at all times of year, and a twice-weekly meditation evening takes place for outsiders, except during retreats. The nearest airports are Exeter and Bournemouth, both an hour away. The nearest station is Crewkerne (four miles away) on the main London Waterloo-Exeter line, from where guests can be collected.

RURAL RETREAT

Middle Piccadilly

🌿 🧖 ♨ ⭕ 🧘 💧 ✳ 😊 📶 **18**

Holwell, near Sherborne, Dorset
T+44 (0)1963-23468
www.middlepiccadilly.com
From £253 per person for 2 nights

A 17th-century thatched cottage surrounded by rolling countryside at Holwell near Sherborne, Middle Piccadilly is a peaceful retreat offering detox and de-stress holistic treatments in a friendly, back-to-basics atmosphere. There's a large front garden with a stone circle leading to the Star House, a wood and glass construction where you can do your own yoga; and there are easy circular country walks from the property.

Generous and laid-back owners, Dominic Harvey and his wife Lisa, a holistic therapist, live here with their two small children and have created a relaxed atmosphere – just ask if you want more one-to-one attention. There is no TV, radio, road noise or light pollution, though you will hear military planes overhead from time to time.

You walk outside to get to the tiny 'aquaspa', which is a room with a deep hot tub, sink, treatment bed, and shower.

Mineral-rich moor mud and seaweed baths are available here in private. Other treatments are carried out in designated rooms in the main cottage, and include ayurvedic massages, reiki, shiatsu, acupressure, clay therapies, reflexology, LaStone therapy and beauty treatments such as the organic fruit facial. Book treatments in advance, as many are carried out by visiting local therapists.

Stay if you can in the Lodge, a converted hay barn with two fair-sized double bedrooms, its own garden area and a high-ceilinged sitting room with a kitchenette. The bedrooms in the Wing, part of the cottage, are small, old fashioned and, when we visited, cluttered – go for the only double in the wing, the Ensuite, or the single room the Lotus, which has its own French windows which open out onto the front garden.

The main house has a cosy low-ceilinged sitting room with open fire, which is dark in the summer, though as rooms are small and there is limited relaxing space indoors, it's best to come here during the spring or summer when you can enjoy the gardens in warmth and sunshine. Passable home-cooked vegetarian meals are eaten communally in the country kitchen around a large wooden table. No alcohol is served.

Most guests are female and travelling alone, a few with friends. The centre arranges group concessions for teetotal hen party visits. Stay for a minimum of two nights, and bring lots of layers, books to read and things to keep you occupied. A basic two-night package includes a consultation, LaStone

massage, and a session in the aquaspa. Mind, Body and Spirit weekends combining yoga with therapies run regularly. Middle Piccadilly is affiliated to **Sura Detox Retreats** (www.suradetox.com), which runs intensive detox retreats in Devon.

RURAL RETREAT

Monkton Wyld Court

🧖 ☀ 🧘 ⭕ 💧 ✳ 🌊 📶 **19**

Bridport, Dorset
T+44 (0)1297-560342
www.monktonwyldcourt.org
From £22 per person per night

At Monkton Wyld Court you have the space to create the retreat you want, be it quiet contemplation, spiritual growth, socializing or exploring the beautiful expanses of countryside that surround it.

Communal rooms sleep up to six; twins, doubles and family rooms are also available, or you can camp. Accommodation is basic but comfortable, and individual heaters fill in for the lack of central heating. There is a sink in each room, but no en suites, although there are bathrooms on all floors. Water comes from a well and there is a reed-bed sewage system; so don't flush the toilet unless you have to. Monkton is about sustainable living and recycling and the conservation of resources is a high priority.

If the gardens, local beaches and country walks are not enough, there is a Thursday hatha yoga class during term time and reiki, reflexology and massages are also available from £25 for an hour. Residential workshops aimed at spiritual and personal development are held throughout the year, including those run by the Eagle's Wing Centre for Contemporary Shamanism (see page 31).

Meals are hearty, organic and vegetarian. Breakfast is a delicious home-made help-yourself affair; lunch and supper are available at extra cost or on a full-board or half-board basis. Special diets can be catered for. There are 15 to 20 people in the resident Monkton community, one of whom will be your 'linker' – the person acting as liaison

CAROLINE SYLGE

Middle Piccadilly.

MONKTON WYLD COURT

Monkton Wyld Court.

between you and the community and ensuring that your stay runs smoothly. Guests are of all ages – couples, singles, young families – and include quite a few repeats. Take the train to Axminster, two hours from Bristol and four miles from Monkton Wyld. Book a taxi in advance to pick you up.

RURAL RETREAT

The Orange Tree

 ⚬ ⚬ ⚬ ⚬ ⚬ 20

Rosedale Abbey, North Yorkshire
T+44 (0)1751-417219
www.theorangetree.com
£179 per person for a weekend

At the end of a remote North Yorkshire dale is The Orange Tree, a family-run retreat that offers day and weekend breaks in a welcoming and homely environment. The setting is truly magical, with views over the lush pasture of Rosedale and the heather-covered moors beyond.

Describing itself as a relaxation centre, this substantial Victorian house is run by Graham and Sue, who both gave up stressful city lives to run the Orange Tree, and their daughters, Cathy and Laura. Sue and Cathy offer a range of treatments, from aromatherapy massages to reflexology, and reiki to hopi ear candling, whilst Graham and Laura prepare the wholesome vegetarian meals.

The house has nine cosy bedrooms, housing up to 17 guests, and the ambience is very much that of a relaxed family home. Decoration is traditional English country style, with a few ethnic touches, and the only sound of the wind, birdsong and the bleating of sheep.

The emphasis is very much on nurturing, with weekend breaks that combine workshops on meditation and a wide choice of treatments with traditional English pursuits such as country walks and afternoon teas. Some guests leave feeling relaxed and grounded; others describe it as a totally life-changing weekend.

Apart from the airy attic studio where the weekend workshops take place, there's a sauna and a sheltered hot tub outside where guests can sit and soak up the surroundings by day, or stargaze by night. If the weather's fine, the garden is the place to sit and enjoy the views down the valley. Whether you come on your own, or as part of a group, you're made to feel totally looked after during your stay. Mobile phone reception is non-existent, so this really is a place to switch off from the stresses of modern life.

Whilst the majority of guests come from the north of England, people do travel here from all over the UK. Your fellow guests will be mostly women, coming on their own for a bit of TLC, or as part of a group for a female bonding session, though increasingly couples are finding their way to this secluded corner of England. The cost is for full board, and includes two relaxation workshops and use of the sauna and hot tub. Treatments cost from £19.50. The nearest train station is York, though you'll really need a car to reach The Orange Tree due to its remote location. Come in the summer if you want to do some walking, winter for long evenings in the hot tub under the stars. You can also rent the whole house.

HOTEL & SPA

Pennyhill Park

 ⚬ ⚬ ⚬ ⚬ ⚬ ⚬ ⚬ 21

Bagshot, Surrey
T+44 (0)1276-471774
www.exclusivehotels.co.uk
From £280 per room per night

An 1800s manor house with three newer stone buildings set in 50 ha, Pennyhill Park hotel boasts a mightily impressive spa with indoor and outdoor swimming pools, hot tubs, herbal saunas, aromatic steam rooms, ice caves, laconiums and hydrotherapy pools. Come for a couple of nights on a residential spa break and soak, steam and pummel yourself back into a brighter state.

For the body-and-soul-weary, the quietest place to stay is the Rugby Wing – especially if you don't want to be bothered by midweek conferences or weekend wedding parties. It's named after the English rugby team, who train here regularly, and the Twickenham Suite boasts a private jacuzzi. Hotel bedrooms are an eclectic mix of the contemporary and

THE ORANGE TREE

The Orange Tree, in the remote North Yorkshire Dales.

the traditional, verging on the old fashioned.

The spa is huge, with (very slippery) marble floors – bring your own waterproof flip-flops, or buy some here. The outdoor Canadian hot tubs are wonderful places to sit on a sunny day as your body is warmed back to life. Also recommended are the large and fabulous ballroom swimming pool, and the rose-scented Aroma Grotto. Tuina and Thai massage, reiki and reflexology are on offer, as well as a wide range of pampering and beauty treatments. The Spa uses the Australian Li'Tya range of products – try the kodo massage, which uses pressure-point and spiralling massage to re-align your energy and release tension (£78 for an hour).

Café Themis offers light meals and healthy smoothies. In the evenings, eat in the intimate Latymer fine dining restaurant rather than the Brasserie, which lacks atmosphere. Food is seasonal and includes healthier options – think seared sea scallops, celeriac and truffle, line caught sea bass and herb risotto, and roasted pineapple.

Pennyhill Park is a 45-minute drive from London, off the M25. The nearest train station is Bagshot. UK-based **Té Wellbeing** (from £1450 for a weekend, T+44 (0)7778-355110, www.te-wellbeing.com), led by health, fitness and lifestyle coach and former world kickboxing champion Cengiz Dervis runs expensive but effective bespoke fitness and detox retreats to Pennyhill.

Qigong Southwest

🌀 ⚠ ◥22

Various locations
T+44 (0)8453-305086
www.qigong-southwest.co.uk
From £140 per person per camp

Qigong Southwest runs a number of retreats and camps in the southwest combining Buddhist meditation with qigong. These include a Buddha Dharma Sangha camp on Dartmoor, Devon, each summer, which is one of the most affordable and fun camps in the UK. Apart from the six daily scheduled

Above: The luxurious Pennyhill Park.
Below: Ragdale Hall Health Hydro.

meditations, there are Dartmoor trips, spontaneous games, final night cabaret, sauna, fireside chats and shared cooking. People come here to relax, or to open up and practise meditation and learn some life skills.

Mornings are silent, apart from children's time, and afternoons are free. Meditation sessions in a magnificent canvas yurt are facilitated by teachers Yanai Postelnik and Catherine McGee from nearby Gaia House (see page 34). They are also available to support your practice on a one-to-one basis, as is camp organizer and qigong teacher, Brad Richecoeur. There's 1¼ hours of qigong with Brad every day.

Participants are allocated supportive base-groups who cook together for the camp and have group time with each of the teachers. Far from being claustrophobic, there's lots of freedom to explore issues or be quiet. There's also an extensive programme of children's activities. Toilets are ultra-clean and there's a great shower tent and a gas boiler for hot water. Expect around 100 people, including perhaps 30 children.

Camps are lively, colourful, inspirational events guaranteed to shake you out of a rut. Others in the UK include **Rainbow 2000** (www.rainbow2000camps.org), which hosts a 'superspirit' event each year, mixing music, dance, crafts, cabaret, drumming and healing workshops, or the eco-friendly will enjoy the **Big Green Gathering** (www.big-green-gathering.com).

Ragdale Hall Health Hydro

🌀 ⚠ ☀ ♠ ◉ ⊕ ⊕ ♡ ⚡ ◥23

Ragdale, Leicestershire
T+44 (0)1664-434831
www.ragdalehall.co.uk.
From £95 per person per night

This sprawling behemoth of a place is part country hotel, part health spa. Make sure to ask for a tour when you first arrive as it's a huge place and slightly baffling for first timers. The overall standard here is very good with a high staff-to-client ratio, friendly service and a good range of facilities.

The aesthetics are inspired by country-house chic: a mix of heavy wooden furnishings with an Asian motif in the bedrooms, through to big comfy sofas and chunky sideboards in the lounge. Surprisingly, given the rather stately, almost austere feel, Ragdale doesn't stand on ceremony, with wine for sale in the bar and smokers even allocated their own den.

Aside from gym-style pool and fitness facilities, Ragdale's whole raison d'être is its extensive range of treatments, which have to be booked well in advance. The spa reception is awash with expectant faces each morning when the battalion of therapists arrives to conduct a roll-call of forthcoming treatments. Miss your slot at your own expense! Many, such as the 'Chakra Journey', are exclusive to Ragdale, and others range from reiki to crystal therapy. There are also dedicated treatments for pregnant women.

A range of just-for-men treatments ensures that, while husbands and boyfriends are not in the majority, guys won't feel like spare parts among the gaggle of hen parties and mother/daughter groupings. With most people in couples or groups, and all meals except breakfast (served in bed) taken in an oak-panelled communal dining hall, this isn't really a place for solo visitors.

Ragdale Hall opens year round, although you will ideally need your own transport as it's a pricey taxi ride to the nearest train or coach stations at Loughborough and Leicester – the hotel will arrange this. They also arrange transfers to East Midlands Airport, 25 miles away.

WELLBEING HOLIDAY

Relaxing The Mind

🌀 ⛰ 🧘 💧 ↘24

Various locations
T+44 (0)845-456 1051
www.relaxingthemind.com
From £175 per person per weekend

Sue Weston runs residential qigong, tai chi and meditation weekends throughout the UK. Sue is principal of the Isleworth School of Tai Chi and has years of experience as an instructor. Courses take place in various locations, including Holy Island (see page 50), and plans are afoot for Sue to have her own

retreat place. All meals are vegetarian and deliciously home-cooked by Sue's sister, Jeanne; you may be asked to help out with the washing up. Sue also runs life coaching residential breaks with CiCi Collins.

Sue's qigong and meditation weekends are extremely relaxing. An early morning outdoors start is voluntary, but a great way to kick the day off. All the techniques offer ways of releasing stress and are easily taken into everyday life. A great communal vibe always develops between guests. The life coaching weekends are good for boosting confidence and communication skills. Sue and CiCi make a space for you to explore your goals and desires, and teach you strategies to achieve them.

Retreats attract men and women from around the globe with an interest in learning to meditate and relax. Sue has spent time in Sri Lanka helping tsunami survivors, and has been awarded a doctorate by the International University of Martial Arts, in Japan. She also runs retreats to Sri Lanka (see page 253).

TAI CHI RETREAT

Revitalise Tai Chi

🌀 ⛰ ☯ 💧 ↘25

T+44 (0)7780-991952
www.re-vitalise.co.uk
From £225 for an all-inclusive 2-night retreat

Revitalise Tai Chi was founded by Andy

Spragg, a Buddhist with a background in Chinese martial arts. Evolving from his interest in the synergy between tai chi and Buddhist meditation, the practice he teaches focuses on health and meditative benefits, with classes tailored to suit all abilities.

Revitalise Tai Chi runs retreats across the country in locations such as Charney Manor in Oxfordshire, one of the oldest inhabited houses in Britain, and Holy Island in Scotland (see page 50). Each is chosen for its inherent beauty and tranquillity – a complement to the peace and energy that are part of tai chi practice. Good food and comfortable accommodation in single or double rooms are also part of the full-board deal.

A typical weekend retreat runs from Friday evening to noon on Sunday, providing informal but thorough instruction through four 90-minute sessions and, in some cases, morning and evening meditation. Two experienced teachers guide the group through a short tai chi form and a set of tau gong exercises – rhythmic movements rather like those of qigong, which promote energy and warm up the body. Revitalise also runs monthly one-day workshops in London.

FITNESS HOLIDAY

The Running Inn

🌐 ⏱ 🧘 🎾 ✤ ✤ ↘26

Eastbourne, East Sussex
T+44 (0)1323-720640
www.therunninginn.com
From £175 per person per weekend

Fiona Bugler and Mike Ovens organize residential courses for runners and anyone with an interest in holistic exercise. Located in the seaside town of Eastbourne, the couple

Top: Revitalise Tai Chi. **Above:** Relaxing the Mind.

A robe by any other name

Like many dedicated health and fitness retreats around the world, those in the UK can be an acquired taste. The clientele hail from all walks of life, but generally take to mooching around in white bathrobes and fluffy slippers within an hour of their arrival. This can seem weird at first, and some people report that wearing only a robe for most of the day makes them feel ill, mad or hospitalized. You can rebel and just lounge about in your own clothes, though there's no greater social leveller than a fluffy robe, and management consultants subsequently rub shoulders with travel writers in perfect harmony. It's also comfortable, stops massage oil from ruining your favourite clothes and saves time. Cheekily, some places charge for their robes, though this is because of the large number that get stolen each year – ask in advance, or bring your own. As for the fluffy slippers, they can be quite lethal to walk in, so it's best to arrive with your own pair of flip-flops.

At their best, health and fitness retreats in the UK are relaxing, friendly, unpretentious places to rejuvenate, usually set in atmospheric converted country houses, where dress code is unimportant, and there's an impressive range of activities and treatments to choose from. At their worst, they are a cross between an old people's home and a holiday camp, with awful airport-style carpets, smoking rooms whose smell pervades the public areas, inexperienced in-house therapists who try to sell you products after each treatment, classes tailored only to beginners, brash guests and gaggles of chattering women on hen parties disturbing the peace.

To make the best of them, it's worth paying more for the best rooms with views, space and privacy, or for 'premier' packages which offer perks. Pre-book any treatment or activity that's important to you. At some of the larger establishments, ask about their visiting therapists, especially if you want decent deep tissue massage, for example, or personalized attention. Be prepared to pay extra for many of the more interesting classes on offer, or for one-to-one tuition.

Say 'health spa' to most people in the UK who have never been to one and they will probably think of **Champneys Health Resorts** (T+44 (0)8703-300300, www.champneys.com, from £160 per person per night at Champneys Springs). The resorts get mixed reports, but their strength is the range of affordable wellbeing weekends and weeks they offer, many led by experts in their field, from weight-loss and detox programmes to weekends dedicated to men's health, Eastern wellbeing, swimming or self-image. Champneys Tring remains the most attractive, a Rothschild mansion set in 70 ha of peaceful grounds, which attracts celebrities, a large number of Arab long-staying guests as well as couples. Forest Mere in Hampshire gets the thumbs up for its lovely lake, and its offer of extensive holistic therapies. There's even a resort in Goa, though we haven't checked it out.

There are many other health spas to choose from in the UK. For those in search of luxury, **Grayshott** is one of the UK's most civilized with a clientele to match (see page 34), or head to the **Monart** in Ireland (see page 58). More affordable offerings include the serene **Cedar Falls** (see page 30), or the relaxed **Temple Spa** in Ireland (page 59), while **Ragdale Hall** has a devoted following of repeat guests (see page 39).

TITANIC SPA

RAGDALE HALL

combine walking and training with yoga, pilates, spa treatments and nutritional advice. Mike is a former 400-m champion, and Fiona has studied pre- and post-natal core stability and body balance. Both are personal trainers.

Courses are individually fine-tuned to any level. You don't have to be in training for a marathon – you can come here to exercise and meet people, or for a healthy break. You'll get a private consultation, with a follow-up plan by email, and nutritionist Lucy Ann will give a talk. One-to-one sessions with her are available on request. Runners will learn to utilize the whole body and will train on hills and speedwork.

Fitness assessments and studio sessions are offered, along with informative talks and workshops. Pilates and yoga are an important part of the course and can be tailored to requirements; discuss your level in advance. The locality offers spectacular sea views and rolling green hills for walking, running and cycling. The shingle seafront is tougher to run on, but invigorating. You'll get a massage after training and, on Saturdays, pick a treatment from their holistic range. Choose from hot-stone massage, organic facials, or hopi ear candling, among others.

Accommodation is in a Grade II listed guesthouse with lots of character and light, and contemporary soft furnishings. Bedrooms are spacious and each suite has a kitchenette, though Mike cooks fantastic healthy meals.

The Running Inn attracts mostly 20-50-year-olds, lots of Londoners, couples and singles. It's good all year round, but summer can be hot and busy. It's around an hour's drive from Gatwick Airport, from where trains run direct to Eastbourne.

You can sink without trace in the Titanic Spa.

Ruth White Yoga

T+44 (0)20-8641 7770
www.ruthwhiteyoga.com
From £298 for 3 days

Ruth White trained with BKS Iyengar himself in Pune, India (see page 203) and has been teaching since her teens. She was the first person to offer yoga retreats in the UK and continues to runs yoga weekends in beautiful country houses, all chosen for their sea or countryside views. She works with her husband John, and has a sense of fun and lots of good energy and enthusiasm.

The magnificent 18th-century Heythrop Park in Oxfordshire is one example, complete with private zoo, indoor pool, 160-ha grounds and luxurious twin, single or double rooms with plentiful buffet meals; you just need to bring your yoga mat. Other locations include Eden Hall in Kent and Cober Hill in Yorkshire. For sun seekers, Ruth also runs yoga holidays on the Greek island of Lesbos (see page 141).

Retreat weekends offer at least two hours of yoga every day, accompanied by yoga nidra and pranayama exercises, all taught by Ruth, John, or one of the other teachers (who they have trained themselves). You can also expect talks on anatomy and physiology, with guest teachers offering guided meditation and massage.

Saol Retreats

T+44 (0)20-8739 0805
www.peteroberts.net
From £1500 per person per week

Saol (Gaelic for 'life') offers bespoke retreat weekends combining the experience and expertise of sports therapist Pete Roberts (who counts Madonna among his clients), yoga teacher Liz Lark and chef Alan Wichert. With an integrated approach to health and

wellbeing, yoga, pilates and an optional detox programme are supported by a variety of bodywork and holistic treatments, nature hikes and organized excursions. Saol is a movable feast, using five-star accommodation in the UK and beyond – their first venue was the **Aghadoe Heights Hotel & Spa** (www.aghadoeheights.com) in Ireland, with plans for retreats in equally inspiring locations in the UK, Costa Rica, Kenya and Morocco.

Pete teaches 'Backworx' – a combination of pilates, Thai yoga therapy, massage therapy and physical and mental conditioning. He focuses on alleviating back pain and creating a sense of fluidity and freedom in the body. Liz is a world-renowned yoga teacher who has worked with performers and artists such as Ralph Fiennes, Donna Karan and Alan Rickman. Her inspiration comes from the ashtanga vinyasa tradition and hatha yoga practice, and she runs retreats around the world (see www.lizlark.com). Alan is a former Four Seasons executive chef, who specializes in detox menus. Both Alan and Liz also work for In:Spa (see Morocco, page 172).

Titanic Spa

Linthwaite, Huddersfield
T+44 (0)1484-843544
www.titanicspa.com
From £130 per double room

Titanic Spa offers day treatments and accommodation set in a textile mill on the banks of a Huddersfield canal. The village of Linthwaite is being regenerated and the mill is superbly renovated.

Titanic attracts people from all over the UK and offers oodles of tempting treatments for men and women. The beauty range is extensive and you can have your hair done at the same time. The spa menu includes massages, mineral therapies, Pevonia Stone therapy, body wraps that make you feel you're being cooked in pine oils, a chakra room with heated stone plinth for four-hands treatment, and a mud chamber. For spiritual wellbeing, you can combine the spa with a holistic treatment such as reiki or Indian head massage.

The sensory 'Titanic Heat Experience' is a must. You'll relax in a variety of heated rooms: sauna, aromatherapy room, crystal steam bath and Scandinavian sauna, and between each heat session you can cool in a reinvigorating plunge pool, ice room, freezing bucket shower or a cold multi-jet shower. Afterwards your skin will be glowing, and you can relax in the beanbag pit in your dressing gown and read, or just absorb the silence. The spa uses its own natural water source, and the chlorine-free, salt swimming pool with bubbling hydrozone bath and underwater music makes exercise a joy.

Decorated in minimalist style with chocolate- and slate-coloured cushions, the spa has an exclusive feel, and staff are discreet. Luxury self-catering apartments continue the spa's modern style. Be as decadent as you wish: sip champagne or enjoy herbal teas and the healthy cuisine. You'll find orange juice, champagne and chocolates in your room to kick-start the indulgence. The spa offers excellent disabled access. Bring your swimsuit, as some treatments require it. Bring your walking boots, too, as you can also walk in the nearby Peak District. It's 30 miles from Manchester airport.

RURAL RETREAT

Tregoddick Farm

Penzance, Cornwall
T+44 (0)1736-361301
www.yogafarm.co.uk
From £45 per person per night

Elizabeth Connolly's organic restaurant, B&B and yoga retreat centre is perched on a Cornish hillside with spectacular views over Mounts Bay and St Michael's Mount. Five-day yoga retreats and occasional workshops are based on the ashtanga vinyasa system with a

Yoga at Treggodick Farm.

strong emphasis on technique and alignment that owes something to the iyengar school.

Guests from all over the world may come for the yoga the first time around, but they surely come back for the food. The conservatory restaurant attached to the centre is something special: it's 100% organic – certified by the Soil Association – and unusual among yoga retreats in that its menus include meat dishes as well as fantastic fresh locally caught fish. Bread is baked on site daily and treats include home-made ice cream and chocolate brownies as well as organic wines and beers. It's a convivial setting for an evening get-together with your fellow yogis and helps to make sure that, while the centre is supremely peaceful and relaxing, this is a break to appeal to more gregarious souls, particularly if your idea of a restorative repast is a steak dinner rather than a mung bean salad.

Bedrooms are light, airy and tastefully decorated – a long way from the chintz nightmare that the words 'bed and breakfast' sometimes evoke. Visitors in search of good food and sea air without the discipline of twice-daily yoga classes can come independently as B&B guests. A recent

addition to the centre itself is the Tregoddick Beauty Clinic, offering relaxing treatments for face and body using organic, locally manufactured products as well as massage, body toning and non-surgical facelift treatments. The area is a haven for hikers, and day trips include surfing at Sennen Beach and visits to the Eden Project.

RURAL RETREAT

The Vale Healing Centre

Stoke Trister, Somerset
T+44 (0)1963-33360
www.valehealing.co.uk
From £16.50 per person per night

Charlotte and Tim MacCaw could have kept their beautiful 600-year-old manor house and grounds to themselves. Instead, they set up the Vale Healing Centre here – a tranquil hideaway offering rest, relaxation and the chance to rebalance among peaceful expanses of Somerset countryside. Vale Healing is both a retreat centre for workshops and a short-break destination for exploring the area and tapping into the therapies on offer.

Accommodation is provided in two self-catering cottages, sleeping four apiece, with views across the valley. Vale Cottage includes two twin rooms, Vale House a twin and a master bedroom with a king-size orthopaedic bed. The non-smoking apartments are simply decorated, comfortable and clean. They are well kitted out with all the necessary mod cons and centrally heated, although this costs extra from October to April. Normally let out in their entirety rather than on a room-by-room basis, although individuals are welcome if there is space.

Although it's about self-catering, lunches and dinners can be ordered in, and hearty pub food is only a few minutes' drive away, as are supermarkets and farmers' markets. If you request it in advance, you can also have a box of organic food delivered.

The Vale Healing Centre is about inspiring people to find new ways of staying healthy in mind, body and spirit. Therapies start at £30 an hour and include satvik energy therapy (see glossary), angel readings from Sarah Cox, co-founder of the Satvik Training School, and one-to-one spiritual fitness training, which incorporates nutrition, relaxation, visualization, and qigong or tai chi.

Charlotte and Tim see themselves as a resource of information on complementary therapies, with a focus on nutrition. Tim works with homeopathy and the QX-SCIO device. Charlotte is trained in satvik healing

and also works with Australian bush flower remedies. Their approach is intuitive, and their aim is to empower guests to investigate alternative therapies for themselves, guiding them to relevant sources of information.

The courses on offer include a combined tennis and pilates workshop, angelic psychic development, yoga and meditation. The centre is also home to the Satvik Training School, which runs its own courses. Costs vary, with some by donation, others at a fixed fee. Accommodation is on top of workshop fees, which allows flexibility for attendees who can stay elsewhere or travel from home if they wish.

Unless they're participating in workshops, most guests stay for a week or long weekend and are generally couples or families. The workshops attract mainly women in their thirties, forties and fifties. It's two hours from London down the M3 and A303, or about 10 minutes by taxi from Gillingham station, or 15 minutes from Castle Cary.

Above: The Vale Healing Centre, a peaceful hideaway in the Somerset countryside.

WildWise

Dartmoor, Devon
T +44 (0)1803-868269
www.wildwise.co.uk
From £50 per person for a wild night

Professional storyteller, Chris Salisbury, runs inspiring courses in the wilds of Dartmoor in Devon to help rejuvenate tired souls. Try Wild Yoga, a long weekend with yoga, holistic therapies, storytelling, and moorland walks, and workshops in partner yoga, acupressure or oil massage, meditational movement and dance (from £295). You'll be based near the river Dart at Brimpts Farm, a 19th-century barn conversion surrounded by woodlands and tors with a sauna, hot tub and large yoga room with wood burning stove. Or stay overnight on the moor with a Wild Night Out, a wildlife camp featuring naturalist activities, sensory awareness, and night and dawn walks (from £50 per person).

Enjoy the wilds of Dartmoor, in Devon, on a WildWise course.

Wales

RURAL RETREAT

Cae Mabon

☀ ⊕ ◐ ⊘ ⏷33

Fachwen, near Llanberis, Gwynedd
T+44 (0)1286-871542
www.caemabon.co.uk
From £425 for a 5-day course

Craftily hidden away in the woods, Cae Mabon is a constantly evolving retreat centre in Fachwen, near the town of Llanberis in Snowdonia. It's the creation of Eric Maddern, an Australian who worked for four years with Aboriginal communities and whose experience of the people, culture and land inspired him to find his own piece of 'sacred space' in the UK. The encampment is five minutes' walk from a lake, within sight of the mountains and right next to an enthusiastic river: a location to transport you away from the stress and noise of everyday life and give you space and time for reflection and peace.

A variety of different courses runs here throughout the year, or you can hire the venue for your own retreat. Activity at Cae Mabon is centred around the studio barn, which has a spacious area for eating, singing, gathering or meeting, and an adjoining well-equipped kitchen. There is also a large roundhouse which can have a fire in its centre and is the hub for storytelling, singing and evening activities.

You sleep in one of Cae Mabon's various buildings, which include the cedar cabin, cob cottage, bunkhouse, barn lodge, straw bale hogan and a chalet, all built from sustainable and natural materials and based on traditional designs from a variety of cultures. Accommodation is shared, and very basic – you'll need to bring your own sleeping bag. There is only one shower (though it is hot), and two composting toilets. The fabulous views, the peaceful atmosphere and the recent addition of a hot tub right by the river almost makes up for the lack of home comforts. Cae Mabon is right next to National

Above: Cae Mabon. **Below:** Pen Pynfarch.

Trust land and there are plenty of walks in the area. The really brave can swim in the lake.

RURAL RETREAT

Gaia Cooperative

☀ ◐ ⏷34

Near Hay-on-Wye
T+44 (0)1981-550246
www.gaiacooperative.org
From £140 for a residential weekend retreat

An outreach and education initiative, the Gaia Cooperative promotes ecological awareness and a healthy lifestyle in harmony with the natural environment. Their retreat venue, set in an expanse of rolling countryside on the Welsh borders, is predominantly a course centre, but personal retreats are possible with prior arrangement.

Although art, poetry and theatre workshops are included in their programme, Gaia's raison d'être is to educate participants

about sustainable living, inviting facilitators who make the scientific and practical information accessible with their own experiences. These include Peter Harper, co-founder of the Centre for Alternative Technology, Tania Dolley, co-founder of the Ecopsychology Network, and Satish Kumar, editor of *Resurgence* magazine.

Guests enjoy homely cottage accommodation in bright twin or double rooms with solar-powered hot water and electricity, and home-grown organic food. There's also a campsite with access to the cottage showers, and an outdoor pool. Weather permitting, courses are held in the garden with a backdrop of lawns, flowers and vegetable patches.

RURAL RETREAT

Pen Pynfarch

☀ ⋔ ◉ ⊛ ⏷35

Llandysul, Carmarthenshire
T+44 (0)1559-384948
www.penpynfarch.co.uk
£130 for a weekend self-catering

A short drive from the beautiful coastline of Ceredigion, and sheltered in a peaceful woodland valley, Carmarthenshire's Pen Pynfarch is a welcoming destination for individual retreats. It also runs body and movement workshops from March to June, and hosts visiting teachers for group retreats.

Nestled into a 16-ha smallholding, the traditional stone-built accommodation, a collection of converted farm buildings, is simple, cosy and homely, with antique furniture, open fires and a wood burner. There is also a caravan and camping in season, with access to hot showers and a compost toilet. Go self-catering or enjoy the organic vegetarian meals on a half- or full-board basis.

The old barns have been given a new lease of life as a clean, bright dance studio with underfloor heating, and a practice and therapy room. Workshops here aim to encourage a deeper understanding of the body and a better ability to care for it,

Northern & Central Europe Wales

through somatic approaches to movement and improvisation, drawing on such work as the feldenkrais method, experiential anatomy, the alexander and skinner releasing techniques, and craniosacral therapy. There is a strong emphasis on helping to restore your connection with the natural environment. The nearest station is Carmarthen, from where it's a 30-minute drive.

YOGA RETREAT
Snowdon Lodge

Near Bethesda, Gwynedd
T+44 (0)1248-602900
www.druyoga.com
From £225 per person for a weekend

Regular dru yoga retreats take place at Snowdon Lodge in Nant Ffrancon, a peaceful haven surrounded by the mountains of Snowdonia, with a sauna and comfortable rooms, and a river only five minutes' walk away. Dru comes from the Sanskrit *dhruva*, meaning still and unchanging, and dru yoga concentrates on helping you retain inner tranquility and strength no matter what is happening in your life.

Courses include detox, vitality and superhealth weekends, which combine yoga with vegetarian cooking demos, gentle detoxing, relaxation and massage, holistic back care (to help you manage and reduce back problems), and introductory weekends to dru yoga and meditation. Each weekend is

RUSSEL LEWINS

led by teachers who are renowned for their good energy.

Dru focuses on energy block release sequences, which help release energy blocked in the mind as well as the body, enabling you to focus on what's important in your life. As the sequences focus on the energy surrounding the heart centre, practitioners report immediate feelings of calm and happiness after just one session.

Dru yoga teacher training is also available at Snowdon Lodge, and there are dru yoga classes and centres around the world. The lodge is eight miles south of Bangor, where you'll find the nearest train station.

MOUNTAIN RETREAT
Snowdonia Retreat

Fron Goch, Dolwyddelan, Conwy
T+44 (0)1690-750471
www.snowdoniaretreat.co.uk
£30 per night self-catering

Mountainous and wild, Snowdonia makes a great place for a personal retreat. Take a tent, stove, yoga mat and a healthy respect for the people and the land, and walk yourself to blissful happiness on a bootstring budget. For a balance between natural and home comforts, stay a couple of nights with Annette Bunning, who offers holistic therapies at her cosy self-catering mountain retreat just three miles southwest of the beautiful valley town of Betws-y-Coed.

Annette has worked as a counsellor for many years and takes a holistic approach to the individual, offering counselling, life coaching and complementary treatments such as reiki, reflexology, Indian head massage and aromatherapy. Her property is a renovated traditional, stone-and-slate Welsh farm cottage. Have a post-hike chat in the cosy sitting area, which has a large wood burner and low ceiling. For those who do not wish to stray far, 18 ha of surrounding semi-wild land offers a variety of nooks in which to lose yourself during the summer.

Bedrooms are basic but comfy. For a short

stay of two or three nights, the upstairs doubles are more spacious and, with roof windows, brighter than the double room off the main kitchen. If you are staying longer, there is separate accommodation in the main house, which comprises a living room and conservatory with a double room above. A self-contained flat is also available. Minumum stay is two nights.

Treatments are given upstairs in a warm, private room. Guests can enjoy their own company or share experiences and thoughts with other guests and day visitors. Wholesome meals are eaten communally. Take the train to Llandudno then the X1 bus to Penygroes, getting off at Pont-y-pant, from where it's a 20-minute walk. Other activities in the area include canoeing, sea swimming, climbing, visiting castles and exploring Celtic culture.

MEDITATION RETREAT
Vajraloka Buddhist Meditation Centre

Corwen, Denbighshire
+ 44 (0)1490-460406
www.vajraloka.com
From £30 per person per night

A cluster of old converted stone farm buildings on the edge of a forest and just a few minutes walk from the River Alwen, Vajraloka makes an inspiring setting for its regular meditation retreats. At least one or two retreats are held every month, each lasting two to 14 days; a few are open to men only, but most to everyone, including beginners. You can also stay for a longer period as a guest.

The centre's two main retreat leaders, Tejananda (author of *The Buddhist Path to Awakening*) and Vajradaka, have taught Buddhism and meditation all over the world. People are encouraged to explore their own experience, with input from the teacher being mainly via discussion groups. Outside of the group activity, the retreats are held in silence, but people have the opportunity to talk one-to-one with a teacher should they wish.

The accommodation is simple but comfortable, in either single or shared rooms, with shared bathrooms. A communal dining area opens out to the richly stocked and terraced gardens. Food is vegan, nutritious, tasty and from ethical sources where possible. Meditation takes place in the main shrine room, a still and peaceful space.

Vajraloka is linked to the **Friends of the Western Buddhist Order** (www.fwbo.org). The retreat attracts all sorts of people, usually between the ages of 30 and 45, and mostly from the UK. The closest train stations are at Wrexham or Ruabon; a taxi from either costs around £8. The closest airport is Manchester, a one-hour drive away. Good idea to bring waterproofs.

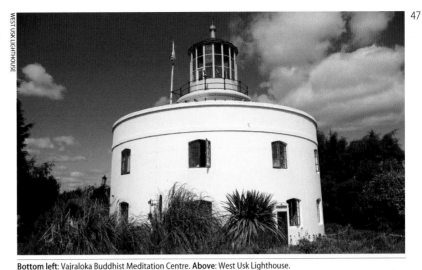

WEST USK LIGHTHOUSE

Bottom left: Vajraloka Buddhist Meditation Centre. **Above**: West Usk Lighthouse.

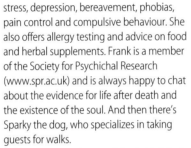

WATERSIDE RETREAT

West Usk Lighthouse

☀ 🐾 ⊚ 🌍 ☍ 🌀 ⊡39

St Brides, Wentloog, near Newport, Gwent
T+44 (0)1633-810126
www.westusklighthouse.co.uk
From £105 per room per night

From the autographed Dalek in the lobby to the Buddisht shrine in the lantern tower, West Usk Lighthouse is one of Wales' more unusual B&Bs. Built in 1821, and lovingly restored by owners Frank and Danielle Sheahan, it occupies a wonderfully lonely spot where the River Usk flows into the Severn estuary.

Short and squat rather than tall and thin, the lighthouse has four guest bedrooms on the first floor, ranged around a central spiral staircase like slices of a cake. All have private bathrooms; our favourite rooms are the two on the south side, which both have four-poster beds and sea views. The decor is homely, a little worn at the edges but filled with endearingly quirky details – an upside-down model ship steaming across a sea-effect ceiling and a traditional red telephone box recycled as a shower cubicle.

Danielle is a qualified hypnotherapist with an excellent track record in getting people to quit smoking; her sessions can help deal with stress, depression, bereavement, phobias, pain control and compulsive behaviour. She also offers allergy testing and advice on food and herbal supplements. Frank is a member of the Society for Psychichal Research (www.spr.ac.uk) and is always happy to chat about the evidence for life after death and the existence of the soul. And then there's Sparky the dog, who specializes in taking guests for walks.

Most guests make use of the hot tub in the roof garden, and the flotation tank, which is housed in a ramshackle wooden summer house in the garden. After your float, you can open the door and breathe in the sea air. A wide range of alternative therapies is also on offer, from aromatherapy and massage to kinesiology.

But perhaps the lighthouse's most appealing feature is its spiritual atmosphere, offering the chance to relax away from the bustle of the city, chat with like-minded people, and just watch the tides come and go with the rhythm of the moon.

There's a two-night minimum stay at weekends. The nearest train station is in Newport (four miles); the nearest airport is Cardiff International (22 miles). Spring and autumn are the top times for birdwatching, while high summer is best for lounging in the hot tub in the roof garden.

COASTAL RETREAT

White Horses Retreat

🌍 ☍ ♨ ☀ 🐾 ⊚ 🌀 ☍ ⊡40

Bontddu, Gwynedd
T+44 (0)1691-648546
www.whitehorsesretreat.co.uk
From £195 per person for 2 nights

Set on the coast with views over the Mawddach estuary, White Horses runs a number of holistic courses from March to November. Hostess Hilary Collins has an aptitude for human interaction and an ability to make each visitor feel special and cared for. The courses emphasize spiritual growth and healing, and draw on a variety of teachings, including yoga, tai chi, qigong and shiatsu, meditation and Celtic spirituality.

You stay in simple, homely accommodation restored with individual touches such as local handmade quilts. Accommodation is mainly in shared rooms in a long wood-panelled outbuilding with a veranda overlooking a field of wild flowers which attract abundant bird-life. Two bedrooms in the main house have the best views – especially the upstairs en suite double, which has a large window and enjoys an uninterrupted view of the estuary. A footpath runs through the grounds and

48 provides direct access to the beach, where yoga and tai chi can be practised.

Plentiful vegetarian food using home-grown and local produce is eaten communally around a large farmhouse-style table – think home-made pâté or soup, followed by vegetarian moussaka and finished with bread and butter pudding with home-grown pears. They are unable to cater to special diets, so bring what you need. Alcohol isn't allowed.

The courses attract a range of people, depending on their content. Most guests come with a friend or partner, although groups generally interact comfortably and a safe environment is assured for the single traveller. Pack waterproof gear and some warm outdoor clothing as the weather can be unpredictable. To avoid the crowds but still enjoy warmth, come in September. The White Horses Retreat lies on the coast, south-west of Snowdonia National Park, between Dolgellau and Barmouth. Fly to Liverpool or Birmingham, then drive or take the train to Barmouth. Pickups can be arranged.

Top: White Horses Retreat, Wales.
Above: Ashwhin Balanced Living Retreat, Scotland.

Scotland

COASTAL RETREAT
Ashwhin Balanced Living Retreat

🧭 🕐 ⛰ ☀ 🏔 🌙 ⚽ 🌀 🌊 🍃 ▶ ↘41

Dunbeg, near Oban, Argyll
T+44 (0)1631-567192
www.ashwhin.com
From £35 per person per night; £220 per week

Surrounded by mountains and secluded beaches near the village of Dunbeg, Ashwhin Balanced Living Retreat is a wonderful place to escape to and reconnect with yourself. Opened in 1999 by holistic therapist Derby Stewart-Amsden and her partner, Peter, it offers a safe, relaxing environment where you can have as much or as little attention as you want or need.

There's just one self-contained studio here, for singles, couples or close friends who don't mind sharing a bed, with its own entrance and a terrace overlooking the huge garden and hills. It's homely and comfortable, with a small kitchenette, shower and toilet, TV for watching DVDs and videos (there's deliberately no aerial), and living room with a double sofa bed.

Come here to slow down and relax, sort out a deep-rooted trauma or condition, or work through a life-changing event. Derby is loving, honest and inspiring, with the knack of helping you open up in the safe environment she has created. On arrival you'll have a consultation with her, and she'll help you devise a programme for your stay. Accommodation is self-catering but Oban is a major fishing port, and there are good farm shops and local organic meat suppliers in the area.

On offer are holistic therapies such as reflexology, reiki, massage, counselling, meditation, sessions on motivation, writing, art, relaxation techniques and life balance, rescue packages for busy and stressed people, and massage workshops for couples. The beach is two minutes' walk away, and is great for walks (take Derby's two dogs if you like).

Three miles away is Oban, from where you can catch the ferry to Mull, Iona or the islands of the Outer Hebrides, where wildlife includes dolphins, whales, seals and golden eagles.

There are occasional group retreats on various holistic subjects such as reiki, when people stay at local B&Bs. There's a one week minimum stay in July and August, and treatments start from £25. No pets or children are allowed. Fly to Glasgow, then hire a car, or take a train to Oban, from where Derby will pick you up.

SPIRITUAL RETREAT
Findhorn Foundation

🧭 🕐 ⛰ ☀ 🌙 🍃 ↘42

Findhorn, Morayshire
T+44 (0)1309-690311
www.findhorn.org
From £345 per person per week

Findhorn was established in the 1960s when three people moved to a small seaside caravan park in Findhorn, on the Morayshire coast, to follow a spiritual path, grow vegetables and start up a self-sufficient community. It was registered as a Scottish Charity in 1972, and today runs over 200 one-week self development courses a year as well as conferences and home training. There are more than 40 holistic businesses and outreach projects connected with Findhorn, and there are around 120 staff and volunteers on site at their two bases: The Park, and Cluny Hill College, in nearby Forres.

Findhorn describes itself 'a place where the eternal truths at the core of all the world's religions and wisdom traditions are explored, experienced and integrated.' The Experience Week programme, run since 1974, is the best way to meet the community. Come with an open mind. You'll spend seven days at one of their bases where you'll be expected to join in with house or garden work, getting back as much energy as you're prapred to give. You'll learn about their spiritual principles, ecological plans, meditation and dance. You may find that the magic of the place will surprise you, open your heart, and leave you

Wellbeing holiday

Yogoloji

UK-based Yogoloji is a young, laid-back company providing decent treatments, good yoga tuition and fun outdoor activities in luxurious surroundings. Its UK trips include a stay at Alladale Wilderness Lodge & Reserve, a pristine lodge set in 9300 ha in the remote Scottish Highlands.

Where you stay Alladale is an elegant, family-owned converted hunting lodge – think luxurious Laura Ashley decor, original fireplaces and tasteful antiques. You sleep in one of seven en suite rooms: some are larger than others, but all are beautifully turned out and have the kind of beds you need on a relaxing weekend, with goose down pillows, fine feather duvets and lambswool over-blankets. The drawing room has a baby grand piano and a big fireplace, which is cosily lit in cooler weather, and the large windows give great views of the glen.

What you do You'll be in safe hands with the kind and energetic co-founders of Yogoloji, Francesca Quaradeghini, a British massage and holistic therapist, and Liisa Halme, a Finnish ashtanga-trained yoga teacher and therapist. Together with Juliet Russell, holistic Chinese physiotherapy and massage practitioner, they offer a daily mix of dynamic yoga, relaxing yoga with meditation, tai chi and qigong classes, and one therapy a day. Choose from ayurvedic abhyanga and marma massage (Fran's speciality), full body holistic massage or acupuncture.

ALLADALE

66 99

Alladale beds are made for lie-ins, and I felt distinctly cosy on my Yogoloji long weekend, a winning combination of clean fresh air, majestic natural surroundings, daily yoga and therapies carried out with love. A ride out to see the stags dotted around the heather-clad and sprawling private estate was a highlight. I stood transfixed by them, oblivious to the cold – an encounter that helped diminish the stresses back home.

Caroline

Yoga is done in a small room, but it's adequate for the limited numbers Yogoloji accepts on its weekends. One-to-one sessions on nutrition, yoga, tai chi and qigong are also available. There's a sauna, steam room and gym, but everything is optional – so lie in if you choose. When you're not in a class or having a treatment, Alladale offers some private walking country, or you can go clay-pigeon shooting, fly-fishing, or mountain biking. There are conservation tours of the reserve, and guided nature walks.

What you eat and drink This is a great time to kick-start a healthier lifestyle, for there's no red meat, dairy, white flour, sugar, processed food, caffeine or alcohol. Tasty fusion meals use lots of fresh fish, organic local fruit and vegetables – think couscous salad and tagine sauce, West Indian curry, warm beetroot and 'funky stuff' salad. Meals are eaten dinner-party style in the large and elegant dining room.

Who goes Anyone of any age who wants to relax and rejuvenate, especially couples, but including stressed-out 30-40-something women and men travelling alone from London.

Essentials Trips to Alladale (T+44 (0)20-7730 7473, www.yogoloji.co.uk) usually run in May, and you can stay four, five or nine nights. Fly to Inverness, where you'll be picked up for the one-hour drive to Alladale. Bring yoga gear, warm layers, waterproofs, good walking boots, books and binoculars. Yogoloji also runs retreats to Grayshott in England (see page 34), Canal Om in Chile (see page 381), Sukhavati in Brazil (see page 380), Ngare Sero in Tanzania (see page 193), Sandy Lane in Barbados (see page 370) and Anassa in Cyprus (see page 147). Alladale also hosts art, photography and cooking breaks (see www.alladale.com).

Breathe deep in Scotland

To meditate in Scotland, head to **Dhanakosa** (from £90 per person per weekend, T+44 (0)1877-384213, www.dhanakosa.com), which is a member of FWBO and offers vipasana meditation retreats for all levels as well as yoga, hillwalking, shiatsu massage and tai chi. The centre sits on the shores of Loch Voil in the Balquhidder valley, and is surrounded by the mountains and forests of the southern Scottish Highlands.

For Tibetan meditation, head to the famous **Kagyu Samye Ling Buddhist Monastery and Tibetan Centre** (from £62 per person per weekend, www.samyeling.org), on the river Esk in the Scottish borders, which as well as running a whole range of fantastic retreats is committed to preserving Tibetan Buddhism, arts, medicine and culture.

a different person than when you arrived.

Accommodation at The Park is varied: environmentally friendly houses sit with caravans and bungalows, all differing in design; some are made of recycled whisky barrels, others with turfed roofs. Cluny Hill College is a large imposing Victorian house.

Weeks run from Saturday to Friday with an optional extra night. During the summer, Experience Weeks are run in other languages; check website for details. After completing the week, other holistic workshops and retreats are available.

Part of the Findhorn community, and a five-minute walk from the centre, lies **Shambala Retreat Centre** (from £25 per person per night, T+44 (0)1309-690690, www.shambala-retreat.org) set in six acres of quiet, secluded grounds adjacent to a nature reserve. Newly renovated and with a Buddhist flavour, this haven is open to everyone and offers coaching, daily meditation with a Buddhist nun, an in-house

sauna and library, as well as massages, complementary therapy sessions, and vegetarian meals on request. There are just eight comfy rooms, and a beautiful decked terrace overlooking the sea.

Findhorn is 25 miles from Inverness airport. Take a bus or taxi from the airport to The Park or Forres (five miles apart) for Cluny Hill.

ISLAND RETREAT

Holy Island Centre for World Peace and Health

🌐 🅿 ⛎ ☀ ⛰ 🐕 ◪44

Lamlash Bay, Isle of Arran
T+44 (0)1770-601100
www.holyisland.org
From £25 per person per night

An unspoilt sanctuary off the Isle of Arran, Holy Island Centre for World Peace and Health offers a relaxing and healing retreat from everyday life. Some come here just to relax and enjoy the serene environment and fabulous scenery, while others are looking for healing, learning and meaning in life. Rooted in the Christian tradition, it's open to people of all faiths, or none, and runs a wide range of courses, from tai chi and meditation to cooking and gardening.

This is a great place to learn to meditate, and there are lots of courses to choose from, as well as yoga, Tibetan Buddhism and vegetarian cooking led by Rob, the chef, whose food is admired and enjoyed by all

who visit. Tai chi retreats include those run by Relaxing the Mind (see page 40) and Revitalise Tai Chi (see page 40). In the Mandala Garden, Sid and Sarah hold organic gardening weeks where you can learn how to grow plants and vegetables in a hostile environment; there's no topsoil on the island, yet they manage to grow an abundant array of flowers and plants here. The island is a great place to explore: there are rare plants and birds, an ancient healing spring, the hermit-cave of a sixth-century monk, and evidence of a 13th-century Christian monastery. If you want a longer retreat, consider staying as a volunteer.

The centre was built around a planted courtyard in 2003. The public rooms open off this area and most of the accommodation is on the first floor, in single, twin or dormitory rooms. All bathrooms are shared. Standing separately is the Peace Hall, where most activities take place. It has a high wooden ceiling and cosy underfloor heating. Further along the shore is the Boathouse, now a small shop/café and a shrine room.

Delicious and generously portioned vegetarian home-cooked meals use organic produce grown on the island wherever possible. Snacks and soft drinks are always

Holy Island Centre for World Peace and Health.

66 99

The short crossing from Arran in an open boat takes me into another, more peaceful world. An unexpected and abundant garden, warm and friendly volunteers, free afternoons spent gently weeding, or going up into the hills with Rinchen and his chainsaw to tackle the encroaching rhododendrons. These simple acts of service are repaid a thousandfold by the feelings of connection with the Holy Island community. Reluctant to leave, one participant extended her stay. My final sight was of her collecting horse manure in a wheelbarrow, her face alight with sheer happiness.

Sue Weston

From cashmere to canvas: health retreats in Scotland

Scotland boasts health retreats for whatever your needs may be. For those in need of a proper detox, expert nutritionist and queen of detoxing, Amanda Hamilton of **Life Detox** (T+44 (0)845-500 7545, www.lifedetox.co.uk), runs five-day retreats (from £1650) at Culcrieff Village, a five-star development in the grounds of the **Crieff Hydro Spa Hotel** in the Perthshire town of Crieff, a one-hour drive from Edinburgh. Amanda will lead your body detox, while life coach and therapist Sandy Newbigging will help sort out any negative thought patterns. Your full-on detox will include colon cleansing, and a full range of activities and therapies to support the detoxing process, including rolfing, yoga, lymph drainage massage, reflexology and sessions on raw food cooking and nutrition. You can use the Victorian spa of the main hotel, but retreat to the peaceful Culcrieff Village, away from hotel guests, who are more likely to be retoxing. You'll stay in twin or double en suite rooms in luxury lodges with great views and comfortable lounges with TV, DVD player and stereo to help you while away those detoxing hours. Life Detox also runs retreats to Spain and Turkey. See page 14 for what to expect from a detox.

Also in Crieff, **Roundelwood Health Spa** (from £45 per person per night, T+44 (0)1764-653806, www.roundelwoodhealthspa.co.uk) was first opened as the Crieff Health Institute in 1945 by Dr Gertrude Brown, one of the first doctors in the UK to combine traditional medicine with natural therapies and treatments. It's a very affordable if old-fashioned place emphasizing health rather than pampering – stop smoking, treat diabetes, or contemplate your life here with the Safari Spa, which involves living outdoors under canvas in the Highlands for one to three days accompanied by

a survival expert, and begins and ends with pampering treatments at the spa. Renovations started in 2006 and continue in 2007 to tart up bedrooms and rejuvenate jaded treatment rooms, but this is a friendly place to be, with a pretty garden, and high-ceilinged, spacious rooms in the main house.

Sybarites who require pampering should head for the lovely 100-year-old **Stobo Castle** (from £99 per person per night in the Castle Lodge including all meals, T+44 (0)1721-725300, www.stobocastle.co.uk), set on a hill overlooking a loch in the Borders countryside, near Peebles, 25 miles outside Edinburgh. The spa includes a mud chamber, aromatic steam room, crystal steam room and a 25-m ozone pool. You can learn about nutrition, detox, get fit, or indulge yourself with beauty treatments, puddings and fine wines. Rooms are traditionally smart – the Cashmere Suite is the best, its walls covered with cream and claret cashmere from Peebles. Outside, go walking along the Southern Upland Way.

STOBO CASTLE

Northern & Central Europe Scotland

available in the dining room – important when there is no shop on the island.

The international mix of visitors ensures you will meet like-minded others and make lifelong friendships. Come alone or with a friend. A single room costs £45, a twin £65 and a dormitory with eight others £25. Getting to the island is part of the adventure – the nearest airports are Glasgow International or Prestwick, from where you can get a train to Ardrossan harbour for a CalMac ferry to Brodick, on Arran, then a bus to Lamlash and the little ferry to Holy Island. Spring and summer are warm and lovely times to visit.

HOTEL & SPA

Isle of Eriska Hotel

Benderloch, near Oban, Argyll
T+44 (0)1631-720371
www.eriska-hotel.co.uk
From £290 per room per night

Scotland has many luxurious hotels with spas, but Eriska offers something special for body- -and-soul travellers. It's a 120-ha family- owned estate on a private island, attached to the mainland by a small bridge. The island looks out across the Lynn of Lorn and

boasts walking and cycle routes and pebbly beaches (good for quiet, contemplative walks), and badgers and stags roam the estate. There's a heated pool, sauna and

DENNIS HARDLEY COURTESY OF ISLE OF ERISKA HOTEL

steam room, pampering treatments with ESPA products, and golf and tennis facilities. Stay in a traditional grand room in the main Victorian house, or in one of the three spa suites. Minimum stay of two nights.

RURAL RETREAT

Lendrick Lodge

Brig O'Turk, Callander, Perthshire
T+44 (0)1877-376263
www.lendricklodge.com
From £76 per person for a weekend

Sitting in the heart of the Trossachs, overlooking the calm waters of Loch Venachar, Lendrick Lodge provides the perfect setting for a peaceful holistic retreat. Formerly a yoga centre, it was taken over in 2000 by Stephen and Victoria Mulhearn, who have created a friendly, home-from-home atmosphere for the range of yoga, reiki, shamanism and other holistic courses on offer. You can also stay here as an individual for a quiet break.

The lodge has standard rooms sleeping three to four people, or go for the River Retreat next door, which offers bright en suite twin and triple rooms and the soothing sound of the river flowing to ease you to sleep. Eating is communal, and the delicious vegetarian meals use delicious home-grown organic produce. No alcohol is allowed.

Highly qualified staff are on hand to help people through whatever course they choose; some of these – such as the shamanic sweat lodges and fire walking –

can be difficult yet enlightening experiences. Numbers on the courses are limited to 30 to ensure guests maintain that community feel and do not get lost in the crowd. Courses include Giant Steps, which is designed to initiate a positive outlook on life and release inner blocks and past negative experiences, and there is also a rebirthing pool used for healing and therapy work.

Staying as an individual on retreat, you are free to enjoy the meditation room, and have treatments, but be sure to book these in advance as the therapists are also used by the guests of a nearby hotel. Choose from reiki, acupuncture, colonic irrigation, aromatherapy, massage and reflexology.

Lendrick Lodge attracts all manner of guests, from the mature spiritual seeker to the city dweller looking for a break, and it's family friendly. Extend your trip with a few days cycling or walking in the glorious surroundings; if you're visiting in the summer, take some insect repellent as the Scottish midges are voracious. Fly to Edinburgh or Glasgow, from where it's a 1½-hour drive. The nearest station is Stirling, then take a bus to Callander, from where it's a 10-minute drive to the lodge.

ISLAND RETREAT

Via House

Sandwick, Orkney
T+44 (0)1856-841207
www.orkneyretreat.co.uk
From £250 per person for a weekend; £395 for a week

A 1900s farmhouse set in over three acres of mainland Orkney's western coast, Via House (via means 'a sacred place' in the Norse language) is set in one of the most rejuvenating locations in the UK. The Orkney islands are celebrated for their spectacular beauty and heritage, with unspoilt golden sands and ancient standing stones. As Orkney writer, George MacKay Brown, put it: "The essence of Orkney's magic is Silence, Loneliness and the deep marvellous

rhythms of Sea and Land, Darkness and Light."

Retreat owners Lynn Barbour and John Brooks organize a wealth of retreats here: tai chi and qigong courses focusing on meditation and breathwork, reiki and massage workshops, and creative courses in communication, Orkney folklore and artistic exploration. Complementary therapies are also available: choose from Chinese massage, creative visualization, reiki or bush essence remedies.

Accommodation is simple yet inviting. Each guest has their own room, which is based on one of the four elements. There's a great atmosphere in the house - you are invited to cosy up in the library for storytelling in front of the open peat fire. The area is steeped in history: step out of the door and you'll find a Bronze Age burial site, or amble a few miles along the coast to Skara Brae, a Stone Age village. Three miles away are the Ring of Brodgar and the Standing Stones of Stenness, both in a designated World Heritage site.

As you'd expect, seafood and fish are fresh and most vegetables are home-grown, and you'll find delights such as Orkney fudge and ice cream. Contrary to popular belief, the weather here is not damp, but can change in the blink of an eye. Sunrise and sunset are stunning, as is the aurora borealis, sometimes visible during winter.

Retreat prices are all inclusive, and can be tailor made to your needs. Via House attracts both men and women of all ages; disabled facilities are available. Students and writers will find it a perfect place to work in peace. Transfers from Stromness ferry port or Kirkwall airport are complimentary.

Left: Lendrick Lodge. **Above**: Via House on Orkney.

Ard Nahoo Health Farm

Mullagh, Dromahaire, County Leitrim
T+353 (0)71-913 4939
www.ardnahoo.com
From €67.50 per person per night

This simple, soulful health farm has a magical location in Yeats country, just a few miles from the Lake Isle of Innisfree, where 'peace comes dropping slow, Dropping from the veils of the morning to where the cricket sings'. Stress and tension start to melt away even as you meander up the single-track road to reach the centre's few wooden buildings, surrounded by fields dotted with sculptures by local artists.

Accommodation is in three fetching little wooden cabins, with sheepskin rugs and electric blankets, and sheltered front porches for sitting out on sunny days   compact and bijou they most certainly are. Cabins are self-catering, although Noeleen Tyrrell, who owns and runs the centre with her partner, Brendan Murphy, often cooks organic vegetarian feasts for lunch. She also thoughtfully stocks the cabins with staples: organic tea and coffee, milk and eggs, local jam and home-made bread.

In the main building, choose from a short no-nonsense list of treatments: simple massages and facials given with Dr Hauschka products and a lot of love. Alongside the treatment room there's a steam room and an Epsom float room (great for those who find a coffin-sized flotation tank too claustrophobic). The whole centre is refreshingly free from mirrors, as if to signal

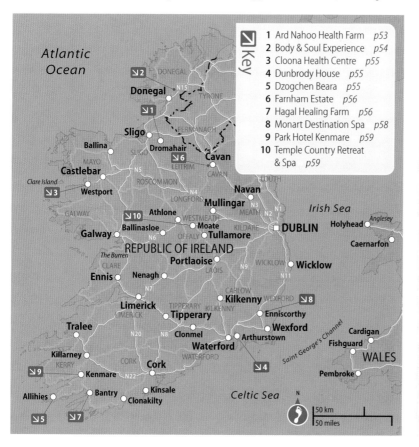

Key

1 Ard Nahoo Health Farm *p53*
2 Body & Soul Experience *p54*
3 Cloona Health Centre *p55*
4 Dunbrody House *p55*
5 Dzogchen Beara *p55*
6 Farnham Estate *p56*
7 Hagal Healing Farm *p56*
8 Monart Destination Spa *p58*
9 Park Hotel Kenmare *p59*
10 Temple Country Retreat & Spa *p59*

The emerald isle has it all, from gorgeous walking country and indulgent spas to island yoga and a Tibetan Buddhist haven.

Fact file

➲ **Visa:** None required for citizens of EU countries, the US, Canada, Australia and New Zealand

🕿 **IDD:** +353

💲 **Currency:** Euro (€)

🕑 **Time zone:** GMT

⚡ **Electricity:** 230v

ℹ **Tourist board:** www.ireland.ie

FRED CORCORAN

that this is a place for cultivating inner rather than outer beauty. The only gripe is that the eco-friendly showers lacked oomph.

From late 2007, Ard Nahoo will boast a new Japanese *osento* (communal bathing area), with an outdoor cedarwood hot tub, detox box (infrared sauna) and rain shower. A group room will be dedicated to yoga classes and a host of other activities, including courses and workshops. And a Celtic nature trail will culminate in a meditation garden.

Ard Nahoo is already the proud recipient of an EU flower symbol, awarded to eco-friendly businesses. This is a genuinely holistic enterprise, where the healing stillness of the Irish countryside is perfectly complemented by the warmth of the welcome and the integrity and simplicity of the approach. Treatments from €45. Fly to Knock, then it's an hour's drive. Or it's three hours from Dublin by car; or take a train to Sligo, from where it's 30 minutes by taxi (€25).

WELLBEING HOLIDAY
Body & Soul Experience

Lough Eske, County Donegal
T+353 (0)87-939 7821
www.bodysoulexperience.com
From €900 per person per weekend

Body and Soul Experience offers weekend and week-long wellbeing retreats combining walking, cycling and yoga with massage, detox baths and a reduced-calorie diet. Donegal boasts spectacular and unspoilt scenery: your walks include a trip to Slieve League, the highest sea cliffs in Europe, and

there are 10-mile cycle rides around the majestic and other-worldly Lough Eske.

Your base is Harvey's Point Country Hotel, set on Lough Eske. It's in an inspiring setting, the staff are friendly, and the bath tubs (and bedrooms) are huge, though some may find the ambience and muted brown interiors rather soulless and corporate for a wellbeing retreat.

Food is delicious vegetarian, with some fish dishes, reduced to 1000-1200 calories a day (if you've a high metabolism, or are here for exercise rather than weight loss, you can ask in advance for larger portions). You eat communally in the dining room, or in a cosy candlelit boathouse by the lake. A strict no smoking, alcohol or caffeine rule applies. Be warned that there will be other guests at the hotel enjoying good food and wine, which may make the detox harder to stick to for some.

Aidan Boyle, co-founder of **Body Soul Adventures in Brazil** (see page 378), is your relaxed if somewhat hands-off host. Two yoga classes a day are taught by Aidan, or teachers from Dublin, depending on the size of the group; American-Portuguese

Though you like the fat and meat which are eaten in the drinking halls, I like better to eat a head of clean watercress in a place without sorrow.

Seamus Heaney,
translation of 12th century manuscript

ashtanga-based yoga teacher, nutritionist and massage therapist Michele Van Valey (www.bodyworks.ie) is particularly good.

As well as walking and cycling, horse riding, sailing and surfing are sometimes on offer. Daily massages are done in your room

BODY & SOUL EXPERIENCE

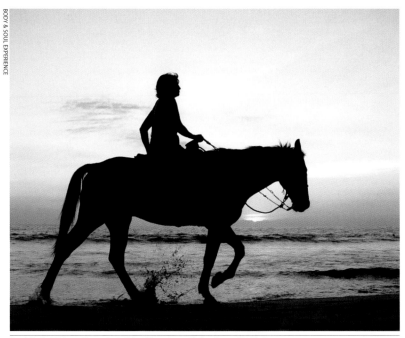

Top left: Ard Nahoo. **Above**: Body & Soul Experience. **Right**: Cloona Health Centre.

by local therapists, who are difficult to find in the area, and can be hit and miss.

The retreat attracts mothers looking for downtime and weight loss, and men and women – from Ireland, England and the US – who want to kick-start a fitness programme or detox. Those looking for an advanced fitness or yoga programme should look elsewhere. Fly to Belfast City or Belfast International airport from where it's a 3-3½-hour drive. Group pickups are included on some flights.

DETOX RETREAT

Cloona Health Centre

🌐 ⓐ ⓞ ⓜ ⓠ ⓧ ⬛3

Westport, County Mayo
T+353 (0)98-25251
www.cloona.ie
From €490 for 3 nights

This is an old-fashioned health farm, and all the better for it. The watchword is simplicity, from the crisp white sheets on the single beds to the structured regime of yoga, massage, walks and light vegan diet. Detox programmes have been on offer here since 1971, long before the concept became so fashionable. The majority of customers are professional Irish women over 40, and many visit every year.

Cloona is a converted watermill, a few kilometres from the Atlantic shore on Ireland's wild west coast. You can get here from central London in under four hours, but the contrast couldn't be starker: there is no television or radio, mobile phones are banned inside the house, and guests are

encouraged to keep contact with home to a minimum. This sounds draconian, but it's actually strangely indulgent – a cast-iron excuse to switch off completely and detox mind as well as body.

Owner and course director, Dhara Kelly, lays down the law with humour and charm. But the regime is strict: breakfast is citrus fruit, and is followed by two hours of gentle yoga and relaxation. Lunch – hearty vegan soup and plentiful salads – is mostly organic, and colourful and appetizing, if light on protein. A bracing 8-12-km guided walk follows – a different route every day through winding lanes, woodland trails or along windswept beaches.

The rest of the afternoon is free, with shiatsu, reflexology and massage available for around €55 a session. Dinner is a plate of fruit, and is followed by an optional sauna and a 20-minute massage (included in the course fee) before bed. Eight glasses a day of Cloona's own spring water are prescribed, and herbal teas stand in for coffee and alcohol.

One of the unexpected benefits of the programme is rediscovering the pleasure of eating when you're really hungry. You leave with skin positively glowing, and although the course is geared towards detox rather than weight loss, it's fairly likely your clothes will hang a little looser too.

Fly to Knock, from where it's an hour's drive. It's a four-hour drive from Dublin, or three hours by train to Westport, the nearest station.

HOTEL & SPA

Dunbrody House

ⓞ ⓜ ⓧ ⓟ ⬛4

County Wexford
T+353 (0)51-389600
www.dunbrodyhouse.com
From €150 per person per night

Ancestral home of the Chichester family, Dunbrody House, on County Wexford's dramatic Hook Peninsula, is all traditional Georgian elegance with its welcoming open fires, dark wood furniture and richly coloured furnishings. The spacious, individually styled

bedrooms and suites are enjoyed by guests from around the world, but it's the sensory experiences as much as aesthetics that seduce them.

Few spas offer champagne and lavender sorbets or chocolate fondues between treatments, but as you emerge from your suede-walled, muslin-draped therapy room, after an organic 'Savage Beauty Facial', an Elemis frangipani body wrap or perhaps the 'Uspa Ritual Body Massage', that is exactly what you can expect. Try the food-orientated beauty treatments too, including potato eye masks and chocolate mud therapy.

If you prefer the sensual experience of eating food rather than having it smoothed over you, the award-winning restaurant serves up a delicious seasonal menu using ingredients from its own organic kitchen garden. The creative flair rests safely in the hands of Celebrity Masterchef Kevin Dundon, who also designed the residential cooking courses that are held here. A sociable experience with a focus on fun, beginners and experienced chefs alike learn the art of creating mouthwatering dishes using the best and freshest Irish ingredients.

MEDITATION RETREAT

Dzogchen Beara

ⓐ ⬛5

Near Allihies, County Cork
T+353 (0)27-73032
www.dzogchenbeara.org
From €155 per person per weekend

Dzogchen Beara is a Tibetan Buddhist retreat centre under the spiritual direction of Sogyal Rinpoche, author of *The Tibetan Book of Living and Dying*. Set on high cliffs looking out to the Atlantic Ocean, on Ireland's lovely Beara Peninsula, it's open to people of all faiths, or none, and is a wonderfully natural and tranquil place to learn to meditate, or to deepen an existing practice.

There's a full programme of courses, seminars and retreats on offer year round on Buddhist subjects such as meditation, listening and developing compassion. All are

Above: Dzogchen Beara. Below: Farnham Estate.

led by respected teachers, many of whom are westerners. For those facing serious illness or death, the centre also runs a highly regarded spiritual care programme.

Accommodation is in three self-catering cottages, or in a dorm in the centre's farmhouse hostel. A registered charity, Dzogchen Beara is the long-term retreat centre for **Rigpa** (www.rigpa.org), an international network of Buddhist centres. The nearest airport, train station, bus station and port are in Cork, 160 km away. The nearest villages are Castletownbere 8 km and Allihies 11 km.

HOTEL & SPA

Farnham Estate

🐾 ⊛ ✪ ✪ ⊘ ↘6

County Cavan
T+353 (0)49-437 7700
www.farnhamestate.ie
From €180 per room per night

In 2006 Farnham Estate opened to the public for the first time in 300 years, when the Radisson SAS group unveiled a brand new resort featuring a 40,000-sq-ft health spa, the largest in Ireland. Come here midweek to create your own retreat, or be a weekender and indulge.

Designed by Heinz Schletterer, the spa complex features a Water Mint Thermal Suite, featuring a pastel green-tiled aroma steam room and a hotter and more intense salt inhalation grotto. There's also a laconium, kneipp walk, Finnish sauna and ice fountain. Work out in the gym, take a relaxation class in the studio, get pummelled in the small hydrotherapy pool or swim in the indoor/outdoor infinity pool, which has country views over Farnham's 530 ha of meadows and woodlands and is wonderful in cooler months, with steam rising off it.

This is a hotel spa, but it's no afterthought. The treatments are consistently excellent, from facials to therapeutic sports massages. Alongside gorgeous-smelling Aromatherapy Associates products, it uses a botanical range by Swedish company Kirsten Florian, which devised Farnham's signature treatment, The Farnham Cure, a two-hour total relaxation ritual involving steam, hydrotherapy 'wildflower bath', mineral mud wrap,

mini-facial and full body massage. The hotel accepts day guests, though the spaciousness here means you won't feel crowded. The spa's Pear Tree restaurant serves elegant and healthy dishes.

It's worth paying a little more for the space and elegant country-character of one of the eight suites in Farnham House (from €100 extra per room midweek). Hotel interiors are contemporary and effectively decked out with giant photographs of the flora, fauna, forests and lakes of the estate taken during different seasons. In the evenings, the lounge bar area makes a more cosy and inspiring eating space than the main restaurant.

Conferences sometimes take place here, so be sure to check in advance that you won't be surrounded by suits. A private residential development opens late 2007, and an 18-hole golf course is planned for 2008, so you will experience building work at some points. It's 90 minutes from Dublin airport; take a bus to Cavan town or a train to Longford, or it's a €145 transfer by car.

RURAL RETREAT

Hagal Healing Farm

🌍 ⊛ 🐾 ⊛ ✪ ✪ ⊘ ↘7

Coomleigh, Bantry, County Cork
T+353 (0)27-66179
www.hagalhealingfarm.com
From €30 per person per night

Dutch expatriates Fred and Janny Wieler offer retreat programmes or accommodation facilities for those who want to create a retreat of their own. Their rural country farmhouse is 13 km from Bantry town and bay, in Mealagh Valley, at the foot of the Maughnaclea mountains in west Cork.

The Wielers have been in Ireland since the late 1970s and Hagal has become a family business. You'll find the atmosphere easy going and welcoming; everyone is invited to join the family in the main house for freshly picked wild herb tea and a chat, which makes the place special. This is a popular retreat, and you'll need to book well in advance to join their weekend and five-day programmes.

Yoga in the Emerald Isle

Remote hideaways in the Irish countryside are perfect for distraction-free yoga and meditation. **Clare Island Yoga Retreat Centre** (from €65 per day, T+353 (0)98-25412, www.yogaretreats.ie) offers residential yoga and meditation courses for beginners and advanced practitioners on a 97-ha farm on Clare Island off Ireland's west coast. Hosts Ciara and Christophe also run an organic guesthouse. Visiting teachers from around the globe bring a variety of practices and philosophies, and Ciara and Christophe also take courses combining ashtanga-based vinyasa flow with pranayama and meditation. Alternatively, try the workshop combining yoga and ayurvedic vegetarian cooking.

The yoga room is peaceful, with views over Clew Bay and Croagh Patrick. Accommodation is in shared homely rooms with solar water heaters and a cosy wood burner. Meals are strictly vegetarian and ingredients are mostly organic or home-grown and totally GM free. Try local farmhouse cheeses and butter with freshly baked bread. Drinking water comes from a private spring. Take relaxing walks to the nearby lighthouse, have a swim in the Atlantic or relax and read. Rates are for full board. The retreat attracts visitors from many countries, but guests are mainly British and Irish women from 25 to 60. Fly to Dublin, take a train to Westport and a taxi to Roonagh Pier.

The remote **Burren Yoga and Meditation Centre** (from €670 for a seven-day retreat, T+353 (0)91-637680, www.burrenyoga.com) is set at the foot of the Burren hills, 8 km from the seaside village of Kinvara, on the Galway-Clare border. It hosts around 40 weekend and one-week courses for beginners, advanced students and teachers. You'll find ashtanga, iyengar, satyananda, and kundalini yoga, and bikram, which is practised in a heated room (40.5°C); beginners need to be reasonably fit as postures require strength. Other workshops offer meditation, detox, vegetarian cooking and Buddhist teachings. Buildings are eco-friendly with underfloor heating. Male and female dormitories have bunk beds; small single rooms are also available. Bathrooms are shared; one has a two-person bath for romantic relaxing. Food is vegetarian, fresh and wholesome. Meals are served in the kitchen or on the patio in good weather and snacks are always available. You'll be expected to do some karma yoga by helping to clear up meals and keep the bathroom and yoga studio clean, which is a good way of meeting fellow guests.

East Clare Yoga Centre (from €290 including transfers from Shannon Airport, T+353 (0)61-640923, www.eastclareyoga.com) is a family-run residential retreat centre set in two acres of gardens and woodland in rural Tuamgraney, County Clare. The focus is purely iyengar yoga with all teachers certified in the iyengar tradition; check the website for specific programmes. The centre offers weekend retreats which include up to 13 hours of yoga along with group meals and country walks; make sure you ramble in their grounds, which host some of the oldest oak trees in Europe. The yoga studio is bright and simple. Meals are home-cooked and vegetarian, and healthy snacks such as dried and fresh fruits and nuts are available throughout the weekend. Water comes from an on-site well. Bedrooms are cosy with either en suite or shared bath. Relax during evenings by the wood burning stove in the living room. Expect to meet British and Irish mostly female, guests. The centre is closed in December and January.

BURREN YOGA (WWW.BURRENYOGA.COM)

CLARE ISLAND

HAGAL HEALING FARM

Above: Hagal Healing Farm. **Bottom:** Monart Destination Spa. **Right:** Park Hotel Kenmore.

If you are not booking a programme, you can choose a treatment in advance, or risk availability and see what you feel like when you arrive. Yoga is thoroughly recommended here: the peaceful landscape and fresh coastal air is the perfect complement to asanas. Other therapies include massages – therapeutic, Indian head, hot stone, Thai and aromatherapy – and reflexology, reiki, and seaweed body wraps and facials. On a detox health retreat you'll get daily yoga and guided relaxation sessions, saunas, walks and four treatments, of which two are your own your choice. Pampering weekends combine treatments and saunas with rest and walking. Packages start from €225. Hagal also offers a variety of training classes and diplomas in reiki, Indian head massage, holistic massage or vegetarian cooking.

The 150-year-old farmhouse is recently renovated and offers some modern rooms with valley views through huge windows to the Atlantic Ocean. Bedrooms are simple and comfortable. There's an open fire in the living room, or retreat to the garden, which is filled with wild flowers during summer months.

You can book full board or just breakfast.

Meals are served in a conservatory festooned with vines and luscious-looking blue grapes in season. A lot of the food comes from their organic vegetable plot and all meals are freshly prepared. Fly to Cork, from where it's a 1½-hour drive.

HEALTH & FITNESS RETREAT

Monart Destination Spa

🏔 🟤 🟢 🟢 🟢 🟢 📶 8

Enniscorthy, County Wexford
T+353 (0)53-923 8999
www.monart.ie
From €130 per person per night

This €30 million development sets a new standard for Ireland's destination health retreats. Announce your arrival at the electronic gates, sweep up the driveway to a handsome Georgian manor house and the red-carpet treatment begins. Your car is parked, your luggage whisked away and you are ceremoniously ushered inside. From the back of the manor house a gleaming glass tunnel leads from the old world to the new. Nestled in a glorious garden, the Monart's

modern extension curves its two arms to embrace a central pond: bedrooms are in one wing, restaurants and spa in the other, all overlooking an enchanting prospect of mature trees, mossy banks, and paths that meander over stone bridges and under ivy-clad bowers. The old house boasts two magnificent suites with claw-footed baths and four-posters, while in the 68 rooms in the new wing the decor is cool and modern; high ceilings and vast picture windows.

The highlight is undoubtedly the thermal spa. With no less than nine different 'environments' – from saunas to scented rain showers, a salt grotto and a hydrotherapy pool – it's a place to linger all afternoon. Thoughtful details like heated sun loungers and free foot massage help to set the tone. It is designed to be 'gender neutral', so as not to alienate the guys. Indeed, the Monart claims its proportion of male guests is 40%.

Beauty treatments use the Pevonia Botanicals range – all-natural products with very high levels of active plant ingredients. As with most UK destination spas, if you need a real therapeutic massage rather than a pampering rub-down, you'll need to ask for a specialist massage therapist. But the regular spa staff – the majority of them local Wexford girls – are charming, professional and extremely well trained. Detox, weight-loss and anti-ageing programmes are available.

MONART DESTINATION SPA

There's a state-of-the-art gym with personal trainers, and golf, horse riding and walking can be organized on request. The restaurant offers food and wine of a very high standard with few concessions to dieters or detoxers, although you will find lighter fare if you choose carefully. In the mornings, a hearty Irish breakfast seems to be the most popular option. A thoughtful raised walkway means you can trundle from your room to the restaurant, to the spa and back again in robe and slippers without even having to cross the reception area. Treatments cost €45-230. Fly to Dublin, from where it's 2½ hours by car. Note that Monart is an adults-only retreat.

HOTEL & SPA

Park Hotel Kenmare

🌐 🅿 ♨ ⊙ ♒ ✿ ✸ ❀ ⌖ №9

Kenmare, County Kerry
T+353 (0)64-41200
www.samaskenmare.com
From €140 per person for 'SÁMAS Experience'

Overlooking Kenmare Bay, Park Hotel Kenmare has an exceptional luxury spa exclusively for its residents. SÁMAS (Gaelic for 'indulgence of the senses') is in an idyllic location, in rich green woodland with picturesque views over the water. Dating from 1897, the hotel is a testament to gracious living, with a wonderful collection of antiques and original oils all accessible for the enjoyment of guests.

SÁMAS offers a variety of activities, from simple spa treatments to a complete holiday agenda. The 'lifestyle' option combines morning woodland walks and daily events with their signature spa treatment, the 'SÁMAS Experience'. Start in the Thermal Suite with a sauna and crystal steam room, after which take a tropical mist shower and a crushed ice fountain. Swim in the outdoor vitality pool, or relax on the edge of the infinity pool. Treatments on offer include massage, such as pre-natal and hot stone, facials and beauty treatments, body polish

and reflexology. To finish, lie back on an olive wood bench, plug yourself into their relaxation music and gaze at the fibre-optic coloured lights drifting in front of you.

Join Oriental arts classes in their light, wooden practice hall: choose from yoga, pilates, tai chi, meditation, qigong and Thai massage. For a romantic break book the couple's day suite, which has two treatment couches, and private spa pool. Retreats take place here, including a Yoga Hikes trip run by the **Power of Three** (see www.tpo3.com) with UK-based yoga teacher Katy Appleton and energy healer Alla Svirinskaya.

The hotel has no meeting rooms, and bedrooms overlook either the water or gardens. Garden rooms have private verandas, or ask for one of the eight rooms with private gardens. The hotel is 43 km from Kerry airport.

RURAL RETREAT

Temple Country Retreat & Spa

🌐 🅿 ♒ ✸ ❀ ⌖ №10

Moate, County Westmeath
T+353 (0)57-933 5118
www.templespa.ie
From €200 per person per night

Declan and Bernadette Fagan have been sharing their quiet brand of Irish hospitality

on the site of a sixth-century monastery in County Westmeath since 1987, when they began to offer their guests yoga and massage alongside traditional Irish country house B&B. The combination proved so popular that these days a purpose-built destination spa stands here, its 23 simply but luxuriously appointed rooms enjoying panoramic views over the couple's 40-ha farm.

Although there are daily yoga and relaxation classes, the holistic element is discreetly downplayed. Classes are aimed at absolute beginners and there's no incense or chanting to frighten off the sceptics – accordingly, the spa attracts a good many older couples and stressed-out businessmen. Most guests come for the peace and quiet, the delicious food and the more than 80 face and body treatments on offer.

Sweet, well-trained, uniformed staff pamper their clients with a range of options. For example, Italian luxury beauty range ISHI is exclusively available in Ireland through Temple Spa. Its products are food-based, majoring on chocolate, fruit, wine and even truffles. The 'Chocotherapy Body Wrap' begins and ends with a square of dark chocolate on the tongue, followed by full body exfoliation, anti-cellulite serum and chocolate orange body wrap, with a chocolate mini-facial thrown in for good measure. If that's not your cup of tea, there's the 'Natural Moor' massage: two sealed bags of peat, moist and hot as though fresh from the teapot, warm the torso while the therapist works top to toe to ease out knots.

For appetites whetted by various food-based treatments, the real food is, fortunately, rather good. You can choose to arrange a session with a nutritionist but rigorous detox is not really the point here: the restaurant menu emphasizes high quality organic ingredients, fresh flavours and modest portions, all beautifully presented. There's also a juice bar and a cosy lounge with an open fire, ideal for afternoon tea. If you can be tempted out of your bathrobe for an hour or so, daily guided walks and a range of classes are included in all spa packages. Fly to Dublin, from where it's a 1¼-hour drive.

Scandinavia

The land of the Midnight Sun and the Northern Lights offers some delightful and unusual retreats in remote, unpolluted environments.

Fact file

- **Visa:** None required for citizens of EU countries, the US, Canada, Australia and New Zealand

- **IDD:** Denmark +45; Finland +358; Iceland +354; Sweden +46

- **Currency:** Denmark Kroner (DKK); Finland Euro (€); Iceland Krona (ISK); Sweden Kroner (SEK)

- **Time zone:** Denmark GMT +1 hour; Finland GMT +2 hours; Iceland GMT; Sweden GMT +1 hour

- **Electricity:** Denmark 230v; Finland 230v; Iceland 220v; Sweden 230v

- **Tourist board:** Denmark: www.visitdenmark.com; Finland: www.visitfinland.com; Iceland: www.icelandtouristboard.com; Sweden: www.visitsweden.com

Denmark

COASTAL RETREAT

Svinkløv Badehotel

Fjerritslev
T+45 9-821 7002
www.svinkloev-badehotel.dk
From €130 per room per night

Picturesque and romantic bathing hotels (*badehoteller*) dot the coastline of Denmark. Built over 100 years ago, before planning restrictions were in force, many are in peaceful surroundings just metres from the sea, and spending time at one is a great way to get back to an easier and purer lifestyle. One of the best is Svinkløv Badehotel, built in 1925 and located in solitary splendour just 200 m from the North Sea in one of the best-preserved wooden houses in Denmark.

With sea views everywhere you look, this is the ideal place to get back to the simple things in life – a long walk on the beach, reading a book in front of the fire, enjoying a rustic meal. The chef buys fresh seasonal local produce on a daily basis, and each day offers a new menu. The 36 bedrooms are relatively small, with minimalist decor in light colours and wooden floors throughout. There are five singles. Half of the rooms have sea views, the other half views of the forest nearby.

The area around Svinkløv is renowned for its long wide sandy beaches. Take a walk in the forest or experience the wild landscapes of the west coast with its hillsides, dunes, forests and ravines. Skagen, an idyllic old fishing village just north of Svinkløv, is famous for its wonderful light and has attracted artists since the 19th century. Check out the work of the most famous Skagen artists, Anna and Michael Ancher and PS Krøyer, in the local Skagen Museum, which was founded by the painters themselves and houses more than 1700 works of art. The hotel is open from April to October. The nearest airport is Aalborg.

Finland

COASTAL RETREAT

Box Tours

Box Gård
T+358 (0)50-500 2248
www.boxtours.com
From €785 per person per day

In a remote and rocky coastal setting, Box Tours offers bespoke three-day or week-long wellbeing retreats on Box Gård, a large and relatively undiscovered island on the Finnish archipelago, 85 km southwest of Helsinki.

Yoga on the Rocks and ayurveda retreats are run for groups of up to six people, and packages are tailored to meet the group's requirements. Hatha-based yoga is taught by Tarja Aalto, who trained under several Indian masters during her travels in Asia, as well as in Finland. Sessions take place in a renovated barn, with its 1½ m-thick rock walls, or in the garden that overlooks the sea. The garden is fenced, but elk and deer occasionally wander in.

Ayurveda retreats include two individual wellness consultations, and lectures to demonstrate how ayurveda can help you personally. You'll also get a massage each day; you can choose from abhyanga, a stimulating head massage, or marma massage. Detox in the traditional sauna, or soak in a hot tub filled with wild flowers. Longer panchakarma detox retreats of two weeks or more, can be arranged if you book well in advance, when treatments are carried

Right: Box Tours, Finland.

out by Indian ayurvedic doctors.

The group is accommodated in a homely environment. A housekeeper takes care of cleaning so you can relax in two large living rooms with working fireplaces and a separate dining area. There are two single rooms and three doubles. Food is mostly organic and locally grown. You'll sample some vegetarian Finnish specialities, cooked using traditional recipes with an ayurvedic twist. Think oven-baked cheese with cloudberries, local green salad, local black sweet bread, and lots of seasonal fresh berries. You can drink their own well water.

In your spare time, walk in the private forest and fields, and gather the wild flowers and herbs used in the hot tub and sauna. You can also pick berries and edible mushrooms. There's a hut in the forest from which you can enjoy nature, and in good weather you can take a boat trip to barren rocky islands. During winter there's a chance to see the aurora borealis at night; you'll experience the midnight sun in summer. Fly to Helsinki airport, from where transfers are extra.

Method Putkisto with Marja Putkisto.

Midnight Sun Ashtanga Yoga Retreat.

MARJA PUTKISTO
STEFAN ENGSTRÖM

METHOD PUTKISTO HOLIDAY

Method Putkisto with Marja Putkisto

🐟 ⊕ ✪ ☒3

Lapland
T+44 (0)20-8878 7384
www.methodputkisto.com
From €1400 per person per week

Marja Putkisto hosts annual week-long Method Putkisto holidays at the alpine **Rokua Health Farm** and Spa (www.rokua.fi), on the edge of Lapland in central Finland. Marja established the method to correct her hip problem, and it aims to improve body alignment through movement, deep stretching, breathing and strengthening muscles.

During daily sessions you'll learn how to control your spine for everyday movements, and you can practise these whilst walking and skipping on alpine moss around the lake. You should find that the exercises boost energy levels and rebalance muscles; Marja recommends the method for relaxing.

Expect nutritious meals and crisp Scandinavian country air. For an additional fee you can have a four-hour Face School course, which teaches you how to utilize facial muscles for reduced puffiness, double chin and other benefits. Spa treatments are available at Rokua. Accommodation is simple, clean and bright.

The trip takes place during the summer, so you can experience the midnight sun, and is aimed at all ages and fitness levels. You should note there are 250 steps at the resort. The rate includes accommodation, meals, unlimited use of Rokua's equipment, a gym, sauna and pool. Rokua is one hour from Oulu and Kajaani airports.

Marja also runs trips to Kumlubuk in Turkey, see page 151.

YOGA RETREAT

Midnight Sun Ashtanga Yoga Retreat

🐟 ♨ ☀ ✪ ☒4

Kadermo, Hanko
T+358 (0)40-502 9811
www.yogaartsmagic.net
From €370 per person per week

Stefan Engström runs yoga retreats from the island of Kadermo, just east of Hanko on the southwest tip of Finland. The island is remote, with no cars or shops, so expect an all-natural, dramatic coastal haven in which to concentrate on yoga.

Stefan has trained with several teachers in India, including Sri K Pattabhi Jois and his retreats focus on ashtanga vinyasa yoga. Stefan performs and teaches fluidly and you'll find you work up quite a sweat, which helps the body detox. Some programmes are combined with dance workshops, such as Bollywood dancing and Argentine tango. Other retreats are occasionally run by guest teachers and lecturers.

The white-wood house is very pretty, with plenty of windows for lots of light. Accommodation is shared; single rooms are extra. All food served is vegetarian. There's a small café on the island where you can listen to piano music, and, in good weather, an island boat tour is recommended.

Courses are designed for beginners and experienced practitioners of all ages. Most are run in English and take place from June to September, with longer retreats during Christmas and Easter holidays, and several weekend and special events throughout the year. You can come and stay for as long as you feel comfortable: a weekend or several months (the weekly rate reduces the longer you stay). Fellow guests are mostly, but not exclusively, women, and the place is popular with Finnish students. Fly to Helsinki and take a train to Hanko.

Iceland

NATURAL SPA RETREAT

Blue Lagoon Clinic

🜂 ⊕ ⊕ ⊕ ⊘ ⊿5

Grindavík
T+354 (0)4-208806
www.bluelagoon.com
From €193 per room per night

Soaking in natural spas is a great Icelandic tradition and locals, young and old, come to the Blue Lagoon all year round to bathe. It's just 40 minutes from Iceland's capital, and en route to the airport. If you're looking for a wellbeing break, however, that's possible too – you can stay at the Blue Lagoon Clinic. Known for offering geothermal seawater as a treatment programme to help serious skin diseases such as psoriasis, the clinic is also open to those who just want to relax and use the lagoon.

Research from Blue Lagoon's laboratory claims that a soak in the milky blue waters could have powerful anti-ageing effects on skin, and that silica mud, found in the lagoon, and various algae could provide skin protection properties. The laboratory has a skincare range, but you can't beat the real thing. Water filters through magma rock at 240°C, before it reaches the lagoon. The air outside is cold, but you'll feel toasty and warm with water temperatures of 37-39°C.

Above: Hotel Glymur. **Right:** Blue Lagoon. **Far right:** Back to basics with Magma Essentials.

You should soak for at least an hour to open skin pores, allow the water's minerals to sink in, and increase your blood circulation. Slather the white silica mud on your face and body as it exfoliates and also stimulates blood flow. The lagoon is surrounded by dark-grey volcanic rock, a barren and moon-like setting alongside the aquamarine waters, and you'll find your soak a multi-sensory experience. For complete indulgence, try a massage or spa treatment such as a body scrub or facial, taken while floating on mats in shallow water. You'll need to book these in advance.

The clinic is a five-minute walk from the lagoon. Bedrooms are spacious and modern, with pale wooden flooring and large windows that let in lots of light. All rooms are en suite and have TV and internet access. There's a fitness room, saunas and a communal area with a cosy fireplace and views of surrounding lava. The snack bar and restaurant, which overlooks the waters, mostly offers fish dishes, but they also have a good range of vegetarian options.

Entrance to the Lagoon is from €15 per person per day, if you're not staying at the clinic. Towels, bathing suits and robes are available to hire. Take a taxi or bus from Keflavik airport (20 minutes).

WATERSIDE RETREAT

Hotel Glymur

☀ ⊕ ⊕ ⊕ ⊕ ⊕ ⊕ ⊿6

Hvalfjordur
T+354 (0)4-303100
www.hotel.glymur.com
From €140 per person per night

Set high on a mountainside overlooking the scenic Hvalfjordur, with open-air hot tubs and creative courses, cosy and friendly Hotel Glymur is an ideal place for a personal retreat.

Hvalfjordur – which means 'whale fjord' – is surrounded by inspiring scenery. The hot tubs contain geothermal heated water and are on the mountainside overlooking the fjord.

Holistic health company, **Icefusion** (www.icefusion.eu), runs creative retreats to enable people to connect with the country's environment and energies, and to meet Icelandic poets, artists and healers. A five-day Sunfusion course in June, for example, combines stretching yoga, laughing yoga, colour meditation and chanting, with visits to a sweat tent in Reykjavík, the Snaefellsnes (an area known for its natural energy), and the Blue Lagoon. Songwriting, film-making, creative writing and fashion and textile seminars are also planned.

The hotel's 22 en suite rooms are arranged over two floors, with bathroom and sitting room on the lower level and the sleeping area upstairs. Wooden floors, wrought iron banisters and painted white walls create a sleek and spacious setting, and all rooms have Wi-Fi access.

The hotel is one big art gallery, and exhibitions by Icelandic artists take place regularly. The menu uses fresh local ingredients such as lamb and fish to create traditional fare with a modern influence. Fly to Reykjavík, from where it's a 45-60-minute drive – take a taxi or rent a car. Summer is best for exploring and walking, or come between September and March for a chance to see the Northern Lights.

YOGA & ACTIVITY HOLIDAY

Magma Essentials

🌐 ☀ 🏔 🎧 ⊘ ↘7

Reykjahlíd, Myvatn
T+354 (0)4-643740
www.magmaessentials.com
Price varies

Ásta Price organizes bespoke retreats in back-to-basics surroundings, combining yoga and massage with Iceland's energizing natural landscapes. Reykjahlíd is a small village with just 250 people located in Myvatn, northeast Iceland, which is known as the 'diamond circle' due to its numerous natural assets.

Ásta's aim is to balance creative and spiritual energies and heighten your sense of self-awareness. Her holidays are a holistic mix of aromatherapy and relaxation massage, art and dance improvisation classes, reiki and yoga. As well as hatha yoga, Ásta teaches ergonomically designed rope yoga based on a technique developed by Icelander, Gudni Gunnarsson. Rope yoga involves energetic body movements that promote strength and stamina, regulate breathing and stimulate blood flow. Another of her skills is deep tissue health massage using the Brandon Raynor Technique: Icelanders drive over 100 km to experience it.

Magma Essentials does not provide accommodation on site; Ásta will organize a hotel, guesthouse, hostel or camping to suit your budget, close to Magma's base. Whether you eat out or in your hotel, you can sample healthy food and local specialities such as Arctic char (a type of trout), home-made cheeses and geyser bread baked in the geothermal ground.

You'll find Icelandic air fresh and invigorating, and the activities you can add to the Magma experience are inspiring. Choose from whale-watching, exploring ice caves, hiking trails, climbing craters or walking through sculptured lava fields. During summer months expect 24-hours of daylight, great for birdwatching on the lake. During winter months it's light for only around four hours each day, so join the locals in hot lagoons to admire the Northern Lights over extensive white horizons. Interestingly, some say Myvatn's location between North American and Euro-Asian tectonic plates gives the region a boost of positive energy.

Price depends on how many are in a group and the package of yoga and treatments you want. Private yoga lessons cost from €54 per session. Magma Essentials offers retreats year round; Iceland attracts most tourists from June to August, winter is quiet – be prepared for extreme cold. Fly to Aukereyri from the domestic airport at Reykjavík (45 minutes). Magma is a one-hour drive from Aukereyri, use a 4WD and drive slowly.

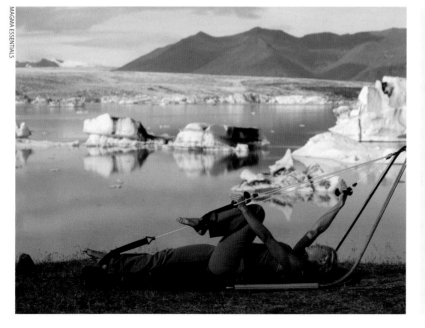

MAGMA ESSENTIALS

🖐 Soul food

Landmannalaugar is Iceland's second-largest geothermal field, a stunning landscape dominated by colourful rhyolite peaks and valleys, blue mountain lakes, and rambling lava flows. The UK-based organization **Charity Challenge** (T+44 (0)20-8557 0000, www.charitychallenge.com) runs two annual long-weekend treks to the region each summer, open to anyone who wants to raise money for a charity of their choice. The trek includes the chance to soothe tired limbs in the naturally occurring hot pools and springs dotting the route, as well as a dip in the Blue Lagoon on the last day .

Sweden

RURAL RETREAT

RURAL RETREAT

Aurora Retreat

Lapland
T+46 (0)97-830061
www.auroraretreat.se
From €71 per person per night

Canadian Maya Rao and her Swedish husband, Mikael Kangas, opened this remote retreat inside the Arctic Circle in 2005. Located in a quiet, tiny village in Lapland surrounded by forests, rivers and wetlands, they offer tailor-made breaks with a creative focus for individuals, and also run a few annual retreats focusing on topics such as yoga and music.

From June to September you can gather Arctic herbs to make pine needle oil and herbal footbaths, pick wild blueberries, lingonberries and cloudberries, and bake your own bread using their wood-fired oven. You can learn felt and textile crafts, visit local woodworkers and watch birchbark craft and willow working. You will also witness the natural phenomenon of the midnight sun during the summer months, and there are several day trips in the area if you have your own car, including to a moose park at the nearby village of Vittangi.

The Northern Lights are visible during the winter months of October to April. One of the winter activities is a cross-country night ski in search of the aurora borealis, which includes a campfire under the stars. You can explore the landscape during the day on skis or kicksledge, or experience a 35-km dog sledge tour. Try your hand at snow sculpture or meet a Sámi reindeer herder who will teach you ancient forest crafts. In December children can visit Santa Claus.

Maya runs weekly yoga sessions in Swedish; private or group sessions can be arranged in English, as can movement classes. You can also enjoy a woodfired sauna, best taken during winter evenings.

Maya is fanatical about cooking and lovingly prepares organic vegetarian cuisine using ayurvedic techniques, with wholesome grains and seasonal vegetables and, on occasion, fresh fish from local rivers.

The guesthouse is a renovated village vicarage. There are just four double bedrooms, which have simple furniture and light wooden flooring; bathrooms are shared. Aurora recycles and reuses as much as possible; even human waste is composted. You are expected to help them by recycling any waste you produce; they sell reusable sanitary towels, nappies and handkerchiefs. Mobile phones are discouraged.

❝❞

Worry gives small things a big shadow.

Swedish proverb

Aurora attracts people from all over, including families, couples and groups of mainly middle-aged women. December to April are the most interesting months to visit, because of the snow, polar night and Northern Lights. Rates are for full board; activities are not included. Aurora only takes advance bookings, and the retreat can also be booked through www.responsibletravel.com.

Haa International Course Center.

YOGA RETREAT

Haa International Course Center

Hamneda
T+46 (0)37-255063
www.yogameditation.com
From €715 per person per retreat

Danish yogi, Swami Janakananda, established the Haa centre as a Swedish base for his Scandinavian Yoga and Meditation School in 1972. It has since become renowned throughout Europe.

The 10- or 14-day yoga and meditation retreats are aimed at beginners and experienced practitioners and teach classical yoga, breathing exercises, deep relaxation and tantric meditation. There is no TV, newspaper, radio or internet access and you have to hand in your mobile phone on arrival (they will pass on emergency calls). You must complete this course if you want to take their advanced four-week course in kriya yoga, which offers deep meditations to regenerate personal strengths and self-development, and is taught during 21 days of silence. There is also a three-month sadhana programme open to everyone serious about yoga.

Single, double and dormitory accommodation is available with private or shared bath. Rooms are allocated according to gender and booking order, but if you request a single room you will get a private bathroom. Houses are light and airy, constructed of brightly painted wood and nestled between trees in the grounds. Rooms are plain and simple, with light pine furniture and big windows.

Meals are served in the communal dining room, which provides a chance to get to know your fellow guests. Food is vegetarian and mostly comes from their organic gardens. Milk, sugar, spices, coffee, chocolate, black tea and alcohol are avoided here. During a 10-day period following the intestinal cleansing day, raw vegetables and fruit are avoided. You are advised to wean yourself off coffee and tea and other toxins before you arrive.

Courses are taught in English. Rates include accommodation and food; you need to buy or bring a string of 108 beads for meditation and a plastic netipot (nasal cleaning pot). Fly to Copenhagen in Denmark and take a train to Älmhult (two hours), Haa is a 25-km taxi ride. Ensure you arrive before 1900.

RURAL RETREAT

The Sun Garden

🌞 ⚕ ♨ ⛷ ⊙ ○ ☯ ☑10

Ljungaverk
T+46 (0)69-133100
www.thesungarden.com
From €60 per person per night

Marie and Jamie set up the Sun Garden in 2003 as a wellbeing retreat for individuals, in a grand, stylish house set in mature parkland at the edge of a village, and overlooking a river. Marie is Swedish and Jamie Scottish, and classes can be held in either Swedish or English. Hatha-based yoga and meditation sessions are on offer, as well as life coaching and a selection of treatments. Occasional talks and lectures run in the grounds.

Treatments include Indian head massage, Thai massage and bio-energy therapy. Jamie offers Egyptian sekhem, an ancient healing art that channels body energies. Reiki master Patrick Zeigler discovered sekhem while meditating in Egypt in 1984 (www.sekhemhome.com).

The Sun Garden.

The house has an imposing marble fireplace downstairs and plenty of places to relax. There is a sitting room, yoga and meditation room, and a reading area with a collection of books on healing (mostly in English). There are just three guest bedrooms, sleeping eight people, and all overlooking the garden; the bathroom is shared. Vegetarian food is cooked with local seasonal produce and is organic where possible.

Take the opportunity to wander the woodland, gardens and along the river; this is a place you can visit just to relax and escape the daily grind. In the grounds is a cosy log cabin with a big fireplace. In high season try the Summer Café where you can buy light snacks and teas.

There is a minimum two-night stay. Fellow guests are usually Swedish career women and mothers, aged between 35-45, who need a break. Fly to Sundsvall airport, where Marie or Jamie will pick you up for a nominal fee.

HOTEL & SPA

Yasuragi

⊙ ⚕ ○ ♨ ❄ ☯ ☑11

Hasseludden
T+46 (0)87-476400
www.yasuragi.se
From €140 per person per night

Yasuragi (meaning 'inner peace and harmony'), is a hushed sanctuary 20 minutes' drive from Stockholm. A sophisticated hotel spa that draws stressed Swedes like a magnet, it was built in accordance with Japanese Buddhist aesthetics to create calm-inducing interiors, with untreated wood, pale stone, simple lines and sleek, low-lying furniture. A feng shui expert regularly reviews the accommodation to maintain a positive flow of energy.

On arrival, you receive a cotton kimono, slippers and swimming costume. Drifting blissfully through Zen meditation, qigong, massage and ritualistic bathing, you won't need much else. The en suite bedrooms and suites, each with views across Höggarnsfjärden

Have an ice day

While you're near Stockholm, and if there's a cold winter, try *bada isvak* – bathing in a hole in the ice – usually done after baking yourself in a very hot sauna. The process is supposed to improve circulation and eliminate toxins though, as the writer Fraser Nelson puts it, 'it is an extreme sport for the ultra lazy, delivering all of the thrills with none of the exertion.' Half way to Stockholm from Yasuragi lies **Hellasgården** (www.hellasgarden.se), an outdoor recreation area with ski tracks, ice skating and a sauna.

Bay, feature tatami floor coverings – thick straw mats – and either a futon or double bed. Dormitory accommodation sleeps up to eight, but the more you pay, the richer the Japanese experience. The minimally furnished Ryokan suites for two to eight people include a hot spring in the bathroom, a wooden tub and a mosaic bath. Aromatherapy, classic Japanese and hot-stone massages are all available in your room.

Lessons in the art of hot spring bathing are held every half hour. You can also enroll on a weekend sushi course or just enjoy the meticulously prepared, beautifully presented Japanese food in the hotel restaurants.

Yasuragi.

Rest of Europe

Soak away the blues or sort your life out on top of a mountain.

Fact file

- **Visa:** None required for citizens of EU countries, the US, Canada, Australia and New Zealand
- **IDD:** Austria +43; Germany +49; Slovenia +386; Switzerland +41
- **Currency:** Austria, Germany, Slovenia: Euro (€); Switzerland: Swiss Franc (CHF)
- **Time zone:** GMT +1 hour
- **Electricity:** Austria, Germany, Switzerland 230v; Slovenia 220v
- **Tourist board:** Austria: www.austria.info; Germany: www.germany-tourism.de; Slovenia: www.slovenia.info: Switzerland: wwwmyswitzerland.com

Austria

YOGA RETREAT

International Sivananda Yoga Retreat House

Reith, Tyrol
T+43 (0)53-566 7404
www.sivananda.org/tyrol
From €57 per person per day

Located on the slopes of Kitzbühel, surrounded by Alpine forests and mountains, this sivananda yoga retreat runs all sorts of courses with long-established instructors, including those tailored to beginners. There is an emphasis on combining yoga with a healthy diet for physical and mental wellbeing, but courses address every aspect of mind, body and soul.

An accessible and spiritual style, sivananda yoga was founded in 1957 by Swami Vishnu-devananda and was introduced to Europe around 30 years ago. There are sivananda ashrams and centres all over the globe. Senior disciples of Swami Vishnu teach here, and retreats follow an ashram-style daily schedule of waking at 0530, meditation, satsang, yoga classes and daily workshops. You must join all your classes, and non-vegetarian food, eggs, onions, garlic, black tea, coffee, alcohol and cigarettes are not allowed on the premises.

Try Indian dance, craniosacral therapy, or a trip combining cross-country skiing with

asanas. Other programmes include detox, stress management, positive thinking, cardiovascular breathing, life flow (prana), Sanskrit lectures, ayurvedic bodycare and cooking workshops. You can tailor courses according to your requirements and you'll get lots of individual attention.

The yoga room is spacious and light with wooden ceiling and floors; take morning meditation on the outdoor yoga platform where the crisp mountain air is uplifting. Open yoga classes are available to all twice daily. Swami Durgananda, a senior student of Swami Vishnu-devananda, runs yoga teacher-training courses.

Bio Hotel Florian accommodates guests; the owners warmly welcome yogis and have built a yoga hall and extra accommodation purely for the retreat. Bedrooms have natural wood furniture and decent beds. Bathrooms are en suite and the hotel has a sauna. Two organic, buffet-style vegetarian meals are served daily.

The surrounding area offers winter sports, hiking trails, cycling and horse riding. Or visit nearby natural lakes, which are good for swimming. Arrive at any time and stay as long as you want, or on an ad-hoc basis; if a room is not available they will find you accommodation at a local B&B. The place attracts an international crowd as well as German-speaking students. Bring a yoga mat, meditation cushion, blanket and meditation shawl, or buy them from the on-site shop. Rate includes two asana classes, two meditations, a lecture and accommodation. Airport transfers are available from Munich or Innsbruck airports.

Left: Sivananda Yoga in Austria. **Above:** Mayr Detox.

Heat and heritage: where to spa in Austria

Austria makes a wonderful place for a wellbeing spa break. It is one of the few places in Europe where affordable doesn't mean sacrificing tranquility and sophistication. The country has many mineral springs and serene unpolluted lakes amongst its Heidi-style villages, great walking and mountain biking trails, clean air, uplifting Alpine scenery, and a bathing tradition that dates back to the Romans. Therapists usually speak English and are assured and experienced rather than young and light-handed and, best of all, most spa hotels have large relaxing hot and wet areas where, refreshingly, you won't have to sweat into your swim suit – you are actually asked to remove it. Therapies range from traditional western massages to a whole host of treatments inspired by the east.

The country is teeming with affordable and well-managed family-run spa hotels. The state of Styria boasts some of the best, with healing mineral-rich thermal waters and high-quality local organic produce which graces most hotel menus. A 45-minute drive from the UNESCO World Heritage city of Graz lies the thermal spa resort of Bad Waltersdorf. You can stay here at **Der Steirehof Hotel & Spa** (€102 per night half-board, T+43 (0)33-3332 1182, www.dersteirehof. com), where most rooms have balconies and views, and there's good walking and mountain biking in the area.

Alternatively, try the **Rogner-Bad Blumau Hotel, Therme & Spa** (from €117 per person per night, T+43 (0)33-835 1000, www.blumau.com), a rather gorgeous place designed by Friedensreich Hundertwasser. As well as indoor and outdoor hot pools, there's access to a pool fed by waters from the nearby Vulkania hot spring. Its impressive range of treatments include sound therapies to treat stress.

The Tirol also boasts some lovely places, including the **Posthotel Achenkirch Resort & Spa** (from €130 per night, T+43 (0)52-466522 wwww.posthotel.at), a large, elegant hotel close to lake Achensee, about 50 km from Innsbruck. Its spa facilities include a Turkish hamam, and its therapists specialize in Chinese remedies, overseen by a specialist in acupuncture and tuina. It's a great place to go horse riding too, for the hotel has the largest privately owned Lipizzan stud farm in Europe.

If you're into skiing but want more from your après ski than a tiny massage room, heavy fondues and too many schnapps, head to **Mavida Balance Hotel & Spa** (from €120 per person per day, T+43 (0)65-425410, www.mavida.at) in the village of Schuettdorf, near Zell am See, next to a large lake and surrounded by mountains. Despite the ugly concrete exterior, the hotel shines on the inside, with muted, stylish interiors and an excellent approach to wellbeing: yoga, qigong and pilates are on offer alongside an impressive range of western and eastern treatments and special packages including a three-day body, mind and soul break. It also employs a caring and approachable 'mental trainer' who'll use hypnosis, meditation, breathing exercises or just a listening ear to help you get back on track. Or try the **Hotel Madlein** (from €120, T+43 (0)54-445226, www.ischglmadlein.com) at Ischgl, which boasts Philippe Starck interiors, a zen garden, a beauty spa and a wonderful fire room, where you can cosy up, chat or meditate around a central open fire.

The Mayr Detox & Health Spa

○ ⚙ ✪ ✪ ◣2

Golfhotel at Dellach, Wörthersee
T+43 (0)42-732511
www.mayr-health-spa.com
From €1080 per person per week

Established in 1976 by Dr Erich Rauch, a pupil of FX Mayr, this detox and health spa is the longest-running Mayr centre in Austria and programmes adhere strictly to the founding philosophy (see page 68). It's based at a modernized 1930s hotel on the shores of the Wörthersee, surrounded by a golf course and woodland, in the small town of Dellach.

Your programme will be devised after an individual consultation, and supporting treatments may include massages, kneipp hydrotherapy, liver wraps and hay baths. There are group morning exercise classes, an indoor pool and a lake to swim in, and tobogganing during snowy months.

❝❞

I felt decidedly bulbous at the Mayr Detox & Health Spa when asked to stand sideways to a long mirror and relax in bra and pants. Then flat out on a couch, the doctor took hand measurements of various parts of my body. To my surprise, it wasn't so much fat that was the problem, but bloating. I was a veritable gasbag. My flabby stomach and bad posture was due to intestinal sluggishness, a build-up of half digested food (my usual vegetarian diet) much of it uncooked. I was prescribed the FXM – Healthy Intestine module. I was told I had 'good life power', but needed to correct my eating habits. Each small mouthful of a bit of day-old bread to be chewed 50 times then, without swallowing, a teaspoon of liquid added and more mastication before swallowing the resultant pap. For seven days. The Mayr cure requires discipline. It is a therapy of character.

Lucinda Carling

Expect cosy, light rooms with voluminous duvets. Some rooms have bathtubs, others showers, so ask for which you'd prefer in advance. Balconies overlook the gardens and dining rooms, which may bother some; rooms facing east get the morning sun.

You'll eat the recommended spelt bread and yoghurt alongside home-grown dishes. There is a strict no talking policy for breakfast and lunch, to enable you to concentrate on your meal and to help you eat and digest calmly. Expect to meet slimmers of all ages alongside people getting over serious illness. Treatments are paid for separately; discuss at the beginning with the doctor exactly what you are signing up for. Take a taxi from Klagenfurt (23 km).

Viva Centre for Modern Mayr Medicine.

◗ Body language

It's all in the gut: the Mayr method

Traditionally based around a diet of milk and day-old bread, the Mayr method of detoxing is not for everyone, but it's based on years of painstaking research by Austrian physician Franz Xaver Mayr, who believed the root cause of most illnesses lay in the gut. Inadequate digestion, our body's intolerance to certain things, eating too much and too quickly, he believed, all help build up toxins that lead to disease.

Eating less helps us heal. Our bodies process food best in the morning, but struggle to do so at night, which is usually when we eat our biggest meals. Eating after 1900, Mayr believed, would lead to food rotting and fermenting in the gut. He also noted that the digestion process starts in the mouth – food should be chewed thoroughly (as much as 50 times), not only to break it down, but to add saliva, integral to digestion.

Mayr prescribed Epsom salts to help cleanse the body, a diet of milk to provide the essential nutrients, and day-old bread to encourage you to chew over and over. The milk is taken by the teaspoon after small chunks of the bread have been chewed for some time. His work proved popular and today his findings are used by some alternative practitioners to help with widespread chronic illnesses such as asthma, hay fever, eczema, painful joints and digestive disorders, all of which could be caused, it is thought, by allergies. Some people are attracted to the weight loss the programme ensures.

Mayr practitioners must first be general practitioners before they train in Mayr diagnostics. You'll find contemporary Mayr institutes offer a mixture of traditional and modern practices. Expect to be served two-day old spelt bread, encouraged to drink lots of water and herbal teas between meals, and to take gentle exercise. You'll have a dose of Epsom salts daily to kick-start the detox – the first of these is powerful, so stay near the bathroom. Your diet is supplemented with vitamins, including EFAs (essential fatty acids), and a vital part of the detox is spending daily self-time sitting quietly doing nothing.

The detox process is supported by hydrotherapy treatments such as herbal baths, and colonics designed to detox the skin, as well as massage and gentle exercise. The indigenous Austrian hay bath sees you wrapped in fermenting hay, arnica, clover and mountain flowers, which is great for purifying your skin, though you may find the sickly sweet smell of hayflower nauseating. You're encouraged to skin brush, repeatedly shower with hot and cold water to stimulate the immune and lymphatic systems, soak in warm baths of baking soda, and do your own detox liver wraps: this involves placing a cold wet cloth on the right side of your upper abdomen, putting a hot-water bottle on top, wrapping up in a towel and relaxing in bed for an hour.

Like most methods of detoxing, the Mayr method is not an easy process, and you may develop strong feelings of anger, boredom and depression. The hunger will make you feel tired and lethargic, and you may get headaches and feel nauseous. To completely clean out the system, therapy can take up to six weeks. Many report it working miracles.

Viva

⚙ 🅰 ⬤ 🔥 ⊙ ✦ ✦ ✦ ⬤ ⊘ ≥3

Wörthersee, Carinthia
T+43 (0)42-733 1117
www.viva-mayr.com
From €1970 per person per week

Viva Centre for Modern Mayr Medicine is located in a beautiful contemporary hotel on a small picturesque peninsula on the Wörthersee. It was established in 2005 by Dr Stossier, who previously oversaw treatments at the nearby Mayr Detox & Health Spa in Dellach (see above).

President of the International Society of Mayr Doctors, Dr Stossier is renowned in Mayr practice and was taught by the legendary Dr Rauch, tutor of FX Mayr. He and his motivated medical team combine the old and proven traditions of Mayr medicine with modern holistic therapies such as applied kinesiology. Whatever your needs, they will customize a modern Mayr therapy for you following a medical consultation. As well as programmes for detoxing, weight loss and infertility, Phytomer beauty treatments and Mayr cooking workshops are also on offer.

En suite bedrooms are elegant and minimalist, with pale wood floors, warm earthy colours and Moroccan berber rugs. Not all rooms have bathtubs – ask in advance if you want one. All rooms overlook the lake, as does the dining room and outdoor terrace. There's a sauna and steam room, and a stylish outdoor infinity pool, or swim in the lake. You can go cycling, walking or running nearby, and the region is steeped in history – Gustav Mahlers' villa is only a short walk away.

Meals are mostly organic; you might have porridge for breakfast, steamed fish for lunch and bread and avocado spread for dinner. Alcohol and cigarettes are not allowed. A two- to three-week stay is recommended. Rate includes accommodation, basic treatments and individual reducing diet plan. Medical treatments start from €120, massage and other therapies from €10. Take a taxi from Klagenfurt airport (23 km).

Spa Czech

With their graceful colonnades and majestic parks, the elegant west Bohemian spa towns of the Czech Republic are a testament to how much the country treasures its rich supply of natural mineral sources. For centuries, people have travelled to the Spa Triangle of Mariánské Lazně, Karlovy Vary and Františkovy Lazně to take the waters, including history's rich and famously creative, from Edward VII to Chopin, Kafka and Goethe.

Czech spas are renowned for alleviating ailments from respiratory and dermatological complaints to digestive and circulatory disorders. Though holistic treatments such as Thai massage, reflexology and shiatsu are now being offered by some, a spa experience here is likely to be based on medical treatment rather than relaxation and pampering, which pushes the average age of visitors into the 50-plus bracket, most of whom are Germans seeking better-value treatments than those in their own country. Expect brightly lit interiors and no-nonsense, expertly performed treatments by therapists whose second language is likely to be German.

Mariánské Lazně boasts neoclassical architecture in fondant icing white and yellow. Its graceful colonnade is the place to sip the local mineral waters, all with different healing properties and a variety of unpleasant aftertastes. For the widest variety of traditional spa treatments, head for the **Hotel Nové Lazně** (from €70 per person per night, T+420 35-464 4111, www.danubiushotels.com). Although the grand exterior belies a more modest accommodation inside, it has a stunning Roman-style spa complex offering sauna, jacuzzi, steam room and various therapies to perk up the circulation. In its original tiled spa cabins, you can experience hydrotherapy, inhalations, peat and mud wraps alongside non water-based treatments such as physiotherapy and even colonics. Book a mineral bath in one of the spectacular Royal cabins and gape at the opulent interior.

At Františkovy Lazně visit the Aquaforum, a large modern pool and wellness complex with pristine white architecture. There are three sleekly-designed apartments at the top and a glass-covered passageway connecting it to the **Hotel Pawlik-Isis** (from €57 per person per night, T+420 35-420 6000, www.franzensbad.cz/aquaforum), two separate buildings offer three- and four-star accommodation with fresh, cheerful and simply decorated bedrooms.

Karlovy Vary is busier and more cosmopolitan. Here you'll find the five-star **Carlsbad Plaza Spa and Wellness Hotel** (from €162 per person per night, T+420 35-322 5502, www.carlsbadplaza.cz) which has a subtly lit, Regency-style decor. Its authentic spa includes Thai massage and yoga. For an atmospheric day spa experience, book a package at the **Castle Baths** (english.edenhotels.cz), where you can also swim, relax and try some traditional hydrotherapy.

All these spa towns are less than two hours from Prague. If you're after some indulgent pampering in the capital, head for the **Mandarin Oriental** (from €249 per room per night, T+420 23-308 8888, www.mandarinoriental.com/prague) where a Renaissance chapel houses tranquil and elegant treatment suites and offers therapies combining techniques from around the world.

Northern & Central Europe Czech Republic

Germany

PARKSCHLÖSSCHEN

RURAL RETREAT

Kloster Gerode

Gerode, near Weissenborn-Lüderode
T+49 (0)36072-8200
www.wegdermitte.de
From €38 per person per night

A secluded, lovingly restored former Benedictine monastery on the edge of the Harz and the Ohm mountains in Germany's unspoilt east, Kloster Gerode is the home of Weg der Mitte, a non-profit foundation for holistic medicine, health education and social services founded by Dr Daya Mullins in Berlin over 30 years ago. It's also the base for the European College for Yoga and Therapy.

The objective of Weg der Mitte at Kloster Gerode is that you should gain awareness of yourself and others and relax into the now. In 10 ha of parkland, gardens and mature trees, you can take a wide range of interesting and creative workshops throughout the year, most of them in English, lasting between three and 14 days up to three months. These include various types of yoga and yoga therapy, chanting and singing, healing with medicinaal herbs, and a special holistic detox based on Azidose therapy, which combines an acid-reducing diet with healing massages to help reduce the acid in your tissues and clear out toxins (from €845 per person for seven days in a single room including appropriate diet).

Whatever courses you choose, you can attend daily yoga and meditation, and there are various therapies available including oil massages, reflexology, lymphatic drainage, acupuncture and naturopathy as well as nutritional advice and lifestyle training. During summer, classes are held outdoors.

Inside, the decor is warm, simple and a touch cloistral, with high-ceilinged yoga rooms and 28 spacious guest rooms with modern toilets and bathroom. The retreat accommodates up to 70, so expect to share,

though singles are available on request. During summer, theatre performances and concerts take place in a beautiful old ruined church in the grounds, which also feature manicured lawns, wooden sun loungers, a medical herb garden, a greenhouse and fields with organic vegetables and old fruit trees.

Food is delicious, organic and vegetarian. A vast selection of fresh organic herb teas and fruit is available during the day. There's a rustic country-style organic café, which serves wonderful home-made cakes and the odd glass of wine.

Guests are usually aged between 20 and 60, and are a mix of nationalities. There are opportunities for volunteers, and the work and study programme includes sharing circles designed to enrich your experience while practising mindfulness.

Prices depend on the number of beds in your room: for three beds in a room it's €38 per person per night, for two it's €48, for a single room it's €65 for food and lodging plus seminar fee. The nearest airports are Frankfurt and Hannover, and the nearest train station at Herzberg, a 30-minute drive away. Pickups can be arranged.

Parkschlösschen is based in the quiet German town of Bad Wildstein.

AYURVEDA RETREAT

Parkschlösschen

Bad Wildstein, Traben-Trarbach
T+49 (0)65-417050
www.parkschloesschen.de
From €920 per person for 2 nights

As most ayurveda retreats across the globe are frequented largely by German guests, it's fitting that their own country should boast one of the best retreats outside India. The hushed, slightly clinical surroundings won't suit everyone, but this is a supremely civilized if unlikely environment in which to detox the ancient Indian way. There are clean lines, white spaces, and delicious smells of ayurveda herbs and spices infusing the corridors.

The elegant art deco building, on the edge of a quiet German town surrounded by vineyards, has a range of spacious, well-designed bedrooms whose colour is tailored to the doshas – green to earth *vata* types, red to fire you up if you're *kapha*, and blue to cool you if you're *pita*. Come here for short wellbeing packages or for proper

Hungary for water

Landlocked Hungary might seem an unlikely destination for water babies, but there are 400 registered thermal springs in the country, and few self-respecting settlements are without a bathing complex.

The aquatic culture stretches back many moons: the Romans established 14 baths in Budapest alone. Turkish bathhouses with gorgeous domed roofs are among the rare remaining signs of 16th- and 17th-century Ottoman occupation, while grand fin-de-siècle confections are ornate markers of Budapest's period of prosperity in the years before the First World War. A spa visit can be as much a dip into history as a wallow in water: in Budapest, check out the **Gellért** (a day spa complete with fountains and fluted columns) and the **Széchenyi** (housed in a neo-Baroque edifice and one of the largest bathing establishments in Europe).

Many mineral-rich springs have medicinal properties, and Hungarians have traditionally used thermal water to treat a range of complaints, from skin disorders to gynaecological problems. As such, some complexes feel more like sanitoriums than places of leisure, and, in a country that shook off communism's shackles less than 20 years ago, Hungary's spa hotels are not yet as polished in look or feel as those in the west.

That said, in the last couple of years hotels have begun to offer beauty and wellness packages designed to recharge batteries rather than treat specific medical ailments. The over-fifties still comprise a considerable chunk of the market, but Hungarians are well-versed in spa therapy, and the country makes for a very affordable body and soul break.

You could start with a short spa break in Budapest, staying at the **Danubius Health Spa Resort Margitsziget** (from €132 per night, T+36 (06)-1889 4700, resind@margitsziget.danubiusgroup.com). Although ugly from the outside, the hotel is well located on tree-heavy Margaret Island in the middle of the Danube, and makes use of the island's natural thermal water, which emerges at 70°C before being cooled to just under 40°C.

The spa facilities include six pools, as well as saunas, steam rooms and aroma cabins. Among the centre's specialities are kneipp therapy (see glossary), hydrotherapy, Cleopatra baths with milk and honey, a full body massage using cream mixed with Hungarian wines and grape seeds, mud packs, and shiatsu and Thai massages. In addition, the spa offers cutting-edge treatments like oxygen therapy. Between massages, wander Budapest's cobbled Castle District, bustling market halls and superb museums and galleries.

A couple of hours southwest of the capital, near Lake Balaton, is the town of Hévíz, situated on the largest thermal lake in Europe. The lake's crater is 39 m deep, and is filled by springs that gush 60 million litres each day; the water remains hot all year round, and you can even bathe in darkest winter as snowflakes dab the steaming surface. Nearby is the **Hotel Európa Fit** (from €139 per night, T+36 (06)-8350 1100, sales@europafit.hu), an inoffensive four-star with two thermal pools and an excellent wellness centre. Among the treatments available are those for anti-ageing and detoxing, stress relief and rejuvenation, as well as seaweed treatments, ayurvedic massage and group meditation.

Across the road is the **Naturmed Hotel Carbona** (from €150 per night, T+36 (06)-8350 1500, hotel@carbona.hu), a four-star offering fewer treatments but a slightly more pleasant ambience. It has several pools (one of them a 'Roman-style' thermal bath drawing on a local spring), saunas and steam baths. Treatments include kneipp therapy, reflexology, a variety of massages including shiatsu, Thai and yumeiho (an energy-harmonizing therapy using acupressure), aromatherapy, thalassotherapy, acupuncture, and herbal packs, and relaxation classes including yoga and tai chi.

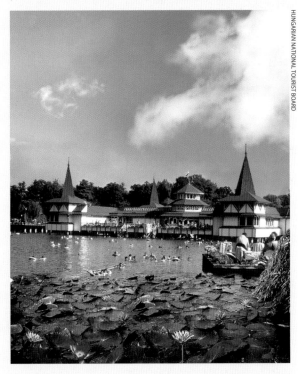

HUNGARIAN NATIONAL TOURIST BOARD

Northern & Central Europe Hungary

"

Parkschlösschen makes detoxing feel indulgent. My morning dose of ghee is served in a pristine sherry glass. During Svedana, lying in a wooden steam box and sweating profusely, my hair is cooled with coconut oil and my heart protected by a pure white towel. The dining room is white-clothed and elegant, and a single white candle burns at dinner. The food is superb, and I am never served the same dish twice.

Caroline

panchakarma of two weeks or more (see page 210 for a full explanation of ayurveda).

Decadent touches will make you feel very well cared for. Hot-water bottles, rose petal eye pads and knee rolls are used during the treatments. Therapists are kind and trustworthy, and every treatment is carried out with expert synchronicity. Saunas are infused with lemongrass, spruce or sandalwood for different constitutions. Yoga classes are taken in a gorgeous wooden-floored room with huge windows.

The main meal is eaten at lunchtime, when your digestive fire is at its strongest, with dessert served first, it being the hardest to digest. Chef Eckhard Fischer cooks up exceptional food that doesn't make you feel you're being deprived – think Asian red lentil soup, sushi, braised endives, spicy carrots, Indian pistachio dessert.

You'll find a wide range of mainly German-speaking guests, from stressed-out businessmen and women to ladies who lunch. Some of the evening lectures are in German; private sessions can be arranged. An all-inclusive 13-night panchakarma package costs from €4970 per person, a two-night 'Taking a Break' package costs €920 and includes three treatments, a doctor's consultation, all meals, use of the spa and accommodation. Wellbeing, slimming, beauty and anti-ageing packages are also on offer. The nearest airport is Frankfurt-Hahn.

Slovenia

Specialized Fitness retreats

Julian Alps
T+44 (0)7957-608167
www.specializedfitness.co.uk
From €2030 per person per week

Respected UK-based personal trainer Jon Orum runs an annual fitness retreat to Slovenia, ideal for those with an above average level of fitness who want to get fitter. Your base is the Triglav-Narodni National Park in the Julian Alps, which boasts inspiring landscapes in which to work out, from large valleys and mountains to wild flower meadows and tranquil woodland.

Witty, motivating and down to earth, Jon is an inspired personal trainer and this is a fun, rejuvenating week with mountain hikes, road and trail cycling, kayaking, wall climbing, circuit training, swimming in the local lake or nearby pool, tennis, coreball training, stretching, horse riding and archery all on offer. There's also sunrise yoga and early morning runs on alternate days. Yoga is taught by Hella Lund, who trained with UK-based Simon Low. Two sports massages are included, and Jon also offers lifestyle & nutritional counselling.

You stay in a contemporary and comfortable restored seven-bedroom chalet-style hotel set on the shores of a lake, where each room has a balcony and there are plenty of areas to relax, plus a bar and sauna. Share a room, or pay more for a single (about €420 per person per week). Food is healthy, fresh and organic wherever possible, and special diets are catered for. Juices and fruit are served as snacks, and there's a packed lunch each day.

You fly to Ljubljana, and it's an hour's drive from there. Jon also runs bespoke and fun countryside fitness weekends in Suffolk in the UK, and will organize trips to Iceland from late 2007. He also works for In:Spa holidays (see page 172).

Switzerland

Clinique La Prairie

Montreux
T+41 (0)21-989 3311
www.laprairie.ch
From €915 per person for 2 nights

Established in 1931 as a private clinic, Clinique La Prairie now has a spa and offers rejuvenating breaks as well as medical health care. Stay for a weekend or a week to sort out an issue in your life, change your diet, kick-start a fitness regime or just relax and be pampered by a friendly, unpretentious, expert and caring team of staff.

The retreat consists of four very different styles of building around a central garden area, all linked by tunnels. The spa and thalassotherapy centre is contemporary and sleek, though some might find its minimalist interiors a little soulless. Stay in Le Château, a renovated 19th-century girls' finishing school, with 24 elegant rooms, 18 of which have balconies and views of the lake. There's also La Résidence, a 1920s building with cosy

Specialized Fitness retreats in Slovenia.

rooms and wooden floors, and the unattractive medical centre, which houses art deco-style suites.

The best views are to be had from the outdoor terrace near the indoor pool. There's a jacuzzi, sauna, steam room and relaxation room, daily classes in the aqua gym, stretching and hydroform, and personal trainers who base their fitness advice on the importance of the core muscles. Expect excellent beauty treatments, thalassotherapy, hydrotherapy, a range of therapeutic massages (and especially good Thai therapists), nutritional advice and one-to-one sessions in yoga and meditation. Various types of counselling are on offer – Fatima Santos, for example, combines reflexology, hypnotherapy, and sophrology to find out 'what the need is behind the feeling', helping to sort out issues ranging from phobias to life-changing decisions.

Clinique La Prairie sold the name of its beauty products range – 'La Prairie' – to the makers of Nivea, and the only product used here now is Swiss Perfection. The clinic is also famous for its Cellular Revitalization Therapy: this involves injections of an extract from the cells of a sheep foetus to stimulate the immune system, which in turn improves energy levels and delays the ageing process.

Meals are taken in the elegant restaurant. Dietetic, vegetarian and à la carte menus are on offer, and food is cooked to perfection and with fresh seasonal ingredients by chef Jean-Bernard Muraro.

The clinic attracts a wide range of guests, usually in their forties and up. More than two-thirds are repeat visitors. Fly to Geneva and arrange a transfer with the clinic's limo, or take the train to Montreux via Lausanne for some lovely lake and vineyard views.

LIFE COACHING HOLIDAY

In Touch

🌐 ⛄ 🏔 🏂 ❄️ 🎿 💧 ↘8

Verbier
T+41 (0)76-516 3447
www.intouchlifestyles.com
From €968 per person for 3 days

In Touch combines fitness activities, self-analysis and a stay in a cabin on a remote Swiss mountain peak above the winter sports resort of Verbier. Created by Niko de Rohan, weekend and week-long retreats are designed as a detox from modern life.

A weekend involves one night in a mountain cabin, from which views are incredible. During winter months you can cross-country ski to the cabin, in the summer you can hike or bike. Arriving in the wilderness after leaving your home comforts can make you feel shaky, but Niko's exercises – and a good communal group vibe – will ease your mind. You leave your belongings (other than essentials) at a base hotel so you can enjoy the surroundings without being weighed down.

The cabin is basic but has warm bedding and hot showers. After a wholesome dinner, staff leave, but a cabin warden stays throughout the night. Use the evening to fill out the personal lifestyle question sheet and stargaze. Next morning, there's optional yoga, and Niko will later guide you through your lifestyle sheets. He is encouraging and supportive and attempts to help you find your own answers. Extra life coaching consultations can be arranged on demand (from €54) and, for a fee, he can provide telephone

consultancy for up to six months after.

During the rest of the time you are encouraged to take long walks and hikes, which are tailored to your fitness level. Included in your package are treatments at the resort-style spa, **Les Bains de Lavey** (www.lavey-les-baines.ch), which has indoor and outdoor pools, Turkish baths, saunas and whirlpools and offers a variety of massage and beauty treatments.

Your base hotel is your choice – In Touch works with a selection, and accommodation is included in the package. **Les Rois Mages** (www.skiverbier.com) is a four-star B&B with light, modern rooms, but if you find the shops and bars of Verbier too distracting, try the **Chill Inn** (www.chillinnverbier.com), in the neighbouring village of Le Chable, which offers cosy, unpretentious hospitality in quiet, traditional surroundings.

For those after some excitement, try a tandem paragliding flight from the Monte Fort cabin to Le Chable – a drop of 1390 m – or a two-hour mountain bike descent to a Rhône Valley vineyard restaurant.

Retreats are popular with workaholics and a young fashionable crowd, but all ages, corporate groups and families are welcome. Bring thermals, a fleece, waterproof jacket and trousers, binoculars and torch. Fly to

IN TOUCH

Keeping In Touch.

Geneva, then take the train to Martigny. Car transfer from Martigny is included in the package, but the 30-minute train ride is fun.

VALLEY RETREAT

Kientalerhof

🔆 ◻ ◻ ◻ ◻ ◻ ◻ ◻ ◻ ◻ ◻ ◻ ◻ ◻ ⏴9

Kiental
T+41 (0)33-676 2676
www.kientalerhof.ch
From €26 per person per night

A remote retreat hidden in the valley below the high peak of Blüemlisalp, Kientalerhof is a centre for the International School of Shiatsu and School of Basic Craniosacral Therapy, but also runs holistic courses which are open to everyone. Its gorgeous natural surroundings include a nearby lake, glaciers, forest, pale-green pastures and crystal-clear waterfalls.

Try dance, spiritual massage, the alchemy of sound, or cooking with wild herbs. Classes are combined with meditation sessions, morning yoga, tai chi and exercise classes. Food and lifestyle counselling are on offer, as well as rejuvenating treatments including shiatsu, Thai massage, craniosacral therapy or colonics.

Students will find the centre supportive as the daily schedule is organized to allow time to relax and socialize. The library has comfy couches and in summer you can sunbathe on

Kientalerhof.

the first floor corridor rooftop – great for a private escape with a book. The little crystal room is a nice suntrap during colder weather.

Take time out in the pool, sauna and whirlpool (most guests use the woodfired sauna nude), and try jumping in the heated outdoor pool after a sauna, especially on moonlit nights, with hauntingly beautiful glaciers looming in the background.

Accommodation is in comfortable single, double or dormitory rooms with private or shared bath. Organic, mostly vegetarian, meals are delicious, and in summer you can eat al fresco.

Outdoor activities include sledging, skating, horse riding, sailing, paragliding, snow walking, rafting, amateur piloting and hot-air ballooning. There are also meals round the campfire (good for glacier gazing) and evening discos. Smoking is not permitted and most people don't drink.

Kientalerhof hosts around 2000 students and independent visitors of all ages annually, from over 40 countries. This is a good place to come alone. Courses are mostly run in German and English but can be translated on request. Fly to Zurich, Geneva or Bern and take trains to Reichenbach im Kandertal, changing in Spiez; a bus will drop you at Kientalerhof. Or take a taxi straight from Spiez.

HOTEL & SPA

La Réserve

◻ ◻ ◻ ◻ ◻ ◻ ⏴10

Lake Geneva
T+41 (0)22-959 5959
www.lareserve.ch
From €224 per room per night

Located under crisp, snow-capped mountains, on the shores of Lake Geneva, La Réserve is a highly contemporary hotel with a luxurious 2000 sq m spa. Designed by Jacques Garcia, its decor is as far from chocolate box as you can get, with animal prints, dark wood and sleek leather chairs. An elephant figure stands in the lobby and perspex parrots in pinks, oranges and blues adorn lamps throughout.

Five-day packages address complete body and soul requirements, and are designed after a lifestyle assessment. They include holistic therapies such as acupuncture, naturopathy and herbal medicine, beauty and body treatments and nutritious meals. Choose from a sumptuous spa menu: slimming wraps, spice and flower baths, ageing-prevention solutions; you'll feel younger just reading about treatments.

Bedrooms are clad in attractive textiles, orchids, velvet bedspreads and Frette sheets. Two restaurants serve Asian and Mediterranean cuisine, or use the hotel's 1950s Venetian water-taxi to lunch in town. Expect to meet a wealthy crowd, perhaps a Hollywood star or two. Non-residents can use the spa. Airport transfers can be arranged.

NATURAL SPA RETREAT

Therme Vals

◻ ◻ ◻ ◻ ◻ ⏴11

Vals
T+41 (0)81-926 8080
www.therme-vals.ch
From €68 per person per night

Switzerland boasts some spectacularly designed spas, but perhaps the most remote is Therme Vals, some 1250 m up, in the small valley town of Vals. The community-owned spa is a contemporary masterpiece, designed as a series of caves set in the hillside and using dark-grey slabs of local Valser quartzite.

The building is an impressive fusion of vast grey rock and glass. The quartzite is polished and shiny inside which reflects the light from large panes of glass. The outside has a turfed roof studded with alpine flowers to match the mountainside setting.

Try every pool at least once. The temperature in the hot pool reaches 42°C, its rising steam creating a sauna-like atmosphere. There's a thermal spring cavern with natural stone walls, a scented flower pool, indoor and outdoor warm pools, even a pool where you can drink the 30°C water straight from the source.

To complement the water therapy, take a

spa treatment such as an aromatherapy massage or invigorating Vals brush massage. More pampering offers include a total body hot kelp pack, hydro-aromatic bath, lymph drainage therapy, reflexology massages and a range of beauty treatments. The 1960s hotel is more stylish inside than out, with three- and four-star rooms. Hotel guests get free entry to the spa, fitness studio, exercise classes and sauna, and can bathe at night. All spa treatments are extra.

The hotel and spa close during some spring months, check websites. Fly to Zurich and take a train or drive to Vals (200 km).

Whitepod

🌐 👥 ❄️ 🔑 ↘12

Les Cerniers, Villars
T+41 (0)24-471 3838
www.whitepod.com
From €176 per night

For an unusual mountain escape try an eco-pod. Swiss founder Sofia de Meyer has created a spa with nine geodesic domes modelled on igloos. At 1500 m in the Swiss Alps, skiers and snowboarders will find this a welcome retreat for tired limbs. Or, for those looking for peace and quiet, there are no cars, roads or shops here, just mountains and your thoughts.

Book yoga or pilates, then move to the treatment rooms in the Alpine chalet and relax. Take rehydrating milk and honey wraps, facial or deep tissue massage, then retreat to the sauna and finish with a herbal tea in front of the fire.

Dogsledding, skiing and other activities can be arranged, or take advantage of the private ski run and Alpine refuge reserved exclusively for guests. Organize a night ski back to your pod: staff tend to the wood burning stove during the day, so you'll find it cosy and warm on your return.

A stay in a pod can be surreal, especially during winter months when the white canvas domes almost disappear in thick snow. Inside, they look homely and are lit with kerosine lamps. Choose from the Pavilion pod with double bed, lounge and en suite toilet, or standard Expedition pod with shared toilet facilities. Both have large windows so you can gaze at mountain peaks from your bed.

Meals are freshly made and breakfast is brought to your pod. Fly to Geneva airport, and take a train to Aigle station, where transfers are provided.

Yogatraveller

🌐 ⛺ 🏔️ 🧘 ❄️ ↘13

Wengen
T+353 (0)86-828 9178
www.yogatraveller.com
From €940 per person per week

Yogatraveller runs ski and snowboarding holidays every February and March to Wengen, a village perched on a cliff with spectacular views, crystal-clear air and no cars. Ski and snowboard newbies are welcome – lessons can be organized with the experts at the local ski school. Your base is the family-run **Alpenruhe Hotel**, set on a sunny plateau a few minutes outside the village. All rooms are south facing with private balcony.

The day starts with a warm-up class of yoga, followed by a hearty breakfast, after which the group divides between those attending ski school and those who can ski or snowboard already. Yogatraveller staff are all extremely familiar with the region and offer guided trips around the many pistes available. You can also go snowshoeing and hiking, visit the local spa, or try sledging – Wengen boasts the longest track in Europe.

A day of adventure is concluded with a warm-down yoga class, and massage and holistic treatments are also on offer. The evenings are kept free – go ice-skating, curling and moonlight sledging. Group meals are organized for those who wish to join in. The price includes accommodation, breakfast, yoga twice daily, meditation, ski-pass for three regions, guided ski and snowboarding trips and optional hikes.

Above: Whitepod. Below: Yogatraveller.

CAROLINE SYLGE

Adler Thermae, set amongst the rolling hills of Tuscany.

Southern Europe

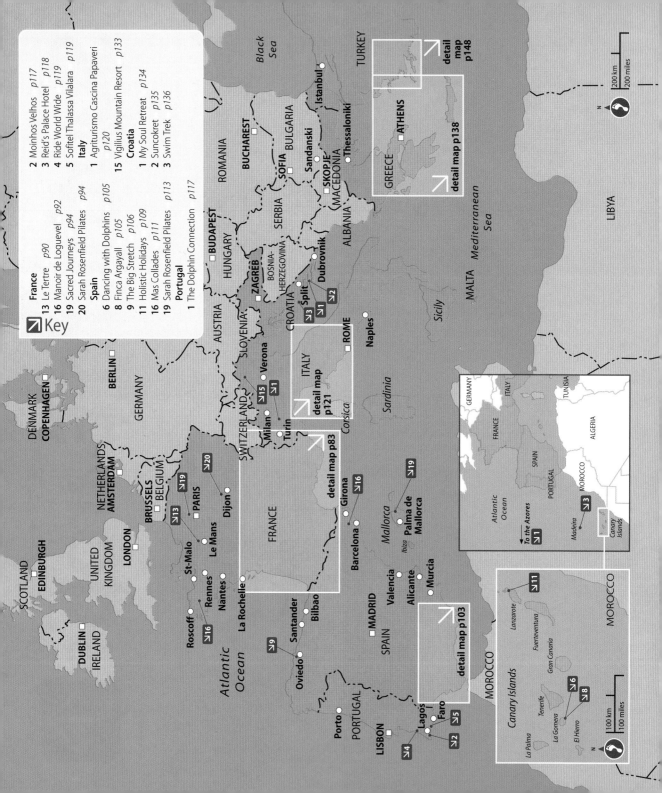

Introduction

With calming countryside and a balmy climate, southern Europe is a summer for the soul, and an especially good region to be healed by water. Tuscany is the place to soak in one of Italy's many thermal hot springs, where Adler Thermae expertly combines wellbeing with style and a lack of pretention. Or heal yourself with seawater and fresh air in Brittany, home of thalassotherapy.

Most people go on a retreat for a reason, be it to reconsider a career or deal with a broken relationship. If you're stuck in a rut but only have a week to spare, this region is the base for two superb life coaching holidays – head for the Picos de Europa with The Big Stretch, or sail the Mediterrean on a gulet in Turkey with The Lifecraft Experience. If you're feeling unhappy, swimming with dolphins has been scientifically proven to lift your spirits by increasing the release of endorphins, and you can do it here with The Dolphin Connection in Portugal. Or just say 'Fuck It' to all your problems at the Hill the Breathes in Italy.

Southern Spain, France, Turkey and Greece are packed with a range of affordable and impressive family-run retreats whose owners believe passionately in a holistic take on life. Pilates enthusiasts can enjoy good food, fine wine and a daily dose of spine work, and you'll find some of the best yoga holidays in the world: try dynamic yoga in a house-party atmosphere at Kali Yoga in Spain, or head for Yoga Hikes in Italy for a more comfortable take on California's The Ashram.

66 99 *Movement is life. Without movement life is unthinkable.*
Moshe Feldenkrais

Travel essentials

CAUDALIE

France

Getting there Air France and all major international airlines fly to Paris Charles de Gaulle. European services, including charter and low-cost airlines, fly to regional airports such as Bergerac, Bordeaux, Carcassonne, Limoges, Lyon, Montpellier, Nice, Nîmes, Paris-Orly, Pau, Toulon and Toulouse. Take the **Eurostar** (www.eurostar.com) from London Waterloo to Lille and Paris, with onward connections on the French rail network, **SNCF** (www.sncf.com). High-speed TGV trains (www.tgv.com) are quick and efficient, linking Paris to destinations like Angouleme, Avignon and Nîmes. Trains from Paris to Bordeaux take three hours. Driving to France from other European countries is straightforward. From the UK, car ferries sail to ports in northern France. For the fastest way to cover long distances, take the toll highways (*autoroutes*).

Best time to visit Given that many places offer outdoor activities such as meditation and walks, visit from May to September for the best weather. Check which months centres are open, since some are closed during the autumn and winter months and courses sometimes run during the summer only.

Spain

Getting there International airlines fly to Alicante, Almería, Arrecife (Lanzarote), Barcelona, Girona, Granada, Ibiza, Jerez, Madrid, Málaga, Murcia, Oviedo, Palma (Mallorca), Santander and Seville. Fly to Tenerife for La Gomera, and to Gibraltar for Tarifa and places inland from the Costa de la Luz. Transatlantic flights arrive at Madrid (with regional connections). Rail and road links connect Spain to the rest of Europe, with a high-speed overnight train between Paris and Madrid or Barcelona. The national rail network, **RENFE** (www.renfe.es) links cities and many provincial towns. From Madrid to Seville the high-speed AVE train takes only 2½ hours. Car ferries operate from Portsmouth or Plymouth in the UK to Bilbao and Santander in northern Spain. Take toll routes (*autopistas de peajes*) for a faster journey, but note that Spain is a big place and getting around often involves travelling long distances (Bilbao to Seville takes around nine hours).

Best time to visit Climate can vary enormously depending on the region. Northern Spain, for example, has similar rainfall and temperatures to the UK, while Andalucía can become uncomfortably hot during the height of summer. Spring and autumn are often the best times to visit, especially in southern and central Spain.

Portugal

Getting there European airlines operate flights to Faro, Funchal (Madeira) and Lisbon, with connections to Horta in the Azores. Transatlantic flights use Lisbon only. Travel from other continents is limited so visitors often have to travel via another European hub. The most convenient way to get around is to hire a car, which is very cheap. If you don't fancy driving, take a train on the rail network run by **Caminhos de Ferro Portugueses** (www.cp.pt), although local trains may be very slow. A daily train links Lisbon with the TGV service to Paris and there is an overnight service to Madrid.

Best time to visit Madeira and the Azores are blessed with a mild year-round climate, with no extremes in temperature. On the Portuguese mainland, the Algarve has pleasant weather all year with plenty of sunshine and mild winters.

Italy

Getting there European carriers fly to Ancona, Bologna, Florence, Genoa, Naples, Rome, Pisa, Turin and Verona. North American airlines fly to Rome and Turin. Travelling by train to Italy, direct services run from major European cities to Naples, Rome and Turin. **Eurostar** from London to Paris and on to Turin takes around 14 hours. Once in Italy, **Trenitalia** (www.trenitalia.com) runs the rail network. Driving from neighbouring countries is easy, with the Mont Blanc tunnel from France, the Simplon Pass from Switzerland and the Brenner Pass from Austria. Tolls operate on all motorways, with additional charges for tunnels and mountain passes.

Best time to visit When to visit depends on the region. Winters are cold in the north, with snow on the mountains, and wet in the south. The heat can be intense in midsummer, particularly in the south. Some centres are closed January and February.

Croatia

Getting there During summer, most European capitals have flights to Split, while charter airlines fly from many regional UK airports. Scheduled airlines operate flights all year round from European cities, including **British Airways** from London. Travel from outside Europe usually involves a transfer via another airport. From Split, there are regular ferries to Hvar and other islands. Alternatively, travel to Croatia by train on direct services from European cities such as Venice, Vienna, Munich and Belgrade. From London, take the **Eurostar** to Paris and then onward trains to Venice and Zagreb. Within Croatia, rail travel is

Eat me

Thanks to days of endless sunshine there's an abundance of fresh, healthy and flavoursome food to be enjoyed in this part of the world. Make the most of the stunningly sweet, plump, ripe tomatoes that are grown throughout southern Europe. Tomatoes are often tagged a miracle food because of the high levels of lycopene they contain, a substance believed to prevent cancer. They're also very low in calories, typically only 10-15 kcals for a medium-sized fruit, and are packed full of Vitamins A, C and E. They can be found on almost every menu: diced into Greek salads, crushed over thick rustic slices of garlic-rubbed ciabatta in Italy's bruschetta, and blended with garlic and extra virgin olive oil in Spain's gazpacho (a detoxer's dream dish owing to the mass of healthy, raw ingredients crammed into every bowl).

The endless supply of sparklingly fresh seafood shouldn't be ignored. Low in fat, high in protein, vitamins and minerals and rich in omega-3 (the amino acid believed to improve memory and prevent heart disease), it's nutritional, flavoursome and diet-friendly. Try freshly caught barbecued sardines in Portugal, grilled fish with a piquant salsa verde in Italy, fresh anchovies in Spain and fish plaki in Greece – a truly tasty yet virtuous combination of baked fish, onions, garlic, tomatoes and lemons. In Croatia try the slow-roast octopus if you come across it.

No self-respecting body and soul traveller visiting the South of France should miss out on the local Agen prunes. It hardly needs to be said that they'll keep your system moving along nicely, but they're also packed with iron and B vitamins. Their sweetness and juicy texture has marked them down as a local delicacy. Try them gently stewed with red wine or steeped in water or tea for a virtually fat-free finish to a meal.

Southern Europe

relatively inexpensive compared to western European countries. See www.hznet.hr for timetable information, available in English. Split is well connected by car ferry and catamaran (for example, www.jadrolinija.hr and www.splittours.hr) to Italy, mainly from Ancona, which is linked to the UK with **Ryanair** flights. Boats may also stop at Hvar and other islands, depending on the season and shipping company.

Best time to visit The Adriatic coast has a Mediterranean climate, with mild winters and warm, sunny summers. To avoid the crowds in summer and enjoy the most comfortable temperatures, visit in spring and autumn.

Greece

Getting there Athens is the main hub, served by most international airlines. Other airports with year-round international flights are Heraklion and Thessaloniki. Many European charter flights operate in summer to tourist destinations on the mainland and islands. Take a domestic flight from Athens or a ferry from Piraeus near Athens to reach the islands. Buses, trains and taxis connect the port to Athens city centre and airport. Intercity buses are the best alternative to driving on the mainland, since the rail network is limited.

Best time to visit July and August are usually hot and busy with tourists, so it's best to visit at a more peaceful time of year, in spring and early summer when wild flowers are abundant, or in autumn. Some centres are closed during winter.

Turkey

Getting there Some international scheduled airlines fly from major European cities to Dalaman (with flight connections to Istanbul), with many charter flights arriving here and at Izmir in the summer.

Milas-Bodrum Airport is served by flights from various UK airports. **Turkish Airlines** operate regular non-stop flights from New York, Chicago and Miami to Istanbul. If driving from western Europe, cross at the Kipi-Ipsala border. Or take a car ferry from Italy (Venice–Izmir, Brindisi–Çesme) or Greece (Lesbos–Ayvalik, Kos–Bodrum). Some boats only operate during the summer. Train travel from other European cities is slow and expensive.

Best time to visit July and August are the busiest and hottest months of the year. Spring and early summer are the best times to visit for the cooler weather, greenery and lack of crowds. The Aegean Sea is warm enough to swim in from late May to October. Autumn is often warm and sunny. Despite being the wettest months, January and February can also have long periods of sunny weather.

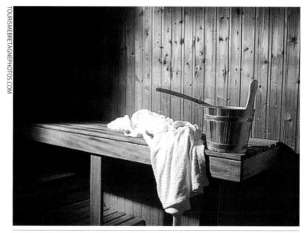

TOURISMEBRETAGNEPHOTOS.COM

Top left: Vinotherapy in France. **Above:** Sauna in France.

France

France has some gorgeous spaces for bien-être, from rural retreats to luxurious pilates weekends.

Fact file

- **Visa:** None required for citizens of EU member states, US, Australia, Canada and Japan
- **Country code:** +33
- **Currency:** Euro (€)
- **Time zone:** GMT +1 hour
- **Electricity:** 230v
- **Tourist board:** www.franceguide.com

MEDITATION RETREAT

Dharmahouse

🌍 ♨ ◎ ↘1

Near St-Ambroix, Languedoc-Roussillon
T+33 (0)8-7798 2899
www.thedharmahouse.com
From €25 per person per night

The Dharmahouse is a Buddhist-inspired permaculture community in the foothills of the Cévennes mountains in the Languedoc National Park. Set in eight acres of olive trees, old vines and fruit trees, interspersed with Buddhist statues and stones carved with inspirational Buddhist sayings, it welcomes people of all faiths, or none, on a meditation retreat, eco-course or holiday.

Summer courses, run by resident and visiting teachers, include vipassana meditation, scaravelli yoga, sustainable building and natural agriculture. At other times, visitors are expected to fit in with daily meditation sittings, work periods and sometimes mindful silence. It suits those wanting a mix of activity, meditation and communing with others.

There's a fabulous straw-bale meditation hall with live turf roof, and for those who want to come on a personal meditation retreat there are individual cob and straw-bale *kutis* (meditation huts) with no road nearby to disturb the peace. The main house accommodates 14 in clean but basic shared bedrooms, all named after Buddhist concepts such as *annica* (the law of impermanence) and *metta* (loving kindness). They're excellent for a personal morning meditation, writing or contemplation, and you step straight onto the adjoining main balcony for yoga. Camping is also available.

Food is mainly vegan, with dairy options. Dining is on the balcony, on triangular Thai meditation cushions at a communal table under a roof of trailing vines. There's an expansive view of rolling hills, villages and old terraces dotted with ruins. A trail heads down to a natural swimming spot in the Cèze river and 25 minutes' walk away is the medieval town of St-Ambroix, which has a lively Tuesday market.

No alcohol is served and smoking is not allowed in the main house. However, although the community is serious about its aims, it's a relaxed, accepting place, where guests are given a gentle welcome and allowed to just be. You're as likely to find an international crowd of keen gardeners or DIY-ers of both sexes and all ages as those interested in the concept of community and eco-living or Buddhism.

Solar power, compost toilets, an outdoor yoga platform and silent dining area shielded by cypress trees are all planned for 2007/8, when the stone ruins will be converted into gîtes for eco-holidays. Walking, canoeing, mountain biking, rock climbing and horse riding are all available nearby. The Dharmahouse is only open from May to September. Fly to Nîmes, 50 minutes away, from where you can hire a car, or take a train or a bus via Alès to St-Ambroix, which is a 10-minute taxi ride away.

Left: 'Gavin's Cottage', Dharmahouse.
Top: Time for contemplation.

RURAL RETREAT

Gardoussel

🌐 ☀ ○ 🕉 ⊙ ⊙ ⊿2

Near St André de Valborgne,
Languedoc-Roussillon
T+33 (0)4-6660 1678
www.thesuncentre.net
From €400 per person per week full board

Set in the steep, unspoiled Cévennes mountains, just 1 km from the village of St André de Valborgne, Gardoussel is a large, converted, stone homing-pigeon station offering various holistic holidays and individual retreats throughout the summer. Reached along a winding mountain road and across an old bridge, this unusual and beautiful retreat is set in 18 ha of secluded holm oak and pine forest, with meadows leading to a stretch of river.

The place was opened in 2006 by Sharon and Alex, a dynamic couple in their mid-thirties who used to run the popular Sun Centre nearby. Their integration of holistic principles into their family life is a large part of the appeal. Alex teaches hatha yoga, leads chanting some evenings and offers ayurvedic consultations. He trained at the European Institute of Vedic Studies (www.atreya.com) and, for 20 weeks a year, the centre is a dedicated venue for courses run by the institute. Sharon offers life counselling and craniosacral therapy.

Yoga is also taught by Frances, who trained at the British Wheel of Yoga. She also gives Swedish or ayurvedic massage in a Mongolian yurt, attractively decorated with ethnic rugs and heated by a wood burning stove. There are ayurvedic cooking, yoga, walking and creative arts retreats throughout the year, and more courses

using the principles of ayurveda are planned. Mountain biking and tennis are also available.

Courses and workshops are held in the loft, which has an open fire, whole trees for beams and a wooden parquet floor, and though there isn't much natural light, it's a pleasant spotlit space. Outside there's a large wooden deck under the trees to practise yoga al fresco. You can walk from the house along quartz crystal-lined paths to meditation benches among the olive groves, and there's a lovely natural swimming hole at the foot of a pretty waterfall.

Vegetarian meals based on ayurvedic principles are a highlight and Alex is on hand to advise about eating for your dosha. The menu may include nutty broccoli soup; spinach, pumpkin, walnut, fresh basil and ricotta lasagne; or green quinoa pilaf; as well as goodies such as chestnut cake or banana

Southern Europe France

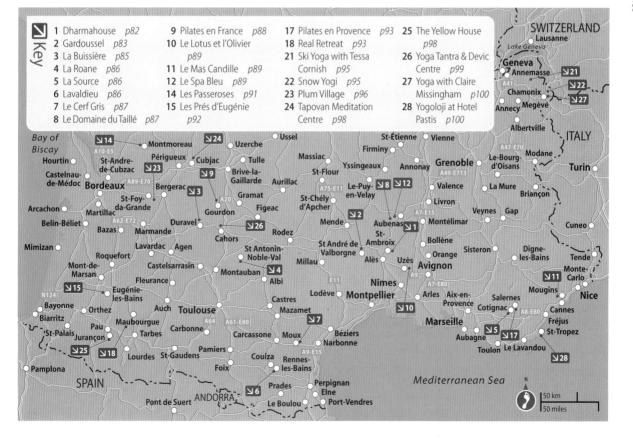

◗ Body language

Grape escapes

Fancy a bathful of Burgundy? Wealthy ancient Romans would have recommended it, though if you tried it today it would just dry out your skin. It's the seeds that are good for you, as they contain powerful polyphenols, a natural plant-made chemical useful for fighting free radicals and repairing the skin. For decades, attempts to use grapeseed polyphenols in cosmetic preparations failed – they were unstable and quickly turned skin creams red and vinegary. That all changed in 1993 when Professor Joseph Vercauteren, from the Bordeaux University of Pharmacy, discovered a fatty acid that stabilized the polyphenols.

On a wine tasting at a Bordeaux château, the professor casually mentioned his discovery to the owner's daughter, Mathilde. Seeing an opportunity to use the mountain of grapeseeds binned at the end of every harvest, Mathilde bought the patent from the professor and went on to found the first wine-based skincare company, **Caudalie**.

Vinotherapie, a trademarked term meaning wine-based skincare, took off in 1999 when Caudalie opened its **Vinotherapie** spa (T+33 (0)5-5783 8282, www.caudalie.com, treatments from €50) in the grounds of Mathilde's family chateau at Martillac, just outside the city of Bordeaux. Local devotees now mingle with savvy European and American clients to create a low-key, welcoming atmosphere, and you'll see almost as many men here as you will women. While waiting for treatments, take a dip in the small thermal pool, relax in a hamam, or hydrate with a cup of the spa's delicious red vine tea and chilled grapes.

You can stay next door at the four-star **Les Sources de Caudalie** (T+33 (0)5-5783 8383, www.sources-caudalie.com), which offers five styles of individually decorated rooms, from the charmingly rustic La Maison du Lièvre (Hare's House) to the romantic Île aux Oiseaux (Bird Island), which sits over a lake. Wine fans might want to opt for one of the beautiful wine-themed suites in the main building. Gourmet meals, including set 500-calorie meals for those watching their weight, are served at one of the hotel's two acclaimed restaurants. It costs from €185 for a double room

Treatments use only Caudalie's own patented products, which are ethically produced, with no animal testing or nasty parabens (a chemical preservative) and, where possible, organic and fairly traded. Choose from a package of treatments to rejuvenate, relax or slim, or select something à la carte: the Crushed Cabernet body scrub (€68 for 35 minutes) will see you slathered in whole grapeseeds, honey, brown sugar and contouring concentrate for baby-bottom skin, while fans of whirlpools will enjoy the wine barrel bath (€51 for 15 minutes).

Caudalie has several more destination spas in wine-growing regions around the world, including the **Relais San Maurizio**, in Piedmont (T+39 0141-841900, www.relaissanmaurizio.it), **Marques de Riscal**, in Bilbao (T+34 945-180888, www.luxury collection.com/marquesderiscal) and **Kenwood Inn**, Sonoma Valley, California (T+1707-833 1293, www.kenwoodinn.com).

Other wine spas using their own wine-based ingredients (Caudalie's are patented) are also worth a trip. Try the **Santé Winelands Hotel and Wellness Centre** in South Africa (see page 187) or the **Patios de Cafayate Hotel and Spa** in Argentina. Back in France, the rustic **Château Vent d'Autan** (T+33 (0)5-6531 9675, www.cahorsaoc.com) is an organic working vineyard in the Lot region, which has developed its own Vino-Cure and offers various treatments; guests stay at **Le Moustans** (from €65 per room per night, www.lesmoustans.com), in one of eight stylish gîtes built in a converted farmhouse and its outbuildings.

CAUDALIE

GARDOUSSEL

LA BUISSIÈRE

Left: Gardoussel. **Top:** La Buissière.

muffins for pudding. Meals are served in the communal lounge at an old farmhouse table, or outside on the balcony. Wine is served, in moderation, but smoking isn't allowed inside.

Gardoussel is comfortable without trying to be luxurious. A maximum of 20 can be accommodated in two gîtes and two new conversions: Le Nid, which has a mezzanine for extra bed space, and a barn conversion with lovely en suite rooms, simply decorated with white, stonewashed walls and light woods. The gîtes are more traditional, with wood burning stoves or open fires. Yurts and straw-bale dwellings are planned for 2008.

Fellow guests are 70% female, mostly professionals in their thirties and upwards, of whom many are already interested in or practising some form of complementary health. Gardoussel welcomes guests on individual retreats in summer, usually for a week, but occasionally a weekend. Families are also welcome. As these mountains receive high rainfall, take waterproofs and warm clothing. Fly to Nîmes, 1½ hours away, or Montpellier. There are trains or buses to St André de Valborgne and shared taxis can be arranged at extra cost, but it's best to hire a car as public transport is limited.

YOGA & ACTIVITY HOLIDAY

La Buissière

🌐 🏔 ☺ ⚽ ⏩ ☑3

Duravel, Lot
T+44 (0)870-490 1461
www.yogafrance.com
From €440 per person per week sharing

Situated on the edge of the village of Duravel, in the picturesque region of Lot, La Buissière is a rustic stone barn conversion in a leafy and peaceful setting, providing week-long relaxation holidays with yoga and guided walks from mid-May to late September. The owners, Brian and Pierette Plews, give their guests a warm welcome and are friendly and helpful without being imposing.

Only nine people can be accommodated here at any one time, which makes for an intimate, restful experience. The grounds are beautiful, with hammocks among the boxwood and cherry trees, a swimming pool with terrace and plenty of quiet places to enjoy some time alone. Guests sleep in four double studios and one single (single guests may be allocated a twin room for a small surcharge). The modern studios have small, well-equipped kitchens and simple, clean bathrooms, though some may find the decor

a little impersonal. Accommodation borders directly onto a road, though it is a quiet one. There are also communal kitchen, dining and sitting areas with comfy seating, and the walls are hung with the owners' artwork and local prints.

Gentle hatha yoga sessions take place three mornings a week. The yoga room is spacious with floor-to-ceiling windows, and the level of the yoga is tailored to the group's abilities. You can also have a rejuvenating massage, and facials, manicures and pedicures from visiting therapists.

There are two guided walks a week with Brian, who has a superb knowledge of the area and its history. Cycling, canoeing, horse riding and wine tasting can be easily arranged. One of the largest palaeolithic caves in Europe, La Grotte de Pech Merle, with paintings dating back 18,000 to 40,000 years, is nearby at Cabrerets

A self-service continental breakfast is included, and the hosts will take guests to the local supermarket on the first day at no extra charge. For eating out, there's a local crêperie, and, for lunch, there's **Marie Colline** (rue Georges Clemenceau, T+33 (0)5-65 355996), a fabulous vegetarian restaurant in Cahors, a 40-minute drive away.

Fellow guests are aged thirties and up, from the UK, and a mix of men and women, singles and couples, who have come to relax, and practise or simply try out, yoga, and explore the local area. Allergy sufferers should note that Brian and Pierette have a dog and two cats. If you're a single traveller, it's €585 per week for a room on your own. Fly to Bergerac, 80 km, or Toulouse, 150 km away.

RURAL RETREAT

La Roane

🌐 🍃 ⛰ ☀ ♠ ❀ ⬡ ⬓4

St Antonin-Noble-Val, near Montauban, Lot/Tarn
T+33 (0)5-6368 2367
www.nigelshamash.com
From €490 per person per week full board

The home of eccentric and likeable Nigel Shamash, who founded Cortijo Romero in Spain (see page 104), La Roane is set in 20 acres of peaceful meadow and woodland, and offers one-week summer holidays with visiting teachers of yoga, tai chi, dancing, singing and personal development. You can also stay here independently – just ask in advance.

The property sleeps up to 20 in the manor house, the cottage and the barn. Rustic but comfortable, each house has a variety of single, double and twin-bedded rooms, shared bathrooms, a kitchen, a sitting room and terraces. Alternatively, sleep in the tree-house, with its compost loo and cold-water shower at ground level.

There's a swimming pool, sauna and ornamental pond in the grounds, a huge swing in the forest, ping-pong tables, croquet and badminton facilities, bicycles to borrow and canoeing in the nearby Aveyron river. Group activities take place in a large room in the barn, with a smooth wooden floor and doors on three sides leading to the garden. Nigel, a warm and open-hearted host, usually offers a daily morning session of do-in and qigong in the meadow. Shiatsu and aromatherapy massages are available from local therapists (€30 per treatment).

Above: Guests strutting their funky stuff at La Roane.
Top right: La Source.

The vegetarian food, cooked by Italian chef Enzo, uses seasonal vegetables and herbs from the garden and is delicious and beautifully presented. Breakfast is a help-yourself affair, eaten wherever you like; lunch and supper are taken on the terrace of the manor house, or in a large room inside.

Fellow guests are usually open-minded British women interested in personal development, mostly in their forties, though the age and gender balance shifts with each course. Many people come alone, a few bring a friend or partner. Fly to Toulouse, from where transfers can be arranged (€28 one way), or take a train from Paris to Caussade (journey time from London about 10 hours).

VALLEY RETREAT

La Source

🌐 ☀ ⬡ ♠ ⬡ ⬓5

Near Cotignac, Provence
T+33 (0)4-9404 6731
www.change-your-life-retreats.com
From €150 per person per night

Nestled in a tranquil hidden valley, La Source is a beautiful 300-year-old house from which British couple, Peter and Gill Coates, run inspirational creative workshops to help you realize what you want to achieve.
It's an intimate, personal place with only four en suite bedrooms in the house, which is full of objets d'art and set in seven acres of gardens full of flowering shrubs, woodland and olive groves. There's a 12-m salt filter pool, and lots of secluded spots in the grounds for writing, meditating and dining al fresco – a stay here includes organic gourmet food, with special diets catered for – and there are also trips to local beauty spots, with pretty walks nearby.

The inspirational workshops are the main reason for coming here. Regulars include Creative Change, Life Coaching, Dealing with Stress, and Painting and Drawing. Peter has 21 years' experience of life coaching and is also a successful artist – he has used creative approaches to help people bring about change for many years. Gill is a qualified

LA SOURCE

nutritionist, masseuse and reflexologist and believes in a holistic approach to wellbeing. La Source attracts a wide range of ages, and both sexes, mostly people seeking lifestyle changes. Beginners are welcome. The price includes all meals, accommodation on a shared room basis, facilitator and course materials and daily four-hour workshops. Fly to Nice, from where there's a free return transfer (1¼ hours).

RURAL RETREAT

Lavaldieu

🌐 ☀ ♠ ⬡ ⬓6

Rennes-le-Château, near Rennes-les-Bains, near Couiza, Languedoc-Roussillon
T+33 (0)4-6874 2321
www.lavaldieu.com
From €36 per person per night half-board

Lavaldieu is an 18th-century guesthouse in a small eco-village of five houses nestled in forested hills 4 km from the popular hilltop village of Rennes-le-Château. Facing the sacred Mount Bugarach, with its standing stones dating back to the Celts, the 51-ha site is known locally for its powerful earth energies. The hamlet is owned by six resident shareholders, and Lavaldieu is run as a guesthouse by British founder members Pat and Russell Cooper. It's an informal, friendly and accommodating place, and the residents are passionate about ecotourism, without being dogmatic.

Guests are welcome throughout the year and informal kundalini yoga classes are offered on request in a pleasant, though slightly dark, wooden-floored studio on the

LA ROANE

Lavaldieu.

first floor of one of the old stone houses, or outside in summer. These are taught by sprightly octagenerian resident Brigit, who has taught yoga for 40 years. Massage is also on offer, and reiki, craniosacral therapy, reflexology and head massage can be arranged in towns nearby (book these in advance).

Lavaldieu also hosts courses year round, including kundalini yoga camp weeks in June and September, held under a large oak tree, a Life Dance camp based around native American dances, and painting courses. You'll find people of all ages here, coming to re-energize, have fun, or just to rest. Daily yoga costs €60 for the week

Accommodation is basic, with four rooms of varying sizes, mixed shared showers upstairs and a toilet downstairs (bring a dressing gown). There are also two self-contained studios with en suite bathrooms, a communal kitchen and a large though unobtrusive campsite that accommodates up to 150 people in summer. The guesthouse has a homely, farmhouse feel with rough stone walls, black oak beams and an eclectic mix of cherry, oak, chestnut and pine wooden panelling and furniture.

Organic vegetarian food is cooked expertly by Pat, bread and jams are home-made and special diets are catered for. Wine is served with dinner and coffee with breakfast for those who want it.

There is lovely walking in nearby scented forest to the thermal town of Rennes-les-Bains, or you can explore local Cathar sites. Lavaldieu is on a plateau and can get cool in the evening, so take warm clothing. Most camps and courses happen

between June and September, which offers the best weather. Fly to Carcassonne, a one-hour drive away, or take the train to nearby Couiza, from where you'll get a free transfer.

CREATIVE RETREAT

Le Cerf Gris

Moux, near Lézignan-Corbières, Languedoc-Roussillon
T+33 (0)4-6843 9883
www.artholiday.com
From €300 per person for a weekend

Mary and Richard run creative residential courses mixing art, cooking and yoga at their home, Le Cerf Gris, a spacious 1860s mansion

Don't just do something, sit there!

Thich Nhat Hanh

decked out with Mary's mosaics and featuring walled gardens, terraces, courtyards and a beautiful big pool. Art, including mosaic and painting, is the main focus, with cookery, yoga, walking and wine tours also on offer.

The courses are held in a house-party atmosphere, with good home cooking. Vegans can be catered for, and wine is on the menu. All abilities are welcome, as well as partners who may not want to participate. Fellow guests are likely to be a mix of singles and couples, generally more women than men, and from the UK, Ireland and North America. Six-day all-inclusive courses run throughout the year, with spring weekend breaks also on offer. Free transfers are available from Carcassonne airport.

RURAL RETREAT

Le Domaine du Taillé

Aubenas, Ardèche
T+33 (0)4-7587 1038
www.domainedutaille.com
From €600 per person per week

Le Domaine du Taillé was built for Zen meditation retreats in the 1970s, on a carefully chosen spot at the crown of a hill, surrounded by 80 ha of beautiful chestnut, oak and pine in a remote part of the Ardèche forest. It's a lovely place that you can visit independently for a few days' rest, or to attend one of the organized courses which run throughout the year. There's enormous energy here, and there are great walks to be had in the surrounding forests.

Courses on offer include tai chi, martial arts, meditation, pilates, rolfing, method putkisto, shiatsu, and holistic therapies such as acupuncture, Chinese medicine, iridology and reiki, as well as various types of yoga. Participants are mostly women, aged 30 to 60. Some courses are geared towards beginners and those just looking for a quiet holiday, while others are aimed more at committed practitioners.

The heart of the centre is a huge, airy dojo with sprung wooden floors and large windows, perfect for practising yoga, and remaining cool even in the July heat. Accommodation is in private rooms (doubles available for couples), most with views of open space and forest, or in little private chalets, all simply decorated but very comfortable, and sensitively designed to blend harmoniously with the natural surroundings.

Meals are served in the original old house, on a high sunny terrace shaded with trees. There are often different groups here at the same time, so you eat together with your own group around big tables. The food is superb: French vegetarian with fresh local produce. No alcohol is served. Prices are for full board and include workshop fees. Fly to Lyon, or take the Eurostar and TGV, and then either the local bus or a taxi.

Pilates holiday

Pilates en France ⚕ 🏃 🏔 ↘9

Pilates en France, at La Roque Haute, offers supremely relaxing pilates weekend breaks in a beautiful country house nestled between working farms and walnut groves, with panoramic views of the Lot and Dordogne countryside. Catering for no more than eight guests at a time, it's run by Melanie Geenty, a qualified British Pilates Foundation teacher, who creates an intimate house-party atmosphere where people can unwind with daily pilates classes, delicious regional food and wines, and good company. Bespoke pilates breaks can also be arranged.

Where you stay Lovingly restored to an extremely high standard, Melanie's stone house, Les Tilleuls, is on the right side of cool and full of character. The house is big enough to find space to relax alone, inside or out, and there's an outdoor pool and plenty of board games. Each of the four twin-bedded or double guest rooms is different in style and decor, luxuriously turned-out with en suite facilities and fabulous views. Two are in the main house and two across the courtyard in a charming, mellow, stone grange, where you'll also find the bright, fully-equipped pilates studio.

What you do Guests on a weekend break have a one-to-one session, a paired session and an optional group class in pilates – people on bespoke breaks can decide how many sessions they want on arrival. With views of the pool, the picturesque pigeonnier and the surrounding countryside, the studio is an ideal environment in which to exercise and Melanie is an excellent teacher who tailors classes to each client's capability. You can walk in the surrounding countryside (where you're very unlikely to come across a car or another person),

> 66 99
>
> Luxury hotels hold decreasing appeal as places for me to recharge my batteries. At Les Tilleuls, Melanie's home-from- home style makes this luxury house-share work, from the welcome hug and constant supply of culinary delights to family-style chats around the kitchen table and expert pilates sessions.
>
> *Claire Dumbreck*

go cycling, canoeing, riding and sightseeing to the nearby pretty villages, or simply stay put.

What you eat and drink Food is locally sourced, plentiful and delicious, served with regional wines. The cocktail hour before dinner is an important part of the day; this is not the place to come for a detox, though specific dietary requirements can be catered for. During the warmer months, breakfast is eaten in a sunlit courtyard, lunch in the shade of the linden tree, and aperitifs are served on the southwest facing terrace watching the sun go down. Cocktails and leisurely candlelit dinners can be enjoyed during cooler months by a huge, log fire in the drawing room, and there's a spacious kitchen at the heart of the house where guests can help themselves at any time to tea, coffee and drinks. The open fridge and wine rack policy means that not one Euro is exchanged during the whole stay.

Who goes Retreats are open to everyone and tend to attract mainly professional women, mostly from the UK, aged between 30 and 60, coming alone or with a friend for a minimum of two days and a maximum of a week. A lot of women running their own companies or in stressful jobs come here to enjoy pilates, good food and wine and get away from everything.

Essentials Pilates en France is near Gourdon, in Lot/Dordogne, T+33 (0)5-5331 9722, www.pilates-en-france.com, and cost from €217.50 per person per night (minimum stay two nights). Bring a swimming costume, walking shoes and losse, comfortable clothing for pilates – hairdryers and bathrobes are provided. All tuition, meals and drinks are included in the price. For guests on the standard weekend, transfers are included, or taxis can be arranged from Bergerac (1¼ hours) or Toulouse (1¾ hours) airport, or from Gourdon, the nearest train station (15 minutes away). It's open year-round but try to avoid the heat of July and August.

PILATES EN FRANCE

WELLBEING HOLIDAY

Le Lotus et l'Olivier

St-Victor des Oules, near Uzès, Gard
T+33 (0)8-7028 9049
www.lotus-et-olivier.com
From €380 per person for 3 days

Le Lotus et l'Olivier runs three- and five-day wellbeing courses mixing yoga with relaxation techniques, a Mediterranean diet and herbal medicine, based at the elegant **Villa Saint-Victor** (T+33 (0)4-6681 9047, www.villasaintvictor.com), a supremely comfortable 17-bedroom hotel set in the heart of a beautiful park and perched on a hill overlooking the city of Uzès.

The courses are aimed at anyone who wants to de-stress, increase their energy levels and learn how to relax and preserve energy when back in the daily grind. Options include The Zen Formula, five days of daily stretching exercises, breathing and relaxation, or The Source Formula, three days of workshops on medicinal plants, essential oils and the health benefits of a Mediterranean diet as well as stretching exercises, breathing and relaxation. In addition to the workshops you can relax in the park, the hotel salons or around the pool. The hotel restaurant offers regional French and lighter fusion food.

The courses attract people of all ages who speak English or French, and are taught by Claire Meisel, who trained at the International Traditional Yoga School in Paris, has taught yoga since 1988 and is an affiliate of the FFHY, the French Federation of Hatha Yoga. Following a passionate interest in herbal medicine, she trained at IMDERPLAM, the Mediterranean Institute for Medicinal Plant Documentation, Teaching and Research. Each workshop takes no more than 10 people, though the hotel may have other guests staying at the same time.

The courses run year-round except in January and February. The hotel is a 45-minute drive from Nîmes airport, 1¼ hours from Montpellier airport, or you can get the TGV to Avignon and Nîmes.

HOTEL & SPA

Le Mas Candille

Near Mougins, Côte d'Azur
T+33 (0) 4-9228 4343
www.lemascandille.com
From €395 per room per night

This 18th-century former olive farm, set on a terraced hillside with views out to the Alpes-Maritime, is an informal, romantic hotel with the first spa in Europe from Japanese company **Shiseido** (www.shiseido.co.uk). It makes a lovely luxurious weekend retreat, surrounded by parkland, with a gastronomic restaurant. A minute's walk away is the medieval village of Mougins, a classy haunt of artists, designers and actresses where the likes of Picasso used to live.

The Zen-like and incredibly stylish spa boasts two beautifully designed heated pools, an outdoor hot tub in peaceful Japanese gardens, four treatment suites, a hydrotherapy pool, a sauna and a lovely outdoor gym with views over the Grasse valley. You can book a personal trainer. Pampering and holistic body treatments (some specially created for men) use Shiseido's delicious product range and are based on the company's chi method, which combines shiatsu pressure point work, oshiboris (Japanese hot towels) and special fragrances to stimulate the flow of your chi and promote wellbeing. The Four Hands body care (€200 for 45 minutes) is especially indulgent, a luxurious massage given by two therapists.

Your fellow guests are likely to be European couples or small groups of friends from their mid-twenties upwards, usually staying for a

Above and left: Le Lotus et l'Olivier.

long weekend. There are meeting rooms and a few business guests do stay midweek, so check in advance if you don't want to hear a mobile phone conversation. Fly to Nice, from where it's a 25-km drive. Transfers can be arranged at extra cost.

RURAL RETREAT

Le Spa Bleu

Blacheyrette, near Aubenas, Ardèche
T+33 (0)4-7539 9375
www.lespableu.com
From €60 per person per night

This 18th-century Provençal farmhouse-meets-spa has gorgeous blue shutters and views of vineyards, fruit trees and the forested hills of the Ardèche. It's a well-run, clean but informal place offering an impressive range of alternative therapies from an international team of therapists. Not everyone speaks fluent English, so ask in advance if you need someone to translate.

German owners, Holger and Anna, really care about their guests but leave them to do as they wish. Smoking is allowed, and guests can help themselves to bottles of wine from the cellar-cum-games room. A domed hammam is heated, ready and waiting for you on arrival, along with a basket of fresh seasonal fruit, bread, cheese and wine. Bespoke breakfasts are served whenever and wherever you want, and you cook your own food the rest of the time. Supermarkets are a seven-minute drive away, and **Valentina** is a good Italian restaurant in the nearby historic

LE SPA BLEU

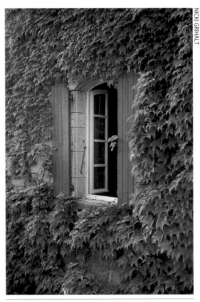

NICKI GRIHALT

Above: Around the pool at Le Spa Bleu.
Bottom right: The relaxed interior at Le Tertre.

Above: The aptly named Le Spa Bleu, with its distinctive blue-shuttered windows, is the epitome of Provençal charm.

RURAL RETREAT

Le Tertre

⊞ ⛰ ☀ ❀ ❀ ◯ ♫ ↘13

Montgaudry, Orne
T+33 (0)2-3325 5998
www.french-country-retreat.com
From €80 per person per day full board

Le Tertre is a converted Normandy farm with an easy, relaxed atmosphere, surrounded by seven acres of the Percheron countryside. It offers a serene environment in which to feel better, either as part of an organized seminar or just by staying on a B&B basis. It's the home of British-American yoga teacher, Anne Morgan, who trained with the British Wheel of Yoga and teaches hatha yoga classes on Mondays and Fridays 1700-1830 (B&B visitors are welcome at no extra charge). Private lessons and meditation may also be arranged for individuals on weekend retreats, and beginners are welcome. Le Tertre also hosts seminars throughout the year run by visiting teachers on subjects such as personal growth, as well as art and writing retreats (some of which are in French).

There are three en suite bedrooms with antique furniture and panoramic views, a

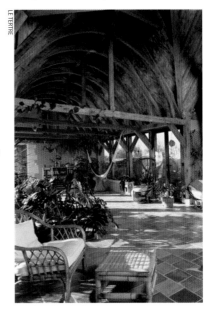

LE TERTRE

village of Joyeuse. You could even hire a cook for €35 per person per meal including drinks. There's an outdoor communal cooking and dining area in summer.

You stay in one of seven spacious self-catering apartments which sleep 2-10 people. Each is decorated in a traditional farmhouse style, with lovely chestnut cupboards, wood-burning Agas and wooden stairs leading to the bedrooms. All have balconies, some more private than others. Esteban, the romantic suite, looks over the courtyard, and one of the two suites on ground level has its own private garden. The Spa suite includes exercise equipment and a massage table for in-room treatments. There are hints of Morocco in the ceramic tables, filigree lampshades and gold lamé curtains, and ceramic sculptures of women peek out of nooks and crannies in the garden.

The farmhouse has an unheated outdoor private pool and a large indoor jacuzzi with whirlpool and jetstream. Most treatments take place in one of two massage rooms, one in the main house and the other in the garden. Treatments range from the traditional to the more esoteric, and include a

huge range of massages, pregnancy and post-pregnancy treatments, reflexology and reiki, as well as very effective and highly unusual 'aquawellness' treatments by local expert, Anne Toulemonde (www.aquawellness.fr), who combines watsu and jahara to ease stresses and strains that have built up over years inside your body.

Private classes with Anna in yoga, qigong, tai chi and do-in can be arranged, as well as guided hikes, biking, kayaking, horse riding and private painting classes with a local artist. Le Spa Bleu is popular with couples, friends and young families from France and the rest of Europe, either on holiday or specifically taking advantage of the spa and treatments. Up to 25 people can be catered for at any one time, and it's open all year, though grape harvest in autumn is the best time to see the local villages come alive. Weekend spa packages are available, with an inventive range of treatments from €80 per person. Fly to Montpellier, from where it's a two-hour drive, or take the TGV from Paris to Montelimar, and then a bus to Aubenas. Transfers from any stage of your journey can be arranged in advance at extra cost.

romantic tower apartment with jacuzzi and, in the summer, an African safari tent in the grounds which sleeps one. Simple country meals are eaten in a spacious and light kitchen-cum-dining room – choose from traditional French or vegetarian dishes using locally sourced produce and home-grown vegetables. Good wines are available at reasonable prices.

The house is surrounded by tranquil nature walks and you're likely to see lots of wildlife, including deer, wild boar, kestrels, sparrowhawks and buzzards. It's also on the pilgrimage route GR22 to Mont-St-Michel. There are quiet places to sit and meditate in the grounds, as well as an indoor winter garden. Guests stay from two days to a week and include anyone looking for a quiet space in which to de-stress and detox body and mind. Le Tertre attracts a wide range of ages and nationalities.

Bring comfortable clothes for yoga, good shoes for walking, rainproof clothing and an open mind. Fly to Paris (275 km northeast), then take a train from Montparnasse to Nogent-le-Rotrou on the Le Mans line, followed by a taxi, or hire a car from the airport. Le Tertre is open all year round except Christmas and January. In May the flowering laburnum turns the whole countryside yellow; in June the garden is a mass of roses.

Les Passeroses.

YOGA & ACTIVITY HOLIDAY

Les Passeroses

🌐 ⛺ ⭕ 🧗 🎧 ⚽ ↘14

Nonac, near Montmoreau, Charente
T+33 (0)5-4561 5518
www.passeroses.com
From €360 per person for a long weekend

Laid-back and lovely Les Passeroses runs yoga, activity and vegetarian cookery weekends and week-long holidays from May to September – individuals can also stay at other times when courses aren't running. Set in a peaceful valley of the Charente surrounded by fields of vines, corn and sunflowers and a 20-minute walk away from the nearest village, this rural retreat is a real

antidote to city living: you may find yourself sharing your outdoor meditation with lizards, tree frogs and the owner's friendly cats, and your evening yoga class with bats and barn owls. Alex and Adrian are very friendly, witty and easy-going hosts.

Accommodation is in a sensitively restored traditional long farmhouse, which retains its original features (oak beams, fireplaces and pigeonnier windows). You sleep in one of five beautifully decorated bedrooms with candles and incense holders in every room. The en suite or shared modern bathrooms have efficient showers and water saving toilets. If you're here on a yoga week, you'll need to be prepared to share a room. Up to 18 people can be accommodated here – 11 in the main house, and the rest in three gîtes which are a minute's walk away.

Outside there are hidden spaces amongst the trees for quiet contemplation, as well as a mature garden with a wild-flower meadow, a lily-covered lake and a Japanese pond. Hammocks are strung under an ancient yew, and there are sunloungers and seating around an unheated pool (a heated one is planned for 2008). Yoga takes place in a 65 sq m barn with solid oak floor and views across the countryside. There's a cosy chill-out space at the back of the barn, with French windows opening out onto a wooden terrace. A yoga deck and a sauna are planned for 2008.

The wonderful range of yoga courses on offer includes iyengar, hatha, kundalini, ashtanga, yin/yang, viniyoga, vinyasa flow and partner yoga, taught by visiting teachers from all over the world. There are also courses in ayurveda, Thai yoga massage and meditation; yoga and activity weeks when you can go horse riding, kayaking, cycling and walking, plus a yoga and vegetarian cookery week. Indian head massage, aromatherapy massage and reflexology are available in your room. A treatment room is planned for late 2007.

Meals are eaten on the outdoor terrace looking out over the swimming pool and countryside, or in an open-plan indoor dining area. Alex and Adrian are brilliant cooks and the food is a highlight; mainly vegetarian,

with an imaginative vegan menu also on offer. Dishes include Mediterranean, Morroccan, Thai and Indian and ingredients are home-grown where possible. A typical post-yoga brunch might be baked figs with goat's cheese and honey, ratatouille, buckwheat pancakes, courgette salad with lemon juice, fresh thyme and parmesan shavings and coconut sorbet with lime sauce. Alcohol is available, at the discretion of the yoga teacher.

Fellow guests may include devotees of a particular yoga teacher from as far afield as Australia and Japan, plus a broad mix of adventurous, chilled-out types in their thirties and forties; beginners are welcome. Fly to Bordeaux or Bergerac, from where transfers cost €50 per person return. Or take the Eurostar and TGV to Angouleme (a 5-6-hour journey from London with one change in Paris). Transfers from Angoulême cost €25.

Southern Europe France

HOTEL & SPA

Les Prés d'Eugénie

Eugénie-les-Bains, Landes
T+33 (0)5-5805 0505
www.michelguerard.com
From €100 per room per night

Les Prés d'Eugénie is a delightful 40-acre spa estate, designed and run by Christine Guérard, owner of her family's thalassotherapy chain, Chaîne Thermale du Soleil, and her husband, chef Michel Guérard, pioneer of haute cuisine minceur (gastronomic spa food). This Relais & Châteaux property is all very lush and country-chic, with lavender bushes, lemon trees and climbing roses.

The hotel's 40 rooms are set in four ancient buildings scattered across the estate, each with its own character, and all the rooms have pretty views overlooking the park or the gardens. The largest suites are in Le Couvent des Herbes, a converted priory, and Les Logis de la Ferme aux Grives. Both are set apart from the main building and offer four-star accommodation. La Maison Rose is a pretty two-star alternative.

There is a busy main spa with its own thermal spring where you can enjoy a pool and thermal water treatments (€130 for five sessions). La Ferme Thermale is a separate, more private farmhouse-style spa offering a range of treatments and massages in rooms with vaulted, beamed ceilings, also open to

day guests. The most requested treatment is the signature, a bath of creamy white kaolin mud, which is buoyant enough to float on (€30).

Guests who want to restrict fat, salt and calories can dine on Michel Guérard's daily fixed cuisine minceur menu, served in the three-Michelin-starred restaurant, where gastronomic menus are also served. Some 60% of the guests are well-heeled French, with the remiander including other Europeans and Americans looking for downtime. Fly or take a train to Pau, 45 km from Eugénie, from where it's a €75 taxi ride.

RURAL RETREAT

Manoir de Loguevel

Locarn near Callac, Brittany
T+33 (0)2-9636 6898
www.manoir-loguevel.com
From €53 per person per night half board

Newly built inside the old walls of an ancient manor house and set in 33 acres of meadows and forest, Longuevel offers counselling, psychotherapy and alternative therapies as well as time and space to de-stress. Guests are mostly women of all ages, from Europe, Australia and Asia, though there is an increasing number of men. Loguevel also runs training courses for alternative therapies such as reiki and crystal healing (see www.iihtvh.com), and so also attracts those with an existing interest in all things holistic.

🍴 Soul food

A cycling trip with **Breton Bikes** (T+33 (0)2-9624 8672, www.bretonbikes.com, from €300 per person per week) offers an active holiday in Brittany and a chance to make a difference to people's lives. When you book, they can supply you with a sponsorship pack for the UK-based **Intermediate Technology Development Group** (www.itdg.org), which specializes in providing training and expertise to developing countries – training local blacksmiths in sub-Saharan Africa to make new ploughs, for example, meant locals could increase food production by 50%. In the past four years Breton Bikes has donated over €8000 to the charity, and their guests have raised well over €20,000.

Accommodation is in modern, comfortable en suite studio rooms (which have their own kitchenette should you choose to be alone and cook for yourself) and food is vegetarian, plentiful and nutritious. On arrival you can have your own retreat tailor-made by UK-trained holistic therapist Anna and an experienced team. There's a sauna, spa bath and a range of pampering treatments on offer as well as yoga, pilates, meditation, detoxes, massage and reflexology – or try something more alternative, such as regression therapy, crystal therapy or Bach flower remedies.

This is an easy place to relax – there are large and well-kept gardens, a swimming pool, two large ponds, and plenty of garden benches and seats in tranquil spots. Guests stay for anything from three nights to two weeks. From the UK take a ferry to St Malo or Roscoff, then a train to Guingamp, the nearest station. Guests can be picked up by request. The centre is open all year round, but avoid mid-July to the end of August when families tend to use the property for their holiday retreats.

Above: Les Prés d'Eugénie.
Right: Manoir de Longuevel.

PILATES HOLIDAY

Pilates en Provence

🔆 ⊙ ⨂ ❏17

Salernes
T+44 (0)20-7284 4044
www.pilatesenprovence.com
From €482 per person for 2 nights half board

Pilates en Provence runs pilates holidays during May, June, September and October, for a maximum of eight people. You can stay for a two- or three-night weekend, or arrange a longer stay on a self-catering basis. The breaks are open to beginners as well as those already into pilates, and are taught by American-born Lynne Gentle, a member of the British Pilates Foundation, level 3 certified by the Register of Exercise Professionals and a qualified gyrotonic teacher.

Your base is Salernes, a 45-minute drive inland from St Tropez. It's a charming French working community famous for its *tomettes* (tiles) and ceramics decorated by local artists; if you opt for a Friday to Monday break, you'll have the opportunity to enjoy the lovely local Sunday market followed by a leisurely Provençal lunch.

You stay at Villa Les Olives, a four-bedroom open-plan single-storey house just 1 km from the village in a quiet rural setting. South facing with wonderful views over open countryside, the villa has a heated swimming pool, an orchard and terraces. The house has under-floor heating and a fireplace, and is simply but comfortably furnished. Amenities include a satellite television, DVD player and stereo system, dishwasher and washer and dryer – there's also a double hammock.

Pilates group classes are conducted outdoors by the pool when weather permits. Massage and beauty treatments can be arranged with local therapists, as well as guided wine tours, outdoor jazz concerts, cookery, art and French language classes and local day trips.

Half-board weekends include accommodation based on two people sharing a twin room, breakfast and either lunch or supper with wine, and a daily pilates matwork and gyrokinesis class. If you're travelling alone, you'll need to pay a supplement. A three-night stay will also give you a one-to-one session including posture assessment. Fly to Marseille, Toulon or Nice – from each airport it's about a 90-minute transfer. Pilates en Provence also run Pilates Caribe! holidays in Antigua.

RURAL RETREAT

Real Retreat

🗺 ⊙ 🔆 ⊙ ❋ ⊙ ❏18

Pontiacq, Pyrénées-Atlantique
T+33 (0)5-5981 5313
www.realretreat.com
From €450 per person, €585 per couple per week including treatments

The Real Retreat is set in a secluded 18th-century farmhouse and run by British couple Danya and Neil, who offer alternative therapies, yoga and detoxing as part of a relaxing holiday in the Pyrenees. Their picturesque house is set in Pontiacq-Viellepinte, a quiet spot which sees just a car or two a day. It's the kind of village where it's quite normal to exchange reiki for bread, and to find people picking figs in your garden.

Most guests come for an all-inclusive holistic week, though if there's a vacancy you can also stay for a shorter time and have à la carte treatments (from €25). Danya, an easy-going, energetic ex-policewoman who gives free yoga classes to the local village children, offers all the therapies herself. These include crystal healing (see below), reiki, aromatherapy, hot-stone therapy, Indian head massage and mud wraps. Danya also offers counselling while trekking in the mountains and takes yoga classes by the river at Lourdes (a 20-minute drive away). Trained in ashtanga yoga in the UK, she incorporates hatha yoga into classes for newcomers.

66 99

A gentle, intuitive technique which uses the natural vibration of crystals to balance problem areas, crystal healing activates the electro-magnetic sheath that surrounds the physical body, using crystals that correspond to the seven chakras. "You may experience burning, freezing or a kind of electric shock if a chakra is out of balance," explained Danya, making me nervous.

She waved a piece of clear quartz above my crown chakra, then passed her hands over it, using reiki techniques which involve a sequence of hand movements to heal your aura. Then came a hunk of the cool stone amethyst, which she placed on my third eye (the point between the eyebrows). A piece of rose quartz put on my throat "to help me speak out" felt a bit warm, the sign of a problem area. Jade on my heart chakra was fine, but as she waved a piece of citrine over the solar plexus, my stomach gurgled and tensed in knots. As she worked her hands above the area, it seemed to ease.

Each stone and chakra has specific properties. Tiger's eye, placed on the sacral chakra (on top of the pelvis) restores confidence and wellbeing. Smoky quartz, now sitting on the root chakra (my pubic bone) eases stress. As Danya passes her hands above the ridge of stones, working until the warm areas had become aligned with the rest, a deep relaxation seeps over me. When she takes them off one by one, I feel inexplicably lighter and calmer, and after spending a few weeks dawdling over my writing work, later that day I let it flow. There may have been no electric shocks, but perhaps crystal healing, with Danya's strong, positive energy, had helped.

Nicki Grihault

NICKI GRIHAULT

94 Dedicated detox weeks are also on offer with organic food and juices and a daily programme of ashtanga yoga, guided hikes, detox treatments and life coaching.

There are two bedrooms with en suite bathrooms in the farmhouse, ideal for single travellers, and three gîtes, each sleeping two people. Each is decorated in a feminine, cottagey style, with exposed stone walls, spotlights and romantic double beds under rustic beams. Lavender soap, candles and soft dressing gowns are provided. Food is self-catering, fresh produce is available locally and every gîte has a fridge stocked generously with pasta and sauce, bread, milk, cheese and ham and good quality jams.

Ancient stone walls partly enclose the garden and morning yoga deck, creating privacy and intimacy. There are three great yoga spaces as well as the deck: an outdoor space shaded by trees near the blackcurrant bushes, a huge space upstairs in the barn with a view over wheat fields, and treatment rooms below. A sunken pool, indoor flotation tank, tai chi classes and a small organic garden are planned for late 2008.

Fellow guests are typically professional couples including practising therapists aged 40-60, groups of younger female friends wanting pampering, and individuals who have come for bereavement counselling (one of Danya's specialities). In the evenings, there's an honesty bar on the yoga deck and guests often sit and chat in the garden until the early hours, to a deafening chorus of tree frogs from the man-made lake nearby. The retreat is open all year round. Fly to Pau, a 40-minute drive, or Toulouse, a two-hour drive away.

YOGA HOLIDAY

Sacred Journeys

🌐 ↘19

Paris and Picardy
T+44 (0)7866-385366
www.sacredjourneys.co.uk
From €700 for 4 nights

Sacred Journeys runs sumptuous yoga weekends to France every Easter combining ashtanga yoga with cultural sights and good food and wine. Led by director Sally Griffyn, author of *Ashtanga Yoga For Women*, the break comprises an overnight stay in Paris at the cosy and eclectic **Hotel Jeanne d'Arc**, followed by three nights at the **Château de Sacy** (www.chateaudesacy.com), a 30-minute drive north in Picardy.

At the château you'll have morning ashtanga classes, with afternoons free to walk in the lovely woods nearby, relax or have a massage. There's a meditation session in the late afternoon before dinner. The yoga caters to all levels: if you're experienced you do self-practice Mysore-style (see page 203), where beginners will be offered a taught class before lunch. If you're new to ashtanga, this is a great place to be introduced to the primary series (see glossary, page 14).

Sally's laid-back nature and welcoming, non-judgemental approach makes for a lively and friendly house party atmosphere. She runs yoga holidays at different stately homes, private villas and châteaux in various countires across Europe.

PILATES HOLIDAY

Sarah Rosenfield Pilates

🌀 ⚡ ↘20

Montbard, Côte d'Or
T+44 (0)20-7722 4373
www.sarahpilates.com
From €590 for the weekend

Sarah Rosenfield runs annual pilates weekends at La Maison du Château (www.lamaisonduchateau.co.uk), a rambling 18th-century nine-bedded mansion in the sleepy Burgundy village of Cry-sur-Armançon. Set in 24 acres with heated swimming pool, grass tennis court, an avenue of chestnut trees and a meadow full

Above: Real Retreat. **Right:** La Maison du Château, the rambling 18th-century mansion used by Sarah Rosenfied Pilates. **Opposite:** The hills are alive with the sound of Tessa Cornish.

of wild flowers, it's a lovely place to come for a house-party-style weekend led by bubbly ex-singer and tour manager, Sarah, who trained at the Pilates Institute and has been running pilates holidays since 2002.

Pilates is on the menu twice daily – two hours in the morning and early evening, including half an hour of relaxation and a guided visualization. UK-based massage therapist Sandie Duncan (www.4getstress.com) comes with the group – one half-hour massage is included, and extra massages cost €34 for half an hour.

Sarah's retreats take a maximum of 12 and tend to attract single women, with some couples and men, aged from 25 to 70, mostly from the UK and including Sarah's existing students from her London classes. The chateau is one hour by fast train from Paris to Montbard, and a 15-minute taxi ride from there. Sarah also holds weekend retreats in Tuscany (www.hotelvillavolpi.com) and Mallorca (www.fincaescastell.com, see page 113), as well as ad hoc retreats in South Africa.

Ski yoga with Tessa Cornish

☀ ⛰ ♿ ◧21

Lullin, Haute Savoie
T+44 (0)845-638 0717
www.yogamorzine.com
From €770 for 4 nights

Iyengar yoga teacher Tessa Cornish lives in the French Alps and teaches daily iyengar yoga classes and workshops in Morzine and Évian. She runs a regular four-night yoga and ski break in the neighbouring village of Essert Romand, where you'll have a yoga class before skiing, snowboarding or snow walking, and a second class before dinner. You stay in the large, comfortable **Chalet les Echos** (www.chaletlesechos.com) in the village. Massage therapy can be arranged in house, and meals are cooked with organic local produce. Beginners are welcome. Both places are in the Portes du Soleil region, which offers brilliant skiing.

Snow Yogi

☀ ⛰ ◉ ⚽ ♿ ◧22

Argentière, near Chamonix Sud
T+44 (0)7753-678 582
www.ayurvedicyogi.com
From €965 for 7 nights excluding flights

UK-based Ayurvedic Yogi offers week-long skiing holidays with a holistic twist in Argentière, near Chamonix Sud, with world-class skiing in spectacular mountain scenery. Run every February and April, the holidays combine skiing, yoga, healthy eating, alternative therapies and massage.

Ayurvedic Yogi founder, Jo Johnston, a sivananda yoga teacher and ayurvedic therapist, devised Snow Yogi when she wanted a healthier skiing trip herself.

Jo teaches a daily 90-minute sivananda yoga class, with an emphasis on asansas, pranayama and final relaxation to allow the body to recharge; beginners and those

On our first night at La Maison du Château, champagne flowed in the lounge in front of an open fire with the wonderful smells of delphines wafting through. I was getting the picture. Pilates doesn't attract tipi-dwelling types, but people who expect comfortable accommodation and a good standard of service. A delicious five-course dinner in the elegant dining room followed. This isn't a place to count calories.

Pilates is technical not spiritual, and my fellow guests reflected this straightforward approach to life. Our group was all women, mostly in the media. One of the participants, Katy, had been unable to move, following an injury, when she came to see Sarah three years ago. She swears by pilates now, which stretches the core, inner muscles. The subtle movements are challenging, requiring intense concentration.

"You're wearing your shoulders as earrings!" laughed Sarah. With her chirpy, attentive but commanding style, Sarah is well-trained, sociable and caring. Afterwards, Sandie the massage therapist banished my stiffness with strong capable fingers and a heaven-sent camomile, black pepper and lavender aromatherapy mix. I've always eschewed 'women's holidays', but here I was on one, and really enjoying it. Best of all, at the end of the weekend, my shoulders were in an entirely new position – down.

Nicki Grihault

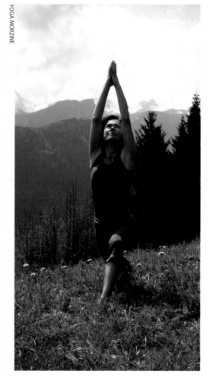

YOGA MORZINE

Southern Europe France

Meditation retreat

Plum Village ☯ ⛰ 🌳 ↘23

Plum Village, or Village des Pruniers, is a Zen Buddhist retreat community set on the hills among vineyards and plum trees at Dieulivol, 48 km from Saint-Foy-La-Grande. It is the home of monks and nuns following the teachings of the inspirational Thich Nhat Hanh (or Thay as he is known), a Vietnamese Zen master, poet and peace activist. The community runs retreats throughout the year, and provides the perfect environment for anyone who wants to experience being part of a Buddhist community (or sangha).

Where you stay This is a popular place and up to 700 people can be accommodated at any one time. Accommodation is in one of four hamlets, depending on whether you are a single man, single woman or in a couple. Rooms are in traditional French farmhouses made of wood and stone, or in modern accommodation blocks. Twin rooms are available for couples, but otherwise it's usual to share a room or sleep in a dorm. Bathrooms are en suite or communal, clean and simple. In the summer, camping provides a cheap and private alternative. Quiet private space can be found outdoors by the lotus pond, in the bamboo grove, or in the woods and fields surrounding the village – over 2500 plum trees have been planted here and there are long lines of poplars to walk among.

What you do The main point of coming here is to learn Vietnamese Zen meditation, and especially 'mindful living': to attempt to be present in the moment, to practise mindfulness in our everyday lives and to develop compassion for ourselves and for others. Thich Nhat Hanh is an expert at making Buddhism accessible to a 21st-century audience, and his inspirational, wise and lucid talks are a main draw.

There are daily meditation sessions, including walking meditation and working meditation, when you'll be assigned a task such as chopping vegetables, cleaning the toilets or gardening. In the mornings and evenings there are sessions of Vietnamese qigong and, with prior permission, you can also use one of the meditation halls to

❝❞

I love Plum Village. Thich Nhat Hanh's teachings encourage you to experience the joy of being alive. The buildings are scattered, so day and night you are going outside, whatever the weather, and experiencing stars and moon, dawn and sunset, heat and cold, mist and rain – and learning to accept things as they are.

June Mitchell

do yoga. You'll be taken through your day by the sound of a bell, which first chimes at 0500. To learn mindfulness, you are encouraged to stop and breathe consciously for three breaths every time you hear the bell. It can seem strange for everyone to suddenly stop at the same time and breathe, but after a while it becomes natural, and a good way of coming back to the present moment.

What you eat and drink Food is vegetarian, and both Eastern and Western tastes are catered for – the dishes are delightful to look at, tasty and healthy. There are three meals a day, and also a small shop where you can buy snacks. Alcohol and smoking are strictly forbidden.

Who goes Plum Village attracts a complete mix – by age, nationality and background – of people interested in meditation and a calmer way of living. It's a particularly open place to come if you have never set foot in a meditation hall before. There are family retreats in late July/early August and at Christmas and New Year. For those looking for something intensive, there's a traditional three-month-long retreat in winter, or a three-week retreat every two years in June when Thich Nhat Hanh teaches for five or six days each week.

Essentials Plum Village is near St-Foy-la-Grande, Dordogne, T+33 (0)5-5661 6688, www.plumvillage.org. It costs from €250 per person per week. To enable you to fully experience mindful living, you are required to participate in all activities, to stay at least a week and ensure you arrive on a Friday, when there is an introduction and orientation session. Bring light shoes for indoors and another pair for outdoors. The nearest airport is Bordeaux, 85 km away. Hire a car or take a shuttle bus to Saint Jean train station, then a local train to St-Foy- la-Grande. Plum Village can arrange transfers to and from the station (only on Fridays) for €5 each way.

It's advisable to book your stay here well in advance. Thich Nhat Hanh occasionally runs retreats in the rest of Europe, and there are sister retreats in the US (see page 339).

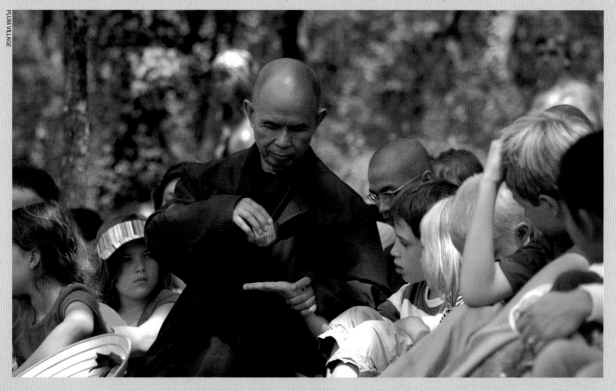
PLUM VILLAGE

already into a practice are taught separately. The aim is to help minimize the risk of injury and maximize skiing performance by increasing fitness, spatial awareness and balance. Holistic sports, Indian head and ayurvedic full-body massages, reiki and indulgent ayurvedic facials are also available from Jo or complementary therapist, Claire Hamilton, who uses Neal's Yard oils.

A maximum of 14 guests stay at the **Chalet Cosmique** (privately hired from www.freshtraxxx.com) in twin or triple rooms; it's a luxurious venue which has an outside hot tub seating eight.

Energy-rich and organic food cooked by Jo is served for breakfast, afternoon tea and dinner and organic wine is included in the price. You can join a local skiing or snowboarding guided group arranged by Ayurvedic Yogi, be guided by local Michelle King, a trained sports therapist and ski guide, or explore on your own. Most guests are in their twenties and thirties, beginners are welcome, and the holiday is open to non-skiing partners.

The price includes shared accommodation, daily yoga and full board. Extras include a meal out (about €42), ski passes (about €210), ski hire (about €105), airport transfers (€70 return) and massages (from €35 for 40 minutes). Fly to Geneva, from where it's a 1¼-hour drive (Ayurvedic Yogi arranges carbon offset for each person flying), or take the Eurostar to Lille, then TGV to Bellegarde, a one-hour drive away. Ayurvedic Yogi also holds ayurveda and yoga retreat weekends in Dorset, UK (see page 28).

MEDITATION RETREAT

Tapovan Meditation Centre

Cubjac, Dordogne
T+33 (0)5-5305 9746
www.dharmanetwork.org
From €22 a day

Tapovan runs very well-organized meditation retreats in beautiful surroundings on the site of a former 19th-century Zen monastery and water mill, on the river Auvézère (where you can swim from mid-May to late September). The centre is set on the edge of a village with a shop, café and bakery, though you feel nicely secluded inside Tapovan's grounds.

Resident teacher Martin Aylward founded Tapovan with his wife Gail and two children, and has been teaching vipassana meditation internationally since 1999. Retreats are open to beginners as well as those who want to deepen their practice, and often feature guest teachers such as the wonderful Stephen Batchelor (see Gaia House entry page 34).

Retreats take a maximum of 40 at any one time, except in July when two weeks are given over to a massive summer retreat hosting more than 200 participants from 25 countries. This opportunity to live and meditate in such a large and peaceful community is a real inspiration for many.

There are also open summer retreats from May to August, when people can arrive and leave any day and stay for as long as they

want (minimum of two nights). During this time mornings are conducted in silence and the daily programme includes four meditation periods, one work period in which you help out in the kitchens or gardens, time for exercise and yoga and talks and discussion on dharma teachings.

You meditate in a wooden Japanese-style meditation hall surrounded by a bamboo grove, and sleep in clean and simple shared or single rooms or secluded cabins set among the trees and bamboo – there are limited single rooms available, which you will need to request ahead. There is also a dormitory, or you can camp if you bring your own tent and sleeping bag. All food is vegetarian, largely organic, and much of it grown in Tapovan's own vegetable gardens. Tapovan is two hours by road from Bordeaux – you could also fly to Bergerac or Limoges. The nearest train and bus station is Périgueux, 20 minutes by bus or taxi.

RURAL RETREAT

The Yellow House

Jurançon, near Pau, Pyrénées-Atlantique
T+33 (0)5-5606 2758
www.yellow-house-services.org
From €56 per person per night

This beautifully restored 19th-century summer residence, painted a sunny yellow and run by ex-organic farmers, is a chambre d'hote with a twist, offering tools to change your life, as well as delicious organic food. Dutchman Johan offers one-to-one life coaching and other guided self-development activities such as autobiographical work, and his partner, German-Canadian Andrea, who started her training by curing her own illness as a teenager, offers nutritional consultation and cookery lessons – sushi is a speciality. You can also learn candle-making, claying, mosaic-making, painting and stonecarving, or walk the 900 km from here over the Pyrenees along the old pilgrimage route to Santiago de Compostela in Spain.

Snow Yogi at Argentière.

Vipassana meditation session at Tapovan.

With just four elegant rooms, The Yellow House is an intimate, nurturing place. Guests can join the family on summer evenings at a long table on the veranda, with stunning views of a leafy valley and hills, and the snow-capped Pyrenees beyond. There's also a small swimming pool. Meals are largely organic and made with local produce, and include home-made bread and soup, heaps of fresh salad, delicacies like fresh artichoke, and hearty dishes such as mushroom and onion cheese tart or home-made ravioli; meat and fish are also on the menu. It's the kind of place where if you mention liking a particular dish, vegetable or fruit, it may appear at the next meal. Breakfast can be brought to your room when you want it.

The house has high ceilings and rich, oiled chestnut parquet floors throughout. Of the four en suite bedrooms upstairs, three have king-size beds with very comfortable mattresses and soft, light duvets; one is south facing with a Hersch designer bath and optional aromatherapy infusion, a large shower and daybed. There are plans to build a bathhouse with an aromatherapy infusion bath and rest room, sauna and outdoor Japanese hot tub by 2010.

This guesthouse attracts mainly British couples, families or individuals wanting life coaching or nutrition consultation and staying for a minimum of three days. Consultations cost €100 a session – it's usual to book a minimum of three. This isn't a place to come if you want a monastic atmosphere; it offers a balance of time alone and company. The location is wonderfully quiet, with no road noise, but the family are full of life: Johan and Andrea have seven children between them, the youngest of whom is 14. The Yellow House is based in wine country, a 15-minute drive from cosmopolitan Pau, and free transfers are provided. Come any time: the summer has the best weather, the wine harvest is in autumn and the Pyrenees look spectacular in winter.

YOGA RETREAT
Yoga Tantra & Devic Centre

Le Vidou, St Matre, near Cahors
T +33 (0)5-6521 7620
www.europeyoga.com
From €400 per person per week (karma yoga weeks free)

This peaceful, chilled-out place run by Dutch yoga teacher Nawajyoti and her team is set in 3 ha of oak woodland packed with wildlife.

Come and stay independently, or join one of the retreats which run throughout the year. These include yoga for beginners (with one class a day), more intensive ashtanga vinyasa yoga holidays (with two classes a day), meditation and psychic awareness. You can also detox, take tai chi classes, enjoy sports massages or have your tarot cards read. There is a nearby lake with a beach which is great for swimming, local village markets with cafés, and great walking and cycling country nearby.

Your fellow guests will be men and

YELLOW HOUSE

YOGA TANTRA & DEVIC CENTRE

Top: The beautiful 19th-century Yellow House, with the majestic Pyrenees looming in the background.
Above: Loosening up at the Yoga Tantra & Devic Centre.

women in their thirties and forties, most travelling alone to enjoy yoga, or to re-evaluate careers or relationships. Mainly European with an occasional American, they include teachers, mothers, journalists and nurses as well as therapists and yoga and pilates teachers. Younger people are attracted to the free karma yoga weeks, during which participants can practise yoga, join local classes and enjoy full board and lodging in return for about 5½ hours' work a day. Longer stays are also available for people who want to live a gently yogic lifestyle and be part of the team (€650 a month).

The centre takes a maximum of 10 guests at a time to ensure individual attention and an intimate atmosphere. Accommodation is in basic but clean and tidy good-sized shared rooms – there are two twin-bedded rooms in the main centre (the larger one in the loft) and three log cabins, one of which can sleep three. Guests share three bathrooms, three toilets and an outside compost toilet. All courses are full board, food is decent vegetarian using produce from the centre's own vegetable plot, and special diets are catered for. Tea, coffee and cake are served, but no alcohol, and smoking is not allowed in the house. Yoga takes place in a studio or on outside yoga decking. There's also a meditation hut and various seating areas within the woodlands.

Fly to Toulouse, then take a train to Cahors, 1½ hours. Pickups from Cahors can be arranged in advance (€30 return).

YOGA HOLIDAY
Yoga with Claire Missingham

Ferme de Montagne, near Chamonix
T+44 (0)79-8943 1818
www.claireyoga.com
From €2000 for 4 days

For anyone looking to indulge and rejuvenate, UK-based yoga teacher Claire Missingham takes long-weekend yoga retreats each summer to Les Ges in the French Alps. You stay at **Ferme de Montagne** (www.fermedemontagne.co.uk), a boutique ski lodge converted from a Savoy farmhouse, with eight luxurious double bedrooms and relaxed, top-notch service.

Down-to-earth and with years of teaching experience, Claire is very good at combining the spiritual aspects of yoga with the physical, and her own Yoga Touch method mixes vinyasa flow yoga with expert hands-on massage to help students go deeper into their practice. Over the course of the weekend you'll get a mix of group and one-to-one classes, and also enjoy the outdoor yoga shala, which is set in the middle of a lovely meadow surrounded by mountains.

Aromatherapy, hot-stone massage and beauty treatments using Guinot products are available with the resident therapist, and you can go on a luscious guided forest walk to enjoy views of Mont Blanc. There's an outdoor jacuzzi to soak in at the end of the day, before a gourmet dinner is served on the terrace. The price includes yoga, food, accommodation, guided walks, transfers and treatments, but not flights – the nearest airport is Geneva. Claire also teaches on In:Spa holidays (see page 172).

WELLBEING HOLIDAY
Yogoloji at Hotel Pastis

St-Tropez, Côte d'Azur
T+44 (0)20-7730 7473
www.yogoloji.co.uk
From €1225 per person excluding flights

Yogoloji run annual three-night retreats at **Hotel Pastis** (www.pastis-st-tropez.com), a quiet contemporary boutique hotel overlooking the sea at St-Tropez. Retreats take place away from the busy tourist season, usually in September when it's still warm, and are designed to help you relax and re-energize.

The retreats take no more than 12 and you'll have exclusive use of the hotel, staying in beautifully designed rooms with an impressive attention to detail. On arrival you're given a daily programme which includes group classes and one-to-one sessions, and treatments tailored to your needs; these may include acupuncture, Chinese medicine, Indian head massage, ayurvedic, holistic and deep tissue massage, reiki and Tibetan hot-stone therapy. There are two daily sessions of yoga and meditation – a dynamic class in the morning and a more relaxing session in the evening.

Food is delicious vegetarian, with an emphasis on helping you understand your relationship to food rather than strict detoxing. You can also pop into St-Tropez for a spot of shopping, and tennis and sailing can be arranged (at extra cost). The long weekend is aimed at couples, friends or people wanting to take time out alone, and you'll be in safe hands with Francesca and Liisa, co-founders of Yogoloji. You fly to Toulon, 45 minutes from St-Tropez – transfers are included. For other Yogoloji retreats, see page 370.

CLAIRE MISSINGHAM

Yoga shala at Ferme de Montagne.

HOTEL PASTIS

Hotel Pastis, home of the Yogoloji retreats.

◑ Body language

A dip in the sea

Thalassotherapy simply means treatments with sea water. 'Thalasso' is the Greek word for 'sea', though the practice actually derives from the Brittany coast where, according to records, Henry III of France took sea-baths to cure his 'torments', and, by 1778, seawater bathtubs had been erected on the beaches in Dieppe. The beautiful people of the day, titled nobility and minor European royalty flocked to 'take the waters', socialize and gossip, and the idea caught on all over Europe – even England's Queen Victoria had a bathing hut erected for daily seawater dips at Osborne House, her Italianate villa on the Isle of Wight.

In 1877, a Dr Joseph de la Bommardière from Arcachon, near Bordeaux, coined the word *thalassothérapie* to describe these water cures, which by then were popular all over Europe. Though they fell out of favour after 1940 when modern antibiotics such as penicillin appeared, they came back into fashion in the 1960s after Louisson Bobet, the winner of three Tours de France, made a near-miraculous recovery from a serious car crash thanks to the healing properties of seawater. So impressed was he, that he led a movement to reintroduce thalassotherapy centres in France.

The treatments are said to boost the immune system and help the mind and body to combat stress and regain a sense of wellbeing. They can also do wonders for people suffering from muscle pain, joint disorders and post-traumatic stress. Bona fide thalassotherapy spas today use only fresh, filtered seawater pumped straight from the sea and warmed to body temperature for a dizzying array of treatments. Thalassotherapy is very functional and results-driven, with little space for niceties. A seaweed wrap feels rather like being smothered in giant rubber tea-bags – other treatments include the rather more pleasant water massage baths as well as affusions showers, underwater showers, jet showers, hydro massages, and spraying with seawater mixed with oils. It's not for everyone, especially those with high or low blood pressure or with sensitive skin.

One of the best places to experience thalassotherapy is on the Brittany coast, where you can also indulge in some bracing sea-air walks. Here, 13 thalassotherapy centres have signed up to the Thalasso Bretagne Association (www.brittanytourism.com), which guarantees on-site doctors and freshly drawn and filtered seawater. They're rather large, austere places, but you'll get expert treatments.

Try **La Thalassa de Roscoff** (T+33 (0)8-2500 4230, www.thalasso.com, from €882 per person for 6 nights, half board) in north Finistère, where the house speciality is 'Le Palper Rouler', a talc massage which involves pinching the skin to encourage blood flow – and yes, it hurts. Or try *algothérapie*, which involves lying on a squishy, pungent bed of seaweed and being blanketed with more, right up to your neck.

At **Les Therme Marins de St Malo** (T+33 (0)2-99 40 7500, www.thalassosaintmalo.com, from €730 per person for 2 nights) has one of the largest teams of therapists in France, offering therapies for weight-loss, back pain, a post-natal programme and a range of pampering beauty treatments. Set on a rocky cliff at Dinard is the **Thalassa Spa** (T+33 (0)2-9916 7810, www.noveldinard.com, from €188 per person per night sharing), with panoramic views over the sea and outlying islands from treatment rooms. You stay at the connected three-star Novotel or in nearby apartments with sea views. Try a marine mud bath, or one of the many inventive treatments such as 'The Sea of Tranquility', a specially designed curen. for insomniacs, and 'Pressotherapy', a treatment to improve circulation.

CAROLINE SYLGE

TOURISMEBRETAGNE-PHOTOS.COM

Spain

Sort your life out trekking in the Picos de Europa, retreat in Andalucía or liberate yourself through dance.

Fact file

- **Visa:** None required for EU passport holders and for US and Canadian citizens staying up to 90 days
- **Country code:** +34
- **Currency:** Euro (€)
- **Time zone:** GMT +1 hour
- **Electricity:** 230v
- **Tourist board:** www.spain.info

YOGA RETREAT

Casa Blanca

Arboleas, Andalucía
T+34 950-439020
www.casablancayogareiki.com
From €600 per person per week

Liz and Paul have made their home from an old Andalucían manor house, and specialize in providing individually tailored yoga and reiki therapy for those needing gentle attention. Liz saved herself from incapacity and painful operations through devising her own yoga practice, and this would be a good place to come for some one-to-one attention for anyone with back problems. You can also join six weekly yoga classes Liz gives to locals and expats. Paul is calm, aware and a qualified reiki master.

The house retains many of its traditional features including beams and arches and large wooden shuttered windows. Only four people stay here at any one time, so you're sure of personal attention. Bedrooms are simple, there's a calm and comfortable sitting area, and the manor enjoys views across an expansive valley, although you can sometimes hear the sounds of a distant industrial plant.

You'll eat home-cooked vegetarian food with Liz and Paul, who can also take you on trips to the mountains or the sea, 35 minutes away. Otherwise, be prepared to be at the house. Come all year round, although July/August can be too hot. Fly to Almería from where they'll pick you up.

Casa Blanca in Andalucía.

DANCE HOLIDAY

Club Dance Holidays

Granada and Vejer
T+44 0870-286 6000
www.clubdanceholidays.com
From €699 per person per week

Express yourself and get back to your basic instincts on a dance holiday with UK-based Club Dance Holidays, who run two well-organized trips every year to Spain. An Oriental dance holiday in the fascinating Moorish city of Granada runs every May/June to coincide with the Spanish fiesta of Las Cruces de Mayo, which you can enjoy on your last two nights. The week includes 10 hours of Oriental dance classes and there are optional classes in salsa, tango and Sevillanas. You stay at the central three-star Hotel Los Angeles, which has a pool, and local trips and evenings out are arranged. Alternatively go in October for a week of belly dancing in Vejer, a whitewashed town in Andalucía not far from the coast. A trip to Morocco is included in the week. Both holidays welcome beginners and those already into dance; most guests tend to be women in their twenties to fifties looking for fun and relaxation.

DETOX RETREAT

The Complete Retreat

Málaga
T+44 (0)7941-214750
www.thecompleteretreat.com
From €2000 per person per week

The Complete Retreat is not a detox holiday for the half-hearted. With views across the stunning Andalucían countryside and a luxurious villa as their home from home, guests are both challenged and rewarded by a retreat formula that has many of them coming back for more.

The beautiful finca provides en suite accommodation for an intimate group of 10 guests. Each room is quite individual and

> If you think you can, or if you think you can't, you're right.

Henry Ford

hike through the countryside follows, before a buffet lunch on the terrace. Afternoons are free for treatments, if you've booked them, or lazing by the pool. Another yoga class takes place in the late afternoon, followed by a nutrition-based talk or a kitchen demonstration. A candlelit meditation session brings the day to a close.

The therapies they provide include aromatherapy and deep tissue massages, reflexology and acupuncture (from €70 for 70 minutes). The shiatsu massage, a deeply healing experience, is also to be recommended. The staff and therapists are exceptional in their specialist areas, working with each guest on a personal level to ensure the experience is the best it can be.

The 'living' or raw food diet and juice detox programme aim to replenish and cleanse the body and strengthen the immune system with superfoods such as wheatgrass,

most have a private terrace. The quirky antique furnishings and Moroccan-influenced bohemian style are luxurious (though you'd expect it at this price).

Days are very structured, beginning with a guided meditation and 90-minute hatha yoga class with a backdrop of mountains. A

The Complete Retreat takes place in a beautiful finca in the stunning Andalucían countryside, near Málaga.

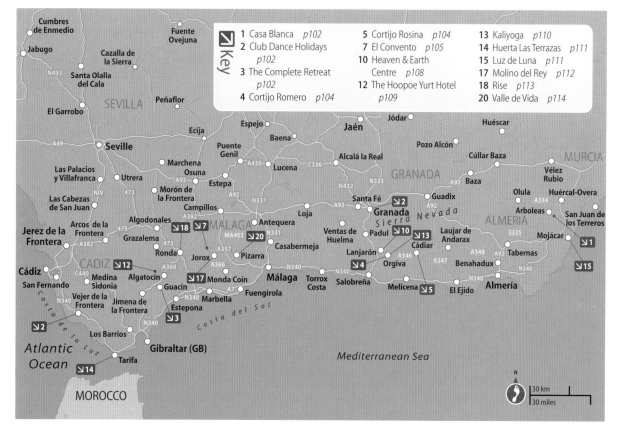

blue-green algae and 'green juices' such as celery and cucumber. Meals are strictly controlled and the calorie intake is around 300-400 per day, but the juices and raw veg are served in abundance, and are delicious and beautifully presented. Hunger pangs are rare, but as toxins are eliminated you may feel dreadful. However, by day seven, most people are converts with bags of energy and about 3 kg lighter.

Those who stay here are mainly in their thirties to fifties, from Europe or the US. Most come alone or as couples, and looking for a challenge and ready for change. They include health fanatics looking for an 'all or nothing' approach, wealthy professionals and those who are simply treating themselves. Other guests are looking to detox as an aid to recovery from illness.

Bring comfortable walking shoes, practical clothing, sarongs and bikinis and plenty of books. Guests stay for a minimum of a week. Single rooms cost from €2700 per week. The Complete Retreat runs from March to December, but you may prefer to avoid the intense summer heat in late July and August or the increased chance of rain at the end of the year. Transfers are provided for all guests from Málaga airport.

Tai chi on the roof at Cortijo Romero.

RURAL RETREAT

Cortijo Romero

Orgiva, Andalucía
T+44 (0)1494-765775
www.cortijo-romero.co.uk
From €600 per week

Just outside Orgiva in the Alpujarras mountains, Cortijo Romero offers a relaxed and safe environment for an impressive and well-organized range of personal development holidays. Ranging from flamenco dancing to Flirting with Confidence, from Tibetan meditation to tai chi, the holidays attract an open-minded fun-loving crowd of people in their late thirties to sixties, mainly from northern Europe, and many of whom are repeat guests.

The centre comprises a set of single-storey buildings with a courtyard, pool and beautiful gardens, and has a calm and uplifting ambience. You sleep in single or shared comfortable bedrooms with cool tiled floors and white walls. There's a meditation room and yoga platform, and good massages on offer, including Swedish, Thai and deep-tissue. Excursions to neighbouring villages and walks in the mountains are arranged. The food is delicious and plentiful, and served with local organic wines.

Staff will help guests choose a course that's right for them. Come for at least a week, many people stay for two. Fly to Granada, or Málaga, from where a pickup can be arranged. Cortijo Romero was founded by Nigel Shamash, who now runs La Roane in France (see page 86). Many guests also enjoy holistic holiday retreats at Skyros (see page 142) and The Grange (see page 33).

Detox International (T+44 (0)845-100 0247, www.detox-international.com) runs annual programmes at Cortijo Romero, from €1400 per person. Set up in 2006 by Midi Fairgrieve, a nutritionist and healer, the company also leads detox retreats at the German-run **Casa El Morisco** (www.morisco.de) east of Málaga, and at Moinhos Velhos in Portugal (see page 117).

RURAL RETREAT

Cortijo Rosina

Sierra Nevada, Andalucía
T+34 958-343036
www.developmenow.com
From €396 per week

Cortijo Rosina is a peaceful place run by trained life coaches, Michael and Rosie Sinclair, with great views of the Sierra Nevada mountains, dotted with whitewashed pueblos, acres of almond, olive and fig trees and carpets of wild flowers.

Michael is a musician and songwriter, and voice and breathing exercises, music lessons and recording are all available, or you could join him for an informal jam session. Rosie is a freelance writer with a host of ideas to aid your creative writing. Both are life coaches.

Accommodation is in two-bedroom self-catering apartments. Come alone or with a friend or partner to undertake life coaching, or just relax, walk or chill out with a book, dipping in and out of the treatments and classes which include massage, reiki and yoga. Fly to Almería or Granada (just under two hours away), from where they'll pick you up if you don't want to hire a car.

The beautiful Sierra Nevada from Cortijo Rosina.

Southern Europe Spain

ISLAND RETREAT
Finca Argayall

🌐 🪂 ⛰ ☀ ♠ ⦿ 🌐 ↘8

La Gomera, Canary Islands
T+44 (0)1273-882778
www.argayall.com
From €525 per person per week

The Finca Argayall is an alternative retreat nestled among plantation palms overlooking the sea on peaceful, unspoilt La Gomera. It's run by a permaculture community, so food is grown on site. Guests are open-minded Europeans seeking relaxation or self-exploration. Come here for a group holiday when care, friendliness and service are guaranteed. You can stay on a B&B basis, though your welcome may be a hit-and-miss affair as most of the community are not part of the staff. **Zen Holidays** (T+44 (0)7957-338525, www.zenholidays.co.uk) runs well-organized yoga trips with inspirational teachers such as David Sye, creator of his own distinctive **Yoga Beats** (www.yogabeats.com), or try a Dancing with Dolphins holiday with **The Dolphin Connection** (see above). There's also access to holistic therapies. There are tents, wooden huts, apartments or standard rooms (choose an en suite for a sea view), as well as a pool, small garden, and rocky beach nearby.

Fly to Tenerife South, then take a taxi to Los Cristianos, and a ferry to Valle Gran Rey (arrange to be met).

DANCE HOLIDAY
Dancing with Dolphins

☀ ♠ 🌐 ↘6

Finca Argayall
La Gomera, Canary Islands
T+44 (0)1273-882778
www.dolphinconnectionexperience.com
From €770 per person per week

Dancing with Dolphins, also called Reflections, is an unusual week's holiday combining encounters with dolphins and 5 Rhythms dance workshops (see glossary). Based at the Finca Argayall (see above right) on La Gomera, you'll have dance workshops for three hours each morning, and free afternoons to explore the ocean for dolphins, have a massage, swim, kayak, walk, or just relax in the sunshine.

The holiday is designed to encourage a sense of mental and physical freedom. Watching dolphins move through the waves inspires you to move freely and gracefully during your 5 Rhythms sessions. It's actually illegal to swim with dolphins off the coast of La Gomera, but it is possible to follow them from a boat – a genuinely exhilarating experience. Dancing with Dolphins is run by The Dolphin Connection, who also run swimming with dolphin holidays in the Bahamas and the Azores (see page 94).

YOGA RETREAT
El Convento

🌐 ⛰ ☀ ○ ♠ ⦿ 🌐 ↘7

El Burgo, near Ronda
T+34 690 681 068
www.ashtangaom.com
From €610 per person per week

A sprawling place set in the heart of La Sierra de las Nieves nature reserve, El Convento is probably Europe's most remote yoga retreat, and certainly one of its most beautiful. It lies at the end of a 9-km dirt track that climbs along a river and disgorges into a deep wooded bowl of 1000 olive and fig trees. The two yoga shalas are set in two restored 16th-century monasteries which once belonged to the Barefoot Carmelites: one is open to a 360° panorama of forested mountains where eagles soar overhead; the other is a cool room of pine floors and whitewashed stone walls. It hosts yoga, dance, meditation and music retreats from June to September, but was up for sale when we went to press. Owners Nic and Gemma are holding out for a buyer who will continue to run the retreat in its current form.

Finca Argayall, on La Gomera.

Life coaching holiday

The Big Stretch ☀ 👤 🏃 ↘9

A beautifully organized life coaching holiday based in the Picos de Europa in northern Spain, The Big Stretch is the brainchild of psychologist Rosie Walford, a charismatic and creative life coach whose techniques have changed many people's lives. With workshops each morning and treks or canoeing through inspirational scenery each afternoon, it's a brilliant break for people feeling restless or stuck in their lifestyles, careers or relationships, and an investment that could stop you wasting time and money pursuing something (or someone) that just isn't right for you.

Where you stay   Your base is La Montaña Mágica, a charming all-wood mountain hotel set on a hill near the hamlet of El Allende near Posada in the Picos. There may be other tourists staying at the same time, but it's still an incredibly peaceful place, with fresh, clear air, lovely views of the surrounding mountains, and the tinkling of cowbells. You get your own simple room with tiled floors, wooden furniture and thick, colourful blankets, should you feel the cold. Most have lovely views and big windows, and each is en suite, with a shower over a jacuzzi bath. Life coaching workshops take place in a private well-lit room painted a cheerful Buddha-orange, with French windows leading to a small terrace with tables and chairs. You can help yourself to tea, coffee and snacks here all day. Staff are friendly and unobtrusive.

What you do   After a simple morning stretch on the terrace followed by breakfast, Rosie and another life coach run intensive group workshops for three to four hours. Afternoons are spent trekking, with a picnic en route, with one afternoon canoeing down the Sella river, and a day at the hotel resting, having one-to-one sessions and enjoying a craniosacral or reiki massage with a local therapist.

The workshops use creative problem-solving, lateral thinking and group brainstorming exercises as well as classic life coaching tools to help you recognize your self-limiting beliefs and turn them around. Rosie trained in creative problem solving at the Creative Education Foundation in New York, and in coaching at Zenergy in New Zealand. She has a background in advertising and management consultancy, and is a writer and photographer too, so she has masses of creative tricks up her sleeve to get you feeling motivated and thinking innovatively, and draws on everything she's experienced, from meditation to medicine men.

Her tools and techniques are designed to cut through the rational side of us that might ordinarily say 'no' to something, and to help us access our intuitive side instead. You're encouraged to move outside your comfort zone to rediscover what you feel passionate about, and

> 66 99
>
> Two months after I attend The Big Stretch, I receive a postcard with my handwriting on it. I'd forgotten we'd been asked to write ourselves cards urging us to keep pursuing our dreams when back in the chaos of daily living. It's typical of Rosie's creative and effective approach. The highlight for me was walking down a beautiful hillside pretending to be at a cocktail party in five years time, talking with the group about what we then did in life. It was a funny and very illuminating exercise – if you're fantasising about a house in the country, a husband and a Harley Davidson but currently live on a beach in Thailand with two cats and a tuc tuc, you know you're on the wrong track. This was a very human trip that woke my consciousness up and got me going again. If I got stuck in life again, I'd go back, no question.
>
> *Caroline*

CAROLINE SYLGE

to pay attention to habits you may have got yourself into which won't serve you in the long term. Whatever your issue, you'll explore your relationships, values, beliefs, health, money and job situation to get to the heart of it. Your behaviour in the group is also monitored: a strong reaction to others is often a sign of something going on inside us. All of which means the week can be emotional, and reveal some unexpected things.

The afternoon treks are very varied, taking you through craggy mountains, majestic gorges and sheltered grassy valleys. They are an important part of the coaching, giving you time to distil all you have experienced that morning. You're encouraged to go at your own pace, to be aware of your natural surroundings, and sometimes to walk in silence.

One afternoon each person gets one-to-one coaching en route, and impromptu roleplay exercises also take place during the treks. You may be asked, for example, to close your eyes on a hillside and imagine meeting your future self at 70 years old – what is he/she like, and what does he/she say to you? Or you get to pretend you are at a cocktail party in five years time, a funny and very illuminating exercise.

Vitally, the week is seen as the beginning of a journey, not an end in itself, so you're provided with all the tools you need to carry things forward on return, including a list of 'easy wins' and harder things that need to be worked on over a longer period of time. You're even coached in how to articulate what you've learnt to others, helping you keep up the commitment and momentum at home and gather support from real life.

What you eat and drink The food at the hotel is simple Spanish fare, with cereals, bread, eggs, cheese and yoghurt for breakfast and a selection of meat and fish dishes in the evenings. For four of the evenings you'll eat out at different local restaurants specializing in local fish and meat dishes. Be prepared to eat after 2100. Lunch is a picnic eaten on the trek, with breads, cheeses, meats, olives and tomatoes – as well as a rather lovely leather pouch full of red wine for those who want it. The Spanish diet is wheat- and meat-based, though good fish is available. If you're a non-wheat eater, bring your own supplies, and if you're a vegetarian, be prepared for a monotonous week.

Who goes The Big Stretch attracts intelligent, professional, self-aware people usually in their thirties, forties and fifties looking to make a real change in their lives. Most come from the UK, together with other Europeans, and everyone comes alone. On return, people have reported achieving all sorts of things, from changing careers to saving a marriage.

Essentials The Big Stretch (T+44 (0)1273-676712, www.thebigstretch.com) runs week-long trips in May, June, September and October. May is a brilliant time to go for the spring flowers. No more than eight attend any one trip. It costs €3290, which includes everything except flights. You fly to Oviedo or Santander airport, depending on the airline. It's a 1½-hour transfer from either one. Bring layers of warm, comfortable clothing and good walking shoes. Rosie offers coaching after the week is over, by phone, email or face-to-face depending where you are based, from €390 a month for three months.

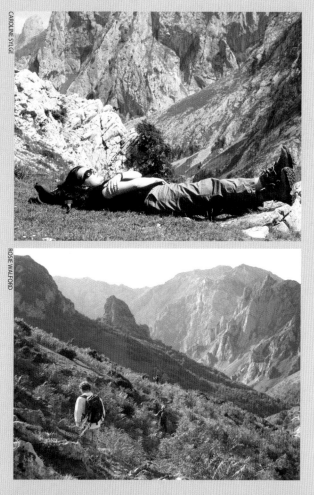
CAROLINE SYLGE
ROSIE WALFORD

Heaven and Earth Centre

Lanjaron, Orgiva
T+34 958-347215
www.heavenandearthcentre.com
From €550 per person per week

This is a back-to-nature retreat in the Sierra Nevada, planted with olive, almond and fruit trees and enjoying fresh mountain air. Run by healer and teacher Richard Waterborn, it's a restorative place to be for those who are in serious need of time and space. It also hosts group retreats in yoga and qigong during the summer months.

This is not a place for those who can't survive without home comforts, but great if you love being close to nature. You sleep in fairly basic twin-bedded chalets with verandas overlooking the mountains, with an unpredictable electricity supply and access to shared outdoor showers, wash basins and toilets. You can also camp during the summer, and there are rooms in the *casita* where all the catering takes place. If you're part of a group, be warned that there's limited space indoors and you may need to share your hut.

The yoga platform has a spectacular view, and watching the sun set or rise over the mountains is an absolute joy. Retreats include those run by the excellent **Yoga under the Sky** team (www.yogaunderthesky.com), whose three English-speaking teachers mix iyengar with breathwork, mantras, meditation and Thai yoga massage.

If you're staying alone or with a friend, massage, acupuncture, yoga and meditation can be arranged, or you can have cellular healing sessions (€120 for two hours) with Richard. He describes these as a "powerful, synergistic approach to healing of the body, mind, heart and soul". Or just enjoy the spectacular view over the mountains, paint, read, write, and be inspired. There are good walks nearby and a pure spring water swimming pool.

There's an organic garden, and Richard buys yoghurt from the local goat man. You can do self-catering, or there are local cafés and restaurants in nearby hippy market town of Orgiva (**Café Libertad**, on Calle Libertad, is a good choice, with seasonal food). It can be cold in the evenings, so bring warm sleepwear, as well as a good torch. Fly to Málaga, from where it's a two-hour drive, or to Granada, from where you can get a bus to Lanjarón. Airport pickups can be arranged.

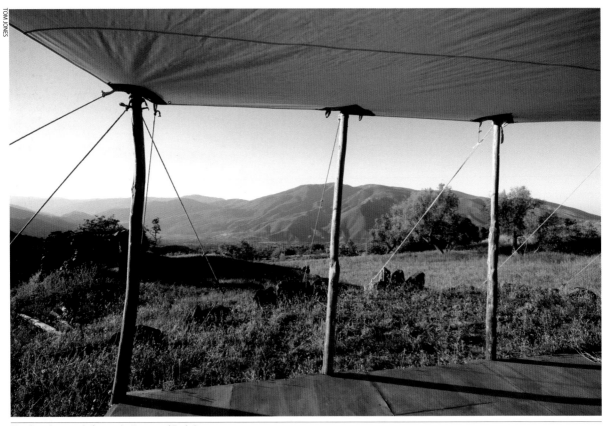

View from the yoga platform at the Heaven and Earth Centre.

Southern Europe Spain

Holistic Holidays, on Lanzarote.

ISLAND RETREAT

Holistic Holidays

🌐 🅟 🛖 ⊙ ❋ ❀ ↘11

Lanzarote, Canary Islands
T+44 (0)20-8123 9250
www.hoho.co.uk
From €390 per person for 3 nights

Hidden away from Lanzarote's tourist bustle, Villa Isis is in the small town of Tías, on a hill overlooking the sea. It's the home of Lynne and Stuart, who welcome guests warmly into their comfortable space to enjoy a relaxing, nurturing break on a beautiful island.

The villa is a great place to kick back and relax. The communal lounge has plenty of books, CDs and DVDs to browse, and very comfortable sofas. There are six guest rooms, simply decorated, but most are en suite and either single, with panoramic views, or twin; there is one double.

Yoga forms the basis of these holidays and, unless you are a B&B guest, some or all of the week's five 90-minute classes are included. Lynne teaches the morning classes herself and has over 30 years experience. Her practice is based on a range of yoga theory rather than one particular type. Up to 12 people stay at any one time and the small classes allow for one-to-one guidance.

The all-inclusive HO2 Formula is value for money: it includes yoga – which otherwise costs €99 – an hour's massage, a 90-minute shiatsu session and an hour of reiki or reflexology, plus a guided walk. Transformational breathwork therapy (see glossary) is also available. Individually bought therapies start at €55 for an hour. There is a beautiful chlorine-free pool on site, and a lovingly tended garden.

Guests are given a buffet dinner on the first day, but the basic package is B&B with some optional lunches. Breakfast consists of cereals, fruit, yoghurt and bread, teas and coffee; other meals are vegetarian-based with accompanying chicken or fish. Special diets are catered for with advance notice. Snacks and drinks can also be bought at the local health food store or supermarket. Guests have access to a fridge. The tapas bars and restaurants in the village are worth exploring.

Holistic Holidays are popular with women travelling alone, but also couples. No under 16s are allowed. Weekly stays are the norm. A hire car is necessary if you want to explore the island, or you can up the tempo with scuba-diving, hang-gliding or windsurfing. Fly to Arrecife, Lanzarote's only airport. Transfers are provided for all guests. Bookings start on Thursdays.

RURAL RETREAT

The Hoopoe Yurt Hotel

🌐 🛖 ⊙ ❂ ↘12

Cortes de la Frontera, near Málaga
T+34 952-117055
www.yurthotel.com
From €110 per double yurt per night

Get back to nature by staying in a yurt at the solar-powered Hoopoe Yurt Hotel, set in 3 ha of olive groves and cork oak forest with spectacular views of the Grazalema mountains. Chill out by the pool, go walking or riding nearby, or have yoga classes led by Alison George, a local ashtanga teacher who trained with Danny Paradise. Ayurvedic massage, aromatherapy, reflexology and reiki are also available, all done on site and in the open air under the shade of the cork trees.

Each luxury yurt is spacious and comfortable, with its own bit of private meadow, hammocks, comfy beds, traditional Mongolian furniture and private bathrooms with hot showers and eco-loos. The Mongolian yurt is hand-painted in burnt orange with traditional motifs in green, blue

Book the yurt of your dreams at the idyllic Hoopoe Yurt Hotel.

Yoga holiday

Kaliyoga ⬊13

Kaliyoga is a high-spirited yoga retreat set on the terraces of the Alpujarras, at Orgiva, near Granada. With colourful boho furnishings overflowing onto terraces outside, the owners have made a comfortable stone farmhouse into a top-notch 'yoga home' which is livelier and more informal than most retreats.

Where you stay Two lucky people sleep in furnished tipis while most share spacious stone-floored bedrooms around a herb-filled courtyard. There are a couple of smallish single rooms, which are not especially glamorous but airy and functional with shared bathrooms. The maximum size of group is 12.

In warm winds, you swing from hammocks and lounge round the pool, gazing across olive groves onto a wild mountainside. The yoga platform faces out onto a different range of hills. There are shaded platforms amongst olive trees and a hydrospa surrounded by fig trees. There's a leafy terrace for aperitifs, with low tables and Moroccan leather cushions. Meals are shared round a big wooden table. The sitting room houses a good library of yoga and massage books, and inviting daybeds. The CD collection and fridge are open to all.

What you do The daily timetable feels leisurely: yoga from 0900 to 1100, followed by brunch and a long luxurious stretch of free time for optional treatments, then restorative yoga from 1700 to 1900. The yoga here is strong. Owners Rosie and Jonathan Miles teach dynamic yoga, a flowing form which has you stretching deep for flexibility, and continuing without pause for stamina and strength.

Rosie directs you clearly into strong restructuring poses at a challenging pace. Jonathan is more theoretical and spiritual, but breaks quite randomly into bursts of laughter. Both teachers care passionately that you practise yoga at that fine point beyond laziness and before aggression. It's demanding at the time, but brings vibrant energy afterwards. Classes end with lengthy peace-inducing meditations serenaded by crickets. By the end of the week, the teachers aim to have given you a routine to practise at home.

During the long, mellow afternoons, you swim, read and pick from a menu of treatments that's wonderfully broad for such an intimate place (Thai and Swedish massage, reflexology, acupuncture, chakra balancing). Serious independent practitioners come in from outside. As guests swap notes of their experiences, it's tempting to choose a new treatment each afternoon.

What you eat and drink Food is satisfying and wholesome – fresh juices, fruits, yoghurts for breakfast, magnificent lunches of home-baked tarts and salads. At supper it's Moorish and Mediterranean. Aperitifs appear with fresh lemonades and herby cocktails, but no one drinks much. On the night off, you can get the finest grilled fish at a local beach.

Who goes Guests range from early twenties to late forties; an international clientele, from near-beginners to keen yogis. Most are women, many on return visits.

Essentials Kaliyoga (T+34 958-784496, www.kaliyoga.com) costs from €740 per person for six days. As well as straight yoga retreats, you can also do a week-long yoga and detox retreat. Fly to Granada or Málaga, from where Kali arranges a private driver (€55 from Granada, €85 from Málaga). Alternatively, hire a car so that you can visit the market town of Orgiva or drive to the coast, which is less than an hour away.

> 66 99
> Many yoga holidays leave you nicely translucent for your return home, but are somewhat po-faced while you're away. Not Kaliyoga. It licked me into vibrant physical shape, yet felt like a gentle house party at the time.
> *Rosie Walford*

and gold, while the Afghan yurt is more romantic, with bent willow poles and a deep- red ceiling. Alternatively, you can opt for the new light and airy yurt, made locally from coppiced chestnut.

Owner Henrietta serves up home-cooked dinners four nights a week and light lunches. Fly to Gibraltar (best for public transport), Jerez or Málaga. April and May are great for the wild flowers; spring and autumn for walking, for the migrating birds and the lovely morning light.

A wooden Turkish-style pergola next to the pool, where guests can drink cocktails, play backgammon or smoke a hookah, is planned for 2007.

COASTAL RETREAT

Huerta Las Terrazas

🐾 🔗 ↘14

Near Tarifa
T+34 956-679041
www.huertalasterrazas.com
From €85 per room per night

Huerta Las Terrazas is a chilled-out place to stay, its mature gardens filled with honeysuckle, mimosa and cypress trees, and with wonderful views across to Morocco.

Owner Amy is a qualified therapist and offers a combination of aromatherapy massage and craniosacral therapy.

The lovely bedrooms blend modern design with traditional furnishings; fresh cotton linen, rich cushions and hints of Morocco. Or self-cater in the *casita*, which sleeps two and enjoys spectacular views to the Rif Mountains. Do your own yoga by the pool or on the casita terrace, sun yourself, swim or go horse riding on the unspoilt beaches of the nearby Costa de la Luz. The room rate includes a breakfast of seasonal organic fruits from the garden. , or from €550 per week.

RURAL RETREAT

Luz de Luna

🐾 🔗 ◯ 🔗 ↘15

Near Mojácar, Almería
T+34 637-469937
www.luzdelunaretreat.com
From €266 per week (per apartment)

A chilled-out place to stay, with mountain views, Luz de Luna is the home of qualified holistic therapists Bruce and Barbara, who offer treatments and workshops all year round. It's also a lovely private place to come and simply chill, just 7 km from Mojácar, with its pretty hilltop village and beach.

You stay in one of two self-catering apartments with en suite bedrooms, one attached to the house, opening onto the pool terrace and the outdoor jacuzzi, the other detached with its own terrace overlooking the grounds. A maximum of six guests can be accommodated at any one time.

There are fruit trees and shaded paths to wander and enjoy, and many therapies on offer including all types of massage, reiki, reflexology, hypnotherapy, EFT (emotional freedom technique) and NLP (neuro-linguistic programming). Workshops and classes may include meditation for beginners in the winter, a healing course run by a qualified healer and shaman with a drop-in healing clinic, and a feng shui

weekend. The facilitators are always experienced in their field; some are local and some from the UK.

Fly to Almería (just 45 minutes away), or Alicante or Murcia (about two hours away). It's best to hire a car, as there are no buses in the area. The region enjoys over 300 days of sunshine, and Luz de Luna is open all year.

RURAL RETREAT

Mas Collades

🔗 🐾 ◯ 🔗 ↘16

Balsareny, Catalunya
T+34 938-396259
www.mascollades.com
From €38 per person per night

Mas Collades is an 18th-century Catalan farmhouse (or *masia*) built of golden stone and surrounded by extensive gardens, fields and hills. Perched on the brow of a hill, far from any neighbours, it offers complete tranquility and relaxation, and a warm welcome from Catalan owner Alex Permanyer and his staff.

Stay on a B&B basis, or join one of the courses hosted here year round. Led by qualified international practitioners, these include alexander technique, reiki, yoga, ceramic-making, regression therapy and life coaching, and attract a varied group, mostly from the UK, who come to enjoy the climate and beautiful countryside while learning.

There are two swimming pools, tennis

Left: Huerta Las Terrazas. **Top right**: Luz de Luna.

Mas Collades.

courts, a football pitch and even a court for *fronton*, a fast and furious Spanish sport which involves hitting a ball against a wall using the bare hand or a special racket. There are outdoor areas for summer barbecues, and pretty wrought iron garden furniture scattered throughout the grounds. Hiking paths snake down to the river or up to the hills, and day trips to the sacred mountain of Montserrat or pretty medieval villages can be arranged.

The main house is a museum of traditional Catalan rural life, with vaulted stone cellars, which were originally stables, and a bodega where wine was once produced for Mass. The large public rooms upstairs are decorated with a quirky mixture of paintings, sculpture, photographs and curiosities. There are six bedrooms in the main house, all individually styled with antique furniture, and sharing three fully equipped bathrooms. Dormitory-style accommodation with bunk beds and separate kitchens and bathrooms is available in the surrounding outbuildings.

The *masia* offers home-cooking by Alex, a trained chef, who prepares delicious vegetarian and non-vegetarian dishes using produce from the kitchen garden. Some course leaders prefer to ask their pupils to cook together in groups, in order to foster their team spirit. Fly to Barcelona or Girona, from where it's a €60 transfer, or take the train to Manresa, from where Alex will pick you up free of charge.

VILLAGE RETREAT
Molino del Rey

🌐 🅿 ♨ 🚶 ↘17

Jorox
T+44 (0)952-480009
www.molinodelrey.com
From €70 per person per night

A true original, owner Anthony has created a unique venue here in the hillside at Jorox. On first impression the main building looks conventional, but you enter an oasis of cool running water amidst the arid, dusty Sierra de las Nieves. A labyrinth of caves has been hewn out of the rock to create meditation spaces, and there's a fantastically serene yoga room that has been designed to exacting acoustic standards, providing a fabulous space for drumming and singing workshops, which Anthony loves to lead.

A small pool lies beneath the exposed rock with lounging areas, and a daybed nestles next to a sauna. People sit around the dining area and patio, where you can enjoy the sounds of running water as a backdrop to gentle conversation. You stay in clean, comfortable and bright individually designed en suite rooms in the main part of the building, each with nice touches such as scented candles.

Above: Time for contemplation at Molino del Rey.
Below: An oasis of cool.

Yoga teachers visit regularly. Once a month there's a visit from local yoga teacher James Jewell (www.yogamoutainyogasea. com), a mellow Englishman with a humorous, relaxing approach to yoga, quite willing and able to step it up if needed. The sun appears a good 1½ hours later than on the coast due to the shadow of the mountains, but this works well for an early

morning yoga session.

Deep inside the caves, stalactites are still forming and the air is cool and fresh. Find your own space to meditate in the silence, or make your way upwards to the meditation room, a wonderful place with a glass front coloured with the seven chakra colours and overlooking

🌀 Soul food

The **World Wildlife Fund** (T+44 (0)1483-426444, www.wwf.org.uk) runs regular environmental and conservation campaigns in Spain. The Iberian lynx, for example, could become the first big cat species to become extinct since the sabre-toothed tiger if damaging developments continue to be allowed. Since 2000, 16 lynx have died on the roads (one of which is illegal) in Doñana in Spain, close to one-third of the total number.

Spain also has over half a million illegal boreholes used to irrigate agricultural land, and this is often supported by EU agricultural subsidies. In a country that suffers from severe water shortages, this degree of illegal extraction makes it impossible for water to be used wisely, and has negative effects on the environment and other water users. To support the work of the WWF, become a member, adopt an animal, support a campaign, volunteer to help or make a donation.

the mountains. The caves are the main source of privacy, for despite its dramatic setting and great facilities, the property is quite small and feels fairly enclosed.

Anthony's Russian partner, Lidiya, offers a range of massages using her own oils made from local plants, including Thai massage, lomi lomi, aromatherapy, Japanese facial massage, foot massage and hot-stone massage as well as private yoga classes (she qualified in 2006). Most visitors are women, but the combination of Lidiya's strong massage treatments and Anthony's direct and vivacious approach to life means that men feel equally at home here.

A local chef prepares salads and healthy dishes, but also beautiful cakes. From late April to June you can simply pick lemons from the laden trees, nourished by some of the best water in Andalucía. Fellow guests are aged from twenties and up, local and from the UK, seeking a deep but relaxing and chilled break. Come alone if you're feeling sociable. A one-week stay costs from €800 including yoga and full board; there's a single supplement of €30 per day. Fly to Málaga, from where it's a one-hour drive, or pickups can be arranged.

RURAL RETREAT

Rise

🌐 ☀ 🌀 🕉 🔊 🌀 ⬇18

Ronda
T+34 610-847731
www.rise-resort.com
From €945 for 5 nights all-inclusive

Set in its own 22 acres with inspirational views towards Ronda and over the Sierra de las Nieves, Rise breaks the mould by offering personal development courses in luxurious surroundings. Opened in 2006, it looks set to become extremely popular. Teachers from all over the world offer courses covering philosophy, psychology, health, spirituality and the arts – ranging from NLP to photography and Mediterranean cooking. A course runs as soon as enough people have registered interest – bookings are made with

Views from the garden at Rise.

individual teachers and prices vary.

There are five bright and airy double bedrooms for up to 10 people, all en suite and with a private terrace. Larger groups stay in the owner's nearby **Hotel la Fuente** (www.hotellafuente.com), a 10-minute drive away, and there are two more simple houses (with their own pool) a five-minute walk away. Activities take place in a central room, big enough for 25 people, with a heated wooden floor and fireplace. There's a comfortable lounge and sitting room with an open kitchen, and an outdoor pool set in a peaceful garden. You'll also have the use of a Turkish bath, and hydrotherapy and various massages are on offer. The centre has its own chef and offers a daily changing menu.

Fly to Seville, Jerez or Málaga; Rise is a 90-minute drive from each.

PILATES HOLIDAY

Sarah Rosenfield Pilates

🕉 ▶ ⬇19

Finca Es Castell, Caimari, Mallorca
T+44 (0)20-7722 4373
www.sarahpilates.com
From €590 for a weekend

Sarah Rosenfield runs long-weekend pilates holidays at Finca Es Castell (www.fincaescastell.com), a pretty and peaceful hotel at the foot of the Sierra de Tramuntana, surrounded by acres of olive,

orange, lemon, fig and almond trees. Twice-daily pilates sessions, relaxation, guided visualization and massage are on offer, in a group of up to 12. The price excludes transport and is based on two sharing. Fly to Palma de Mallorca, from where it's a 45-minute transfer. Sarah's retreats attract single women, with some couples and men, aged from 24 to 70, mostly from the UK and including Sarah's existing students from her London classes. Sarah trained at the Pilates Institute and has been running pilates holidays in France, Tuscany and South Africa since 2002 (see also pages 94 and 188).

VALLEY RETREAT
Valle de Vida

Pizarra, Málaga
T+34 951-238614
www.valledevida.com
€230 for 3 nights (minimum stay)

A very affordable, isolated retreat set in a peaceful valley just 30 minutes from Málaga airport, Valle de Vida is run by charming husband-and-wife team, Robi (who is an exceptional osteopath with his own practice in London) and Keri.

The place attracts a mainly UK-based, thirties-plus clientele who are here to enjoy the relaxed ambience, do yoga, or for osteopathic treatment, plus an increasing number of expats and Spanish.

With wooden furniture, white walls and tiles, shuttered windows, subtle lighting and a wood burner in the main living area, the finca offers clean and uncluttered homely accommodation. You stay in one of seven double or twin rooms, and share two stylish and spacious shower rooms: Rama or Ganesh in the main finca are the most peaceful rooms with the greatest natural light. To be closer to nature, however, it's best to opt for one of the tipis (there are seven) set around the hillside in the olive groves; each has electricity, some storage, very comfortable beds and an individual outdoor space where you can sit under the shade of a tree.

Top: Finca Es Castell. **Above**: Yoga platform at Valle de Vida.

Retreat to party island

Ibiza may be a party island, but it's also stunningly beautiful, with a surprising amount of rural space to enjoy and a free-spirited nature. April to October are warm and lovely months, but avoid July and August for the heat and the crowds. If you want to be nurtured, book a week with UK-based **In:Spa** (T+44 (0)20-7229 3064, www.inspa.co.uk), who run regular weeks in the northwest of the island mixing yoga with walking, cycling and hiking. You'll be based near the tiny village of Santa Agnès at Es Cucons, a family-run bohemian-chic converted farmhouse with pretty rooms. Yoga is done on a terrace overlooking almond groves, and you'll be served delicious toxin-free organic meals and enjoy regular massage. It costs from €2790 per person per week based on two sharing including everything except flights. In:Spa also run trips to Seville on the mainland and to Morocco (see page 172).

For something more affordable, the alternative **Ibiza Moving Arts** (T+34 637 269884, www.ibizamovingarts.com) is based in a lovely 400-year-old country house in the north of the island, with a dance studio, pretty gardens, swimming pool and rooms for up to 12 people. It costs from €650 per person for a five-day workshop. Ibiza Moving Arts offers individual wellness weeks combining massage, craniosacral therapy and hatha yoga, or choose a Healing Week, which includes healing dance, meditation and creative expression. The team includes Volker, a movement teacher and anthropologist, Nicola Marcesi, a psychotherapist, and Sandra Morrel, an experienced dancer, yoga teacher and craniosacral and massage therapist who teaches her own Total Dance, which encourages you to dance spontaneously and from the heart. Sandra also runs trips to Peru (see page 383).

Set in a valley surrounded by forest, at San Miguel, also in the north of the island, **The Garden of Light** (www.thegardenoflight.net) hosts group retreats, including detox weeks led by Dhara Kelly of the Cloona Health Centre in Ireland (see page 55).

If you're feeling sociable, **Ibiza Yoga** (T+44 (0)20-7419 0999, www.ibizayoga.com) offers ashtanga yoga weeks in a party atmosphere, where you stay in one of two villas five minutes' walk from the stunning Benirras beach on the north of the island. Two three-hour classes run each day simultaneously at each villa, one for beginners and one for experienced practitioners. Villa Palmas is the more luxurious of the two, sleeping eight people, while Villa Roca sleeps up to 30 and can feel crowded. Both have lovely sprung wood yoga decks imported from Indonesia. The weeks cost from €350 per person in a shared room at Villa Roca, up to €1680 per person for your own room in Villa Palma. They attract a youngish crowd and run

from mid-April to end-October.

Alternatively, take your own clifftop villa with **Ibiza Body and Soul** (T+44 (0)701-071 8162, www.ibizabodyandsoul.com), which offers two villas in the south of the island at San Augustin. Husband-and-wife team Gary and Claire host holistic holidays here from April to October. Led by visiting teachers, they include yoga, creative writing, pilates and karate (which Gary teaches). You can also stay as an individual just to chill out, enjoy yoga sessions with Claire, who trained as a sivananda teacher in Quebec, and indulge in massage, holistic therapies and beauty treatments with local therapists. One villa sleeps 17 and houses a spacious outdoor yoga deck, the other is more intimate and sleeps nine. There are two swimming pools, an outdoor jacuzzi and shaded tropical gardens, and it's a 15-minute walk to the beach. Holidays start from €979, villas cost from €2639 per week in low season (November to March), when you'll still enjoy warm days, and peace and quiet.

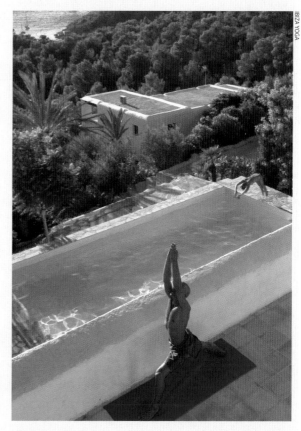

IBIZA YOGA

Southern Europe Spain

TOM JONES

Though only half an hour from Málaga's busy airport, Valle de Vida is a real back-to-basics retreat, where guests can stay in tipis in the wilds of the Andalucían countryside.

Visiting yoga, pilates, art and tai chi teachers bring their own students, but all are welcome. The wooden hilltop yoga platform enjoys a spectacular vista across the Andalucían mountains and valley below, and there's a good-sized swimming pool, hammocks to lounge in, and a large daybed on the veranda.

As well as osteopathy (€50 per session) you can enjoy lots of different treatments (from €35) by hand-picked therapists including Indian head message, reflexology, Thai, Swedish and deep tissue massage, shiatsu and acupuncture. Keri is trained in beauty treatments such as manicures, pedicures and facials. If you're suffering from back pain, this is a great place to come, where a programme of osteopathy with Robi

will be supported by recommended massage, hydrotherapy, gentle exercises and a daily steam in the hammam.

Water, herbal teas and juice are available all day. Meals are is generally a buffet served on the front patio, with fruit, yoghurt and muesli for breakfast and a good range of healthy supper dishes such as pulses and fish. Special diets can be catered for, and local wines are available.

Weekly stays cost from around €600 per person including food, drinks and accommodation. The venue can be hired out as a whole during the summer. Late spring or late summer enjoy the most comfortable climate. Bring a torch and warm sleepwear if you're staying in a tipi. Fly to Málaga; it's a 30-km drive from there via the A357.

66 99

Robi at Valle de Vida certainly knows what he's doing. Within 20 minutes he'd worked out how my spine had got out of position, and with a gentle click here and there, I was standing properly, possibly for the first time since I was knocked over aged eight.

Tom Jones

VALLE DE VIDA

SWIMMING WITH DOLPHINS HOLIDAY

The Dolphin Connection

Pico, Azores islands
T+44 (0)1273-882778
www.dolphinconnectionexperience.com
€1540 for 9 nights

The Dolphin Connection runs annual swimming with dolphins and whale-watching trips to the Azores, a beautiful group of islands in the mid-Atlantic, west of Portugal. Scientifically proven to help you feel happy by increasing the release of endorphins, encountering wild dolphins underwater is an exhilarating experience. You're likely to discover a renewed passion for life and a refreshed perspective.

You'll be hosted and supported by two well-organized and friendly guides hand-picked by founder Amanda Stafford, a psychologist, shiatsu practitioner and body therapist who has spoken worldwide on the human-dolphin connection. Her studies in Australia have revealed that people show more 'theta' in their brains after being with dolphins, the same chemical that is released when we dream or meditate. Her company operates a policy of minimum impact on the dolphins and the environment, and staff approach the animals with sensitivity.

The islands enjoy an abundance of dolphins and whales, and sightings are very common. Six boat trips of three hours in total are included in the holiday, and you'll sometimes see schools of 500 swimming with the boats. There are also land-based lookouts from which to view them close up,

Swimming with dolphins.

slide shows about marine life from local experts, nature walks and downtime for relaxing or socializing.

You stay at a comfortable four-star hotel on the island of Pico, with a dramatic cliff-side setting looking out to sea. There are aromatherapy and Swedish massages on offer and a swimming pool. Food is home-cooked, with meat and vegetarian options. Come alone, with a friend or your family. The trips run in July and August, and take up to 24 people, with eight on each boat. Fly to Lisbon, then it's another 2½-hour flight to Horta, on the island of Faial. Transfers are included.

DETOX RETREAT

Moinhos Velhos

Lagos, Algarve
T+351 282-687147
www.moinhos-velhos.com
From €1400 per person per week

Set in a peaceful valley with lovely wild gardens and surrounded by unspoilt countryside, Moinhos Velhos runs dedicated juice fasting retreats supported by relaxed, knowledgeable and friendly staff. If you're in need of a serious detox, bring lots of books and hole up here for 10 to 14 days.

Though just 20 minutes from the beach at Lagos, this is a remote location, with few outside distractions. There's a morning yoga class and evening meditation in a spacious glass-walled room, a sauna and hot tub for you to use on alternate days, and a saltwater swimming pool surrounded by loungers.

Moinhos Velhos was founded by two Norwegians, Frank and Annkarine, who devised the fasts based on years of experience and continue to provide a nurturing environment where the spiritual and emotional aspects of fasting are addressed as much as the physical. Both live nearby, and Frank teaches yoga, leads the meditation and does some of the therapies.

Depending on the length of your fast, you'll usually have juice for breakfast, juice for

Detoxify, indulge at a spa or swim with dolphins.

Fact file

➲ **Visa:** None required for EU, US, Canadian and Australian citizens staying up to 90 days

ⓘ **IDD:** +351

ⓢ **Currency:** Euro (€)

ⓦ **Time zone:** GMT

ⓔ **Electricity:** 230v

ⓘ **Tourist board:** www.visitportugal.com

THE DOLPHIN CONNECTION

66 99

I arrived at Moinhos Velhos totally burnt out and left 10 days later feeling like a different person. The chronic back pain my London osteopaths hadn't been able to sort out had gone, and the combination of the juice fast, meditation, walking in gorgeous countryside and brilliant, affordable therapies left me feeling totally rejuvenated.

Zoe Stebbing

lunch and vegetable broth for supper. A betonite clay mixture is drunk with the juices to aid detoxification and keep hunger pangs at bay. All the vegetables and most of the fruits are grown on site. You perform your own daily colonics using a 'clysmatic' – a gravity colonics unit set up in your own bathroom (an uncomfortable process but easy once you know how). The whole programme is fully supported and you'll receive two nutrition consultations during your week.

The main house is a converted mill, and there's a separate building for treatments. A steep five-minute walk away are pleasant en suite rooms in a converted barn, each with two single beds, wooden floors, Indian wall hangings and cushions, and a private outdoor patio where you can chill out. You can share a room, though it's worth paying extra to have your own (from €1945 to €2150 per week) as detoxing is an emotional experience and you'll be glad of the privacy. For even more space, go for one of the two wooden cottages. There's also one room in the mill.

Treatments on offer to help the detoxification process include salt scrubs, lymph drainage massage and a detox foot bath. There's also a massive range of relaxation and holistic treatments to choose from including Thai yoga massage, craniosacral therapy and reiki.

The detox programmes run from February to December. Most guests come alone, and most are female, from Europe and America. Bring lots of books, and warm clothing for the evenings, especially outside the summer months. Fly to Faro, from where it's an hour's drive. Arrange to be picked up at the airport (€45 each way) as the train journey to Lagos takes over three hours and is complicated. See page 7 for more information on what to expect from a detox.

HOTEL & SPA
Reid's Palace Hotel

Madeira
T+351 291-717171
www.reidspalace.com
From €469 per room per night

An elegant, relaxing place to stay, where you'll feel utterly cosseted, this is a wonderful weekend destination where you can enjoy pampering treatments and complimentary yoga and pilates between walks along the *levadas* – 2 km of paths that run along a network of ancient irrigation channels.

The spa has five treatment rooms looking over the bay of Funchal, and offers signature treatments from Ytsara using indigenous products such as lemongrass, orange, papaya, aloe vera and banana leaves. There are three swimming pools, one of which is a tidal pool at the foot of a steep path, and lush subtropical gardens to wander through. On Saturdays take some tango lessons in the art deco cocktail bar. Most of the 164 rooms are all clotted-cream walls and traditional furniture. Stay in the main building if you want character and the newer garden wing if you want to be secluded. Suite 980 has glorious views across the ocean. Madeira enjoys a gorgeous climate all year round. Fly to Funchal airport, from where it's a 30-minute transfer – or hire a car to explore more of the island.

Above: Fasting is the name of the game at Moinhos Velhos.
Right: You'll be pampered to within an inch of your life at Reid's Palace Hotel on the Atlantic island of Madeira.

YOGA & ACTIVITY HOLIDAY

Ride World Wide

Milfontes, Alentejo province
T+44 (0)1837-82544
www.rideworldwide.com
From €1240-1440 per person for 7 nights

Ride World Wide runs annual riding and yoga holidays, usually every July, in the beautiful Alentejo province. As well as a full programme of riding through spectacular coastal scenery, you'll get twice-daily yoga sessions taught by US-based Kate Olafson (www.kateolafson.com), a yoga instructor, personal trainer and Thai yoga massage practitioner. The course includes group and one-to-one Thai massage sessions.

Your base is the riding centre **Caminhos do Alentejo** (www.cdaportugal.com), a 15-minute drive from Milfontes. Its clubhouse has a bar and lounge area, a shaded terrace for meals, a sun terrace, garden and pool. You sleep in modern twin rooms with en suite bathrooms and private terrace, or in comfortable semi-permanent East African safari-style tents set up in woodland within the grounds; these are spacious, carpeted and furnished with comfortable double beds, and you'll have use of shared hot showers and loos in the clubhouse. Prices include all riding, guiding and accommodation. The holiday is aimed at keen riders of all ages. Fly to Lisbon airport, from where group transfers are included.

HOTEL & SPA

Sofitel Thalassa Vilalara

Praia das Gaivotas, Alporchinhos
T+351 282-320000
www.sofitelvilalara.com
From €295 per room per night

The first thalassotherapy centre in Portugal and one of Europe's best, Sofitel Thalassa Vilalara, was designed in 1989 with advice from expert, Jean Bobet . Approached

through streets of new buildings, it's a welcome 25-acre oasis of subtropical gardens leading down to a well-kept beach, with unobtrusive, terracotta buildings and a considerate and friendly staff.

Come alone or with a friend or partner to relax and take advantage of the excellent thalassotherapy treatments. There are five seawater and freshwater swimming pools, and the Thalassotherapy Centre boasts extensive equipment for marine hydrotherapy. Treatments are prepared by the centre's doctor and include a full range of baths, pool treatments, showers and wraps. The resort uses the Accor Thalassa Institute produce range from France.

Watsu, shiatsu, osteopathy, pilates, reiki and tai chi are also on offer, and there are fitness and gym rooms, a rest area, saunas and Turkish baths for you to use, plus regular classes in stretching, muscle toning, modern jazz dance and Portuguese. A free hatha yoga class takes place each morning under the shade of huge pine trees, looking straight out to sea. The gardens are beautifully laid out for peaceful, contemplative walks, and are stuffed to bursting with subtropical plants, fruit trees

and colourful bougainvillea.

Rooms are decorated in restful blues and yellows with elegant marble en suite bathrooms. The junior suites have small terraces where you can meditate or do yoga, though you aren't allowed to venture onto the lawn outside. Packages of four treatments per day cost from €110. Fly to Faro, from where it's a 45-minute drive.

Sofitel Thalassa Vialara.

Italy

Recharge in the mountains or soak up the vibes of a Tuscan hideaway.

Fact file

- **Visa:** None required for citizens of EU countries, US, Canada or Australia and New Zealand
- **Country code:** +39
- **Currency:** Euro (€)
- **Time zone:** GMT +2 hours
- **Electricity:** 230v
- **Tourist board:** www.italiantouristboard.co.uk (UK and Ireland), www.italiantourism.com (North America)

PILATES HOLIDAY

Agriturismo Cascina Papaveri

Costigliole d'Asti, Piedmont
T+39 0141-962044
www.cascinapapaveri.com
From €989 for 4 nights

Cascina Papaveri (or Poppy Farmhouse) is a stylish agriturismo in the Piedmont region of northern Italy which hosts regular three-, four- and seven-night pilates breaks led by visiting teachers from the UK and the US, as well as cookery holidays. The property enjoys 360° views of vine-covered hills, hilltop villages and valleys and, with only 10 guests at any one time, is a lovely, comfortable place to relax, alone or with a friend or partner.

It's run by Robyn and John, who offer a warm welcome and excellent food using fresh local ingredients, most of which are grown in the organic gardens and amongst the vines (which also provide some very palatable wines). There's an indoor pool, and a fully equipped pilates studio with en suite steam room and sauna. Bedrooms are en suite and luxuriously appointed, with finest Quagliotti Egyptian cotton sheets, mood lighting, flat screen TV and satellite and Wi-Fi connections.

Highly experienced teachers are from the UK and US and include Jessica Hope, a dancer from New York, and a teacher of great charm and ability, and Sophie Lyske, who runs **So Pilates** in Leeds (www.so-pilates.co.uk). Cooking lessons are on offer with local master chef Pietro Baldi, who has a lovely sense of

> It is not because things are difficult that we do not dare, it is because we do not dare that they are difficult.
>
> *Seneca*

humour and a very calm but commanding approach to his craft.

There's a single supplement of €379. The nearest airport is Turin, which has excellent airport bus and train services to Asti from where there is a free pick up to the resort. Transfer costs are under €20.

RURAL RETREAT

Agriturismo Perucci di Sopra

Grosseto
T +39 0564-580138
www.peruccidisopra.com
From €55 per person per night

A converted 400-year-old farmhouse in a nature reserve set high up in the hills with spectacular views across countryside and out

Agriturismo Cascina Papaveri.

Yoga by the pool at Agriturismo Perucci di Sopra.

to sea, Agriturismo Perucci di Sopra is a chilled out place to stay, from where, on a clear day, you can see the islands of Elba and Corsica. UK-based yoga teacher Carl Hargreaves runs relaxing annual holidays here (see page 123), or stay as an individual to go walking and enjoy shiatsu and ayurvedic massage with local therapists, which owner Marina Kummer can arrange.

The huge, light and bright yoga studio is in a converted barn. There's also a garden with a hammock, a (small) swimming pool, and a comfortable dining room and living room in the main house. You sleep in one of six spacious and comfortable rooms. There are also two converted pig pens outside the main house – Casa Rosa, with two rooms and a shared bathroom, and La Porcellaia, great for couples, with a double room and bathroom and its own private terrace with view.

Most meals are served on the outdoor terrace, and Marina is a superb cook. If you're here on Carl's yoga holiday, you'll be served mouth-watering vegetarian soups, salads and main dishes all sourced from their own vegetable garden or local farms – think pecorino cheese with chilli, delicious little concoctions made from spinach and ricotta, big platters of fresh vegetables, fluffy omelettes and home-made desserts. If you're here as an individual and eat meat, try the speciality, a wild-boar stew cooked with the local wine.

Marina's farm is open all year round except for January and February. Fly to Rome or Pisa and take the train to Grosseto, from where a taxi costs about €45. There are no villages within walking distance, and the beach is a good drive away, so restless souls should hire a car for exploring.

PILATES HOLIDAY

Aurora Gercke pilates holidays

Massa Marittima, Tuscany
T+44 (0)1223-563615
www.cambs-pilates.co.uk
From €840 per person per week

A body control pilates instructor with five years' teaching experience, UK-based Aurora Gercke runs three- and five-day pilates holidays in her home region of Tuscany. You stay at Domus Bernardiniana, the farmhouse on an olive oil and wine producing estate surrounded by countryside near the medieval town of Massa Marittima.

There's a tranquil small lake and swimming pool here, and traditional and wholesome Tuscan food is served, with vegetarian

Southern Europe Italy

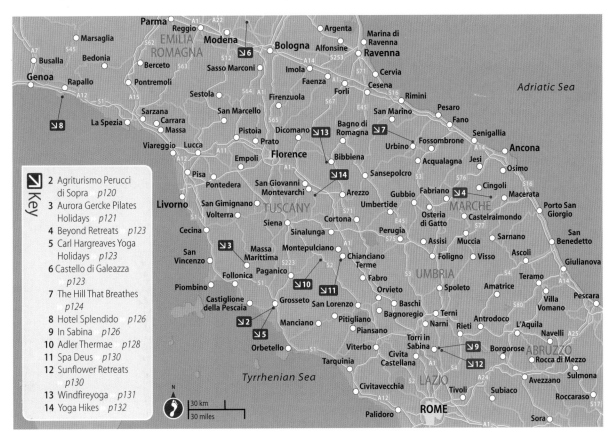

◑ Body language

Healing waters

The Italians have a long tradition of using their thermal waters in baths, showers, inhalations and mud wraps as a cure for everything from backache to asthma, and there are thermal springs dotted throughout the country. The waters' heat, and various mineral properties, are good for rebalancing stressed immune and nervous systems, for easing stiff joints and for exfoliating and softening the skin. They're great for all-round relaxation, and no health trip to Italy would be complete without a dip.

Tuscany is a good place to start. Like everywhere in Italy, the thermal waters here are public property, and private hotels need licences to be able to use them in their treatments and pools. If they are bona fide medical thermal spas, they are also legally obliged to make the waters available for locals to use, by offering treatments subsidized by the government, and a doctor on site. They will also have a pool separate from those used by guests, which acts as a kind of lido for locals (and visiting tourists), especially during the summer. If you're on a road trip, this can be a fun way of easing tired muscles, but if it's genuine relaxation you seek, you'd be better off investing in at least a weekend's stay.

The **Terme di Saturnia** (T+39 0564-600 0111, www.termedisaturnia.it) is a contemporary, relaxed place to be for a weekend, set in the untouristy Maremma region of Tuscany, a two-hour drive from Rome (from €180 per room per night). There's a wide range of medical, holistic and beauty treatments on offer here, but you'll be most satisfied with simply soaking or gently swimming in the giant natural crater alongside many a returning Italian guest. The pool was used by the Romans and Etruscans and has been here for 3000 years. Water flows into it at a rate of 800 litres per second, and keeps at a near constant temperature of 37°C. Its eggy, sulphurous smell pervades the whole resort, but you do get used to it (sort of). There are also Roman baths with steam rooms and saunas, an outdoor juice bar, and two restaurants – choose the Mediterranean over the Tuscan if you want lighter meals.

To enjoy the benefits of thermal waters during a longer stay, head for the wonderfully relaxing **Adler Thermae** (see page 128), which shares its thermal water source with the beautiful medieval village of Bagno Vignoni (where the bathing pools are no longer in daily use). As a wellness resort rather than a thermal hotel, Adler Thermae doesn't have to offer a pool for locals, and it's a sumptuous place to stay.

Other thermal hotels in Tuscany are luxurious, slightly old-fashioned places set in beautiful, historical buildings, aimed at well-heeled Italians and offering an impressive range of medical and pampering treatments. The **Fonteverde** (T+39 0578-57241, www.fonteverdespa.com) costs from €220 per person per night. It is partly based in a former Medici villa, has an Indian-born, Italian-raised ayurvedic massage therapist, Dipu, who is favoured by celebrities, its own product range, and (you guessed it) a separate thermal pool for its guests' pampered pooches. It's a member of the Italian Societa Terme e Benessere or STB (Society for Bathing and Wellbeing).

Its sister hotels are the 18th-century **Bagni di Pisa** (T+39 050-88501, www.bagnidipisa.com, from €120 per person per night), and **Grotta Giusti** (T+39 0572-90771, www.grottagiustispa.com, from €170 per person per night), which boasts its own natural thermal cave and is set in the 19th-century former home of Italian poet, Giuseppe Giusti.

ADLER THERMAE

Bagno Vignoni.

options available. Aurora is a member of the Body Control Pilates Association, Europe's largest pilates professional body, and she'll teach two sessions a day for five days, with classes tailored to beginners or intermediate and advanced.

Two days are left completely free so you can explore the surrounding area; Florence and Siena are an easy drive away, and there will be daytime excursions to the coast and local thermal baths. Massa Marittima is 45 miles from Pisa and Rome airports – the price excludes flights.

YOGA & ACTIVITY HOLIDAY

Beyond Retreats

Le Marche
T+44 (0)20-7226 4044
www.beyondretreats.co.uk
From €2095 per person per week

UK-based luxury adventure and yoga company Beyond Retreats runs annual cookery and yoga holidays at Santo Stefano, a marvellous restored Italian country house which feels more like a boutique hotel, with views out to the rolling hills of Le Marche and the medieval hilltop village of Treia.

Designed to help you relax and revitalize your approach to cooking and food, the core of the trip is three creative cookery lessons with expert chef Sera Irvine, who'll share her philosophy of food with you. You'll learn how to prepare many of the scrumptious Italian dishes you're served at mealtimes, as well as how to make your own focaccia and other breads. There's also a visit to the local market,

a chance to understand the importance of seasonal shopping.

Relaxing and energizing daily yoga sessions are taught by iyengar yoga teacher Geraldine Ross, who has studied with Mr Iyengar himself in Pune, in India. You'll stay in supremely comfortable en suite rooms with Molton Brown toiletries and personal bathrobes, and there's a small swimming pool. Therapeutic treatments are also on offer from a visiting therapist, including Thai yoga massage, reflexology and Indian head massage.

The holiday takes a maximum of 12, and the price includes everything except flights and massages (€63 per hour) – it's €2515 if you want your own room. Fly to Ancona, from where transfers are included. Beyond Retreats also runs trips in the UK – see page 29 for an account.

YOGA HOLIDAY

Carl Hargreaves yoga holidays

Near Grosseto, Tuscany
T+44 (0)20-8444 3178
www.mapayoga.com
From €450 per person per week

UK-based yoga teacher Carl Hargreaves runs annual yoga holidays to two rural farms near Grosseto in Tuscany – Agriturismo Perucci di Sopra, otherwise known as Marina's farm (see previous spread), and a nearby biodynamic farm run by Gemma and Tonino.

Relaxed, welcoming and dedicated to yoga, with a background in dance and martial arts, Carl's teaching has a strong emphasis on correct alignment and synchronizing movement with the breath. Together with his Italian-speaking wife Ruth and their young daughter Fleur, he facilitates a relaxed and convivial atmosphere at each retreat.

There's yoga twice a day, with plenty of time for siestas, walks and pool time, as well as two optional afternoon excursions to local attractions including the hot springs at Saturnia. Carl offers a one-to-one session for

Above: Carl Hargreaves yoga holidays.
Bottom left: Beyond Retreats at Santo Stefano.

each person before or during the week, so he can create a personalized programme specifically for you, and massages with local therapists can be arranged.

Come to Marina's farm for more of a holiday, Gemma's for more of a retreat. Gemma and Tonino (a cook and musician) are a welcoming couple whose farm is a rustic, friendly place overlooking rolling hills. There's a small plunge pool and well-lit wooden-floored studio for yoga. You can stay in a simple room in the main house and share a bathroom, camp or opt for the circus caravan, which has two rooms, one with bunk beds. There are walking paths around the farm and simple, fresh home-made meals using biodynamic ingredients are eaten alfresco, with home-made bread and cheese and jugs of local wine.

Carl's yoga trips usually take 12 guests and attract a range of people, usually in their thirties to fifties, looking to improve their yoga, some of whom are Carl's students from London. Beginners are welcome. Fly to Rome or Pisa and take the train to Grosseto. One pickup and drop-off is included in the price.

CREATIVE RETREAT

Castello di Galeazza

Near Crevalcore
T+39 0519-85170
www.galeazza.com
€40 per person per day

Set in the enervating flatlands between Bologna and the river Po, Castello di Galeazza

CASTELLO DI GALEAZZA

Chamber music concerts, art exhibitions, parties and various workshops are staged throughout the year, mainly in the summer months. Artists who exhibit here leave a sample of their work on permanent display, and the gardens, undergoing a slow renaissance, provide peaceful surroundings. Bring your art equipment, musical instruments, cameras, binoculars, or a notebook in which to start that elusive first novel.

Accommodation in the 14th-century castle is homely, with four bedrooms, one of which is single. Furniture is more mix than match and a bit creaky, and there is no central heating, but there are abundant frescoes, fraying fabrics, 3000-plus books, old bicycles to borrow, and pianos to play.

Meals are literally what you make of them, as catering is a shared activity. You may find yourself going to the market, harvesting herbs in the courtyard, or conjuring up new recipes out of local produce. There's always pasta to be cooked and washing up to be done in the true spirit of communal living. All this is lubricated with vino di tavola and a wide choice of music.

There's a compulsory membership charge of €10 to stay here; guests come back from all over the world to benefit from this

is a laid-back, creative place to stay, run by Clark Lawrence, a young American who originally set out to provide a residential book club experience but now offers a wider range of cultural activities under the banner of Reading Retreats in Rural Italy. There is no compulsion to read in this browser's paradise, but a book, in a hammock with a glass of wine, is difficult to resist.

🅞 Soul food

Scale three of Italy's famous volcanoes and raise money for children with leukaemia. **Classic Tours** (T+44 (0)20 7619 0066, www.classictours.co.uk) run regular global adventure charity trips, and in 14 years has helped 30,000 participants raise £30 million for over 100 UK charities. Their Italy trip comprises a four-hour trek to Vesuvius, a tough, six-hour climb to Stromboli, and a gentler seven-hour trek on the slopes of Mount Etna in Sicily.

uniquely memorable retreat. Fly to Bologna Marconi, from where it's a 40-minute drive, or Bologna Forli, an 80-minute drive away. The nearest train station is Crevalcore – a bus from the station takes 30 minutes (and costs €2), or it's a 15-minute taxi ride (€20).

RURAL RETREAT
The Hill That Breathes

🌐 🅖 🅐 ☀ 🅝 🅠 🅞 ⑰

Urbino
T+44 (0)870-609 2690
www.thehillthatbreathes.com
From €99 per person per night

The Hill That Breathes feels thoroughly remote, yet is only 20 minutes' drive from Urbino and 90 minutes from Ancona airport. The site, chosen for its excellent feng shui, is a horseshoe-shaped hill, surrounded by mature woods of pine, oak and beech, with running water on three sides. Although the summer months are hot and dry, there's a near-constant breeze around the hill, which really does appear to breathe.

People come here to attend a course; those on offer include various styles of yoga, qigong and shamanism as well as the popular

66 99

"It's time to say 'Fuck It' to all your problems and concerns, your biggest issues and your deepest fears." As I read the brochure, my heart sank. The people who dreamt up this course, I thought to myself grimly, used to work in advertising. It's not big, clever or in keeping with my idea of spiritual development to swear at things, I thought. But I arrived in Ancona with an open mind. Sort of.

John Parkin and his wife Gaia did meet while working for an advertising company. But I was wrong about everything else. The jaunty marketing concept is a front for some thoughtful, serious and incredibly subtle healing practice. When John (a qigong teacher) and Gaia (a breathwork therapist)

opened The Hill That Breathes in 2004, they had a clear ethos from the start, to offer light-hearted holidays and serious energy work – what John calls "spiritual hedonism". The Fuck It week celebrates this paradox, and involves deep soul-searching and inner healing but lots of trips to town, local Puglian

THE HILL THAT BREATHES

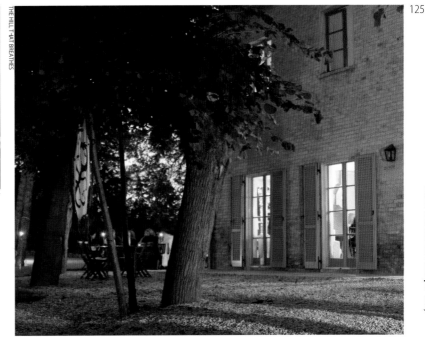

Left: Castello di Galazzea. **Above and right:** Style and substance at the Hill that Breathes.

Southern Europe Italy

Fuck It weeks (see below) run by The Hill's owners, John and Gaia. The average client is English, female, mid-thirties and travelling alone, though the non-yoga weeks tend to attract a higher proportion of men as well as a greater age range (from 25 to 70), and there's an occasional yoga week for families.

Accommodation is in a tastefully renovated traditional Italian farmhouse. Be prepared to share a room with two others, though there are some singles available for a supplement. Classes take an average of 18 people and take place in a huge tipi on top of the hill, and on a wooden platform jutting out over the valley. There's an irresistible salt water pool, and various bodywork treatments (around €40 for 50 minutes) are given in smaller tipis hidden in the woods.

Communal meals are taken on the terrace – plentiful delicious vegetarian food with a pronounced Italian influence (special dietary requirements are catered for on request) – and local wines are available to buy.

wine and plenty of cakes, too.

So what actually happens on a Fuck It week? Well, it's hard to say. You'll certainly learn the rudiments of qigong (the Chinese 'art of energy' that underpins tai chi and Chinese medicine). But mostly you will learn that you are your own best teacher. You will start to tune in more readily to your energetic body, and learn to listen to its considerable wisdom. Once you've spent 24 hours there, it will all make perfect sense. It's OK to laugh until you cry. Or cry until you're sick. Everybody here is on a journey: some are simply curious, but others are at a turning point in their career, or dealing with bereavement, illness or romantic meltdown. This can make group sessions intense – and

that's when your new-found ability to say 'fuck it' comes in handy. Besides, John and Gaia put a great deal of care into creating a safe space for people to simply be themselves. They lead most of the sessions together, which seems to diffuse the hint of guru-worship that often surfaces when this sort of course is built around one charismatic teacher.

If you don't feel like joining in, that's fine. You can lie in a hammock reading Jilly Cooper all day, only resurfacing in time for a Pinot Grigio and a gossip over dinner, and nobody will look askance at you. Or you can indulge in your own personal primal screaming, tree-hugging, trance-dancing barefoot re-birthing odyssey, and nobody

will take any notice of that either. The relief at being free of rules and peer pressure is palpable. By day three, everybody looks five years younger.

Don't be put off by the confrontational name. The Fuck It philosophy is about fun and friendship, not nihilism and delinquency. Go on the course if you're interested in shaking things up, challenging your preconceptions and booting yourself into the next chapter of your life. You may get nothing more from it than a tan and a lot of sleep. On the other hand, you may well wake up on the last day, as I did, with the joyous realization that you're head-over-heels in love with life again.

Lucy Greeves

Most courses incorporate one day off, with optional excursions such as shopping and culture in Urbino, the beach in Faro or a walk in the mountains with a local guide. But with 100 acres of fragrant pine woods, there's plenty of room to escape without leaving the centre. Animal life abounds – deer and hare, wild boar and porcupine – as does life of the insect sort. Daytime sessions are serenaded by the mechanical whirr of cicadas; mosquitoes are rare but not absent. The centre is managed sustainably (green waste treatment facility, solar-heated water, recycling and an emphasis on local produce and labour), adding to the sense of living in harmony with nature.

Fly to Ancona, from where it's a 90-minute minibus transfer organized by the centre (€30 each way). Or take the train from Rome to Ancona or Urbino then a taxi. Early July generally sees the hottest two weeks of the season. Christmas and New Year retreats are about as cold as the UK, but sunnier. A second farmhouse is planned for 2008, offering 10 further single rooms and a meditation hall.

HOTEL & SPA
Hotel Splendido

Portofino
T+39 0185-267801
www.hotelsplendido.com
From €1350 for 4 nights

Frequented by movie stars and thespians since 1901, the Hotel Splendido is a glamorous, luxury villa perched on a hillside in semi-tropical, terraced gardens with views of Portofino bay. It offers wellness programmes in April and October, outside the busy tourist season, aimed at single travellers, couples or friends looking to take time out.

Choose from Herbs and Health, which offers lessons on 'phytotherapy' and 'phytocosmesis' treatments and their ancient technique in using medicinal plants for therapeutic purposes. Participants also get the opportunity to walk in the verdant greenery of Monte do Portofino, to discover

herbs with an expert botanist and have a lesson on Mediterranean cuisine and the use of Ligurian herbs and spices. Or go for the Ayurvedic Immersion, when you'll get the lowdown on ayurvedic philosophy and the chance to explore your own 'dosha', or imbalances in the body and diet (see page 210 for more information on ayurveda).

The Splendido's Wellness Centre is located below the pool and surrounded by fragrant pine and olive trees, with panoramic views of the Mediterranean below. You can have outdoor massages here, and a pilates teacher is on call for one-to-one or group sessions. A gym and other holistic treatments are available in three indoor therapy rooms.

Courses are held in English and Italian and take a maximum of eight people. The price includes four nights accommodation in a double sea view, breakfast and lessons. Fly to Genoa, a 45-minute drive away (transfers €125) or take the train to Santa Margherita Ligure, 5 km from the hotel.

YOGA HOLIDAY
In Sabina

Near Torri in Sabina
T+39 340-387 6028
www.insabina.com
From €700 per person per week
B&B from €100 per room per night

Converted from two stone farmhouses in seven acres of olive groves and gardens, In Sabina is a tranquil retreat hosting yoga holidays by teachers from all over the world. If there's space, you can stay as an individual on a B&B basis, when yoga classes can be arranged. Sabina is a quiet, untouristy area of Italy, despite being just 45 minutes' drive from Rome, and you're unlikely to hear anything more than birdsong and the occasional tractor.

Grassy pathways lead to the large outdoor wooden yoga deck, set in a valley below the main buildings with a white canvas roof. In

66 99

Expert iyengar yoga teacher Glenn Ceresoli (www.actionyoga.com) is based in Australia but runs workshops and retreats all over the world. I'd done a weekend with him at The Barefoot Barn in Devon, and, despite finding it gruelling, felt physically taller and mentally lighter after just one day. The masochist in me decided to try a week with him at In Sabina in Italy. A system devised by BKS Iyengar with a strong attention to detail, iyengar yoga uses blocks and straps to help you get into and stay in asanas. Glenn, who has trained with the man himself and been teaching it for over 20 years, must be one of its toughest teachers. His classes are a subtle mix of the physical and the philosophical: dealing with bodily pain on the mat, he says, helps you deal with a difficult world. He's right, of course, and this isn't an easy week.

We have a three hour class at 0600 every morning, and a two hour class at 1630 every afternoon. I stretch and test my body in ways I'm very unused to, but because of Glenn's tough-love manner and obvious knowledge of anatomy, I feel utterly safe doing so. His attention to detail is oddly catching. 'Monitor, Measure and Manage,' he says, urging us to analyse where our bodies are at. 'Pull the skin of your outer groin down, and the skin of your inner groin up', he'll repeat, whist we're trying to breathe in a particularly challenging pose.

The rest of the group are supportive and friendly, though I find myself wanting more peace and quiet during down time, and restlessly take myself off with one or two others most afternoons. By the end of the week, though, my energy has started to rise, my body feels like Tank Girl's and mentally I am as bright as a new born babe. A few months on, and I'm thinking Australia might be my next trip. After a little rest.

Caroline

cooler weather there's a (much smaller) indoor yoga room at the top of one of the buildings. There's a reasonable sized pool with loungers and a kitchenette, and areas for lounging in or meditation in the grounds, including hammocks slung between linden trees. Cactuses in pots, flower beds of pansies, and the prevalent sweet smell of jasmine add to a rustic feel.

A highlight of In Sabina is the delicious and varied vegetarian Italian food cooked by local Elide d'Artibale. Think basil, mozzarella and sweet freshly picked tomatoes from the garden, home made houmous, bread from the pizza oven, light and scrumptious panacotta – wheat- and dairy-free diets can be catered for. Meals are eaten at a long wooden table shaded by bamboo on the front veranda with a view to the hills beyond, and the table is always set beautifully with vibrant flowers and tall green bottles of the local red wine in the evening for those who want it.

If you're on a yoga week, you'll need to be prepared to share one of the eight rooms – sometimes single rooms are available (for €200 extra a week). The beds are tiny, but the rooms are spacious and airy, with simple white and wooden furniture and window shutters. Noise travels from the dining terrace, so if you want guaranteed quiet, ask for a room nearer the pool area or opt for one of the five yurts.

Every kind of yoga is on offer here throughout the year: regular visiting teachers include iyengar expert Glenn Ceresoli (see box) and John Stirk, who specializes in scaravelli yoga. Some yoga weeks are open to everyone, others only to the students of the teacher. Songwriting, poetry and photography courses are sometimes on offer too. Local hikes and trips, such as the hot springs at Viterbo or the lovely village of Casperia can be arranged, and it's a 40-minute walk to the medieval hilltop town of Torri in Sabina; if you're a restless soul, hire a car. Bring layers of clothing to deal with a varied climate, your own pool towel and flip-flops. Fly to Fiumicino in Rome, from where it's a 1½-hour train ride to the nearest station, Stimigliano. It's a €20 transfer from here, or a €100 transfer from the airport.

Southern Europe Italy

CAROLINE SYLGE

Above: In Sabina
Below: Yoga session at In Sabina

Natural spa retreat

Adler Thermae 🏃 🏔 👨‍👩‍👧 👐 🎯 🌸 🏃 🤸 ↘10

This relaxed and gorgeous spa and wellness resort, set in a dream-like Tuscan setting, lies in the World Heritage site of the Val d'Orcia and shares its thermal water source with the nearby medieval town of Bagno Vignoni. Owned by two German brothers, it was built from scratch in 2004 and has been beautifully designed to fit in with the surrounding countryside; you can't even see the resort from the approach road.

Where you stay From the pools, your room or the terrace you'll enjoy restorative views of the Tuscan hills, long lines of cypress trees and the pretty hilltop village of Castigliano d'Orcia. The main thermal pool is full of strong massage jets and waterfalls, and part of it is covered for cooler days. There's an attached large swimming pool surrounded by lush garden areas with rose bushes and sun loungers. The spa has a spacious reception area with 20 modern, well-lit treatment rooms including a quieter corridor of rooms for holistic treatments and massages, two levels of relaxation beds looking over a small lake, a small watsu pool and an amazing range of saunas and steam rooms (see below).

There are 90 rooms here, though the design of the building means that you never feel crowded. The en suite rooms are modern, many split level and each with a balcony or terrace overlooking the pool or

the hills. The signature colours of subtle greens and yellows make for a refreshing, clean-looking decor to complement the mainly light wood furniture – ask for a room away from the pool area with a valley view if you want to be quieter.

What you do Enjoy the relaxing and purifying effects of the main warm thermal water pool, which contains curative sulphur compounds, bicarbonates and sulphates (see Healing Waters box on page 122). There's also an impressive selection of saunas and steam rooms to help detoxify your skin, stimulate your circulation and promote relaxation. These include the Salino, an Etruscan sauna in which you inhale a refreshing salty steam to help clear out your nose and lungs; the Artemisia, a herbal steam room; the Philosopher's Cave, a steam room built into a tastefully man-made grotto, and the Olivae, an olive wood sauna set on a small lake. It's also curiously relaxing to float in the underground salt bath, the Grotta Salina (€10 for 20 minutes).

The treatment list is vast and will satisfy you whether you want to come here for deeper, longer-lasting holistic treatments or just to feel nurtured and pampered. It includes ayurvedic treatments, every type of massage you could think of from craniosacral and deep tissue to shiatsu and Thai, physiotherapy, thalassotherapy and holistic treatments such as reiki and Bach flower essences. A wide selection of beautifying baths, wraps and facials is also on offer, many using local Tuscan ingredients such as grapeseed oil, olive cream, sheep's milk and honey. The on site Dr Thomas Platzer, can tailor a health programme to suit your diet and lifestyle needs, both during your stay and for you to take home with you.

There's a gym, spacious studios for classes and a daily programme of activities for you to tap into at will, which vary according the season, with more water-based sessions during the summer. They include yoga and pilates (both in the thermal water and in the studio), hydrobike (on the underwater bikes in the swimming pool), various stretch classes and mountain biking. There are daily guided countryside walks, though it's easy enough to take yourself off alone. The coast is an hour's drive away, and there are lots of nearby villages and vineyards to explore. Two minutes' walk from the resort is Bagno Vignoni, a gorgeous picture-postcard medieval village great for pottering around.

What you eat and drink You can eat as little or as much as you like here; food intolerance, nutrition and body composition check-ups are available, and special diets can be catered for, including weight-loss, wheat- and dairy-free. A sumptuous and healthy buffet

ADLER THERMAE

breakfast is served in the elegant courtyard restaurant with retractable roof at the top of the main building, and healthy salads and simple fish and meat dishes are available for lunch at the poolside Osteria (€15 per person). It's in the evenings that the restaurant comes into its own, with expert service and a brilliant atmosphere, especially at weekends. The Italian menu includes indulgent dishes (shank of beef with Brunello wine sauce, parsley potatoes and French beans with fennel seeds) as well as lighter and vegetarian options (from a tuna tartare with sweet peppers to crêpes with onions, Batavian endive and black olives), and comes complete with an extensive list of local and international wines.

Who goes The resort attracts couples, families and groups of friends coming to relax and recharge or get fit, but you'd be well looked after if you were alone (there are five single rooms available, for a daily supplement of €50). Thirty-something, sassy Italians come here at weekends to escape city life. During the week and in high season you're likely to find a complete mix of guests from all over the world, though most are Europeans, as well as occasional honeymooners. This would be a good place for stressed parents – there's a daily programme of activities for children, a small children's pool and lots of post-natal treatments on the menu. To preserve the peace, a maximum of 25 children is allowed at any one time.

Essentials Adler Thermae (T+39 (0)577-889000, www.adler-thermae.com) is very good value, costing from €1145 for seven nights, which includes accommodation, half board and access to all the facilities and daily classes. A three-night stay (outside August) is from €507 all inclusive. You can choose from a set programme of treatments (from €388) or just pick and mix from the à la carte menu on arrival. Spring and autumn are warm and balmy, though winter would be a great time to escape any gloom back home (except in January, when the resort is closed). August is packed with Italians on holiday, so avoid it if you want a quieter time. Florence is the nearest airport, from where it's a 1¾-hour drive by road. The nearest station is Chiusi-Chianciano Terme. You could also fly to Rome or Pisa. Hotel Adler (T+39 (0)471-775000, www.hotel-adler.com) is the sister hotel in the Dolomites, with a strong emphasis on skiing and outdoor sports.

❝❞

This is an elegant pleasure palace, with no sign of tackiness or pretension. After a particularly soothing session in the thermal pool, my boyfriend and I decided we could happily live here permanently, so relaxed did we feel. Our room was large and well balanced with Feng Shui - we didn't feel boxed in like you can do in some health resorts. I had an expert shiatsu massage by a strong male therapist which brought a stillness to my body and mind I hadn't felt in weeks – but I equally enjoyed a pedicure, carried out with an efficiency I've rarely seen during pampering treatments. Dressing up in the evenings to be served tasty and tender Italian dishes by expert staff only added to the feeling of being nurtured. They do play a somewhat interesting mix of 1970s and 1980s 'prog rock' music around the hotel, and there are cigar and cocktail evenings we decided to avoid, but I could quite happily go back here every year to rejuvenate, especially for long weekends off season.

Caroline

Southern Europe Italy

SPA DEUS

SPA DEUS

Above and top: Open-air massage at Spa Deus. **Bottom right:** Sunflower Retreats.

Sunflower Retreats

🌱 ♨ ○ ♦ ◉ ✛ ✖ ↘12

Casperia
T+44 (0)116-259 9422
www.sunflowerretreats.com
Frm €449 per person per week

Tucked away along the winding streets of a medieval hilltop village 40 minutes from Rome, Sunflower Retreats offers a respite from the pace of 21st-century living. Guests can join a 90-minute hatha yoga class before breakfast, given by owner Lucy, or go on walks led by husband Alan, who gives an introduction to the area's rich natural history.

The yoga studio features a flowing freshwater spring which can be seen through glass in the floor. One-to-one tuition and meditation classes can be arranged on request, including chakra meditation, affirmations, visualization and breathing exercises. Canoeing, climbing, horse riding and skiing are on offer at extra cost, along with cookery courses, and treatments such as reiki, aromatherapy, Bach remedies, LaStone and crystal therapies, and aloe vera facials.

Accommodation in three renovated, self-catering properties varies from spacious and stylish to more basic and less polished, though the character of each makes them appealing. For the generous country kitchen and spectacular views, Casa Bella Vista is worth paying extra for. After a continental breakfast served in **Il Dopolavor**, a café where guests and locals meet and socialize, the day is your own.

OLIVIA MACKINDER

HEALTH & FITNESS RETREAT

Spa Deus

○ ♦ ✛ ✛ ✖ ↘11

Chianciano Terme
T+39 0578-63232
www.spadeus.it
From €270 per day

A Californian-style health spa on a hill just outside Chianciano Terme, Spa Deus offers serious health and fitness programmes with an Italian twist. You'll be based in an art-filled hotel and have morning walks through the pristine Tuscan hillsides of the Val d'Orcia, a UNESCO World Heritage site. Food is made with local produce and lots of fresh herbs but without salt or sugar – and is served formally, by waiters dressed in white jackets.

Drinking and smoking aren't allowed, and everyone is here to de-stress, get fit or lose weight – a lot of the clientele are American. There are wake-up stretches to Handel's Hallelujah Chorus, an Olympic size, heated indoor pool, and a huge range of exercise classes from aquaaerobics and boxercise to gyrotonics, pilates and spinning. Treatments include shiatsu or hot-stone massage, rolfing and reflexology, loofah rubs and mud wraps, thalasso and ayurvedic treatments and a variety of facials. Juice fasts (from €1960 for seven nights) and quit smoking weeks (from €1975 for seven nights) are also on offer. Early-evening excursions to nearby villages when the tourists have gone home are also included.

Fly to Fiumicino Airport in Rome, from where it's a two-hour drive, or take the train from Roma Termini (Rome Central Station) to Chiusi-Chianciano Terme.

Excursions are managed informally, often on request, and at extra cost. They include trips to nearby villages and restaurants, and to the thermal pools at Terme dei Papa, but they feel expensive for what they are. A hire car makes sense if you want more flexibility.

Sunflower Retreats attract individuals, couples and friends in their thirties, forties and fifties, drawn by the yoga and a love of the great outdoors. Avoid the intense heat of mid-summer. For those who love snowy mountains, long-weekend breaks from January to March are an alternative. The cheapest and easiest way to reach Casperia is by train from Rome's Fiumicino Airport to Poggio Mirteto, where a free bus operates to the village. Sunflower Retreats also plans to run holidays in Sardinia.

There is more in you than you think.

Anon

Southern Europe Italy

Top: Sunflower Retreats. **Above**: Windfireyoga.

YOGA RETREAT

Windfireyoga

🎯 ⛰ ↘13

Near Bibbiena
T+39 (0)349-435 3445
www.windfireyoga.com
From €450 per week

A genuine retreat in a gorgeous remote location, Windfireyoga was set up by expert yoga teacher, Godfri Dev, who teaches his own Dynamic Yoga Training Method based on the original Eight Limbs of Yoga. This is a place to come and be peaceful, explore yoga and enjoy the natural surroundings. All the founders require is that you be "as honestly and fully yourself as you can".

Based on the slopes of the holy mountain where St Francis is said to have received his stigmata, this is an incredibly rejuvenating location set high up in a national park. You'll often see wild boar and deer, and there are wonderful long forest walks to be had nearby. The main house is surrounded by oak, beech and maple trees and supplied with water from natural springs, and there's a river running nearby where you can swim, temperature permitting.

A morning class is taught by Godfri Dev; his classes are of the highest standard and include pranayama and meditation as well as asanas based on vinyasa flow. Godfri himself is witty, genuine and relaxed.

Afternoon classes are taught by his senior apprentices, and all levels of experience are welcome. As well as yoga there is an intensive mediation retreat at the end of the season.

There are no home comforts here; you sleep under canvas in tents pitched around the land, and share outdoor showers. Food is wholesome, tasty grains, beans, vegetables and fruit, sourced organically wherever possible – special diets can be catered for if you tell them in advance. Windfireyoga is open to everyone, but tends to attract a younger set of men and women who are into yoga, as well as volunteers devoted to Godfri's yoga style.

The retreat is open during the summer months. Bring warm clothing, a torch and any other home comforts you feel you can't do without when camping, and don't rely on your mobile working. There's a sleepy village a 10-minute walk below, with a simple pizzeria, and the town of Bibbiena is a bus ride away, but if you come here, come here to stay. Fly to Bologna, Pisa, Florence or Rome, then take a train to Bibbiena; Windfireyoga can arrange pick ups from various points.

YOGA & ACTIVITY HOLIDAY

Yoga Hikes

🌀 ✳ ▨14

Bucine, Tuscany
T+44 (0)7768-117413
www.yogahikes.com
From €2310 per week

Yoga Hikes is the brainchild of UK film producer Ian Flooks, who was inspired to set it up after loving his experience at the Californian boot camp The Ashram (see page 342). Though challenging, this is a deliberately less austere break – you get your own bathroom, and you'll stay in a beautifully restored farmhouse on a 400-ha olive and wine estate.

Your base is Iesolana farm, a hilltop agriturismo (www.iesolana.com) with luxurious rooms and inspirational views across the Tuscan countryside. Your day starts with yoga, then after breakfast there's a challenging two-hour hike through the hills. This is done in silence, as an extension of the meditative element of the yoga. After lunch you can do an optional shorter hike, or just lie by the pool, read or have a massage. Evening yoga is 1800-2000, followed by dinner.

Alexa Harris, who teaches at The Life Centre in London (see page 29), offers a mix of vinyasa flow, iyengar and hatha, and her classes are designed to accommodate all levels. Beginners are welcome, but it's best to have done some yoga before you come.

Expect delicious organic vegetarian Tuscan fare cooked by private chefs, and no alcohol or caffeine. The holiday attracts men and women from their twenties to their sixties, mostly from the UK and America – there's a high return rate. Fly to Florence, from where it's a 50-km drive – flights from the UK and transfers are included in the price, as well as full board, yoga and two massages.

Windfireyoga deck.

Alexa Harris does triconasana at Yoga Hikes.

Mountain retreat

Vigilius Mountain Resort ↘15

This superb south Tyrolean mountain retreat is 1500 m up and accessible only by cable car. Go hiking through the larches, dine extravagantly, be massaged into happiness, or curl up on a cushion in front of the log fire and do absolutely nothing.

Where you stay An architect's dream, the hotel itself is built from wood and glass and has an uncluttered, calming and contemporary feel. The spacious, open-plan bedrooms are all clean lines and smooth pale wood, with white bedlinen and splashes of warm colour on the walls. From the bed, through a floor-to-ceiling window, you look out across the mountains. Alternatively, step onto your private balcony and breathe the exceptionally fresh air. Even the cheapest accommodation includes a panorama bathroom with shower and bath – there are 35 rooms, or go for one of the six suites.

As the light fades, candles and fires are lit in the public areas. Suites have their own log fires. The communal lounge or Piazza is the central hub of the building and a library offers music as well as books for fireside relaxation. There's a beautiful Mountain Spa which has treatment rooms with refreshingly huge windows, and a swimming pool looking over the south Tyrolean mountains.

What you do Keep a healthy heart rate with mountain biking, archery, Nordic walking, hiking, tobogganing or skiing, depending on the season. These, along with yoga and autogenic training (a form of self-hypnosis, see glossary) are free as part of the Move & Explore programme. Skis and ski boots are available for a fee and you can hire a guide (€55 for 50 minutes). Try paragliding while you're here, a liberating experience, and take advantage of sessions in pilates, feldenkrais and spinal gymnastics with expert teachers.

Enjoy a gentler pace in the outdoor whirlpool, sauna and steam bath, or indulge in the spa, which offers watsu, shiatsu and body treatments devised by the Japanese company Shiseido. Massages, masks, scrubs and facials (from €20 for 20 minutes) use the active power of natural ingredients such as apples, polenta, honey and the Sarn mountain pine. Have foot reflexology enhanced with pine cones, try kneipping in the open air, or have a one-to-one session in the meditation room.

What you eat and drink The emphasis is on fresh local ingredients, vegetarian and gluten-free options come as standard, and the service is impeccable. The Parlour Ida provides delicious, south Tyrolean specialities – a typical menu (€42) would be a sweet herb risotto, courgette soup, saddle of lamb and buckwheat roll with blueberries.

Or indulge in a gourmet menu at the more elegant, Mediterranean-inspired 1500 restaurant. You won't go hungry.

Who goes Men and women in their thirties and forties, from across Europe. It's a favourite destination for couples, but anyone with a passion for nature and the good life will be happy here. In the Italian family spirit, children and babies are welcome.

Essentials Vigilius (T+39 0473-556600, www.vigilius.it) costs from €225 per room per day. The price includes breakfast and cable car, and packages of treatments are available. Suites cost from €565 per night. Pack layers for the mountains, and bring smart casual gear for evenings. Fly to Verona or Innsbruck airport, from where transfers to the cable car station at Lana can be arranged.

> 66 99
> If there's anywhere I would go back to, this is it.
> I haven't felt so relaxed in years – I had a sense of being borne aloft, away from worldly worries. I am good at doing nothing, but there was a natural progression here from doing nothing to doing something. I was so relaxed, I actually felt like going for a walk!
>
> *Lucinda Carling*

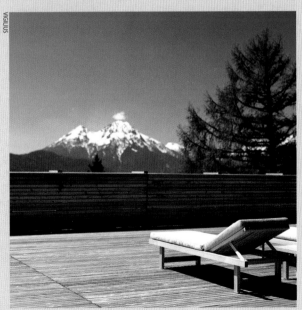

VIGILIUS

Croatia

ISLAND RETREAT

My Soul Retreat

🌐 ⛺ 🏔 🧘 ⭕ ✈1

Ivan Dolac, island of Hvar
T+44 (0)7789-813481
www.mysoulretreat.com
From €750 per week

My Soul Retreat lies in a small hillside village overlooking the sea on the south side of Hvar. This strip of coast is blissfully isolated, accessed solely through a narrow, unlit, 1400-m tunnel carved through the rocks. Backed by rugged mountains planted with vineyards, it looks out over a stunning seascape punctuated with secluded coves, pebble beaches and other distant islands.

Guests come here to do ashtanga yoga weeks, or to stay and receive individual one-to-one attention for anything from back pain to lifestyle counselling. It's run by charismatic German-born former model, Simone, a therapist and yoga teacher, and her Canadian-born partner, Tobias, a nutritionist and life coach trained in therapies such as emotional freedom technique. Both Simone and Tobias are warm, open and highly capable, and this is a wonderful retreat for anyone suffering from a lack of direction. Bespoke detox weeks and counselling for couples in crisis are also on offer.

The ashtanga yoga weeks include a morning session in ashtanga Mysore-style (see glossary), and an evening workshop to improve technique. You can also have reiki sessions with Simone, who is a reiki master, while skilled masseur Bruce melts knotted muscles and tension points with blissful Thai and Indonesian massages. Apart from yoga, visitors are introduced to the island's unspoiled nature through hiking, swimming and boat trips, but if you prefer to be on your own, that's encouraged too. Sundays are free and can be devoted to silence and fasting, or visit the sophisticated, Venetian-style urban centre of Hvar Town.

Guests stay at **Spila** (www.spila.hr), a modern seafront villa comprising eight airy apartments (sleeping from two to six people) with terracotta tile floors, wooden furniture and cheerful primary-coloured fabrics. Each unit has a living room with basic cooking facilities, a bathroom, and a balcony with a sea view. A restored old stone cottage (complete with a bio-toilet) on the hillside above the sea is available for individual guests who really want to retreat.

Downstairs, the Spila restaurant occupies a spacious terrace looking onto the water. Tobias is an excellent cook, and conjures up flavoursome organic vegetarian dishes based around ayurvedic principles, using plenty of fresh herbs and spices. Alcohol, coffee and cigarettes are all prohibited.

Simone also teaches yoga in Glasgow, Scotland (www.myoneonone.com), and works with hospital patients suffering from physical injuries, so this is a good place to come for help with back pain or to recuperate after an injury. My Soul Retreat draws a loyal following of her Scottish clients, many of whom are dedicated yoga enthusiasts. Groups are limited to eight participants; expect an age range from 25 up to 55, mainly singles, postgraduates and

Retreat to an island or swim between them.

Fact file

➲ **Visa:** None required for citizens of EU countries, US, Canada or Australia and New Zealand for visits of up to 90 days

🕐 **Country code:** +385

💲 **Currency:** Kuna (HRK)

🕜 **Time zone:** GMT +1 hour

🔌 **Electricity:** 220v

ℹ **Tourist board:** www.croatia.hr

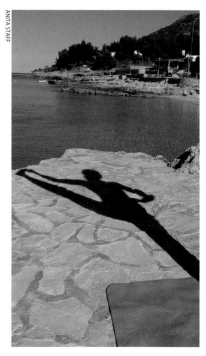

ANITA STAFF

professionals, with equal numbers of men and women.

Ashtanga weeks take place in early June and late September, when the sea is warm enough to swim in and islands aren't packed with tourists. Arrange individual visits in advance for any time over the summer.

Fly to Split, then take a ferry or catamaran to either Stari Grad, Hvar Town or Jelsa on the island of Hvar. Pickups can be arranged in advance.

YOGA HOLIDAY

Suncokret

🌐 ⛰ ☀ ⭕ 🚶 ⊚ ↘2

Dol, Island of Hvar
T+385 (0)91-739 2526
www.suncokretdream.net
From €375 per person per week

Suncokret is an easy-going, friendly retreat based in the peaceful village of Dol, an old-fashioned settlement of scattered stone cottages and farm buildings set amid vineyards and pine woods. It's run by yoga teacher,

Evening, a New Yorker, and her partner Stipe, who grew up on Hvar island and is a chef by training. Both are enthusiastic hosts who adore the island and its way of life.

Come here for a yoga week, where you trek regularly to isolated beaches for a suryashakti (sun-power yoga) session by the sea, followed by meditation and a swim. You can have reiki with Evening or attend a 'life-path' workshop, intended to help you move forward if you're feeling stuck in life. Stipe leads hiking trips across the island, introducing guests to flora and fauna, and folk customs. Workshops in natural therapies and fine arts, including painting and jewellery-making, are also available. Each autumn Suncokret offers special five-day retreats where visitors can help with grape collecting and the olive harvest.

Small groups are accommodated in single or double rooms in old cottages adjoining the family house. The decor is basic but homely, with colourful Indian bedspreads and vases of fragrant, freshly-picked herbs. Living space is shared and each house offers fully equipped kitchens, bathrooms with washing machines, plus patios and large

tables for indoor and outdoor communal meals. A farmhouse atmosphere prevails, with the family's cats and dogs checking out newcomers, and a neighbouring cockerel delivering his sunrise call each morning. Additional accommodation can be arranged in guesthouses in the village.

Stipe cooks delicious Dalmatian specialities for dinner, with an emphasis on local seasonal produce using vegetables and herbs from the garden, freshly caught fish, and the family's own organic olive oil and wine. Cooking classes can be combined with yoga.

Guests are from all over the world including Europe, Canada and America, from their 20s to early 50s, mostly professionals here to relax, de-stress and rejuvenate. Special retreats for families with young children can also be arranged. Suncokret is 6 km from the main ferry port of Stari Grad. Fly to Split, then take a ferry or catamaran to Stari Grad, Hvar Town or Jelsa – pickups can be arranged. Retreats run from April to New Year's Eve. Avoid the tourist-packed months of July and August if you want more peace.

Southern Europe Croatia

SONJA MOIOLI

Opposite page: My Soul Retreat. **This page:** Suncokret.

Swimming holiday

Swim Trek

Swimming in open water is a liberating experience, a kind of meditation, when you cannot help but be in the present moment. It's also a real mood lifter, and a healthy alternative to swimming pools with all that lane rage and chlorine. UK-based Swim Trek runs safe, well-organized six-day trips to the Dalmatian coast, where you swim between just a few of the (mostly uninhabited) islands, reefs and islets which make up the Sibenik archipelago and Kornati National Park.

Where you stay You'll be based at Hotel Maestral (www.hotelmaestral.com) on Prvic Luka, a charming, laid-back island which sees just a few Croatian and Italian tourists. The three-star hotel is small with limited lounging areas, but it has exposed stone walls and clean white rooms, and looks out over the pretty harbour and island square. The outdoor restaurant is open to outside guests and can get noisy, so if you are a light sleeper, ask for a room at the back.

What you do You are taken to a different stretch of water each day by local boatman Jadran and your two professional Swim Trek guides. Smeared with Vaseline to prevent chafing, you then swim through lovely deep blue open water, sometimes along the coast, sometimes between bays, and once along a river, covering around 4 km a day, usually swimming for about two hours at a time. A safety boat is with you all the time, slower swimmers go first so that everybody keeps together, and flippers are available for those that want them. The guides will video your strokes during the week and give you some useful tips – everybody finds they improve by the end of the week. Downtime is spent lounging on the boat, reading, playing in the water or walking across some of the islands on which you land.

What you eat and drink A basic breakfast of fruits, breads, jams and cheese is included – non-wheat eaters will want to bring their own supplies. Lunch is usually tasty salads and pulses made by the guides and eaten on the boat, and dinner is eaten out and paid for separately. There are only a few restaurants on the island, most with lovely sea views and serving similar fare, including great ice cream. The fish is surprisingly pricey, but good. One night you eat out in the buzzy town of Sibenik.

Who goes A real mix, men as much as women, in their twenties to fifties, from teachers to city boys. Most people swim regularly, often as part of a club, and are reasonably or very fit, but if you're less experienced you'll find the group supportive and encouraging. Come if you enjoy swimming and a challenge.

Essentials Swim Trek (T+44 (0)20-8696 6220, www.swimtrek.com) costs from €910 per person per week. Before you come, you should be able to swim comfortably for an hour without stopping, and Swim Trek will give you an easy-to-follow training plan when you book. The price includes breakfast, lunch and accommodation, and the trip takes a maximum of 14 people. Fly to Split, take a taxi to the harbour and then a ferry. Swim Trek also runs trips to the Hellespont in Turkey, the Greek Cyclades islands, the Bavarian lakes in Germany, Malta, Australia, New Zealand and various locations in the UK.

> 66 99
>
> I adore swimming – not to swim fast, but to lose myself in the motion and the water. This holiday was still a challenge, but if at times I didn't quite want to face all that blank wet space, I always emerged later feeling light and liberated, with a smug grin on my face. Seeing dolphins dance with the boat midweek was a wonderful highlight, the group was laid back and supportive, and my boyfriend loved it as much as I did. By the end of the week, our bodies and hearts were singing.
>
> *Caroline*

SWIM TREK

Fitness in Malta

Inhabited even before Stonehenge and the Pyramids were constructed, the pretty island of Malta and its little sister Gozo offer a healing Mediterranean climate and mild winters, and there are places to escape the tourist crowds.

First off, liberate yourself from land and go swimming between Malta, Gozo and the tiny island of Comino on a **Swim Trek holiday** (T+44 (0)20-8696 6220, www.swimtrek.com, from €910 per week), which combines lovely long swims with walking and downtime based at Mellieha Bay and St Paul's Bay on the quieter, northern side of Malta.

Alternatively, get fit or lose weight safely with down-to-earth personal trainer and life coach Michele Hart, who runs six holistic weight management weeks and two fitness weeks each year at the **Fortina Spa Resort**, in Sliema (T+44 (0)7956-314093, www.fitspirit.co.uk) from €990 per week. It's a huge hotel with four- and five-star sections and no fewer than eight restaurants, but the facilities are mighty impressive and it's in a superb setting on the waterfront facing the UNESCO World Heritage town of Valletta. Michele's holistic weight management courses use NLP, life coaching and relaxation sessions and focus on

nutrition as well as health and fitness. The fitness weeks combine hard-core exercise with downtime and can be as easy or as gruelling as you want. If it's a rest you need, just come with a friend or partner and book into one of the 32 spa bedrooms here, from €224 per person per night (T+356 (21)23-460000, www.hotelfortina.com). Personal therapists and chefs are available to give treatments or prepare meals in your room, and you can enjoy your own balcony (ask for one with a seawater plunge pool). The rooms are filled to bursting with equipment to make you feel good, including a therapeutic bath (choose from seaweed, salts or essential oils), a high-pressure massage shower which doubles as a steam sauna, and a Dermalife machine, which combines steam therapy and vibrating massage for the good of your skin. If you venture out, there are four interlinked spas offering a staggering array of treatments from a 'Cleopatra Bath' to colonic irrigation to a course of Chinese medicine with visiting professor Dr Minrong Kang.

The smaller neighbouring island of Gozo, a 30-minute ferry ride from the north of Malta, is a great location for a long weekend and a quieter, more serene place to stay. Check into the five-star **Kempinski San Lawrenz** (T+356 (21)22-110000, www.kempinski-gozo.com), from €290 per room per night, which, as well as a spa offering marine facial and body treatments, houses a world-renowned ayurveda centre led by Dr Vijayakumar, who studied in Kerala and has been treating patients for over 16 years. He'll tailor a package to suit you, and you can enjoy an ayurvedic menu in the restaurant, as well as beginner's yoga and pilates. See page 210 for more information on ayurveda.

Left: Indian therapist performing chavutti thirumal at the Kempinski San Lawrenz.
Above: Michele Hart fitness class at the Fortina Spa Resort.

Southern Europe Malta

Greece

Gaia Visions

Vassilikos, Zakynthos
T+44 (0)20-8401 8319
www.gaiavisions.co.uk
From €580 per person per week

Gaia Visions is a restorative retreat set in a small enclave of villas on the peninsula of Vassilikos, which is graced with stunning beaches and virgin forest in the south of the island of Zakynthos. It was founded by Frances Englehardt, a respected NLP practitioner (see glossary) and life coach who changed her life when she was diagnosed with ME following a career in management training. Frances is also a trained sivananda and scarevelli yoga teacher, a reiki master and holistic therapist, and has sent many a person home feeling nurtured and full of positivity.

Come for the week and enjoy daily yoga with two meditation classes, one given at dawn on the beach followed by a morning swim. A basic week's package also includes reiki healing or a head and shoulder massage, but you can add to that whatever you like, Thai and Swedish massage or aromatherapy. You could also do a course in reiki, or receive one-to-one life coaching with Frances, who uses NLP to transform the way you think of yourself and help move your life forward.

There are mountain bikes you can use, and an optional sailing trip. A few visiting teachers take week-long holidays – programmes vary annually but may include dance and writing or different types of yoga, including kundalini, and raw food retreats with Julie Cuddihy (www.anaharta.com), who has an easy-to-understand teaching style for this challenging form.

The retreat takes just eight guests at any one time and you sleep in a traditional stone villa set amid olive groves with a sea view. As well as bedrooms with exposed stone walls, there's a fully equipped kitchen, living

'Holistic' comes from the Greek 'holos' meaning 'whole', and Greece boasts some superb holistic retreats: express yourself creatively, practice island yoga or just chill out by the sea.

Fact file

- **Visa:** None required for citizens of EU countries, US, Canada or Australia and New Zealand
- **Country code:** +30
- **Currency:** Euro (€)
- **Time zone:** GMT +2 hours
- **Electricity:** 220v
- **Tourist board:** www.gnto.gr

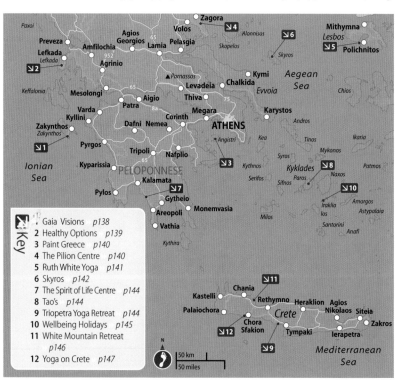

50 km
50 miles

room, veranda areas and two bathrooms. Book early if you want a room to yourself, and be prepared to pay a single supplement. Bikes are available, as well as easy-to-follow maps of good island walks. Visiting teachers occasionally bring their own groups, which others can sometimes join.

A simple breakfast of fruit, muesli, Greek yoghurt and breads is provided, plus two evening meals during the week – one after a vegetarian cooking lesson with Frances' Greek assistant Daniella, the other at an atmospheric local restaurant where musicians play Zakynthian music. For other meals, guests can either eat out in the many restaurants on the beach or in the village, or buy food in the village and prepare it in the kitchen.

Gaia sees a mainly British and northern European crowd with the occasional American, and a huge age range, from people in their mid-twenties to mid-sixties. People come alone or bring a friend or partner; some have never done yoga or meditation before, others are yoga teachers on holiday. Frances tailors her classes to suit all levels of experience and ensure everyone makes progress.

Bring cash with you, as there is no ATM in the village and the nearest is in Agassi, a 15-minute bus or taxi ride away. You fly to Zante from Athens, from where transfers are included if you arrive between 0800 and 1830, otherwise it's a €22 taxi ride one way. The Mediterranean weather is lovely from May to early October, with the hottest and busiest months in July and August. Frances intends to move venue in 2008, to continue with her retreats in a larger space.

GAIA VISIONS

Villa, Gaia Visions

YOGA & ACTIVITY HOLIDAY

Healthy Options

Lefkas
T+44 (0)1920-484515
www.healthy-option.co.uk
From €559 per person per week

Healthy Options holidays are based in the water sports mecca of Vassiliki on the Ionian island of Lefkas. With so many varied activities on offer, this is a holiday you can easily tailor to be as busy or relaxing as you want, and it's a great opportunity to enjoy a full, rejuvenating package of exercise, pampering, fresh air and a taste of adventure.

The Healthy Options programme includes five 90-minute hatha yoga classes, normally held in the evening. This may be followed by a visualization-based meditation session. The price also covers one 30-minute massage, a herbal walk with the entertaining Brigitte, a herbalist and phytotherapist, a boat trip to spot dolphins, a sailing taster session on a catamaran and two guided cycling tours through the flat and scenic countryside. Additional workshops are available most weeks and start at €63. These include nutritional consultations, reiki, an introduction to yoga teaching and seven-day exercise packages with aqua aerobics in the sea and a fitness test.

Guests stay in two adjacent pensions with pleasant, simply furnished, en suite rooms. Ground floor accommodation is cheaper but doesn't have air conditioning or the views afforded by the first floor. Melas pension is the prettier and more expensive of the two, but both are surrounded by beautiful landscaped gardens. Rooms are cleaned six days a week, but bedding and towels are replaced weekly so sand and salt from the beach will linger unless you pay extra for a midweek change.

Of the two bar-restaurants at the resort, the poolside one is the healthier option with soups, salads and delicious smoothies. Breakfast is a mixed buffet of hot and cold food. Barbecue and curry nights are hosted

---

Healthy stopovers in Athens

If you're just staying a night before catching a flight to an island and want to save the hassle of the 45-minute bus ride into Athens, your only option is the **Sofitel** (T+30 210-354 4000, www.sofitel.com), from €267 per room per night. It's just across the road from the airport, has friendly staff, a small pool on its ninth floor, a sauna (ask in advance for it to be switched on), a gym, and a salon for beauty treatments and massages. In the city centre, try the **Fresh Hotel** (T+30 210-524 8511, freshhotel.gr), a surprisingly affordable design hotel (from €130 per room per night) in the buzzy night-time district of Psirri. It has a sauna, gym, small open-air rooftop pool, and massages, beauty treatments and one-to-one personal training and yoga sessions can be arranged in advance. If you've more than a night to kill, head for **The Athens Yoga Retreat** (see Triopetra entry, page 144).

on a weekly basis, but if loud music and drunken revelry don't appeal, escape into Vassiliki for the catch of the day or drive to **Maria's restaurant** for some of the best Greek food around; organic and from her own garden.

Although quite a few single women stay here, Healthy Options is also popular with couples. The atmosphere is friendly, with

JOE CONSTABLE, HEALTHY OPTIONS

Healthy Options holiday includes a taster session on a catamaran.

sailing types and yoga fans gathering in the evenings for food on site or in town. Most are British, mainly between 30 and 55, and staying for a week.

Single supplements start at €63. Fly to Prevesa airport as part of a package from the UK with Islands in the Sun or travel to Athens and take an internal flight with Olympic Airways. Transfers can be arranged in advance.

CREATIVE RETREAT

Paint Greece

☀ ⊠3

Angistri
T+44 (0)1424-712968
www.paintgreece.com
From €665 per week

Paint Greece runs three art and yoga holidays a year based on the island of Angistri, an hour's ferry ride from Athens. You stay in a small family-run hotel overlooking the Aegean Sea, with a lovely terrace on which you can paint. Workshops are complemented by optional yoga classes twice a day and downtime.

Led by UK-based artist and teacher, Sandy Adey, the main aim of the holiday is to help you interpret the landscape around you in your own way. It's open to anyone with an interest in painting and art, including beginners, and is designed for you to go at your own pace.

There's a gentle morning yoga class, and an evening session focused on relaxation. The price includes accommodation, tuition, breakfast and dinner. Bring your own materials. Fly to Athens, take the bus to the port of Piraeus, then a ferry or catamaran to Angistri or Aegina.

FOREST RETREAT

The Pilion Centre

🌿 🍃 ⚠ ☀ 🐴 ◉ ✴ ⊠4

Anilio, near Volos
T+30 24-2603 2173 (May-Oct)
www.pilion.org
From €230 per person per week full board

View from the hotel terrace on Angistri.

Set in forest on the side of a mountain above the Aegean Sea, The Pilion Centre is incredibly good value and offers the chance for some relaxed time away from everyday life in a friendly, chilled-out community. It's set in three acres of cherry, fig and walnut trees, grape vines, wild flowers and herbs, on the coast of the Pilion peninsula, northeast of Athens.

The centre is staffed mainly by volunteers, and as a guest you help out with tasks such as chopping vegetables, gardening or washing up. This is easy, light work and helps foster a spirit of community.

You sleep in basic but bright and clean rooms, dressed with vases of flowers and attractive white stones. Be prepared to share one of seven bedrooms. To be alone, opt for

Yoga on the beach, The Pilion Centre.

one of their roomy tents pitched under the cherry trees – or bring your own tent – and there's a friendly local pension minutes away along a donkey track (€200 extra). There are four hot showers to share indoors, and a shower block outside for campers. The grounds of the centre are on three levels and include a circular meeting house, a yurt for massage, reflexology and other treatments, a lovely dance floor open on all sides to the trees and wild flowers, and a cabin in the woods.

Most people come here to attend a workshop week (from €420 full board) led by visiting teachers, which include dance, creative writing, singing, painting, NVC (non violent communication) as well as pilates, massage and reflexology. You can also stay for a 'home from home' week (€320 full board) to relax, read, paint, write, take photographs, experience some treatments and connect with people. The whole region is criss-crossed by ancient donkey tracks, and it's a 45-minute saunter to the nearest beach. Each day starts with an optional 'Awareness Circle', which many people unexpectedly find to be one of the most positive experiences of their stay.

Basic, tasty, local vegetarian food is served for a buffet breakfast, lunch and hot evening meal – fruit from their own trees is used to

❝❞
I was a little nervous about the communal aspect of the Pilion Centre, but I needn't have worried. It felt really good to share the easy work with the staff, who foster an atmosphere of warmth, openness, acceptance and authenticity. I left feeling rested, healthy and renewed.

Mike Aidallbery

make pies and jams. Special diets can be catered for, you can have your lunch in a picnic box for the beach and you can bring your own wine to drink at meal times. The local water is from mountain springs fed by Mount Pilion snow-melt, and is safe to drink.

Fellow guests will be a real mix of different ages, backgrounds and life stages. Most are from the UK, some from the rest of Europe (including Eastern Europe), Australia and the US. Many come alone for the workshops, and stay two weeks. The centre is open from May to October, and closed in August. The nearest airport is Volos, from where it's a scenic 40-km drive. You can also fly to Skiathos, Thessaloniki or Athens – transfers can be arranged in advance.

YOGA HOLIDAY

Ruth White Yoga

⚐ ⇘5

Lesbos
T +44 (0)20-8641 7770
www.ruthwhiteyoga.com
From €760 per person per week all inclusive

Expert yoga teacher Ruth White runs annual yoga holidays from mid-May to June aimed at all levels of ability, from teachers in training to beginners. You'll stay on the island of Lesbos at the idyllic **Milelja**, a guesthouse and retreat centre beautifully run by a German Buddhist monk and his wife. Surrounded by flower-adorned hills scattered with castle ruins, monuments and traditional Greek houses, near the ancient village of Molyvos, it's a calm and quiet place to enjoy warm sunshine and dedicated yoga teaching.

Ruth trained with BKS Iyengar himself in Pune, in India and has been teaching since she was in her teens. Classes are split to accommodate all levels, and the day starts with stretching and pranayama, followed by a short break before the main morning iyengar-based class. In the cool of early evening there's an ashtanga class. Sessions take place in an octagonal glass-sided practice room framed by fragrant wood – it's feng shui-ed into a rock basin with 360° views of the garden, the sea, the hot springs and the hills.

Local sounds add to the atmosphere – owls hooting at night, waves breaking on the beach, goat bells and the local farmer singing as he milks his sheep. During the day you can hike, cycle, soak in the nearby natural hot springs, swim in the pool or hang out by the beach, an eight-minute walk away. You can also use the larger pool in the nearby

☻ Soul food

The international environmental charity **Earthwatch** (T+44 (0)1865-318831, www.earthwatch.org) runs regular nine-day trips to Greece between May and September, when you can follow Greece's bottlenose dolphins and help marine biologists understand and protect them. The trip takes place on the Amvrakikos Gulf, where the 150 dolphins who live here face increasing environmental pressure from fishing and pollution. Following dolphins and recording and inputting data, your days will start early, but you will have the traditional siesta each afternoon to rest, or enjoy the small village of Vonitsa and the Greek coast. The trip costs from €1275.

Delphinia hotel, where people with families wanting to attend the holiday sometimes prefer to stay – ask Ruth for details. Thai massage is also available.

A healthy vegetarian brunch is included (you can be wheat- and dairy-free if you want). Everyone eats out in the evenings, usually at a seafront taverna serving great local fish and local wines of varying quality. Fly to Mytilene (there are flights from Athens and direct flights from the UK) or take the overnight ferry from Athens and wake up in the port. Pick ups can be arranged in advance (€14 per person each way).

A group at The Pilion Centre.

Yoga room at Milelja, base for Ruth White holidays.

Southern Europe Greece

Wellbeing holiday

Skyros

Skyros, an island in the northern Sporades, is the most talked about holistic holiday destination in Europe since it was founded in 1979. It offers a multi-layered experience which, at its most gentle, means relaxation, socializing and great food, and, at its most profound, the confidence and insight to change your life. You can stay at the Skyros Centre, in the main town, or by the sea and surrounded by pine forests, at Atsitsa.

Where you stay Accommodation at the Skyros Centre is either with local landlords in the town, or around the centre itself in modern en suite rooms or apartments which offer peace, quiet and air conditioning. Generally, two people share each simply furnished, generously sized room. A mezzanine level creates a great sense of space, with one bed upstairs. If you are staying in town, you will be in a room in, or attached to, one of the traditional houses overlooking the busy streets. It's a less polished, more authentic slice of Greek island life. Sharing a room is part of the Skyros experience, but a single supplement will buy you more privacy.

Atsitsa is bigger, accommodating around 90 people – as opposed to the Centre's 40 – and has a bohemian feel. Accommodation is in the spacious stone villa, with up to five per room, or in very small, rustic, two-person bamboo cabins. It is more basic than anything at the Centre, but staying here is about getting back to nature, with showers open to the sky and meals eaten outside (if it rains heavily, those in the cabins will get a little damp). Single cabins are bookable in advance, or you can upgrade to rooms at the Atsitsa Taverna, purpose-built accommodation with 20 en suite rooms with balconies – it's not owned by Skyros, so you'll need to pay €30 a night extra.

What you do The courses on offer are many and varied, working around the themes of creativity, healing, psychology, spirituality, music and dance, treatments, yoga and meditation. They include personal development groups, qigong, pilates, creative writing, film-making, art, massage and singing. There are plenty of opportunities to learn new skills, have fun and 'find yourself' or rediscover what really makes you tick.

Skyros holidays are run in two-week blocks, but course changeovers happen after the first week to allow people to try as many activities as they want. The calibre of facilitators is high, including leaders in their fields and recognized names such as Sue Townsend and Steven Birkoff. Your experience will depend on the course, the teacher and the group: come with an open mind.

Atsitsa puts greater emphasis on physical activities – such as sailing, windsurfing and different kinds of yoga – suited to anyone who wants to embrace an active, healthier lifestyle, while those staying at the centre focus on creative courses and in-depth personal development. This can be an emotional road and a profoundly powerful experience as they discover what it is to 'let go'.

The day begins with yoga or qigong, then, after breakfast, there is an hour for *demos* (Greek for people's assembly, from which the word democracy comes), when the facilitators outline the day's itinerary and guests can offer feedback and comments. At 1030, the morning courses begin and continue for three hours. Afternoons are free for relaxing on the beach, having a massage or reiki treatment, going on a boat trip, exploring the island on foot, or simply doing nothing. To bring the day to a close, there are movement and meditation-based courses which begin at 1830.

Evenings are free for meals in town or a trip to the cheesy disco for the sort of dancing you only ever do on holiday. Alternatively, moonlit walks, midnight skinny-dipping or staying up to watch the sun rise with new friends rate high on the agenda. There is also an end-of-holiday cabaret during which volunteers can show off their new skills. The chance to see pale, tired, shy individuals transformed before your eyes with new-found confidence is a wonderful experience.

What you eat and drink The food is all freshly prepared vegetarian fare and there's plenty of it. Special diets can be catered for, with advance warning. There is a focus on health and vitality, as well as locally sourced produce. For those staying at the Skyros Centre, generous breakfast and lunch buffets are provided; the evening meal is taken wherever you want – in the town or along the beach – and there are plenty of great restaurants from which to choose. In the more remote Atsitsa, guests have all meals on site and are treated to the same exceptional cooking. There is also a café-bar.

Who goes Most people come to Skyros alone; the majority at the Centre are female. Atsitsa is more family-orientated and welcomes young children. Overall, the age range is younger there and due to the outdoor, sporty activities on offer, it attracts more men. Although all ages are welcome, most people are in their mid-thirties and upwards, but age becomes rather immaterial – it's often the oldest who are the most adventurous and young at heart.

Guests come from different backgrounds and are looking for different things from the experience. Some are here just to enjoy the location, others want to get creative and quite a few are looking to push boundaries in their personal development. Many are embracing new-found spirituality in their lives, others are at a crossroads and need something to nudge them in the right direction.

Essentials A week on Skyros (T+44 (0)20-7267 4424, www.skyros.co.uk) costs from €665 per person for one week half board, excluding flights and transfers. Although people do book for one week only, particularly if they're not sure they're going to enjoy the experience, 99% go for the two-week stint (and are glad they did). You can opt for a transfer, which is organized by Skyros and provides a

> **❝ ❞**
> Before I went, people said to me "Things happen on Skyros". I felt that you couldn't go somewhere with that kind of expectation, but emotionally and spiritually, the impact of the holiday was enormous. It was inspiring. Surprising. More than I could have expected. Against the odds - namely my own cynicism, doubts and reserve - I gained an insight into me and the way I want to live my life. Back in the real world, this sort of thing gets lost all too easily under everyday stresses and other people's expectations, but having had that clarity once, I knew I could have it again: I knew I had it in me. What you give to the holiday, you get out. It's as simple as that, so pour your heart into it.
>
> *Olivia Mackinder*

chance to start getting to know people. This costs €160 and includes the seven-hour coach and ferry to and from the island, and one night in the **Dorian Inn**, an average hotel in the centre of Athens with a rooftop bar and views. Alternatively, arrange to stay somewhere else and just take the coach and ferry part of the transfer, or book a domestic flight from Athens to Skyros (twice a week with Olympic Airlines). Skyros also runs holidays in Cambodia in January and February (see page 286), and in Cuba (see page 370).

SKYROS

SKYROS

Opposite page far left: Atsitsa House. **Left centre:** Writer's workshop.
This page left: Accommodation on Skyros. **Above:** Boat excursion.

COASTAL RETREAT

The Spirit of Life Centre

Agios Nikolaos, Messinia
T+30 272-107 8240
www.thespiritoflife.co.uk
From €545 per person per week

Set between the Taygetos mountains and the Mediterranean, Spirit of Life runs yoga, healing and detox retreats, or you can just stay for some downtime. The area has a temple dedicated to Asclepius (the god of healing), and it feels a very restorative place to be. As it's set high above the little fishing village of Agios Nikolaos, it's very peaceful, yet easy enough to walk to the bars and restaurants in nearby Stoupa.

You stay in comfortable rooms in the main house, or there are two twin self-contained apartments. There's also a quiet room with a library of books on personal and spiritual development, a large shaded pergola, and a fragrant garden full of crickets, butterflies and bees. Yoga and meditation are taught in a lovely studio with oak flooring, French windows opening on to the terrace and 360° views of mountains and sea. The hatha yoga classes are often open to locals, so you feel as if you are part of island life rather than a tourist.

Guests fill in a questionnaire before they visit, from which the director, Kyriacos, tailors everyone's stay to their own needs and interests. The approach is personal, but never intrusive. If you're on a personal retreat, you can enjoy the daily meditation and yoga classes, book some holistic therapies and body treatments – including shiatsu and Thai yoga massage – and spend the rest of the time

Beach and mountains near The Spirit of Life centre.

relaxing, reading or swimming in the many coves and beaches.

Kyriacos used to run a restaurant and has a passion for good healthy cooking. The Mediterranean vegetarian meals are always imaginative and interesting, and use produce from the centre's own garden and the local farmers' market, as well as wild herbs from the surrounding hills, and olives and olive oil from nearby Kalamata.

People come from the UK and Europe to recharge here, some with friends, often alone, and the average age is between 30 and 55, with a 3:1 ratio of women to men. Stay for at least a week: courses run throughout the year but April, May, June, September, October and November are best, when the countryside is green and alive with wild flowers. Fly to Kalamata from Athens, or travel by coach, hire your own car or have a pickup arranged direct from Athens airport (€85).

MEDITATION RETREAT

Tao's

Naoussa, Paros
T+30 228-402 8882
www.taos-greece.com
From €5 per session

Tao's is a meditation and self-development centre on a small hill on Paros with gorgeous sea views. It's the creation of Zen master, Nissim Amon, whose daily Zen stories and twice-weekly Zen life management sessions are a main draw. There's also daily yoga and tai chi, and a whole host of personal development courses.

Through the Zen story sessions and workshops you'll get a good introduction to how to approach life situations with a more balanced attitude; you can also try the Japanese tradition of zazen (or sitting) meditation. Come with an open mind – it's a happy, laid-back efficiently run place with no rules and lots of opportunities to learn.

You stay at various family-run hotels based in surrounding villages, which the centre can arrange on your behalf. **Margarita Studios**

(from €30 per room per night, T+30 228-405 2362, www.margaritastudios.com) in Ambelas is a welcoming place a two-minute walk from the sea with a swimming pool, while **Petres Hotel** is 10 minutes from the centre and has sea views of Naoussa bay (from €70 per room, T+30 228-405 2467, www.petres.gr). Avoid the high summer months if you want a more peaceful island.

Treatments, including Thai massage, shiatsu, rebirthing and reiki, are on offer as well as personal counselling and group therapy. There are verandas and terraces to sit on and enjoy the view over the Aegean Sea. This isn't a place to detox – there's a good Thai/oriental restaurant, bar and internet café on site, and spontaneous jam sessions and parties often take place in the restaurant.

The place attracts a real mix of nationalities and ages, from people on a five-day self-exploratory Walking Through Walls workshop (from €350) to passing tourists and locals. Come between April and December. Fly to Paros via Athens, or get a bus, train or taxi from Athens airport to Piraeus port and then a ferry to Paros. Hiring a car or moped is recommended.

YOGA RETREAT

Triopetra Yoga Retreat

Agios Pavlos, Crete
T+30 694-471 1725
www.astanga.gr
From €750 per person per week

On a small cliff overlooking a long sandy beach and backed by hills and mountains, Triopetra is serene place to learn ashtanga yoga or advance your ashtanga practice. It's in an untouristy pocket of the south of Crete, just next to the bay of Agios Pavlos, and enjoys spectacular sunsets.

Their regular yoga teachers have studied under Sri K Pattabhi Jois in Mysore, and include Greek-born Kristina Karitinos-Ireland, Canadian Mark Darby (director of the Sattva Yoga Shala in Montreal), American

Guy Donahaye (co-director of the Ashtanga Yoga Shala in New York) and London-based Florence Graham and her daughter Sam.

There are two yoga classes a day, a morning practice and an afternoon workshop in the philosophy of yoga or pranayama. The rest of the time you can explore, go caving, walking, or mountain biking nearby, or just laze in a hammock. Massages are on offer, and private yoga sessions can be arranged. Tripetra also runs an artist-in-residence programme, and artists will occasionally lead painting and art workshops in the afternoons.

The delicious vegetarian and vegan meals use locally sourced Mediterranean ingredients perpared by chef and practising ashtangi, Chris Clark. He bases all his cooking on macrobiotic and ayurvedic principles (think steamed vegetables with tahini lemon sauce, burdock and carrot kinpira or tempeh chilli-baked millet). No smoking or alcohol is allowed. Fish and meat dishes are available at local tavernas nearby.

There are 11 large and comfortable double rooms and four single rooms, all with verandas overlooking the sea, en suite showers or bathrooms, and a fridge. You eat in one of two outdoor sheltered dining areas – there's also an indoor space used for creative workshops, with a library, piano and guitars.

The retreat takes no more than 22 guests, mostly Europeans at different levels of yoga ability, some travelling alone, some with friends or family. Sessions run from May to October. From Crete's main airport it's just under a two-hour drive (€80 transfer, or hire a car, which costs on average €30 a day). Don't confuse Triopetra with **Yoga Plus**, a longer- running ashtanga yoga retreat based on Agios Pavlos bay (see www.yogaplus.co.uk).

Triopetra also runs the **Athens Yoga Retreat** (from €800-1100 per week), which opened in late 2006. It has rooms and terraces facing the Acropolis, a large yoga room, and a vegetarian, macrobiotic and raw food restaurant and café-bar on the roof terrace. You stay in comfortable double rooms or a penthouse suite and, as well as yoga, enjoy visits to local archaeological sites and markets, as well as trips to local beaches in the summer.

Kristina Karitinos-Ireland co-directs **Yoga Practice** with fellow ashtanga teacher Michael Anastassiades, and runs summer retreats at Limeni bay, on Mani in the southern Peloponnese (from €550 per person per week). Yoga Practice also runs workshops in London, UK (T+44 (0)207 928 7527, www.yogapractice.net).

LIFE COACHING HOLIDAY

Wellbeing Holidays

◑ ↘10

Iraklia, Small Cyclades
T+44 (0)7747-103502
www.wellbeing-holidays.co.uk
From €525 per person per week

This is an opportunity to cast yourself adrift from everyday life and experience neuro-linguistic programming (NLP) on a tiny Greek island. This system of life coaching, devised in America, can help people understand how their negative thought processes have got in the way of them achieving what they want in life, and offers tools and techniques to help people get 'unstuck' and move forward.

Wellbeing Holidays is the brainchild of Pam Rigden, a master practitioner and trainer of NLP and a member of the International NLP Trainers Association (www.inlpta.co.uk). Pam is dedicated and has helped many a person deal with an issue on her Greek isle. She offers bespoke one-to-one coaching or organized weeks in small groups of no more than eight, exploring how to get the most out of life, stress management, weight management or relationships.

Iraklia is a small, quiet island of whitewashed houses, and a population of only 60. You stay at **Villa Glafkos**, in one of four pleasant blue-and-white painted en suite studio rooms off a small courtyard, in a tiny hamlet just off the island's only road. Foodies beware: there are only a few average restaurants on the island, and you eat out for every meal. Breakfast is included at nearby **Nikolas'** (eggs, white bread,

Triopetra – yoga class.

Villa Glafkos, Wellbeing Holidays.

yoghurt, fruits, nuts and honey), and you buy your own lunch and dinner. Most restaurants serve local fish and meat dishes, Greek salads, and a small selection of vegetables and potatoes. There is a kettle and a fridge in the studio rooms. Those with special dietary requirements should bring their own snacks.

Workshops take place on the roof of Villa Glafkos or on the terrace at Nikolas' – both looking out to sea. Your first day, Sunday, is a day of rest, so workshops start on Monday with one day off later in the week. The schedule is flexible and the pace slow. Something physical is sometimes on offer such as a morning fitness class with Pam's colleague Michele Hart (www.fitspirit.com), who offers an effective mix of yoga, pilates and tai chi to music. Restless souls will want to take themselves off for runs or walks, or for regular swims at the nearby beach. If you're into yoga or pilates, bring your own mat.

The price includes accommodation, breakfast, group workshops and three one-to-one coaching sessions: further sessions are available for €70 per hour. Fly to Athens, then take the ferry to Naxos, or stay a night in Athens and take a flight. Iraklia is a 1½-hour ferry ride from Naxos. The weeks run from March to October, avoiding the busy month of August, and one-to-one coaching available by arrangement off season. Pam also runs wellbeing weekends in Cornwall in the UK during January, February and March. For more information on NLP, see glossary.

VILLAGE RETREAT

White Mountain Retreat

Plaka, Chania, Crete
T +30 282-503 2028
www.whitemountainretreat.com
From €320 per person per week

On the outskirts of the sleepy village of Plaka, in the Chania region of Crete, White Mountain is set in five acres, with olive groves, at the end of a long track. Run by two Brits, Julie and Kate, it's a nourishing place to take much-needed time out.

White Mountain Retreat on Crete.

Each day starts with a gentle get-together, when you'll find out who is doing what and whether there might be a lift into Almyrida, a slightly livelier local town. There's also a blackboard on which you are asked to write where you are going when you go off alone. Flowers are everywhere, inside and out, and there are lots of lovely seats in personal spaces, often with sea views.

The property fully embraces all things alternative – there's a stone circle and a labyrinth in the grounds, and Julie is a reiki practitioner who offers sessions with Bach flower essences, making her own olive flower essence from the surrounding groves. Aromatherapy, crystal healing, homeopathy, hopi ear candling, and shiatsu are all available from local therapists, or you can have a naked in-house massage on a private terrace with lovely sea views, weather permitting.

Come to enjoy a calm, Mediterranean pace and do your own thing, or join one of the organized weeks, which may include yoga, meditation, gardening, creative writing, drumming and dance, cookery or pilates. Work and Play and Willing Hands weeks are also on offer, when you get a reduced rate for helping out around the property. There's a drop-in yoga class once a week (€10), and

Tiziano Calabrese, an Italian with excellent English, gives drop-in classes in the Japanese martial art of aikido.

Activities take place in Eagle, the main house, which has a large living space with sunken floor area and a quiet room for meditation and therapies. You sleep in the second building, Phoenix. Both properties are ongoing projects and feel slightly unfinished, though they provide everything you need. Bedrooms are simple, with colour-washed walls, painted floors and rag rugs; night lights and matches are provided, but bring your own toiletries. Sheets are not always 100% cotton, and you will need to share a bathroom, though these are spacious and clean. A total of 12 guests can sleep in six rooms – Sapphire is the only room without a door to a terrace or patio. You can also bring your own tent, or sleep under the stars.

Guests are mainly British, of all ages, and mostly single travellers. Be warned, you will hear the twice-daily air force training flights overhead, and there are dogs and cats, which may trouble allergy sufferers. Good swimmers can swim in the sea on calm days; there are plans for an eco-pool in late 2007/8. Bring your own towel, and mosquito repellent. Changeover day is Tuesday to suit the arrival time of flights from the UK. Fly from Athens to Chania, from where it's a 45-minute drive – pickups can be arranged in advance, or get a boat to Souda port, which is a 25-minute drive away.

YOGA HOLIDAY

Yoga on Crete

✈ ↘12

Chora Sfakion
T+30 210-801 1529
www.yogaoncrete.gr
From €600 per week

Yoga on Crete is an ideal holiday for beginners or intermediate yoga students who want small classes, one-to-one attention and a private house party atmosphere. It is based at Chora Sfakion, a mellow Cretan fishing village with whitewashed houses tumbling down to the sea, and a harbour clean enough to swim in.

Started in 2006, the holidays run each summer and are led by dance student and dedicated sivananda yoga teacher, Eugenia Sivitou. You stay at Eugenia's 200-year-old spacious parental summer home, which enjoys lovely coastal views on the unpopulated south side of the island. Eugenia's mother does the cooking, and her partner Marcus assists her classes.

You'll be far away from other tourists, though there's sometimes noise from a nightclub in town. No alcohol or smoking is allowed, but the atmosphere is relaxed. Ask for a room with a roof terrace if you want some space. A single room costs €200 extra and won't be in the main house. Fly to Chania, from where pickups can be arranged.

Yoga on Crete.

Cyprus for the stressed

Cyprus's most exclusive resorts offer respectable rejuvenating breaks outside the main tourist season, when the island still enjoys plenty of sunshine and the sea's still warm enough to swim in. Particularly good for stressed parents who need to bring the kids, they entail far more than a lie-in with a facial.

UK-based wellbeing company **Yogoloji** (T+44 (0)20-7730 7473, www.yogoloji.com, see page 49) run annual family yoga retreats in February and November at **Anassa** (T+357 26-888000, www.thanoshotels.com), a hang-out for the rich and famous on Asprokemnos beach, backed by mountains and pine forest (from €202 per room per night). Run by a relaxed and hands-on team, the Yogoloji retreats include daily classes for children and adults and a choice of holistic treatments, from €3528 for a couple for four nights.

Anassa also boasts a Thalassa Spa offering holistic and therapeutic consultations, acupuncture, a healthy eating menu and treatments using 100% natural products from London-based The Organic Pharmacy. Four- and 10-day detoxifying programmes are available, including an annual retreat led by Margo Marrone, founder of The Organic Pharmacy. For great sea views, stay in the garden studio suites, set in small white buildings among the bougainvillea-filled gardens. Fly to Paphos, 40 minutes away, or Larnaca, two hours.

Alternatively, head for the huge but tastefully built **Aphrodite Hills Resort** (T+357 26-829000, www.aphroditehills.com), set 15 minutes from the secluded Avdimou beach near Paphos, with an 18-hole golf course, from €270 per room per night. It offers regular five-day packages for stress relief and detoxing, based at its rather lovely spa, The Retreat. These include a mix of hammams, facials, scrubs and massages, a fitness programme, and meals from the Plaisir Santé menu (from €1055 for treatments, meals and classes). Reiki, aromatherapy and reflexology are also on offer, and treatments use the full range of Pevonia Botanica, which have very high levels of active plant ingredients (also used by the Monart in Ireland, see page 58). There are twice-weekly yoga sessions given by Christina Vassiliadou, a qualified physiologist and yoga teacher who trained in England and America. Yoga weeks are planned from 2007. For peace, rent a villa with a pool. Fly to Paphos, 15 minutes away, or Larnaca, 1¼ hours away.

Anassa.

Aphrodite Hills – on the daybed.

Southern Europe Cyprus

DETOX RETREAT

Detox weeks with Jason Vale

Montenegro, Göcek
T+44 (0)845-130 2829
www.thejuicemaster.com
From €1300 per person, excluding flights

'Juicemaster' Jason Vale offers detox weeks at the Montenegro four or five times a year. Set in the remote Taurus Mountains with fresh clean air, the Montenegro is an exclusive property with only six main rooms, five of which have spectacular mountain and woodland views. There's a small dedicated spa room for massages and facials, a pool, purpose-built yoga platform and small sauna.

Led by Jason, a charismatic and passionate advocate of juicing and healthy living, or by a member of his staff, the week will include

Montenegro Hotel.

yoga, tai chi, meditation and lymphatic breathing classes, and a diet of juices and supplements, as well as life coaching, addiction counselling and massage. Courses take a maximum of 18 people during the spring and autumn. Jason also runs retreats in Bordubet, in southern Turkey.

Retreat to an east-meets-west culture and a breathtaking coastline, with everything from life coaching on a gulet to beach and mountain yoga.

Fact file

- **Visa:** UK citizens require visas, but other EU passport-holders do not; see www.disisleri.gov.tr or check with the Turkish consulate. US, Canadian and Australian citizens need visas, obtainable on arrival, for stays of up to 90 days
- **Country code:** +90
- **Currency:** Euro (€)
- **Time zone:** GMT +2 hours
- **Electricity:** 230v
- **Tourist board:** www.tourismturkey.org/

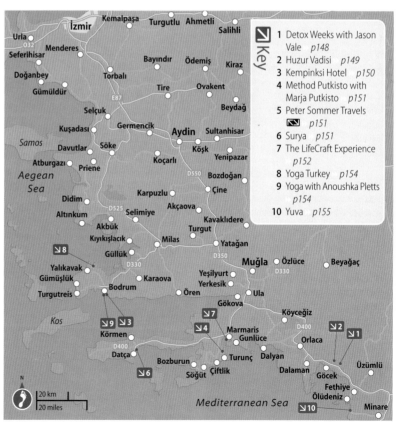

Key

1. Detox Weeks with Jason Vale *p148*
2. Huzur Vadisi *p149*
3. Kempinksi Hotel *p150*
4. Method Putkisto with Marja Putkisto *p151*
5. Peter Sommer Travels *p151*
6. Surya *p151*
7. The LifeCraft Experience *p152*
8. Yoga Turkey *p154*
9. Yoga with Anoushka Pletts *p154*
10. Yuva *p155*

Valley retreat

Huzur Vadisi 🛫 ☀ 🏄 ↘2

Huzur Vadisi means 'Peaceful Valley' in Turkish, and that's what it is; an entire valley has been specifically landscaped over 15 years to provide a true retreat environment amongst the whispering pine forests that flank the Turquoise Coast. Virtually the whole week is spent outdoors, in a perfect balance of rustic simplicity and comfort, sociability and space.

Where you stay Accommodation is in very civilized yurts spaced out across the valley. They have hardwood floors, high domed ceilings, electric lights and fans, with none of the drawbacks of a tent. Most are shared, or pay extra to be alone. You eat at a long friendly table on the terrace, swim in a stone-built pool, and lounge at night on a *kösk* – a kilim-carpeted giant tree house. You wash in screened outdoor showers which have quirky Ottoman tiles and hand-cast taps. Everything is functional but the artistic detail makes the difference.

What you do Various yoga teachers run weekly retreats here from May to October. They include the likes of Simon Low, Tuesday McNeill (T+44 (0)20-8898 0978) and bikram yoga teacher, Michele Pernetta

❝❞

Founder of London's smart Triyoga centre, Simon Low (www.simonlow.com), is a yoga Name, with 15 years teaching experience. He has a following, and I brace myself for guru-esque arrogance, but Simon's near-shyness and depth of teaching catch me unawares. He teaches hatha yoga, both dynamic and restorative, using slow, soft language, such as "cascade your body down… allow limbs to soften…". He's often lyrical, sometimes wry. It's not stressing musclework and, on the first few days, I find the pace so soporific that I am half-dreaming while following instructions into deep twists. The best part is the evening 'yin' yoga, inspired by Paul Grilley. Supported on bolsters we sink into postures for 10 or 15 minutes. As our muscles yield (or protest) ever further, Simon speaks to us, weaving Sufism and Buddhism amongst classical yoga concepts to challenge our minds. I ask where defensive tightness in my thighs comes from emotionally and I encounter – in spiritual terms - my 'flee' reactions at the first sign of pain. But patient endurance leads to floaty, out-of-body bliss, and I sleep like a baby every night. Thanks to Simon, I end my week with my emotions as well as my muscles opened up.

Rosie Walford

(T+44 (0)20-7692 6900). Generally you do yoga twice a day, with time off between. The week includes a glorious day out sailing along the sparkling Lycian coast, dropping anchor to swim in clear seas and eat fresh fish. You can also come here for certain weeks during May and September to simply chill out and relax.

What you eat and drink Every meal is a generous buffet of Turkish goodness – a big variety of vegetables, pulses, nuts and yoghurt-based dishes, all extremely freshly made. There's a small self-service bar which operates on trust.

Who goes A mixture of students dedicated to the particular yoga teacher, and others who have chosen Huzur for the place. Mostly women, mostly British, in their thirties and forties; the crowd reflects the style of yoga and personality of the teacher who's there that week. Talkative British owner, Ian, who created this retreat with his bare hands after years of interesting eco-projects in Sikkim and Ladakh, acts as your entertainer and host.

Essentials Huzur Vadisi (T+90 (0)252-644 0008, www.huzurvadisi.com) costs from €490 per person per week, and most yoga weeks cost €850 per person. Stay in one of the yurts rather than a room. Göcek marina, over the hill, is good for quality shopping and eating. Fly to Dalaman, from where minibus transfers (€20 per person) or taxis (€40 for 4 people) can be arranged. Change taxi at Göcek as airport drivers don't know their way. It's very hot in August.

Kempinski Hotel

🌐 🏠 👤 ⚙ 💠 ❂ ≥3

Barbaros Bay, Bodrum
T+90 (0)252-311 0303
www.kempinski-bodrum.com
From €400 per room per night

Set in an idyllic private bay overlooking the sea, with a peaceful ambience and spacious rooms, the Kempinksi Hotel and its Six Senses spa is a great location for a relaxing and indulgent break. Special offers are available year-round.

Just 30 minutes from Bodrum airport but far away from the noise of the town, this luxurious hotel has an infinity pool overlooking the bay, a private beach and a multitude of comfortable lounging areas. The Six Senses spa is the largest in Turkey: the 16 treatment areas include three pools, a dedicated watsu pool, a jacuzzi with uninterrupted views of the coast and three beautifully designed hammams (see box on page 154) where you can indulge in luxurious versions of the traditional scrub and massage. Other treatments on offer include reiki, hopi ear candling and reflexology as well as Thai and hot-stone massage. Small group classes in yoga, pilates and tai chi are often on offer, or you can arrange for one-to-one sessions. The best time of year for a wellness break is between mid-September and May, when the weather is still pleasant but not hot. Three- to five-day detox programmes are available, or the hotel will customize a programme to meet your needs. Fly to Bodrum.

"If a stone can change its shape, then so can you." Marja Putkisto's words gave me a great deal of hope, when I'd given up on improving the poor posture which had caused me backache for years and cost me a fortune in massages. I was at the lovely Dionysos Hotel with 16 other women, and while we all expected to stretch, I don't think any of us realized we would be going back to school. Marja and her assistants used photos, diagrams and demonstrations to show us in detail how our bodies are constructed and how we've been misusing them, so we could set about changing the habits of a lifetime. It seemed an awful lot of hard work, but looking at the fabulous postures of Marja and her two assistants, I felt inspired.

The first class was challenging, physically and mentally. I struggled with the quantity of information and the visualization exercises, but Marja's assistants were on hand to help us find the correct positions for the movements and stretches. Marja uses stretches from yoga and pilates, but they felt very different because of the detail that Marja goes into. Working with each other also helped, and was a great way to bond with the rest of the group.

After one particular stretch, I felt myself lift up like a puppet that has had all its strings pulled taut. And after my first class, I felt lighter and more aligned, and thought how wonderful it would be to feel like that all the time. Alas, by the time we had dinner, my body had returned to 'normal'. The idea is that with regular method putkisto work, it will eventually find a new, healthier position. A few months on, the course has brought about a physical awareness that I've never experienced before. I can also now isolate muscles that I didn't know existed, and I believe I am already standing straighter and taller. It's going to take a lot of work, but I'm hopeful that if I followed the 30-day programme book – free with the course – I would see some lasting change.

Ruth Rosselson

Above: Kempinski Hotel. **Right:** Method Putkisto.

Method Putkisto with Marja Putkisto

Dionysos Hotel, Kumlubuk
T+ 44 (0)20-8605 3500
www.exclusiveescapes.co.uk
From €1500 for 7 nights

Exclusive Escapes organizes three week-long method putkisto holidays a year at the **Dionysos Hotel**, a lovely complex of cottages and rooms set on top of a canyon overlooking the bay of Kumlubuk. Classes are taught by founder Marja Putkisto (www.methodputkisto.com), a dance and movement teacher who developed the method to correct a lifelong hip problem . A blend of yoga and pilates, it combines deep-breathing and stretching routines which can help realign muscles and reshape the body.

There are two two-hour classes a day, in the morning and evening, which take place outside on a specially constructed platform next to the tennis courts, with a view of the beach and valley below. There's also ample time to enjoy the venue's gardens, socialize with your fellow guests, swim in the 25-m infinity pool, indulge in a treatment at the small Clarins spa, or chill on the Dionysos' stretch of private beach. There's also an air-conditioned gym.

The holiday takes a maximum of 16 guests, attracts mainly women from the UK travelling alone, and of all ages, fitness levels and professions – beginners are welcome. General tourists may well be staying at the hotel as well as method putkisto guests. The holidays run in May, June and October, and the price includes half board, lessons, flights, transfers and a luxury gulet cruise. Fly to Dalaman airport, a two-hour drive away. Method Putkisto also runs courses in the UK and Nordic walking trips in Finland.

Peter Sommer Travels

Turquoise Coast
T+44 (0)1600-861929
www.petersommer.com
From €2895 per person for 2 weeks

If you fancy organizing your own group, specialist tour operator Peter Sommer Travels can arrange for his archaeological and cultural trips to include walking and yoga for parties of up to 16. You'll cruise beautiful stretches of the Turquoise Coast aboard a luxury 8-cabin gulet, stopping off at different sites along the way.

The undeveloped pine-clad coastline makes for a trekkers' paradise, particularly along Turkey's first national long-distance footpath, the Lycian Way, and the fresh salty air, lovely light, and peace aboard a gulet at sea are a natural setting for yoga. There's also fine food and superb swimming.

The price includes full board, transfers, accommodation and entrance fees to sites, but excludes flights.

PETER SOMMER

Cruise the Turquoise Coast aboard one of Peter Sommer's luxury gulets.

Surya

Datça
T+90 (0)252-712 2287
www.yogaturkey.com
From €660 for a yoga week; from €45 per person per night

Set in the sleepy, cobbled village of Datça Eski (old Datça), Surya was an abandoned old olive mill before its owners, Alex and Seda, brought it back to life. Tastefully refurbished, the pension is comfortable and unpretentious and, as the couple's year-round home, has a positive, personal ambience. Seda is a trained sivananda yoga teacher, ayurvedic health consultant and massage therapist, and Alex is an expert walking guide with great knowledge of the local area. You can stay here independently for a minimum of two nights, to relax, enjoy yoga and ayurvedic treatments, or you can attend one of the holistic weeks that run from May to October.

The spacious living room has comfortable

Life coaching holiday

The LifeCraft Experience 7

A life coaching holiday set aboard a traditional Turkish gulet, this is a wonderful trip to take if you're in a rut and need space, time and a new perspective.

Where you stay The 95-ft boat is well laid out and staffed by an expert crew with a captain, cook and two deck hands. You share one of eight cabins, which are surprisingly spacious with en suite facilities. Yoga, massage treatments, eating and workshops all take place on deck in the open air; you can even sleep out under the stars.

What you do Boats set out from Marmaris and along the Turquoise Coast, sailing for four hours each day. A typical day starts with yoga on deck, followed by breakfast. After the first part of the daily sail comes the first of two workshops: interesting and inspiring, they are run by fully trained life coaches on topics such as health, diet, values, relaxation, setting goals, self-limiting beliefs and managing pressure. In between times you receive one-to-one coaching sessions. A month before leaving you're asked to fill in self-analysis profiles to kick-start your week, and there's three months of life coaching after the holiday. The trip is led by psychologist and facilitator Heather Girling, and accompanied by a complementary therapist who offers Indian head massage, full body massage and reflexology throughout the day. All the staff are on hand for support. There's plenty of time for quiet reflection, as well as conversation. You'll also have the opportunity to visit local sights, try water sports, sail, swim, fish or just lounge around reading and sunbathing.

What you eat and drink A wide range of traditional Turkish dishes are freshly prepared and cooked on board by a dedicated cook. Breakfasts include fresh melon, omelettes, tomatoes, traditional breads and honey. Lunch is mainly Turkish vegetarian with fresh salads, couscous dishes and fruits, and supper features delicious meat and fish dishes. Allergies are catered for, and also any special occasions.

Who goes LifeCraft takes a maximum of 12 guests and attracts a wide range of people from all walks of life. Aged 25-65 and mainly British, they may have been bereaved, made redundant, or simply want to take stock. Workshops and games allow you to bond quickly with the group, and the whole atmosphere is positive.

Essentials LifeCraft (T+44 (0)800-389 4672, www.thelifecraftexperience.com) organizes cruises in May, June, September and October. The cost, from €3780 for a week, includes food and accommodation, workshops, materials, flights, treatments on board and three months coaching following the trip. Note that this isn't for those who get seriously seasick. LifeCraft also runs life coaching weekends in the UK.

LIFE CRAFT

66 99

I had always been sceptical about yoga, life coaching and touchy-feely type solutions to personal issues, but I had recently lost both my parents in a short period of time and my wife encouraged me to go on LifeCraft. I was into sailing, so I figured that if I didn't benefit from the course, then at least I would enjoy the boat journey. With everything so brilliantly taken care of, there was time and space to focus on personal issues, and at the end of the week I was prepared for my future and looking forward to the challenges that I set myself. Having little contact with the outside world and being with others going through similar issues helped a great deal. If you want to provide yourself with the tools and techniques to enable you to move forward in a happy and contented way, there's no better starting place.

Nigel Packer

Top, left and above: Surya.

> 66 99
>
> For my first class with Seda in Surya, I stumbled, stiff and sleepy, at 0645 into the garden pavilion. The sivananda yoga lesson started with a number of different breathing exercises, many of which were new to me, and I found myself struggling. I felt the benefits later in the day, however, as my blocked nose – the tail end of a heavy cold – gradually eased. Following a short meditation, Seda warmed us up with stretches. I felt my whole body being gently massaged, and my mind prodded awake, and by the end I was ready for the delicious breakfast laid out for us on the veranda. Three days of these early morning classes were enough to convince me that daily breathing and stretching wasn't just desirable, but essential. I've done a fair amount of yoga classes, but Seda is the only teacher who has had enough of an effect for me to want to try and practise at home. She is patient and calm, and clearly passionate about yoga and its importance in her life.
>
> *Ruth Rosselson*

> 66 99
>
> # A ship is safe in harbour, but that's not what ships are for.
>
> *William Shedd*

cushions spread out along the walls and a small sound system. Rooms are small but comfortable, and bathrooms shared. The house can accommodate 10, but be prepared to share if you come on a yoga week. If a course takes more than 10, some people stay in local village B&Bs; check in advance.

Your fellow guests will be in their thirties and upwards, and from the UK, northern Europe and also Istanbul. Breakfasts and evening meals are eaten on the delightful

veranda overlooking the garden. Food is largely vegetarian and tends towards traditional Turkish home cooking using fresh seasonal ingredients.

Classes during the yoga weeks take place in a spacious tented pavilion in the corner of a well-kept garden, or on the roof of the pension. Courses on offer include ashtanga, tantra kriya, kundalini and sivananda yoga, some incorporating other activites such as Thai massage, qigong, tai chi and avuryedic medicine, and there are also yoga and

walking weeks. Many courses are open to beginners. Classes run twice a day so there´s plenty of time in between for exploring this relatively untouched region of Turkey, and Alex is an excellent walking guide.

As Datça is on a peninsula, you can swim in either the Mediterranean or the Aegean, or head to Knidos, on the tip of the peninsula, to see where these two seas meet. The nearest airports are at Dalaman, a three-hour drive or €90 taxi ride away, or Bodrum, from where there is a ferry to Bodrum (from €18 per person, €38 with a car, T+90 (0)252-712 2143). Buses run regularly from Dalaman to Marmaris, and from Marmaris to Datça.

YOGA HOLIDAY

Yoga Turkey

🌐 📅8

Ece Hotel, Gölköy
T+44 (0)20-8699 1900
www.yogaturkey.co.uk
From €585 per week

Yoga Turkey was set up by couple, Pervin and Michael, who offer a variety of health and yoga holidays in the small town of Gölköy. Yoga classes take place on a bamboo-shaded terrace overlooking the olive trees in the beautifully landscaped garden of Pervin's house, and you stay at the friendly Ece Hotel, run by the delightful Mr Erkam. It's a nice 20-minute walk to the yoga classes, or lifts can be arranged.

The hotel is 10 minutes from the sea, and set just off the main road in a mandarin grove with a small pool, restaurant and bar. The rooms are small but comfortable and many have a living area with TV. Hand-painted murals, Turkish rugs, embroidered bedspreads and cushions give the place a comfortable yet slightly quirky feel. Bear in mind that other guests will be staying at the hotel, not just those on the yoga weeks.

Courses take up to 20 people and are taught by Pervin or a variety of visiting teachers. They include hatha yoga and deep relaxation, yoga and creativity, okido yoga and walking, and flow yoga and feldenkrais. As you are not staying where the yoga classes take place, the morning session doesn't start until 1000, so try not to eat too much at breakfast. Most days also include another two-hour class of yoga or pranayama in the afternoon.

Lunch is provided as well as evening meals on the days when there are afternoon classes. The food is a delicious variety of home-cooked, traditional local dishes, usually vegetarian. Meals are eaten communally and are a good way to get to know your fellow guests, who are likely to be beginners or those in need of a kick-start to a rusty yoga practice.

When you're not doing yoga, you can relax by the hotel pool, visit the beach, or Pervin can help you arrange local sightseeing and trips to the local Turkish bath. Gölköy gets extremely busy in the summer with Turkish tourists, so if you're after peace and quiet, avoid July and August. Fly to Bodrum, an hour's drive or €35 taxi ride away.

YOGA HOLIDAY

Yoga with Anoushka Pletts

🌐 📅9

Atami Hotel, Bodrum
T+44 (0)20-8946 6694
www.anoushkasyoga.com
From €725, excluding flights

London-based sivananda yoga teacher, Anoushka Pletts, runs annual yoga holidays

🌙 Body language

The Turkish bath

The Turkish bath or hammam is the Middle Eastern alternative to the European steam bath, and has been an important part of traditional Turkish life since medieval times. Usually set in fabulous marble-clad ancient buildings, these public bath houses are fascinating places in which to be scraped and pummelled into a clean and relaxed state. The most accessible hammams are in Istanbul, but on the south coast it's also possible to find local places near Fethiye and Bodrum that will accept foreign visitors. It's a good idea to ask your host for their local knowledge – for example at Yuva and Yoga Turkey. Alternatively, indulge in a luxury version of the scrub and massage at the likes of the Kempinksi Hotel. For a complete low-down on the hammam, see Morocco, page 174.

at the Atami Hotel in Bodrum. The Atami is a four-star resort in a quiet cove away from the town, with pretty gardens and a delicious menu of fusion food. French-born Anoushka has a foundation diploma from the British Wheel of Yoga, and trained at the Sivananda Yoga Vedanta Dhanwantari Ashram in Kerala (see page 225).

HILLSIDE RETREAT

Yuva

Faralya
T+44 (0)1760-755888
www.yuvaholidays.com
From €360 per week;
courses from €490 per week

Set in 16 ha of private, peaceful woodland on a steep hillside right next to the sea, Yuva's very special atmosphere makes it a great place to re-energize. Owner Atilla Sevilmis clearly loves the area and is passionate about conserving the local environment as well as promoting eastern Turkish food and culture.

You'll stay in simple, traditional rustic houses, built from natural materials. Each house has two spacious twin or double rooms, and there are four log cabins for single rooms. Each room has an en suite bathroom and its own veranda facing out to sea. They are basic, but clean and comfortable, and have a lovely homely feel. The wooden floors are covered with a multitude of rugs and throws, cool during the day, but warm at night. As the accommodation is nicely spread throughout

the property you won't feel overcrowded, even when Yuva is fully booked.

There are two outside *kösks* (cushioned seated areas), a beautifully constructed yoga platform with stunning views of the mountainous coastline and out to sea, and a private rocky cove with excellent swimming. The nearby forest is filled with fragrant wild thyme and sage, and is a relaxing place to walk.

You can stay here as an individual all year round to relax, walk, swim and enjoy the good food, or attend one of an inspiring mix of courses run by Yuva's UK agent **Vegi Ventures**. These include yoga and detox breaks, creativity breaks (yoga, art, alternative therapies, cookery and Turkish language and song), and walking trips along the Lycian Way. Atilla can help arrange sightseeing trips, and you can treat yourself to a Turkish bath in nearby Fethiye.

Meals are eaten round large wooden tables on a covered terrace with views of the pine trees, the sea and wonderful sunsets. Food is cooked by one of Atilla's extended family and served buffet-style. A typical breakfast includes corn porridge, yoghurt, cheeses, and homemade flatbread with Atilla's wonderful organic mulberry and tahini combination. All the food is Turkish vegetarian, using locally

⬤ Soul food

SOS Children, T+90 (0)212-257 0911, www.soschildrensvillages.org.uk) the world's largest charity for orphans and abandoned children, provides homes for over 60,000 children in 124 countries. It worked with the Foundation for the Protection of Children in Turkey to set up a children's community in the 1980s at Bolluça, about 35 km from Istanbul, and now works to maintain it.

sourced and organic ingredients where possible. You can buy local wine, and teas are made with freshly picked herbs.

Fellow guests are likely to be singles or couples, in their thirties or older, and ecologically aware. The nearest airport is Dalaman, a 1¾-hour drive; transfers cost €23 each way per person if you are in a group, or €60 each way if you are alone. Independent breaks cost as little as €236 per week from November to March. Take a torch to help you find your way at night.

Top: One of the traditional rustic houses at Yuva.
Right: Sea views at Yuva.

CAROLINE SYLGE

Bedouin in the Sinai Desert, Egypt.

Africa & the Levant

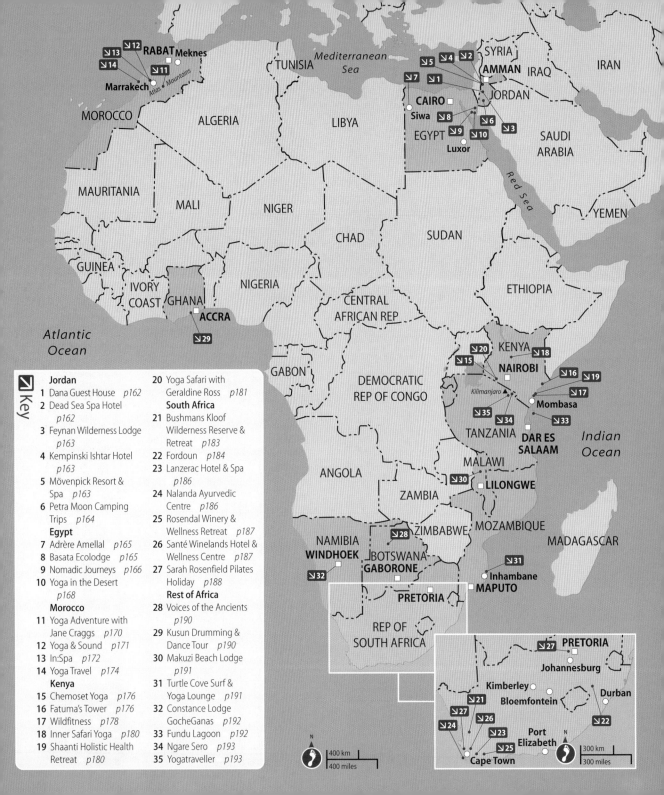

Key

Jordan
1 Dana Guest House *p162*
2 Dead Sea Spa Hotel *p162*
3 Feynan Wilderness Lodge *p163*
4 Kempinski Ishtar Hotel *p163*
5 Mövenpick Resort & Spa *p163*
6 Petra Moon Camping Trips *p164*

Egypt
7 Adrère Amellal *p165*
8 Basata Ecolodge *p165*
9 Nomadic Journeys *p166*
10 Yoga in the Desert *p168*

Morocco
11 Yoga Adventure with Jane Craggs *p170*
12 Yoga & Sound *p171*
13 In:Spa *p172*
14 Yoga Travel *p174*

Kenya
15 Chemoset Yoga *p176*
16 Fatuma's Tower *p176*
17 Wildfitness *p178*
18 Inner Safari Yoga *p180*
19 Shaanti Holistic Health Retreat *p180*

20 Yoga Safari with Geraldine Ross *p181*

South Africa
21 Bushmans Kloof Wilderness Reserve & Retreat *p183*
22 Fordoun *p184*
23 Lanzerac Hotel & Spa *p186*
24 Nalanda Ayurvedic Centre *p186*
25 Rosendal Winery & Wellness Retreat *p187*
26 Santé Winelands Hotel & Wellness Centre *p187*
27 Sarah Rosenfield Pilates Holiday *p188*

Rest of Africa
28 Voices of the Ancients *p190*
29 Kusun Drumming & Dance Tour *p190*
30 Makuzi Beach Lodge *p191*
31 Turtle Cove Surf & Yoga Lounge *p191*
32 Constance Lodge GocheGanas *p192*
33 Fundu Lagoon *p192*
34 Ngare Sero *p193*
35 Yogatraveller *p193*

Africa offers replenishing activities in landscapes made for reflection: practise pilates or yoga at dawn looking across the Kenyan savannah before a morning game drive; meditate by the shores of Lake Malawi; go on a healing tour in the footsteps of the bushmen in Botswana. There are plenty of top-notch places to stay for a DIY retreat, from the hammam hotels in Marrakech to hideaways in South Africa. Choose treatments that feature indigenous plants and techniques that have been used for centuries by Africans to calm and cure.

This region is the base for some of the best body and soul programmes around: the inspirational Wildfitness uses the natural assets of Kenya to get the unfit fit and the very fit even fitter, while In:Spa's wellbeing holidays at the gorgeous Jnane Tamsna in Morocco are a real tonic for the time-poor and stressed out.

Nomadic Journeys run inspirational spiritual trips through the deserts of Egypt, and work with the Bedouin to help preserve local communities. Head to Jordan and the spectacularly situated Dana village in the Dana Nature Reserve, the peace and beauty of which you'll find as spiritually and physically nourishing as any spa treatment in a Dead Sea hotel. Africa and the Levant offers you life-changing journeys through some of the earth's most beautiful spaces – journeys to stay with you long after you return home.

66 99 *There is nothing like returning to a place that remains unchanged to find the ways in which you yourself have altered.*
Nelson Mandela

Travel essentials

CAROLINE SYLGE

Jordan

Getting there International flights arrive at the Queen Alia International Airport, Amman. Some charter flights arrive at Aqaba. Flights from Aqaba and Tel Aviv arrive at Amman's Marka Airport. A cheaper option may be to fly to Tel Aviv or Eilat and continue overland. There are no direct flights North America or Australia. From Egypt, boats run from Nuweiba in the Sinai to Aqaba. Travelling overland to Jordan through Europe is a costly and lengthy journey. The Dead Sea is about an hour's drive from Amman and Dana Nature Reserve is 2½-hours' drive. Aqaba is the closest airport to Wadi Rum.

Best time to visit The best time to visit is generally during spring or autumn. Summers are scorchingly hot throughout most of the country, with temperatures frequently higher than 40°C and high humidity on the Red Sea coast. Winters in Aqaba, the Dead Sea and Wadi Rum are warm and pleasant, although in Wadi Rum it gets very cold at night and the Dead Sea has higher humidity than in summer.

South Africa

Getting there The three main international airports are Johannesburg, Cape Town and Durban. Johannesburg is the regional hub with numerous daily flights to Europe, North America, Asia and Australia. Although most flights arrive in Johannesburg, a fair number of carriers fly directly to Cape Town. **British Airways, Virgin and South African Airways** (SAA) are the main operators with daily flights between London Gatwick or Heathrow and Johannesburg or Cape Town. Flying time is 10½ hours to Johannesburg and 11 hours to Cape Town. Nationwide is a regional carrier in southern Africa but also has one daily flight between Johannesburg and London Gatwick. Indirect flights from other airlines can also be good value. **Kenya Airways** flies between London and Johannesburg, via Nairobi; **Air Namibia** flies between Frankfurt and London to Johannesburg and Cape Town via Windhoek; and **Emirates** flies daily to Johannesburg via Dubai from just about anywhere else in the world.

Best time to visit Generally the summers are hot and wet and winters are cool with clear sunny days. The coast around Cape Town and the Garden Route is at its best during the spring and summer months. The best time of year for game viewing is during the winter months. Winter is also the best time for hiking, avoiding the high temperatures and frequent thunderstorms of the summer months. December and January are the busiest months for tourism, as they coincide with the long summer holiday. Be sure to book your car hire and accommodation well in advance during these periods.

Kenya

Getting there All international flights either go to Jomo Kenyatta International Airport in Nairobi, the capital (about nine hours from London), or Moi International Airport in Mombasa on the Indian Ocean coast (about 11 hours). The cheapest plane tickets are in the off season, from February to June and from October to early December. **EgyptAir, KLM, Emirates, Ethiopian Airlines** and **British Airways** all have surprisingly good deals. **Kenya Airways** (T+254 (0)20-3207 4747, kenya-airways.com), the national airline of Kenya, handles most internal routes as well as regular flights to Europe.

When to go It's obviously best to avoid the rainy seasons if you want to be active and out and about, even though during these there is still an average of four to six hours of sunshine each day. There are two rainy seasons; the long rains fall in March to April and the short rains fall in October to December. Kenya's daytime temperatures average

---

Healthy stopovers in Dubai

If you've a long weekend and lots of cash to spare, join the Jumeirah Janes and indulge all your spa fantasies at **Madinat Jumeirah** (T+971 (0)4-386 8888, www.madinat jumeirah.com), Dubai's most extravagant resort at US$800 per room per night. The superb range of treatments on offer at the **Shangri-La Dubai** (T+971 (0)4-343 8888, www.shangri -la.com) are carried out by some of the most experienced therapists in the city; all for a mere US$420 per room per night. For something a little more affordable, stay in your own apartment and dip in and out of Dubai's hotel and day spas. **Pearl Residence** in Bur Dubai (www.pearlresidence.com) has spacious apartments and studios, a rooftop swimming pool with sundeck, a gym, and daily beach transfers (from US$180 per room per night with breakfast). One of the best day spas is the **Tranquillity Spa** at the Oasis Centre (T+971 (0)4-338 3426, www.tranquility-spas.com), which offers a wide range of modestly-priced alternative health treatments from homeopathy to reiki.

CAROLINE SYLGE

via Paris and **KLM** (www.klm.com) via Amsterdam. From New York, **EgyptAir** flies direct to Cairo (11 hours), while BA and KLM serve the major cities on the west coast.

Best time to visit The best for visiting Egypt is between October and April, though the sun shines year round and rainy days are the exception. The south is significantly warmer than Cairo and in April and May be prepared for the khamseen – the wind of 50 days – which blows sand and heat and is uncomfortable for those caught in the open.

Morocco

Getting there There are direct flights daily from most European capitals to Casablanca-Mohamed V, Marrakech and Agadir. The cheapest flights are to Marrakech from London airports with **easyJet** and **Ryanair**, though **Royal Air Morocco** (www.royalairmaroc.com) and **KLM** also offer good deals. An alternative to flying would be to take the Eurostar from London to Paris, then a train hotel to Madrid and another train from there to Algeciras, from where ferries depart to Tanger. Journey time is under 48 hours, including connections and you can spend some time in Madrid on the way. For full details of train and ferry times and prices, check out the superb www.seat61.com.

Best time to visit Morocco is a good destination all year round though January and February can be a bit cold. Note also that in Fès and Marrakech the heat can be oppressive during the day from July to late September. March and April are probably the best months for visiting the south.

between 20°C and 25°C, though it is cooler in the highlands and hotter on the coast. The high season in safari country is from July to November, and on the coast it's September to January, though February and March are still fine to visit, and year-round temperatures are cooled by ocean breezes. Christmas is busy on the coast and best avoided if you're looking for peace and quiet.

Egypt

Getting there **British Airways** (www.britishairways.com) and **EgyptAir** (www.egyptair.com.eg) fly daily from London to Cairo (four hours). There are also direct flights with **Lufthansa** (www.lufthansa.com) via Frankfurt, **Air France** (www.airfrance.com)

Africa & the Levant Travel essentials

Eat me

There's no point trying to forego good food in this part of the world as you'll smell it, see it and hear it being prepared, eaten or displayed on every street corner. For those dedicated to detox there are plenty of dishes that are good for you, and some stunning ingredients that will cleanse, soothe and protect your body.

Tahini, the paste made from crushed sesame seeds, is best known as the key ingredient in hummus. You should also try it combined with roasted aubergines in the smoky dip bhaba ghanoush, and mixed with lemon juice in simple dressings and dips. It's a good source of calcium, protein, B vitamins and vitamin E, and is particularly good if you're detoxing, because it contains the amino acid Methionine which helps with liver detoxification.

Other popular and healthy Middle Eastern dishes include tabbouleh, a salad packed with fresh parsley and mint, bulgur wheat, tomatoes and lemon juice, and fattoush, similar to tabbouleh, but using torn pitta bread in place of the bulgur and more salad ingredients such as lettuce and cucumbers.

Ras-el-hanout contains dozens of spices that can soothe, cleanse and protect, from the antiseptic properties of cloves to iron-rich cumin seeds. You'll find it used in meat, fish and poultry dishes.

Pomegranates are a staple ingredient in the Middle East and are brimming with vitamins A, C, E and iron. Packed full of antioxidants, they're believed to help reduce the risk of cardiovascular disease. They'll also cool and cleanse the system. Pomegranate seeds are also sprinkled over meat dishes or salads such as batinjan raheb (aubergine and tomato salad) and batinjan bil rumman wal laban (aubergine with pomegranate, yoghurt and tahini).

The ever-present fresh mint tea is great for the body and soul traveller. It makes a fantastically cleansing alternative to coffee and black tea, aiding digestion and giving you a zingy fresh feeling as you sip it. Mint tea can also help calm the symptoms of irritable bowel syndrome – though make sure you order a sugar-free version. Also look out for Salep, a tasty and unusual drink made from powdered orchid root, which is believed to stimulate the immune system and nourish and strengthen the body.

Jordan

Nourish your soul in a nature reserve or indulge beside the world's largest natural spa.

Fact file

- **Visa:** Citizens of most EU countries including the UK, US, Canada, Australia and New Zealand can obtain visas on arrival in Jordan
- **IDD:** +962
- **Currency:** Jordanian Dinar (JD)
- **Time zone:** GMT+2 hours (Oct-Mar), GMT+3 hours (Apr-Sep)
- **Electricity:** 220v
- **Tourist board:** www.visitjordan.com

VILLAGE RETREAT

Dana Guest House

Dana village
T+962 (0)6-461 6523
www.rscn.org.jo
From US$60 per person per night

Perched on the very edge of Dana village overlooking the breathtaking head of Wadi Dana, Dana Guest House is a restored, rustic-style building in the glorious Dana Nature Reserve. It has exposed stone walls and hand-woven kilims on the floor contrasting with stylish, modern furniture made of natural materials. In the centre of the sitting room is a vast, wood-burning stove for the cool nights when the wind whistles up the valley, carrying with it the faint jingle of distant goat bells.

You sleep in one of nine bedrooms, most with private terraces. Food involves a healthy buffet of traditional Jordanian dishes, such as *mezze*, and plates of rice and meat, with lots of fresh vegetables. Next door to the guesthouse is the visitors' centre with an exhibition on the flora and fauna of the wadi, a shop selling the village's organically grown produce, and silver jewellery made by the village women.

From Dana village you can hike round the dramatic head of the wadi to Rummana Camp, or down the valley to Feynan, where you can stay at the Feynan Wilderness Lodge (see below). Dana Guest House is open throughout the year, though it's recommended that you book well in advance – up to 12 months if you plan to travel in high season.

Dana occupies an area that has been inhabited since c 4000BC, although most of the village dates from the Ottoman period. Its peace and tranquility make it a spiritually nourishing place to be, and it's great for treks, which are organized by Jordan's Royal Society for the Conservation of Nature, who run Dana Guest Hosue and Feynan Wilderness Lodge.

VISIT JORDAN

Above: The healing waters of the Dead Sea may float your boat. **Below right:** Creature comforts in the Feynan Wilderness Camp. **Bottom far right:** Dead Sea salt scrub at the Mövenpick Hotel.

HOTEL & SPA

Dead Sea Spa Hotel

Dead Sea coast
T+962 (0)5-560 1554
www.jordandeadsea.com
From US$140 per room per night

The Dead Sea Spa Hotel is an unpretentious place that deals in cures rather than pampering. It was established for guests with diagnosed medical conditions such as skin complaints, rheumatism and circulation problems, and its client base is still those who come primarily to use the fully-equipped medical centre, with its proper white-coated doctors and nurses and clinical surroundings. The treatments, such as the traditional Dead Sea wrap where you're smothered in warm mud, wrapped in plastic and left to bake for 20 minutes, are efficiently rather than indulgently administered. This family-run hotel prides itself on the personal relationship it builds with its guests, many of whom know the staff by name, and who appreciate the tranquillity and friendly personal service – and many return year after year. It also appeals to people – mostly Germans, Austrians and other Europeans – who don't want to pay the lofty prices of its swankier neighbours. Built in 1991, the hotel's simple yet comfortable rooms were being renovated when this book went to press, and the ambience is delightfully unfussy.

DESERT RETREAT

Feynan Wilderness Lodge

🌐 🅿 ↘3

T+962 (0)6-461 6523
www.rscn.org.jo
From US$ 62 per person per night

Set among the arid mountains of the wadi, the Feynan Wilderness Lodge lies on the remote western border of the Dana Nature Reserve, where the Great Rift Valley pushes through Wadi Arabah. This is one of the most archaeologically rich – yet least discovered - areas of Jordan.

This remote lodge was designed by a renowned Jordanian architect in modern Arabic style on sound envirnomental principles. It has stone walls to keep it cool in summer, and, powered by solar energy, is lit only by hundreds of candles, giving the lodge a deeply magical atmosphere at night. Inside, the 'desert-chic' feel continues through the public spaces and 26 bedrooms, with sand-coloured walls, spice-red sofas and natural calico fabrics. At night you can sit on the roof terrace and admire the starriest skies you'll ever see, unpolluted by artificial light. The staff are from the local Bedouin

community and, with their long robes and red-and-white headdress, they complete the romantic desert ambience.

Food is served buffet-style, with a good selection of fresh salads, vegetables, rice and Jordanian stews - the vegetable stew is particularly good. Go trekking from here, do your own yoga, meditate, write, read, be at peace. The lodge is closed during July and August.

Life is not a mystery to be solved, but a mystery to be lived.

Thomas Merton

HOTEL & SPA

Kempinski Ishtar Hotel

🌐 🅾 🌐 🌐 🅿 ↘4

Dead Sea coast
T+962 (0)5-356 8888
www.kempinski-deadsea.com
From US$395 per room per night

This contemporary lush oasis set in an arid landscape is right next door to the **Mövenpick** (see below) on the Dead Sea coast. The cool, airy interior is decorated in soothing blues and greens, a contrast to the parched-earth colours of the surrounding mountains, creating a restful ambience complemented by verdant gardens, water features and an infinity pool that seemingly merges with the Dead Sea beyond. The hotel recycles as much water as possible, an absolute environmental necessity in a country where water is at such a premium. As well as 114 gorgeous rooms, suites and private villas there is the luxury Anatara Spa which, combined with the largest natural spa in the world, aims to combine time-honoured Dead Sea therapies such as

mud rubs and salt scrubs with modern services like herbal facials and beauty treatments. All the therapists are Thai, with traditional Thai massages amongst their specialities. The spa offers 'Journeys of Wellbeing' – a selection of tailor-made packages up to five days long, and aims to become the biggest spa in the Middle East, with light cosmetic procedures as part of the whole holiday experience. The hotel has a selection of restaurants, serving excellent Jordanian and international cuisine, cooked by an award-winning chef. Fellow guests are wealthy Jordanians and Europeans, plus the odd celebrity.

HOTEL & SPA

Mövenpick Resort and Spa

🌐 🌐 🌐 🅿 ↘5

Dead Sea coast
T+962 (0)5-356 1111
www.movenpick-deadsea.com
From US$180 per room per night

Though this is a resort as well as a spa, with the amenities and clientele that go it, Mövenpick has gone to great trouble to create a traditional Jordanian ambience here. The standard accommodation is in the main building whilst the low-profile 'village houses' are finished with golden local stone and plaster. Each of the cosy rooms is furnished in oriental fashion with warm, natural colours and antique-style wood furniture, plush fabrics and rattan chairs. Beyond the accommodation blocks is the village square, planted with gnarled, 2000-year-old olive trees moved here from Bethlehem, around

◐ Body language

Glorious mud

The Dead Sea is the largest natural spa in the world. At 410 m below sea level it's the lowest place on earth, a vast lake where only about 50 mm of rain falls each year. People have sung the praises of its thermo-mineral springs for millennia, and it remains as enticing to visitors today as it was to kings, emperors, traders, and prophets in antiquity. King David used it as a place of refuge, and King Herod built a fort overlooking the water as a place of retreat. The Dead Sea was also the site of the Qumran community which produced the Dead Sea Scrolls, Hebrew texts written around the time of Christ, which were accidentally discovered by a Bedouin shepherd boy in 1947. And if you drive along the salt-encrusted shores you can still see Lot's Wife, who famously turned into a pillar of salt, now a craggy pinnacle of stone overlooking the water.

The main attraction of the Dead Sea is the ozone-rich air, the ultra-violet filtered sunshine (330 days of it a year) and the soothing, abnormally salty water itself. The salt content of the water is 31.5% making the water so dense and buoyant that it is impossible for bathers to sink (or even to swim properly). The water also contains 21 minerals, including high levels of magnesium, sodium, potassium, and bromine, 12 of which are found in no other body of water in the world. People have valued its medicinal properties as long as they have lived around here, covering themselves with the rich black mud to treat numerous conditions. Now there are more sophisticated treatments on offer as well, as Jordan begins to catch onto luxury spa hotels, with new ones appearing along the shores each year: for an intimate, affordable experience, try the long-established **Dead Sea Spa Hotel**, or for a spot of luxurious pampering, head for the **Mövenpick** or the lush **Kempinski Ishtar**.

which you can find most of the restaurants and cafés as well as the Zara Spa. It is the largest spa operation in the Middle East and offers a range of treatments using the therapeutic resources of Dead Sea: mud wraps, salt scrubs, hydro-pools and algae facials. A new therapy centre offers remedies for various conditions such as skin problems. There's a buffet-style restaurant serving international cuisine in the main hotel, plus a good Italian trattoria in the village square. The

clientele are largely groups and families from Russia, Switzerland and the rest of Europe, many of whom come to spend up to a week in the spa as part of a wellbeing package.

DESERT RETREAT

Petra Moon camping trips

⚜ ▶ ◥ 6

Wadi Rum
T+962 (0)3-215 6665
www.petramoon.com
From US$45 per person per night

Lawrence of Arabia famously described Wadi Rum as "vast, echoing and god-like", and indeed a night camping on its immense swathes of apricot sands, encircled by towering pinnacles of rock under a canopy of stars, is one of life's great spiritual experiences. Petra Moon organises trips - as night falls your Bedouin hosts light candles in the sand, and cook up a delicious meal which they serve under the traditional black woven

bayt char (house of hair) tent. After dinner you sit around the campfire listening to the magical music of the oud before retiring to your own private tent, which can range from simple to luxurious (furnished with proper beds, sheets and blankets, and laid with kilims) according to your budget. Meditate, do your own yoga, or just allow yourself to be nourished by the quiet surrounds.

Food involves simple dishes such as unleavened bread, rice, meat and salads, eaten Bedouin-style on cushions in a communal tent. Prices vary according to just how private you want to be – a private camp set up in a remote part of Wadi Rum away from all lights and noise costs from US$180 per person per night for two people, and gets cheaper the more people there are. Alternatively, Petra Moon has a small fixed campsite at the confluence of Wadi Um Ashrin and Bara Canyon which costs from US$ 45 per person per night – the camp is not accessible by car or coach, so it is still relatively remote.

PETRA MOON

The "vast, echoing and god-like" Wadi Rum.

Egypt

DESERT RETREAT

Adrère Amellal

Siwa
T+20 (0)27-381327
www.adrereamellal.net
From US$ 400 per room per night

Siwa, an oasis in Egypt's remote western desert, boasts salt lakes surrounded by date palms and countless hot and cold springs. The place to stay is Adrère Amellal ('White Mountain' in native Berber), an astonishing ecolodge with walls of rock salt and a palm roof, melding beautifully into the surrounding landscape. There is no electricity, and the enchanting rooms ooze desert calm. Meals use herbs and vegetables from the organic garden, there's a majestic cold bubbling spring-fed pool and you'll have access to horses. With ancient olive and palm groves and breathtaking views over Siwa lake, it's the perfect place to lose yourself in meditation. As well as exploring Siwa, you can take an overnight trip into the desert,

Siwa is famous for its sand baths.

where a Bedouin guide will brew you a sugary tea, share a story, or bang out belly dancing beats on a local drum. Alternatively, take a sand bath, or *hammam ramal* for which Siwa is famous. Adrere Amellal is 16 km outside Siwa, and an eight-hour drive from Cairo.

● Body language

In the heat of summer, travellers come to Siwa to experience a sand bath, or **hammam ramal**. Some 400 years ago, according to legend, a Danish man travelled to Siwa to bury his crippled daughter in the sand. On the first day of treatment, she stood, and on the ninth day, she walked. Today people still come to experience this ancient healing ritual, to sweat out whatever is troubling them, looked after by Bedouin caretakers and staying in local 'sand hotels'. Though most seek relief for rheumatic pains, locals say the sand treats lots of different ailments. Many, however, will find it a bizarre experience, and you should consult a doctor before you set out.

COASTAL RETREAT

Basata Ecolodge

Nuweiba, Red Sea coast
T+20 (0)69-350 0481
www.basata.com
From US$12 per person per night

Set up 20 years ago by Egyptian civil engineer Sherif El-Ghamrawy and built slowly hut by hut, Basata (meaning 'simple' in Arabic) is the only ecolodge on the Red Sea coast. It's a wonderful place for a DIY retreat, with great snorkelling (no diving allowed) over a pristine coral reef, and an intimate, bohemian vibe. Basata's reputation has grown by word of mouth and it now attracts a varied international crowd, a mix of the young eco-beautiful and expats, families and alternative older people. Many stay for an

Be a nomad in the desert, belly dance or do yoga by the Red Sea.

Fact file

- ● **Visa:** Citizens of EU countries including the UK, US, Canada, Australia and New Zealand can obtain visas on arrival in Egypt. Travellers entering via Taba for the Gulf of Aqaba coast are issued a free 14-day permit instead
- ● **IDD:** +20
- ● **Currency:** Egyptian pound (EGP)
- ● **Time zone:** GMT +2 hours
- ● **Electricity:** 220v
- ● **Tourist board:** www.touregypt.net

NICKI GRIHAULT

Africa & the Levant Egypt

extended period and are repeat guests. Sherif doesn't accept any groups from mainstream tourist companies. He is a hands-on owner, offering hospitality in person, and employing local Bedouin staff. You can camp, stay in one of 18 bamboo huts (with no electricity) on the beach, or in one of 10 spacious and individually decorated traditional beehive adobe houses.

An honesty system operates in the kitchen (and gift shop); you can self-cater, or there's an evening meal on offer in the open-sided restaurant, which has low tables in nooks and crannies, and areas separated by horizontal palm trunks. Pizza is served from the on-site

◉ Soul food

On the Go Tours (T+44 (0)20-7371 1113, www.onthego tours.com, from US$585 per person) runs a 10-day Eco Egypt trip twice a year which enables you to explore Egypt's best-loved sights and give something back to the environment and its people. During the trip there are special initiatives in which you can take part such as spring-cleaning the banks of the Nile, organizing activities at one of Cairo's many children's homes and supporting the women's cooperative at 'rubbish city' in Cairo. Half the proceeds from the tour go directly to On the Go Tours' initiative 'Change for Children', which supports local children's orphanages in Cairo.

bakery at lunchtime, and there are fresh rolls for breakfast. Beers are available in the fridge. There's a small library, no music or television, and mobile phones are discouraged. Although solar-heated showers are available, water conservation is promoted and there are compost toilets. Bring a sleeping bag and torch. It's a 2½-hour drive along the coast from Sharm El-Sheikh airport, or a half-hour ferry ride from Aqbar in Jordan.

66 99

A powerful longing towards Sinai seized me, and neither with my bodily eyes nor with those of the spirit could I find joy in anything, so strongly was I attracted to that place of solitude.

St Nilus of Sinai

DESERT RETREAT
Nomadic Journeys

☀ ⓟ ⊕ ⓟ ⏁9

Sinai Desert
T+44 (0)1242-544546
www.nomadicjourneys.org
From US$1800 for 7 nights

Hosted by the Bedouin of the Mouzeina tribe who came to the Sinai from Saudi Arabia 600 years ago, these amazing journeys into the desert offer the chance to live as the Bedouins do, sleeping in a tent or under a blanket of stars, eating meals cooked over an open fire and travelling by foot or camel. Whether you choose an eight-day Desert Retreat or a 10-day

Mountain Journey, your trip will help support the **Makhad Trust**, which works with Bedouin leaders to improve living conditions and generate income through a craft centre, digging wells, and garden restoration projects.

On the Desert Retreat an open-sided goat-hair tent acts as base camp – foam mattresses and blankets are provided. You spend two nights alone in a secluded spot under the stars, and the final night is spent around the fire. On the Mountain Journey the group stays in eco-accommodation in a succession of desert gardens before open-air camping on Mount Sinai. Accommodation on the final night for both journeys is at **Basata Ecolodge** on the Red Sea (see above). Both trips encourage spiritual recharge and a shift of consciousness, and are hosted by Danny, th founder, a down-to-earth but spiritual visionary born in Galilee.

The Desert Retreat mixes camel treks with guided walks to pick out historic, ecological and spiritual aspects of the Sinai, and there's plenty of time to chat with the Bedouin about life in the desert.

The focus of the Desert Retreat is a two-day water-only fast, when you pick a special spot near enough to base camp, but isolated enough to enjoy the silence and solitude of the desert. Retreating at first light, the group returns two days later for a special herbal wash and breakfast. The staff stay wake all night, in case someone needs to return to the camp.

66 99

As a chatterbox and someone who always seems to be hungry, I wasn't sure how I'd fare for two days and two nights with just silence and water for company, or how secure I'd feel sleeping alone under a blanket of stars. But as I sank into the silence, meandered alone across the plain looking at rocks and plants, wrote in whatever shady nook I fancied and baked unselfconsciously in the sun, I found I was enjoying the solitude.

Nicki Grihault

The Mountain Journey is an eco-pilgrimage, involving two to three days in the desert and visits to ancient gardens. It includes working alongside the Bedouin in the remote walled Amran garden. On your final day at Mount Sinai, you camp overnight, watch the sun rise, then enjoy exclusive entry to the 0500 service at St Catherine's Monastery before going to the hanging gardens for breakfast.

The Sinai provides 70% of the world's herbal medicines and you can stay on for a one- to three-day treatment in the healing garden. Workshops in Bedouin dancing and music, painting and photography are sometimes offered.

The day starts early and soon after first light the Bedouin will be boiling a comforting tea, coffee or *kakadae* (hibiscus tea). Food is mainly vegetarian; breakfast is local porridge and pancake-style bread with feta cheese, eggs or honey. Lunch is a similar bread, or, on special occasions, *liba* – a thicker bread baked under the ash of the fire – is served with tomato and cucumber, tuna and bean salad, humous, tahini, feta cheese and sometimes eggs, followed by halva and dates. Dinner is a local soup, and rice with a variety of vegetables. On the Mountain Journey, fresh fruit and vegetables from the hanging gardens are available. The Bedouin are Muslim and there is no alcohol available in the desert. On the last night, you can drink beer at Basata Ecolodge, which also serves pizzas from its bakery.

Nomadic Journeys attracts a wide range of people, including families, single travellers, friends and couples, mainly from the UK, aged 30-plus, seeking an authentic experience of the Sinai. Most arrive through a personal connection or word of mouth. Bespoke trips are arranged – prearranged group trips range in size from eight to 18, with an average of around 12 people. The price is all-inclusive and money is only needed for the mobile desert shop. Journeys run all year, except in July and August. The best time to go is October to March. Bring thermals, sleeping bag, a large mug, books and writing materials. Nomadic Journeys also runs trips to Finland, Tibet and Namibia.

Left: Basata Ecolodge. **Above**: Nomadic Journeys.

◗ Body language

Shake your belly

Belly dancing is an ancient art of self-expression for women of all ages, and a wonderful way to move that puts you into a blissed-out state. It can be slow and sensual, or fast and commanding, and you don't have to wear tassled tops or diaphanous veils to do it – a willingness to learn and a skirt that's easy to move in will do. The name 'belly dancing' was coined at the 1893 Chicago World Fair, when not many people were coming to the Algerian Village display to see the *danse du ventre*. When it was translated into English, the Victorian visitors flocked to the display in droves. The Egyptian name for belly dancing is *raqs sharqi*, which many serious practitioners prefer to use, believing that its change of name helped cause the corruption and over-sexualization of the dance form.

UK-based belly dancer and teacher **Jacqueline Chapman** (T+44 (0)208-300 7616, www.bellydancer.org.uk) runs annual belly dancing holidays to Egypt, spending three nights in Cairo and five in Luxor at four- or five-star hotels. This energizing holiday includes three four-hour belly dancing workshops given by professional Egyptian dancers, accompanied by a tabla drummer. You'll learn cabaret belly dancing in Cairo, a more traditional form in Luxor, and get to see (and sometimes participate in) evening dance shows (from US$1500 for 8 nights, workshops from US$80). Jacqueline also runs belly dancing holidays to Morocco and Turkey.

Alternatively, **Club Dance Holidays** runs belly dancing weeks in the Sahara Desert in Morocco, to Bodrum in Turkey and to Vejer in Spain (from US$1485, T+44 (0)870-286 6000, www.clubdanceholidays.com), whilst **Jasmine Journeys** (T+216 (0)72-278665, www.jasminejourneys.com) run regular belly dancing trips to Tunisia which also include yoga and trips to the hammam.

Yoga holiday

Yoga in the desert 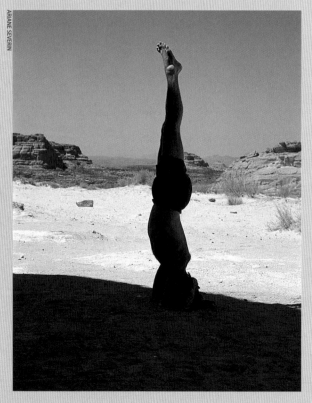 🏔️ ⛺ 🧘 🧘‍♀️ ❀ 🏃 🏄 ↘10

Dahab (meaning 'gold' in Arabic) is a laid-back hippy-chic town an hour's drive, but a lifetime away in spirit, from the soulless resort of Sharm El-Sheikh. Dahab suffered a terrorist attack in April 2006, but security has since tightened up and the vibe of the town has not been dented. A coastal strip of small and independent bars, cafés, al fresco restaurants, dive centres and shops, it's easy to kick back here with a tropical fruit smoothie and dip into the developing yoga scene. There are drop-in classes year-round on the roof of the Desert Divers centre and at the Blue Beach Hotel twice a week, attended by a mix of travellers and locals. Better still is to book onto one of the many excellent and affordable week-long yoga holidays on offer.

Overlooking the Red Sea with the desert mountains as a backdrop, Dahab is an incredible setting for asanas and meditation, but better

still is the desert, and every company featured here offers trips into the Sinai, where you'll have the chance to camp overnight with the Bedouin. It's an experience not to be missed. You'll also have the chance to go horse riding in the mountains or along the beach, snorkel, scuba-dive and camel-trek. Massages and a visit to the local hammam can easily be arranged.

Yoga Travel offers regular eight-day Red Sea Paradise trips throughout the year (from US$655 per person per week, T+44 (0)870-350 3545, www.yogatravel.co.uk). Based at the Bedouin-run Coral Coast Hotel, you do yoga on the lovely rooftop terrace. Every room has a private balcony overlooking the sea. Your trip is led by experienced tour leader Will Cottrell, and the overnight desert trip during this week includes a climb up Mount Sinai the following morning. Yoga is taught by Dahab-based sivananda teachers Monica Farrell and Ali Gilling. Yoga Travel also runs a 10-day Wonders of the World yoga adventure (from US$945) taking in Cairo, the beach retreat Ras Sudr, Mount Sinai and Dahab, as well as a trip to Morocco (see page 174).

Also including a morning climb up Mount Sinai as part of its desert trip, **Yoga on a Shoestring** (from US$370 per person per week, T+44 (0)20-8690 0890, www.yogaonashoestring.com) offers good-value holidays from October to May based at the Bedouin-run Hotel Amanda. A simple, intimate hotel with a cushioned chill out area right on the beach, there's a choice of simply decorated single or double rooms inside the hotel or in wooden huts. Yoga is done in a studio right on the seafront, overlooking the Red Sea with the mountains in the background. There is meditation and pranayama every morning for early risers, followed by a two-hour yoga session and an early evening class. Teachers include local Ali Gilling and Yoga on a Shoestring's founder Sue Pendlebury, who fuses her creative background in music, dance and theatre, and her bodywork, into her classes.

The popular **Blue Beach** (from US$25 per day, T+20 (0)69-640411, www.bluebeachclub.com) is a clean and friendly beachside alternative with a lovely purpose-built rooftop yoga room with a black and white tiled floor and desert and ocean views. For six months of the year it hosts an impressive range of week-long holidays in most styles of yoga, from vinyasa flow to sivananda to iyengar, with mainly UK-based teachers and organized by **Free Spirit Travel** in the UK (from US$585 per person per week, T+44 (0)1273-564230, www.freespirituk.com). Overnight desert trips are part of the course, you can learn Arabic with the owner and the hotel has its own dive centre and riding stables, though the bar area is frequented in the evenings by divers, who may not be as chilled out as you want to be on a yoga week.

ARIANE SEVERIN

❝❞

I did my first yoga holiday in Dahab and loved the mix of exoticism and accessibility. The highlight was an overnight camel trek into the Sinai, a staggering landscape of craggy sandstone mountains and long stretches of rock-strewn desert that invigorates and calms all at once. It's one of the most tranquil environments on earth to do yoga, but simply lying on my back looking at the stars was a nourishing experience. Its haunting solitude stayed with me for months after and provided me with a little piece of calm in my heart, which I still tap into whenever life gets too busy back home.

Caroline

Come with a friend and have two daily sessions with **Sara Campbell** (from US$360 for 14 sessions of yoga, T+44 (0)20-8133 0380, www.radiantbeingyoga.com), who teaches kundalini yoga either in her garden in Dahab, or on the terraces and rooftops of whichever hotel you choose to stay in. Sara trained with the School of Kundalini Yoga (www.ssense.co.uk/sky/) and has been teaching since 2003. She can help you arrange accommodation according to your budget: try the boutique Hotel Alf Leila (from US$30 a night, www.alfleila.com), where you can also enjoy a sandalwood smoke sauna, body scrub and massage with a local Sudanese therapist using handmade natural ingredients.

If you want more action, **Zen Holidays** (from US$675 per person per week, T+44 (0)7957-338525, www.zenholidays.co.uk) runs an annual yoga and pilates week with celebrity personal trainer, yoga teacher and reiki healer Christianne Wolff, combining pilates and budokon, and a horse riding holiday. You'll be based at the clean and comfortable Daniella Hotel, and have a chance to climb Mount Sinai. If you stay for two full weeks, Zen can arrange day or overnight trips to Luxor or Cairo.

For something a little different, try a yoga diving holiday taught by sivananda teachers and dive instructors **Monica Farrell** and **Barbara Gordon** (from US$980 per person per week, T+44 (0)20-8677 1957, www.yogadiving.com). Base is at the British-run Reef 2000 diving centre (www.reef2000.org) at the Bedouin Moon, a lovely whitewashed Bedouin-run hotel 3 km from central Dahab. Here you'll learn diving as a meditation rather than a sport, using yoga breathing and meditation techniques to focus and still your mind, and enhance your experience underwater.

Finally, UK-based vinyasa flow teacher **Claire Missingham** (T+44 (0)7989-431818, www.claireyoga.com) who teaches at the Blue Beach, plans to run bespoke luxury yoga holidays in 2007/8 to Dahab's Hilton, which boasts a lovely sandy stretch of beach. Whichever holiday you choose, this a great week to meet like-minded people, and you'll be comfortable alone or with a friend. Fly to Sharm El-Sheikh, from where it's a 40-minute drive by jeep or bus – each company arranges pickups. Holidays usually run when the weather's at its best, from October to May.

Left: Yoga in the desert. **Top:** Dahab. **Above:** Sara Campbell teaching kundalini yoga.

Morocco

JANE CRAGGS

YOGA HOLIDAY

Yoga adventure with Jane Craggs

Marrakech and the High Atlas
T+44 (0)7764-963138
www.janecraggs.co.uk
From US$1100 for 12 days

Explore Morocco on and off the mat with Jane Craggs, who is committed to working with venues which are truly sustainable for the local people and ecologically sound. This (quite deliberately) isn't luxury – you'll get a real travelling experience as well as excellent yoga teaching.

A highly approachable, witty and nurturing teacher, Jane runs the **Manchester Yoga Shala** in the UK (www.manchesteryoga shala.co.uk) and teaches yoga according to the eight-limbed path of Patanjali's Yoga Sutras. Her classes are deep but accessible and creative, and draw on her extensive experience of all the yoga styles including iyengar, ashtanga and yin yoga – she is especially influenced by Donna Farhi (www.donnafarhi.co.nz).

After a night in a riad in Marrakech, a seven-hour drive will take you to **Kasbah Itran** (www.kasbahitran.com) high in the Atlas Mountains, an eco-project run by a Berber family who have created a very relaxed, easy-going atmosphere where nothing is too much trouble. They use their profits to support the local community: for many villagers, the kasbah is their only source of water, and they often join the staff for mint tea and a chat.

Traditional in style, the kasbah is made of adobe bricks and straw with a bamboo roof, and decorated stylishly with lots of quirky little details such as baskets of rose petals bought from local farmers, which are strewn across the pathways every evening. Twice-daily yoga classes are held on the terrace overlooking the mountains and the M'goun delta, sometimes watched by curious children. Three vegetarian meals are served each day and, after dinner, the chef Mohammed usually leads a session of traditional Berber music.

JANE CRAGGS

Above: Yoga Adventures with Jane Craggs.
Right: Riad Ifoulki, location for Yoga and Sound.

There's a three-day guided trek in the middle of the trip through mountain villages and the desert, when you camp out and have the chance to meet local Berber families. During the trek you'll have one yoga class a day. The last two nights of the holiday are spent exploring the delights of Marrakech.

Treat yourself to an In:Spa holiday, get pummelled in a hammam or explore mountains and coast on and off the yoga mat.

Fact file

⮕ **Visa:** None required for citizens of EU countries, US, Canada, Australia and New Zealand

ⓘ **IDD:** +212

Ⓢ **Currency:** Moroccan dirham (MAD)

◷ **Time zone:** GMT

⚡ **Electricity:** 127/220v

ⓘ **Tourist board:** www.visitmorocco.org

◉ Soul food

The **Global Diversity Foundation** is an international charity that promotes the richness and diversity of local cultures around the world. In rural areas of Morocco, it creates opportunities for young people to continue their education while developing their own cultural traditions and knowledge of the environment. In Marrakech, it supports the creation of gardens to ensure locals have access to nutrition-rich food and green urban spaces. If you would like to contribute, visit www.globaldiversity.org.uk.

JOAO SILVEIRA RAMOS

MADELEINE CEMM

makes a distinctive shape whose frequency can be translated into sound. The sound in turn makes it easier to get into the posture, creating a kind of spaciousness to help people experience themselves in the moment. Letting the body speak through yoga, in the presence of others, is believed to develop a gentle self-confidence which helps us to face the negative aspects of ourselves and begin the journey of self-acceptance. It sounds strange, but the sessions are powerful and liberating.

Riad Ifoulki (chosen for its harmonious architecture) was once a royal home, and is in a discreet and quiet corner of Marrakech. It is run like a private home rather than a hotel, so retains an intimate, friendly atmosphere. Each room is different – most have access to a courtyard or balcony, some have their own. You can breakfast in the courtyard gardens or on the roof terrace before the two-hour yoga class.

The yoga takes place among orange trees and fountains sprinkled with rose petals in one of the riad's five beautifully tiled courtyards. There are two sessions a day, with optional evening meditation before a rooftop candlelit dinner. The rest of the time you are free to relax or explore the wonders of Marrakech – the souks and Jemmaâ el Fna are a few minutes' walk away – or book a body scrub and massage in the riad's fine hammam (see box page 174) and lounge on divans in its gardens and courtyards. Local musicians come to play on one evening.

The retreat attracts an equal mix of men and women, couples and singles in their thirties to late sixties, some newcomers, some Judith's regular students. The holiday cost is split into US$250 for the yoga teaching, and from US$250 to US$385 for bed and breakfast for four nights at the Riad (whom you pay direct), depending on the size of the room you choose. Dinner is around US$32 a head. You arrange your own flights, and can choose to stay on longer at the riad – transfers are included. Judith is based in the UK, and also runs Yoga and Sound retreats in France and Hawaii, as well as workshops in London and retreats at **Earth Spirit** in the UK (see page 32).

Flights are not included; Jane encourages guests to make a donation to the Carbon Trust according to the distance travelled by air. Jane also leads retreats in West Bengal in India (see page 230), and at Les Passeroses in France (see page 91) and she is planning a yoga and surfing trip to Morocco for 2008.

YOGA HOLIDAY

Yoga and Sound

Marrakech
T+44 (0)20-8450 2723
www.yogaandsound.com
From US$500 per person for 4 nights

Inspirational and charismatic healer and teacher Judith Seelig runs annual four-night yoga and sound retreats at the sumptuous **Riad Ifoulki** (www.riadifoulki.com) in Marrakech. Designed to accommodate beginners as well as experienced practitioners, her sessions will give you a very deep and slow, introduction to hatha yoga with sound.

Judith studied the healing powers of vibration, and her yoga and sound teaching is based on the idea that each yoga posture

The sounds Judith makes range from clucking to a booming sound that feels like it will shatter the windows, from North American Indian shaman chants to screeching like a witch and growling like a bear. I'm not sure whether to feel frightened or to laugh. The sounds, as they are meant to, bypass the logical rational mind and I notice that it shifts me into different feeling states, from sadness to elation. As a teacher, Judith can be both a terrifying force or incredibly gentle - depending on what she feels a person needs. She obviously decides I need the full cannon treatment as she hisses into my downward dog, 'Soften your mouth, its full of all the things you haven't said!' It's a powerful experience, which gets only deeper on the second day. I leave feeling enriched, nurtured and deeply relaxed.

Nicki Grihault

Wellbeing holiday

In:Spa ⟨icons⟩ ↘13

In:Spa runs regular week-long luxury wellbeing retreats led by a hand-picked team of experts including a nutritionist, yoga teacher, two personal trainers and a private chef. The hot dry heat and stark plains of Morocco provide an exotic setting in which to concentrate on yourself. Based at the marvellous Jnane Tamsna, the holiday features three treks in the foothills of the Atlas Mountains as well as a full programme of yoga, massage, personal training, nutrition consultations and tasty but healthy food.

Where you stay The stunning boutique hotel Jnane Tamsna is in the Palmeraie, a quiet, flat enclave strewn with palm trees a 15-minute drive from the centre of Marrakech. This gorgeous place has 24 bedrooms spread over five buildings, each with rooftop views of date palms, mountains and neighbouring burnt-orange buildings. Exquisite-smelling rosemary lines the main entrance path, which is lit with candles every evening. Co-owner French-Senegalese Meryanne is an interior designer and the place is beautifully decked out with artefacts, furniture and soft furnishings from all over the Islamic world. You won't need to share your room here unless you come with a friend or partner. For extra privacy, it's worth paying more for one of the five rooms in Moussafir (or house of the traveller). There are five pools to swim in, plenty of nooks and crannies where you can bed down with a book, and a hammam is planned for late 2007.

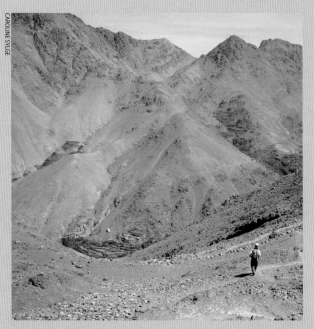
CAROLINE SYLGE

66 99

I was mightily impressed with the positive energy of the In:Spa team on my week in Morocco. They were witty, encouraging, friendly and down-to-earth. I learnt a lot, especially from the nutritionist, New Yorker Lorraine Perretta – that bananas are high in sugar, that hazelnuts offer more nutritional benefit than cashews, that Tamari sauce is a wheat-free alternative to soy. Personal trainers Jon Orum and Nick Cook made a very funny and highly effective team, and Alan Wichert created some of the most delicious healthy meals I have ever tasted. A particular treat was the vinyasa flow yoga with Claire Missingham, who used her own hand-blended massage lotions to rub our necks and shoulders during the class, and played haunting sounds of deep-throated Indian chants and songs at every session. I ended my week clear-headed, clear-eyed, slimmer and a lot more relaxed. I'd do the In:Spa Intense next time – cash flow permitting.

Caroline

What you do You'll be warmly hosted by one of In:Spa's founders, Kathryn Brown or Gillian Crotty, with a team hand-picked from a pool of experts which includes personal trainers Stephen Price and Jon Orum, founder of UK-based **Specialized Fitness** (www.specializedfitness.co.uk), yoga teachers Claire Missingham (www.claireyoga.com, pictured right) and Liz Lark (www.lizlark.com), expert nutritionists Alli Godbold (www.feedyourhealth.co.uk) and Lorraine Perretta, and chefs such as Alan Wichert and Charles Amos.

Though there's a full programme of events, you're encouraged to listen to your body; if you need to sleep, sleep, if you want to take yourself off one afternoon away from the group, do it. In addition to the group activities of three hikes, regular yoga, two cross-training sessions and a cycle ride through the Palmeraie, your week includes a one-to-one session with the nutritionist and personal trainer, three 45-minute massages (given by local therapists) and three small-group yoga sessions tailored to your level. These personal sessions will help you use the week to great effect, whether you want to work on your posture, your fitness, your stress levels or your diet.

The three hikes take you through the villages and desert-like landscape of the High Atlas. The 1½-hour drive to the starting point won't appeal to everyone, but the walks are invigorating and a lovely contrast with the activities back at the hotel. Yoga is usually in a large room with rich terracotta walls, dark wood floors and French windows opening onto a terrace. Evening meditation sessions occasionally take place in the cool of the night on the roof.

Cross-training sessions will have you warming up on the tennis court, jogging around the grounds, then working in pairs on a fitness circuit. There are occasional nutritional talks in the evening, and a short cooking workshop towards the end of the week. Dinner is at 2000, after which most people feel like going to bed.

For those who want to push themselves more, you'll find the pace a lot more challenging on an In:Spa Intense week. The hikes and circuit classes are longer and tougher, you'll have two personal training sessions, four massages and the option of an extra fitness or yoga class each day.

What you eat and drink You're encouraged to reduce or cut out caffeine, alcohol, bread and snack foods a week before you arrive on an In:Spa holiday. You're then served gourmet breakfasts, lunches and dinners which somehow manage to taste staggeringly wonderful yet contain no sugar, salt, caffeine, alcohol or red meat. Dairy is on the side – so you can help yourself to goat's cheese and yoghurt if you desire.

The hotel has wonderful orchards and organic vegetable gardens on which the chef draws. Breakfasts are buffet-style with salmon and poached eggs, passion fruit protein smoothies, mueslis and wheat-free fruit crumbles; lunches include a wide range of delicious salads with interestingly cooked fish, chicken and turkey dishes. Freshly squeezed vegetable juices, ginger, lemon and mint teas, nuts and crudités are served at 1600 as a snack.

Dinners are a treat here – served outdoors by candlelight at a long table dressed with a gorgeous white table cloth and white roses in coloured Moroccan glasses. Alan Wichert, for example, creates inspired fusion dishes – think Vietnamese ricepaper rolls with marinated chicken, guava, papaya and mango, or smoked trout from the Atlas Mountains with fresh garden roccolla.

Who goes In:Spa attracts intelligent, high-earning professionals from London but also the rest of Europe, usually in their thirties and forties looking to de-stress in luxurious surroundings. Most are travelling alone, some are couples. The price bracket also attracts a fair number of upbeat and reasonably fit 'empty nesters' and retirees. The In:Spa Intense weeks are for those who are already into fitness.

CAROLINE SYLGE

Essentials T+44 (0)845-458 0723, www.inspa-retreats.com. Fly to Marrakech, from where it's a 30-minute drive. Transfers are included with group flights from the UK, otherwise a pickup is €20 one way. Bring your own rucksack – the ones they provide are not comfortable to walk with. There's an afternoon trip to the medina in Marrakech, which some may find rushed – better to plan a weekend before or after your In:Spa trip and enjoy Marrakech at a more leisurely pace (see next spread for where to stay).

A one-week In:Spa holiday in Morocco costs from US$3700 per person based on shared occupancy in a small room to US$5300 for single occupancy in a large suite. In:Spa also runs holidays on the coast in Morocco at the stunning Ksar Massa, south of Agadir (www.ksarmassa.com), at Es Cucons in Ibiza and Trasierra in Seville (see page 115), and in the UK. Bespoke private fitness holidays can be arranged, and you can join an In:Spa club to enjoy health and fitness events, discounts and a monthly newsletter (US$ 225 a year for UK members, US$100 for members overseas). Jnane Tamsna (from US$380 per room per night, T+212 24-329423, www.jnanetamsna.com) also hosts cooking, pilates and adventure holidays.

CAROLINE SYLGE

● Body language

Sweating it out

Being scraped and pummelled in a hammam is one of the most rejuvenating things you can experience. The tradition of the hammam, Arabic for 'spreader of warmth', dates back to the Romans and Byzantines, and has been adopted by different cultures across the region since medieval times. These gorgeous public steam bath-houses are an important part of Middle Eastern culture as washing and cleanliness is such an essential aspect of Islam. They were usually built next to a marketplace or mosque and evolved to become a place for socializing and an intrinsic part of everyday life.

Public hammams comprise a series of marble-walled cave-like rooms of varying temperatures – the *sogukluk* (cool room), *tepidarium* (warm room) and *sicaklik* (hot room) – and are usually staffed by strong-handed local massage therapists who will pummel you into a clean, calm state. Private hotel hammams are smaller, but the best ones replicate the traditional architecture and treatment, which starts with you sitting naked on just-bearable hot marble to sweat for a good ten minutes to open your pores. You're then doused with water from the washbasins in the room, and covered with a traditional black soap, made from 100% natural ingredients. It doesn't lather, but instead turns into a cream as soon as you add warm water. Cleansing and hydrating, it's great for the skin and also helps to strengthen the hair. It's usually massaged in and left on for about ten minutes.

Your skin is then scrubbed with an exfoliating mitt; you'll see your dead skin cells stripped away in tiny rolls of dirt. It's an exquisite feeling, like a chemical peel without the chemicals. This is followed by a long rinse with plenty of hot water, usually buckets of it poured over your head. Afterwards, you feel cleansed from the inside out, deeply

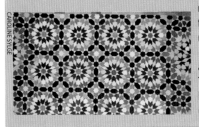

CAROLINE SYLGE

relaxed, and with baby-soft skin. Put your feet up in a cooler place, and enjoy a sweet mint tea.

You can experience authentic public and hotel hammams in Dubai, Jordan, Tunisia, Morocco, Turkey (where it is spelt hamam), and Egypt; try a *hammam ramal* (sand bath) at Siwa (see page 165).

YOGA HOLIDAY

Yoga Travel

⊙ ⊗ ⊘ ↘14

Marrakech and the coast
T+44 (0)870-350 3545
www.yogatravel.co.uk
From US$980 for 7 nights

If you want to enjoy the coast as well as Marrakech, Yoga Travel runs two eight-day yoga holidays a year which include two nights on the beach at Sidi Embarque and two at funky Essaouira. On Hendrix's Trail offers twice-daily yoga and the chance to get close to local Berber culture. In Marrakech you stay in the Moroccan-owned 18th-century Riad Omar (www.riadomar. com), where you explore the markets and sights, including quirkier ones such as a traditional Berber pharmacy. Sidi Embarque is a vast, empty Atlantic beach, where you stay at a riad belonging to a local sculptor. This romantic, untouristy area is full of olive groves and crumbling kasbahs. You then move on to Essaouira, whose popularity hasn't dented its laid-back, hippy-chic vibe and where you can enjoy a café au lait and pain au chocolat in a bustling café in the ancient medina. You sleep at the **Riad Al Medina** (www.riadalmadina.com), where Jimi Hendrix stayed when he lived here in the 1970s. The trip attracts people of all ages, and beginners are welcome. Yoga is taught by expert kundalini teacher Julie Cuddihy (www.anaharta.com), and you'll be guided by Will Cottrell, an experienced tour leader who also freelances for adventure travel company **Explore**. Yoga Travel also runs trips to Egypt (see page 168).

Make it a hammam hotel

If you're extending your body and soul escape in Morocco with a long weekend in Marrakech or the Atlas Mountains, stay at a hotel with a hammam, where a cleansing sweat, scrub and massage will keep you in a relaxed state (see box on facing page) and you'll be able to go back to your own room to chill straight after.

Owned and designed by Vanessa Branson, **Riad El Fenn** (T+212 24-441210, www.riadelfenn.com), in the Mouassine area of the Medina, is a calm, exquisite oasis with individually designed rooms and costs from US$410 per room per day. The gommage treatment here ends with two halves of a fresh orange being squeezed over your body, and a jar of gorgeous-smelling rosewater poured over your head and face. Afterwards, sit in a cool courtyard by a pomegranate tree sipping mint tea. Holistic and beauty treatments are also available, and there are two pools.

Riad Farnatchi (T+212 24-384910, www.riadfarnatchi.com) has only five suites and an elegant but intimate homely atmosphere. It costs from US$360 per room per day. You can use its gorgeous white marble hammam for free from 1600 to 1900 every day. There are gommage, massage or beauty treatments on offer, and a small pool with an underwater jetstream (heated in the winter).

The hamman at the funky **Riad El Cadi** (T+212 24-378655, www.riadelcadi.com) has rich red walls, and there's a small solar-heated pool and a jacuzzi you can dip into afterwards. It costs from US$140 per room per night. Or try the lovely **Riad Ariha** (www.riadariha.com), from US$80 per room per night, which provides bed and breakfast in a tucked-away corner of the city. Use the small but perfectly formed hammam, or arrange to have an exfoliation followed by a massage. There's a plunge pool in a vibrant white courtyard, and the owner,

Barbara Abu-Zahra, is a yoga teacher with 18 years experience of sivananda, iyengar and vinyasa flow. If she's here when you visit, you can have a one-to-one class with her. 'Jasmine' is the nicest of the six rooms, at the top of the riad.

Alternatively, drive 1½ hours from Marrakech into the Atlas Mountains, to the **Kasbah du Toubkal** (T+44 (0)1883-744392, www.kasbahdutoubkal.com), whose rough and ready hammam uses rubber tyres as water buckets and features an ice-cold plunge pool. Perched above the village of Imlil and only accessible by donkey track, this Berber hospitality centre ploughs its profits back into the local community and has won a string of awards for sustainable and responsible tourism. Rooms from US$ 200 per night. You won't be blown away by the erratic service or the mediocre food (ask in advance if you don't want red meat, wheat or dairy), but it's a perfect base for well-guided treks and boasts staggeringly romantic views over the mountains. A room in the tower gives you easy access to its small rooftop, which is ideal for doing your own yoga or meditating in private.

For a more upmarket experience of a kasbah, head to the village of Asni and Richard Branson's eclectic **Kasbah Tamadot** (T+44 (0)20-8600 0430, www.virginlimited edition.co.uk), where the hammam is a step away from a lovely dark blue swimming pool; it costs from US$430 per room per night. Back nearer Marrakech, **Kasbah Agafay** (T+212 24-368600, www.kasbahagafay.com) costs from US$515 per room per night and offers gloriously expansive desert views despite being just off a road, as well as a roomy hammam set next to a courtyard garden and a pretty spa with muslin drapes and water features. Its star feature, however, is its cookery school, set in an organic herb and vegetable garden, where you can learn some exotic yet easy recipes to take home.

Africa & the Levant Morocco

Left: Riad El Fenn. **Above**: Kasbah du Toubkal.

Kenya

From a fitness course on the Watamu coast to a chilled-out yoga safari, Kenya's natural habitats are a brilliant place to recharge.

Fact file

➲ **Visa:** Required by citizens of the EU, US, Canada, Australia and New Zealand

ⓘ **IDD:** +254

Ⓢ **Currency:** Kenyan shilling (KES)

◷ **Time zone:** GMT +3 hours

⚡ **Electricity:** 220v

ⓘ **Tourist board:**
www.magicalkenya.com

YOGA & ACTIVITY HOLIDAY

Chemoset Yoga

🌐 🏠 ⚙ 🧭 ↘15

Various national parks
T+254 (0)73-345 0224
www.chemoset-yoga.com
From US$390 per person per day for a minimum of 10 days

Chemoset is a small private company specializing in personalized mobile yoga and pilates camping safaris throughout East Africa. Run by Tor Frost, a third-generation Kenyan, the safaris can be tailor-made for your needs and take place in remote locations such as the Meru National Park, the Aberdares National Park and the Masai Mara.

Pilates, yoga and meditation sessions are held wherever and whenever you feel like it: at dawn under a thorn tree looking across the savannah before a morning game drive, at sunset to help ease tired muscles, or later by the campfire. Mats are carried for you wherever you go. The pilates is taught by Natasha Abrahams, who trained with American expert David Brown, while yoga is taught by Kenyan-born Katie Wedd, who trained with the British School of Yoga. Katie adapts her sessions with a mix of hatha, iyengar and kundalini yoga.

Guests sleep in very comfortable large dome tents, and Tor's crew of three do everything, from setting up camp to cooking. Food is prepared before departure and all preferences are catered for, from wheat-free diets to the type of wine. Everything is designed to enable you to move from place to place at will. Chemoset is for anyone interested in pilates and/or yoga (you can choose to do one or the other, or both).

The airport you fly to depends on where you want to go on safari, but it's usually Nairobi. Arrange your own itinerary with a group of friends, or join an organized 14-day trip for a maximum of six. Bring your own yoga mat – blocks and straps are provided. The price is inclusive of everything except flights. Chemoset also run yoga and pilates safaris in Tanzania and Uganda.

ISLAND RETREAT

Fatuma's Tower

🌐 🧭 ↘16

Shela village, Lamu island
T+ 254 (0)42-632079
www.lamuyoga.com
From US$55-75 per person per night full board

Fatuma's Tower is an enchanting retreat in a secluded position in Shela village, with its tangle of narrow sandy lanes and lovely beach. It was renovated from the ruins of an 18th-century Arab house by English yoga teacher Gilles Turle, who has lived in Kenya for over 40 years. The yoga room follows the lead of traditional mosques by using slanted windows to deflect direct sunlight and keep it cool. Gilles trained to be a sivananda yoga teacher at the **Sivananda Yoga Vedanta Dhanwantari Ashram** in Kerala (see page 224), and teaches a mixture of sivananda and ashtanga. Another resident teacher, Monica, teaches every morning, and private classes can be arranged. Those not into yoga are also made welcome; this is the kind of place where you could come for a few nights and end up staying several weeks. Snorkelling, walking and dhow trips can all be arranged.

Left: Chemoset Yoga. **Above and below**: Inside and out, Fatuma's Tower makes the ideal place to come and relax, even for those not into yoga.

Africa & the Levant Kenya

In the tower there are six bedrooms, all with bright African curtains, cushions and bedspreads, wooden shutters, fans and mozzie nets. The two rooms on the top floor make an ideal retreat for friends or a couple, as they share their own veranda with two chill-out daybeds. There's also The Sand Castle, a small three-bedroom apartment beside Gilles' house, and The Cottage, which has one double bedroom and sitting area. Decor throughout is simple with a touch of the bohemian - whitewashed walls, engraved dark wood furniture, painted tiles and corners stuffed with antiques from all over Lamu. The breakfast room looks onto a secluded courtyard dominated by a mature acacia tree; there's also a rooftoop from which to stargaze. You dine in a candlelit open-air courtyard shaded by a mammoth tamarind tree. Food is tasty vegetarian, with fresh fish whenever possible – expect little surprises, such as home-made passion fruit tart in the shape of a heart. You can bring your own wine, and non-residential guests sometimes come to eat here too.

Fatuma's Tower attracts an international crowd of all ages who are into yoga or just in need of time out. You'll feel comfortable here alone, or it's a lovely place to come with a friend or partner. Fly to Lamu Island from Nairobi or Mombasa. All flights land on the airstrip on Manda Island, from where it's easy to catch a boat to Lamu Island.

UK-based ashtanga vinyasa yoga teacher **Liz Lark** (www.lizlark.com) leads yoga retreats to Fatuma's Tower once or twice a year, followed by yoga safaris in the Masai Mara, from US$1700 per week excluding flights. Yoga twice a day is complemented by swimming, hiking, boat trips and chilling out.

Keep your face to the sunshine and you cannot see the shadows.

Helen Keller

Fitness holiday

Wildfitness 🦶🧗🍎🏃🪂 ↘17

Based on an isolated, pristine stretch of the Watamu coast, Wildfitness uses natural habitats to help get you fit. You'll find yourself sprinting up sand dunes, swimming across creeks and jogging through sweet-smelling eucalyptus forest in a non-competitive environment designed to increase your body confidence. It's the brainchild of Tara Wood, a competitive kite surfer and all-round athlete who grew up in Kenya.

Where you stay Your base is Baraka House ('blessing' in Swahili), set right on the beach and angled to catch the Kaskasi monsoon breezes. It's open and spacious with shaded lounge areas and two rooftops with 360° views. Each of the five en suite bedrooms has a veranda or balcony with ocean views. Furniture is made of painted natural wood, walls are washed cinnamon and there are handmade cushions and embroidered bedspreads in greens, blues and purples. Reading lamps and light switches *inside* the mosquito nets mean you won't have to risk random mozzie bites just to turn out the light. The house accommodates 10 people sharing; a five-minute walk away is a three-bedroom villa to accommodate any overflowing with a pretty garden, huge veranda and small cooling-off pool, though it's not as special as Baraka.

What you do Run by a changing rota of personal trainers from the CHEK Institute (Corrective High-Performance Exercise Kinesiology, devised by Paul Chek, www.chekinstitute.com), Wildfitness is all about helping to break the negative thought patterns which make us say too often, "'I can't do that". Depending on the length of your stay, you'll be encouraged to jog 6 km through the local Sokoke forest, walk for five hours along a deserted beach, swim through the sea, play football with the locals, compete in a triathlon or swim 3 km across the local Meda creek, accompanied by your own canoe and boatman. Nothing is compulsory, most things are lots of fun, and the most strenuous activities take place in the early morning and late afternoon.

There are also group sessions drawing on the interests of the personal trainers running your week, including free-weight training,

> ❝❞
>
> Wildfitness got me to remember how good sport made me feel before I hit 14, school sport got competitive and I lost interest. It was incredibly inspiring to be in such natural surroundings – swimming across the Meda Creek was the highlight, fantasies of crocodiles aside, and inspired me to go on a Swim Trek holiday shortly after (see page 136). I thought my heart would explode after sprinting up and down a steep sand dune six times – but I slept like a log that night and felt so good the next day the pain began not to matter. Our group included a comedian, lawyer, management consultant, broker and drill supervisor of an offshore oil rig, though what we did and where we were in life became refreshingly irrelevant when we were all sweating together. Nine days got rid of so much tension I felt more chilled out than I had done in months. I'd certainly go back, and for longer.
>
> *Caroline*

working on your core muscles using a softball and sports such as Thai kick-boxing (a little daunting at first, but actually a surprisingly good mental release). Daily circuit training uses subtly painful (and so very effective) exercises devised around swiss boards, wobble boards, skipping ropes, free weights and medicine balls, and free exercises to help increase your movement, flexibility and strength. The Primal Move circuit is especially powerful, getting you to lift, bend, twist, push and pull in ways most office-bound bodies have forgotten.

It's not a problem if the last time you did anything like this was in your school gym when you were five – you're encouraged to go at your own pace, and to stop whenever you need to. Lots of 'active recovery' is built into your programme, such as barefoot acrobatics on a sand island, and snorkelling in the Watamu Marine Park (which is just offshore from Baraka House and teeming with coral fish). A favourite with many is floating through the local mangrove swamps on rubber rings – a highly meditative experience in the mellow afternoon light.

Once or twice a week there'll be more stretchy classes in pilates or yoga – and those wishing to do their own practice can have a mat in their room. You can also have regular massage from very good local masseuses in Baraka's dojo, where you'll be accompanied by a collection of fascinated Sykes monkeys who live near the house. Deep-sea fishing, scuba-diving, catamaran sailing, windsurfing,

CAROLINE SYLGE
CAROLINE SYLGE

kite-surfing, bike riding to the local Gede ruins or a spot of shopping in Malindi can also be arranged.

What you eat and drink Organic food is served five times a day to keep your energy levels up and stop you binge eating after all that exercise. Breakfast is home-made muesli, yoghurt, fresh fruit, home-made brown bread and a choice of eggs, while lunch and dinner are a mix of salads and vegetable dishes with lots of protein, especially fresh fish. Snacks at 1100 and 1600 could be anything from fruit and nuts to raw fish pieces, or a bowl of soup. Raw food is offered, and vegetarians are catered for. Caffeinated tea and alcohol are on offer for those who desire them, but most people resist. There are talks on nutrition, when you are encouraged to start eating according to your metabolic type. Dinner conversation is mellow; without the stimulus of alcohol, and nicely exhausted by the day's activities, most people feel like going to bed by around 2100. Those who do drink find themselves getting tipsy after just one glass, and going to bed just after 2100 too. There are local clubs and restaurants if you get an energy kick, and one group night out a week.

Who goes A mix of men and women, mostly in their thirties and forties, and mostly from the UK. Most people are reasonably fit and wanting to get fitter, but if you hate exercise and are not very fit at all, you'll find Wildfitness to be a very supportive environment. Quite a few people are travelling alone to reassess their options in between jobs or relationships, or just to de-stress and get some much-needed sunshine. Wildfitness also makes a great holiday for friends or a couple – ask for room three on the ground floor of Baraka, a lovely huge room with two walk-in wardrobe spaces and a large veranda.

Essentials Wildfitness (T+44 (0)845-056 8343) takes a maximum of 10 people at any one time. Nine-day (from US$4300), two-week, 3½-week and five- week courses run throughout the year except May, June and July. As the week progresses you're likely to want to push yourself harder, so try for a minimum of two weeks if you can. This is an expensive course, so make sure you come when you're in the right frame of mind to make the most of it, and if you're alone, share a room. Organic toiletries, beach towels and dressing gowns made of kikois (African sarongs) are provided. Take sports and casual clothes, a rash vest, earplugs, goggles, sturdy sandals you don't mind getting wet and two pairs of worn-in running shoes. Fly direct to Mombasa (a two-hour drive away and a US$70 transfer) or take an internal flight from Nairobi to Malindi (a 20-minute drive away and a free transfer).

YOGA & ACTIVITY HOLIDAY

Inner Safari Yoga

🌿 ☀ ⛰ ✈ 🧘 ⬇18

Masai bushland and Watamu coast
T+44 (0)845-056 8343
www.innersafariyoga.com
From US$3500 for 14 nights

CAROLINE SYLGE

Inner Safari Yoga started in 2007 and is run by Checkie, a bodyworker and yoga teacher who has lived in Kenya all her life and who is the mother of Tara Wood, who founded Wildfitness. Two-week holidays combining yoga, meditation and safari treks run eight times a year, seven based at a local private game ranch, Tumarin, in January-April, August and November, and one based at Baraka House on the Watamu coast (see previous spread) in October. Tumarin Ranch is 1½ hours' drive from the Nanyuki township near the equator line in Kenya and surrounded by bushland full of elephants, giraffe and other game as well as flocks of domestic camel. The highlight of the holiday is a three-day camel trek through the bush with local Masai tribesmen, with two nights spent sleeping out under the stars – Checkie has planned most of the trips to coincide

CAROLINE SYLGE

with a full moon. On the trek you'll get a chance to do group meditation, nature walks and learn about shamanism.

The rest of the time you camp at the private ranch, where silent sitting and walking meditation is taught and explored. There are two sessions of sivananda-based yoga a day; an energizing class at sunrise, and a more relaxing class later. Beginners and those already into yoga are welcome, as everyone is encouraged to go at their own pace. The ranch has a river for swimming, rocky outcrops for stargazing and lots of areas for biking, hiking, bird and animal watching, and you can also snorkel or take boat trips. Friends or partners who don't want to participate in yoga or meditation are welcome.

Also timetabled in are creativity workshops and sessions on mind/body subjects such as massage, simple healing techniques and understanding the chakras.

A masseuse accompanies the group, and there is ample time to read, write and

unwind. Evenings are spent around a camp fire, star gazing, listening to a guest speaker, playing games, strumming a guitar – or take yourself off and go swimming by moonlight.

There's a dojo for yoga, and accommodation is on the riverbank in comfortable private tents divided from one another by vegetation. Food is fresh and delicious, with fish complementing a mainly vegetarian diet. At Baraka House, you'll do yoga on the rooftop or in the dojo, and sleep in the main house or the nearby pool house (see under Wildfitness).

COASTAL RETREAT

Shaanti Holistic Health Retreat

🌿 ⛰ ○ 🏠 ⊙ ✦ 🧘 ⬇19

Diani beach
T+254 (0)40-320 2064
www.shaantihhr.com
From US$140 per person per night including full board and yoga

Healthy stopovers in Nairobi

If you need to stay overnight in Nairobi, **Fairview** (T+254 (0)20-271 0090, fairviewkenya.com from US$90 per night per room) has a swimming pool, pretty gardens, a gym and a secluded feel. The **Serena Hotel** (T+254 (0)20-282 2000, serenahotels.com, from US$320 per night per room) has an outdoor pool and the Maisha Health Club with steam rooms,

jacuzzis, and health and beauty treatments – try the African Coffee Scrub to cleanse your skin. Or blow the budget at **Giraffe Manor** (T+254 (0)20-891078, giraffe manor.com, from US$300 per night per person), a lovely grand house with giraffes wandering the grounds where massage and private yoga sessions can be arranged in advance.

Opposite top: Inner Safari Yoga's Baraka House. **Above:** Shaanti Holistic Health Retreat.
Bottom: A room at Kizingo.

natural yoghurt and honey facials, and indulge in a serene 'star bath', soaking in a sunken bubble bath tub on the lawn under the stars, surrounded by candles.

Fellow guests include expats, aid workers and an increasing number of Europeans. Bring your own flip-flops, and avoid walking alone on the beach at night after 2000. The resort is 1½ hours from Mombasa airport, or eight minutes from Ukanda domestic airport.

Yoga Safari with Geraldine Ross

Masai Mara and Lamu
T+44 (0)20-7722 5511
www.gerry4yoga.net
From US$3800 excluding flights

UK-based iyengar teacher Geraldine Ross runs a two-week yoga safari in Kenya twice a year, in October and March. The first week's base is Fisherman's Camp on Lake Naivasha, when you'll enjoy walking safaris to see giraffe and impala, and a three-day jeep safari with local guides into the Masai Mara National Reserve to see the big five, all complemented by daily yoga to ease your aches and pains. In the second week you'll be based on Lamu island, where Geraldine hires out in its entirety **Kizingo** (kizingo.com), an eco lodge only accessible by boat and graced by deserted beaches. There are just eight hand-built *bandas* (traditional huts) here with uncluttered interiors, solar panels and eco-toilets. Geraldine takes a maximum of eight people on each yoga safari, so privacy and individual attention are guaranteed.

A set of eight smart chalets set on a peaceful beach in Diani, Shaanti is a good place to come for a few days' rest; it also runs stress-buster, wellbeing and weight-shifting programmes lasting up to two weeks. The complex is small, but there's enough space to find solitude, including a meditation and chill-out area with comfy sofas, and 'peace pavilions' by the beach where you can go for privacy. There are optional daily yoga and meditation classes, on an open yoga platform with wooden floors looking directly over the beach – styles vary according to who is teaching. There's no alcohol on sale here, and no smoking allowed.

Each en suite chalet overlooks the beach from its own veranda and is decorated in neutral creams and browns, set off with vibrantly coloured cushions and fabrics. Facilities include an outdoor pool, an aromatherapy steam room, a flotation tank and an indoor hot jacuzzi with an oval window looking out over the beach. You can use the jacuzzi 24 hours a day – ask the porter if it's late at night. Food is mainly vegetarian with some fish from the nearby Diani fishing village, all served in a pleasant shaded treetop house on the front lawn overlooking the beach.

Treatments include basic ayurveda sesame oil massages and sirodhara, though there is no ayurvedic doctor here and they don't run courses of ayurvedic treatments. Reflexology, homeopathy, dance therapy and nutrition consultations can also be arranged. There's a strong focus on pampering: you can beautify yourself with body wraps and

🌀 Soul food

Watamu Turtle Watch

(watamuturtles.com) on the Kenyan coast educates local fishermen and hoteliers to practise a sustainable way of using their marine resource. Since it was set up in 1997 it has saved over 2000 turtles accidentally caught in fishing nets, and protected over 300 nests from which over 28,000 hatchlings have successfully made their way to the ocean. You can adopt a sea turtle nest or make a donation.

Safari and spa

As well as awe-inspiring safari country, Kenya has a growing number of places which offer indulgent treatments for your wellbeing. UK-based specialist safari company **African Safari Roots** (T+44 (0)1736-367635, www.africansafariroots.com) runs tailor-made wellness safaris to lodges throughout Africa, including Loisaba Lodge in Kenya's Laikipia plateau. Game drives and walking, horse and camel safaris are followed by massages and beauty treatments in the safari spa. You can choose to sleep out under the stars in special 'star beds', and there's an open-air bubble bath with a tranquil view of the Karissia hills (from US$2800 for 5 nights per person sharing).

The luxury ecolodge **Saruni Camp** (www.sarunicamp.com) just outside the Masai Mara game park employs a mainly Masai staff and contributes to local community projects. The small Masai Wellbeing Space here offers massages and facials using local African plants and seeds, from a Masai therapist trained in Italy (from US$300 per person per night, www.sarunicamp.com, see box on page 185).

If there's a group of you, **Hippo Point** (T+254 (0)733-333014) is an impressive house for rent in the middle of its own wildlife

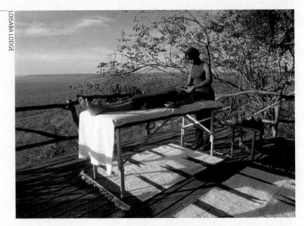

LOISABA LODGE

sanctuary on Lake Naivasha in Kenya's Rift Valley. It has gorgeous grounds complete with watchtower and swimming pool, with six bedrooms in the house and five in the tower. You can actually walk amongst wildlife here, which includes zebra, giraffe and a variety of antelope. A visiting therapist gives full-body aromatherapy massages and reiki in a lakeside gazebo, and private yoga sessions, facials, manicures and pedicures can be arranged in advance (from US$500 per night for the whole property).

Alternatively, divide your time between two different venues with UK-based agent **Wellbeing Escapes** (see Resources) which offers a 10-day Spa & Safari Escape with seven nights at Shaanti Holistic Health Retreat (see previous spread) followed by a three-night/four-day safari at Galdessa (www.galdessa.com), a luxury tented camp in Tsavo East National Park. Indulge in massage, reflexology, a facial, twice-daily yoga classes, a daily meditation class and a daily pranayama class at Shaanti, then hang out with the big five on game drives, exploring birdlife and wild fauna on foot (from US$3299 per person excluding flights).

AFRICANSAFARIROOTS.COM

LOISABA LODGE

South Africa

RURAL RETREAT

Bushmans Kloof Wilderness Reserve & Retreat

Cederberg mountains
T +27 (0)21-685 5210
www.bushmanskloof.co.za
From US$270 per person per night

Bushmans Kloof, a four-hour drive from Cape Town, has stunning views across the Cederberg mountains and rugged plains of the Great Karoo. Set in a remote World Heritage site renowned for its ancient rock art, it offers real luxury in the wilderness. You can explore the area's fascinating rock art sites with expert guides and the resident archaeologist. Visit the 10,000-year-old rock art in the early morning, when the light is best and you can feel the energy of the landscape.

For a pampering fix, there's a spa offering facials and Moya therapies, which use aromatic, therapeutic and native South African essences such as Cape snowbush, buchu, zinziba, Cape chamomile and lanyana to heal, nourish and soothe. Reflexology, aromatherapy, Swedish and deep tissue massages are also available.

There is a gym and three pools at the lodge, one of which is heated, plus plenty of hiking routes and the chance to swim in natural rock pools; mountain biking, rock climbing and canoeing are also available, or take a game drive to spot antelope, zebra and wildebeest then watch the sun set from a nearby hilltop with a glass of wine.

Guests stay in thatched cottages styled in the Cape Dutch tradition. A superb five-course table d'hôte menu is served at dinner, and special diets can be catered for. Eat on the outdoor terrace, which is situated in a natural sandstone amphitheatre. Fly to Cape Town, from where it's a 270-km drive. Make sure your fuel tank is topped up.

Above: Bushman rock art painting.
Below: Bushmans Kloof homestead.

Be healed by Africa's herbs, plants and vines, or retreat and be pampered in the bush.

Fact file

- **Visa:** Not required for citizens of EU countries, US, Canada, Australia and New Zealand
- **IDD:** +27
- **Currency:** Rand (ZAR)
- **Time zone:** GMT +2 hours
- **Electricity:** 220/230v
- **Tourist board:** www.southafrica.net

HOTEL & SPA

Fordoun

🟢 🟢 🟢 🟢 🟢 🟢 🟢 🟢 🟢 🔲22

KwaZulu Natal
T +27 (0)33-266 6217
www.fordoun.com
From US$210 per room per night

The low-lying buildings of this former settler homestead and dairy farm are almost lost amongst the green pastures and gently rolling hills of KwaZulu Natal, but this destination spa should not be overlooked. Its roots are firmly planted in ancient African healing traditions, giving it a spirituality that other hotels with spas lack.

The conversion from dairy farm to boutique hotel has transformed the original buildings with high-quality, colonial-style furnishings and plenty of interesting memorabilia. There is a village feel about the place that creates a relaxed space, enhanced by the friendly and welcoming staff. History is echoed in the interiors of the 17 double suites, which are comfortable rather than overtly luxurious, with private verandas, huge mirrors and a deep, oval double bath.

There are forest canopy tours, fly-fishing and plenty of walking trails. Closer to home, you can investigate the indigenous herb garden, use the gym or dip into the pool with its jacuzzi, fountains and water jets. However, once you have experienced the beautiful softly-lit steam room with floor-to-ceiling mosaics, and nearly fallen asleep in the fantastic candlelit flotation pool, the desire to be anywhere else may well have left you.

African traditional healer Dr Elliott Ndlovu, a *sangoma* (spiritual healer), *inyanga* (medicinal healer), herbalist and ethno-botanist, is the inspiration behind the spa's healing therapies, many of which use traditional plant remedies such as African

The former settler homestead of Fordoun.

potato, marula, aloe vera and artemesia as well as local red and white clay to sooth and uplift the body and soul (see box opposite). Book a consultation with the doctor and he will advise you on plant medicine and, on request, predict your future with animal bones. His consulting room and two of the treatment rooms are designed in Zulu style, and his intriguing and deeply luxurious treatments can be easily combined with the

---

Healthy stopovers in Cape Town

Cape Town has some lovely restorative places to stay for a night or two. If you're flush, **Cape Grace** (from US$490 per room per night, T +27 (0)21-418 0495, www.capegrace.com) is right on the V&A waterfront with a full view of Table Mountain, and offers some lovely treatments that draw on African healing traditions (see box opposite). You can have mats, stretch bands, even trampolines delivered to your room, and there's a communal steam and jacuzzi in which to soak. A 15-minute drive away is the much-publicized **Twelve Apostles Hotel & Spa** (from US$400 per room per night, T +27 (0)21-437 9000, www.12apostleshotel.com), worth a stay for its spectacular location overlooking the rolling Atlantic and backed by mountains. There are expert treatments here, but be prepared for a disappointingly dark and cave-like spa.

For a more affordable option, **Four Rosmead** (from US$200 per room per night, T +27 (0)21-480 3810, www.fourros mead.com) is a quiet boutique guesthouse in a listed building with just eight lovely rooms, a saltwater pool, a vegetarian-friendly menu and a treatment room for massages and reflexology. **An African Villa** (from US$120 per room per night, T +27 (0)21-423 2162, www.capetowncity.co.za), is a contemporary B&B in a leafy neighbourhood with stunning interiors, plunge pool, courtyard and chilled-out ambience.

For drop-in yoga classes in Cape Town, there's **Moksha**, on the third floor of Thebe Hosken House on Mill Street (T +27 (0)21-465 1733, www.moksha.biz) who also arrange regular retreats and host international teachers such as ashtanga guru Danny Paradise and Rema Datta. Beginners pilates and yoga classes can be arranged at **Stillness Manor & Spa** (US$84 per room per night, T +27 (0)21-713 8800, www.stillness manor.com), a 20-minute drive from town, with a large and beautiful garden, welcoming staff, a wide range of treatments and views over Constantia valley.

Cape Town boasts some wonderful places to spend a night or two before catching a flight home.

◑ Body language

African healing

Africa has a wealth of indigenous herbs and plants that have been used for centuries to calm and cure. Meet Africans who know their stuff, and they'll offer you pieces of botanical wisdom – that the leaves from the leleshwa tree have similar properties to tea tree oil and are used as a natural deodorant, or that acacia bark can be ground up to make a soup to aid digestion. Different tribes have traditionally drawn on the natural world for whatever they need, be it clay for fertility rituals or desert sand for a natural body scrub, and used plants and massage to ease pain and cure diseases rather than pamper or beautify. The best treatments for westerners to be found across the continent draw on this rich heritage.

Traditional African healer Dr Elliott Ndlovu at **Fordoun** hotel and spa in South Africa's KwaZulu Natal (see previous page), for example, has a large garden of traditional medicinal plants which include a crop of African potato (*inkomfe* in Zulu). Resembling giant black turnips, these are reputedly very good for the immune system and have anti-cancer properties. They're used in treatments at Fordoun, and sold in pepper mills so you can take them home and grind them onto salads. Dr Ndlovu also blends indigenous herbs into his massage oils, such as detoxing artemesia, used locally as a decongestant for coughs, colds and sinus troubles, and as a remedy for malaria, or de-stressing leonotis leonorus, Africa's wild cannabis plant traditionally used to treat stress-related disorders such as skin diseases and itching. The signature treatment, 'Umcako Lungis', features the local white clay, apparently gathered at midnight by maidens and post-menopausal women and then boiled in a large pot for many hours. Applied at Fordoun after a good steam bath, it's an extremely slimy but effective way to soften and purify the skin.

If it's knotted muscles you want to cure, the signature treatment at **Mount Grace** in Magaliesburg (see page 189) and its sister hotel **Cape Grace** in Cape Town (see box opposite) is the thaba massage. Sotho for mountain, the thaba is based on the Zulu ideal of 'strengthening for the fight ahead'. Two therapists apply *intelezi*, a soothing gel of aloe vera and eucalyptus, to the ankles, wrists, arms and head, and then use a *knopkierie* – a Zulu fighting stick with rounded ends – to work deep into tense muscles. Other treatments draw on the healing and cleansing rituals of South Africa's desert-dwelling hunters, the Khoi San – the 'African Cape' massage includes an effective circular stomach motion, drawing on the Khoi San's belief that the stomach is the centre of one's being, and the 'African Way' treatment uses a dry scrub to exfoliate your skin, mirroring the Khoi San cleansing ritual which has them rubbing their bodies with sand. Heading north on the continent to the Masai Wellbeing Space at the **Saruni Camp** in Kenya (see page 182), a Masai therapist will give you an invigorating wallop with a back massager. Traditionally used to ease the muscles of the Masai women who carry huge piles of firewood on their backs, the massager is made from local olmurmura seeds packed tightly into a cloth and attached to a wooden stick. Or you can indulge here in a facial using a compress of leleshwa leaves, which help exfoliate the skin.

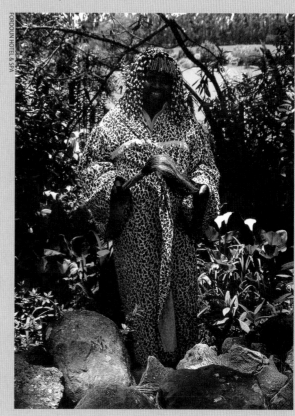

FORDOUN HOTEL & SPA

more familiar aromatherapy, thalassotherapy, reflexology and massages.

The food and service are excellent. For dinner you can pre-order a healthy alternative with grilled or steamed chicken and fish and the spa juice bar offers a good selection of healthy options and smoothies. Most guests are South African and you'll meet couples, groups of friends and conference delegates who bring their partner for the spa.

Use of the flotation pool, gym, sauna and steam room are included in the rate, and treatments are extremely good value. The cheapest package, The Couple's Delight, costs from US$ 145 per person and includes a night's bed and breakfast. Fordoun is 150 km from Durban and pick ups can be arranged.

HOTEL & SPA
Lanzerac Hotel and Spa

🐟 ⭕ 🧖 ⓥ ❄ ✳ 🅿 ⎣23

Stellenbosch, Western Cape
T+27 (0)21-887 1132
www.lanzerac.co.za
From US$360 per room per night

The Lanzerac, a 300-year-old traditional Cape Dutch wine estate with an excellent reputation as a hotel, started to offer wellness programmes in 2006. With giant oak trees, spacious grounds and lovely mountain views, these are inspiring surroundings in which to kick-start a healthy lifestyle.

The spa and wellness centre is light, modern and airy, with its own separate and secluded pool area, and a garden jacuzzi

Lanzerac Hotel and spa.

● Soul food

Project Play (www.projectplay.net) is dedicated to enriching the lives of children and adults in African nations through the world's most popular sport, soccer. Set up by Mike Mitchell, founder of Body and Soul Adventures in Brazil (see page 378), the charity has so far provided 5000 soccer balls as well as other soccer equipment to the Republic of Niger. Project Play, in collaboration with the Peace Corps, aims to provide educational incentives, promote self-esteem and foster community pride while generating confidence and hope for those in impoverished African nations.

looking on to the vines. There are saunas, steam rooms, wet rooms, four treatment rooms and a fitness sudio with yoga, pilates and spinning classes on offer. It's all very modern and high-tech – there's even an ATM – and the spa café is more like a cocktail bar than a health bar, serving Lanzerac's own wine and beer and gourmet sandwiches.

That said, the therapists here are very good. Book a massage with François, who is partially sighted and has an excellent sensitive touch. If you're a couple, you can do a massage workshop and learn how to massage each other. There's a doctor on site who offers health and lifestyle assessments under the South African Blueprint Health programme (www.blueprinthealth.co.za), and the hotel draws on a wide pool of very good freelance therapists including a nutritionist, physiotherapist, personal trainer, reiki practitioner and chiropractor.

The hotel is a restored old manor with whitewashed walls and gabled roofs, with new buildings built in the same style. Choose from 48 very large en suite rooms or three pool suites, all individually decorated with antiques and period furniture. The gourmet food served here is superb, and the menu

changes seasonally from French to South African to Italian – special diets can be catered for. The Lanzerac is 4 km outside Stellenbosch, and a one-hour drive from Cape Town.

AYURVEDA RETREAT
Nalanda Ayurvedic Centre

🐟 🌀 ⭕ 🧖 ⓥ ✳ 🅿 ⎣24

Hout Bay, Cape Peninsula
T+27 (0)21-790 4200
www.nalanda.co.za
From US$1135 per person per week

Set in the most beautiful part of Cape Town, surrounded by mountains and sea, Nalanda has been running as a day centre since early 2000 but moved location in 2006 to enable people to come and retreat. Uniquely, the centre's staff includes African women and men from local township communities, who have been well-trained in ayurveda by founder Margit Gilliot.

In a homely atmosphere you can do vegetarian cooking courses, have one-to-one sessions in ayurvedic diet and lifestyle counselling, listen to talks by the ayurvedic doctor, undertake short retreats or do a full-on two-week ayurveda detox, or panchakarma. As well as a host of ayurvedic treatments (from US$25 for a foot, hand or head massage), yoga is available daily.

For those on a retreat, there is one en suite double bedroom and several other rooms with shared bathrooms in a beautiful thatched farmhouse with an open-plan kitchen and big shady garden with saline pool. The centre is non-smoking, vegetarian, and alcohol- and drug-free in order to create an atmosphere conducive to healing. Meals are made using ayurvedic principles, and are mostly egg- and dairy-free, though ghee is sometimes used.

Nalanda attracts mainly women in their twenties to fifties, though everyone is welcome. Fly to Cape Town (45 minutes away), from where pickups can be arranged. The weather is warm from November to March, but the rainy season is also very

beautiful, when everything is green and the sea can be stormy and dramatic.

RURAL RETREAT

Rosendal Winery & Wellness Retreat

⊕ ⊘ ↘25

Voogds West, Robertson, Western Cape
T+27 (0)23-626 1570
www.rosendalwinery.com
From US$105 per room per night

Set in the heart of the countryside and surrounded by vineyards, this is a peaceful and isolated place with unobtrusive, friendly staff. It's quite feasible to do absolutely nothing here for a several days, and is a particularly good spot to rest up at the end of a holiday before the flight home.

Rosendal is a restored 1800s farm, all Cape

Top: Santé Winelands. Above: Rosendal.

Dutch whitewashed architecture, thick walls and cool rooms, surrounded by established vines of table grapes which guests are invited to pick for themselves, green lawns and lots of rose bushes attracting butterflies. The main building and room terraces have lovely views over the (unheated) pool, a farm dam with ducks and herons, and open countryside. There are lots of loungers around the pool, tables and chairs set up at quiet, peaceful spots, an outdoor jacuzzi and cold pool with loungers, and an indoor steam room and treatment room where you can indulge in facials, scrubs, wraps and massages using Theravine, a local product made in Stellenbosch incorporating vine extracts, red wine and grapeseed oil as antioxidant treats for your skin.

You sleep in one of eight large rooms, each with high ceilings, enormous beds and a curtained two-person bath. They are all very romantic, with chaises longues, flowers and throw cushions, startlingly white linen, huge ornate mirrors, distressed colonial antique furniture and French windows with satin curtains. Be warned, the walls are a little thin so you may hear the guests in the next room.

There are walks around the immediate vineyards and to neighbouring farms, and Rosendal can arrange game drives to see some smaller African mammals at the nearby **Pat Busch Nature Reserve**. Have a picnic or go fishing on the nearby Breede

River, or just sit on the stoop and watch the birds and the sunset.

Meals use home-grown fruit and vegetables, though don't expect gourmet dishes – vegetarians need to pre-book. You can drink the local mountain stream water, and Rosendal's home-grown Merlot is very good. Come in the summer to make use of all the facilities, and bring a partner or friend. Rosendal is a two-hour drive from Cape Town in the heart of the Robertson winelands.

HOTEL & SPA

Santé Winelands Hotel & Wellness Centre

🧭 🍴 ☕ 👪 ⊙ ⊕ ⊛ ⊗ ⊘ ↘26

Klapmuts
T+27 (0)21-875 8100
www.santewellness.co.za
From US$420 per room per night

Sheltered by mountains and nestled in the tranquil Paarl-Franschhoek valley, Santé Winelands is on a picturesque wine estate 40 km from Cape Town. It's a destination spa as well as a hotel, offering relaxation and rejuvenation treatments, state-of-the-art equipment, and medically supervised stress-management and health programmes, all overseen by wellness director Dr Geraldine Mitton, health guru and author of *The Anti-Aging Handbook*.

The hotel's Bergan style of architecture, with its arched windows, red-tiled roofs and plastered walls, complements the landscape. The interiors are stylishly minimalist, with an African influence in the art and the rich earth tones. You can stay in a manor room, spa suite or self-catering villa – all are luxurious with great views and baths big enough for two. In the Wellness Centre spa, 24 rooms open out from candlelit, stone clad corridors, and highly-trained therapists provide a comprehensive range of therapies including Thai, ayurvedic and hot stone massages, aromatherapy and thalassotherapy using African marine algae.

Santé specializes in vinotherapy, using different products to those launched under the Vinotherapie trademark by Les Sources de Caudalie in France, but based on the same idea of using wine grapes for their antioxidant health-promoting properties (see page 84). Santé's signature treatment starts with an invigorating Shiraz body scrub using grape seeds, followed by a Chardonnay cocoon wrap to make the skin receptive to the massage; this takes place on a waterbed with internal 'pounders' that run up and down the body. It's gentle, but the machine is noisy and you might not find it as thorough as a hands-on massage. The experience ends in the soothing Cabernet Sauvignon wine casket bath, with colour, liquid-sound, and magnetic field therapy to create a feeling of balance and calm.

Yoga, tai chi and pilates enhance the feel-good factor, along with a state-of-the-art gym. After pounding the treadmill, mountain biking or following a fitness trail through the vineyards, ease yourself into the pool, steam rooms or sauna to relax tired muscles, or book a nutrition consultation or cardio-vascular profiling. Spa packages offer a complete health and wellbeing experience, including indulgent treatments alongside wine tasting, cookery classes and full body and lifestyle assessments, involving medical staff as well as therapists.

The bright and airy Cadeaux restaurant serves contemporary organic dishes and will cater for specific dietary or nutritional

requirements. Or you can indulge at the Sommelier restaurant, which has a gourmet menu featuring local delicacies.

Santé draws a younger, mainly South African crowd, in their thirties and forties, half of whom are couples, perhaps with one attending a conference in the hotel. Europeans come for the weight-loss, anti-aging and detox packages. It's also popular with post- and pre-op clients or those recovering from illness. The minimum stay is normally three days. Santé is a 40-minute drive from Cape Town International Airport.

PILATES HOLIDAY

Sarah Rosenfield pilates holiday

Welgevonden and Cape Town
T+44 (0)20-7722 4373
www.sarahpilates.com
From US$4410 for 10 days

Ex-singer and tour manager, Sarah Rosenfield, who trained at the Pilates Institute, runs a luxury safari and pilates trip to South Africa, including game drives, gourmet meals, sightseeing and daily pilates. The holiday starts at the luxurious **Shibula Lodge Bush and Spa** (www.shibulalodge.co.za) on the small Welgevonden private game reserve in the Waterberg Biosphere north of Johannesburg, which has nine sophisticated suites blending

lace and crystal with an ethnic decor, and a small spa offering massages and facials. Here you'll combine daily game drives with bush walks and pilates classes. Book in a massage during the day if you want to relax even more.

On leaving the game reserve, you take an internal flight (included) to **The Clarendon in Bantry Bay** (www.capestay.co.za/clarendon -bantrybay), a boutique hotel with fabulous views over the ocean. Daily pilates classes will be combined with additional trips to Cape Town's monuments, museums and wineries.

The trip takes between eight and 12 people, and runs once or twice a year depending on demand; a nutritionalist and fitness trainer can also be arranged if desired. The price includes pilates, accommodation, internal flights and transport. Sarah also leads retreats in Italy, France (see page 94) and Mallorca (see page 113).

Top: Interior of the Clarendon in Bantry Bay.
Above: On safari with Sarah Rosenfield.

Get nourished in the north

For a nourishing experience in the northern provinces of South Africa, head somewhere you can hole up for a good few days in private. An hour's drive from Tambo International Airport at Johannesburg, **Mount Grace** at Magaliesburg (T+27 (0)14-777 1350, www.mountgrace.co.za) is a very affordable country-house hotel (from US$85 per person per night), which offers the solace of a mountain location and a spa with fresh, modern interiors, all set in 10 acres of lovingly tended gardens. A magnet for frazzled city dwellers and couples seeking a stylish hideaway, the main house is decked out with gilt mirrors and lavish cloth wallpaper, and guests stay in individual thatched cottages with country-style furniture (if you're feeling flush, ask for a room with a heated splash pool). As well as a gourmet country restaurant, there's a spa café offering huge bowls of salads, pulses and grains, which can provide a detox menu for the virtuous. Some of the spa's treatment rooms are in separate thatched huts, and the tranquil hydrotherapy garden is a blissful experience with its jacuzzi, reflexology stream, waterfall pool and the wonderful flotation pool. Try the signature thaba massage (see box on page 185).

The exceptionally private **Cybele Forest Lodge & Spa** (T+27 (0)13-794 9500, www.cybele.co.za) costs from US$200 per person per night full board and is enclosed by a 120-ha pine forest full of monkeys and birds in the stunning Mpumalanga Panorama region. The converted 1800s hunting lodge has crackling fires in the evening and interesting antiques dotted about. Guests are accommodated in individual cottages with fireplaces and private walled gardens, and some have been known not to emerge from their rooms for whole weekends. Delicious meals are cooked by a friendly chef, and you can dine

CYBELE FOREST LODGE & SPA

under giant jacaranda and blue gum trees in fine weather. There are lots of flowering trees and benches for peaceful dreaming outside. Have a picnic at a pretty spot along a forest walk, or join a guided horse ride. There's a heated swimming pool, and a black slate and white-walled spa with two therapy rooms, a steam room fragranced with eucalyptus, and a sauna. Luxuriate in an outdoor sunken granite bath with lavender and milk and watch the stars, ease out tired muscles with a sports massage or indulge in a body wrap using French Algologie products. It's a 40-km drive to an entrance of the Kruger National Park, and 50 km from Kruger Mpumalanga airport.

Alternatively, head west of Kruger to **Garonga Safari Camp** (T+27 (0)82-440 3522, www.garonga.com) on the banks of the river Makhutswi, where you'll feel no need to rush off for a game drive; instead bed down in a hammock or soak in an outdoor bush bath; from US$260 per person per night full board. There are reiki treatments available in an open-air sala, and various holistic massages such as lomi lomi, Indian head, hot stone and aromatherapy. This is a calming, well-run, friendly place with gastronomic but healthy meals using home-grown and locally sourced ingredients wherever possible. With no single supplement and communal meals, it's also one of the few places in South Africa's game lands where you'll feel comfortable travelling alone. There's an infinity pool, and you sleep in close-to- nature half-tented en suite rooms, each with its own deck and fabulous hammock raised on stilts with views across a water- course. Choose the Hambleden suite for your own four-poster bed and a pool. It's a five-hour drive from Johannesburg, or take an internal flight to Hoedspruit or Phalaborwa.

GARONGA

Africa & the Levant South Africa

Rest of Africa

Get back to your roots and in touch with your body in the desert, on safari or by the coast.

KUSUN STUDY TOURS

Botswana

SPIRITUAL HOLIDAY

Voices of the Ancients

☀ ⊘ ↘28

T+267 71-510997
www.voicesofancients.co.bw
From US$4550 per person excluding flights

Head to Botswana, where you can spend seven days following in the footsteps of the ancient bushman with Voices of the Ancients. Its programmes mix music and craft workshops, meditation, yoga, healing rituals and medicine walks with the chance to experience local communities and their sacred rituals including a healing trance dance. You'll also have a chance to see bushman paintings of whales, penguins and sharks thousands of years old in an area surrounded by desert. The trips are led by Louise Claassen, a qualified clinical hypnotherapist and practising transpersonal psychotherapist, and Charmaine Freeman, a reiki master and holistic therapist who runs two businesses in Botswana. The programmes started in 2006, and for anyone feeling a little stuck in life who needs to get a different perspective, this looks set to be a highly rejuvenating experience for those with an open mind. You even get your own medicine bag, complete with journals, crystals, totems and other appropriate articles you'll need on your bushman journey.

The Kusun drumming and dance tour was a life-changing month. The classes were hard work, but there was plenty of fun too, and even more rewarding than the funky dance moves was experiencing life in a Ghanaian village and getting to know people and their way of life.

Kayla Mindarl

Ghana

CREATIVE RETREAT

Kusun drumming and dance tour

☀ ⊘ ◐ ↘29

Nungua, near Accra
T+61 39-593 9598
www.ghanadrumschool.com
From US$2680 for 4 weeks

For a full-on cultural immersion in one of Africa's safest countries, Australia-based Kusun Study Tours runs an annual four-week intensive trip to Ghana each autumn where you can learn traditional drumming, dance and song. The tour is centred on the fishing village of Nungua, only a 15-minute drive from the capital Accra.

Led by musicians and dancers from West Africa, workshops are held in a specially laid out area near the beach and run for four hours a day, five days a week. In a group tailored to suit your level of experience, you'll learn everything from simple chants to complex percussion, as well as the social context of Ghana's art forms. Private sessions can also be arranged. In addition, there are village performances, ceremonies and festivals and a final show in which to take part.

You'll be based at the Kusun Centre, a specially built guesthouse with simple single or double rooms with showers and toilets. Three delicious Ghanaian meals a day are prepared by village women, and usually involve fish – for example, grilled with a garlic and ginger crust with boiled yam and a tomato stew. Special and vegetarian diets can be catered for.

The trip takes a maximum of 20 and attracts people of all ages, from all over the globe. You need to bring your own *djembe* and *kpanlogo* (traditional Ghanaian drum), or have them made locally (both together cost US$120). The price includes everything except international flights, visas and insurance. Fly to Kotoka, from where transfers take about 45 minutes.

Malawi

COASTAL RETREAT

Makuzi Beach Lodge

🌐 👤 🏠 🧘 ⛵ 📶 ↘30

Chintheche
T+265 1-357296
www.makuzibeach.com
From US$61 per room per night

Makuzi Beach Lodge is a laid-back collection of 10 chalets, in its own private cove, a few yards away from the white-sand beaches of Lake Malawi and surrounded by lovely gardens. It was started by sivananda yoga teacher Lara Pollard, who runs regular five-day yoga and meditation retreats (from U$900 per person for five nights). A group of six (minimum), you can also come for a private retreat, or you can stay as an individual to chill out.

Lara trained at the Sivananda Yoga Vedanta Dhanwantari Ashram in Kerala, and is also a reiki master and includes reiki attunements as an extra on her retreats. With over 10 years' experience, she's a dedicated teacher whose retreats focus on pranayama, diet, relaxation, positive thinking and meditation as well as asanas. Delicious vegetarian meals are served, smoking and alcohol are not allowed, and each retreat takes no more than 20 people.

If you're into horse riding, you can extend your retreat with another five days on the rolling plains of the Nyika plateau, where **Nyika Safaris** (www.nyika.com) runs daily horse rides through one of the last explored areas of Southern Africa; the plateau's rolling grasslands stretch as far as the eye can see, and in spring and summer become a gorgeous carpet of wild flowers. You'll be based at Nyika Safari's Chelinda Lodge, and have a yoga class once a day with Lara.

You can book the 10-day yoga, riding and beach retreat through **Ride Worldwide** in the UK (from US$3750 per person for 10 nights including transfers, T+44 (0)1837-82544, www.rideworldwide.co.uk). To get to Makuzi Beach Lodge, fly to Malawi's capital, Lilongwe, from where a private charter flight or road transfer can be arranged – road transfers cost from US$150 for three people one way, flights considerably more.

Mozambique

COASTAL RETREAT

Turtle Cove Surf & Yoga Lounge

🌐 ⛵ 📶 📶 ↘31

Tofo Beach
T+27 (0)82-563 9744
From US$40 per person per night full board

One of the few places in the world where you can swim with whale sharks, Tofo Beach is a laid-back palm-strewn surfing destination a short drive from the Mozambican town of Inhambane. Turtle Cove Surf & Yoga Lounge is a base for regular yoga and surf holidays, and you can also stay here as individual to enjoy yoga, dance and surf lessons as well as personal development workshops led by visiting teachers.

Halo Gaia, a holistic tourism company based in Johannesburg, runs a yoga centre here with daily classes as well as 10-day surf and yoga holidays (from US$500 per person). Regular instructors include British hatha yoga teacher Clara Woodburn, an Oxbridge graduate who trained with Cyndi Lee in New

Africa & the Levant Mozambique

Far left: Drumming in Ghana. **Top left**: Meditating on Lake Malawi. **Bottom left**: Makuzi Beach Lodge. **Above**: Clara Woodburn at Turtle Cove.

York and now runs **Yoga Warrior** studio in Johannesburg (www.yogawarrior.co.za).

Turtle Cove offers a personal, relaxed, home-from-home feel rather than hotel luxury. The main building is an attractive blend of African and Arabic architectural styles. You stay in one of 10 comfortable chalets in amongst the palm trees, each with en suite bathroom and decorated in rich blues and reds, with interesting doorways and high grass ceilings. If you want to be somewhere quieter during the yoga holidays, you can also choose to stay at Anastaseá in Tofinho, self-catering accommodation with four individual en suite chalets.

The lodge offers a warm community atmosphere, with a relaxed lounge bar and a restaurant specializing in seafood and sushi and serving up very tasty fruit smoothies. There's an in-house professional surf instructor, and you can also take samba classes, go diving or enjoy a sunset cruise in a dhow. Workshops led by visiting teachers run regularly and include bio dancing, pilates and kahuna massage, or just lounge on the beach and soak up the local culture.

The place attracts all ages and nationalities, mostly single travellers for the 10-day holidays, at other times couples interested in the surfing or the yoga. Family surf holidays run during the school holidays. Yoga mats are supplied, and you can hire foam and fibreglass boards. Inhambane is within a malaria area (see Essentials for details on how to protect yourself). The best time to visit is from March to July, when the weather is sunny and warm and the risk of malaria is lowest. Fly to Johannesburg, then via Maputo to Inhambane (flights operate every Monday, Wednesday, Friday and Sunday), from where it's a 20-km drive. Or hire a car and travel through Kruger National Park. Halo Gaia can help you arrange accommodation en route. Optional bus transfers from Johannesburg are included in the 10-day holidays. Halo Gaia runs various alternative safaris throughout Africa including an Essence of Africa Soul Safari led by holistic health therapists; see website for details.

Namibia

DESERT RETREAT

Constance Lodge GocheGanas

🌐 🌿 🔥 🏠 🌀 🌀 🌀 🗺32

Windhoek
T+264 (0)61-224909
www.gocheganas.com
From US$260 per room per night

GocheGanas consists of 16 luxurious thatched rondavels overlooking miles of rolling hills covered with the camel thorn trees from which it takes its name. The last thing you expect is a spa in the middle of the desert, but GocheGanas offers a wide range of treatments in its wellness village, set in its own thatched rondavel at the top of the hill, just below the round open-sided Toko Bar - the place for a stunning 360° view at sunset.

The 11 treatment rooms here encircle a heated swimming pool, and a cave-like sauna with high vaulted ceiling. There is a whole range of massages on offer, from aromatherapy and reflexology to Indian head and Thai, and an extensive range of beauty treatments from facials to body masks and wraps, as well as hydrotherapy. Try the local marula oil healing massage, or be driven into the bush to have a massage alone under the vast blue skies (from US$70).

If you're not too hot, you can have a personal training session; yoga is sometimes on offer and there are nutritional consultations available. The restaurant, where you can eat under the stars, has a special wellness choice. On game drives through the 2500-ha site you'll have a chance to see the 21 species of wildlife here, from baboons to springbok to white rhino, which were introduced as part of a conservation programme. Although only one hour's drive from the capital's airport, the place feels very remote, and it's an ideal beginning or end to a journey through Namibia.

Tanzania

HOTEL & SPA

Fundu Lagoon

🌀 🌀 🗺33

Pemba
T+255 (0)747-438668
www.fundulagoon.com
From US$335 per person per night

Only accessible by boat and set amongst indigenous mangrove forest on a pristine beach, Fundu Lagoon has 16 en suite tented rooms dotted over the hillside. The brainchild of designer Ellis Flyte and co-owned by

Top: Constance Lodge GocheGanas. **Above:** Yoga teacher Stacia, doing the camel pose at Ngare Sero. **Right:** Walking safari with Yogatraveller.

westerners, it is staffed by locals and part of the profits are regularly ploughed into projects for the local community.

There's a double-decker infinity pool facing the ocean, and Swedish and Indian head massage and pampering facials, manicures and pedicures are on offer. Do your own yoga on the platform, on a hilltop overlooking the lagoon, and an excellent location for sunrises and sunsets. You can go snorkelling, diving, take a dhow trip, explore the mangroves in a canoe or just enjoy the simple things, like sitting on the jetty watching the boats. This is a very relaxed and easy-going place without any stuffiness, where plentiful meals are made from fresh local produce, most of it grown by a local women's cooperative. Fly to Dar es Salaam, then to Chake Chake airport on Pemba, from where it's an hour's transfer by jeep and speedboat.

YOGA TRAVELLER

MOUNTAIN RETREAT
Ngare Sero

🌐 ⛰ ◉ ❋ ✎ ↘34

Mount Meru
T+255 (0)27-255 3638
www.ngare-sero-lodge.com
From US$160 per person per night

A peaceful mountain lodge set on the slopes of Mount Meru with views over Kilimanjaro, Ngare Sero has a resident hatha yoga teacher, Stacia, and Swedish and Chinese massages are available. There's also a lovely lake fed by cold springs in the nearby forest, a 30-m swimming pool set in colourful gardens and a sauna.

Regular yoga retreats take place here, including an annual 10-night yoga safari combining yoga, treatments, and overnight trips to the bush (from US$ 4200) run by UK-based luxury wellbeing company **Yogoloji** (see page 49). Yoga is done on the lodge's lovely outdoor platform under a forest canopy overlooking a lake.

A converted colonial farmhouse built at the turn of the century, the lodge has two suites with views of Kilimanjaro, or there are 10 attractive and simply furnished garden rooms. Food is organic whenever possible

and vegetarian-friendly. There are over 30 ha of forest and gardens to explore, horses and camels to ride and the option of trout fishing in the extensive grounds. Or take a game drive through the Arusha National Park to see elephant, buffalo and giraffe.

Overnight or longer safari trips to the lodge's bush camp on Lake Natron, which boasts panoramic views of the Rift Valley, can easily be arranged. The lodge generates its own power from a hydroelectric turbine, and originates tree planting and community projects. Fly to Kilimanjaro International Airport, from where it's a 20-minute taxi ride.

YOGA & ACTIVITY HOLIDAY
Yogatraveller

🌐 ⛰ ◉ ❋ ✎ ↘35

Various safari parks
T+353 (0)86-828 9178
www.yogatraveller.com
From US$2500 for 10 days

Yogatraveller runs two yoga safari holidays a year to Tanzania, taking in several national parks and wilderness reserves including Manyara National Park, Ngorongoro crater, the Nou Forest, Mbulu highlands, Tarangire National Park and the Oldonyo Sambu. You stay at luxury lodges or comfortable camps along the way – think campfires, canopies of stars, and wonderful African savannah.

Two daily classes mixing hatha, sivananda and ashtanga yoga will be taught by Michelle Riordan, founder of Yogatraveller, and classes are designed to help soothe tired muscles after jeep game drives. You'll also have access to complementary therapies, meditation and various types of massage. As well as seeing the big five – lion, cheetah, leopard, elephant and rhino – there are bush walks and animal tracking, treks and a kayaking trip when you can spot game from the water.

The company uses **Greenfootprint** (www.greenfootprint.co.tz), an eco-friendly Dutch company which trains and educates local staff. They have licences to do night drives and walking safaris where other companies do not, and are heavily involved

in helping the local community. Food is vegetarian- friendly, and made from local organic ingredients wherever possible.

The trip takes a maximum of 15 people, and the price includes camping, all meals, park fees, transfers, internal transport, two yoga classes a day, an English-speaking guide and animal expert. Yoga mats are provided. Fly to Kilimanjaro International, where you will be met by your guide and yoga teacher. Yogatraveller can also arrange an extension to visit the Serengeti and Zanzibar island, or to climb Mount Kilimanjaro or Mount Meru. The company also runs trips to Thailand (see page 285) and Switzerland (see page 75).

🛈 Soul food

African Initiatives is a UK-based social justice organization that promotes the rights of all people to a life of dignity. It works with local communities in Tanzania and Ghana on projects promoting sustainable agriculture, girls' education, women's rights and economic empowerment, and land rights. Twice a year, they organize a sponsored safari trek through Tanzania's wild landscapes including Lake Natron, the Serengeti and the Ngorongoro Crater, to raise money for the local communities. To take part, or to donate, T+44 (0)117- 915 0001, www.african-initiatives.org.uk.

Africa & the Levant Tanzania

AGE FOTOSTOCK / SUPERSTOCK

Sunset at Colva beach, Goa.

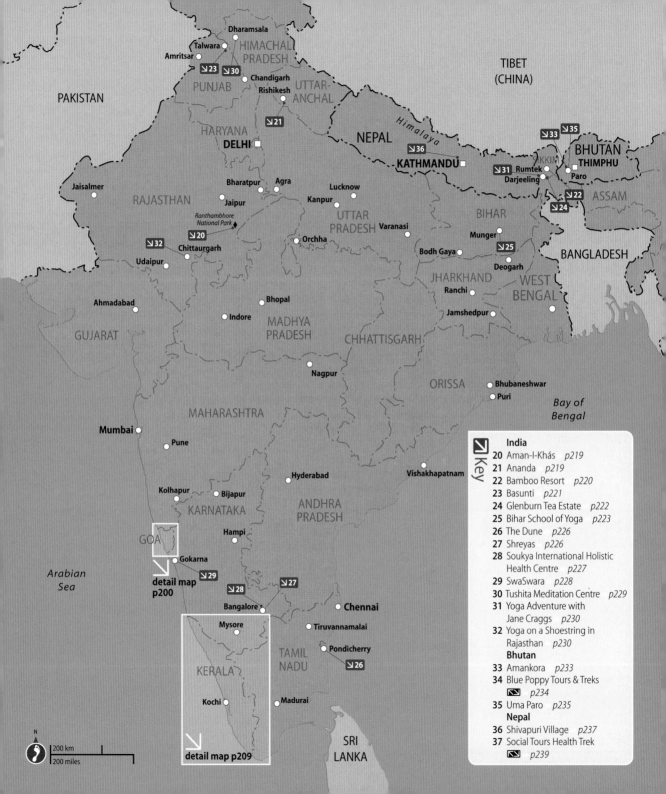

DHARAMSALA
Talwara
Amritsar
HIMACHAL PRADESH
⬊ 23   ⬊ 30
PUNJAB
Chandigarh
Rishikesh
UTTAR-ANCHAL
HARYANA
⬊ 21
DELHI

TIBET (CHINA)

Himalaya

NEPAL

⬊ 33   ⬊ 35

KATHMANDU

⬊ 36

BHUTAN
THIMPHU

SIKKIM

⬊ 31   Rumtek
Darjeeling
Paro

⬊ 22

ASSAM

⬊ 24

Jaisalmer
RAJASTHAN
Bharatpur   Agra
Jaipur
Lucknow
Kanpur
UTTAR PRADESH
Varanasi

BIHAR

BANGLADESH

Ranthambhore National Park
⬊ 20
Orchha
⬊ 32
Chittaurgarh
Udaipur

Munger
Bodh Gaya   ⬊ 25
Deogarh

WEST BENGAL

PAKISTAN

Ahmadabad
GUJARAT
Indore
Bhopal
MADHYA PRADESH
CHHATTISGARH
JHARKHAND
Ranchi
Jamshedpur

Nagpur

ORISSA
Bhubaneshwar
Puri

Bay of Bengal

Mumbai
Pune
MAHARASHTRA

Hyderabad

Vishakhapatnam

Arabian Sea

Kolhapur   Bijapur
KARNATAKA
Hampi
ANDHRA PRADESH

GOA
Gokarna
⬊ 29
detail map p200
⬊ 28   ⬊ 27
Bangalore
Mysore
Tiruvannamalai
Pondicherry
⬊ 26

Chennai

TAMIL NADU

KERALA
Kochi
Madurai

SRI LANKA

N
200 km
200 miles

detail map p209

India is as chaotic as it is beguiling, so it's fitting that the body and soul escapes on offer here should deal in extremes. Get back to basics at an ashram, do a DIY retreat at contemporary havens such as Panchavatti in Goa, or sample decadent pampering in luxury at the Aman-I-Khás.

In a country with such an enormous gap between rich and poor, be prepared for some discomforting sights and for a certain amount of (albeit good humoured) tourist hassle. But don't hide yourself away in an air-conditioned room or jeep; India is an amazing place to get out of your comfort zone and get a better perspective on life.

Home to two of the oldest and most effective systems of health and personal development, India has increasing amounts to offer a stressed-out Westerner looking for more than a quick fix. Detox through ayurveda in Kerala, enjoy yoga with a Western teacher on a beach in Goa, or go deeper into yogic philosophy at renowned schools such as The Krishnamacharya Yoga Mandiram in Tamil Nadu or The Bihar School of Yoga.

For cooler climes and wider perspectives, head for the hills and enjoy your own time at Glenburn tea estate near Darjeeling, on a mountain retreat in Nepal, or an inspirational trek around the monasteries and mountains of Bhutan, one of the world's most remote and spiritual countries, which only opened its doors to the outside world three decades ago.

66 99 *Emptiness is infinitely satisfying to the human mind. Art and architecture are simply the concrete externalisations of our attempts to understand that void.*

Charles Correa, architect

Travel essentials

India

Getting there The main gateways to India for international flights are Delhi, Mumbai, Chennai or Kolkata. The cheapest airfares to India are usually with central European, central Asian and Middle Eastern airlines. Good discounts are also available from Australasia, Southeast Asia and Japan. Onward travel is mainly by domestic flights (**Air India, Indian Airways**, **Sahara Airlines**, **Jet Airways** and **Air Deccan**) or for shorter distances, by rail (see www.seat61.com).

Goa No scheduled flights go to Goa's Dabolim Airport. Domestic flights link Goa to the nearest international airport at Mumbai, as well as Delhi, Chennai, Bangalore and Thiruvananthapuram. Direct charter flights operate to many European cities from November to April. Alternatively, fly to Mumbai and travel onwards to Goa by train, a 12-hour journey.

Kerala International airlines serve Cochin, Thiruvananthapuram and Calicut/Karipur airports. Trains run between Mumbai and Trivandrum, although this is a 35-hour journey.

Best time to visit For most of India, the weather is most conducive from the end of the monsoon in October to late March. Places in the Himalayas and Darjeeling in West Bengal enjoy a pleasant year-round climate, especially notable from April to early June, when it is intensely

Whatever you do will be insignificant, but it is very important that you do it.

Mahatma Gandhi

hot in many other parts of the country. Nights can be very cold in December and January in the mountains. Around Bangalore, temperatures are moderated by altitude. The best time to visit Tamil Nadu is mid-December to early March; heaviest rainfall is between October and December.

Goa The best months to visit Goa are October to March and most retreats and courses run only during this time. Goa's climate is generally comfortable but from mid-April to the beginning of the six-week monsoon season in mid-June it gets increasingly hot and humid, culminating in torrential rain and strong winds.

Kerala There isn't an extended dry season as in the rest of India, but it is especially wet from June to September. Maximum temperatures

Eat me

The ancient Indian system of ayurveda teaches that a balanced diet is one of the first steps to good health. Learning what suits your body, and eating accordingly is the secret to inner wellbeing (see page 210). It's not hard to eat well in this region of the world. Look out for dishes made with lentils and chickpeas, full of fibre, protein, and low in fat. Chana dal is perhaps the most famous of the lentil dishes. There's plenty of choice for vegetarians: look for avail (spicy vegetable curry with fresh coconut) and subz khada masala (spicy vegetable stir-fry). If you're craving a plain, light meal then order a bowl of coconut rice. Depending on where you are, your food will almost certainly include cardamom and may also be flecked with ginger, chillies, coriander or mustard seeds.

Both ayurvedic and yogic diets teach the importance of eating breakfast. Fruit drinks are a good option if you're not much of a breakfast-eater. Try panna, a chilled drink made with green mangoes, sugar and cardamom, or ananas sharbart,

pineapple punch with cardamom and cloves – make sure you're ordering the non-alcoholic ananas sharbart, because vodka is sometimes added. Lassis are perfect whenever you need a refreshing yet soothing drink. Made with natural yoghurt they come in sweet, salty or fruit varieties. Try a mango or banana lassi for a fruit and vitamin fix or a lassi masala made with coriander seeds, black pepper and cardamom for a spice fix that will help cleanse your system too. Almost all spices have therapeutic and medicinal properties, of course, and they're used copiously in India. Turmeric helps detoxify the liver and stimulate digestion, as well as boosting the immune system and fighting allergies. Cardamom is excellent for the digestion and can be found in many of India's dishes, from the deeply aromatic kathirikai kara kulambu (sweet and sour aubergines) to the ever-present Chai ka masala (spiced tea). Cardamom pods can also be chewed whole after a meal to aid digestion and freshen breath.

Healthy stopovers in Delhi

If you need to stay in Delhi for the night, **The Imperial** (T+91 (0)11-2334 1234, www.theimperialindia.com) is a decadent but friendly hotel with a knowledgeable concierge. There's a lovely terrace for outdoor dining overlooking a lawn, a giant atrium for afternoon tea, a glamorous bar and a huge pool. A much-delayed Six Senses spa opens late 2007.

For something more affordable, **Master Guesthouse** (from US$23 per room per night, T+91 (0)11-28741089, www.master-guesthouse.com) is run by a reiki master, Urvashi, and her husband Avnish, a pranic healer. You can have therapy sessions and do yoga on their rooftop. This is a clean and calm place to stay in a non-descript building in Delhi's suburbs, 20 minutes from the centre by taxi.

Alternatively, head south out of the city and get some peace at **Tikli Bottom** (US$150 per person per night including all meals and drinks, T+91 (0)12-4276 6556, www.tiklibottom.com), which is just 45 minutes from the international airport. There's organic food, a large pool, four rooms, and full body massage and reflexology are on offer from Muna and Rachna, the housekeepers who are also trained therapists (US$9 for an hour). Sleep out on a *charpai* under a mosquito net on hotter nights.

---

rarely rise above 32°C, while minimum temperatures at sea level are never below 20°C. The monsoon season, from June to mid-August, is a particularly good time to visit ayurveda retreats (see page 210).

Bhutan
Getting there Bhutan has no long-haul flight connections so travellers have to fly first to Delhi, Kathmandu, Bangkok, Dhaka or Kolkata. The most competitive fares can usually be found to Delhi and Bangkok. Paro is Bhutan's internatonal airport and **Druk Air**, Bhutan's national carrier, is the only airline operating flights in and out of the country. There are frequent delays due to bad weather in the rainy season and occasional strong winds in the spring.
Best time to visit Late September to November is the best time for clear mountain views and trekking. Spring is more overcast, but offers abundant wild flowers and the chance to experience Paro festival. Winter has some sunny and warm weather with very cold nights and snow on the higher peaks above 2500m. Despite causing landslides and floods, the summer rainy season is also when the landscape is at its greenest.

Nepal
Getting there All international flights go to Kathmandu. Several international airlines have direct flights from London and other European cities, Singapore, Bangkok, New Delhi and Mumbai. **Royal Nepal Airlines** is the national carrier, with **Druk Air**, **Indian Airlines** and **Thai Airlines** being among those that fly regularly to Kathmandu. Flights from North America operate via London or Bangkok. Cheap flights from Australia and New Zealand are usually via Bangkok.
Best time to visit Peak time for tourists is between September and November, when the air is clear and mountain views are at their best. However, many trekking routes are also very busy with travellers. The coldest months are December, January and February. March and April are warmer, but these months are also popular with trekkers. By May and June, temperatures are rising and views may be obscured by haze, with the monsoon arriving around mid-June and continue until September. Despite the monsoon rains, travel during these months is the cheapest and the landscape at its most lush.

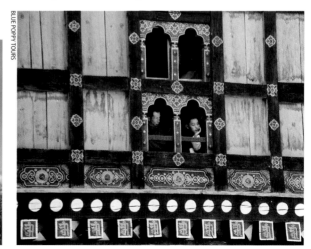

India & the Himalaya

India

Home of yoga and ayurveda, India is a colourful chaotic delight of a country to uplift jaded souls.

Fact file

- **Visa:** Required by citizens of EU countries, US, Canada, Australia and New Zealand
- **Country code:** +91
- **Currency:** Indian rupee (INR)
- **Time zone:** GMT+5½ hours
- **Electricity:** 230v
- **Tourist board:**
  www.incredibleindia.org

Goa

DETOX RETREAT

Ananda Health & Yoga

Ashwem Beach
T+44 (0)7786-363553
www.jivahealing.com
From US$540 per week

As India's most laid-back state, it's not surprising that Goa is one of Ananda's chosen retreat destinations. The venue on Ashwem Beach remains wonderfully peaceful, even during the peak season, and here the friendly team offers guests an educational approach to health and rejuvenation. Combining detox, yoga, meditation and massage with classes in sustainable living and nutrition, they provide you with the tools to continue a healthier lifestyle after the holiday comes to an end.

Your home from home, in the small resort of Meem's Arabian Sea, is a fairly primitive and sparsely furnished bamboo bungalow with an en suite outdoor bathroom and a small porch with seats or hammocks from which to contemplate the wonderful views across the beach.

Ananda specializes in juice fasting programmes, including a one-to-one session with a nutritional adviser, hatha yoga, and twice-daily classes which cover a range of subjects from food combining and natural remedies to setting up a health food kitchen. With a maximum of 12 people on each holiday, you receive plenty of personal

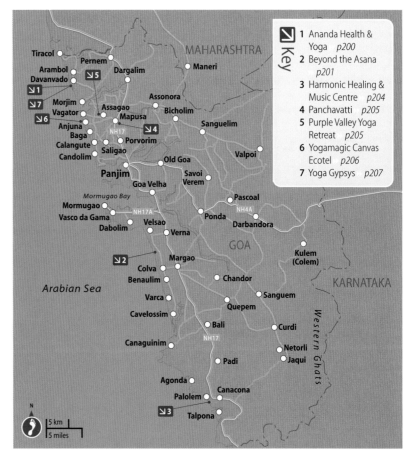

Key

1. Ananda Health & Yoga *p200*
2. Beyond the Asana *p201*
3. Harmonic Healing & Music Centre *p204*
4. Panchavatti *p205*
5. Purple Valley Yoga Retreat *p205*
6. Yogamagic Canvas Ecotel *p206*
7. Yoga Gypsys *p207*

attention, including nutritional counselling. This helps to reinforce the theory behind the detox, giving you the rationale to continue along the healthy path when you return home. You also have access to holistic therapies such as Thai and aromatherapy massages, reflexology, meditation, pranayama and spiritual group healing.

Afternoons are free for swimming, treatments or exploring the famous Anjuna flea markets – a highlight of many people's trip to Goa. There is plenty of wonderful food at the resort and it's mainly organic, which is unusual in India. If you're on the detox, you are given fresh organic juices, mineral broths, chlorophyll drinks, herbs and fibre to support the cleansing process.

Those who stay at Ananda retreats are generally in their mid-thirties and professionals from Europe or North America, seeking a healthier lifestyle, for themselves and the planet. Ananda is a strong advocate of sustainable living – it takes travel details in order to compensate for those emissions by supporting CO_2 reduction programmes – and sound advice is offered on reducing your own environmental footprint too.

Most guests follow the detox programme, but healthy eating and yoga weeks are also available. Many return year after year and because of these repeat visits, Ananda prefers

to vary its retreat locations, with destinations in Europe and Thailand. For the Goa trip, fly to Dabolim airport and take a taxi to Ashwem Beach for about US$15. With advance notice, and at extra cost, Ananda can organize transfers. Co-founder Rebecca Andrist also runs a retreat in Hawaii (see page 347).

(see page 347)

YOGA RETREAT
Beyond the Asana

Verla-Parra, north Goa
T+44 (0)20-8690 0890
www.beyond-the-asana.com
From US$1125 per person for 14 days

If you're looking to understand more about yoga than just the physical postures, this popular two-week yoga retreat is a carefully thought-out combination of ancient yogic techniques and contemporary practices, and attracts people from all over the world.

The retreat is led by Sue Pendlebury, dancer, musician, theatre artist, yogini and founder of Yoga on a Shoestring, and Asia-based Emil Wendel, scholar, philosopher, meditation teacher and adept yogi; both assist participants in their journey of letting go and discovering 'that which they truly are'.

Presently this annual intensive retreat is held during the last two weeks of January at the **Satsanga Retreat Centre** at Verla-Parra in north Goa, a lovely comfortable place where some very tasty vegetarian food is served up by chef Lizzie Jones.

Travelling in India

Wonderful as the sub continent is, travelling in India can be exhausting and, if you are not careful, you will undo all the good you have done on your retreat just by getting home. Take it slow, travel light, and with lots of patience – you'll experience real kindness everywhere you go, and find people on hand to give you directions or carry your bags (for a tip, naturally).

◗ Body language

From the Sanskrit meaning 'wheel' or 'circle', **chakras** are the seven energy centres or vortices in the body that are concerned with the body's psychic energy flow. Ascending in a line from the base of the spine to the top of the head, each chakra has its own colour and is associated with different parts of the body and different emotions. They are muladhara (root, red), swadhisthana (sacrum or lower abdomen, orange), manipura (solar plexus, yellow), anahata (heart/lung, green), vishuddha (throat, light blue), aina (third Eye, indigo) and sahasrara (crown, white or violet). It is through the chakras that a person's spirit connects with universal energy. Carl Jung called them 'gateways of consciousness'. Balancing the chakras promotes wellbeing.

India & the Himalaya India – Goa

ANANDA HEALTH & YOGA

Ananda Health & Yoga.

◗ Body language

Bandhas and back bends: yoga in India

Yoga, the world's oldest system of personal development, began in India over 5000 years ago. It is first mentioned in The Vedas, or scriptures, which provide the main foundation of yoga teaching and the yogic philosophy known as Vedanta. Vedanta says that there is one absolute reality, or consciousness, which underlies the universe. The underlying purpose of any type of yoga is to reunite the individual self (Jiva) with this consciousness (Brahman), freeing us from the illusion of separation and allowing us to see our true nature – hence the word 'yoga', which means to yoke or join. It is this Brahman that many yogis call on when they invoke the name of God.

In essence there are four main paths of yoga: karma (the path of selfless action), bhakti (the path of devotion), jnana (the path of self-knowledge or wisdom) and raja (the yoga of physical and mental control). Raja is the yoga that most people in the West practice in one form or another, and it is based on the Eight Limbs of Yoga, set down by the sage, Patanjali, in the *Yoga Sutras*, which are thought to have been written in the third century BC. This is where ashtanga yoga gets its name – ashtanga is Sanskrit for 'eight limbs' (see glossary).

The Eight Limbs of Yoga map out a whole programme of living to purify the body and mind (see glossary). These include such things as non-violence, telling the truth, moderation, non-possessiveness, positive thinking, meditation and awareness of self and others, as well as the asanas, pranayama and relaxation that most classes in the west include. The goal is to eventually attain the state of superconsciousness. As earnest as this may sound, for most of us, it makes sense that bodily control, breathing, relaxation, positive thinking, self-awareness, a healthy diet and respect for others will help us lead fuller, more nourishing and less stressful lives. In the West, most yoga classes concentrate on bodily control and tend to neglect the rest, so what better place to get a handle on what yoga's really all about, than in the land of its birth?

Yoga holidays

Wherever you are in India, you'll find a plethora of yoga classes – in shacks, ashrams, beach huts and upmarket hotels – all aimed at westerners. Some classes will be taught brilliantly, others not very well at all, and most will be nothing like the classes you get back home: choose carefully. If you have limited time and are

new to yoga, or you're looking for a guaranteed escape in inspiring surroundings, it's best to book onto one of the yoga holidays that are featured in this section, where daily yoga classes focus on pranayama, meditation and a healthy diet as well as asanas. Try a holiday with Appleyoga at **Yoga Gypsys** (page 207), **Ananda Health Yoga** (page 200) or **Yoga on a Shoestring** (page 230), or head to an established retreat centre such as **Purple Valley** (page 205) for a two-week course. **Go Differently** (T+44 (0)1799-521950, www.godifferently.com) runs an impressive on-the-move eight-day yoga holiday exploring ashrams, yoga, meditation and holistic therapies on a journey that takes you from Delhi to Haridwar, Dhanolti and Rishikesh, costing from US$1585. To go deeper, try **Beyond the Asana** (page 201) or a yoga adventure with **Jane Craggs** (page 230).

Ashrams

Many travellers curious about experiencing yoga in India head to Rishikesh in the northern state of Uttaranchal (see feature on ashrams on page 224). An international yoga festival takes place here every year, usually in March. The brave spiritual warrior may like to spend some time at an ashram here, or one of the many more around the country. You'll find the asanas taught in ashrams to be softer and gentler than what you may experience in a yoga class back home, but the emphasis on meditation, chanting and karma yoga (selfless service) will be just as nourishing.

Luxury retreats

Of the upmarket retreats, **Ananda in the Himalayas** (page 219) and **Shreyas** (page 226) offer some impressive workshops in vedanta, all taught by a representative from the Vedanta Institute in Delhi or the Vedanta Academy in Pune. **Kalari Kovilakom** (page 215) and **SwaSwara** (page 228) were set up in consultation with Swami Yogaratna Saraswati, a very talented and accessible swami who trained at the Bihar School of Yoga, and both now teach yoga in the satyananda style, which combines gentle, stretching postures with practices such as yoga nidra (deep relaxation). Many of the best yoga and meditation teachers in India have no set base: Swami Yogaratna moves about, for example, and now holds regular workshops in Bangalore on yoga nidra, as well as hosting yoga and meditation retreats at Om Beach Resort (www.ombeachresort.com).

Yoga schools

The **Krishnamacharya Yoga Mandiram** at Chennai in Tamil Nadu (www.kym.org) runs excellent regular courses for westerners on every aspect of yoga, including a four-week intensive introduction and a two-week advanced course. The centre was founded by yoga guru, TKV Desikachar, in 1976, to transmit the teachings of his father T Krishnamacharya, the grandfather of modern yoga, whose students included two of today's most influential teachers, Sri BKS Iyengar and Sri K Pattabhi Jois.

Ardent ashtanga yogis will head to the **Ashtanga Yoga Research Institute** in Mysore, Karnataka (www.ayri.com), which costs from US$500 a month. It is home to Sri K Pattabhi Jois, whose version of yoga has most permeated contemporary Western practice. This is where the Mysore-style of ashtanga vinyasa yoga comes from, which has students working at their own pace and level within one class, the teacher offering help whenever it is needed. A steady flow of international students – many of them teachers themselves – make the pilgrimage here throughout the year to wake up before dawn and take Jois's uncompromising instruction in downward dogs, bandhas and ujjayi breathing. Jois, who is in his nineties, shares the burden of teaching with his grandson Shirat and his daughter Saraswati. There is a strict pecking order which first-timers can find alienating, and there are times when it's ridiculously busy, sweaty and cramped, with just about enough space for your mat.

For hatha yoga in Mysore there's Venkatesha (www.atmavikasa.com), whose own practice is formidably advanced. He picks up numerous awards at international yoga competitions and students are evangelical about his back bend workshops.

Hardcore iyengar students will head south to the **Ramamani Iyengar Memorial Yoga Institute**, headquarters of the BKS Iyengar school (www.bksiyengar.com) in Pune, Maharashtra. To study here you need certified proof of having studied the iyengar method for eight years, and application forms require a qualified iyengar teacher's signature as reference. Iyengar's strain of yoga focuses on a quiet and focused mind and body alignment, often using props like belts and blocks. Teaching is now done mostly by his daughter, Geeta and son, Prashant.

VEENA AT SVYC

ROSIE WALFORD

Expect an inspiring programme which includes meditation, pranayama (breath work), asanas, mantra (the work with sound vibration), mudra (ritual hand or body gestures), chanting, philosophy, and the practice of mouna (silence) with creative expression, through dancing, singing and writing. It is hard work, yet the workshop halls are always full of laughter and friendship. The retreat is for people with some experience of yoga or meditation. Sue and Emil also run introduction workshops in different locations around Europe, and there is a plan to offer full retreats in additional locations in the future; check website for details.

COASTAL RETREAT

Harmonic Healing and Music Centre

🌐 🅿 ♿ ☀ 👁 ↘3

Colomb
T+91 (0)98-2251 2814
www.harmonicingoa.com
US$350 for a 2-week course

This healing retreat by the sea at Colomb is run by English couple, Natalie Mathos and Marc Clayton, and inspired by Indian culture. Natalie specializes in reiki classes and treatments, Marc in tabla and Indian classical music workshops. This isn't a residential retreat; you can stay at various local family-run hotels, which Harmonics can arrange on your behalf.

Natalie offers courses and treatments in reiki, the ancient art that channels energy to synchronize body and mind (see glossary). There's a commitment to individual attention, and Natalie is a member of the Practitioners Register for Alternative Therapies and the British Complementary Medical Association. Treatments are taken inside a bamboo hut, or in a secluded shady area by the water's edge.

Harmonics offers three levels of reiki initiation (training): levels one and two include around 26 teaching hours and cover practical work, theory and guided meditation, opportunities to exchange treatments with others, a massage, guidebook and ongoing email support. You will be rewarded with a certificate from the British Complementary Medical Association.

Another Harmonic retreat combines classical medical consultation and a holistic diagnosis from Dr Johnathon Dao, a government registered doctor of alternative medicines in India and Australia. It's a good way to self-rejuvenate and includes eight hours of reiki, acupuncture, Thai yoga massage, shiatsu massage and ongoing guidance. Yoga sessions are also available as well as tai chi, qigong, guided meditation sessions and, on Sundays, Bollywood and belly dancing for adults and children. You can also try a course in quantum touch, a form of energy healing.

Marc teaches a five-day course in Indian classical music and the tabla, an instrument consisting of two goatskin-covered drums. He uses contemporary north Indian Hindustani songs, which sound magical. Lessons costs from US$45 and include printed notes, an interactive DVD and Marc's tales of ancient Indian music and myth.

Accommodation options include **Green Park**, a lively place to stay with pleasant huts

---

❝❞

I first discovered sivananda yoga on a weekend at Gaunt's House in Devon. At first I was a little shocked to walk into the dining room and find a group beginning to link hands, with two orange-robed swamis in the circle. Their beatific smiles made me feel strange, as if I could never be as happy as they seemed to be. But I joined in, and listened while they sang, feeling vaguely uncomfortable. It was somebody's birthday and, later that evening, after singing happy birthday, some people in the room sang their own version, with the lyrics, "May you realize yourself". How wonderful, I thought, for that to be a goal in life.

Over the course of the weekend I found the asana classes and chanting sessions deeply rewarding, and especially enjoyed the talks given by the lead swami, Swami Krishnadevananda, who heads up the Sivananda centre in London (www.sivananda.co.uk). He turned out to be a very wise, witty and intelligent man, who used to get just as stressed as the rest of us, and sit on his sofa eating too many Chinese takeaways.

VEENA AT SYVC

He inspired me to go to the sivananda ashram at Neyyar Dam in India (see page 224), where the two-week yoga 'vacation' turned out to be a lot of very hard but richly rewarding work in intense heat. The teachers were kind and expert, and the surroundings very inspiring. Yoga is done out of doors, or in a spacious airy meditation hall. Chanting under the stars was an amazing experience, as was rising before dawn to see the sun come up from the top of a hill. This wasn't beach yoga – it was something much more profound.

Caroline

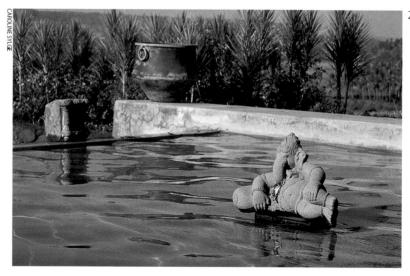

Above: Harmonic Healing & Music Centre.
Right: Ganesh in the pool at Panchavatti.

on the shore and a good restaurant and bar, and **Laguna Vista**, which is a little more basic with bamboo huts and good Goan health food. Retreats generally run between November and March. For US$68 Harmonic can include transfers to the hotel of your choice from Dabolim airport.

India & the Himalaya India – Goa

WATERSIDE RETREAT

Panchavatti

Corjuem
T+91 (0)98-2258 0632
www.islaingoa.com
From US$180 per room per night

A simply stunning place to stay overlooking the Mapusa river on the island of Corjuem, Panchavatti will suit those seeking peace and quiet. The focus of this stylish and rejuvenating 10-ha property is a glorious house with a long veranda, built around a large plant-filled courtyard by Loulou Van Damme, an elegant Belgian woman who has made her home here. She offers daily practice in satyananda yoga, the meditative style of asanas from the Bihar School of Yoga (see page 223). You can join her, or if you're a beginner, she will happily give you lessons. If you're advanced, she can arrange for her own

guru from the Bihar School of Yoga, Swami Priya, to take a few sessions.

Relaxing or toning ayurvedic massages are on offer from a therapist trained in Kerala, or you can have a one-to-one ayurvedic consultation with Dr Ganesh, who studied in Bombay alongside his wife – she gives a wonderful facial cleanse using fresh fruit and vegetable concoctions.

There are four elegant rooms to choose from, each in its own contemporary style with an Indian twist – stone floors, ornate mirrors, shuttered windows, rich reds and yellows. The writer's room has a four-poster bed and lovely views across the countryside. Antiques and bowls of fresh flowers are liberally dotted around.

Come here to get away from everything. You can relax in the sitting room, which has ornate rugs and tables, interesting artwork and a library full of fascinating books. Loulou also has a lovely collection of music, from sacred chants of Siva to Chopin, which you can listen to while watching the light change over the paddy fields from the veranda.

Outside there's a hammock, lots of places to sit, a great swimming pool with a cute stone statue of Ganesh sunbathing at its end, and a garden of lush lawns, fruit trees and tropical plants. If you want a little action, there are walks in the countryside, three good bicycles

to borrow, and Loulou can give you a one-to-one exercise class in the pool.

The rate includes all meals, which you eat with Loulou or alone. A table is often set up in the garden, lit only by candles. The food here is a real treat, cooked by the resident chef, Maria, and using only locally sourced fish and herbs, salads and fruits from the garden.

Some of Goa's main beaches are a 30-minute drive away. There are yoga mats to choose from, or bring your own. Corjuem is just across a bridge from the mainland, a 9-km drive from Mapusa. Fly to Dabolim and it's a 1¼-hour drive from there.

YOGA RETREAT

Purple Valley Yoga Retreat

Assagao
T+91 (0)83-2226 8364
www.yogagoa.com
From US$600 per room per week

This secluded Goan retreat, set amongst flowers and palms about 2 km from the sea, offers an excellent choice of holistic and yoga retreats at very affordable rates.

The main focus is ashtanga yoga, and Purple Valley hosts leading teachers such as Sharath Rangaswamy, grandson of Sri K

PURPLE VALLEY YOGA RETREAT

PURPLE VALLEY YOGA RETREAT

Pattabhi Jois, David Swenson and Nancy Gilgoff, two of the first to introduce ashtanga to the West during the 1970s. Yoga lessons take place in a lovely shala at the end of delightful gardens.

On-site massage is available, and there are occasional guest therapists such as Alan Reynolds from the Esalen Institue in the USA (see page 337), who offers Esalen massage, deep tissue massage, craniosacral therapy and rolfing for an incredibly reasonable US$30 for 1½ hours. Plans for late 2007 and 2008 include ayurvedic massages, meditation classes, beauty treatments, Indian cooking, hot-stone massage and Bollywood dancing.

Public areas are decorated with Indian textiles and ornaments. Relax in quiet spaces on purple and gold cushions or in hammocks, and there's a swimming pool in the garden to keep you fresh between classes. The beach is a short taxi ride from the hotel, and the Anjuna craft markets are nearby.

Bedrooms have mosquito nets, wooden shutters and embroidered throws. All are en suite, but some toilets are Indian style, so ask if you have a preference. Students can share rooms cheaply – workshops can hold as many as 40 so there are plenty of opportunities to meet people. Purple Valley likes to create a friendly, communal atmosphere and gets visitors talking to each other from the outset.

Meals are vegetarian, a fusion of Indian and international cuisine, prepared by local and Western cooks. Food is organic where possible and all sourced locally. Breakfast and dinners are buffet style and are served on a breezy open-air patio decorated with palms.

In true Goan style your fellow guests will be a wide variety of people from around the globe between the ages of 24 and 70. The retreat is open between November and April. Fly to Goa Dabolim, from where Purple Valley will arrange transfers. These are included in the rates, along with accommodation, yoga classes and two vegetarian meals per day. A two-week break is recommended.

RURAL RETREAT
Yogamagic Canvas Ecotel

Anjuna, Bardez
T+91 (0)83-2562 3796
www.yogamagic.net
From US$348 per week per person

A peaceful retreat surrounded by paddy fields and coconut palms, Yogamagic is an environmentally friendly resort with a luxury feel, a 30-minute stroll from the beaches and famous markets of Anjuna.

Make use of the jacuzzi and picturesque natural swimming pool and waterfalls, meditate alone under neem trees and indulge in a series of remarkable ayurvedic massages with Vishnu, fondly dubbed the 'Grandad of Yogamagic'. Vishnu also runs massage training sessions for two students at a time (from US$230 for 21 hours).

Reflexology, ozone therapy, iridology and astrology readings are available on request.

There's a grass-thatched yoga hall with mosquito netting and soft, woven bamboo flooring; one-to-one yoga classes can be arranged, or you can sometimes join a visiting group. Alternatively, just dip in and out of the regular yoga and holistic therapy workshops and classes run by **Brahmani Yoga** (www.brahmaniyoga.com), which has two lovely white airy yoga shalas in the grounds of Hotel Bougainvillea, a five-minute walk across a paddy field.

Buildings fuse bamboo, stone, jute and coconut leaf, and you can choose to sleep in the Rajasthani Hunting Tents, the Tipi Garden or the Maharani Suite. The spacious white canvas tents have silk bedcovers and cushions, and low reading tables with bowls of floating flowers. Open-air bathrooms have curved palm-leaf walls, clay pots for washing and eco-composting toilets. Hot water is available each evening, but open-air solar heated communal showers are also available. Biodegradable ayurvedic body wash powder is provided along with dressing gowns.

The split-level stone Maharani Suite is decked out in sand and terracotta colours, with lots of wood features. There is a sunken bath in the en suite, a veranda overlooking the pool, waterfalls, and hibiscus and frangipani trees. The Tipi Garden is close to the pool, surrounded by banana and papaya plants and with a separate lounge, dressing shack and open-air eco-bathroom. The 16-ft wide tipi can be a double or twin and is decorated in cool creams, with coconut rugs, antique chests, cushions, bolsters and solar lighting.

Fruits, vegetables and herbs used for cooking are grown organically in the gardens. Breakfast consists of fruit (including wheatgrass shots), muesli and omelettes, while lunches and suppers are a delicious fusion of Indian and Mediterranean salads, mezzes and hot dishes. Fresh juices and lassis are a speciality. Dinners are eaten under oil lamps, with Sufi or classical Indian music, sometimes live, in the backround.

Warm-hearted owners Phil and Juliet will make sure you have your chai on your veranda each morning, and giant incense sticks lit outside your tent flap each night. Your fellow guests will be yoga devotees, or couples and single travellers here just to relax.

Bring a torch (in case of power cuts) and a refillable glass water bottle – plastic is not allowed. The resort is open between mid-November and April; book early for Christmas and New Year. Fly or take the train from Mumbai to Dabolim, where Yogamagic can pick you up for a nominal fee.

Not far from Yogamagic, you can experience the amazing healing power of watsu at **Watsu Goa** (www.watsugoa.com) a custom-built luxury heated pool set in the exotic garden of Guggenheim, a private house near Anjuna.

Left: Purple Valley. **Above**: Ashwem Beach.

YOGA RETREAT

Yoga Gypsys

Ashwem Beach
T+91 (0)93-2613 0115
yogagypsys@yahoo.com (no website)
From US$40 per room per night

Yoga Gypsys sits in a peaceful palm grove close to a Hindu temple, on an unspoilt stretch of beach. Group yoga retreats run here from November to March.

Five rustic terracotta bungalows provide shared self-catering accommodation, each with its own garden space. If you don't mind a minute's walk to the bathroom, octagonal wooden tree huts are the next best thing to sleeping outdoors, and offer sea views and a veranda big enough for a hammock.

Apple Yoga (from US$ 890 per person for 10 days excluding flights, T+44 (0)20-8788 8892, www.appleyoga.com) holds 10-day retreats here, led by UK-based Katy Appleton, who is trained in sivananda, ashtanga and vinyasa flow. Your day begins with pranayama and meditation, followed by a session of vinyasa flow yoga. The evening session is a gentler practice, to bring the day to a close. Owner Cathy Richardson teaches scaravelli yoga at the beginning and end of every season, in November and March. Other teachers include UK-based Scaravelli teacher Marc Woolford, who runs intensive retreats each January (from US$ 855 per person per week excluding flights, T+ 44 (0)7866-512885, www.yogawithmarc.co.uk), and Sophy Hoare (www.sophyhoare.co.uk) who was taught directly by Vanda Scaravelli.

There are usually yoga sessions twice a day. Afternoons are free to explore the beaches and flea markets, or try your hand at Indian cookery with lessons from the resident chef, Gaba, who provides two enticing meals a day; a breakfast of organic fruit, juices, curd, a bhaji dish and masala chai and a vegetarian dinner with the occasional Goan fish dish on the side. Self-caterers can order food to be delivered, or try one of the numerous local restaurants. Fly to Dabolim, from where it's a 90-minute transfer.

☺ Soul food

If you want to help out in communities in Asia but don't have the time to commit to long-term volunteering, **AidCamps International** (www.aidcamps.org) organizes three-week-long voluntary work placements in Nepal, India and Sri Lanka. You live and work with local people in parts of the world where tourists rarely go, and experience their culture first hand, while funding and helping to build and renovate local schools and resource centres for children. All ages and level of experience are welcome, and itineraries include local awareness visits and trips to heritage sites and national parks. Other individual short-term placements are also available.

Kerala

ISLAND RETREAT

Emerald Isle Heritage Villa

○ ⊙ ⊘ ⊘ ⊠ 8

Alleppey
T+91 (0)47-7270 3899
www.emeraldislekerala.com
From US$90 per person per night

Emerald Isle Heritage Villa, ancestral home to the Job family, is a utopia for relaxation on the shores of a floating island. You can wander through seven acres of lush jungle, or lie in a hammock looking out across a long stretch of sunken paddy field, reading, or just listening to the birdsong and the hum and whirr of exotic insects. There's a toddy tree to tap, you can learn how to cook Keralan food, take a boat trip, or indulge in an ayurvedic massage, but chances are you'll be just as happy to slow your internal tempo to the snail's pace of village life and do precisely nothing. Food is delicious, and vegetarians and meat eaters are equally well catered for. The four double rooms are comfortable, though the lights can be a little dim.

It's a 10-km drive from Alleppey. Your holiday really begins as you pass through the arable land leading up to the Manimala river, carpets of Indian paddy whistling in the breeze, with goats picking their way along the threads of walls between fields. Next step is the ferry across the Manimala river, a

dugout that seats a handful of people at a time and is paddled by a villager for a rupee a head. You'll share the bench with local families, schoolkids and men in dhotis back from a day in Alleppey town. Nearest airports are Cochin or Trivandrum.

RURAL RETREAT

Friday's Place

⊙ ⊙ ○ ⊘ ⊠ 9

Poovar
T+44 (0)14-2874 1510
www.fridaysplace.biz
From US$170 per room per night

This remote, watery hideaway offers a rustic retreat in the backwaters of the Neyyar estuary at Poovar. Just 30 km from Kerala's capital, this tiny cluster of four cottages is set on an isolated sandbank amid rows of windswept virgin palms.

British couple Mark and Sujeewa decided to turn it into a retreat after seeing friends fall in love with the place. Sujeewa studied yoga at the sivananda ashram in Orleans, France, and teaches both beginners and intermediate students (from just US$5 a class). As a complement, take advantage of one of her reiki sessions. Meditation, life coaching and emotional healing are also on offer.

You can kayak the maze of canals and enjoy a sunset on tranquil Poovar beach, 1 km away and accessed by traditional Thai longtail boat. Mark and Sujeewa can organize trips to Dravidian temples, markets, Tamil

Nadu, Kodaikanal, the tea gardens of Munnar and the old spice port of Cochin.

Each palm-thatched cottage sits on an individual island, giving you ample privacy. The traditional teak and mahogany cottages have simple rooms, which are surprisingly cool. Guests share one spacious communal bathroom, electricity is solar powered and bio-sewage treatment techniques are used. Gardens are full of hibiscus, frangipani and bougainvillea. Bridges connect the cottages with a communal area used for yoga, dining and conversation.

Sujeewa's Sri Lankan roots influence the cuisine with dishes such as aubergine and bitter gourd salad. She and Mark take the boat out each day to shop for the daily menu. Dishes consist of tropical fruits, Indian porridge and chai for breakfast, light thali meals for lunch, and vegetarian, chicken or fish dishes for dinner.

Expect to meet easy-going, down to earth singles and couples; conversation may include New Age philosophy and academic theories. The area is rural, so also expect the occasional rogue guest such as a palm spider, mouse or snake – all are harmless.

Friday's Place is open during the dry months from October to April. Fly to Trivandrum, from where Friday's will organize a pickup. Transfers are included in the rate along with all meals and some alcoholic evening drinks, plus a 10% service charge.

Below: Life on the Keralan backwaters.
Above right: Friday's Place.

FRIDAY'S PLACE

Map Key

8	Emerald Isle Heritage Villa *p208*
9	Friday's Place *p208*
10	Harivihar Ayurvedic Heritage Home *p209*
11	The Indian School of Martial Arts *p212*
12	Kadappuram Beach Resort *p212*
13	Kailasam Yoga & Ayurveda Holidays *p213*
14	Keraleeyam *p213*
15	Leela Kovalam Beach *p214*
16	Kalari Kovilakom *p215*
17	Serenity *p216*
18	Somatheeram & Manaltheeram *p216*
19	Surya Samudra Beach Garden *p217*

Map locations include: Puttur, Maddur, Madikeri, Mandya, Bekal, Kanhangad, Hunsur, Mysore, Kollegal, Virajendrapet, **KARNATAKA**, Cannanore, Manandavady, Gundlupet, Thalassery, Mahe, Kalpetta, Udhagamandalam (Ooty), Bhavani Sagar, Vyttiri, Kappad, Coonoor, Mettupalayam, Avanashi, Calicut, Beypore, Nilanbur, **KERALA**, Malappuram, Perintalmanna, Tiruppur, Coimbatore, Shornur Junction, Palakkad, **TAMIL NADU**, Kunnamkulam, Kollengode, Pollachi, Trichur, Nemmara, Udumalpettai, Peruvanum, Angamali, Parambikulam, Kodungallur, Munnar, Nedumbassery, Aluva, Devikulam, Ernakulam, Muvattapuzha, Cochin, Vaikom, Payikad, Gudalur, Alleppey, Kanjirapalli, Ambalapuzha, Changanacherry, Thiruvalla, Chengannur, **Lakshadweep Sea**, Puliangudi, Kilakkarai, Kovilpatti, Kayankulam, Vadckkeula, Vallickavu, Kollam, Tenmalai, Tirunelveli, Tuticorin, Varkala, Palayamkottai, Nedumangad, Thiruvananthapuram, Tiruchendur, Kovalam, Nagercoil, Kanniyakumari

Malabar Coast, NH17, NH47

N, 50 km, 50 miles

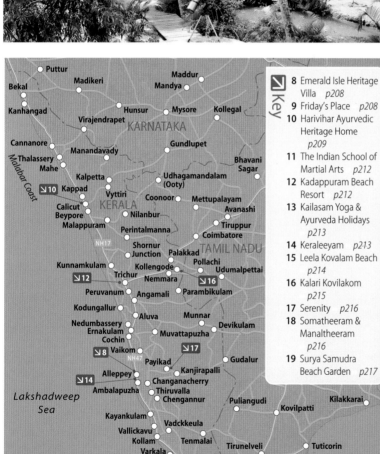

Harivihar Ayurvedic Heritage Home

Calicut
T +91 (0)49-5276 5865
www.harivihar.com
From US$110 per room per night

Calicut is the biggest of the cities along the lesser-visited Malabar stretch of Kerala's coastline, a vibrant area steeped in Muslim and Hindu culture. In its pretty Brahminical suburbs lies Harivihar, an immaculate former royal home which offers you the chance to undertake authentic ayurveda in a small, guesthouse setting.

The super-soft lawn leads down to a beautiful green water tank in which you can bathe. There are mango and jackfruit trees in the garden and, inside, cool and calming rooms with dark wood furniture and plantation chairs; ask for a room with a garden view. There are just five doubles and three singles. The retreat is run by traditional medics, Dr Srikumar, a neurologist, and his wife Dr Neetha, a consultant dermatologist, who will make sure you're well looked after. Though some people will be staying on a

66 99

Life in India has not yet withdrawn into the capsule of the head. It is still the whole body that lives.

Carl Jung

India & the Himalaya India – Kerala

◑ Body language

Ayurveda in India

Ayurveda, a Sanskrit word meaning 'the knowledge (veda) of life (ayur)', is an Indian holistic system of health dating back over 5000 years. Indians see it as a divine gift from Lord Brahma, their Hindu creator God, which has been developed by sages and holy men over the centuries. In contrast to the Western system of medicine, which is geared to treating an already-diseased body or mind, ayurveda seeks to help the individual strengthen and control both mind and body in order to prolong life and prevent illness. In today's world, it's a brilliant complement to western medicine and, as well as detoxing the body and mind and relieving stress, has been used to treat ME, high blood pressure, allergies, asthma, rheumatism, back pain, skin diseases, migraines and insomnia, and is also employed as an effective follow-up treatment to chemotherapy.

How it works

In essence, ayurveda combines body treatments and detoxification therapies with a balanced diet, gentle exercise and meditation to promote wellbeing. The type of treatments and therapies we receive will be dictated by our individual constitution, which is defined by a balance of three bodily energies or 'doshas': vata, pitta and kapha. Composed of the five elements – earth, water, fire, air and ether (or space) – these doshas govern our bodily processes: vata controls circulation and the nervous system, for example, pitta the metabolism and digestion, kapha bodily strength and energy. When we feel out of kilter, our doshas are likely to be out of balance, which a course of

ayurvedic treatments will seek to remedy. If we're uptight and prone to do too many things at once, it will calm us down and help us focus. If we're sluggish and suffer from bad digestion, it will energize us and get our bowels moving again.

An experienced ayurvedic doctor will diagnose your dosha type by taking your pulse, and observing such things as how quickly you speak and move, your build, the colour of your eyes and the quality of your skin. You'll also be asked lots of questions about your preferences (for example, do you prefer hot or cold climes, like mild or spicy food, prefer to be alone or with other people). The more open and honest you are, the more accurate a judgement will be, though it's uncanny how the best doctors will read you just right, whatever you tell them.

What you do

Any programme of ayurveda will include preparation treatments and elimination (or detox) therapies. The former include soothing, synchronized oil applications and massages, and swedana (purifying steam and herbal baths), while the latter involve ingesting or retaining herbal medicines, medicated oils and ghee (or clarified butter), inhalations, bastis (or oil enemas), therapeutic vomiting and bloodletting. Preparation treatments often include sleep-inducing shirodara, when a wonderful continuous stream of warm oil is poured across your forehead, choornaswedana, where hot herbal or lemon poultices are massaged all over you to induce sweating, and the supremely nourishing four-handed abhyanga and marma massage (see glossary). Pizzichilli is often regarded as the 'Marmite' of ayurveda. Gallons of cleansing sesame oil are poured continuously over your body and massaged in by two therapists as the oil increases in heat. You'll slip about like a sardine in a tin, but this treatment is very effective. Look at the oil afterwards, and you'll be shocked at just how dirty you were. If you're a smoker, it's likely to be black.

Any hotel or retreat venue that offers only ayurvedic massages is offering only a part of what ayurveda is all about. You need time for ayurveda treatments to have any real effect. A proper course of ayurveda needs at least two weeks to be effective and offer any real lasting benefit, and rest between treatments is vital. Most people who undertake a course of ayurveda have a 'panchakarma' – which literally translates as five therapies, and which also refers to a general ayurveda detox lasting two weeks or more.

VEENA AT SYVC

Where to go

As pure ayurvedic treatments can take up to three therapists working together, India makes an affordable place in which to try it. Most people head to Kerala, which is absolutely teeming with ayurveda centres, some of them not very good at all, so choose carefully. Where you go depends on just how rustic and earthy you want your experience to be. Despite its over exposure in recent years, Somatheeram (see page 216) and its sister resort, Manaltheeram, offer bona fide ayurveda programmes, while Kadappuram (see page 212) and Keraleeyam (see page 213) are even more affordable. Many fellow guests at all three resorts are likely to be earnest, Birkenstock-wearing Germans, Swiss and Italians, countries where ayurveda evangelists have been promoting the ancient Indian system for longer than in the UK. You can also take a programme of ayurveda with expert doctors at the Sivananda Yoga Vedanta Dhanwantari Ashram in Kerala, where you'll find a supportive, yogic environment (see page 224). For an upmarket experience, Kalari Kovilakom (see page 215) is exceptional, or head out of Kerala and north to the Himalaya to Ananda (see page 219).

What to expect

As with any kind of detox, allow at least three days for your body and mind to get into the process. Treatments are often preceded by rituals and prayers, when the crown of your head is rubbed with herbs, or your forehead is smeared with sandalwood paste. You're often given herbal medicine to drink straight after, or whatever you might need at that time – if you have a headache, for example, a thick herbal paste is sometimes applied to your forehead after a treatment and you're encouraged to keep it on for the rest of the day. Whilst constantly having ayurvedic oils rubbed into your hair will be good for your locks, you're likely to be mighty sick of the smell after a few days. Most good ayurveda retreats will have natural products to help remove the oils, but it's a good idea to bring an organic shampoo with you so you can wash your hair properly halfway through your treatment. A bandana or any cotton material will keep hair tucked away during downtime or at dinner. Be prepared for some strong daily herbal drinks, powders and pills, many of which taste pretty disgusting, and for your fellow guests to have that wan expression that comes with fasting. Bring lots of books and an open mind.

What you'll eat

During an ayurveda programme all the food you eat will be designed to remove *ama* (Sanskrit for toxins blocking the body). Usually light and very delicious, ayurvedic dishes avoid meat and fish, mainly because of the time they take to digest, when your energy is needed for the cleansing process. Food is classified according to six different tastes, each of which influences the doshas – these are sweet, salty, sour, pungent, bitter and astringent – and each meal will attempt to stimulate all of them to create a balance in the stomach. Taking a class in ayurvedic cookery during a course of treatments is an excellent way to learn how maintain this balance when you're back home.

When to go

Though India's warm, humid climate makes it a good place to undertake ayurveda year-round, the monsoon, which usually runs from June to the middle of August, is an especially good time to go. Not only does the clean and moist air help to loosen the skin, the cooler climate means your metabolic rate increases, making digestion and blood circulation more efficient. It's also the time they call *athanakal* in Sanskrit, which is when our bodies accept nature's energy more readily. An intensely romantic season with short heavy bursts of rain followed by long spells of sunshine, it's a lovely time to meditate on the rain, enjoy the quiet and smell the ayurvedic herbs in the air.

VEENA AT SYVC

India & the Himalaya India – Kerala

Harivihar Ayurvedic Healing Home.

All that is not given is lost

Indian proverb

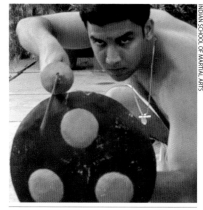

Kalaripayattu at the Indian School of Martial Arts.

B&B basis, most will be here for proper ayurvedic treatments of at least a week, and fellow guests are likely to be middle aged and settled rather than travellers.

The ayurvedic treatment team is led by Dr Mali, a graduate of the Coimbatore Arya Vaidya Pharmacy, with more than 12 years personal experience – he is also the son and grandson of ayurvedic practitioners. The team will diagnose your dosha type and prescribe the course of treatment you need to get yourself back in balance: stay for at least seven days to enjoy the full benefits. Gentle sivananda yoga is taught by a fully qualified teacher. Food is traditional vegetarian ayurvedic cooking and will be tailored to your need; no alcohol is served. Bespoke courses can be arranged two months in advance, though you may also wish to join some of the talks and workshops that are going on: these include Indian philosophy, culture and aesthetics, astrology, Sanskrit, sivananda yoga and vasthu, India's answer to feng shui. All are taught by authorities in their subjects.

The price includes accommodation and food – ayurveda packages cost from US$140 per day. You can fly to Calicut – 28 km away – from Dubai, Sharjah, Kuwait and Colombo, and most major Indian cities. Pickups can be arranged. Local dance and elephant festivals are wonderful affairs in Malabar, so ask in advance if one is happening during your stay. The main

season is November to March. See previous pages for more information on ayurveda.

RURAL RETREAT

The Indian School of Martial Arts

Parasuvykal
T+91 (0)47-1272 5140
www.kalari.in
Payment by donation

For something a little different, the Indian School of Martial Arts is set in a lush landscape in the village of Parasuvykal. It's run by guru Balachandran Nair, otherwise know as 'Baba', who is a master in kalaripayattu, India's traditional martial art. Kalari warriors were healers as well as fighters with an intricate knowledge of the body, and Baba's knowledge has been passed down over 12 generations.

Guests can stay at Dharmikam ashram, where they will witness or learn kalaripayatt, as well as kalarichikitsa, an ancient Indian healing tradition combining ayurveda with marma therapy, which manipulates the vital pressure points of the body to ease pain. A fighter would have had an intimate knowledge of these points to know what to harm or how to heal, and the massage that stems from this knowledge is a truly sensational physical, emotional and psychic release.

This is a warm, welcoming and fascinating place to stay, where you'll be able to make your own oils using herbs from the ashram's extensive garden. Food is excellent, and all the water is filtered and comes from a well 100 m below the Namaskara Mandapam, an

open-air meditation centre.

The school is 20 km from Trivandrum. If you go on to stay in or near Kovalam, you can experience a wonderfully healing 10 days of massage with one of Baba's students, Padma Nair, at her village home. The 10 days cost from US$180 and can be booked at 'Karma', TC6 /2291 Kundamankadavu, Trivandrum 695013, T+91 (0)471-363038.

AYURVEDA RETREAT

Kadappuram Beach Resort

Nattika Beach, Trichur
T+91 (0)48-7239 4988
www.kadappurambeachresorts.com
From US$40 per person per night

Kadappuram is a peaceful, self-contained complex of rustic cottages built in traditional Keralan style. Set in Kerala's more conservative and quieter north, it's a refreshingly untouristy spot in which to undertake ayurveda.

Most guests are from Europe, and are here for a full-on two-week panchakarma, either alone or with a friend or partner. Built to accommodate a large number of guests, the ayurveda centre is functional not luxurious, but massage and medical attention is excellent.

After treatments, you walk across a bridge over a pretty river to get to a large garden of coconut trees and hammocks that leads to the sea. The yoga shala is here too, and you're welcome to do your own practice. Basic yoga sessions are available on request.

A 14-day panchakarma programme costs from US$720, and the resort is a 60-km drive north of Cochin airport. See page 210 for more information on ayurveda.

Yoga at Kailasam.

India & the Himalaya India – Kerala

YOGA & ACTIVITY HOLIDAY

Kailasam Yoga and Ayurveda Holidays

🌍 ⚤ ☀ ⊙ ↘13

Kovalam
T+91 (0)47-1248 4018
www.yogaindia.co.uk
From US$711 per person for 2 weeks

The peaceful oasis of Kailasam was set up by UK yoga teacher Diana Shipp, and her partner Mohan, an ayurvedic physician. Here, amongst the coconut groves, tropical gardens and white sandy beaches, you can have a genuinely restorative holiday with yoga, holistic therapies and, if the exotic landscape, lively festivals and colourful markets inspire you, watercolour painting.

You stay in purpose-built accommodation: five singles and three twin or double rooms. These are cool, comfortable en suites with Western-style toilets and showers and mosquito nets. The newest rooms are the most luxurious, and couples will love room six, which has an attractive, terracotta-tiled ceiling and a balcony overlooking the coconut groves.

For company and conversation or a post-massage snooze, make for the veranda or peaceful relaxation roof. Yoga classes are held in tiled areas under coconut-leaf roofs, surrounded by trees and open-sided to catch the sea breezes. Diana – with diplomas from the British Wheel of Yoga and the Sivananda Yoga Vedanta Dhanwantari Ashram (see page 224) – teaches two optional yoga classes a day: a hatha yoga class in the morning and a shorter, more meditative session in the late afternoon. She focuses on awakening awareness and finding a quiet

centre within, rather than mastering complicated postures, which suits all abilities.

The yoga is complemented by Mohan's ayurvedic treatments, which aid relaxation, detoxify and increase flexibility. His speciality is chavutti thirumal, during which he massages your body with his foot, providing deeper, more thorough pressure than the traditional hand massage. Hypnotherapy is also available and, for the artistically inclined, a two-week painting holiday led by professional landscape artist Susan Beaulah.

Breakfast is the only meal that Diana provides, but the delicious Western-style selection of hot and cold food will keep you going until afternoon. Head out to nearby restaurants on the beach or in the coconut groves for tropical fruit juices – including red banana, a local delicacy – chai and cake, fish, seafood and plenty of fresh Indian specialities.

Your fellow guests are likely to be British women of all ages, though there's normally at least one couple. It's a safe, friendly environment for single travellers and you'll probably find at least one person has been before. If you're there for yoga, you'll need to bring your own mat and go for loose, cotton clothing rather than lycra. Kailasam holidays run from November to March to make the most of the sunshine. Christmas is the busiest time. Fly to Trivandrum – also the nearest train station – a 30-minute taxi ride away. Transfers are included.

AYURVEDA RETREAT

Keraleeyam

○ ⊙ ◐ ↘14

Alleppey
T+91 (0)47-7223 761
www.keraleeyam.com
From US$15 per person per night

Housed in a traditional 70-year-old wooden Keralan home, Keraleeyam sits on one of the prettiest parts of the backwaters, and is a rustic, peaceful and very affordable place to undertake ayurveda – especially a longer programme of treatments – as well as a quiet and restful place to chill out.

The service is excellent, doctors are on hand daily and the whole outfit is a subsidiary of SD Pharmacy, which is one of Kerala's most respected ayurvedic medicinal factories.

Painting at Kailasam.

Some of the therapists do not speak fluent English, but the doctor supervising your treatment will. As well as a full-on two-week (or more) panchakarma, packages of ayurvedic treatments range from slimming and anti-ageing body purification to beauty care and stress management.

All the en suite rooms are on the lake, their walls made of coconut leaves, with simple dark wood furniture and comfortable beds. Only 11 people can be accommodated here at any one time. Food is tasty, and chicken and seafood are on the menu if your diet plan allows it, though no alcohol.

You won't need to do much here – just sit and watch as the village life plays out before your eyes: neat schoolgirls with bright bows in their pony tails getting the water-bus to school, coir weavers paddling past, and boys practising for their boat races. Bring your own books, paints, reading materials – whatever you need to entertain yourself, as it's remote and Alleppey town is a fairly sleepy place. Trips on houseboats and to local sites can easily be arranged if you're up to it.

Fellow guests are likely to be French, German and Swiss, and mostly women or

Kalari Kovilakom has an integrity that is rarely found in upmarket destinations. I laughed easily here, and learnt a lot about my body, especially what real rest can give back to a stressed-out person. The palace is an elegant and uplifting place in which to wander barefoot. There are painted shutters on windows, carved doorways and hand-painted frescoes depicting romantic legends. Though this is a luxurious place to stay, the balance between comfort and the calm cool air of discipline has been expertly struck.

Caroline

couples, though many travel here on their own. Packages cost from US$253 for four nights including all treatments, meals and transfers; a month costs from US$1652. The resort is a three-hour taxi ride from Trivandrum airport, or two hours from Cochin.

HOTEL & SPA

Leela Kovalam Beach

🌐 ⭕ ♨ ⦿ 🅿 ⛵15

Samudra Beach, Kovalam
T+91 (0)47-1248 0101
www.theleela.com
From US$300 per room per night

The Leela is an upmarket chain hotel which uses golf buggies to take its guests from A to B. If that doesn't put you off, the service is immaculate, and the Divya Spa has one of the loveliest yoga shalas in India: a long low pavilion with polished wood floors in a lush garden overlooking the sea.

Accommodation-wise, the Leela sank a whopping US$5 million into a new wing in 2006, and 'The Club' has a series of presidential suites with beautiful views out over the Indian Ocean, 24-hour butlering, and a personal library and living room stocked with every pretty coffee-table book ever published on the subcontinent. The 25-m infinity pool is peerless.

For lesser mortals, the retreat element of the spa is not carried through into the design of the main hotel. Beds are a bit over-plump for any extreme treatment or yoga but, as with Surya Samudra (page 217), the accent here is on luxury beach resort holiday, with a bit of ayurveda on the side.

That said, the ayurveda is extremely professional, with doctors and software programmes to detect your ayurvedic type. They can accommodate any dietary requests, and you won't be starved or kept in a wooden chamber like the more militant retreats in Kerala.

There are eight massage rooms, a hybrid of massage chamber and swish hotel suite – six for massages, one for couples and one for foot massages which is open to the beautiful landscaped gardens and gives you views through coconut trees down to the sea.

Gentle sivananda yoga is taught, and every last need has been pre-empted: floors are granite to compensate for after-oil slipperiness, and there's even a music menu offering you a choice of chakra-balancing acoustic sounds

Left: Backwaters at dawn. **Above**: Keraleeyam.

Ayurveda retreat

Kalari Kovilakom ✈ ☯ ⛰ ⊙ ↘16

A beautiful rich-red and sage-green maharaja's palace built in the 1880s, Kalari Kovilakom was converted into an ayurveda retreat in 2004 by the India-based hotel company CGH Earth. Set on the edge of the village of Kollengode in the foothills of the Annamalai range of mountains, it's well off the Kerala tourist trail and a wonderfully different place to undertake ayurveda.

CAROLINE SYLGE

Where you stay There are a few lovely rooms in the original palace, where the Vengunad suite has stained-glass windows and a daybed suspended from the ceiling. Most rooms are in a tastefully designed guest wing, with elegant dark wooden furniture, cool floor tiles, and four-poster beds with firm mattresses, all decked out with an uplifting use of mellow and welcoming yellows, reds and greens. The spacious grounds are planted with ayurvedic herbs, and contain an authentically designed yoga and meditation hall, and buildings with light and airy treatment rooms. There is also a kalari, where experts train in Kalaripayattu (see glossary).

What you do The minimum stay here is two weeks, the time required for ayurveda treatments to have any real effect (for more on ayurveda, see page 210). Packages include traditional panchakarma (which they call 'rejuvenation'), stress relief, weight reduction or anti-ageing. There are ashram-like qualities to Kalari Kovilakom – your day starts early with hot water, lemon and ginger, and you're then encouraged to go to a session of yoga, which may include chanting and meditation, and which is gentle, with slow, focused stretches and yoga nidra (psychic sleep) in the Bihar School satyananda style (see page 223). When you're not having a treatment, wander the grounds, read in your room, go for a

CGH EARTH

walk in the nearby paddy fields or commission the tailor to copy some of your favourite pieces of clothing.

What you eat and drink Eating is communal, at long wooden tables in a simple open dining room, which means guests bond in a way they rarely do at five-star hotels. All food is vegetarian, and cooked by a chef who practises what he preaches, getting up at 0400 to do yoga, and carrying his energy through to the kitchen. Meals are cooked according to ayurvedic principles with minimal oils and spices: think gram-and-sprout salad, organic vegetables served on a banana leaf, red rice, lightly spiced mango curry, served on giant thali dishes with vata, pitta or kapha tea. Alcohol is not permitted.

Who goes Kalari Kovilakom's price tag attracts professional men and women travelling independently and as couples, to de-stress, detox, or cure genuine aches and pains, including physical disabilities. You're as likely to meet wealthy Indians here as you are well-heeled women from the UK.

Essentials Kollengode, T+91 (0)48-4301 1711, www.kalarikovilakom.com. From US$5378 per person for 14 days. Programmes run for 14, 21 or 28 days, and the palace is open all year round – the monsoon (June to mid August) is a particularly good time to receive treatments. The nearest international airport is Cochin, about a 2½-hour drive away. Palghat is the nearest railway station, on the Mumbai-Trivandrum route. CGH Earth (www.cghearth.com) also runs SwaSwara in Karnataka (see page 228).

(although what perceptible difference namaste, samsara and chakra music makes on Western ears is difficult to say). The atmosphere is classy and a bit ethnic. Russians and British are starting to come for the longer-term retreats here, with packages of de-stress, detoxification or rejuvenation.

To experience this rather lovely place on retreat, come on an organized yoga holiday with wonderfully open and down-to-earth American teacher, **Bridget Shields** (www.bridgetshields.com), who is also a brilliant reflexologist. Bridget also teaches at Amansala in Mexico (see page 352).

MALABAR HOUSE

RURAL RETREAT

Serenity

🌐 🏔 ⊙ ◉ ↘17

Payikad
T+91 (0)48-1245 6353
www.malabarescapes.com
From US$195 per room per night

A gorgeous 1920s five-bedroom spice plantation house on a hilltop in an ancient rubber tree estate, Serenity makes for a lovely hideaway in Kerala. Peaceful and private, it comes complete with a butler and a personal chef, as well as a resident yoga teacher.

The house has a spice garden, a swimming pool and a massage room – a range of rejuvenating ayurvedic massages are available from a local therapist. The friendly yoga teacher has taught all over the world and, as well as optional asana sessions, he can talk to you about yogic philosophy and local culture. Alternatively, just use the grounds to do your own practice whenever you want.

Learn to cook with spices, go cycling in the local village, walk through the spice plantations, or just chill on a hammock. All the bedrooms are stylishly decked out – rooms three, four and five have views across the landscape towards the Blue Mountains.

Fly to Cochin – it's a three-hour drive from there – or take the train to Kottayam from Palghat, Cochin, Quilon, Trivandrum or Chennai, followed by a one-hour drive.

CAROLINE SYLGE

Pickups can be arranged. You can rent the entire house for US$975 plus 15% taxes.

AYURVEDA RETREAT

Somatheeram & Manaltheeram

🌐 🏔 ⊙ ◉ ↘18

Chowara Beach, south of Kovalam
T+091 (0)47-1226 6501
www.somatheeram.org
From US$820 per person per week

Set up in 1992, Somatheeram was Kerala's first ayurveda resort, and still regularly wins the Keralan government's award for the best ayurveda centre in the state. It has also received lots of press coverage in recent

CAROLINE SYLGE

Top: The aptly named Serenity.
Above left and right: Manaltheeram.

years, which means this popular place becomes less tranquil with each year that passes. That said, it continues to offers authentic, expert programmes of ayurveda in a rejuvenating coastal setting: from the bedroom to the treatment room you'll hear waves crashing on expansive Chowara Beach and feel a welcome breeze.

Somatheeram's cottages are dotted over quite a steep hill above the beach with lush plants and vibrant flowers everywhere. The more expensive cottages are based on the design of traditional Keralan houses, or go for cottages 201 or 202 which, despite being labelled 'ordinary', are in a lovely location with a superb view.

If you want more peace on level ground and the use of a swimming pool with whirlpool, stay at the sister resort of Manaltheeram, a five-minute walk away across the beach. The brick and coconut palm thatch cottages have all you need but are decked out with little pizzazz; it's worth paying extra either for a front row special cottage with a proper sea view, or for a side cottage to get more privacy.

Both resorts share the ayurvedic treatment facilities, where 14 doctors and 90 therapists will attend to your needs. Expect thorough

There's no chance of being irritated by weak-handed therapists at Somatheeram – the signature rejuvenation massage is a dream, starting with a very thorough head and shoulder massage, and followed by a chavutti thirumal, where I'm splayed on a plastic mat and my muscles are eased by the feet of a therapist holding onto a ceiling rope to control her weight. This is topped off with a superb abhyanga, a four-handed massage, and the oil-on-the-forehead treatment of shirodara. After which I am so zoned out that I can barely move.

But this is a mixed place. My free shampoo was of the toxic variety, the walls of my treatment room needed a good clean, and my neighbours smoked. The yoga was also a disappointment. I arrived at the appointed 0700 at Manaltheeram to find no mats laid out or anyone waiting. Five minutes later, an Indian man in suit trousers and leather shoes arrived, and offered to talk me through a guided meditation. I declined, not feeling very yogic. Still, I found peace here, and the staff were kind and friendly.

Caroline

India & the Himalaya India – Kerala

Soul food

City of Joy Aid (www.cityofjoyaid.org) is a non-profit humanitarian organization dedicated to helping India's most underprivileged in Kolkata and rural Bengal. Founded and funded by French author Dominique Lapierre and his wife, the charity provides a network of clinics, schools, rehabilitation centres and hospital boats that has brought relief to the poorest of the poor since 1981. The organization has rescued 9000 children suffering from leprosy and other diseases that result from malnutrition and poverty, dug 541 tube wells for drinking water, provided medical assistance to over five million patients, and taught the women of a thousand villages to read and write.

consultations, firm massages and no-nonsense treatments in back-to-basics rooms. The full range of ayurvedic treatments is mixed and matched according to your needs – come for a panchakarma of two weeks or more, or, if you've less time, do a stress management or rejuvenation programme.

After each treatment you're offered a drink of coconut milk, and herbal water is available around the clock, as well as flasks of lemon, honey, ginger and hot water. They make their own oils and liquid medicines, mostly using herbs from their own garden. There's a weekly lecture on ayurveda, and longer courses in ayurvedic massage and philosophy. Somatheeram has a yoga hall, though the standard of teaching and the schedule varies: find a quiet spot on the lawn at Manaltheeram to do your own practice, or check in advance who will be teaching.

Two restaurants offer tasty Keralan food, which you choose from a set menu of dishes labelled according to their suitabiliy for a vata, pitta or kapha constitution. You'll sometimes find people smoking here, and you are able to get a drink, though both are discouraged.

Your fellow guests are Europeans in their thirties and up, predominantly German, with quite a few Russians in recent years, and 40% are repeat guests. Most are here for two-week treatments, some are here just on

holiday, dipping in and out of treatments and sightseeing during the day.

Retreats led by outside teachers often run at Somatheeram. If you want a little hand-holding, UK-based holistic health and beauty therapist, **Bharti Vyas** (T+44 (0)20-7935 5312, www.bharti-vyas.com), leads 10-day retreats, or join a yoga retreat with uplifting American vinyasa flow teacher, **Shiva Rea** (www.yogaadventures.com). Fly or take the train to Trivandrum, and from there it's a 21-km drive; pickups can be arranged. See page 210 for more information on ayurveda.

HOTEL & SPA

Surya Samudra Beach Garden

Near Kovalam
T+91 (0)47-1226 7333
www.suryasamudra.com
From US$120 per room per night

Just 100 m from the beach, Surya Samudra is a delight. It's up on a rocky bluff at the end of a winding path leading from Pulinkudi village, between the backpacker resort of Kovalam and sacred Kanniyakumari, with Asia's largest wooden palace in between.

These 9 ha of jackfruit, bamboo, cinnamon, mango, palm and hibiscus trees are an elite

SURYA SAMUDRA

SURYA SAMUDRA

Top: Poolside at Surya Samudra Beach Garden.
Above: One of the bedrooms at Surya Samudra.

retreat for holidaymakers rather than those in search of a lengthy ayurveda programme, though you can take your rejuvenation here as seriously as you like. The spa is a tranquil and palatial treat lying inside a bespoke pavilion of long corridors, polished wood, teak pillars and hand-carved heavy wood Keralan doors.

This is a sleek place to relax and be pampered. There are eight spotless treatment rooms with little nooks for gods (a plump Ganesh has beautiful blooms tucked behind his elephant ears) and steam baths on the side of each treatment room. Couples can have synchronized massages in one of the specially designed double rooms, there's a room with a Cleopatra-style milk bath and a beauty room for body wraps, manicures and pedicures where pretty nymphs pout down at you from the frescoes.

Attention to detail is second to none. Two top-notch consultant medics have designed the treatment plan and are on hand to give advice, daily from 0900 till 1300, on problems from digestion to arthritis. Medicines have been devised from ancient texts and include lemon and salt and garam (lentil) scrubs, or red sandal powder, turmeric, coriander, banyan tree seeds, egg white and saffron seeds. The accent is on wellness; don't expect chronic diseases to be cured between flights.

Yoga tuition in the sivananda style, with a maximum class sizes of two, takes place in a pavilion that's open to the sky and has views of the Keralan coastline. The Octagon bedroom is the only room with a TV. As well as ayurvedic dishes, north Indian, south Indian and even spaghetti bolognese are all up for grabs at the lovely Octopus restaurant. Those wanting to detox will need self control to resist the fish curries, home-made pickles and ice creams.

Your fellow guests will be chiefly British or continental European honeymooners, retirees and the well heeled. Pack a posh floaty kaftan, and bring a friend or partner – this isn't the place to get chatty.

Most visitors stay between five days and two weeks. Special and very affordable packages are on offer during the monsoon, one of the best times to undertake the treatment (see page 210 for more on ayurveda). Fly to Trivandrum airport, 22 km away, and book a pickup with the hotel.

Rest of India

Aman-I-Khás.

HOTEL & SPA

Aman-I-Khás

Ranthambhore, Rajasthan
T+(0)7462-252052
www.amanresorts.com
From US$900 per tent per night

Aman-I-Khás translates as 'Special Place' in a combination of Sanskrit, Urdu and Hindi, and you will find this Aman property to be an exceptional luxury wilderness camp. Ten stunning tents nestle in the environs of Ranthambhore National Park in Rajasthan, against a backdrop of tall grasses, trees and the Aravalli hills.

There's a spa tent offering various massages, scrubs and facials using local herbs and spices (from US$65). The ayurvedic choornasweda massage treatment with poultices uses organic herbs from the garden; or try some temporary henna body art. Complimentary yoga is available on alternate days; private yoga, meditation and reiki sessions start from US$45.

The large mogul-style canvas tents are set on concrete plinths among well-manicured grounds. A cotton screened dining area in the entrance of each tent leads through to a central space where you can lounge on a large daybed and marvel at the 6-m-high roof. A bedroom, dressing room and bathroom are separated by cotton drapes, the wooden furniture is stylish and offers ample storage, and there's even a sunken stone bath. All tents have air conditioning and a drinks cooler.

Indian and Western dishes are served either in the privacy of your tent, or in the central dining tent, many of the ingredients coming from the camp's organic vegetable garden. After dinner you'll be invited to recline around an outdoor fire, gaze at the stars and chat. There's a lounge tent with a library full of books on Indian culture and wildlife. Real wildlife is on hand in the neighbouring national park, and Aman offers unforgettable day trips – tigers are occasionally spotted – for US$60.

The tents are available between October and April. A minimum two-night stay is required. The rate quoted excludes a daily food and beverage charge of US$75 per person. Aman provides a portered train journey from Delhi and car journey back for US$150 per person each way. Packages incorporating a stay at Aman's Garden Haveli suite at its sister property in Amanbagh are available.

MOUNTAIN RETREAT

Ananda

Near Rishikesh
T+91 (0)11-2656 8888
www.anandaspa.com.
From US$430 per person per night

You cannot fail to be uplifted by the setting at Ananda, a 40-ha pampering palace estate which sits high up in the clear, crisp air of the Himalayan foothills with inspirational views

❝❞

The highlight at Ananda was the daily vedanta sessions with Janki Chopra from the Vedanta Academy. An ancient Indian philosophy packed with common sense, vedanta forms the bedrock of yoga, promoting self-awareness and self-control. It's a little earnest, but infinitely wise. I attended various sessions, including one on relationships and non-attachment, which made more sense to me than any theory I've listened to before or since. Not bad for a philosophy that's thousands of years old.

Caroline

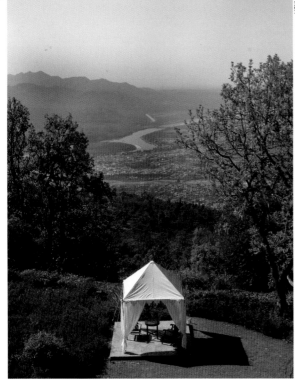

Above: Ayurvedic massage at Ananda. **Left:** Views to soothe even the most jaded of souls at Ananda.

down to the Ganges and Rishikesh. You stay in a modern, tastefully designed block five minutes' walk from the main palace (get a room with an even number for a valley view – all odd numbers have a view of the palace). The Vice-regal suite has the best of both, and three private villas with pools and valley views are new for 2007.

Maroon and orange fabrics are set against creams and browns; there's wooden furniture, rush matting on the floor, and meditation mandalas framed on the walls. It's the little things that make the difference: a hot-water bottle placed inside your bed at night; little nutty almond cakes left on your pillow instead of chocolates; camomile tea served with tiny, white ceramic cups – one for honey, one for lemon.

There's a resident vedanta teacher from the Vedanta Institute in Delhi, who teaches daily classes in this ancient Indian philosophy (see yoga feature, page 203). These teachers are unpaid disciples of their guru, Swami Parthasarathy, the world's foremost vedanta philosopher who founded the Vedanta Academy in Pune (see www .vedanta-edu.org). There are daily vedanta sessions in the morning, and sometimes in the evening as well, and in every bedroom there's a copy of Swami Parthasarathy's book *Vedanta Treatise*.

Lifestyle and ayurvedic consultations and a host of treatments are on offer in a stunningly designed palatial spa building. These include beauty treatments inspired by ancient Indian traditions as well as more serious programmes in nutrition, exercise, stress management, anti-ageing and detoxification. There's an ayurvedic doctor on site and efficient, unflappable therapists.

There's a large outdoor pool, daily set activities, including yoga in the open stone amphitheatre, and power walks. Local treks and whitewater rafting can also be arranged. You may feel a little cut off from the real India here so take a trip into Rishikesh by day, or there are organized trips to an evening ceremony of arati (see glossary) on the Ganges in the evening.

The restaurant serves a delicious and nutritious mix of Asian, India, ayurvedic and European dishes – you're as likely to find a miso soup and wasame salad on the menu as you are fusion curries and bespoke ayurvedic meals. Ananda attracts well-heeled Indian and Western professionals of 35 and above. There are two daily flights from Delhi to Dehra with Air Deccan, or it's a four-hour journey from Delhi by train to Haridwar, an hour's drive away.

MOUNTAIN RETREAT

Bamboo Resort

Sajong Village, Rumtek, Sikkim
T+91 (0)92-3251 3050
www.bambooresort.com
From US$85 per room per night

Set in three acres of paddy fields with wonderful views of the Himalayan mountains bordering Tibet, Bamboo Resort is a quiet and interesting place to base yourself for treks, with creative workshops, meditation and herbal soaks on offer.

The star of the show is a wonderful top-floor meditation room, complete with traditional Buddhist altar and windows looking out to the mountains – the perfect place for your own yoga or meditation practice. An introduction to meditation can also be arranged.

Above right and left: The lush, verdant foothills of the Himalaya are the perfect setting for yoga or meditation at Bamboo Resort.
Below: The lakeside retreat of Basunti.

There's a special room for herbal baths: soak in one infused with lemongrass from the garden, lit by candles and with a relaxing herbal tea. Foot massage is also on offer, and workshops available on request include basket weaving, cooking and Sikkimese language classes, and Tibetan mandala painting with a Thangka Master. There's a library with a good selection of books and videos on the Himalaya.

Swiss-born owner Helen Kampf runs Greenwood Travels and can help you plan some inspirational treks or mountain bike rides in the surrounding area. Visits to local Buddhist monasteries with expert guides can be arranged.

The main house is built on the principals of feng shui. All 10 rooms are painted a different colour and cover the four elements. Chic lamps from Switzerland sit on locally made bamboo tables, beds are raised futons and all rooms have en suite bathrooms and iron balconies with enriching mountain views.

Meals are served buffet-style inside the marbled dining area or on the terrace, using ingredients from the organic herb and vegetable garden. There's locally sourced poultry wherever possible, and Sikkimese, Tibetan, Swiss and Indian dishes are all available, as well home-made pizza cooked in the wood fired oven. Locally produced items including bamboo handicrafts can be bought from the small shop.

Fly to Kolkata or Delhi, then take an internal flight to Bagdogra, from where it's a 4½-hour drive. Pickups can be arranged (US$65 per car). The best time to come for the flowers is from April to June, and for good mountain views from September or October to December. The resort is open year round, but you need to book in advance.

WATERSIDE RETREAT

Basunti

Near Talwara, Himachal Pradesh
T+44 (0)20-7691 0910
www.basunti.com
From US$45 per person per night, full board

Newly opened in 2007, Basunti is a lovely lakeside retreat set in a wildlife sanctuary with views of the Himalaya, and an inspired Balinese-style thatch-roofed yoga shala. Retreats are on offer here, or come as a guest to go walking, swimming, canoeing, fishing and birdwatching, visit local rock temples and forts or just chill out.

There's a pristine lodge with four twin-bedded rooms and a main house with two self-contained maisonettes which each sleep three. Indian and Western veggie dishes are on offer, plus fish caught fresh from the lake. Indian head and neck, full body, aromatherapy and ayurvedic massages can be arranged in advance.

Italian Sandra Sabatini studied for 17 years with the late Vanda Scaravelli, and runs two five-day scaravelli yoga retreats here each year. Plans are afoot to host other yoga retreats by visiting teachers, as well as tai chi and pilates – check website for updates. There are residential workshops in landscape painting and pottery, as well as Indian cookery led by Rachel Demuth, owner of Demuth's Restaurant in Bath, England.

Basunti is about 25 minutes from the village of Talwara. The nearest international airport is Amritsar, from where it's a three-hour drive. The nearest local airport is Pathankot, a 90-minute drive away. There are daily flights to Pathankot from Delhi.

India & the Himalaya Rest of India

Mountain retreat

Glenburn Tea Estate ⛹ ◉ 🏃 ⛷ ↘24

Set in the hills of Darjeeling with brilliant views of Mount Kanchenjunga and the Himalaya, Glenburn Tea Estate is an ideal place to get away from everything – with a friend, a family group or alone. Established in 1860 by Scottish tea planters and now owned by the Prakash family, it is still a working tea estate, so you won't feel like a tourist, and you'll be taken care of by your local host, Neena, and the Nepalese staff.

Where you stay You sleep in Burra Bungalow, an immaculately restored tea planter's bungalow which sleeps 12 in four suites; the pretty Rose Suite has hand-embroidered linens from West Bengal while the elegant Tea Planter's Suite boasts a Spanish mahogany four-poster bed. For a little adventure, stay overnight by the river Rungeet in Glenburn's river cabin, lit only by kerosene lamp and with no electricity, where staff still manage to supply you with some delicious nosh. Eight forest cottages are planned for 2008.

What you do You may just want to chill and read, write, paint, go for long walks, or practise your own yoga or tai chi. Whatever you're into, the attention to detail will see you right in just a few days. Creator of Glenburn, Husna Tara Prakash, can custom-make a rejuvenation week, with daily yoga given by a local teacher, and daily forest and riverside treks across the estate's 650 ha of private forest, tea plantations and tea pickers' villages. You can enjoy a foot soak with fresh mint and camomile from the organic garden, and a foot massage on the veranda, or have an in-room Swedish body massage using Darjeeling green-tea massage oil. There's an orangery and convent to visit on site, or take a jeep ride out to Meera's Buddha, an inspiring 4-m bronze statue created by a European sculptress on the opposite hill to Glenburn.

> ❝❞
> Nothing quite beats sipping a cup of the home-grown Darjeeling tea lounging on a plantation chair, especially if you're watching a pink sun rise and no one else is yet awake.
>
> *Caroline*

What you eat and drink Healthy juices are a speciality – as of course is the anti-oxidant Darjeeling tea. The sit-down evening suppers are inspired by Nepali, Tibetan and Indian cuisine – green-tea ice cream, *thugpa* (a Tibetan soup) and tea leaf pakoras are just some of the morsels on offer. Herbs and vegetables all come from Glenburn's organic garden.

Who goes The place attracts families, friends and couples mainly from Europe, Australia and North America, usually staying for three to five nights, though artists and writers have been known to stay for up to a month.

Essentials Glenburn Tea Estate is in Darjeeling District, West Bengal, T+91 (0)33-2288 5630, www.glenburnteaestate.com. The cost is from US$400 per room per night, and is inclusive of transfers, all meals, soft drinks and accommodation and access to a jeep and driver. It's a 2½-hour drive from Bagdogra airport or New Jalpaiguri station; your hosts will pick you up with a picnic hamper.

GLENBURN   GLENBURN

YOGA RETREAT

Bihar School of Yoga

🌐 ⛰ 🌀 NJ25

Munger, Bihar
T+91 (0)63-4422 2430
www.yogavision.net
US$1500 for a 4-month course

Founded in 1964 by Paramahamsa Satyananda, Bihar is renowned amongst those who wish to explore themselves spiritually and physically. It is presently under the guidance of Swami Niranjanananda, the successor to Swami Satyananda. Its sister institute in the same location, the Bihar Yoga Bharati (BYB) institute of advanced yogic studies, runs an annual four-month yoga course here in English from October to January.

You stay within the gates of the **Ganga Darshan Yogashram**, sitting on a green hill overlooking the Ganges, its cloistered building is surrounded by gardens and paddy fields. The ashram is professionally run, and a clean and safe oasis in one of the poorest and most lawless states in India.

Expect the rigours of ashram life, with no luxuries. The experience is designed to address your strengths and weaknesses and overcome the ego. You'll rise at 0400 for meditation and then follow a full daily schedule of yoga and yogic philosophy classes, karma yoga (selfless service), chanting and evening satsangs (see page 224). Lights go out at 2030 and silence must be observed all night.

Satyananda yoga combines an effective set of uncomplicated stretching and meditative movements to exercise every joint and muscle in a methodical way, with practices like yoga nidra, kirtan, mouna and karma yoga. Asanas are taught by experts in the inspiring grounds or the meditation room – Jyoti Mandir (Hall of Light) – and you're encouraged to keep a journal to chart your reactions to the experience.

There is lots of karma yoga: chopping vegetables, making chapattis and meticulously picking stones from rice, helping to proofread the books the school publishes. Expect to wear a uniform, eat only what is put in front of you, to sit on the floor a lot and have little communication with the outside world. After four months, guests report transformed lives or feeling stronger emotionally and physically.

Meals are taken in silence. The food is bland, vegetarian and consists of basic rice and vegetables and plenty of black tea; bring a travel kettle for your own beverages. Accommodation is simple and can be shared or private; bathrooms are mostly shared, and there is no hot water. Couples should note that men and women stay in separate accommodation.

Bihar attracts a wide variety of Western and Indian guests; the average age is between 20 and 50. Don't travel at night or by bus; group travel is safest. September to March are good months to go; it is very cold during December and January, so bring a sleeping bag and warm clothes. Also bring eating utensils, plate, mug, bowl, rechargeable lamp and torch.

Application forms for the four-month course are available from www.yogavision.net or www.yogamag.net; apply early as this is a very popular course. You can sometimes stay as an individual, but this needs to be arranged in writing beforehand. Fly to Delhi or Kolkata and connect with trains to Jamalpur station – it's safer to travel in air-conditioned compartments.

It's a six-hour taxi drive from Munger to Bihar School's ashram at Rikhia Dham in Jarkhand where Swami Satyananda now resides (see ashram feature, page 224). Courses run here and you can stay at any time, but you need to apply in advance in writing. You can experience satyananda yoga worldwide: there is an academy in Europe (www.saye.org) that runs one-year courses and a satyananda yoga retreat in Australia (see page 315). See the highly informative yoga magazine at www.yogamag.net for more details.

Below left and right: Funky eco-hotel, The Dune, is a great place for a DIY retreat (see page 226).

India & the Himalaya Rest of India

THE DUNE

THE DUNE

◑ Body language

Get thee to an ashram

Derived from the Sanksrit word *aashraya*, meaning shelter, an ashram in ancient India was a hermitage in rural surroundings where sadhus, or holy men, found the peace to explore their spirituality. Today they are places of solace in towns and cities as well as the countryside, where a community drawn by a common (usually spiritual) goal lives, works and studies together, usually led by a guru. Some Indian ashrams today are open to Western guests of all faiths, or none, for a small daily donation, and, if well chosen, offer a nourishing experience for anyone interested in exploring the true meaning of yoga (see page 202). A stay at an ashram can also offer real time out, a chance to re-evaluate your life and to find out what is important to you.

What to expect

India's best ashrams are welcoming, clean, calm complexes of gardens and buildings where a guru, though revered, does not have too tight a grip on the thought processes of its members. Choose carefully, and don't allow yourself to be put off by your first encounter with an ashram's spiritual practices, which most westerners with an open mind usually find very enriching. These may include group chanting (usually from the ancient Indian texts, the Vedas), daily puja (a Hindu religious ritual), and evening satsang (Sanskrit for 'true company', a kind of spiritual

gathering where you chant, meditate, listen to a reading or a talk on an essential aspect of yoga philosophy). Expect to participate in an ashram's set daily schedule, which involves early starts, fixed periods of meditation, chanting and yoga, and a few hours a day of karma yoga, or selfless service. This is work is the bedrock of any ashram: you help out the community with whatever needs to be done, including preparing meals, cleaning, gardening, repairing, even teaching local children. Most ashrams will have a number of community projects on the go, some feeding hundreds of people a day for free.

Meals consist of (usually very delicious) spicy and non-spicy vegetarian dishes which are eaten communally at set times, often in silence – a surprisingly relaxing experience which gives you the chance to appreciate your food and digest it better. People from all over the world and of all ages visit ashrams, and it can be very inspiring to be with a large group of people who are all behaving calmly and kindly to one another. You'll often meet other people having similar experiences to you, so friendships can be very meaningful.

Smoking, alcohol, drugs, mobile phones, iPods and sex are (obviously) not allowed, and men and women sleep in separate quarters. Single rooms are often available – just ask. Bring your own towel and toiletries, and loose, comfortable and discreet clothing, including warm layers if you're visiting at a chilly time. A small pillow will make meditation and sleeping more comfortable, and your own yoga mat will also come in useful. Sometimes you're required to bring your own bedding – ask in advance. With some ashrams, you can simply turn up, while with others, you need to book months in advance – it's always wise to check through a website.

Where to go

Many travellers looking for an authentic yogic experience go to the spiritual supermarket of Rishikesh where the city's largest and most renowned ashram, **Parmath Niketan** (www.parmarth.com), offers an escape from the traffic and noise with a lovely courtyard garden full of wild flowers, and regular courses from visiting teachers in yoga, meditation and holistic therapies. It's set on India's holy river, the Ganga, and celebrates an aarti ceremony (see glossary) every evening on the riverbank.

Alternatively, head out of the city to **Aurovalley**

(www.aurovalley.com), a warm, welcoming ashram set close to the Ganga in rural surroundings at Rishidwar, between Rishikesh and Haridwar. The ashram follows the celebrated guru Sri Aurobindo Ghose, a Bengali philosopher and freedom fighter who set up the Sri Aurobindo Ashram in Pondicherry in 1926, and whose collaborator set up the experimental international community, Auroville, in 1968.

Any ashram connected to the Bihar School of Yoga in Munger (see page 223) will offer an authentic experience of satyananda yoga: the Rikhia Dham ashram, near the pilgrimage town of Deoghar in the state of Jharkhand, is a clean, calm place where the inspirational Swami Satyananda has adopted a hundred villages and educates the village girls and women; or try the Atma Darshan yogashram in Bangalore (www.atmadarshan.org). There are satyananda ashrams and centres all over the world – go to www.yogamag.net.

In Tamil Nadu, head to **Sri Ramanasramam** ashram, a three-hour drive from Chennai, for a taste of the most challenging yoga of all, jnana, the yoga of self-knowledge or wisdom. It's based on the works of Ramana Maharshi, who invented a method of self-inquiry in which the mind is used to dismantle the mind by asking the question, 'Who am I?' The idea is to come to the knowledge that we are nothing but awareness. Don't expect any lessons in this, however – you just go and meditate with that question in mind (see page 226 for a first person account). Don't expect any asana practice here either; the Maharshi didn't believe in it.

In Kerala, most people head to **Amritapuri** and the ashram of one of India's few female gurus, Mata Amritanandamayi, otherwise known as Amma (mother), who doles out all-embracing hugs during her daily darshan (audience). Amma has set up hugely impressive educational and medical programmes all over southern India, and travels for about eight months of the year, so check in advance if a hug from her is important to you. The ashram is a huge, buzzy but inspiring place to be (www.amritapuri.org).

For something a little different in Kerala, stay at **Dharmikam** ashram, part of the **Indian School of Martial Arts** (www.kalari.in) run by guru Balachandran Nair, where you can try kalaripayattu and kalarichikitsa (see page 212). Or experience the power of group chanting at Ananda, in **Kanhangad**

(www.anandashram.org), where the name of the Hindu god Ram Nam is chanted from 0600 to 1800. The ashram is open to all, and the incantation is seen as a way to get closer to universal consciousness. Just listening to the mesmerizing "Om Shree Raam, Jay Raam, Jay Jay Raam" and its vibrations is a nourishing experience – taking part is even more so. Founded in 1931 by Swami Ramdas (otherwise known as papa), the ashram doesn't run courses, but you can come here to stay and help out with some karma yoga: they feed more than 100 people every day.

For a programme aimed specifically at westerners, the **Sivananda Yoga Vedanta Dhanwantari Ashram**, on the edge of Neyyar Dam in Kerala, is a brilliant place to experience yoga in its truest form. It runs regular two-week 'yoga vacations' which start on the 1st and 16th of every month (from US$10 per person per night). As well as an open class (not for the faint-hearted), there is a beginners programme which will accommodate those who are unfit or who have never done yoga before. You can also visit the ashram for ayurveda, fasting and cultural programmes throughout the year, or for the month-long sivananda teacher training course (from US$1550), though it gets extremely busy at these times. There are sivananda ashrams and centres all over the world. In India, you'll also find them in the Himalayas and Madurai (visit www.sivananda.org).

ROSIE WALFORD

❝❞

Sri Ramanasramam is a hermetically sealed world of peaceful elegant simplicity, where ancient sadhus clad in orange waddle silently along the raked sand walkways, and milk-white peacocks fan their tails on the temple roof.

I was there to practise jnana yoga, the most challenging of all yogas. Sri Ramana Maharshi, the guru in whose honour the ashram was built, believed that repetition of the question 'Who am I?' destroys all other thoughts, leaving behind only sat-chit-ananda-existence-consciousness bliss.

I began my quest at 0600 with the morning milk offering to the Maharshi. A bare-chested swami bearing armfuls of orange, pink and white garlands conducted a prayer ceremony, scattering leaves and petals as he chanted, filling the air with a heady mixture of flowers, citronella and incense. Breakfast was eaten off a banana leaf, which I was told to sprinkle first with water – I wasn't sure if this was devotional or hygienic but I gave it a good dousing. A pot-bellied sadhu with a huge tin bucket turned the leaf dirty side up, threw the contents of his ladle upon it and beamed. I beamed back, practising non-attachment to cleanliness. I spent the rest of the day exploring Arunachala, the hill that the Maharshi called his 'guru', where I found his cave, and the little house that he lived in for many years before the ashram was built. The Maharshi would lie for hours in silence, surrounded by every form of life - from Jackie the dog who would sit on an orange cloth and stare at him, to Lakshmi the cow, which he believed to be an incarnation of the old lady who used to feed him when he lived in the cave.

Cave and house were both full so I retired to the ashram's own meditation hall. I settled down and soon I was sinking deep into the infinite blackness. I sat listening to my breath – deep and steady – with nothing to worry about. In that weightlessness I found stillness, an awareness of a bigger reality; pure existence, consciousness, and yes, bliss.

I don't know how much time passed before the cleaning lady's sudden entry awoke me. Had I experienced jnana yoga? Who cared? For the first time in the yoga schools of India, I had felt the potential of a merger with cosmic bliss. For this miracle I award it the title of Ashram of the Year and highly recommend you give it a try.

Lucy Edge, author of Yoga School Dropout (Ebury)

COASTAL RETREAT

The Dune

🌐 ⭕ 🏔 ⊘ ↘26

Pondicherry, Tamil Nadu
T+91 (0)41-3265 5751
www.thedune.in
From US$75 per room per night

A funky eco-hotel set on a lovely stretch of beach on the Coromandel coast in southern India, The Dune offers daily yoga, reflexology and ayurvedic massage, organic food and optional detox programmes. There are bicycles to borrow, plus a swimming pool and tennis court, or just walk on the beach where sadhus have come for centuries from the nearby temples to meditate.

Organic meals, often using raw food, are based on a 'hypotoxic' (or toxin-free) diet plan devised by a French biologist, Dr Jean Seignale. Bedrooms are colourful, clean and peaceful, and the public spaces are often hung with some inspirational artwork (the hotel is a base for an artists-in-residence programme).

The Dune is just 15 km from Pondicherry, one of India's more peaceful towns, which still retains some of its elegant French buildings and charm (it was a French colony until 1954). Fly to Chennai, from where the Dune is just over a two-hour drive; pick ups can be arranged. After your stay, head to the hills and the **Elephant Valley** (www.elephantvalley.com), The Dune's sister retreat, a 40-ha organic farm 20 km from Tamil Nadu's hill station Kodaikanal, and a great base for trekking, horse-riding or just chilling out.

The Dune is also a short 10-km drive from **Auroville** (www.miraura.org), the experimental international community set up in 1968 by Frenchwoman Mirra Alfassa (known as 'The Mother'), where a group of people from various countries has been living for nearly 40 years. After obtaining a guest pass, visitors can explore the complex and participate in activities open to Aurovilians, which include all sorts of things from Indian dance to ashtanga yoga. There's also a Quiet Healing Centre on the nearby beach, well known for its underwater body treatments.

The hydrotherapy treatment tank is a little public so it's best to stick to the ayurvedic massages, which are good.

YOGA RETREAT

Shreyas

🌐 ⭕ 🏔 ⊚ ⊘ ↘27

Bangalore, Karnataka
T+91 (0)80-2773 7183
www.shreyasretreat.com
From US$296 per night, double occupancy

Set in 10 ha of landscaped grounds on the outskirts of Bangalore, Shreyas is an ideal place to come if you want to experience peace and yoga in five-star luxury.

Various hatha yoga lessons by Indian teachers run (usually) twice daily, though those already into yoga may not find these challenging. The staff often join in, adding to the community spirit. The yoga studio floor is tiled, which is a little unforgiving, but the open-sided building allows for lots of fresh air and the architecture is calming.

There are daily silent meditation sessions,

when everyone can benefit from quiet, and a wellness consultant, trained in Vedanta philosophy, is available for advice. An occasional Spiritual Awakening retreat includes yoga, life coaching and meditation, and hosts several high-profile Indian guest speakers. But Shreyas is also about pampering: Balinese massage and exotic fruit body scrubs are invigorating extras along with the steam room, jacuzzi and pool.

Though the main buildings are plain, the de luxe stone cottages are impressive with canvas ceilings and private patios. Internal decor is neutral with beige and white sheets, a small desk, telephone and internet connection. Tall palm trees and superbly maintained gardens surround the rooms.

One of the most appealing features is the organic garden, where aromatic herbs and vegetables are grown. The vegetarian cuisine is exceptional, and is enhanced by the silver service and tables festooned with flower petals. Alcohol is not allowed on the premises. There's a gym, library, home theatre with DVD selection, and outdoor amphitheatre where music recitals are sometimes held.

Expect to meet mainly single women, some couples and a few Indian business travellers. It can feel empty when there are no retreats running. Though accessed by a picturesque road lined with ancient trees, Shreyas is very near a train line, which can be noisy. November to January are the best months to visit. Six-night packages cost from US$2000 and include accommodation, meals, yoga classes, five rejuvenation massages, interactive philosophy sessions and airport transfers. Fly to Bangalore, from where it's a 50-km drive.

Top: The tiled yoga studio at Shreyas. Above: The landscaped grounds at Shreyas make for a peaceful and attractive setting.

HEALTH & FITNESS RETREAT

Soukya International Holistic Health Centre

🌐 🎧 ⚗ ○ 🏃 🎧 ⚙ ⏩ ↘28

Bangalore, Karnataka
T+91 (0)80-2531 8405
www.soukya.com
From US$135 per person per night

East and West unite at Soukya, a tranquil, friendly healing centre in 12 ha of beautifully cultivated countryside east of Bangalore. The centre offers a range of highly personalized programmes – ranging from seven to 28 days – and promotes wellness; not just being free from illness, but living life fully in mind, body and spirit. Come here to relax and rejuvenate, or work more deeply on a psychological or physical level.

Individual cottages are situated around lawns, flowers and trees and house 12 en suite single and double rooms, and four suites richly decorated with silk-draped four-poster beds. You have your own private garden, and there are plenty of places to find space between treatments. There is a maximum of 25 guests at any one time.

The day begins with the first of two yoga classes in a large thatched hut with coloured glasswork on the walls. The yoga teacher is also a trained naturopathic doctor, with whom you can take one-to-one sessions. Although these cost extra, they allow the doctor to guide you on the asanas and movements that suit your physical and emotional needs for the short and long term.

The wellness programmes combine modern medicine with the healing traditions of ayurveda, homeopathy, naturopathy and a wide range of complementary therapies. Choose to detoxify, de-stress, lose weight or relax and rejuvenate. There are medical

programmes to treat asthma, diabetes, hypertension and addictions such as smoking, and the consultants will work in tandem with your own doctor back home if necessary. Each programme includes a health evaluation that allows a bespoke treatment package to be created. This may draw on hydrotherapy, homeopathy and therapies such as zero balancing, acupuncture and reflexology.

Meals are organic, delicious and traditional Indian with a few options for a Western-style breakfast. The food is vegetarian, low fat, low salt and non-spicy. Herbal teas and refreshing coconut water replace alcohol, which is not permitted.

The price is for accommodation and meals;

treatments and programmes cost extra, and range from US$40-300 per day. People come to Soukya from all over the world. Older guests and women in particular visit for the anti-ageing and rejuvenating programmes, and many guests are repeat visitors. Bring warm clothes for the months of November to February. Fly to Bangalore, which is 17 km from Soukya.

SwaSwara

Om beach, Gokarna, Karnataka
T+91 (0)83-8625 7131
www.cghearth.com
From US$300 per villa per night

Set in 12 ha along the curve of gorgeous Om beach, SwaSwara (sound of the self in Sanskrit) offers 'yoga for the soul', with daily yoga classes taught by Indian swamis, and ayurvedic massage. It may look a little like a housing estate, but the staff's gleaming smiles testify to a their care and attention, and it's ideal for both individuals and couples.

There's a wide of range of different yoga classes on offer, including ashtanga, hasya or laughter yoga (a simulated laughter which relaxes the mind, increases the blood flow and strengthens the immune system), and kundalini art yoga (understanding the effect of colour and patterns on the mind). You can also enjoy yoga nidra (psychic sleep), yajna (interactive cooking), and tratak meditation, which involves focusing on an object such as a candle flame and chanting mantras.

The 27 traditional Konkan stone, clay and

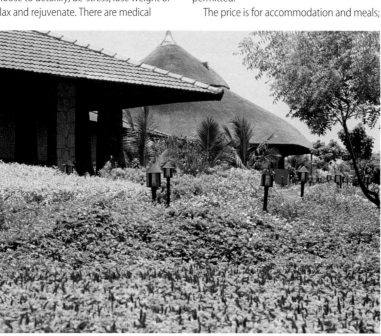

Above and below: Soukya International Holistic Health Centre.

Jane Craggs has the knack of balancing yogic philosophy with expert tuition on breathing and postures, so you get a lot of depth from her lessons. Very approachable and down-to-earth, she used to work as a comedian, and can be very funny – a combination which made our week a simply lovely, heart-warming experience.

Caroline

thatch villas are set around walled private gardens, with air conditioning (or fan), oriental-style floor to ceiling glass doors and cream muslin drapes around a bed which is strewn with flowers in the day and philosophical quotes in the evening. The bathroom – part outside – has curved walls and superb lighting, sweet basil soap and ayurvedic shampoo, and crisp white cotton bathrobes. The roofed patio has a writing desk with a view of a lake and monkeys in the treetops, and there's an ocean view from the beautiful thatched yoga room on the top floor.

Healthy breakfasts and tasty Indian lunches washed down with masala chai are served in the open-sided restaurant with a palm leaf roof and amazing views. Candlelit dinners are eaten in the coconut grove by Om beach, and wine and beer are available.

Healing, relaxation and rejuvenation therapies are offered, accompanied by a tailor-made ayurvedic diet. Ayurvedic massages are given in treatment rooms surrounding the magnificent mandala-shaped blue meditation dome, though, when we visited, there was too much oil and not enough intuition, and the brand-new therapists needed to grow into their role. One-to-one sessions with the yoga master and personalized yoga therapy programmes are at no extra cost and guests can also go through a cleansing programme.

Om beach has strong undercurrents and is not safe for swimming – there's a swimming pool in the grounds and other beaches are a short walk or boat ride away – and it can become overrun with busloads of local families. The temple town of Gokarna is 15 minutes by taxi. Other activities include archery, kayaking, trekking, butterfly and birdwatching, and jungle walks.

Fly to Goa's Dabolim airport, from where it's a 2½-hour drive, or take a train to Kumta, the nearest station on the Konkan railway. The best times to visit are June to August, or September to December when it's pleasant and dry. SwaSwara's sister resort is Kalari Kovilakom (page 215). For more information on ayurveda, see page 210.

MEDITATION RETREAT

Tushita Meditation Centre

McLeod Ganj, Dharamshala, Himachal Pradesh
T+91 (0)18-9222 1866
www.tushita.info
Payment by donation

Tushita (Pure land of the future Buddha) is a Tibetan Buddhist meditation retreat reached by a steep walk through the pine-clad hillsides of McLeod Ganj, hometown of the exiled Dalai Lama. It's a peaceful haven of natural beauty that attracts experienced dharma practitioners as well as beginners who are keen to find out more about Mahayana Buddhism and meditation.

All accommodation is on a shared basis, usually three or four to a room during the courses. Although basic, the rooms are clean and pleasant. There are some brighter, newer rooms, but many of the original ones feel more atmospheric and have a view out over the lawns. The shower blocks are outside, on the edges of the grounds. The walk to your morning ablutions will be accompanied by birdsong, misty mountain air and maybe a few early rising monkeys.

Tushita is well known for its 10-day Introduction to Buddhism courses. Run as a silent retreat by Western and Tibetan teachers, participants are required to follow a clear discipline which includes not leaving the site, attending all sessions and observing silence. The days consist of guided meditation, teachings, karma yoga and discussion groups.

The teachers are all highly experienced, and breathe life and enthusiasm into the study of Buddhism, helping students to understand the practical applications in today's world. They convey a deep understanding of both the dharma and the challenges of staying on a retreat, which ensures that students feel well cared for and emotionally supported throughout.

Simple, wholesome vegetarian food is served in the dining hall (but take care if you decide to sit outside as the monkeys are quite likely to snatch it off your plate). The courses attract a real mixture of people travelling around India, of all ages, nationalities and backgrounds. As the retreat is run in silence, it's easy to pitch up on your own.

The weather in McLeod Ganj is unpredictable and it can rain at any time, so bring waterproofs, and a torch in case of power cuts. You are only given one blanket and it can get very cold during the winter months, so bring lots of warm layers.

The nearest international airport is New Delhi – from here, take an overnight train to Pathankot and either a taxi or bus to McLeod Ganj. An alternative would be to go to Majnukatila, the Tibetan Colony in New Delhi, and get an overnight bus (a rattling 10-12-hour journey). On arrival arrange for a rickshaw to carry your luggage up the hill.

Tushita is open from mid-February to the end of November. The main season is from February to May, when it will definitely be busier, so it's important to book well in advance. See Essentials for what to expect on a meditation retreat.

Soul food

Awake & Shine T+91 (0)35-5225 5204, www.gurudongma.com) is an integrated village tourism project which offers a stay in the beautiful Himalayan hamlet at Samthar hosted by village people. Income goes directly to the village hosts and it supports an English speaking class for local children. You stay in a specially constructed cottage with all modern amenities, enjoy a laid-back lifestyle and get back to basics with chemical-free agriculture, cattle herding, and local cookery and village handicraft sessions. It costs from US$65 per person per day.

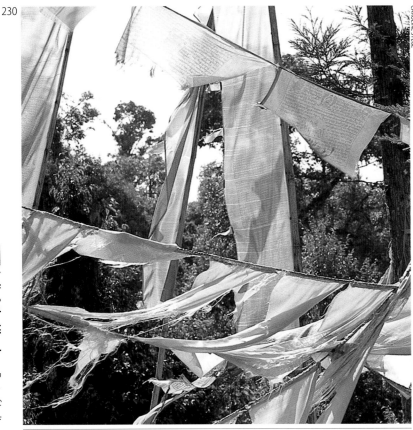

Above: Prayer flags in West Bengal. **Right**: Yoga in the beautiful surroundings of 16th-century Castle Bijaipur.

YOGA HOLIDAY

Yoga adventure with Jane Craggs

🌐 ⛰ ☀ ↘31

West Bengal
T+44 (0)7764-963138
www.janecraggs.co.uk
From US$1350 for 14 days

UK-based yoga teacher Jane Craggs has an intimate knowledge of India, and her yoga adventures are a great way to explore local cultures as well as yourself. Her annual 14-day trip to West Bengal includes a night in Darjeeling, after which you move to the family-run Karmi Farm, a homestead high in the Darjeeling hills, where twice-daily yoga classes are taught on the veranda, with amazing views across the valley.

Karmi is a converted dairy farm built with local timber, decorated with locally made handwoven rugs and run by direct descendants of the ancient Sikkimese Lepcha tribe. There's a 200-year-old family monastery on site, which is home to a group of Tibetan lamas, and visitors are welcome to meditate in the shrine room. The highlight of the trip is a three-day trek in the surrounding foothills, staying with Sherpa families and in trekkers huts, and arriving on the last morning to see the sun rise behind Mount Kanchenjunga, with Everest in the distance.

Jane Craggs is committed to working with venues which are ecologically sound and truly sustainable, and Karmi Farm is no exception. All work is carried out by local people, and any food which is not grown on the farm is bought from neighbours. There is also a regular free clinic for locals, staffed by volunteer health professionals.

Food is organic Nepalese, Sikkimese and Indian vegetarian, and you can enjoy the Indian tradition of tea in bed each morning. The water supply is piped from the nearby spring. Fly to Kolkata; Jane encourages guests to offset the carbon emissions from their flight. Flights are not included.

Jane also leads retreats to Morocco (see page 170) and Les Passeroses in France (see page 91). She is planning yoga adventures in Peru, Thailand and Ibiza, and a yoga and surfing trip to Morocco for 2008.

YOGA HOLIDAY

Yoga on a Shoestring in Rajasthan

🌐 ⛰ ☀ ↘32

Castle Bijaipur, near Chittaurgarh
T+44 (0)20-8690 0890
www.yogaonashoestring.com
From US$1172 per person for 12 days

Yoga on a Shoestring runs affordable yoga holidays to the restored 16th-century **Castle Bijaipur** (www.castlebijaipur.com) in Rajasthan three times a year. Each trip includes 10 days at the castle and two days luxury camping at Pangarh Fort and Lotus Lake.

Restored and run by its Indian prince resident owner, Maharaj Rao Saheb Narendra Singh, Castle Bijaipur is perfect for yoga escapes and peaceful meditation, with vast domes, and balconies adorned with ornate archways, lanterns and beautiful tiles; there's even a lawn in the courtyard. The internal decor is elegant; spice-coloured silk cushions and bolsters lie on invitingly low sofas and the white walls add a sense of calm. Narendra is a very relaxed and welcoming host.

Two of the annual trips are taught by Sue Pendlebury, founder of Yoga on a Shoestring, who fuses her creative background in music, dance and theatre and her bodywork into her classes. The third trip is taught by Clive Sheridan, a wonderful yoga and meditation teacher who works regularly in Europe. Yoga is practised twice a day in the gardens or on the castle roof, where you are surrounded by minarets, domes and a backdrop of valleys

> All yoga should be practised on the roofs of Rajasthani palaces. It is clearly what they were built for.
>
> *Tracy Jeune*

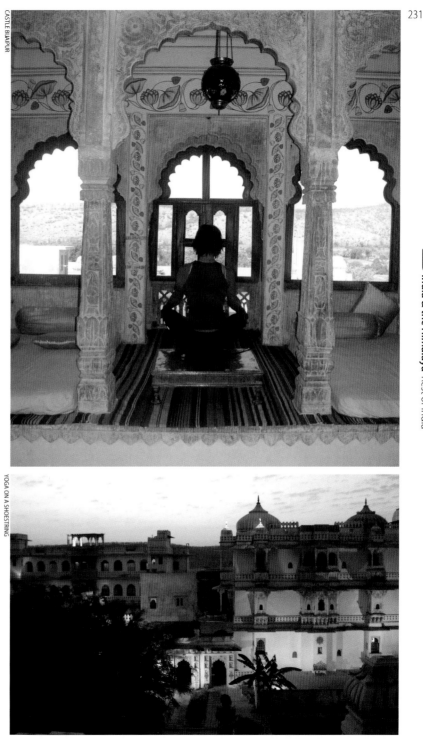

CASTLE BIJAIPUR

YOGA ON A SHOESTRING

and lakes. Early morning sessions last around three hours and are an invigorating start to the day. The session includes meditation, pranayama and asanas. Evening sessions last about half the time and incorporate restorative postures, visualization, dancing, singing and chanting. One day a week is yoga-free, but the castle is an incredible place to practise, so you should take advantage. Creative workshops can also be arranged.

Well-tended flowers surround the courtyard and large swimming pool, which looks idyllic at night when it is lit up with lanterns. Vegetarian Indian food is served al fresco under a white canvas roof, followed by delicious spiced tea. Accommodation is understated but luxurious. The Royal family suite is the most plush, with sitting and dressing rooms, and a black and white marbled en suite with sumptuous fluffy white towels. The two-day camping trip takes place by a lake covered in lotus flowers with water chestnuts growing on the banks – ideal for meditation and silent yoga.

The group meets in Udaipur; you can fly direct from Delhi or Mumbai. Prices include accommodation, meals, yoga, and a wildlife safari. Yoga on a Shoestring also runs holidays to Egypt (see page 168), and to Kerala at the Oceano Cliff Ayurvedic Resort (www.oceano cliff.com). Sue Pendlebury also co-runs a two-week Beyond the Asana retreat in Goa (see page 201).

The Himalayas with a twist

VEENA AT SYVC

Life coach Sue Glanville from UK-based company **Journeying** (T+44 (0)1225-866787, www.allaboutthejourney.co.uk) runs a 17-day India trek each April, from US$2520 per person. As well as visits to the Taj Mahal, the Golden Temple at Amritsar and McLeod Ganj, the home of the exiled Dalai Lama, the trip includes a five-day camping trek in an unspoiled part of the Himalayan foothills.

Your packs, tents, food and water are all taken care of by local Sherpas, leaving you free to take in the incredible surroundings and enjoy one another's company. Sue is skilled at creating a safe space for people to explore the larger questions in life, and has an infectious sense of fun. You stay in four-star hotels when you're not camping. The trip takes a maximum of 16 and is especially good for those who haven't visited India before.

For more challenging trekking in a remote area, the highly efficient India-based **Gurudongma Tours & Treks** (T+91 (0)35 5225 5204, www.gurudongma.com) runs a bespoke 14-day trek along the ancient trail of the Monpa herdsmen in Arunachal Pradesh, a remote and beautiful state of India, which you need a special permit to enter. The scenery is inspirational and you're unlikely to see other tourists. The trek takes in a selection of Buddhist monasteries, ending at Tawang Monastery, the largest in India. Established in the 17th century when the area was part of Greater Tibet, Tawang is perched dramatically at around 3500 m and looks out onto a semicircle of high peaks. The trips take a minimum of four people and cost from US$130 per day.

The Adventure Company (T0870-794 1009, www.adventurecompany.co.uk) runs a regular challenging trek through the sacred Hindu territory surrounding Nanda

Devi, India's highest peak, which includes visits to remote village temples as well as to Rishikesh (see ashrams page 224). Refreshingly, the company doesn't allow guests to bring mobile phones, and you camp or stay at locally owned hotels. The trip costs from US$1530 per person excluding flights, and ends at Corbett National Park, an important tiger reserve.

For a more spiritual take on things, the swamis of the European **Sivananda Yoga Vedanta Centres** (T+44 (0)20-8780 0160, www.sivananda.org/europe) lead an annual trip to experience some of the spiritual sources of yoga in India, costing from US$612 per person. The North Indian Pilgrimage to Sources of Ancient Wisdom starts at the Jai Sing Ghera ashram at Vrindavan, a holy city in a stunning setting on the banks of the Yamuna river. Here you'll have recitations from ancient Indian scriptures and talks on the classical meditative music of India, while asana classes take place on the rooftop overlooking the houses of Vrindavan.

The second part of the trip takes you to other pilgrimage towns such as the temple city of Haridwar, where you can experience an evening arati (see glossary) on the banks of the Ganges; Rishikesh, where you stay at the sivananda ashram, and Uttarkashi, home to hundreds of sadhus from all over India. Accommodation is in simple rooms in various ashrams and lodges along the way, and food is Indian vegetarian. See glossary for more information on sivananda yoga. It's a good idea to attend a term of yoga classes at your local centre before you book.

CAROLINE SYLGE

Top: Combine spirituality with a tough physical challenge on a trekking holiday in the Himalayan mountains. **Above:** En route to Tawang Monastery.

HOTEL & SPA

Amankora

🏠 ❄ ✪ 🌀 🅿 ↘33

Paro Valley
T+975 2-331333
www.amanresorts.com
From US$1000 per room per night

Set in the tranquil pine-clad Paro Valley, Adrian Zecha's Amankora was the first luxury hotel in the country, and shocked the Bhutanese with its minimalist style (the only other undecorated building in the country is the prison).

The views are wonderful from the glass-fronted lounge-cum-honesty bar with live traditional music in the evening. Directly in front are terraced rice fields leading to the romantic ruin of a 17th-century Dzong, or monastery, and, on a clear day, uou can see Tibet's 7300-m-high Mount Johomolhari.

The 24 open-plan suites, all with a view of the mountains, have roll-top baths, rammed-earth walls and wood burning stoves, though when the lovely wooden shutters close for the night, it can feel a bit claustrophobic.

Aman resorts always have that little extra something to offer: a lute plays from behind the pines on arrival; the traditional hot-stone bath treatment is taken by candlelight; you can dine al fresco by the river; and a picnic or moonlit dinner for two can be arranged in the ruins of the old monastery. It's a romantic experience, and it's mostly wealthy older couples who come here, as well as celebrities. The staff, from eastern Bhutan, are gentle and softly spoken.

Aman's restaurant is light and airy, serving gourmet organic food focusing on fresh, natural unfussy meals, such as tofu with wild mushrooms and spinach, with elements from Bhutanese cuisine also incorporated.

The main activity in Bhutan is walking, and a 15-minute daily climb to the monastery is ideal to get acclimatized. Walks radiate straight onto the hillsides from the door, and mountain biking and longer treks can be arranged.

The five-room spa offers treatments such as zu kenyam, or full body massage. An al fresco traditional stone bath is attached to every room, and local herbs and indigenous plants such as khempa – which is known to be good for circulation – are used in the bath and in scrubs. There are silk bags to put your valuables in and white flip-flops instead of slippers. All the spa staff are native, and trained from scratch, as massage isn't a Bhutanese tradition.

The Aman Journey allows guests to experience the Bhutanese countryside in style, staying in satellite hotels in the varied

This spiritual country is home to two upmarket retreats and some great trekking.

Fact file

- ➲ **Visa:** Required by all nationalities except Indians; prior booking needed through travel operators
- ① **Country code:** +975
- ⑤ **Currency:** Ngultrum (BTN)
- ⊕ **Time zone:** GMT +6 hours
- ④ **Electricity:** 230v
- ① **Tourist board:** www.tourism.gov.bt

Bhutan travel tips

Nestled in the high ranges of the eastern Himalaya and largely covered in virgin forest, Bhutan is a spiritual and beautifully remote place, which welcomed its first tourists only 30 years ago. Its tiny capital, Thimphu, is the only one in the world without traffic lights, and people still wear national dress and paint their houses with traditional motifs. The sale of cigarettes is banned here, as are plastic carrier bags, though mobile phones and TVs arrived in the 1990s. In early 2000 the Amankora and Uma Paro hotels opened in Paro.

Contrary to popular belief, Bhutan doesn't have a tourist quota. Anyone is welcome, as long as they pay US$200 a day and can get a seat on Druk Air, the national airline which flies via Bangkok, Kathmandu, Delhi, Kolkata or Dhaka to Bhutan's international airport at Paro.

Limited capacity ensures Bhutan will continue to receive a small volume of high-end visitors, even during festival times (March and September).

Spring is a good time to go, for the Paro festival in April and rhododendrons in bloom in May. Autumn has clear skies and great views of the mountains. Changes of temperature are common, so bring warm clothing for evenings and proper walking boots. Expect to spend three days acclimatizing at altitude.

To get help with visas and local flights and to secure a good deal, it's best to book with a tour operator such as Blue Poppy, while the Amankora and Uma Paro are offered by **Western & Oriental** (T0870-499 1111, www.westernoriental.com) using local agent Chambula Dorji Tours.

locations of Punakha (which has a famous dzong and whitewater rafting), Thimphu (the capital and royal palace) and Gangtey (a remote glacial valley and winter home of the black crane). It's not cheap, with prices starting from US$1000 per person per night.

ADVENTURE HOLIDAY

Blue Poppy Tours & Treks

T+44 (0)20-7700 3084
www.bluepoppybhutan.com
From US$4800 per person for 21 days based on 2 sharing the trip; excluding flights

For a physical and spiritual tonic in the glorious mountains of Bhutan, Blue Poppy Tours & Treks runs a bespoke Mountains, Meditation & Monasteries 21-day trip, mixing visits to centres of Buddhism and religious festivals with invigorating physical treks. Shorter trips can happily be arranged.

Blue Poppy is run by Choki Dorji and is the only specialist tour operator run by a

Left: Blue Poppy take you into the mountains of Bhutan for a spiritual and physical tonic.

We can gradually drop our ideals of who we think we ought to be, or who we think we want to be, or who we think other people think we want to be or ought to be.

Pema Chödrön

Bhutanese based in the UK. Choki's business partner, Karma Wangdi, is based in Bhutan, so your trip will be arranged solely by local people with expert knowledge. Your tour guide will be particularly well-versed in Buddhism and will introduce you to meditation techniques.

There will be the opportunity to meditate and seek spiritual comfort in some of the most sacred locations in Bhutan. You'll journey to the beautiful valley of Bumthang, the spiritual heartland of Bhutan, where you'll have two nights camping and trekking through villages, and past temples and monasteries.

The trip also features a four-day trek along the Druk Path, a tough trek with some hard climbs but offering beautiful views of the mountains and inspiring walking through blue pine and fir forests. The amount of hiking per day varies depending on the

terrain and the altitude, but time is allowed for acclimatization and trek times can be tailored according to physical ability. Tents, dining tents and mattresses are all provided, but you will need to bring your own sleeping bags and the food will be more Western (porridge and cornflakes for breakfast).

You can choose to spend a night with a local farmer and his family to experience village life, and sample the local cooking: the national dish is chillies with cheese, while other favourites are *phaksha paa*, a dish made of pork, chillies and vegetables; and *tukpa*, a kind of noodle soup.

A highlight of the trip is to experience one the Bhutanese festivals – in September, for example, this would include the Wangdi and Thimphu festivals, where masked dancers portray historic events and tell stories of good triumphing over evil. Local people come to pray and receive blessings, but also to socialize and have fun.

Some of the fascinating places you'll visit include the Cheri Gompa, where Bhutan's first body of monks was established in 1620, the National Institute of Traditional Medicine, and the 'Tiger's Lair', the sacred Taktsang monastery which clings to the rock face 900 m above the valley floor, to which Guru Rinpoche is said to have flown riding on a tigress. It is one of Bhutan's most holy sites and draws pilgrims from neighbouring Buddhist countries as well as Bhutan.

● Soul food

In Himalayan countries such as Bhutan, economic pressures on rural families mean that around a quarter of children will not receive a primary school education. Of those who do, even fewer go on to secondary school and by university or college level there are not enough places to fulfil demand. The **Loden Foundation** (www.loden.org) aims to promote education and learning in the Himalayan region, through scholarship schemes, vocational training programmes and the provision of resource centres, mainly in the Kingdom of Bhutan. The Foundation also co-ordinates programmes to raise awareness of the Himalayan religion, culture and environment in other parts of the world.

HOTEL & SPA

Uma Paro

🏵 🏔 ◎ ❂ ❂ ❂ ❂ ⎘35

Paro
T+975 8-271597
www.uma.como.bz
From US$250 per person per night

Genuine smiles are the first thing you notice at Uma Paro, perched on a hilltop in a forest of blue pines and overlooking the medieval-looking town of Paro in western Bhutan. Modelled on a traditional Bhutanese farmhouse made of stone, wood and tiles and painted with ancient geometric motifs in vegetable dyes, the place has a warm yet contemporary interior, making you feel instantly at home.

The glass-walled octagonal restaurant, filled with the scent of burning pine cones from a traditional stove, has spectacular 360° views of the Paro Valley, and serves rich, organic Indian and traditional Bhutanese dishes. There are imaginative interpretations such as chilli-spiced hot chocolate and yak burgers, and plenty for vegetarians. Alcohol is served, but smoking is banned in Bhutan.

Uma Paro offers three- to 10-day luxury retreats with spa treatments, yoga classes and guided outdoor activities, which include walking to temples such as the sacred Tiger's Lair monastery or an equally unforgettable bike ride from Bhutan's highest road pass. With a high staff-to-guest ratio, it attracts mainly well-heeled, well-travelled American and European professional couples or mature single women.

Guests stay in 18 medium-sized airy rooms with views of the mountain, forest or valley, some with balconies, and a mix of mod cons with homely touches such as handwoven Nepalese rugs. Oversize bathrooms have frosted glass walls and the signature Shambhala Spa's gorgeous organic products. Nine private villas have their own spa and butler. Chill out, read or write in the lovely cobbled inner courtyard over a herbal tea, or around the romantic dugout fire which is lit at sunset. Peaceful spots for meditation are found on the pine-clad hillside and the pool has a lovely outdoor sundeck.

A wide range of quality Asian-based treatments, ranging from facials to ayurvedic massage, is offered at the restful Shambhala Spa (or in-room). Try the stress-relieving traditional Bhutanese hot-stone bath where wood-fired river stones crack and release minerals in the water.

Twice-daily vinyasa flow-style classes are held in a wooden-floored pavilion overlooking the valley, its floor-to-ceiling windows open in summer – pranayama will help you adjust to the high altitude. Classes are free, though individual yoga sessions fit better around the activities which require early starts. Dedicated yoga weeks are also on offer.

Uma Paro is a 10-minute drive from Bhutan's only international airport. The Como hotel group has properties all over the world including the Como Shambhala Estate and Uma Ubud in Bali (see page 259), Parrot Cay in the Caribbean (see page 372) and Cocoa Island in the Maldives (see page 264). All-inclusive packages at the hotel, such as the three-day Himalayan Escape, are better value, and Bhutan is a destination best booked through a tour operator (see box on previous spread).

Right top and bottom: Um Paro; outside looking in, and inside looking out.

India & the Himalaya Bhutan

Nepal

MOUNTAIN RETREAT

Shivapuri Village

🌐 ⛱ ✪ ✿ ⛰36

T+977 (0)1-437 1725
www.shivapuri.com.np
From US$60 per person per day, full board

KENNETH ASHLEY-JOHNSON

Above and below: Shivapuri Village.

Just 1½ hours' drive from Kathmandu but a world away in spirit, Shivapuri Village is a peaceful place to hole up for a while, with spectacular 180° views of the Himalayan mountains, and friendly Nepalese owners dedicated to helping the local community.

Lord Buddha and Hindu sages are said to have meditated in the surrounding forests here, and the place has great energy. It's also within the borders of a national park, in an area protected by Gurkhas, so you'll feel safe and there won't be many tourists.

There are 11 comfortable huts made from the local stone, with traditional, red painted clay walls and thatched roofs, and tiled en suite bathrooms with solar-powered showers and flush toilets. There are also three Asian-style bungalows that sleep up to six people – ideal for friends and family groups.

Do your own meditation and yoga, or the hosts can arrange for sessions with a local Buddhist monk or a Hindu yoga teacher. There are over 20 different nature trails to walk and, as no hunting is allowed in the area, you'll see lots of wild animals, including the yellow-throated Himalayan martin (a Nepalese otter), deer, eagles, hawks, boar and, if you're lucky, even leopard and bear.

There are hammocks to lounge in, a telescope, badminton area and table tennis table, and lots of maps and books donated by other travellers. From October to December, days are crystal clear and the evenings cold, and this is a lovely time to enjoy open fires under the stars. Alternatively, there's a traditional wood burning stove inside the main dining hall.

This is also a good place to immerse yourself in Nepalese culture. The actual village is 15 minutes away and Shivapuri is run by the Singh family, high-caste Nepalese who employ a lot of local women who find it difficult to work in Kathmandu. Profits are ploughed into the local community. You can also have one-to-one

KENNETH ASHLEY-JOHNSON

Trek or retreat to the birthplace of The Buddha.

Fact file

➲ **Visa:** Citizens of EU countries, US, Canada or Australia and New Zealand need visas, obtainable on arrival or in advance from a Nepalese consulate or embassy

ⓘ **Country code:** +977

Ⓢ **Currency:** Nepalese rupee (NR)

◉ **Time zone:** GMT +5¾ hours

⚡ **Electricity:** 230v

ⓘ **Tourist board:** www.welcomenepal.com

◐ Body language

Buddhism in India and Nepal

The Buddha was born as Siddhartha Gautama into a wealthy family in Lumbini in present-day Nepal, around 566 BC. Brought up as a prince and a Hindu, he married early and lived in luxury. Aged 29, he renounced his family life, confused by the glimpses of death and suffering he had seen outside the palace walls.

After years of wandering and meditation, he settled under a bodhi tree at Bodhgaya, in India's northeastern state of Bihar. After a night of battling with inner demons, that he called *mara*, he attained Enlightenment, seeing for the first time the way things truly are. Shortly afterwards he gave his first sermon at Sarnath, near Varanasi, and went on to teach the dharma, or the way things are: that the present moment is the key to liberation, that our egos blind us to reality, that impermanence and suffering are characteristics of existence. Mapping out the Four Noble Truths and the Noble Eight-fold Path (see glossary), he then set up a sangha, a community of monks and nuns, to develop and practise his teachings. He died in about 486 BC in Kushinagar, in Uttar Pradesh.

Buddhism is a way of living rather than a religion, and holds much appeal in these times of stress, overwork and focus on the individual. All four towns associated with the Buddha's life are now major pilgrimage centres. Bodhgaya is packed with international temples and monasteries running short and long-term Buddhist meditation courses. It's an authentic place to discover this science of the mind. Choose from courses in Theravada Buddhism, practiced in Sri Lanka, Thailand and other parts of Southeast Asia, which centres around vipassana, or insight meditation, or a course in Mahayana Buddhism. This is practised by refugee Tibetan Buddhists who now comprise a thriving community of over 100,000 in northeastern India with the exiled Tibetan government and the Dalai Lama.

Christopher Titmuss, former Buddhist monk and co-founder of Gaia House in Devon (see page 34), has organized three vipassana retreats, run totally on a voluntary donation basis, at the peaceful Thai monastery in Bodhgaya every January and February since 1975. Together with Jaya Ashmore and other dharma teachers, he also leads a 12-day dharma gathering every February at the **Thai monastery in Sarnath** (www.insight meditation.org). The **Root Institute** (www.rootinstitute.com),

based in pleasant, calm grounds, offers a range of excellent Tibetan Buddhist meditation courses to foreign visitors from October to March. Bear in mind that Bihar is one of the poorest states in India. Bodhgaya is a basic with few facilities, and there is evident hardship amongst the local population, which some people may find difficult to cope with.

At the Dalai Lama's home in McLeod Ganj, in Himachal Pradesh, you can take an excellent 10-day Introduction to Buddhism course at the Root Institute's sister retreat, Tushita (see page 229). A smiling, calm and wonderful presence, the Dalai Lama sometimes gives dharma talks in the town – listening to him is an inspiring experience. The Tibet Museum in McLeod Ganj details the recent history of Tibet, or enrol on a course at the **Library of Tibetan Works & Archives** (T+91 (0)18-9222 2467, www.tibet.net) at nearby Gangchen Kyishong, which offers regular courses in Tibetan Buddhist philosophy and the Tibetan language.

In Nepal, head to Kopan monastery in the Kathmandu valley, home to hundreds of Nepalese and Tibetan monks and nuns, where you can take a seven-day, 10-day or month-long course in Tibetan Buddhism (www.kopan-monastery.com). Experienced practitioners can stay year round at the Panditarama Lumbini International Vipassana Meditation Centre in the place of Buddha's birth, which also runs two retreats a year for beginners. For more information, visit http://web.ukonline.co.uk/buddhism/lumbiniv.htm.

CAROLINE SYLGE

cooking lessons, and the son gives talks on local customs and culture.

All the vegetables are grown organically on site. Breakfast is locally produced honey, porridge and fruit – or go European and have omelettes, tomatoes and chips(!) Lunches are delicious traditional Nepalese vegetarian dishes, while supper can be pizzas and chicken dishes.

Shivapuri attracts student backpackers as well as artists and writers, who mainly get to hear about it by word of mouth. Sometimes there are adventure tour groups here, so if you'd rather be alone, check in advance. Bring warm clothes, a torch, batteries, and good walking shoes – you won't be able to buy anything up here, so bring everything you may need, including medications.

India & the Himalaya Nepal

ADVENTURE HOLIDAY

Social Tours health trek

🌐 ♨ 🔵 🌀 🅿 ✈37

T+977 (0)1-441 2508
www.socialtours.com
From US$1760 per person for 14 days

Social Tours runs bespoke 14-day health treks through the mountains of Nepal, combining six hours of walking a day with healthy organic food, yoga and meditation. Treks are tailored to your level of fitness, and as the company is based in Kathmandu, you'll have a chance to experience the local culture and contribute directly to the local economy.

The start of the trek is geared to your level of fitness, then it gets progressively harder, with some parts at high altitudes. A warm-up session kicks each day off, when you can enjoy yoga with meditation in sensational settings, breathing pristine mountain air. A medically controlled nutritious daily diet ensures that the effects of the exercise during the trip will be long lasting. Most of the food in the villages of Nepal is organic. Breakfast consists of Tibetan bread, which is a kind of chapatti, with mountain honey. Lunch and dinner is either stir-fried vegetable noodles or the Nepali *dal bhat* (rice with lentils and vegetables). You can eat as much as you

I look at every human being from a more positive angle; I try to look for their positive aspects. This attitude immediately creates a feeling of affinity, a kind of connectedness.

The 14th Dalai Lama

want, but the low-fat diet can produce dramatic effects. Yoga and meditation is taught by local teachers from Kathmandu and caters to different levels of experience. The yoga during the trek is more focused on stretches – in the morning to limber up, and at the end of the day to wind down and improve recovery for the next day, though the teachers will support learning and advancement of your personal yoga practice.

You will stay in comfortable family-run lodges which have been housing trekkers in Nepal for years. Your trek ends with an elephant safari trip and a stay at the comfortable Jungle Resort in the Chitwan National Park. The basic package includes the popular Langtang trek, which is rich in culture

and natural beauty. Optional treks to Annapurna or the Everest region are also available, at an additional cost. Your trek can also be expanded to include rafting, mountain biking, paragliding and rock climbing.

The trek attracts stressed-out professionals and health enthusiasts from around the globe, usually aged between 25 and 50, as well as active older people. Trips are custom-made, for groups of three to six people. The price increases as group size shrinks. The trek runs all year round, but Nepal has a distinct tourist season, which peaks between September and May. This trip can also be booked through www.responsibletravel.com, see Resources.

ANNAPURNA RAJ GUJAWALI

Indian Ocean

CAROLINE SYLGE

Even stormy weather couldn't make you feel blue in the luxurious, all-pampering atmosphere of the Maldives.

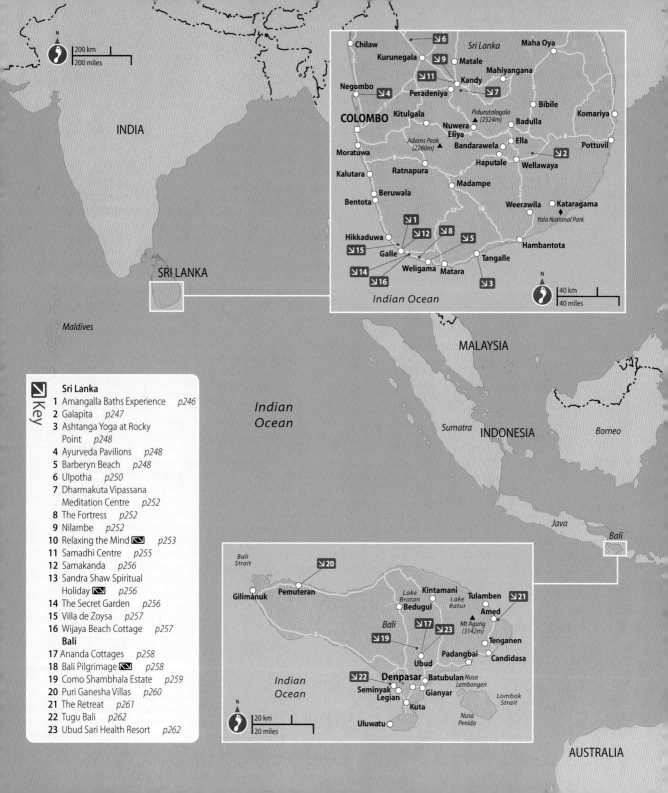

INDIA

Chilaw

Sri Lanka

Maha Oya

Kurunegala ⬂9 Matale

Mahiyangana

⬂6

⬂11 Kandy

Negombo ⬂4 Peradeniya ⬂7

Bibile

Komariya

COLOMBO Kitulgala

Nuwera Eliya

Pidurutalagala (2524m)

Badulla

Moratuwa

Adams Peak (2260m) Bandarawela Ella

⬂2 Pottuvil

Kalutara Ratnapura Haputale Wellawaya

Madampe

Beruwala

Weerawila Kataragama

Bentota Yala National Park

⬂1

Hikkaduwa ⬂12 ⬂8

⬂15 ⬂5

Galle Tangalle Hambantota

⬂14 Weligama Matara

⬂16 ⬂3

Indian Ocean

N 40 km / 40 miles

MALAYSIA

SRI LANKA

Maldives

Indian Ocean

INDONESIA

Sumatra

Borneo

Java

Bali

 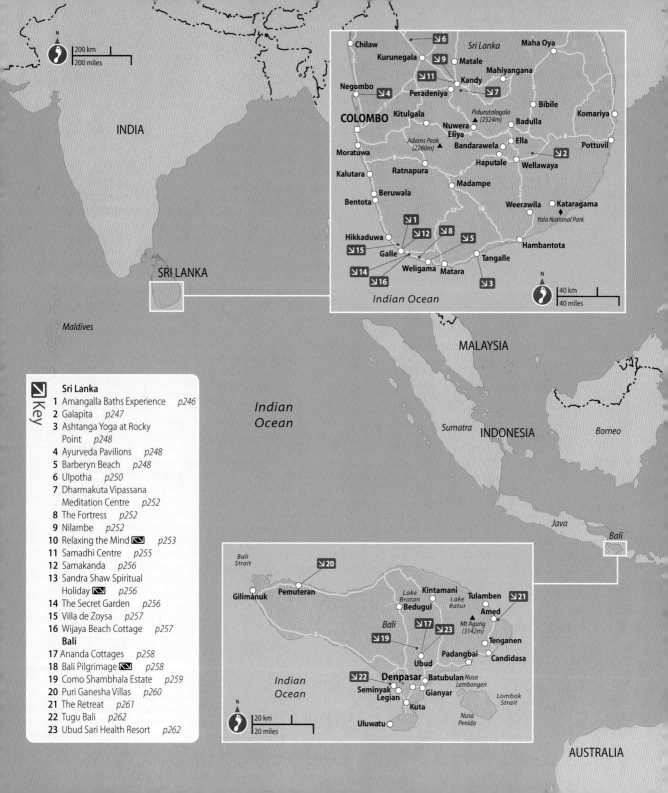
Bali Strait

⬂20

Gilimanuk Pemuteran

Kintamani

Tulamben

Lake Bratan ⬂21

Bedugul *Lake Batur* Amed

Bali

⬂17 Mt Agung (3142m) Tenganen

⬂19 ⬂23

Ubud Padangbai Candidasa

Indian Ocean

⬂22 Denpasar Batubulan *Nusa Lembongan*

Seminyak Gianyar

Legian *Lombok Strait*

Kuta *Nusa Penida*

Uluwatu

N 20 km / 20 miles

AUSTRALIA

Introduction

The Indian Ocean is a relaxed place for a retreat, with a lovely balance between exoticism and unpretentiousness. If there's a group of you, hiring a private villa on Bali or a 'residence' at the Como Shambhala Estate could work wonders, while couples who want to reconnect in style should head to the fantasy islands of the Maldives. For more serious retreat-goers, Bali offers some great places to detox: do it in the warm and friendly atmosphere of the Indonesian-run Ubud Sari, or with expert state-of-the-art techniques at The Retreat, where there's a strong focus on detoxing the mind as well as the body. Alternatively, cleanse with raw food, and in style, at Puri Ganesha villas, which can also arrange bespoke pilgrimages with a Hindu priest to Bali's temples.

Sri Lanka is a tranquil place to undertake a course of ayurveda treatments: take your pick from jungle locations or a coastal retreat such as Barberyn Beach. Galle in the south of the island is a sybarite's haven, while ashtanga vinyasa devotees can head to a yoga retreat in Tangalle; if you're a beginner but are serious about learning this style, you can pitch up here for a month and be taught from scratch. If you've time on your hands and want to get back to nature, longer stays at the Samadhi Centre, Galapita, or Ulpotha will give you the time and tools to replenish and rethink. Indeed, the calm and sheer beauty of this part of the world makes it easy to stay in one place and nurture yourself back to life.

66 99 *The more still, more patient and more open we are when we are sad, so much the deeper and so much the more unswervingly does the new go into us.*

Rainer Maria Rilke

Travel essentials

Sri Lanka

Getting there International flights arrive at Colombo airport. Direct flights operate from London with the national carrier, **Sri Lankan Airlines**, although cheaper deals can be found on Middle Eastern and central European airlines. From the east coast in the US, it is best to fly via London and from the west coast, via Hong Kong, Singapore and Bangkok. There are no direct flights from Australia and New Zealand.

Best time to visit Sri Lanka enjoys a tropical climate, with average temperatures of 29°C. In Colombo, the best time is late October to early March, after the southwest monsoon has passed, although even outside this time, widespread rain can occur.

Bali

Getting there Bali's international airport is Denpasar, with direct flights to Auckland, Brisbane, Melbourne, Sydney, Bangkok, Singapore and Hong Kong. Travel from Europe to Bali currently involves a change in Singapore, Kuala Lumpur or Bangkok.

Best time to visit Bali has a tropical year-round warm climate with a relatively high rainfall. The dry season is June to October and the wet season is November to May. However, rain can fall throughout the year, especially in Ubud and the mountains.

Maldives

Getting there The Maldives is served by Malé international airport – there are scheduled flights with **Emirates**, **Indian Airlines**, **Qatar Airways**, **Singapore Airlines**, and **Sri Lankan Airlines**. Direct flights operate to Bangkok, Kuala Lumpur, London, Singapore and Tokyo. There are also direct charter flights from some European cities including London: check out www.monarchcharter.com, www.mytravel.com, and www.firstchoice.co.uk.

Best time to visit With a tropical climate, the Maldives is blessed with warm and sunny weather all year round. Daytime temperatures average 30°C. Generally, April is the hottest month and December is the coolest. Of the two monsoon seasons affecting the Maldives, the southwest monsoon from May to September is the wettest. The northeast monsoon is December to April, but January to April is comparatively dry, with the lowest rainfall in February and March.

Travel tip

Kandy is a 2½-3½-hour bus or taxi ride northeast of Colombo airport, and Galle is a three-to-four-drive south, depending on whether you travel by day or by night when the roads are far less busy. Taxis are relatively cheap, or arrange a pickup with the venue you're visiting. If you've more money than time, consider chartering a Sri Lankan air taxi (from US$200 per person one-way). **Sri Lankan Airlines** (T+94 (0)19-733 3355, www.srilankan.aero/airtaxi). also runs a scheduled three-day-a-week floatplane service from December to April, flying from Colombo to the Cultural Triangle, Kandy, the Hill Country, Yala National Park, Tangalle, Galle and Bentota – the round trip can be taken in four legs and costs from US$1000 per person.

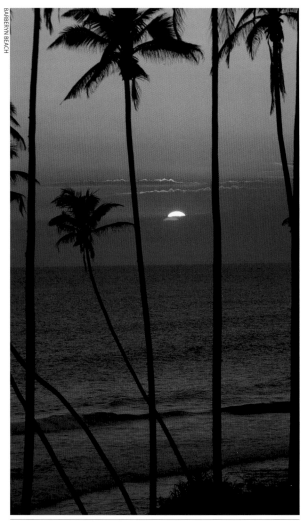

BARBERYN BEACH

Above: Barberyn Beach, Sri Lanka.
Opposite top: The Maldives. **Opposite left:** Woman bathing. **Opposite centre:** foot reflexology chart, Bali. **Opposite right:** water glasses, Bali.

66 99

Nothing can bring you peace but yourself.

Ralph Waldo Emerson

MALDIVES TOURIST BOARD

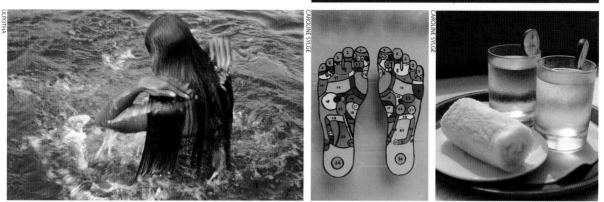

ULPOTHA

CAROLINE SYLGE

CAROLINE SYLGE

Eat me

This beautiful, spiritual part of the world has food that makes your insides smile. Sri Lanka has hundreds of different curries to offer, while in the Maldives the seafood is some of the best you'll ever eat. In Bali try the local rice dishes and, wherever you are, make the most of the fresh, ripe exotic fruit that sells for next-to nothing.

In Sri Lanka the local dish is 'rice and curry'. Far from being as simple as it sounds you'll almost certainly be served a vast selection of different curries to try alongside one of the numerous varieties of rice grown on the island. Most of the dishes will be packed with a mixture of fresh vegetables, lentils, coconut, herbs and spices. Try and find dishes that contain karapincha (curry leaves). Used widely in Sri Lankan curries, ayurvedic medicine teaches that they're highly medicinal and good for the digestion. Vegetarianism is smiled upon by many Sri Lankans so it's easy to eat a wholesome, nutritious diet during your stay. Another must-taste is Kolakenda, a detoxer's dream drink. Made with brown rice, coconut and the juice of green leaves or herbs which are brimming with vitamins,

minerals, fibre and antioxidants, it's served hot and has a porridge-like consistency.

In Bali try some of the different rice dishes for a lighter meal. Nasi kuning is a light, healthy option if you come across it. The rice is cooked in lightly seasoned coconut milk and chicken stock and flavoured with lemongrass (which has antibacterial, antifungal, and fever-reducing properties) and pandan leaves (a natural diuretic).

The Maldives offers stunning seafood - try tuna, jobfish, grouper and octopus. Octopus salad is the perfect dish for the body and soul traveller as it's almost fat-free and high in iron and vitamin B 12. As well as being served fresh, tuna's also popular smoked or dried, thinly sliced and mixed into salads and rice dishes – a low-fat delicacy that's high in protein and omega-3. Breadfruit's a staple ingredient in the Maldives too, and is rich in potassium. Try it boiled, fried, roasted or simmered in curries. Maldivian desserts can be overwhelmingly sweet for many people so try fresh fruits such as papaya and mango instead. Eat them as they come or enjoy them in freshly squeezed juices for a quick vitamin fix.

Sri Lanka

A jungle island steeped in Buddhist history, Sri Lanka is an ideal place to retreat to for meditation, yoga or traditional ayurveda.

Fact file

➡ **Visa:** Citizens of EU countries, US, Canada, Australia and New Zealand can obtain visas on arrival

➡ **IDD:** +94

➡ **Currency:** Sri Lankan rupee (LKR)

➡ **Time zone:** GMT +5½ hours

➡ **Electricity:** 230v

➡ **Tourist board:**
www.srilankatourism.org

HOTEL & SPA

Amangalla Baths Experience

Galle
T+94 (0)91-223 3388
www.amanresorts.com
From US$500 per room per night

Amangalla is an colonial hotel in the centre of the 400-year-old Galle Fort, the mellow old quarter of Galle, with quiet streets and boutique shops. Originally the Dutch army headquarters, the hotel traded as the New Oriental for over 140 years before Amanresorts bought it, and its walls sing with stories. Amangalla runs a regular four-night 'Baths Experience' package which includes daily yoga, meditation and treatments. You'll also have the opportunity to be blessed by a monk at nearby Yatagala, which features a 2000-year-old rock temple surrounded by Bo trees and caves

The spa – known as The Baths – is based where the New Oriental's parade of shops used to be. A calm, whitewashed, arched hallway leads to five treatment rooms, and there's a small but perfectly formed wet area with hydrotherapy pool, cold plunge pool, steam room and sauna, softly lit by candles in recesses. Pampering treatments draw on various cultures: for a luxurious alternative to traditional ayurveda try 'The Complete Ayurvedic' and be gently moisturised by pure sesame oil; or experiment with 'The Healing', which uses craniosacral therapy and coloured crystals on your chakra points to balance your energies. Daily yoga classes take place in the wooden-floored pavilion,

Amangalla.

set in the hotel's mature gardens. Private meditation and qigong can be arranged, and there's a large pool with shaded *ambalamas* (daybeds). You'll sleep in beautiful teak-floored bedrooms, elegantly designed to retain their historical heritage, with very comfortable dark wood four-poster beds, planter's chairs, antique writing desks and pettagama chests. Softer touches include throws covered in rich red flowers, complimentary navy-blue woven cloth bags and huge glass vases filled with fresh lilies.

Healthy stopovers in Colombo

Colombo airport is about 40 minutes from the city – if you need to stay overnight, **Havelock Place** (from US$100 per room, T+94 (0)11-2585191, www,bungalow.lk) is a calm and private colonial home a leafy cul-de-sac with a small pool, jacuzzi and just six rooms.

Massages can be arranged. Respected kundalini yoga teacher **Anoushka Hempel,** who trained with Shiv Charan Singh at the **Karam Kriya Centre** in London, gives Kundalini yoga classes at her home in Colombo (T+94 (0)77-790 7321).

Jungle retreat

Galapita

Bordering Yala National Park in Uva province, this extraordinary jungle retreat is set on ancient rocks and paddy fields and split by the Menik Ganga, or River of Gems. It's a great back-to-nature place to relax, detox and indulge in some DIY hydrotherapy with the river's natural whirlpools. You'll also be comfortable here just doing nothing.

ROMMAN DE FONSECA

Where you stay A wonderfully wobbly suspension bridge takes you into a jungle with lotus ponds and rock gardens. The birdlife is fantastic here, with kingfishers and parrots swooping the skies and peacocks roaming about. Chill out on cushioned clay daybeds, in home-made hammocks and tree houses or on the ancient rocks, which are soothing to walk on in the evening when they are still hot. Up to six people can sleep in each of the six traditional *maluwa* (open-sided pavilions), which use whole dried-up tree trunks as pillars and have roofs thatched with *illuk* (rice straw). Surrounded by cane blinds, each *maluwa* has a comfy lounge area, bed linen, mozzie nets and antique wooden chests. Four share showers and toilets in separate thatched pavilions with solar-powered hot water. Kumbuk Maluwa, by the river, is the most private.

What you do Galapita's ayurvedic mineral spa, opened in 2007 and run by a 12th-generation ayurvedic physician, is a great place to try ayurveda. Set in an alluvial gem field on a 20-m lotus pond, the small spa uses minerals from various gemstones in its treatments. Try a herbal bath with lemon grass, tamarind leaves and uncut sapphires. Ayurvedic massages use a base oil pressed on site from sunflowers in the nearby plantation. Spirulina baths, traditional saunas, Thai massages and Bali-inspired facials, scrubs and body wraps are also on offer.

Yoga lessons can be arranged on demand with visiting teachers, and are taught in a spacious yoga sala built on a platform in the centre of a lotus pond. You can learn to meditate with a local Buddhist

monk (the ancient caves surrounding the retreat were reputedly used by Sri Lanka's aboriginal people, the Veddas, for meditation). You can also go walking, biking, or tubing down the river, take a safari in the nearby Yala National Park, visit the pilgrimage site of Kataragama, star gaze from a telescope or pan for your own gemstones (any you find are yours to keep).

What you eat and drink Nutritious vegetarian curries are cooked in clay pots over an open fire and eaten in a riverside dining pavilion or in the paddy field under the tree house. You can have chicken and fish on request, and the chef will even prepare Western snacks. The home-grown tomatoes, mangoes, watermelons and pineapples are particularly tasty.

Who goes Fellow guests are likely to come from all over the world and range from health-conscious and well-travelled 30- to 40-somethings to adventurous families. Come alone, or with your partner or a group of friends; it's a great environment and atmosphere for bonding.

Essentials From US$80 per night, T+94 (0)11-250 0215, www.galapita.com. Stay at least a week, more if you want a serious detox. It's a seven-hour drive from Colombo airport, or charter a Sri Lankan air taxi (US$200 per person one way, www.srilankan.aero/airtaxi) to Weerawila, a one-hour drive from Galapita. Be prepared for jungle insects and rain; you can buy Galapita's citronella and neem oil insect repellent once there, and they supply umbrellas, but do bring covered shoes.

> ❝❞
> I love to bathe in the river at sunset, when you get the most awesome revitalising jungle smell. In the morning my favourite meditation spot is Galapita Gala, with its views across Yala National Park – after 0800 when you are less likely to bump into wild boar.
>
> *Puma Hammar*

YOGA RETREAT

Ashtanga yoga at Rocky Point

↘3

Tangalle
T+94 (0)472-240834
www.ashtangaworld.com
Rooms from US$27 per night

Sri Lanka's very own dedicated ashtanga yoga retreat is run by Anthony Carlisi from October to March. Based at Rocky Point Beach Bungalows on the glorious Tangalle coastline in the south of the island – a five- to six-hour drive from Colombo airport, or a two-hour drive from Galle – the retreat is aimed at ashtanga devotees who want to deepen their practice in a chilled-out environment. You can also learn the style from scratch, but will need to commit to a month-long stay. A doctor of ayurvedic medicine, and yoga teacher to the likes of Gwyneth Paltrow, Anthony is inspiring and the retreat atmosphere friendly and relaxed. Yoga is practised in a dedicated room with a cool polished cement floor and large windows. The ashtanga is Mysore-style (see glossary), and students get one-to-one attention from Anthony whenever it's needed. Group sessions run from 0700-0900, every day except Saturday, and full moon and new moon days (from US$50 per person per week). Set in pretty gardens with an open restaurant overlooking a rocky bay, Rocky Point has simple but pleasant en suite rooms or bungalows, each with its own veranda. Food is home-cooked vegetarian with a Sri Lankan twist, and fresh fish is served at supper. There are classes once a week to learn more about yoga-related subjects, such as vinyasa and ayurveda.

There are usually a few therapists on the course, and people tend to swap massages in their free time. There are local temples and beautiful beaches nearby for swimming, including Silent Beach, where you'll find the chic, air-conditioned bar and restaurant of the Amanwella Hotel (www.amanwella.com).

CAROLINE SYLGE

CAROLINE SYLGE

AYURVEDA RETREAT

Ayurveda Pavilions

↘4

Negombo
T+94 (0)74-870764
www.ayurvedapavilions.com
From US$250 per night

An easy hour's drive from Colombo airport, Ayurveda Pavilions is a small but attractive ayurveda resort with frangipani trees, tiled walkways and a 12-m swimming pool. The main reason to come here is to receive a programme of ayurvedic treatments from expert staff in the privacy of your own villa, each of which has its own private garden and a veranda which doubles as a treatment area – it's also a good place to come for some nourishing treatments if you've some days to kill before a flight. There's also an ayurveda centre with eight treatment rooms on site, staffed by doctors with years of experience, and also used by guests from two **Jetwing** sister hotels nearby. A visiting teacher gives beginner's yoga lessons twice a week. The restaurant serves alcohol for partners not having treatments, and food is tailored to your dosha type (see glossary) using ingredients from the in-house herb and vegetable garden.

Be warned that Negombo has developed considerably over the last few years into an unattractive town – you need to cross the road to reach the rather bland if spacious beach, and the main road on which Ayurveda Pavilions sits can be noisy with traffic. Ask for a room near the pool area and avoid those right next to the road (including rooms 110, 111 and 112). Better still, go for one of the King villas, set right back from the road and graced by huge gardens.

AYURVEDA PAVILIONS

AYURVEDA RESORT

Barberyn Beach

↘5

Weligama
T +94 (0)41-225 2994
www.barberyn.com
From US$140 per person per night; ayurveda from US$80 per day

Barberyn Beach is a residential ayurveda resort set in 6 ha of landscaped gardens overlooking the Indian Ocean at Weligama, in the south of Sri Lanka. It's a safe and secluded place to undertake a course of authentic ayurvedic treatments and most people come for a two-week panchakarma.

There's a large saltwater swimming pool surrounded by coconut trees, a huge tiered yoga pavilion and a garden full of trees, restful water features and lots of birdlife. Large mustard-yellow buildings house the restaurant, meeting rooms and ayurveda centre and, in a separate block, 60 bedrooms. Lots of wood and tawny orange cushions soften an otherwise slightly dated decor. Each of the bedrooms has a basic en suite bathroom with a shower, large comfortable double bed with mosquito net and fan, cool polished floors, simple wooden furniture and a balcony with views over the gardens and out to sea. If you're staying for two weeks, however, you'll welcome the extra space you get from a more luxurious split-level room or one of the four studio rooms. The treatment centre rooms are clean and bright, and open at the top to cooling breezes and birdsong. There's a special area for steam and herbal baths, and a peaceful herb garden.

Classes in meditation, tai chi and ayurvedic cooking take place regularly, and there are occasional talks on Buddhist philosophy and astrology, as well as excursions to local sights and evening trips to temples. Two gentle yoga classes in basic asanas and pranayama run daily in the pavilion. A public beach is a short walk from the gardens, though it is rather marred by the large brick wall put up to stop locals wandering the grounds. Food is adequate, mainly vegetarian with some fish; they're particularly good at Sri Lankan curries. Your meals are tailored to suit your particular course of treatment and a doctor is present

every mealtime for advice. No alcohol is served and there are fresh flowers at your table every day.

Like most ayurveda resorts in Sri Lanka, 85% of the guests are German-speaking, though there are an increasing number of guests from the rest of Europe as well as

Japan. Staff are friendly and efficient; all the Sri Lankan doctors speak English, and yoga and tai chi classes are taught in English.

It's a 3½-hour drive south from Colombo airport, so best to arrange a transfer on booking. See page 210 for more information on ayurveda.

66 99

I spent most of my time at Barberyn Beach dressed in a faded green sheet with a headscarf covering my sticky, ayurveda-oiled hair, wandering the gardens aimlessly, or sleeping. I certainly felt I was in expert hands. The ayurvedic doctors don't diagnose your dosha type as vata, pita or kapha until a week into your stay, so a person has time to adjust to the new climate and settle back to their natural state after travelling – which is, one of the resident doctors told me, a very "vata increasing activity". Each treatment was expertly carried out by therapists dressed in rather quaint blue and white striped uniforms. My favourite part was being taken to a peaceful herbal garden after each massage, where pads warmed with essential oils were placed on the parts of my body that ached the most. I'd lie on a lounger and watch giant iguanas climb the trees, and butterflies flit about. A little later, in a huge, old-fashioned tiled bath, I was firmly doused with buckets of herbal water by a motherly therapist; a nourishing, if surreal, experience. I needn't have brought half the clothes I did – though I'm glad I brought knickers I didn't mind getting soaked with oils, as they didn't provide disposable ones and didn't encourage nakedness. The atmosphere was friendly and calm, though there was a slight institutional feel to the place; the piano played at supper was more school hall than concert, the stone buildings looked a little stark in the midday sun, and the potions and pills I took each day tasted awful. I'd go back, but with a friend for company, or take a lot more books to read.

Caroline

Left: Ashtanga Yoga at Rocky Point.
Above and right: Barberyn Beach.

BARBERYN BEACH

BARBERYN BEACH

Ayurveda and yoga holiday

Ulpotha 🗡 ⚕ 💧 ❀ 🌳 🏄 ↘6

A traditional working village at the foot of the Galgiriyawa mountains in the Kurunegala district, Ulpotha is a tucked-away haven open to guests six months of the year for yoga and ayurveda retreats. A jungle village with no electricity or hot water, it is an ideal place to be close to nature – tortoises cross the clay pathways, giant red and black butterflies dance around lake pools and ancient vegetation shades stone Buddhist statues.

Where you stay You sleep in one of 10 traditional huts spread out across the village. Made of wattle and daub with sloping palm-leaf roofs to keep them shaded and private, the huts are cosy and simple, with stone water jars, coloured cushions, rush mats, a dressing area with handmade drawers and mosquito-netted single or double beds. Incense-scented toilet huts with Western toilets and copper sinks are nearby, and for every two huts there's a large open-air shower enclosure, where cold water runs out of a giant bamboo pipe (most people find this refreshing in the near-constant heat). Each hut is looked after by a local, who will make your bed, light joss sticks in the mornings and offer you a lamp at night to help you find your way. If you don't fancy the jungle, there are two rooms in the *walauwwa*, a communal manor house built around an open courtyard with burnt-orange walls, dark wood furniture, interesting artworks and a small library and kitchen for guests to use.

Ulpotha takes a maximum of 19 people at a time and, though you can request to be alone when you book, it's more than likely that you will share your hut if you come on your own. For some people this isn't a problem, and it can be reassuring to have someone close by when you're sleeping in the wild, but for others it may take a night or two to get used to sharing – the beds can be quite close together and the nights can be stuffy and hot.

The glory of Ulpotha is its tank, or lake, an incredibly clean and cool place to swim where golden orioles swoop over the water and herons sun themselves on nearby rocks. It's surrounded by vegetation and volcanic rock mountains, on one of which rests a bright white Buddhist temple. You can read in woven flatbed hammocks hanging from trees around the lake, or in a lakeside chill-out hut filled with cushions. There's also a romantic lake hut only reachable by boat, and a tree house overlooking the water.

What you do Yoga retreats run continuously for two weeks at a time, led by teachers from all over the world. In any six-month period you're likely to be able to try iyengar, scaravelli, ashtanga, kundalini, core or dynamic yoga, as well as pilates. Two classes of yoga a day are taught in a spacious pavilion, and the two-week retreats are a brilliant opportunity to deepen your practice or learn yoga from scratch.

Ulpotha is also a secluded and close-to-nature place to experience a full course of traditional ayurvedic treatments (paid for separately) – especially if you have two weeks or more, which is enough time to do a full panchakarma (see page 210). The *wedegedera* (or healing centre) is led by Dr Srilal Mudunkothge, a batchelor of ayurvedic medicine. Set in its own garden near the *walauwwa*, it has different huts for different treatments, and features a dry herb sauna.

Ulpotha cast its spell quite quickly over me. Everything electronic I owned broke down, and it was easy to do nothing in the mesmerizing heat. Our diverse group included a nurse from Saudi Arabia, an IT manager from the Lake District, a film producer from Paris and a mix of people from London. We were taught a strong but gentle yoga by the mellow and friendly Will Young, who trained with Jenny Beekan of the Inner Yoga Trust (www.inneryoga.org.uk), and has a reassuringly strong knowledge of body mechanics. The cacophony of insects, frogs and monkey calls at night and in the early morning was enough to make even the weariest of souls listen in wonder.

Caroline

ULPOTHA

If you want to undertake a full course of ayurvedic treatments, you'll be advised to attend only one of the two yoga classes a day and to avoid Ashtanga yoga, as you'll feel too weak to do such a strong practice. Anyone on a yoga retreat can go to the centre and enjoy a traditional steam and herbal bath, a shirodara (see glossary) and a clay facial free of charge whenever they want. The village produces its own herbs and tonics, which you can buy.

This is also a great place to take off alone, sit and chat with the group or lie around and do nothing. Two massages a week with resident therapists recruited from all over the world are included in a two-week retreat – anything from shiatsu to deep tissue massage could be on offer. You can hire bikes to visit nearby villages, and there's a tailor who visits daily – if you've a particular favourite piece of clothing, take it with you and he'll copy it. Chilled out impromptu parties with local music and singing sometimes take place, especially if it's a villager's birthday. Every two weeks there are two optional excursions (paid for separately) to ancient places of interest such as the forest monastery of Ritigala, the World Heritage site of Sigiriya with its palace, frescoes and water gardens, and Sri Lanka's medieval capital, Polonnaruwa.

What you eat and drink Most of the food you eat will be grown in the village. It's vegetarian, wheat- and dairy-free and absolutely delicious. Breakfast is usually a mix of rice porridge, Sri Lankan cakes, coconut water and home brewed herbal tea, served in a little hut called the *kade*. A changing array of tasty Sri Lankan dishes is laid out on huge bamboo and banana-leaf mats for lunch and dinner in the *ambalama*, a shaded wooden building with hip-high seats on which to perch. You help yourself to curries, salads, pulses and sambals together with the indigenous and extremely delicious rice grown by local farmers. Desert is fresh fruit with buffalo curd and kittul palm treacle. No alcohol is available, though you can bring your own, and it sometimes emerges at impromptu parties. Ulpotha means 'water spring' in Singalese, and there are several wells here with drinkable spring water.

Who goes Ulpotha attracts a lively and interesting group of people from all over the world looking for a relaxed and holistic experience. There is mostly an equal mix of men and women – some will be beginners, others will be devotees of a particular yoga style. For many a stay here is a precious two-week holiday – others are taking time out in between jobs or relationships and staying longer. Most people come alone, but couples and friends are also welcome.

Essentials Ulpotha (T+44 0844-888 5050, www.ulpotha.com), costs from US$1175 per week. It's a 3½-hour drive inland from Colombo airport. Transfers cost from US$50, or are free if you come on the group flight – ask at the time of booking. Try to arrive in daylight so that you can orientate yourself – once night falls the village is lit only by candles and lamps, and it is very difficult to see anything properly. Bring thin cotton clothing, a comfortable bag for carrying around your stuff, a pair of flip-flops and a torch. There is a small plug in the library where you can recharge camera batteries and mobile phones. Ulpotha opens its doors for eight weeks in the summer months of June, July and August, and then again from December to March. In between, it reverts to being a full-time organic farm. Most people stay for two weeks or more, though it is possible to visit for just a week. If you're looking for peace and quiet, avoid Christmas and New Year.

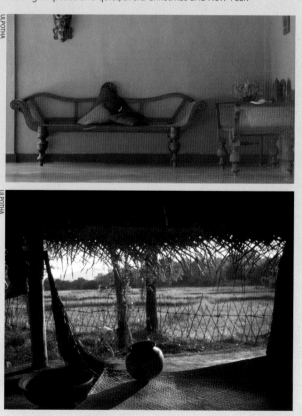

ULPOTHA

ULPOTHA

MEDITATION RETREAT

Dharmakuta Vipassana Meditation Centre

Hindagala
T+94 (0)81-238 5774
www.dhamma.org
10-day courses by donation only

This centre runs hard-core SN Goenka retreats where you live in silence and follow a strict daily timetable, which includes 10 hours of seated meditation and a daily lecture to encourage an insight into 'noble silence'. Tucked away in the countryside above Kandy, the views across the hills are very conducive to quiet contemplation, but don't expect any creature comforts – accommodation is spartan, and you will eat only two meals a day. For more information on meditation retreats, see Essentials.

HOTEL & SPA

The Fortress

Koggala beach, near Galle
T+94 (0)91-438 0909
www.thefortress.lk
From US$370 per room per night full board

Guest yoga teachers and other wellbeing consultants can be enjoyed on a regular basis at The Fortress, a state-of-the-art hotel modelled on Galle's historic Dutch fort. This luxury hotel is located next to the Indian Ocean, and boasts relaxing water features and a free-form pool that curves its way through the gardens, where you'll find day beds and hammocks on which to chill. The spa has a dedicated yoga room and offers a huge range of healing therapies with an holistic bent, including traditional ayurvedic treatments from a qualified ayurvedic doctor. There's also a homeopathic doctor on call, the approachable and expert South African Ivy Dieltiens. Visiting yoga teachers include Sri Lankan-based kundalini teacher, Anoushka Hempel who

teaches in Colombo (see page 246) and Australian Jessie Chapman (www.radianceretreats.com). The Fortress is owned by **Per Aquum Resorts**, who also created Huvafen Fushi in the Maldives (see page 264).

MEDITATION RETREAT

Nilambe

1 hour's drive from Kandy
T+94 (0)077-775 7216
www.nilambe.org
From US$3.95 per day, including accommodation and food

This vipassana Buddhist meditation retreat centre is perched on the side of a mountain amid tea plantations. As well as experienced meditators looking for few distractions and a long-term stay, beginners are welcome.

Though there are no organized retreats here, instruction in insight meditation and metta – or loving kindness – is given in English on demand. Established by the late buddhist teacher Godwin Samararatne,

Better to light one small candle than to curse the darkness.

Chinese Proverb

Nilambe encourages 'noble silence', where you refrain from talking to others except during given times such as the tea break. Some residents observe this strictly, others are more easy-going, but for most of the time you'll find the peaceful environment restful and useful. Despite the strict timetable there is quite a relaxed approach to things, so if you want to skip the odd session to stay in bed, or read and write, you can. The timetable includes yoga, though there is not always a teacher available, so check in advance if this is important to you.

RUSSELL LEWINS

Nilambe.

Accommodation is very basic, in shared or single *koutis* (huts) with stone beds and foam mattresses. Men and women are separated. Food is simple vegetarian, and there's a library of books on spirituality. It's a great place to feel close to nature - you'll hear jungle noises at night, including wild cats, and there's time for outdoor meditation if you so choose. An hour a day is given to 'working meditation' where you're expected to help out in the kitchen or garden. Sunset meditation overlooking the inspirational surroundings is a favourite time for many. There is no electricity here, so bring a torch, warm clothes for the evening and be prepared for cold showers. The leeches during the rainy season can be a hard test of loving kindness. Teaching is free; resident westerners are charged just 400 Sri Lankan rupees per day for food and accommodation. You don't need to book in advance, but you may feel more comfortable making contact before you go.

It's an hour's taxi ride from Kandy. The hard one mile walk up from the main road with your bag feels like an appropriate beginning to your retreat; if you don't want to walk, you need to call ahead and arrange to be picked up. Stay for a minimum of three days. For more information on meditation retreats, see Essentials.

WELLBEING HOLIDAY

Relaxing the Mind

🌓 ♨ ↘10

South coast and near Kandy
T+44 (0)20-8560 9347
www.relaxingthemind.com
From US$1500 for 10 days excluding flights

UK-based tai chi and meditation teacher Sue Weston runs 10-day meditation retreats twice a year in Sri Lanka, with five days on the southern coast and five days inland near Kandy. The course is co-taught with Sri Lankan actress, Anoja Weerasinghe, and inspired by both teachers' experience of acting and the theatre. They met when Weston taught Weerasinghe at LAMDA and

🌓 Body language

Ayurveda in Sri Lanka

Ayurveda, meaning the 'science of life' in Sanskrit, is a holistic system of healing that originated in India over 5000 years ago (see page 210). It was reputedly brought to Sri Lanka from India in the 6th century BC by Prince Vijaya, the first king of the island. Over time the Sinhalese added elements of their own treatments, using indigenous wild plants. During the reign of the last king of Sri Lanka in the 1790s, a monk, the son of the king's personal physician, began practising indigenous ayurvedic medicine in Neelammahara village. The Neelammahara tradition of ayurveda continued to pass from generation to generation, until most villages had an ayurvedic practitioner who held a leading position in the community.

Though ayurveda has always been a way of life for the local population, it wasn't until the late 20th century that it became available to foreign visitors following the West's renewed interest in alternative forms of therapy. Many of Sri Lanka's largest hotels built dedicated ayurveda centres, and in 1982 the Barberyn Reef at Beruwala opened, the island's first dedicated ayurvedic healing resort for overseas visitors. Its sister resort, Barberyn Beach (see page 248), has a more intimate setting and is better geared to independent travellers; at both, 85% of guests are German-speaking. Retreats such as Galapita (page 247), Ulpotha (page 250), and Samadhi (page 255) all began offering Ayurveda in 2006, led by local practitioners with generations of knowledge behind them; these are destined to be the most tranquil and remote settings for those seeking ayurveda and international companions.

BARBERYN BEACH
BARBERYN BEACH

◑ Body language

Buddhism in Sri Lanka

Nearly 70% of Sinhalese are Buddhists practising Theravada Buddhism, which became the dominant form in Sri Lanka and Southeast Asia in the 11th century. There are hundreds of beautiful Buddhist temples dotting the island, many of which can be freely visited; be sure to take off your shoes before you enter, and cover up. In daily life many Sinhalese Buddhists visit temples at least once a week on *poya* days, which correspond with the four quarters of the moon. Full moon days are declared national holidays, when Hindu deities are also worshipped – they have become part of popular Buddhist religion, and inside the temples you'll often see replicas of Skanda, the Hindu god of war, and Vishnu, who is seen the island's protector. Buddhism has lived side by side with Hindu belief in Sri Lanka for over 2000 years, and 15% of the Sinhalese population are Hindu, the rest being Muslims and Christians.

Sinhalese Buddhists place particular emphasis on the sanctity of Buddha relics, which they believe were brought to the island from India. The most important of these is the tooth of Buddha, now enshrined in a casket at the Dalada Maligawa in Kandy, and the sacred bo tree, in the holy city of Anuradhapura. This is believed to be a cutting from the original Bo tree under which the Buddha achieved Enlightenment at Bodhgaya in Bihar, India. When the Bodhgaya Bo tree was cut down, it became the only one in existence associated with the original, and is now visited by Buddhist pilgrims from all over the world.

Relics were not always important on the island. The Pansukulika or Tapovana sect of ascetic Buddhist hermits, who practised between the seventh to 11th centuries in Sri Lanka, shunned ritualistic forms of worship associated with Buddha images and relics. They lived a simple life of deep meditation in forests and caves, wore minimal clothing and immersed themselves in seeking the Truth. One of their forest monasteries can be found at Ritigala, which you can visit from Ulpotha (see page 250). Or try a spiritual journey to Sri Lanka's Buddhist sites with Sandra Shaw (see page 256).

SUE WESTON

now work together in Sri Lanka with those affected by the tsunami and twenty years of civil war, using drama as a path of healing.

On the retreat, breathwork, tai chi and relaxation exercises as well as meditation help guests connect with their body and spirit. Teaching is usually done in the mornings, with afternoons free to be alone or explore sacred sites. The idea is that, once relaxed, you'll be able to really experience a place rather than trying to see everything at once. You meet again in the evening for meditation and group discussions.

Fellow guests are likely to be busy careerists who want to combine the retreat experience with a visit to a new culture. Accommodation is in five star hotels – you'll need to pay extra if you want a room alone. Sue Weston has a calming voice, years of experience and bags of integrity. She spent a year living in the closed Buddhist community of Holy Island and runs week-long retreats there (see page 50), as well as popular weekend retreats in Dorset (see page 40). The fee includes a donation to the **Abhina Foundation UK**.

VALLEY RETREAT

Samadhi Centre

🌐 ⓘ ⛰ ⊙ ↘11

40-min drive from Kandy
T+94 (0)77-771 0013
www.samadhicentre.com
From US$37 per person per night

This very peaceful hideaway is set in a steep valley of the Knuckles mountain range, bordered by two rivers. It's the creation of Waruna, who, along with his Japanese wife, Yumi and a staff of local villagers, looks after guests very well. It's a calm and nourishing place and you can tap into a schedule of yoga and meditation or just come and do your own thing.

Waruna has set out to create the perfect environment in which to calm your mind. There are meditation spaces with staggering views over the valley, and group meditation, pranayama and chanting are also on offer. When you want to be active and still have a specific focus, there's bronze casting and silver, terracotta and carpentry workshops, you can even make your own incense sticks and candles, or you can help out in the vegetable and flower gardens.

Yoga takes place in a 185-sq-m yoga hall, where you can practise alone or take private classes with Yumi, a Sivananda-trained yoga teacher who spent two years living at Neeyar Dam ashram in Kerala. A small ayurveda centre for therapeutic massages opened in late 2006 and is led by local expert, Dr Angela Kulupana. Accommodation is in one of 16

Left and above: Samadhi Centre.

simple adobe huts, carved into the mountains and of varying sizes, some with four-poster beds. There are also two dormitory rooms. A calming neutral decor is brightened by painted yantras and mandalas on the walls. The door columns are over 100 years old, and interesting antiques dot the public spaces. Food is delicious: traditional Sri Lankan, cooked by a local chef using organic vegetables and fruit. No alcohol or meat is served. Kundalini master teacher, Shiv Charan Singh, founder of the Kriya Centre in London (www.karakriya.eu), runs a challenging and upliting annual yoga retreat at Samadhi.

RURAL RETREAT

Samakanda

Nakiyandeniya, Galle
T+94 (0)91-222 2855
www.samakanda.org
From US$60 per person per night

Samakanda, or 'peaceful hill', is a working organic farm with self-catering cottages set up by Rory Spowers, author and founder of

The Web of Hope, a UK-registered charity specializing in environmental education. Developed on the site of an abandoned tea estate, it's in the cool hills with inspirational jungle views, so it's a lovely place to stay for a few nights or longer, and you'll feel comfortable doing whatever you want.

Relax, bike, walk, read, do your own yoga, tai chi or pilates in the thatched yoga hall or meditate under the banyan tree. You can take advantage of a itinerant community of therapists, including masseurs, naturopaths and homeopaths as well as yoga teachers. Organic food is available in abundance: Samakanda grows a staggering array of stuffs from tea, fruit trees and spices to exotic herbs, vegetables and salads.

Accommodation is self-catering. You can stay in a spacious stone bungalow, or in a cottage in the 'bowl', which has been turned into a tropical forest garden growing everything from fruit trees to root crops. By the end of 2008 there will also be a choice of 12 comfortable 'eco-pods', made from different natural materials such as bamboo or compressed mud brick, and built into rock faces or boulders.

SPIRITUAL HOLIDAY

Sandra Shaw Spiritual Holiday

T+44 (0)845-456 1007
www.spiritualholidays.com
From US$1050 excluding flights

If you are drawn to Sri Lanka and also interested in exploring yourself, Sandra Shaw runs spiritual trips to many of the country's Buddhist sites. As well as learning about their cultural and historical background, you'll have a chance to meditate at the sites and participate in energy work with Sandra if you so choose. Sandra has taught spirituality and personal development for over 15 years, and trained with the likes of Deepak Chopra, Louise Hay and Tony Robbins. Her trips are open to anyone, and attract a real mix of mainly British people of all ages. Sandra Shaw runs spiritual holidays around the world.

VILLAGE RETREAT

The Secret Garden

Unawatuna
T+94 (0)91-224 1857
www.secretgardenvilla.lk
From US$54 per person per night

A peaceful, pretty place to stay in the popular village of Unawatuna, the Secret Garden's main asset is a bright white dome where yoga and meditation classes are taken daily from April to November. A menu of treatments from reiki to ayurvedic massage is available, given by visiting practitioners. Classical music concerts are held regularly here, as well as workshops and classes in dance and meditation. You stay in airy and

Above: Samakanda. **Right:** The Secret Garden. **Far right:** Wijaya Beach.

attractive whitewashed rooms with antique furniture and interesting artwork – the two suites have open-air bathrooms. The beach is just 30 m away, though you need to cross a small road to reach it.

YOGA RETREAT
Villa de Zoysa

Boossa, near Galle
T+94 (0)91-226 7123
www.villadezoysa.com
From US$750 for 2 weeks

A white house set on the beach, 10 minutes from Galle, Villa de Zoysa is the ancestral home of Devinda de Zoysa, a third-generation Sri Lankan. He has been hosting yoga holidays here since 2000, and his house makes a peaceful retreat with an intimate relaxed atmosphere. Devinda also runs karma yoga programmes, where you can do post-tsunami work in the nearby villages.

Yoga classes run twice a day and are small, with lots of individual attention. Devinda recruits his teachers carefully – they include iyengar-inspired Paddy McGrath and Florian Palzinsky, a former monk who also teaches meditation. Massages and beauty treatments including natural flower facials can be arranged in a small therapy room – they're expertly done and great value.

Guests eat meals together around one large table, where conversation may move from art and history to Buddhism. Devinda's knowledge of Sri Lanka is encyclopaedic, and this is an excellent opportunity to find out more about the country you're in. Food is traditional spicy Sri Lankan curries and fresh seafood, with lots of fruit for breakfast. You sleep in one of seven spacious en suite double rooms, four of which are very large and have balconies.

Most guests are women between 25 and 40, with a sprinkling of men, and have been doing yoga for a few years but have got rusty. Most come for a full two-week retreat, though it is also possible to stay for just one. The peace and quiet of the house is taken

seriously and arrivals need to be planned in advance, so do book ahead.

COASTAL RETREAT
Wijaya Beach Cottage

Unawatuna
T+94 (0)77-790 3431
www.wijayabeach.com
From US$18 per person per night

A simple, relaxing place set on lovely Dalwella beach, Wijaya Beach Cottage is run by Sri Lankan couple Elizabeth and Mahendra, who spend six months in England. The beach is great for chilling and has good waves for surfing, and Wijaya offers a mix of treatments from a range of itinerant therapists – anything from massage to naturopathy could be available. Rooms are clean if basic, some with only cold-water showers. The delicious food is a real pull: seafood, traditional Sri Lankan dishes and organic vegetables served in the open restaurant a step away from the beach, plus juices and smoothies.

Wijaya also sells **Arcania Apothecary**

Soul food

Friends of the South (www.friendsofthesouth.org) is a Charitable Association which aims to improve lives in the south of Sri Lanka in whatever way is needed. So far they've built fishing boats, sponsored children's education, taught kids to swim, built a new kitchen for an old people's home and replaced a sewing machine, a bicycle and a tuk tuk.

products from England (www.arcaniaapothecary.com), and acts as the base for Shamble Tours. Join a group of no more than eight on 'The Complete Shambles' (from US$50 per person, T+94 (0)77-790 6156), where Alex Barrett leads a day-long 35-km bike ride which starts with an organic brunch at Samakanda (see previous page) and bikes through rainforest, protected reserve, tea country and flat paddy land to finish at sunset over a drink at Wijaya.

CAROLINE SYLGE

Bali

A Hindu island with a rich history of ritual and belief, Bali is a nurturing place where you can retreat to your own villa or detox by the sea.

Fact file

- **Visa:** Citizens of EU countries, US, Canada, Australia and New Zealand can obtain visas on arrival
- **IDD:** +62
- **Currency:** Indonesian Rupiah (IDR)
- **Time zone:** GMT +8 hours
- **Electricity:** 220v, in some rural areas 110v
- **Tourist board:** www.balitourismauthority.net

RURAL RETREAT

Ananda Cottages

Campuhan, near Ubud
www.ananda-cottages.com
From US$69 per room per night

A set of traditional bungalows surrounded by rice paddies with pretty gardens and a swimming pool, Balinese-run Ananda Cottages hosts a number of yoga retreats by visiting teachers throughout the year, or just come and chill out alone. The yoga is done in an open-air studio, with a great view of rice paddies, paddling ducks and distant mountains. It's just outside Ubud town, Bali's hippy cultural capital with traditional buildings, museums, little shops and art galleries, and there are temples and shrines nearby.

Australian yoga teacher **Louisa Sear** (from US$1120 for 10 nights, T+61 (0)2-6684 9346, www.yogarts.com.au) runs a yoga holiday here, usually every June. Director of Yoga Arts in Byron Bay, Australia , Louisa has over 20 years' teaching experience. Her holidays are open to beginners and experienced practitioners, and attract an international crowd. They feature two classes a day, and include pranayama, meditation and asanas. The morning asana session is an energizing dynamic vinyasa-style class, the afternoon session focuses more on alignment. The rest of the time you're free to enjoy affordable massages, beauty treatments, great restaurants and downtime.

Asia-based yoga teacher **Emil Wendel** (US$950 per person, T+62 (0)36-197 5376, www.beyond-the-asana.com, also see page

201) runs a more intensive 10-day yoga retreat at Ananda Cottages each summer, which includes a detailed look at yoga philosophy. All levels are welcome, but this is not for the faint hearted; the retreat will feature seven hours of yoga a day. For other affordable yoga and wellness retreats in Bali, check out www.balispirit.com.

SPIRITUAL HOLIDAY

Bali Pilgrimage

T+62 (0)36-294766
www.well-keptsecrets.com
US$1850 for 5 nights

Explore Bali's nine most important temples accompanied by a specially chosen Hindu priest as your guide. The regular five-night trip is organized by Bali-based company **Well Kept Secrets**, set up by Diana von Cranach who owns Puri Ganesha Villas (see page 260) and has an in-depth knowledge of the island.

You can meditate, pray and submit offerings at Uluwatu temple, one of the most sacred sites on the island, which is perched on the top of a crag overlooking the Indian Ocean. This is the place where Balinese sage Niratha was supposed to have left the temporal world. By contrast, the buzzy Pulaki temple of commerce is visited by Balinese from all over the island on a daily basis. Alternatively, climb the 300 steep steps to Pura Lempyuang, which has an amazing energy surrounding the temple and stunning views of Mount Agung.

After immersing yourself in Balinese culture during the day, relax at selected luxury hotels every evening, including

Above: Yoga with Louisa Sear. **Right:** Bali pilgrimage.

Begawan Giri is an inspirational setting. So breathtaking is it and so full of an eerie energy, that it somehow felt wrong to have a five-star set-up here. Forget the spa treatment rooms – I had my massage in a delightful muslin-shrouded massage bed overlooking the gorge. And after trying to swim in the (very cold) pools, I soaked and stretched instead in the large crystal-clear rock pool down the valley. I loved climbing down the steep steps to find a tiny wooden meditation hut, and to hear the rush of the river from all over the estate – even if it did include the screams of whitewater rafters at regular intervals.

The yoga teacher raced through a set of instructions as if we were in an exercise class, and at dinner we had to endure a photographer talking loudly to his two young models about a pending shoot. But, as I sat on a white-sheeted daybed sipping ginger and honey tea and surveying the view, I didn't really care: the air was incredibly fresh, and I felt as if I were borne aloft into the tree tops, surrounded by an awe-inspiring jungle peppered with bright-red African tulip trees. There's a six-hour trip you can do here which has you climbing a volcano on foot, and descending it on a bike. If I came back next time, I'd bring a group of friends, hire a residence to ourselves, and get stuck in.

Caroline

Luxurious daybed at Como Shambala.

Sarinbuana, (www.baliecolodge.com), an eco-lodge set in the mountains, the tranquil **Como** hotel **Uma Ubud** (www.uma.como.bz) and coastal hotel **Alila Manggis** (www.alilahotels.com/manggis). Good food and massages are available at every stop, and Uma Ubud and Alila Manggis have their own spas where you can indulge in signature treatments. The rate includes all transfers, accommodation, breakfast, guide and temple entrance fees, Balinese offerings, and the sarongs and sashes you need to enter the temples.

JUNGLE RETREAT
Como Shambhala Estate

Begawan Giri, near Ubud
T+62 (0)36-197 8888
http://cse.comoshambhala.bz
From US$347 per room per night

In a simply spectacular setting above the Ayung gorge and surrounded by massive trees and thick jungle, the Como Shambhala Estate at Begawan Giri styles itself as "a retreat for change", offering treatments, classes, counselling and outdoor pursuits to the well heeled. Many visitors are here just to relax on holiday – the estate even offers a dedicated honeymooners' programme – but the setting and energy make this a perfect place for complete rejuvenation.

There are all-inclusive programmes on offer for three, five or seven night, from US$1188, US$2018 and US$2773 respectively. It isn't worth coming here just for a night's rest and relaxation. Complimentary daily activities include morning estate walks, climbing, circuit training, tai chi, pilates, dance classes, yoga, tennis and stress management coaching. There are good six- to seven-hour guided treks, and great mountain biking. Soak in the steam room and hot tub outside the main spa, where you'll also find the swimming pool, and daybeds with great views. There's a separate yoga pavilion and a pilates studio and you can choose to have your massage in the *kedara* (water garden), a set of four treatment rooms in the jungle valley.

A questionnaire is sent out in advance to find out various personal details as well as your goals. You'll have access to an ayurvedic doctor, a psychologist, a nutritionist and naturopath, and a resident nurse with a background in complementary therapies

In the end what matters most is, how well did you live, how well did you love, how well did you learn to let go.

Guy Burgs

CAROLINE SYLGE

who offers reiki, reflexology and crystal healing. There are stress management, detox, anti-ageing and ayurvedic programmes, as well as a whole host of massages and á la carte beauty treatments. Dedicated yoga and pilates retreats are also sometimes held here, including ones by US ashtanga teacher, David Swenson (www.davidswenson.com).

You can stay in one of 21 immaculate wood and glass suites within five different 'residences', which share a pool and communal lounging areas. If you want to be more private, opt for one of the 10 stand-alone villas in the grounds. Food is healthy and sophisticated, and special diets can be catered for. Fusion-style soups, wraps, salads and grills are served at Glow, which feels rather impersonal and needs a view. Kudus House, a traditional wooden Javan dwelling, has far more atmosphere and sits perched over the jungle-clad valley. Here you can eat contemporary Indonesian cuisine, with dishes such as spice-flaked grilled tuna with shallot, lemon grass and chilli salad, followed by braised chicken with green papaya.

Fly to Denpasar, from where it's a one-hour drive. The estate is part of the **Como** hotel group, which includes **Parrot Cay** in the Caribbean (see page 372), **Cocoa Island** in the

Maldives (see page 264), **Uma Paro** in Bhutan (see page 235) and **Uma Ubud** (www.uma.como.bz), a 15-minute drive from the Shambala, in the town of Ubud.

COASTAL RETREAT
Puri Ganesha Villas

⏱ ○ ⛰ ⚙ ⬎20

Desa Pemuteran
T+62 (0)36-294766
www.puriganeshabali.com
From US$484 per villa per night

A stylish yet unpretentious set of four villas set back from a volcanic sand beach, Puri Ganesha Villas is run by charismatic Diana von Cranach, who lives here with her Balinese husband Gusti and a family of dalmatians. It takes three and a half hours from the airport over high mountains to get here, so it's deliciously quiet and untouristy. Come to learn about food, detox or just chill out.

The four uncluttered, comfortable villas feature wooden furniture brightened by Diana's brilliant fabrics. Sleeping two, four or six, each has its own veranda, a good-sized swimming pool and garden with a small rice barn ideal for private meditation or yoga. There are outdoor bathrooms, hand-crafted

antiques from Java and large straw sunhats and baskets for you to use.

Diana has devised her own 'RAWfully Good Living' menu of soups and salads, nut milks and cheeses, and meal-in-themselves juices. Her concoctions are unusually light and beautifully presented, and include locally grown superfoods such as coconuts, cocoa beans and goji berries, as well as herbs, spices and vegetables from an organic mountain farm. You can attend a course in raw food nutrition and preparation, or try a 'Rice & Spice Adventure' featuring Balinese cooking workshops and visits to local markets, spice farms and herbalists.

This is also a great place to detox with a friend. Together with Australian nutritionist Susan Famularo, Diana will devise a cleansing menu of juices and salads; the local volcanic spring water is a perfect accompaniment to a good cleanse.

Head gardener-cum-priest Putu gives a very good deep tissue massage, and private yoga classes can be arranged in advance with a local Nepalese teacher. There's optional evening meditation at the local Melanting temple, or go for invigorating guided treks in the mountains.

Annual retreats include a yoga week with Lance Schuler, head of **Inspya Yoga** in Byron

Bay, Australia (www.inspyayoga.com) and a healing retreat mixing yoga, raw food and holistic therapies, which is hosted by Diana with yoga teacher Stella Yfantidis and therapist Jodie Downes from **Whatever Yoga** in Singapore (www.whatever.com.sg, see page 295). You'll spend four of the 10 nights at the lovely **Uma hotel** in Ubud (wwwuma.como.bz).

As well as the raw food menu, there are lunch and dinner menus featuring locally caught fish and free-range chicken dishes. Order on your own veranda or eat in the sociable space of the quirky restaurant. Diana is a gourmet who smokes and drinks – so you'll find a good wine and champagne list here in amongst the vegetable juices.

Fellow guests include actors, artists and the odd celebrity as well as families, couples and groups of friends – you can be as private or as sociable as you like here. It's open all year round. Arrange a pickup from the airport – you can even arrive on a Harley-Davidson.

The Retreat

🌐 ⏱ ♨ ☁ 🕉 ⓦ ⓢ ⊘ ⏩ ⌁21

T+44 (0)1923-291066
www.theretreatbali.com
From US$220 per night

On the east coast of Bali, beneath the dormant volcano Mount Agung and away from the tourist crowds, The Retreat is a small centre for detox and rejuvenation set up in 2006 by the brilliant English meditation teacher **Guy Burgs** (www.justletgo.org), who runs meditation retreats in UK. It is now staffed by a qualified team of 12 Balinese staff, and Burgs visits at various times throughout the year.

The Retreat is for anyone interested in detoxing their body and mind, for stays of from three days up to 30. Those suffering from diseases such as cancer and MS can also come here to cleanse and recuperate. It attracts expats, as well as visitors of all ages from around the world, especially the UK and US. Meditation, qigong and yoga are used to

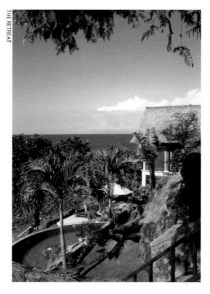

THE RETREAT

help cleanse the mind as well as the body.

A personal programme is devised after an in-depth consultation comprising a questionnaire and live blood analysis together with tests to check your pH balance, blood pressure, heart rate and oxygen saturation. As well as nutrition consultation, supplements and a specially tailored fasting diet, you'll have access to an infra-red sauna

and herbal steam room, ozone therapy, oxygen therapy, bio-magnetic resonance and the use of a trampoline as well as massage, enemas and infusions.

You stay in spacious, well-lit houses with a sitting room and bedroom on two floors – each one opens onto a balcony with soothing sea views. They have en suite bathrooms with open-air showers – decor is minimalist, in calming sandstone colours. There's a communal sitting area with a dining table and rattan chairs, and secluded spots to meditate, including the Golden Rock, built to face the sun and align with the nearby Lumpuyang temple and Mount Agung. There's also a small raised meditation platform, a lovely place to watch the sun rise over distant Lombok. Daily yoga and qigong takes place in a specially built sala overlooking the pool and ocean. The detox clinic with treatment rooms is behind the bungalows.

The Retreat is near Bali's most important complex of Hindu-Buddhist temples, Besakih, and surrounded by a rich spiritual history with unspoilt countryside to walk in. You can also swim or snorkel off the beach, though there are sometimes strong currents.

Fly to Denpasar; if you arrive in the

Indian Ocean Bali

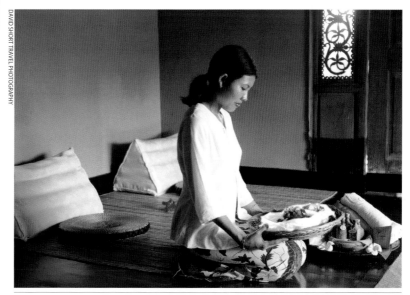

DAVID SHORT TRAVEL PHOTOGRAPHY

Top left: Puri Ganesha. **Top right**: The Retreat. **Above**: Hotel Tugu Bali.

evening, The Retreat will book a room at the **Hyatt** or the **Sanur Beach** hotels, then pick you up the next day. It's a three-hour drive from the airport (US$100 return).

HOTEL & SPA

Tugu Bali

Canggu Beach
T+62 (0)36-173 1701
www.tuguhotels.com
From US$250 per room per night

Bali is full to bursting with hotels offering Balinese and Javanese treatments, but Hotel Tugu Bali stands out.

The Tugu's main feature is a traditional all-natural Javanese apothecary (Waroeng Djamoe), where age-old recipes for herbal massage oils and beauty lotions are made from the frangipani, magnolia, rose, jasmine and ylang-ylang growing in the gardens.

Public spaces are decorated with traditional Javanese art and artefacts and rooms are cool and spacious with garden or ocean views (ocean view suites are bright and airy, while those on the ground floor have private plunge pools). You'll get a complimentary foot massage on arrival, and your oversized beds will be scattered with fresh petals and Balinese poetry each night.

Food is sourced locally and served in the flamboyant blood-red 300-year-old Kang Xi period Bale Sutra temple dining room – or eat on the beach under the stars or in your room, where you'll get 24-hour room service. The current on the beach is too strong for swimming, but there's an outdoor pool, and bikes for hire (cycle to the stunning 15th-century Nirartha sea temples at Tanah Lot, 10 minutes away).

Most treatments offered at the Tugu are inspired by ancient Indonesian therapies, while others reflect the Tugu owner's Chinese heritage. Choose from a wide variety of massage oil recipes at the Waroeng Djamoe, and have a treatment in the 100-year-old open-air massage pavilion. The signature treatment, the Keraton Leha-Leha, combines Javanese massage with a spice scrub and milk splash. Or try samedhi or tapa Javanese meditation, which existed in Java long before the introduction of Buddhism in the 8th century. Your session is preceded with a ginger, lemon and honey infusion, and followed by a 30-minute ayurvedic massage.

Classes such as yogalates (a hybrid of yoga and pilates) are on offer, and workshops on Balinese handicrafts, which can be arranged for groups or on a one-to-one basis. Staff are graceful and unflappable, and the hotel attracts a range of Asian and European guests, usually couples in their thirties and upwards. Fly to Denpasar, a 30-minute drive away – pickups can be arranged.

DETOX RETREAT

Ubud Sari Health Resort

T+62 (0)36-197 4393
www.ubudsari.com
From US$45 per room per night

A relaxed, down-to-earth family-run health resort where you can come to do serious detox cleansing programmes or just de-stress, Ubud Sari is based off a quiet road in the town of Ubud.

The resort was founded by Indonesian doctor and chiropractor Tony Dawson, who was inspired to set it up after witnessing his father's life long migraine and back pain being cured by Balinese healers in the 1970s. He now lives what he preaches, and leads a team of caring Balinese and Indonesian staff.

Healthy food with a Balinese twist is served in the vegetarian restaurant, which,

Ubud Sari Helath Resort.

unusually, only serves (deliciously prepared) raw food. Juices are also on the menu, as well as elixirs such as the traditional Indonesian herbal medicine, Jamu.

You stay in one of the specially built wooden 'zen' villas, minimalist in design and decorated with traditional wall hangings, some with views over the treetops. The property has tropical garden spaces, an outdoor yoga space, a swimming pool, whirlpool, sauna and a herbal steam room. Decor is homely and relaxed, not luxurious.

There's a daily morning yoga class (US$5), and a selection of relaxing massages and beauty treatments on offer, including a traditional Javanese massage and a volcanic mud bath. You can also have a session with Dr Dawson (US$30) and shiatsu, reflexology, reiki and craniosacral therapy.

Most people come here for one of the four- to seven-night cleansing and relaxation programmes. The full seven-day cleansing programme (from US$1480) includes rice field walks, yoga, skin brushing, colonic irrigation, hydrotherapy, juices, meditation and 10 appropriate treatments as well as workshops, private consultations, and use of the facilities.The place attracts a youngish international crowd, mostly in their thirties. Fly to Denpasar, from where it's about a one-hour drive – pick ups can be arranged.

☉ Soul food

YKIP (T+62 (0)36-175 9544 or go to www.ykip.org) is a Balinese charity that was set up in a hospital by a group of emergency volunteers the day after the October 2002 terrorist bomb attacks on the island. Its mission is to improve the lives of everyone who lives in Bali as a tribute to those who were killed, injured or lost their livelihood following the attacks, and they have health and education programmes all over the island.

Retreat to a villa in Bali

Hiring a villa in Bali which offers in-house treatments is an effective way to retreat, especially if there's a group of you. There are plenty of gorgeous properties all over the island and prices are often negotiable, particularly for longer stays, last-minute bookings and off season. Bali has a six-month dry season from June to October but is a lush, quieter place to visit the rest of the year. The busiest tourist areas are Kuta and the beaches west of it, Legian and Seminyak; head east or north if you want to avoid the crowds.

Bali Homes Management (T+62 (0)36-173 0668, www.bhmvillas.com) represents a set of privately-owned luxurious villas staffed mostly by local Balinese. From 0900 till 2100 you can have in-house treatments at most of their villas. The visiting therapists are trained at spas in Ubud and give a decent aromatherapy, Swedish and traditional Balinese massage as well as foot treatments and wraps – try the Balinese wrap mixing pepper, clove and ginger to help clean your system and stimulate circulation. You get your own butler and chef, who'll prepare you healthy Balinese meals with a Western twist on request.

East of Denpasar, at Gianyar, lies the Majapahit Beach Villas (from US$ 750 per night, www.majapahitbeachvillas.com), a complex of four three-bedroom villas set on a breezy but quiet black-sand beach. A spa with a jacuzzi and café are planned for 2008. Villa Samudra is one of the villas, a well-designed, spacious, wood-and-glass house with Balinese antiques and an outdoor lap pool, daybeds and a hammock. There's also a wooden deck overlooking the beach that's perfect for your own yoga, pilates or tai chi practice and meditation. Or try the wonderful Ylang-Ylang (www.theylangylang.com), set between coconut trees and a landscaped garden with six bedrooms; from US$1000 per night for up to six people.

For other repleneshing villas in Bali, interior designer and environmentalist Linda Garland has a few treats (www.lindagarland.com), as does Indigo Lodges' Summer Collection (www.indigolodge.org).

Indian Ocean Bali

The Maldives

Fantasy Islands

The Maldives is an other-worldly seascape of islands and atolls, a staggeringly still and spacious place to rest body and soul. Each of its 90-odd resorts takes up its own private island, tapping into the desire in all of us to play Robinson Crusoe. You'll want to take all your clothes off and walk naked on an empty beach, disturbed only by the gentle sound of waves out on the reef. The islands are destined to be overwhelmed by water in about 150 years as global warming continues to make sea levels rise, but eye-wateringly expensive resorts with spas still open here regularly. Get the right one, and it might just be worth saving to visit while you still have time.

Chic, contemporary **Huvafen Fushi** (from US$1100 per villa per night, T+960 (0)4-44222, www.huvafenfushi.com), has a resident 'wellness mentor' offering naturopathy and live blood analysis, a gorgeous spa built on stilts above the ocean, underwater treatment rooms with sweeping views of tropical fish and a selection of inventive rituals using wraps, scrubs, facials and massages. You can do one-to-one yoga and meditation classes, swim in the infinity pool lit up by coloured fibre-optic lights at night and float in the *lonu veyo*, an outdoor Malaysian saltwater pool. There are annual retreats with experts such as Sri Lanka-based kundalini yoga teacher Annoushka Hempel, Australian yoga teacher Jessie Chapman and beauty therapist-to-the-stars Anastasia Achellios. One of its restaurants specializes in raw food, and all the spacious water bungalows have giant sketch pads on which to unleash your creativity. Choose one

with a full-size jacuzzi in the bathroom, or a glass-bottomed sitting area so you can gaze at the fish below.

One & Only Maldives at Reethi Rah (from US$750 per villa per night, T+960 (0)6-648800, www.oneandonlyresorts.com) boasts 6 km of private coastline. Choose a water villa so you can lie in your over-water hammock and enjoy uninterrupted views of the tropical fish. The world's largest ESPA spa here takes a holistic approach, with therapists, fitness instructors, nutritionists and chefs on hand to provide bespoke programmes for detoxing, de-stressing or just plain pampering: if you like getting your nails done, world-renowned pedicurist and manicurist, Bastien Gonzalez lives in. Reethi Rah also offers kundalini yoga weeks, with resident teachers trained by kundalini expert Maya Fiennes. Buy a programme for three, five, seven or 10 days, or just have ad hoc one-to-one sessions in the stunning Chi Pavilion facing the sea.

Soneva Fushi (from US$530 per room per night, T+960 (0)6-600304, www.sixsenses.com) is set on a large island in the northern atolls, and has a range of visiting consultants including life coaches, acupuncturists and watsu specialists such as UK-based Hilary Austin. The Maldive's first luxury resort, it has a comfortable, lived-in feel and a luscious Six Senses spa. Have a Maldivian sand massage right on the beach, or indulge in a Sodashi facial in a jungle 'champa'. Stay in a villa on the east to enjoy the sunrise – those on the west face an inhabited island.

Cocoa Island, in one of the quieter southern atolls, is a relaxed and lovely place with just 33 rooms, most of them based on

---

❝ ❞

The supremely spacious water bungalows at Huvafen Fushi were designed to make people want to take their clothes off whenever possible – and I kind of saw what they meant. Padding across mahogany wooden floors, who needed clothes on to experience my uninterrupted (and very private) view of the ocean? I lost myself for hours in the Maldives, staring out at the pea-green line where the tranquil lagoon met the horizon, watching the colours of the sky shift with the time and weather from pink to baby blue, from saffron yellow to ink-black. I skinny dipped with parrot fish and baby sharks, swum out to a hammock suspended in the middle of a lagoon, ordered green tea from a private butler at an obscene hour of the morning when I should have been asleep. It wasn't cheap, but it was extremely pleasant. You wouldn't think you needed to spend money to enjoy the colours of the sky, and I did try one of the island's three star resorts, but its busyness led me to conclude that if you are going to come here, save to come here in style or not at all. Forget facing your demons and self exploration for now – this is the place to come for pure escapism, where reality isn't something that will penetrate your skull until you're back home making your own hot drinks. *Caroline*

STEVE HANDLEY

traditional *dhoni* boats. The **Como Shambala** spa here (T+960 (0)6-641818, www.cocoaisland.como.bz) offers fabulous treatments with a holistic approach, and week-long retreats with visiting yoga teachers and health specialists, and costs from US$680 per room per night. For a dedicated programme of ayurveda, head to the **Taj Exotica resort** (T+44 (0)800-282699, www.tajhotels.com), whose Jiva Grande Spa was specially set up for ayurveda with consultants from India, and has dedicated ayurveda treatment pavilions. From US$670 per room per night.

A destination spa where you stay for a minimum of three nights, The Spa Retreat at the **Hilton Maldives Resort and Spa** on Rangali Island (from US$775 per villa per night, T+960 (0)6-680629, www.hilton.co.uk/maldives) is as far from a Hilton as you could get. An over-water complex on stilts set between the Hilton's two islands with an impressive range of health and beauty packages, it has 21 luxurious water villas, each with soothing sea views and its own treatment room, so you don't have to get up after your massage. Being in one of the villas feels as though you're living in the middle of the ocean, and in the evenings you can watch stingrays swim underneath. The Power of Three, with UK-based yoga teacher, Katy Appleton, and energy healer, Alla Svirinskaya (www.tpo3.com) run annual retreats.

If you're keen to get out here at a more affordable rate, the **Sen Spa at Full Moon** (from US$200 per villa per night, T+960 (0)6-641976, www.fullmoonmaldives.com) is run by Per Aquum, the same company that runs Huvafen Fushi, and it offers equally delicious treatments at a fraction of the price. The spa has a split-level infinity pool and a relaxation room looking out to sea with floor-to-ceiling glass walls.

To get the best deal, book an all-inclusive week including flights with tour operators such as **Wellbeing Escapes** (see Resources. **Trailfinders** (T+44 (0)845-058 5858, www.trailfinders.com) often has good deals, or go through an operator with specialist knowledge of the Maldives such as the **Ultimate Travel Company** (T+44 (0)20-7386 4646, www.theultimatetravelcompany.co.uk).

Asia

AGE FOTOSTOCK / SUPERSTOCK

Prayer flags at the foot of Mt Everest.

PAPUA NEW GUINEA

Pacific Ocean

TOKYO
Yokohama
Nagano
Kyoto
Sado Island
JAPAN
Sapporo
↗21
↗19
↗20

Sea of Japan

NORTH KOREA
SEOUL
SOUTH KOREA
Taegu
Fukuoka
↗25

East China Sea

Shanghai
Ningbo
Wuxi
Nanjing
Taipei
TAIWAN
Fuzhou
Shantou

Qiqihar
Harbin
Jilin
Changchun
Fushun
Anshan

RUSSIAN FEDERATION

BEIJING
Tianjin
Tangshan
Jinan
Datong
Zhengzhou
Luoyang
Wuhan
Nanchang
Guangzhou
Hong Kong
Macau
↗18

Baotou
Xi'an
Suizhou
Yueyang
Changsha
Liuzhou
Nanning

PHILIPPINES
MANILA

South China Sea

Lanzhou
CHINA
Chengdu
Chongqing
Neijiang
Guiyang
Kunming
↗16
↗26

Lake Baikal
MONGOLIA
↗24
Gobi Desert

Kyzyl

Quy Nhon
↗27
Ho Chi Minh City

South China Sea

Borneo

INDONESIA
JAKARTA

MALAYSIA
KUALA LUMPUR
SINGAPORE

HANOI
VIENTIANE
VIETNAM
LAOS
Siem Reap
CAMBODIA
PHNOM PENH
BANGKOK
THAILAND
Luang Prabang
MYANMAR
YANGON

Langkawi
detail map p272

Bay of Bengal

SRI LANKA

Indian Ocean

INDIA
DELHI

BANGLADESH
NEPAL
Himalaya
(TIBET)

PAKISTAN

500 km
500 miles

N

Introduction

Thailand and its unflappable people have long been a calming influence on many a stressed-out soul. Home to one of the world's great massages, it also has some great places to detox, and a warm climate to make the process a (slightly) more comfortable experience. There's Chiva Som, of course, or try a newcomer such as Kamalaya, which is breaking the mould in providing affordable holistic alternative therapies and activities in luxurious surroundings.

Across Asia, you'll be able to dip in and out of impeccable places to stay where the service and treatments are second to none. Get back in touch with yourself through unfamiliar cultural experiences: learn tai chi in China, stay in a temple in Korea, horse ride through the unpopulated landscapes of Mongolia, or find out more about Tibet's spiritual heritage on a pilgrimage with Buddhist master Amnyi Trulchung Rinpoche. Japan makes an unusual place to de-stress, with off-the-beaten-track ryokans where you can soak in an *onsen*, the Japanese version of the thermal hot spring, back-to-basic temples which teach Zen meditation, and the amazing Earth Celebration Festival on Sado Island, where you'll find that connecting to others comes easily.

Whatever you choose, this area of the world is the place to experience travel in its purest sense.

66 99 *One does not discover new continents without consenting to lose sight of the shore for a very long time.*

André Gide

Travel essentials

Thailand

Getting there Bangkok is the country's main gateway. From the UK, Qantas, **British Airways** and **THAI** offer non-stop flights from London Heathrow (12 hours). **Finnair** flies daily from Helsinki, **KLM** from Amsterdam, **SAS** from Copenhagen, **Swiss International Airlines** from Zurich and **Lufthansa** from Frankfurt. Chiang Mai in the north and Phuket in the south also have international airports, both with flights from Düsseldorf and Munich. **THAI** offers a non-stop flight from New York (16 hours), but usually flights from the US involve at least one stop. Flights from Los Angeles take around 21 hours. **Qantas** and **THAI** fly from Sydney, Perth and Melbourne (nine hours), as well as Auckland. If you have at least three weeks to get there, travel overland by train from Europe on the Trans-Siberian railway; see www.seat61.com.

Best time to visit In much of Thailand, the best time to visit is from December to February. April and May are the hottest months of the year. The wet season runs from May to October in most regions, although between the heavy showers there are clear skies and it can be cheaper to travel during this time. September and October are the likeliest months for flooding. For Bangkok, central, northern and northeastern areas (including Chiang Mai and Hua Hin), the best time is November to February after the rainy season. November to April are the best months for the southwest (including Phuket, Krabi and Koh Phi Phi) and May to October are the driest months in the southeast (Koh Samui and Koh Phangan).

Japan

Getting there Japan's international airport is Tokyo Narita. **Virgin**, **British Airways**, **Japan Airlines** and **All Nippon Airways** fly direct from major UK airports to Japan (11-12 hours). From the US and Canada, **All Nippon Airways**, **Japan Airlines**, **United Airlines**, **Northwest** and **Korean Air** offer regular services (14 hours). **Cathay Pacific**, **Garuda**, **Qantas**, **Air New Zealand** and **JAL** fly from Australia (10 hours), while **Malaysian Airlines** and **Thai Airlines** also serve the New Zealand route (11 hours). If you don't fancy flying, see www.seat61.com for travel from Europe via the Trans-Siberian railway.

Best time to visit Winters on the coastal plains are generally mild, with temperatures above freezing. The warmest weather is in

Eat me

Eat like the locals when you're in North and Southeast Asia and it's almost impossible not to follow a healthy diet. Look around you and you'll notice two things: how petite so many of the population are and the fact that they always seem to be eating. There's an abundance of fresh, healthy and incredibly flavoursome food to be enjoyed here. From the familiar, such as Japan's sushi and sahimi, to the lesser known but equally detox-friendly bowls of virtually fat-free miso soup that sustain the Japanese from dawn till dusk. In Japan, also look out for dishes containing *kombu* (kelp seaweed) which is considered by many to be a miracle food. It's rich in protein, calcium, iodine, magnesium, iron and folate and is virtually fat-free. *Kombu*, and other varieties of seaweed such as wakame and nori, appears in numerous dishes including soup and *kombu* with beans.

Ginger, and it's relative galangal, appear in endless dishes all across Asia. In Thailand and other parts of Asia it's often added to curry pastes while in China it's popular with steamed or grilled fish. Also try Thailand's hot and sour soup, tom yum. Ginger's believed to warm the internal organs, aid digestion and strengthen the immune system. It's even said to ease depression.

In Southeast Asia you should also seek out green papaya salad – possibly Asia's favourite dish. Often eye-wateringly hot, there are countless variations of this virtually fat-free favourite that's full of gloriously healthy ingredients including raw green papaya, chillies, lime juice and packs a flavour punch that will leave you replete. But be warned, it's addictive.

southern Japan. To enjoy the magnificent cherry blossom, visit in spring. Rain falls in early June for a few weeks, followed by hot and humid weather in July. Come in autumn to see the show of changing colours and for cooler weather.

China and Tibet

Getting there   China's main hubs are Beijing, Hong Kong and Shanghai. **British Airways** and **Virgin** fly direct to Hong Kong and Shanghai from London (12 hours). From the US, **Continental** flies direct from Newark to Hong Kong (13 hours); flights via Bangkok may be cheaper. **Air China** flies direct to Beijing from LAX. **Air Canada** flies non-stop from Toronto to Hong Kong (16 hours) and Vancouver to Beijing. Most flights from Australia and New Zealand go via Bangkok or Singapore, though **Cathay Pacific** and **Air New Zealand** fly non-stop to Hong Kong (11 hours).

Best time to visit   China has a continental climate and, given its huge size, large regional variations. Southern China is in a tropical zone, with hot and humid conditions from April to September. Winters are short, lasting from January to March. Spring and autumn have comfortable temperatures but can also be very wet. Tibet is characterized by huge variations in temperature day and night.

Rest of Asia

Getting there   Bangkok is the main international gateway to Laos, Cambodia and Vietnam. Along with Bangkok, Singapore is one of Asia's main transport hubs, offering onward flights to China, India and countries in the Indian Ocean such as Indonesia. For long-haul flights to Asia, it is often cheaper to go via Bangkok or Singapore than fly to a destination non-stop from Europe, North America or Australasia.

Healthy stopovers in Bangkok

The very affordable **Shanti Lodge** on Sri Ayutthaya Road (US$11 per room per night, T+66 (0)2-281 2497) is down a quiet soi next to a flower market and the river, but just one stop by river taxi from the Khao San Road. The rooms are filled with gorgeous Thai touches, and the larger air-conditioned ones at the front have nice bathrooms, large windows and great views of the nearby temple. The garden restaurant serves exceptional Thai and Western veggie food, and there's a breezy space on the second floor for self-practice yoga and Thai massage.

Phranakorn Nornlen Hotel (from US$59 per room per night, T+66 (0)2-628 8188, www.phranakorn-nornlen.com) is a very special little boutique hotel in the heart of the old city with artistic, airy, Thai-style rooms complete with wooden shutters and beautiful rooftop views. There's an intimate, relaxed atmosphere, a small peaceful garden, and amicable staff offer a range of creative pursuits such as cookery classes to assimilate guests into the Thai way of life.

The luxurious **Baan Thai Wellness Retreat** (from US$320 per room per night, T+66 (0)2-258 5403, www.thebaanthai.com), on a quiet soi off Sukhumvit Road, is a collection of traditional Thai teak houses with a spa. Excellent detox scrubs and massages to cure jet lag are on offer (with 24 hours' notice), and you can even have a colonic. There's a steam room, pretty gardens, and a tiny pool. The teak-panelled rooms are cosy if a tad dark. Apple cider vinegar is served before breakfast to kick-start your digestive system, and the Thai food is fantastic, with plenty of nutritious juices on offer.

Wherever you stay, there are plenty of day places in Bangkok to rejuvenate. The **Balavi Natural Health Centre** (191/3 Soi Ranong 1, Praram 6 Rd, T+66 (0)2-615 8822, www.balavi.com)

offers acupuncture, hypnosis and Thai massage, with a natural health fitness centre opposite featuring an iced pool and classes in tai chi, yoga and 'music for health'. **Rasayana Retreat** (41/1 Soi Prommitr, Soi Sukhumvit 39, T+66 (0)2-662 4803, www.rasayanaretreat.com) offers detox programmes, pilates and yoga classes and an excellent raw food café and spa. **Anotai** (976/17 Rim Klong Samsaen Rd, Rama IX, T+66 (0)2-641 5366) is an exceptional organic vegetarian restaurant serving Thai and fusion dishes and delicious desserts, with a peaceful yoga centre above offering drop-in classes and courses. **TRIA Integrative Wellness** (T+66 (0)2-625 6699, www.triaintegrativewellness.com) offers a holistic approach to health in a five-star set-up on Rama IX in the heart of Bangkok. For meditation sessions, contact **The World Fellowship of Buddhists** at Sukhumvit Sois 22-24, Benjasiri Park, T+66 (0)2-661 1284, www.wfb-hq.org.

CAROLINE SYLGE

Thailand

An anything-goes haven with some of the worlds tastiest and healthiest food, Thailand offers everything from exclusive pampering to total detoxing and silent meditation retreats.

Fact file

⮕ **Visa:** Not required for citizens of the US, Canada, Australia, New Zealand and most EU countries including the UK. Visas for citizens of Eastern European countries issued on arrival

ⓘ **Country code:** +66

Ⓢ **Currency:** Baht (THB)

🕑 **Time zone:** GMT+7 hours

⚡ **Electricity:** 220v

ⓘ **Tourist board:**
www.tourismthailand.org

HOTEL & SPA

Evason Hideaway & Spa

🌐 🅿 ♨ ⭘ 🏃 ⊛ ⊗ ⊕ ↘**1**

Pranburi, Hua Hin
T+66 (0)3-261 8200
www.evasonhideaways.com
From US$447 per room per night

If you're jaded but flush with cash, hole up in a private villa at the Evason Hideaway and be eased back to humanity at its Six Senses Earth Spa. Hua Hin beach isn't as wondrous as most Thai beaches, but this is a serene and easy place to focus inwardly and be spoilt rotten by dedicated stuff who take meditation and reiki courses as part of their staff training.

The Earth Spa is a collection of circular domed buildings made of mud mixed with rice husks and straw, surrounded by ponds and linked by wooden walkways. Refreshingly for a top-notch spa, it has no air conditioning, but has been carefully built to keep treatment huts cool. It offers exceptional sleep-inducing treatments with a holistic element, and a whole host of massages including jet lag recovery and lomi lomi. 'Spa Journeys' are delicious facial and massage combos given by two therapists. Treatments use ingredients grown on site, such as aloe vera, lemongrass and papaya.

The restful meditation dome has silver dots of light in the ceiling and giant green cushions on which to sit. Five-day lifestyle programmes such as Meditation De-mystified or De-stress & Balance are on offer, which include one-to-one consultations, health and wellness workshops, signature therapies, and group classes such as yoga and tai chi. Visiting consultants include psychologist,

---

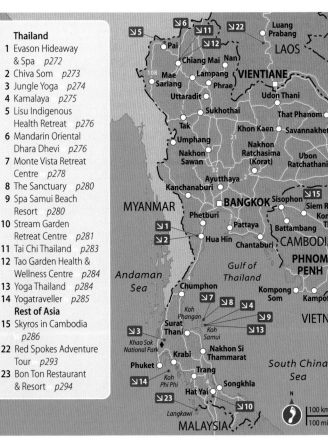

Health and fitness retreat

Chiva Som

Thai businessman Khun Boonchu Rojanastein set up this exclusive hideaway in 1995 inspired by his regular trips during the 1970s to the original Champneys in the UK. Celebrities and Thai royalty come here to hole up – but whoever you are, you'll be treated like a king or queen.

Where you stay The resort is serene and minimalist, with handkerchief lawns and huge banyan trees. Public spaces are dotted with gorgeous displays of orchids, and staff are dressed in traditional costume. Concrete pathways lead to immaculate Thai pavilions with stylish interiors. Some rooms overlook the sea, others are inland. There are indoor and outdoor pools and exercise rooms, a giant hammam, and male and female water suites with steam rooms, saunas and hot tubs. Thoughtful touches make the difference: as you sit in the steam, you're handed a glass of cold water and a cold flannel for your face; fresh red rose petals are strewn across the women's ice-cold plunge pool daily; for a DIY morning cleansing drink, rooms have kettles, lemons and jade stone cutting boards; the oil in your room's burner is changed from lemongrass to lavender if you have difficulty sleeping.

What you do Chiva Som has regular visits from an wide range of international consultants, so tailor your visit accordingly: give up smoking with Deborah Marshall-Warren, learn to meditate with Venerable Phra Mettanado Bikkhu, or have a crystal healing session to unblock your emotions with Sally Forest from Soul-2-Soul in Singapore. Delightful resident anti-ageing consultant, Dr Karl J Neeser, leads retreats for those who want to grow older gracefully.

Every package includes three meals a day, a choice of Thai, Chiva Som or invigorating massage, a health and wellness consultation, and daily group classes in everything from yoga to Thai boxing. Various themed retreats are available, from simple spa and de-stress to special programmes for insomniacs, and a physiotherapy retreat for chronic injuries or back pain. The detox programmes are recommended – Chiva Som therapists are experts at colonics and the Thai abdominal massage, chi nei tsang. For pampering, Chiva Som signature facials and cocoons use products derived from indigenous Thai herbs and ingredients such as wild organic honey.

What you eat Delicious unprocessed food using herbs and vegetables from the organic garden. The Taste of Siam serves Thai dishes and overlooks the beach (you pay extra to eat here on a package). The main restaurant serves more Western-style fusion foods.

> ❝❞
> Much of what I loved about Chiva Som was what makes it special to be in Thailand – the Thai massages in the open-air pavilion, an enlightening chat with a consultant Thai Buddhist monk, my expert abdominal massage, and the serene atmosphere. Chiropractic doctor Philip Parry was the most impressive consultant I saw; his expert manipulation sorted out a painful 'computer' ache in my arm I'd been carrying around for months. I was less convinced by my iridology treatment; somehow I couldn't accept that the 'linen constitution' of my irises showed that I was 'sufficiently in touch with my energy to know when to stop'. At Chiva Som, however, 'stopping' was easy.
>
> *Caroline*

Who goes The rich and famous, couples, lone men and women, some getting over serious illness or sorting out a personal issue, others detoxing or rejuvenating, of all ages and from all over the world.

Essentials Chiva Som (T+66 (0)3-253 6536, www.chivasom.com) is at Hua Hin. The beach isn't Thailand's most beautiful, but it's great for walking along. The minimum length of stay is three nights, which costs from US$1095 per person based on two sharing an Ocean View room. Be sure to book treatments in advance. The nearest airport is Hua Hin – take a shuttle plane from Bangkok, or arrange a three-hour transfer by car. Chiva Some opens a second resort in northern Thailand in 2009/10.

CAROLINE SYLGE

● Soul food

Hands Up Holidays (T+44 (0)20-7193 1062, www.handsupholidays.com) offers you the opportunity to enjoy well-organized cultural and adventure holidays where a third of your trip is spent giving back to the local community through volunteer work. Cultural trips through Thailand with tours of Bangkok and Chiang Mai, trekking, rafting and a Thai cooking class are combined with tsunami relief work in orphanages, teaching English or assisting with wildlife conservation. You can also experience homestay trips in northern Thailand when you can teach, carry out environmental surveys or lay water pipes for the community.

Albert Schmaedick, who runs The Lisu Indigenous Health Retreat (see next spread).

Pristine villas have their own pools, outdoor baths and landscaped gardens – ask for one with a beach view if this is important to you. You can have treatments in your villa, or dine there with your own chef in attendance. A butler will look after your every need. Such decadent privacy makes this a particularly romantic destination (a certain travel writer was even proposed to here).

There's a beachside restaurant, or dine in the open-air living room with seating areas set around a pool of gorgeous pink and purple water lilies (matching the cushions). There's a separate menu for Evason Balanced Cuisine dishes such as roasted red pepper soup, baked snow fish with tomato and olives, wasabi and potato mash, chargrilled tuna steak in salsa verde.

The more affordable **Evason Hua Hin** resort is a five-minute walk away with its own Six Senses Spa. To get a cheaper deal at either resort, book through a tour operator such as Wellbeing Escapes (see Resources). It's 30 minutes from Hua Hin town – you can fly from Bangkok to Hua Hin, or arrange a three-hour transfer by car. There are also Evason Hideaways on Koh Samui and Koh Yao Noi.

YOGA RETREAT
Jungle Yoga

🛶 ⛰ 🏔 ⛵ 🌀 ↘3

Rai Lake, Khao Sok National Park
www.jungleyoga.com
From US$1720 per person for 7 nights

Deep in the heart of Khao Sok National Park, miles away from civilization, Rai Lake offers an idyllic venue for back-to-nature yoga. An impressive range of yoga teachers leads retreats here for practitioners of varying styles: international teachers include Claire Missingham, Simon Low, Clive Sheridan , Danny Paradise and Mary Niker. Courses are booked through individual teachers.

Jungle Yoga is a tiny floating 'village' of bamboo bungalows and an open yoga shala over the lake, surrounded by huge limestone cliffs cloaked in mist makes for a beautiful backdrop to the daily practice. There is no electricity, no phone service or internet, and no real contact with the outside world apart from the occasional delivery of necessities.

Accommodation is very basic. Bathrooms are traditional Thai style with squat toilets, bathing in the lake is popular and the owners ask that guests bring biodegradable toiletries and insect repellent where possible. Bungalows are sparsely furnished, with thin mattresses, but there are plenty of hammocks for stargazing and wildlife spotting. The best way to explore the surroundings is by kayak, although guided jungle treks are possible.

The only drawback is the occasional unwanted spider and unavoidable leeches, but mosquitoes are a rarity. Bring leech socks, repellent and cigarette lighters and contact the owners for advice on seasonal patterns.

Fly from Bangkok to Surat Thani or Krabi, where group transfers are available to the wildlife sanctuary headquarters. From here it's a one-hour boat ride, followed by a half-hour hike to Rai Lake and a 10-minute raft ride to the bungalows. Also check out Golden Buddha Beach Resort (www.goldenbuddharesort.com) on Koh Phra Thong (see page 277).

Above: Evason Hideaway & Spa. **Right top and bottom:** Jungle Yoga.

Island retreat

Kamalaya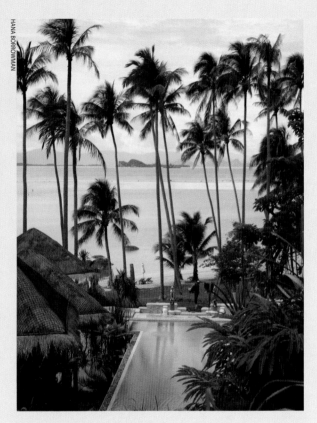

Nestled in a boulder-strewn ravine with luscious tropical gardens trickling down to an idyllic lagoon and vanilla-coloured beach, Kamalaya's wellness sanctuary offers a different kind of retreat experience for soul-seekers and self-indulgent sybarites.

Where you stay Kamalaya is a powerfully rejuvenating space. The settlement is centred round a tiny cave temple that once served as a place of meditative retreat for Buddhist monks. At the heart of the site is the holistic spa, whose majestic views over the bay add an extra edge to the treatment rooms, yoga pavilions and dramatic Yantra Hall where seminars and workshops are held. Sensitively designed villas, bungalows and suites are tucked into the natural landscape down the steep hillside and feature modern interior design with an emphasis on serenity and comfort. Boulders form part of bathrooms, pools straddle lotus-studded ponds, trees grow in communal spaces and the spectacular steam room and plunge pools are set into natural rock.

What you do As much or as little as you want. A variety of relaxation and rejuvenation programmes draw on Oriental and Western holistic healing practices, each beginning with a medical and personal wellness consultation to assess your needs, prescribing anything from gentle nurturing to fitness motivation. Expert help is at hand from all manner of doctors and therapists, from acupuncturists to visiting spiritual gurus.

Detoxing here involves feasting not fasting, and the menu features an imaginative range of detox dishes. The spa menu also offers an array of unexpected and exotic pampering treats, including traditional Chinese medicine, naturopathic and even ayurvedic therapies.

Alongside the modern equipment in the gym, a daily programme of complimentary classes is available, often taking place outdoors. They include yoga classes, expressive dance, pilates, adventure hikes, sound therapy, chakra balancing, kayaking and martial arts.

What you eat and drink Detox dishes include Thai soups bursting with herbs, steamed green vegetables with reduced herbal ragouts and huge raw salads, or distinctly indulgent dishes like lamb chops with mashed potato, and apple pie. Breakfast is a gloriously healthy buffet of tropical fruits, freshly prepared juices and imaginative muesli and salad ingredients. Breakfast and dinner are served in the restaurant atop the hill, while a sumptuous barbecue or à la carte lunch is served in romantic shalas by the pool.

HANA BORROWMAN

Who goes A colourful variety of upmarket, well-travelled, both super chic and plain eccentric soul-seekers. Also spiritual tourists, as well as self-indulgent hedonists with an eye for style and substance.

Essentials Kamalaya (T+66 (0)7-742 9800, www.kamalaya.com), Laem Set Beach, Koh Samui, costs from US$250 per person per night. It's fairly remote and peaceful so don't expect to see any evidence of Samui's party scene. Most packages are three days minimum, and you need this to really feel the effects of the surrounds. The hillside settlement makes for steep climbs as well as beautiful views. Try the paths winding through the foliage, your thighs will thank you for it. International flights fly direct to Samui; from there take a taxi, minibus or songtaew (shared taxi), 45 minutes.

❝❞

I arrived feeling travel sick, and not remotely in the mood for forging new spiritual paths or serious soul mining. But things evolve fast at Kamalaya. Even as I stepped onto the cool stone floor of my bungalow and took in the coconut-plantation panoramas, the magic was tangible. This is no ordinary spa. Plenty of gentle nurturing at the hands of my reassuringly informed wellness consultant and encouraging nurse, along with some intense hands-on healing on the massage bed and deep breaths in the steam room, and I gently floated down to earth three days later, gypsy spirit fully intact.

Hana Borrowman

VILLAGE RETREAT

Lisu Indigenous Health Retreat

🜨 ☀ ○ ⋔ ◉ ✿ ○ ♒ ⛌5

Non Thong, near Soppong
T+66 (0)8-9998 4886
www.lisuhilltribecrafts.blogspot.com/
From US$8 per person per night

Lisu Indigenous Health Retreat is the creation of American holistic health therapist, Albert Schmaedick, and his wife Susanan, a member of the Lisu mountain people. Located in a traditional Lisu village, one hour north of Pai (see box on next spread) in northern Thailand, it was set up in late 2006 to help preserve the Lisu's lifestyle and traditional ways of healing. Originally from Tibet and the far north of China, the semi-nomadic Lisu are generous and warm, with a great sense of humour, and this is a wonderful opportunity to get back to grassroots level.

Come for a night or several weeks – there are lots of interesting things on offer for the jaded and world weary. Trek into the mountains with a Lisu villager and English-speaking guide to pick edible wild foods and learn about traditional herbal medicine. Have a daily Lisu massage, which is gentler and more intuitive than Thai massage, and similar to acupressure. Learn jewellery-making with Albert, make and play traditional Lisu instruments such as the gourd flute, take dance and chanting workshops, learn to sew and weave, or try your hand at earth home building and grass roof construction.

If you're toxic and confused, there are also health programmes available. Albert is a clinical psychologist, practising Buddhist and professional lifestyle consultant and nutritionist who ran his own detox retreat in California for five years. Take one-to-one lifestyle and emotional clearing sessions with him, or embark on a full week's detox (US$400 per person for seven days all inclusive). Three- and ten-day meditation retreats are also on offer, when you can learn and practise vipassana meditation with a Thai Buddhist monk. You'll also have a chance to find out more about Lisu spirituality, which is a mix of animism and Buddhism with some Christian influence.

There are four guest rooms, each sleeping twoin a newly built lodge. Decor is traditional Lisu with a few added creature comforts. You can also stay in a local village bamboo home if you choose. Food is traditional Lisu fare, mostly vegetables grown in the surrounding forest with home-produced pork and chicken, and local freshwater fish. Vegetarian and special diets are easily catered for.

Local buses from Chiang Mai to Soppong take about four hours, or fly from Chiang Mai to Mae Hong Song, and take a two-hour bus ride to Soppong. Book at least a day ahead and you'll be met at the bus stop. Workshops cost from US$25 per day. Albert works as a regular consultant to upmarket resorts such as the Earth Spa at the Evason Hideaway (see page 272).

ALBERT SCHMAEDICK

Lisu Indigenous Health Retreat.

HOTEL & SPA

Mandarin Oriental Dhara Dhevi

🜨 🜨 ☀ ⋔ ◉ ✿ ❁ ⛌6

Chiang Mai
T+66 (0)5-388 8888
www.mandarinoriental.com
From US$390 per room per night

Amid a host of holistic hideaways and wellness centres around north Thailand's capital, the Dhara Dhevi offers a traditional northern Thai experience with a hedonistic twist. The ambience is fantastically serene but in no way forced, and despite the emphasis on luxury, nature still dominates. Birdsong and the farmers' flutes in the paddy fields create a soundtrack to your stay.

Inspired by a Lanna palace, the attention to detail is apparent from the start. Guests can arrive in a horse-drawn carriage or be pedalled in a silver rickshaw over cobblestones, through a village of shops, past a fairy-tale landscape of chuckling rivers, temples, exquisite carved wood structures and up a sweeping driveway to a palatial reception.

Accommodation is in two-storey teakwood villas based on Thai-style high-gabled homes, with interiors crafted by artisans, and personal butlers on hand. Each villa is set in its own grounds around working paddy fields complete with buffalo, lakes, meandering streams and tropical gardens with private swimming pools. One villa nestles in a cottage garden. Verandas overlooking these idyllic views feature whirlpool tubs and wooden massage beds. The Colonial Suites, which opened early 2007, offer marginally less luxurious, European-style accommodation.

The spa and ayurveda centre is set in stunning Thai buildings which reach for the heavens and offer an extensive range of therapies and treatments based on regional

Privacy in Phuket

Long established as a destination for more glamorous tropical getaways, Phuket's beautiful beaches still draw in the tourist hordes, despite the devastation wreaked by the 2004 tsunami. But away from the crowds and building work, Phuket's wilder charms and lush tropical landscapes make a prime location for relaxing resorts to pamper and rejuvenate body and soul.

The first of the world-renowned chain of Amanresorts, Amanpuri's **Aman Spa** (from US$525 per pavilion per night, T+66 (0)7-632 4333, www.amanresorts.com) is a superbly stylish hideaway in an awesome beachside location that offers the ultimate in exclusivity. The resort's traditional Thai architecture has contemporary minimalist touches, and the vast tropical grounds create a sense of spacious seclusion. Top-end villas have their own pools and outdoor living areas as well as separate quarters for the personal live-in maid and chef. The spa itself, which is only open to residents, is an oasis of chic serenity. Regal teakwood shalas and open-sided yoga/meditation pavilions sit on a tree-shaded hillside overlooking the Andaman Sea, and a range of unique holistic bodywork and spa treatments is available.

Phuket is also home to the first of the worldwide chain of exclusive Banyan Tree hotels, and Phuket's **Banyan Tree** (from US$550 per villa per night, T+66 (0)7-632 4374, www.banyantree.com/phuket) has won numerous awards for its combination of extravagant accommodation and Asian spa expertise. Privacy is prioritized over the prettiness of the resort, with the walled villas packed fairly tightly together, but the ostentatious interiors, private gardens and landscaped spa make up for the lack of aesthetic appeal. The spa is also home to the chain's Spa Academy, where 300 hours of training are undertaken by all Banyan Tree therapists. Complimentary yoga, pilates and meditation are offered, though the emphasis here is on perfecting the art of pampering rather than life-changing spiritual pursuits.

Though far less upscale, the **Atsumi Healing Resort** (T+66 (0)8-1272 0571, www.atsumihealing.com) fasting and detoxing retreats offer relaxed and exceptionally personal services in a tranquil tropical garden. Accommodation is in peaceful homely villas and studio apartments surrounded by rubber trees and gardens. To support the fasting programmes, facilities and treatments available include yoga and qigong, meditation and massage as well as purpose-built private colon hydrotherapy rooms. Guests are offered a range of physical, spiritual and emotional support and there are resident therapists for osteopathy, acupuncture, shiatsu and NLP. Expect to pay from US$140 for a four-day fasting programme including accommodation.

For something more remote, the eco-friendly **Golden Buddha Beach Resort** (www.goldenbuddharesort.com) re-opened on Koh Phra Thong at the end of 2006 after being destroyed by the tsunami. Reached by longtail boat from Kuraburi on Phuket, it offers a place to chill out as well as yoga retreats and voluntary work placements.

BANYAN TREE

◐ Body language

Thai massage

One of the most effective and stimulating massages around, Thai massage is based on the theory that we have 10 major life energy lines running through our bodies, known as *sen sib*. To balance energy and release blocks, the therapist uses her palms, fingers, elbows, forearms and feet to perform intense stretches and pressure-point massage along these 10 lines, pulling, pressing, lifting and loosening muscles and joints. Also called Thai yoga massage, it is sometimes referred to as a 'lazy person's yoga', but it is actually far from a lazy experience, and can hurt like hell, depending on how stiff you are. You lie on a wide mat, dressed in loose, comfortable clothing, and the more you relax and give yourself up to the pain, the more effective the massage will be.

Though the Thais are experts at the art, its origins can be traced back to India and an ayurvedic doctor called Shivago Komarpaj, who is said to have treated the Buddha himself. Thousands of years later, some of his notes still remain intact, and Thai King Rama III commissioned the carving of them onto the walls of Wat Po temple in Bangkok, which was founded in 1788 as Thailand's first university.

At the temple today you'll find life-sized figurines of devotees in pretzel-like yoga and massage shapes pulling pained faces, but it's not all agony at the **Wat Po School of Thai Massage** (www.watpomassage.com). Set in the grounds of the temple, it offers authentic and affordable massage in communal, fan-cooled rooms by practitioners who are trained on site. If you want to master the fine art yourself, you can also learn massage here – you'll be black and blue by the end of it from each other's mistakes but you'll become a pretty good masseuse. The **Institute of Thai Massage** in Chiang Mai (T+66 (0)5-321 8632, www.itm.infothai.com), offers 13 different courses, including a five-day foundation in Thai massage for US$150.

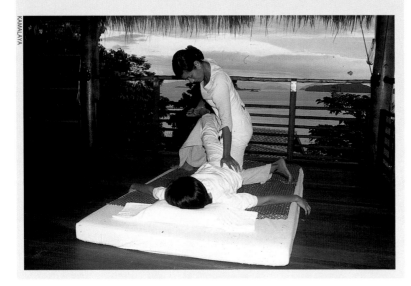

KAMALAYA

and ancient healing techniques. The 'Lanna Signature Experience' combines a body scrub, oil massage and gentle tapping technique performed with a wooden stick which sounds slightly tortuous, but is in fact subtly soothing and a sure cure for insomnia. The region's holistic experts have helped to develop the varied spa menu and the centre caters for all kinds of pampering from herbal hammams to lymphatic drainage massage and watsu.

Alongside yoga and meditation, craft workshops and demonstrations are carried out every morning. There is also a Thai cooking school with daily market tours, and various excursions into the surrounding countryside. Among the several restaurants, bars and cafés in various beautiful settings, Le Grand Lanna gets the ultimate stamp of approval with regular visits from Thai royalty.

The best time to visit Chiang Mai is between October and April. Fly from Bangkok and then take a taxi or request a pickup for the 15-minute drive from Chiang Mai airport.

ISLAND RETREAT

Monte Vista Retreat Centre

🍃 🌿 🌱 ✺ ☀ ○ 🌀 ⊚ ❂ ⬈7

Thong Sala, Koh Phangan
T+66 (0)7-723 8951
www.montevistathailand.com
From US$200 per person for 3 days

A small healing centre among the rocks and trees, in a peaceful spot overlooking the sea, Monte Vista was set up in 2003 by Norm and Mohanie Brown. With a warm, family feel and just nine simple wooden bungalows, it offers a friendly, safe, supportive environment for individual development and exploration. A relative newcomer to Thailand's spa and fasting scene, Monte Vista has already established a word-of-mouth reputation for its magical atmosphere.

Although best known for its 'Cleansing and Self-healing' programmes, which consist mainly of fasting and colonic treatments, the centre also offers a huge variety of self-development courses, including

A slice of Pai

A sleepy little town in Thailand's far north, Pai holds a host of opportunities for travellers looking to bolster body and soul with a combination of stunning natural surrounds, spiritual ambience and healthy attractions. Despite a bustling community of free-spirited expats and a steady flow of backpackers, it is still a laid-back haven compared to more hectic tourist enclaves elsewhere.

Pai's relaxed alternative atmosphere encourages plentiful yoga and meditation sessions, vegetarian restaurants, quiet afternoons and chilled evenings where people gather around campfires with guitars. The tourist hordes are possibly kept at bay by the three-to-four-hour roller-coaster bus ride over the mountains from Chiang Mai or Mae Hong Song – but the breathtaking tropical rainforest views make the long and winding roads just about bearable.

The small riverside town is easy to explore on foot, and noticeboards on the street or in the multitude of cool little cafés, bars and tea shops advertise the latest activities and independent teachers and holistic practitioners. **Mam's Yoga School** (T+66 (0)8-9954 4981) offers quirky daily hatha yoga classes and courses in the exotic home of a former Thai beauty queen and Indian-trained yoga teacher. More serious yogis are advised to plan their trip in the first week of February to coincide with the annual anusara yoga retreat (www.shantaya.org). Held at the picturesque hot spring-fed **Spa Exotic Home**, it offers an intensive introduction with five hours of daily practice including pranayama (breath work) and the 'universal principles of alignment'.

Among the plethora of places to get pummelled and indulge in a variety of cheap body treats, is **Mr Jan's Massage**, set in a heavily foliaged herb garden in the centre of town (see below). The much-lauded **Pai Traditional Massage** is on Sukhaphiban 1 Road, T+66 (0)5-369 9121 (training courses also available).

Other daytime activities can be found just outside of town: hire a bicycle and head out to enjoy waterfalls and wildlife, temples, hot springs and more physical activities such as trekking and rafting. By night there is a handful of popular jazz cafés, veggie restaurants and curative herbal whiskies to experiment with. Adventurous types can also trek to nearby ethnic villages, or to Doi Inthanon, one of the country's most famous peaks and national parks.

Among the plentiful and cheap accommodation options are thatched huts sitting directly over the river at **Baan Tawan** on the east side of town (117 Moo 4 Viangtai, T+66 (0)5-369 8116, rooms from US$14), beds among the branches at **Pai Treehouses** (T+66 (0)5-369 3271, www.paitreehouse.com,

rooms from US$18), little inexpensive houses in the herb gardens of **Mr Jan's Massage** (Soi Wanchanloem, T+66 (0)5-369 9554, rooms from US$8) and simple adobe homestays set deep in the valley among paddy fields at **Amy's Earth House** (T+66 (0)8-6190 2394, www.amyshouse.net, rooms from US$9). There's even a nearby spa camping resort complete with pretty wood and stone villas and hot mineral-water showers at **Tha Pai Spa** (T+66 (0)5-369 3267, www.thapaispa.com, rooms from US$16). See www.paitown.com for more information on Pai itself, as well as travel details, accommodation, attractions and events.

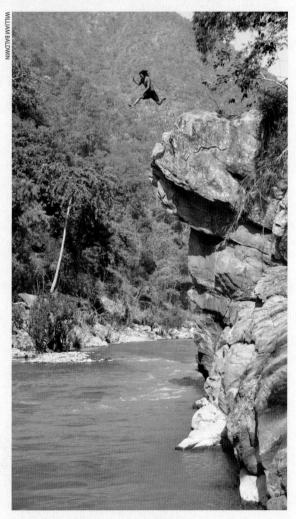

WILLIAM BALDWIN

Asia Thailand

Shamanic Journey and Spiritual Initiation 'Life Flow' courses. These entail living and working as part of the Monte Vista community, individual counselling and daily tailor-made exercises designed to act as catalysts to aid personal change. Guidance in the form of counselling, palm readings and psychic exploration is also on offer.

Programmes are designed specifically for each individual, and the team of holistic health practitioners, together with Norm and Mohanie, offer 24-hour hands-on support for their guests. There are daily morning yoga sessions on a platform overlooking the sea, healthy home-made meals eaten together (for non-fasters), group sunset meditation and evening activities such as storytelling, watching films or spontaneous dance sessions.

There are direct international flights to Koh Samui. From there, ferries take about 45 minutes to Thong Sala pier on Koh Phangan. Monte Vista is a 10-minute walk from the pier.

Above: The Sanctuary. **Below right**: Spa Samui.

ISLAND RETREAT

The Sanctuary

⊕ ⊕ ⊕ ☀ ⊙ ⊛ ⊚ ⊕ ⊕ ⊕ ⊠8

Haad Tien, Koh Phangan
T+66 (0)1-271 3614 (limited hours)
www.thesanctuary-kpg.com.
From US$22 per room per night

Set in a beautiful jungle environment above a rugged beach on Thailand's wildest party island, The Sanctuary sells itself on a unique 'detox, retox' philosophy. Guests can opt to spend their time fasting on one- to seven-day cleansing programmes, or feasting on a variety of self-indulgent treats and lounging in the tropical surrounds.

The detox area offers a wellness centre with cleansing programmes focusing on fasting, relaxation and self-administered colonic irrigation, while the upbeat bar and restaurant's retox space offers chill-out sounds, great food, beer, cocktails, fine wine and a distinctly bohemian beachside vibe. Both areas are blessed with stunning sea views and plenty of options for horizontal

contemplation in the multiple hammocks and scattered floor cushions.

The selection of goodies on offer is varied. Two yoga teachers provide daily classes in separate halls (US$7.50 per session). Free meditation classes are offered four days a week. A separate area houses a herbal sauna built into a rock, a somewhat murky plunge pool, and a therapy room offering exotic-sounding massages using natural local ingredients. A variety of self-development workshops and courses is also on offer, from yoga retreats to group-rebirthing sessions.

Once a simple hippy-style haven, the hammocks and boho atmosphere remain, but now feature more than a dash of practical and beautiful design. Accommodation is secreted away in the jungle, much of it built into the natural rock. The best is in beautiful, huge open-plan houses exposed to dramatic sea views – cheaper accommodation is less spacious and with fewer charming frills. There's cheap-as-chips dormitory accommodation, and a separate yoga space set apart on the hillside, with a sea-view pavilion, eight rooms and shared kitchen and bathroom facilities, which can be rented out for group retreats.

The extensive menu of healthy and self-indulgent delights features over 300 items, including Asian and Western dishes, and a comprehensive selection of healthy and raw meals for pre- and post-fasters. The restaurant is a big draw for The Sanctuary's army of return visitors, seduced by the allure

of the home-baked bread and cakes, home-made yoghurt and home-grown garden delights such as the hydroponically grown salad, as well as the excellent seafood. Fasters be warned.

The Sanctuary attracts a self-consciously funky mix of people, from hip new experience-seekers to fun-seeking expats with a taste for the alternative. International carriers fly direct to Koh Samui, and regular boats run from Samui to Koh Phangan. From Hat Rin or Thong Sala pier charter a longtail boat to Haad Tien (45 minutes).

DETOX RETEAT

Spa Samui Beach Resort

⊕ ⊕ ⊕ ☀ ⊙ ⊛ ⊚ ⊕ ⊕ ⊕ ⊠9

Lamai Beach, Koh Samui
T+66 (0)7-723 0855
www.spasamui.com
From US$200 for a 3-day fast

Holding the prestigious title of the island's original spa, Spa Samui opened over a decade ago with six simple bungalows. Now a famous, funky, holistic haven, it has stuck to its ethos of simplicity with its 'self-help, clean-me-out' health programmes which combine fasting, tropical resort-style relaxation and self-administered colonic cleanses to give a whole new meaning to the term 'beach bum'.

The small bustling beach resort, with its pool, three yoga and massage shalas, communal relaxation areas, herbal steam room, beauty salon and large health centre, is friendly, well-tended and clean, with a charmingly laid-back community feel. Several different styles of accommodation are scattered among the trees around a fairly compact and hotchpotch beachside setting. Snazzy wooden A-frame bungalows are set around the pool and hotel-style rooms sit above the health centre. Simpler beach huts, with slightly weathered interiors and ancient electrical appliances, might be a little too basic for the fussier faster.

A little further down the beach are two private luxury villas with their own pools. Unfortunately the sea at the spa end of this

“ ”

When I first visited Spa Samui, I hadn't intended to flush, twice daily, 16 litres of water mixed with vinegar and coffee through my colon, using a suspended bucket and a piece of tubing. But everybody else seemed to be doing it, so I gave it a try. By day two I was getting bored with constant trips to the toilet. By day three I was looking a little thin in the face. By day four I was dragged down by all sorts of anxious achy feelings. By day five, however, I started to feel a whole lot better. After seven days, I felt more alive than I had done in a long time – possibly years – and this feeling lasted for many months. Detoxing with colonics is not for everyone, but it certainly worked for me. Daily Thai massage, herbal steams, and the spa's gentle ambience also helped.

Caroline

long beach gathers the bay's debris so is not ideal for swimming. The sister 'village' resort up in the mountains offers similar accommodation, along with a change of scenery, views over the island, raw food restaurant and workshops.

Fasts involve a daily routine of detox drinks and herbal supplements every three hours, and twice-daily colonic cleanses. Colonic irrigation is not for everyone, and you can do a fast without it if you choose. Contrary to popular thought, you won't go hungry – the bentonite clay included in your detox drinks keeps the pangs at bay. Optional daily yoga, qigong and (free) meditation sessions are available, as well as daily Thai massages and herbal steams. Health talks and other gatherings such as tea ceremonies encourage a social atmosphere.

Spa Samui is a mecca for the island's numerous holistic health practitioners, and services from reiki and craniosacral therapies through to hypnotherapy and palmistry are available. Plenty of free information and support is offered in the form of literature and videos on health and nutrition. A fasting manager is on call daily from 1300 to 2000.

Spa Samui attracts singles, couples and families from around the globe. Expect a mind-boggling mix, everyone from British backpackers to Thai celebrities. Non-fasters can enjoy the amazing and extensive restaurant menu specializing in healthy Thai vegetarian dishes, salads and imaginative raw food. The menu also features excellent seafood, meat and alcohol, and smoking is allowed outdoors. A 3½-day semi-fast is US$200, while a seven-day fast is US$300.

For a touch of luxury during your fast here, head up the hill to **Tamarind Springs** (T+66 (0)7-742 4221, www.tamarindretreat.com), which has an airy colonial-style wooden café, a steam room based in a hollowed out boulder, and a lagoon under a waterfall where you can take a dip. Expert massages, wraps and facials are carried out in thatched pavilion treatment rooms on the hillside.

WATERSIDE RETREAT

Stream Garden Retreat Centre

Hat Yai
T+66 (0)1-328 7132
www.anveekshana.org
From US$64 per person in shared room

The only Krishnamurti retreat in southeast Asia, the Stream Garden Retreat Centre, in Thailand's deep south, offers a space for individual development and discussion of the renowned Indian philosopher's teachings while staying in forest huts alongside a river. Krishnamurti advocated self-sufficiency, self-reliance, solitude, free reflection and in-depth self-enquiry, and his work has inspired writers, artists and thinkers around the globe. The relaxed ambience and serene riverside setting creates the perfect place to contemplate his teachings.

The retreat centre is owned by the **Quest**

Asia Thailand

SPA SAMUI

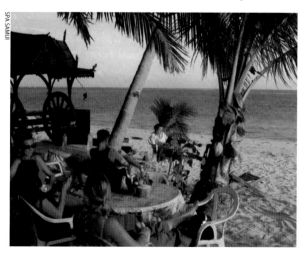

SPA SAMUI

◑ Body language

Breathe deep: meditating in Thailand

Theravada Buddhism became the dominant form in southeast Asia in the 11th century, and its followers practise vipassana or insight meditation (see glossary). Thailand offers many retreats where you can learn to meditate in this tradition, with a warm climate and serene environment to boot.

For vipassana in the forest, **Suan Mokkh Buddhist Monastery** (www.suanmokkh.org) at Chaiya, north of Surat Thani, runs popular 10-day silent meditation retreats every month at its International Dharma Hermitage, starting on the first day of each month. You can't book in advance – turn up the morning of the day before to register. See opposite for a first-person account.

Wat Kow Tahm International Center(www.watkowtahm. org) on Koh Phangan, offers 10- and 20-day meditation retreats, as well as longer work retreats, led by resident Western teachers Rosemary and Steve Weissman, who have been teaching vipassana meditation for nearly 20 years. During the 10-day retreat there are three one-to-one, as well as group, sessions.

The **Northern Insight Meditation Center** (www.watrampoeng.org), at Wat Rampoeng, is tucked away in a leafy suburb of Chiang Mai, with a beautiful old stupa and attractive central ceremony hall. It runs 10- or 26-day basic courses, and a maximum stay of six weeks is allowed. Along with the relatively high number of overseas guests at the temple are plenty of Thai practitioners of all ages and backgrounds.

KAMALAYA

I haven't spoken a word in eight days. From my agonizing half-lotus position in the meditation hall, I watch William the English monk draw finger-circles on the table in front of him. "Life is an uncomfortable business, but we suffer because we turn it into a 'me' experience", he says. Intense, wiry and intelligent, he is determined to demolish our egos and follows his hour-long talk on how ludicrous we are by wishing we "have a nice day".

I am nearing the end of a 10-day meditation retreat at Suan Mokkh. To take away distractions and free the mind to learn to meditate, we're not allowed to read, write, draw, smoke, listen to music or drink anything other than herbal tea. Men and women are segregated. We sleep on straw mats with wooden pillows. We are woken at 0400, wash by communal pools, eat only two meals a day and do daily domestic chores. On top of a vow of silence.

There are 65 of us, mostly Europeans, with a few Thai students and some earnest-looking Americans. Over a hot chocolate before 'going into silence' I discover we're a pretty mixed bunch: a stressed-out marketing director, a woman recovering from ME, a sprinkling of year-out backpackers and a painter in his sixties.

Every day we meditate in 30- to 45-minute sessions, for a total of five hours. During my first session, I develop an intense ache in the centre of my spine, an irritating itch at the side of my neck, and a numb left foot. As I try to concentrate on my in and out breath it feels like someone is pushing their thumbs very hard into every stiff inch of my body. My mind jumps about like a monkey. I reorganize the furniture in my house, chuck out half the contents of my wardrobe, and worry about the obscene amount of money I've just spent in Bangkok. Once I have shifted, itched, rubbed, twisted and rotated my body to get comfortable again, the bell chimes and we can stop. Lovely, I think. Time for a cup of tea.

When we're not sitting to meditate, we're walking. As I tread six feet, turn around and walk back across the same six feet, I am painfully aware of everybody around me doing the same thing. I hallucinate that I am in a home for the mentally unsound aimlessly wandering about coconut groves in floaty clothing. Except that I am aimlessly wandering about coconut groves in floaty clothing.

I learn that desire, aversion, sleepiness, restlessness and doubt will all collude to stop me from meditating. I want to see a stand-up comedy show and down a bottle of champagne. I make wildly unrealistic plans to build my own house on return to the UK. People I haven't thought about in years pop unwelcome into my head.

During yoga I lie down while everyone else does sun salutations. I drink a lot of tea – the peak experience on offer.

During this time my daily chore saves me, by giving me the opportunity to swear out loud. I choose the rather tranquil-sounding task of 'offering water to the young plants by the third pond'. What this actually involves is me carrying heavy buckets of water under the pelting sun to plants that are buried in thigh-high grass, which is full of red ants that climb inside my clothing and bite.

On day four I develop a bout of hiccups, much to the amusement of my neighbour and myself, which is just as well, for at that stage I am in dire need of a good laugh – and I am not the only one. That afternoon after a particularly gloomy talk from William, one of the women swiftly crosses the sand towards a lone tree. Is she crying, we all think in horror? No, she is laughing! The rest of us stare after her, rather affronted that she has dared to express a personality.

That evening, however, I sit through a whole 45-minute session without fidgeting. The next morning, I find myself mesmerized by the movement of my leg dangling over a concrete slab. I notice the bananas growing ten feet away from the dining room – while I'm eating a banana. Keeping silent is, I find, actually quite refreshing. No need to bother with small talk – and it feels great to be smiled at by someone when you haven't exchanged a word for days.

In the dining hall it's unnerving at first to eat opposite someone without speaking, but by day five we are more comfortably spread out, and, instead of spooning great mounds of vegetable rice into our bowls and gobbling it up too quickly, our appetites have dwindled and we need smaller helpings to fill us up. Our embarrassed silence turns into a peaceful one. I start to feel kind of good.

Wandering a meditation hall on day six, I come across a sketch of a seated Buddha inscribed with the words, "Oh boundless joy, to find at last there is no happiness in this world." It sounds like a line from a comedy sketch, but then I recall William's words: we exist as perfect beings regardless of our families and personal hang-ups, and are much more than the 'me' that feels happy and sad. We're ok, whatever we experience. Buddhism starts to make real sense.

Three people leave early. I feel strangely uplifted that someone has had the guts to walk out. But every time my craving for release hits desperation point, a nun or monk changes my mind. Their talks are soothing, witty, highly intelligent and especially candid when it comes to their own life stories. William used to be a psychotherapist, the monk who teaches Pali chanting entered the monastery after discovering his girlfriend was pregnant by another man, the nun who teaches yoga turned to meditation at 27 after stomach cancer and a successful career in advertising.

Tonight, as every night, we have a group walking meditation around two of the ponds. We walk one behind the other, lit by candlelight and the moon, accompanied by the sound of soft pad of bare feet on sand. I think what a miracle it is that all of us can co-habit quietly together for so long, and take a long deep drag of what the monks call 'Buddha's cigarette'. It may just be the sweltering heat that has stunned us all into silence, but that's ok by me.

Caroline

Foundation Thailand, who hold retreats here to discuss Krishnamurti's work and themes. Expect simple accommodation. There's an on-site restaurant and library, international guests are warmly welcomed and talks are given in English and Thai. An annual international gathering provides discussions and video viewings related to Krishnamurti's teachings, along with plenty of time for self-reflection, sightseeing, trekking, yoga and various cultural programmes.

Fly from Bangkok to Hat Yai. The retreat centre provides bus/car transfer to and from the airport.

TAI CHI RETREAT

Tai Chi Thailand

Chiang Mai
T+66 (0)8-1706 7406
www.taichithailand.com
US$418 for 10 days

Although this intensive 10-day tai chi course is conducted in a simple, understated spot in the outskirts of Chiang Mai, it has earned itself an impressive reputation for its life-changing qualities. The Introductory Training Program in The Essential Postures of Tai Chi Chuan runs on the first and 16th of every month and is open to beginners as well as those already practicing tai chi.

The course is taught by American-born Keith Good who has over a decade of teaching experience. He shares the teaching with co-instructor, Mrs Tubtim Khumsing, who has six years experience in the programme. Far from simply offering tutoring in the postures of tai chi, students also study philosophy and theory, including ancient Taoist texts, such as the I-Ching and the Tao Te Ching, as well as Chinese medical chi theory.

Most classes take place on a simple roof-top garden where the breeze and jumble of mats and plants make for a friendly, relaxed environment. The training schedule includes sitting and walking meditation, qigong and relaxation techniques. Classes are limited to just 12 students, guaranteeing some

With silent mind one hears even the leaves of grass counselling each other with this beautiful, witty fact: all beings may dance at ease in the breeze with minds left silent by laying to rest all things.

Tan Ajarn Buddhadasa

one-to-one attention. The relatively isolated location lends itself well to the course, which is intensive; there's only one break in classes on day five. The atmosphere is relaxed and sociable and students are encouraged to develop at their own pace.

The accommodation and rooftop practice area are located in an apartment-style block, originally built as an overflow dormitory for university students, in a non-tourist area approximately 3 km from the centre of Chiang Mai. Accordingly, the en suite single or double occupancy rooms are basic, but clean, and homely.

Plenty of fresh fruit, coffee, herbal tea and bottled water is included in the course fee but meals are not, so guests are encouraged to explore the nearby inexpensive local restaurants and foodstalls. A Chinese doctor provides acupuncture and herbal treatments, and a craniosacral therapist and Shaolin masseur also offer treatments on site.

The course attracts a vibrant, open-minded mix of students from around the globe, with most aged between 20 and 45. Although an ideal introduction to tai chi, the course also tends to attract individuals who want to deepen their practice and study the fundamentals. You can stay on in the accommodation and continue to practise for about US$7 a night. Fly from Bangkok to Chiang Mai and take a 30- to 45-minute taxi ride to Naisuan House.

RURAL RETREAT

Tao Garden Health and Wellness Centre

Chiang Mai
T+66 (0)5-349 5596
www.tao-garden.com
From US$62 per person per night

This secluded retreat set among banana groves, papaya plantations and organic rice paddies on the outskirts of Chiang Mai was initially established as a training facility for the students of Taoist meditation and qigong master Mantak Chia. A decade on and the garden retreat now provides a holistic hideaway for guests seeking out spa treatments with a spiritual edge. Therapists from Chiva Som train here in the Thai abdominal massage, chi nei tsang.

The Tao healing system developed by Master Chia combines Taoism, Chinese, Thai and ayurvedic medicine with more technical facilities such as infrared and ozone-based therapies. Guests have access to a variety of health specialists and doctors, and can sample a huge range of massage techniques, therapies and treatments, including daily qigong, tao yin (Chinese yoga) and six healing sounds meditation.

Accommodation options include fairly spartan but comfortable and clean en suite

rooms, or more luxurious townhouses, which contain three guest rooms. The spa's health restaurant offers a Tao nutrition diet, mainly consisting of food organically grown on the premises. Fly to Chiang Mai airport and take a 30-minute taxi ride to Tao Garden.

YOGA RETREAT

Yoga Thailand

Bang Po beach, Ban Tai, Koh Samui
T+66 (0)7-744 7245
www.yoga-thailand.com
From US$50 per room per night

Although situated on an island best known for its dizzying mix of hedonism and holistic health, the Yoga Thailand retreat centre has built a strong reputation for its intensive ashtanga holidays and yoga teacher training. Occupying a secluded spot on Bang Po beach, well away from the tourist masses, this small resort is owned and run by a husband and wife team, Paul and Jutima Dallaghan.

Classes and retreats are led by Paul along with a handful of resident and guest teachers, and yoga workshops on topics such as anatomy and pranayama run regularly. The daily schedules consist of self-practice six mornings a week, with each student working independently at his or her own level and pace, overseen and guided by the teacher. Restorative stretching classes take place in the afternoons and guided meditation in the evenings. There's a large hand-built wooden yoga shala set in pretty gardens looking directly over the beach. The shala's sliding glass doors open onto a terrace where ayurvedic meals are served. Guests stay in simple but spacious en suite concrete bungalows which surround the shala, and sharing a room is the norm.

The beach here is attractive though not ideal for swimming at low tide, but to loosen the muscles there's an on-site steam room (at extra cost) and a massage shala overlooking the ocean.

The self-contained nature of the resort and all-inclusive packages make for an authentic

retreat atmosphere with little distraction from the outside world. Guests include a fairly equal mix of men and women at all levels of yoga experience, although most have some knowledge of ashtanga. The yogic guidelines of the environment include no smoking or alcohol, and keeping noise levels low at all times. Retreats start at three days. Weekly and fortnightly courses are also available, from US$600 per person per week all inclusive. The month-long teacher training courses are popular so early booking is recommended. International airlines fly direct to Koh Samui, then take a taxi (around 15 minutes) from the airport to the resort.

YOGA HOLIDAY

Yogatraveller

🌐 🅿 ⛰ 🧍 ⚽ 🧘 ↘14

Koh Phi Phi
T+353 (0)8-6828 9178
www.yogatraveller.com
From US$600 per person for 7 nights.

Yogatraveller provides healthy holistic holidays in a picture-postcard setting for those who like to do a little more than lounge in paradise. Breaks from the more typically serene beach routine include the fantastically fun, twice-daily yoga sessions, as well as diving, rock climbing and a number of other adventurous pursuits.

The day starts early with a fairly lively session of wake-up yoga in a fan-cooled glass gazebo overlooking the Andaman Sea (used for Thai massage throughout the day). This is followed by an optional daily meditation on the beach (or floating in the sea). Guests are then free until the sunset yoga session, although the day's activities usually take shape over communal breakfasts. The evening yoga sessions are gentle, sociable and relaxed, taking place on pretty woven mats on the beach under dramatic sunset skies.

Company founder and yoga teacher Michelle Riordan's passion for Phi Phi, as well as her endless enthusiasm for yoga, travel and adventure, makes her an expert hostess. Group sessions and gatherings are cleverly tailored towards the preferences of individuals and each group, making for balanced breaks that are as likely to include sunrise meditations on the beach as evening cocktails at the beach bar. Group bonding is easy as they are no more than 12 in number, and there's a weekly en-masse sunset snorkelling trip to the cove where Leonardo Di Caprio cavorted in *The Beach*.

Accommodation on Phi Phi can be cramped and blighted by construction sites since the tsunami, but Yogatraveller have found one of the quieter corners still within reach of all the action. The large air-conditioned rooms on a hillside have balconies with coastal views and are spacious and clean, with big comfortable beds.

The holidays tend to attract singles, friends travelling together and couples (in that order), mostly from the UK and Ireland, with a few more women than men. The warm atmosphere and wide variety of activities above and below the water make it ideal for the less gregarious solo traveller.

Guests come here to take advantage of the combination of yoga and diving, with yoga's emphasis on breathwork and concentration enhancing both the meditative and physical challenge of diving. The attached eco-friendly dive school **Blue View Divers** also offers a high standard of friendly individual service.

Fly to Phuket or Krabi airports, then take the 1½-hour ferry to Koh Phi Phi, where you'll be met at the pier.

For guaranteed sun and cooler weather opt for between November and February. April is the hottest time of year, and you may experience some rain and choppier seas from June to October. Yogatraveller also runs holidays in Tanzania (see page 193) and Switzerland (see page 75).

Top right and left: Yoga Thailand.
Above: Yogatraveller.

Rest of Asia

Adventure into unknown territories on foot, by bike on horseback or inside the mind.

Fact file (China and Japan)

⮕ **Visa:** China: Required for citizens of EU countries including the UK, US, Canada, Australia and New Zealand. Japan: None required for citizens of EU countries including the UK, US, Canada, Australia and New Zealand

⊙ **Country code:** China +86 ; Japan +81

⑤ **Currency:** China: Renminbi (RMB); Japan: Yen (¥)

⊙ **Time zone:** China GMT +8 hours; Japan: GMT +9 hours

⊙ **Electricity:** China: 220v; Japan 100v

ⓘ **Tourist board:** China: www.cnto.org/; Japan: www.jnto.go

Cambodia

ADVENTURE HOLIDAY

Skyros in Cambodia

T+44 (0)20-7267 4424
www.skyros.co.uk
From US$2025 per person for 10 days

For a soulful experience of Asia, UK-based holistic holiday company Skyros offers a 10-day overland tour to Cambodia. Starting in Bangkok, you spend two nights at a jungle lodge in northern Thailand and four nights at Siem Reap in Cambodia, where you'll explore the ancient Khmer temples of Angkor Wat, a UNESCO World Heritage site and an architectural delight.

To ensure a community feel and enable you to get more out of the trip, creative and personal development workshops are woven into the programme. Michael Eales, manager of Skyros, and a writer and psychologist, leads sessions on meditation and working with dreams; or try sketching, painting and photography with fellow tour leader and artist, Kel Portman.

As well as visits to markets and a school of fine art, you'll see temples in Phimai Historical Park, which pre-date Angkor Wat, and have a chance to visit the 'killing fields' of the Khmer Rouge. The price includes half board, a shared room, ground transfers, entrance fees and guides, but not flights.

Skyros also runs an impressive holiday programme of bodywork, creative and personal development courses every winter, based at the Aiyapura spa resort on Koh Chang in the Gulf of Thailand. For more on Skyros, see page 142.

Wherever you go,
go with all your heart.

Confucius

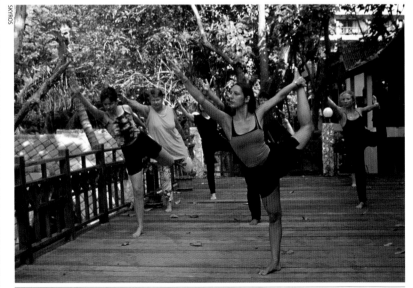

Above: Skyros in Cambodia. **Top right:** Banyan Tree. **Bottom right:** Intrepid China Mind Body Spirit.

China

HOTEL & SPA

Banyan Tree

🛇 ⊛ ⋔ ⊕ ⊛ ⊘ ↘16

Ringha Shangri-La, Yunnan
T+86 (0)887-828 8822
www.banyantree.com
From US$310 per room per night

Reached along a mud track and surrounded by high peaks and scented forests, the Banyan Tree Ringha in Shangri-La may be a chain hotel, but it's brilliantly in keeping with its environment, comprising a set of immaculately reconstructed Tibetan farmhouses made of original timber and packed earth. Tibetans govern the community and Banyan Tree works with local groups to help preserve and promote Tibetan culture. Come here to trek, visit temples and monasteries, and watch the local lamas' daily prayer ceremonies.

A sublime and unspoilt corner of Asia, the state of Zhongdian was officially named Shangri-La in 2001 by the Chinese government. The name comes from James Hilton's 1933 book *Lost Horizon*, in which he described Shangri-La as a utopian valley with no precise location. A marketing ploy it may be, but this is a remote and fascinating region in northwest Yunnan province, part of Greater Tibet (the area with a Tibetan diaspora). Tibetans work as trekking guides at the hotel, so ask about local history during outings – trekkers can stay the night in a village lodge.

Some 90% of Tibetan medicinal herbs and 60% of Chinese medicinal herbs are grown in Yunnan, and the Banyan spa offers body and beauty treatments that reflect local medicinal and spiritual traditions. Try the hand-carved river stone massage and warming spice wraps. The linen pouches of tea dipped in sesame oil and daubed on the body are divine. After a trek take the 'Tibetan Tiptoe', a herbal foot soak and reflexology, in a softly lit red and cream treatment room. Hawaiian

lomi lomi, Swedish massage and individual yoga sessions are also available.

Inside the reconstructed farmhouses there are cosy, wooden roof-beamed interiors and sumptuous soft furnishings. Bedrooms are a contemporary take on traditional Tibetan decor, with vibrant drapes, woven rugs and artefacts. There are 32 huge two-storey suites, with one floor of each devoted entirely to the bathroom. Couples will love the spa suite's wooden bathtub with ladles, and the private treatment room. Expect a mix of Asian cuisine: try bubbling Tibetan hotpots, served

in a terrine, with a glass of sake. At Jakhang Tea House sample tea leaves, buds and brews by the open fire.

You're 3800 m above sea level, so give yourself time to acclimatize – free oxygen is available from the mini-bar. Five hours' drive south of Ringha will take you to sister hotel **Banyan Tree Lijiang** – the ancient city of Lijiang is a UNESCO World Heritage site known as 'the Venice of the Orient' because of its picturesque canals and bridges. If you're flush, this is a good place to acclimatize before you head for Ringha.

Bring sunscreen, and thermal clothing for icy winter months, which are extremely cold (steps get slippery). Fly to Bangkok, then Kunming (two hours), then Diqing (50 minutes), and the hotel is a 30-minute drive.

ADVENTURE HOLIDAY

Intrepid China Mind Body Spirit

🌐 ⭕ 🐒 ✈ ✕17

Hong Kong to Beijing
T+44 (0)1373-826611
www.intrepidtravel.com/trips/CSY
From US$1555 per person for 14 days

This 14-day Mind Body Spirit trip takes you from Hong Kong to Beijing and combines Chinese medicine and cooking with martial arts, massage and cycling. It's a great way to see a different side of China if you've little time, yet want to be replenished.

Starting in Hong Kong, you'll take tai chi classes with a Chinese master and learn a basic set of moves that you can repeat each morning: even better, you'll have lots of opportunities to take local advice, and learn more postures along the way.

You'll go on to explore Hong Kong's food markets to familiarize yourself with the roots and herbs used for Chinese medicine, and the traditional herbs you'll use when at the **Yangshuo Cooking School** (www.yangshuocookingschool.com), which is housed in a rustic farmhouse by the Li river and limestone mountains, in Guangxi Province. The experience is enjoyable and communal; the group shop together in the local market, cook and enjoy the final results together.

The trip requires lots of stamina. You'll learn kung fu and qigong, and take three-hour shaolin sessions with the monks at the famous **Shaolin monastery** (www.shaolin.com). Other highlights include cycling round the traditional quarters of Beijing, and massage from expert blind masseurs. Blind masseur groups practise all over China and are renowned for their high level of sensitivity to an individual's needs. Their sense of touch is heightened to compensate for sight.

As you travel you'll sample different regional foods, and meet lots of locals, making it a very rich experience. Guides can be Chinese or westerners with Chinese knowledge, and groups are no larger than 12. You'll stay in a variety of accommodation, mostly guesthouses, in good locations. Two nights are spent on the train.

Spring and summer are good months to travel in China as June and July can be hot. On top of the price stated, you'll need US$200 local payment; also budget US$150 for food allowance and US$200 for activities. Intrepid will supply detailed instructions on how to reach the designated meeting hotel in Hong Kong.

◐ Body language

Finding the chi

Usually referred to as simply tai chi, tai chi ch'uan is an ancient, non-competitive Chinese martial art that originated with the Chen clan. A martial art it may be, but it's a soft one – there are no belts or grades and the emphasis is on balancing the body and mind rather than combat. At its heart is a belief in the Taoist philosophy of yin and yang, the primal opposing but complementary forces found in all natural things. For devotees, the discipline is intricately linked to Chinese philosophy, culture and medicine.

In practice, tai chi is a mobile meditation combining slow, gentle, graceful movements with the breathing to stimulate 'chi', or qi, the life force or vital energy of the body and the universe. There are various forms, and a whole series of moves, which can take years to perfect in their entirety. The basic form is a continuous sequence of movements with 24, 48 or 108 steps. Be prepared to feel a little silly when you first start – but done properly, it is a liberating, dance-like practice which will calm the mind, keep the body supple, reduce stress, improve circulation and prevent illness. Suitable for people of all ages and levels of fitness, tai chi is usually practised in light, loose fitting clothes and socks or bare feet.

INTREPID

Mountain Yoga

🌏 ⓘ ⛰ 👥 ☑18

Beijing
T+86 (0)10-6259 6702
www.mountainyoga.cn
From US$60 per person per night

Mountain Yoga is the first and only yoga retreat centre in China. Established in 2003, this tranquil holistic mountain hideaway is the product of a passion for yoga, and all profits are ploughed back into the project. It offers one- to five-day yoga and tai chi retreats at three centres: Fragrant Hill, a Buddhist temple, and a tipi yoga camp in a valley close to the Great Wall.

Traditional yoga from the Bihar School in India is followed here, though retreats also include hatha and ashtanga – there is a mix of foreign and Chinese teachers, and senior satyananda yoga teachers from India are invited to give guest lectures. All levels are welcome. You'll also learn about traditional Chinese medicine, and be able to practise calligraphy and ink painting.

The Fragrant Hill centre is in a small village in the Fragrant Hill mountains northwest of Beijing. It's rustic and simple with Chinese furniture, bamboo detail and goldfish pools. There are two en suite bedrooms (one of which is heated) and two dormitories. You can stay here on a B&B (all vegetarian) basis and practise yoga and Taoist tai chi. The area is best during the autumn, when leaves on trees turn red and the hillside is blanketed in spectacular colour.

A stay in the Buddhist temple centre, one hour's drive from Beijing, is unique. The 500-year-old temple is extremely tranquil and is not open to the public. It has 14 bedrooms, each with private toilet and shower, and is surrounded by quiet gardens and trees. You practise yoga at the temple, which has a lotus centrepiece lit with candles and opens on to a courtyard. Meditate under the 600-year-old gingko tree. For something more remote, the tipi camp, a four-hour train ride from Beijing, is a back-to-roots experience.

Mountain Yoga.

Mountain Yoga also runs Yoga Vacations, combining yoga practice with treatments at a local hot spring resort. Depending on the length of your stay, you'll be introduced to traditional Chinese medicine, Taoism and Zen meditation, and have the chance to visit ancient temples such as the 14th-century Azure Clouds temple, a beautiful example of Chinese Buddhist architecture.

Fellow guests include Chinese, expats, diplomats and yogi travellers aged 18-60. There are openings for volunteers in exchange for free accommodation. Retreats and vacations run from March to December. The rate quoted is for a stay at the Fragrant Hill retreat; the Buddhist temple retreat costs from US$100, and the tipi camp from US$50 – and includes yoga, tai-chi, meals and activities. Fly to Beijing.

Asia China

Japan

TEMPLE STAY

Hosen-ji Zen Centre

Kameoka, near Kyoto
T+81 (0)77-124 0378
www.zazen.or.jp
US$82 per person for 3 nights

A stay in a Japanese *shukubo* (temple lodging) is probably one of the most unlikely but effective ways of getting away from it all: think remote, rural locations, ancient shrines and a back-to-basics lifestyle. There are numerous *shukubo* across Japan run by local monks, but Hosen-ji is one of the best known, with ability to introduce first-timers to the ways of Zen. It has an open-door policy to short-term residents and a friendly attitude to potential converts.

Visitors come from all walks of life, with a mix of Japanese and other Asian nationals, plus a handful of guests from further afield, all dedicated to learning the art of zazen (sitting) meditation. Some go on to enroll in monasteries but most simply go back to the rat race feeling better for having taken some time out. To this end, the location is perfect, with fresh mountain air and a large garden for silent contemplation.

Less compelling is the accommodation, which is – at best – basic. Futons are slung out over the tatami mats in spartan dormitories, a single hot shower is

Hosen-ji Zen Centre.

designated for communal use, and two meals per day are taken with the head monks in total silence. Temple rules forbid alcohol and smoking, and the vegetarian diet is based around bland dishes of watery rice, seaweed and soup. Thankfully, dinner, taken in the kitchen, is a more relaxed affair with guests encouraged to chat and cook together, rather than obey a strict silence.

Expect a 0500 wake-up call, sutra chanting and work around the grounds for an hour before breakfast, while each night there is a compulsory two-hour zazen meditation session. It's not everyone's idea of a holiday but, in terms of getting away from it all, the experience takes you to a whole new level. Calligraphy sessions are also offered.

There's a minimum stay of two nights, and you must book in advance. The price for three nights includes all meals and each

Soul food

A registered Not-For-Profit company, **Second Harvest Japan** (www.secondharvestjapan.org) distributes tasty, nutritious food to soup kitchens, orphanages, the elderly, emergency shelters, single mothers, the homeless, migrant workers, and many others throughout Japan, where an estimated 460,000 people don't have access to good food on a daily basis. Get involved by donating time, food, money or equipment.

additional night costs US$25. A month-long stay costs US$650 per person. The centre opens year round but the cold Japanese winter would probably test the nerve of the most devoted student. It is located near JR Umahori station on the Sagano line running out of Kyoto JR station. From there to Hosen-ji Zen Centre it's a 15-minute walk.

The students at the Hosen-ji Zen Centre filed in silently while a monk beat a staccato rhythm on a block of wood and, after a short reading from Buddhist scripture, the peal of a small handbell signalled the start of zazen time. I closed my eyes and tried to tune in to the moment but I had already dropped off before most of the faithful had even finished arranging their feet in contortionist-like positions. After five minutes, my legs felt numb and painful. The only distraction came when, at the 20-minute mark, I had an overwhelming urge to sneeze. After a short break, the second session was only interrupted when the Zen master came around with a large wooden stick (the *keisaku*) to administer voluntary thwacks to anyone nodding off during the pursuit for inner peace. I bowed and accepted my thwacks gratefully. This was starting to feel like Buddhist boot camp.

David Atkinson

Earth Celebration Festival

Sado Island, in the Sea of Japan, requires a bit of a trek, but will reward curious travellers and seekers of soulful adventures. In centuries past, it was home to convicts and gold miners, but is now a floating treasure chest of traditional culture and rich natural beauty, with a handful of beautiful *onsen* (natural hot springs), pristine beaches, and verdant hills through which to hike. It's also home to the world renowned Kodo drummers, and site of the annual Earth Celebration, a three-day music, dance and arts festival held during the third week of August, and a creative and rejuvenating experience for all visitors.

The main events feature the Kodo drummers who have toured the world with their outstanding *waidaiko* compositions incorporating Buddhist ceremonial instruments. In addition to a solo performance, Kodo invites an international guest to accompany them for a collaborative concert on the final evening, and the musical fusion that results moves participants from ecstatic dance to tears. Past guests have

included Galician bagpipe players, Irish folk musicians, Urban Tap dancers, and Botswana drummers and dance troupes.

The festival is based in a multitude of venues, from grassy fields to temple gardens, and also offers lots of dance, music and craft workshops ranging from Miyake *taiko*, traditional Japanese drumming, to hula dancing, dictated by emotions. For artists and musicians, there's a fringe stage where you can showcase your work and collaborate with other performers.

The Earth Celebration workshops tend to fill up fast. If you would like to participate, it is recommended that you buy tickets by early June. Many of the events are free. There are more than 200 places to stay on the island, from beachfront campsites to traditional Japanese ryokan – book early. Sado lies off the coast of Niigata prefecture. It's a two-hour bullet train ride from Tokyo to Niigata, from where there are regular daily hydrofoil and ferry services to the island. For accommodation more information go to http://www.kodo.or.jp/ec/en/index.html.

Origin Arts Program

☀ ○ ⊘ ↘20

Kyoto
T+81 (0)75-352 0211
www.kyoto-machiya.com
From US$290 per person per day

If you're travelling as a family or with a group of friends, consider a visit to the Origin Arts Program, which runs bespoke traditional workshops covering the 'four pillars' of traditional Japanese arts: Noh drama dance, calligraphy, the tea ceremony, and martial arts.

These are each taught by Japanese masters, with English translation provided. The courses are very much a hands-on experience, emphasizing the spiritual roots of each of the arts. *Waraku* is taught – a sword-based martial art related to aikido. Flower arranging, ceramics, and *kyogen* comic theatre workshops are also on offer.

Though the workshops are city based, you stay in an immaculately restored Iori *machiya* townhouse, many of which feature small *tsuboniwa* gardens, and large cedarwood baths for soaking. It's easy to experience some real nature in the city's surrounding mountains, which are filled with shrines and temples and have good walking paths. Classes are held in the tearooms of one of the *machiya*, and in a large adjoining

Everything passes. Nobody gets anything for keeps. And that's how we've got to live.
Haruki Murakami

Japanese hot soak

For an authentic Japanese experience spend some time at a ryokan, a traditional Japanese guesthouse. Many of them have been built on Japan's many mineral-rich *onsen*, or natural hot springs. Most offer good massage services and serve local organic dishes in a style of cuisine known as *kaiseki* – a series of exquisitely presented dishes based around a single ingredient such as crab, apple, mushroom, eel or mountain vegetables. Japanese hot springs are enjoyed naked, and you're expected to shower beforehand. You're given a small towel to wear outside the water, which many Japanese simply place on their heads while soaking. Temperatures range from 40-44°C – take it easy getting in. The best time to visit is during late autumn or early spring, so you can be outside and enjoy the hot waters in clean cool air – if snow falls, it's an even cosier experience. Avoid weekends and holidays, when the locals descend on their *onsens* in droves.

Sekitaitei, at Achi village in the Nagano prefecture, is a luxurious and especially untouched ryokan (see opposite page), and you'll find other upmarket ryokan at www.ryokancollection.com. For a more affordable option, head north to Tazawako in Akita prefecture, where people have been bathing at the **Tsurunoyu** *onsen* (T+81 (0)18-746 2139, from US$66 per person per night including breakfast and dinner) for over 350 years. There are 30 Japanese-style guest rooms with shared bathrooms in dark wooden rural buildings. Soak in square wooden tubs for four inside, or in the large outdoor public bath, set amongst rocks and lit at night with kerosene lamps. Nearby you'll find Kakunodate, which has a beautifully preserved street of 200-year-old samurai houses, and there's good forest country for walking. Tazawako station can be reached from Tokyo by direct bullet train in around three hours. There is no website, but this and many other *onsen* can be booked through www.japaneseguesthouses.com.

warehouse which has been converted into a martial arts dojo and Noh drama stage.

Workshops are held in groups of 10 and prices include a traditional bento lunch. Smaller groups can be accommodated for a higher price pe rhead. A stay in a *machiya* costs US$60-150 per person per night. The courses are the brainchild of American author Alex Kerr, who also runs traditional Asian arts courses in Thailand (see www.alex-kerr.com). For more details on the programme contact Bodhi Fishman at bodhifish@gmail.com.

Sekitaitei

Achi village, Nagano prefecture
T+81 (0)26-543 3300
www.sekitaitei.com
From US$330 per person per night

Situated in a quaint mountain village, Sekitaitei is an elegant and traditional Japanese ryokan with an exquisite *onsen*. Run by Takako and Naoki Henmi, a charming young couple, the inn has managed to stay off the tourist map and out of most foreign guidebooks. Everything about the experience here oozes local beauty, culture and grace, and you come to understand why the Zen tradition originated in Japan.

A wander through the ryokan delights all the senses, and makes it easy to pay attention to the present moment: there are soothing sounds of fountains, crackling fires, birdsong and breezes, and delicious scents of smokeless incense waft through the public rooms. Takako-san is an accomplished student of ikebana (traditional Japanese flower arranging) and there are artful flower arrangements throughout.

You choose a cotton kimono (male or female) to wear during your stay. The traditional tatami mat suites each have their own private garden view of Japanese maple trees, water fountains or Zen rock gardens, or all three, and are exquisite places to sit in quiet contemplation over a cup of green tea. The traditional futon beds are hidden away during the day and made up in the evening, and kept warm on cool nights with a hot-water bottle.

All rooms have a Japanese-style bath with heated floors, though few guests opt to bathe in their rooms. The indoor and outdoor baths, for men and women, as well as a family bath for couples and people with children, invite endless hours of soaking in the soft and sumptuous natural waters, which leave the skin silky and the mind calm and refreshed. There is a vast menu of massage available, ranging from deep, rigorous shiatsu, to more soothing oil massage. You can opt for a session in your room or in the spa.

The food is a highlight, the menu changing with each of the 24 seasons – in traditional Japan, winter, spring, summer and autumn were each divided into six sub-seasons. Multiple courses come out one by one, each a canvas of beauty and a delight to the palate. Take the chance to dine in a private tatatmi mat room.

There's a beautiful stage featuring a traditional Japanese act every evening, such as bamboo flute, puppetry, the koto and the *shimasen*, and calligraphy and ikebana classes are on offer a few times a month. Stroll along the nearby river, cycle through town, or visit a local mountain village with Naoki-san for an authentic country dining experience overlooking the high Japanese Alps. This is an extraordinary experience, especially in autumn when the trees paint the countryside with gold and rust. Sekitaitei is a five-hour bus ride from Shinjuku, Tokyo's largest train station.

Top left: Origin Arts Program. **Above**: Sekitaitei.

Laos

Red Spokes Adventure Tour

T+44 (0)20-7502 7252
www.redspokes.co.uk
From US$1300 per person for 14 days

The tiny Buddhist country of Laos only opened its doors to the outside world in the 1990s. Landlocked between Thailand and Vietnam, it's increasing in popularity with each passing year, but remains a mellow slice of Southeast Asia, with friendly people, little traffic and gorgeous scenery. Most Laotians get about by bicycle, and the 14-day Red Spokes Adventure Tour is an appropriately active way to see this lovely country. Massages to soothe tired limbs can be had en route from local therapists, and there are trips to Buddhist sites and temples.

Company founder and tour leader, Dermot MacWard, works hard to build relationships with local communities, and his trips are a treat for those who want to explore another culture and take time out from their own. You'll stay in local houses, and clock up about 50 miles a day, beginning in northern Thailand and ending in the Lao capital, Vientiane. The trip includes a visit to Ban Faen village, where Red Spokes has ploughed some of its profits into the local economy, and you'll have a chance to take part in a village animist festival.

Northern Laos in particular is a land of rustic villages, where monks ride past on bicycles and hill tribes attend daily morning markets in traditional dress. Your trip includes a boat ride on the chocolate-coloured Mekong, and a visit to the Pak Ou caves, filled with a thousand Buddha images. You'll have a rest day in the increasingly cosmopolitan Luang Prabang, former home of the Laotian royal family and a UNESCO World Heritage site with French-Indochinese architecture. Of the bejewelled and beautiful Buddhist temples,

RED SPOKES

RED SPOKES

Red Spokes Adventure Tour.

Malaysia & Singapore

Bon Ton Restaurant & Resort

Langkawi
T+60 (0)49-551688
www.bontonresort.com.my
From US$140 per room per night

For a laid-back escape in Malaysia away from the tourist hordes, head for Australian-owned Bon Ton Restaurant & Resort on Langkawi, an island of ancient virgin rainforest and serene blue waters. Just 10 minutes from the airport, Bon Ton is near the sea but overlooks tranquil wetland, full of birds, fish and otters. It has just eight restored 100-year-old Malay villas facing a pool and surrounded by tall swaying palms. Intricate details in each have been preserved, and silk throws and traditional textiles keep rooms warm.

This is a great place to reflect and rejuvenate. Island hop on the hotel's ancient yacht, take long jungle walks, or enjoy serene sunsets over the wetlands, cocktail in hand. The fusion of Asian and global cuisine includes mezzes with feta and pine nuts, white bean puree, sweet and sour capsicum and Turkish bread or spiced meatballs in curry coconut sauce. The resort also runs an artists-in-residence programme. Note that the on-site animal shelter may trouble allergy sufferers.

Bon Ton can arrange for an Indian ayurvedic masseur to visit. Guests can also use award-winning Bali-style spa facilities at nearby **Datai** (www.thedatai.com), a luxurious complex on private sands. On-site naturalist, Irshad Mobarak, gives inspiring jungle walks from here. Alternatively, dip in and out of other spa offerings in the area: traditional Thai massage or holistic body treatment at **The Andaman** (www.theandaman.com), tailor-made treatments at **Alun Alun** day spa (www.langkawi-spa.com), or yoga classes at the **Sheraton Langkawi Beach Resort** (www.starwood hotels.com).

the most enchanting is Wat Xiang Thong, with its elegant roof and colourful mosaics.

The French influence in Luang Prabang and Vientiane means cafés au lait and delicious pastries are to be found easily in local cafés, though Laotian food is some of the tastiest in the world (try a glass of rice wine with some *khai paen*, a nutritious river moss lightly fried and sprinkled with sesame seeds). Cycling is on easy, quiet roads, with a few challenging climbs, though rest vehicles are on hand if you should tire. You meet in Bangkok, from where a short flight takes you to Chiang Rai (Thailand) where the trip begins. Red Spokes runs four trips a year to Laos, and leads other cycling trips across the globe, including a challenging 24-day tour through the Tibetan Himalayas.

Healthy stopovers in Singapore

Singapore citizens are fast paced – *kiasu* is a local word for a dynamic desire to get ahead – yet there's a sub-culture of locals and expats who embrace all things holistic, and you'll find a magic mix here of east and west while en route to other destinations.

Where to stay? For airport stopovers try **Changi Village Hotel** (from US$85 per night, T+65 6379 7111, www.changi village.com.sg) at Changi International Airport. The attached Retreat Spa and Thalasso Centre offer therapeutic treatments, and it's conveniently located for ferry access to Indonesian islands such as Bintan, where many expats head for relaxing beach weekends out of the city.

In the city, art deco-styled **Hotel 1929** (from US$84 per night, T+65 6347 1929, www.hotel1929.com) has kitsch and fun, though rather small, rooms and a rooftop hot tub. It's on Keong Saik Road, near Whatever Yoga (see below) and popular late-night food courts. The famous Raffles Hotel has a hip sister, the **Raffles Plaza** (US$205 per room per night, T+65 6339 7777, www.raffles.com), on Bras Basah Road, which has a top-floor bar with views all the way to Malaysia. Enjoy luxurious treatments, plunge pools and gym in the Amrita Spa, exclusive to Raffles guests. The riverside **Fullerton** (from US$368 per night, T+65 6733 8388, www.fullertonhotel.com) has elegant rooms and suites, an outdoor infinity pool and gym; the Asian Spa has a tempting menu.

Alternatively, head for the **Sentosa** (from US$156 per night, T+65 6275 0335, www.sentosa.com), a family-style resort on Sentosa island boasting the Spa Botanica, set on its own with a pool and gardens, offering holistic and beauty treatments as well as traditional Chinese medicine. The island beaches may be man-made, but you'll feel like you're well away from the city here.

For respite in the city, **Whatever Yoga and Healing Space** (T+65 9180 6914, www.whatever.com.sg) in Chinatown was Singapore's first holistic hub and has a vegetarian café and New Age bookstore, and offers reiki, homeopathy and therapeutic massage as well as drop-in ashtanga yoga classes. The **Earth Sanctuary** (T+65 6324 7933, www.earthsanctuary.com.sg) is a day spa on Club Street; therapies include Australian Aboriginal and Hawaiian treatments using herbal products and colour therapy oils.

If you're in Singapore for more than a few days, visit **True Yoga** (T+65 6733 9555, www.trueyoga.com.sg) for classes from flow yoga to yogalates, in the Pacific Plaza on Scott's Road, or in the Raffles Plaza (see above). Or try **COMO Shambhala** (courses from US$82, T+65 6735 2163, www.comoshambhala.bz) for yoga and pilates classes on Orchard Road. For alternative

healing, **SoulCentre** (T+65 6738 4009, www.soulcentre.org) on Balmoral Road offers reiki, crystal therapy and spiritual workshops. Therapists Sally Forrest and Vikas Malkani are visiting consultants to Thailand's Chiva-Som.

CAROLINE SYLGE

WHATEVER

Asia Malaysia & Singapore

Mongolia

PANORAMIC JOURNEYS

ADVENTURE HOLIDAY

Panoramic Journeys

T+44 (0)1608-811183
www.panoramicjourneys.com
From US$3950 per person for 18 days

The most sparsely populated country in the world, Mongolia makes a fantastic place to explore if you want to escape and get a new perspective on life. Vast areas of the country are uninhabited and the land feels wild, rugged and limitless.

Panoramic Journeys specializes in trips to remote spots, and donates part of its annual profits to sustainable projects supporting Mongolia's people and culture. In 2006 they funded a tree-planting project in the Gobi Desert and helped build a Buddhist school in Kharkhorin. Trips take in winter ice festivals, Buddhist monasteries, encounters with monks, shamans and nomads, exploring ancient sites and sand-surfing in the Gobi Desert.

Their 18-day Reindeer Ride is a horseback trip to the isolated Khoridol Saridag mountains where the remote Tsaatan people live. These reindeer herders live off the land, and will often invite you to join their families in the tipi to share reindeer milk and cheese. During the ride you can also meet nomadic people, visit their *ger* (yurt) homes and try their yak's milk yoghurt, delicious served with fresh wild blueberries from the forest. Warm your toes around a fire each night, and camp under infinite starlit skies.

Guides and horses bring all the equipment and provisions you require. You do not need to be an experienced rider, but confidence with animals helps. For a longer experience, add the five-day Beijing extension, which includes a trip on the Trans-Mongolian train. Prices are based on two sharing and include domestic flights and train tickets, accommodation, meals, activities, English-speaking guides, park and museum entrance fees and airport transfers. Fly to Beijing.

PANORAMIC JOURNEYS

Western laziness consists of cramming our lives with compulsive activity, so that there is no time at all to confront the real issues.

Sogyal Rinpoche

South Korea

TEMPLE STAY

Haeinsa temple

⚫ 🔲25

Near Deagu, Gyeongsangbuk-do province
T+82 (0)55-934 3110
www.80000.or.kr/eng/info/temple_stay.html
From US$32 per person per night

A UNESCO World Heritage site, the Haeinsa temple is a serene, sloping-roofed complex of buildings set amongst forests, mountains and streams in the Gayasan National Park. Like many Buddhist temples in South Korea, it offers three-day temple stays to introduce foreign guests to aspects of Korean Buddhism and culture. These are not conventional meditation retreats, but they offer a peaceful environment and a chance to witness life and etiquette in a thriving monastery.

Korean Buddhism is a take on Zen Buddhism, less ritualized and more open to foreigners than the Japanese form. You'll learn both sitting and walking Zen meditation, and be able to have discussions with a temple monk. There's a chance to experience the Zen martial art of sunmudo, or try your hand at worshipping by performing 108 bows, said to eliminate desire and purify the body. Take part in traditional tea ceremonies, or *balwoogongyang*, the four bowl ceremonial meal consisting of rice, soup, temple-grown kimchi, and water.

South Korean temples only started to welcome foreign visitors in 2002 when the country hosted the Football World Cup. Guests wear monks' clothing, stick to a daily routine, and eat vegetarian meals. Monks do not take a vow of silence but loud behaviour is forbidden. English translators are usually available but this should be confirmed when booking.

One of South Korea's most important Buddhist temples, Haeinsa is especially famous for housing the Tripitaka Koreana, one of the country's most important national treasures. It comprises over 81,000 exquisitely carved printing blocks that are one of the oldest and best-preserved collections of Buddhist scriptures in the world.

The temple stay is available all year round, but you can't visit for longer than three days. Bring warm clothing for pre-dawn activities. Fly to Seoul and take the bullet train to Deagu, or fly to the city of Deagu and then take one of the Haeinsa temple buses from Seobu bus terminal, which takes about an hour. The temple is the last stop and it is a 10-minute walk to the entrance gate.

Left: Panoramic Journeys.
Above and below right: Tibet Pilgrimage.

🍲 **Soul food**

About 90% of blind people live in the developing countries of Africa, Asia, Latin America and the Pacific Regions, and nearly six million of them are children. **Braille Without Borders** (www.braillewithoutborders.org) was set up to empower blind people in developing countries so they themselves can set up projects and schools for other blind people. In the Tibet Autonomous Region, for example, where blind children don't have access to education and have few chances of social integration, Braille Without Borders set up a rehabilitation and training centre.

Tibet

SPIRITUAL HOLIDAY

Tibetan Pilgrimage

⚫ 🌀 💧 🔲26

Dzachuka, eastern Tibet
T+44 (0)796-289 0332
www.rigdzintrust.org
US$2500 per person

For anyone with a strong interest in Tibet and its cultural and spiritual heritage, Buddhist master Amnyi Trulchung Rinpoche leads an annual trip to his home region of Dzachuka in eastern Tibet each summer. Explore a magnificent landscape, encounter the fierce and friendly Khampa people, and experience a taste of Tibetan life in a remote nomadic community. The trip includes a five-day meditation retreat at Ju Mohar monastery, which has been home to many great Buddhist masters. Amnyi Trulchung Rinpoche, the abbot of Ju Mohar, has established several meditation centres in New Zealand and teaches throughout New Zealand, Australia, Asia and Europe.

Shamans in Siberia

Shamanism in Siberia is concentrated on Tuva, a tiny mountainous republic to the southwest of Lake Baikal, where the Tos Deer Clinic in Kyzyl is based. Here shaman Ai-Churek Oyun runs courses, and welcomes beginners. To arrange a visit in advance, contact US-based healer and counsellor **Debra Varner** (T+1 415-922 0137, www.purplemedicinewoman.org), who now works in collaboration with the California Institute of Integral Studies in San Francisco. Varner also leads annual group trips to experience the work of the modern-day shaman and the sacred lands of Tuva and Buryatia, as well as to Mongolia (from US$4600 per person for 18 days). For shamanism trips around the world, UK-based Eagle's Wing runs workshops in the UK and trips to Peru (see page 31), US-based Nicki Scully of **Shamanic Journeys** runs trips to Peru, Egypt and Greece (see www.shamanicjourneys.com), or try the EcoTribal Tour to Peru (see page 382).

66 99

When a friend told me about a gathering of Siberian shamans on Olkhon island, in the middle of Lake Baikal, it was hard to resist.

This was to be the first ceremony performed on the island for 80 years. Although it now houses just 1500 farmers and fishermen, it used to be known as 'Shaman Island' before communist repression, and is even rumoured to be the birthplace of Genghis Khan.

The day of the ceremony came and the shamans gathered around a wooden yurt wearing cloaks - a colourful silk and wool riot of men and animals, cloth spirit totems, hanging from their back. Other essential tools they had with them were the *toli* – a gold coloured healing disk worn around the neck – and the sacred shamanic drum, used to call up the gods.

Shamans act as mediators between gods, nature spirits and people, and attempt to heal the body through healing the soul. This can involve soul retrieval, when they journey to another realm in a trance-like state. Theatricals are all part of the work: witnesses have seen shamans walking across ceilings, leaping between trees or appearing as animals. As the first drum beat of the day started from deep in the dark yurt, in front of offerings of tea, sweets and plastic toys, the sheep is led inside and flicked with vodka. I watch in horror and fascination as outside on the grass, they lay it down gently and, cutting a slit in its chest, pluck out its heart, without a

bleat. Everything, except the trotters, goes into the pot, and appears later, cooked, on the altar.

Plaintive, nasal singing rises above the drumbeat and I can feel the intensity as, suddenly, the shaman's voice changes and he clatters out of the yurt, moving like a clumsy bull around the birch grove. Everyone squats down. As you're not allowed to look a shaman in the face, we peer through spread fingers, and as he falls to his knees the villagers press forward with question for the gods – usually help for sickness or delicate questions about marriage or children. The shaman lays his hand gently on their hair and slurs an answer, or beats their bowed heads with the stick he's holding. What's clear, when they suddenly snap out of the trance, is that they are in an altered state of consciousness, and remember nothing about it.

As the day wears on, the shamans go into the yurt one after another and drum themselves into a trance. Some come out giggling like schoolgirls, others thundering like a storm. Clutching my question, translated into Russian, it's now my turn to push forward. I bow before the fearsome looking shaman, but just then, he goes limp. The god has left and my question will have to wait. My questions about shamanism, however, have been answered.

Nicki Grihault

The itinerary weaves together audiences with Tibetan masters and visits to key pilgrimage sites. These include the little-known Mani Dungkar, a spectacular wall made out of hand-carved *mani* stones inscribed with mantras and images, and Derge, home of the famous printing house where Buddhist texts have been produced since the 18th century. There is also a visit to Yachen Gar, a vast encampment of students of HH Achuk Rinpoche, perhaps the greatest living Buddhist master in Tibet. You don't need to be a practising Buddhist to attend the trip, which takes a maximum of 20 and attracts a wide mix of people, from their twenties to their seventies, from North America, Europe, New Zealand and Australia.

You'll travel mainly by 4WD, and accomodation will vary from hotels in the towns, to an authentic Tibetan tent whilst at the majestic Mani Dungkar site. Be prepared for simple food, long journeys and unreliable roads. The Tibetan plateau is above 3000 m, and some people may suffer altitude sickness. The trip begins and ends in Chengdu, China and is organized by the Rigdzin Trust, which raises money and leads projects to help the people of eastern Tibet.

TIBETAN PILGRIMAGE

Tibetan Pilgrimage.

Vietnam

COASTAL RETREAT

Life Wellness Resort Quy Nhon

Quy Nhon
T+84 (0)56-840132
www.life-resorts.com
From US$132 per person sharing

Dutch-owned Life Wellness Resort Quy Nhon is Vietnam's first wellness centre, situated in extensive private grounds with its own beach. This is a quiet, informal and relaxed place to be, with unfailingly friendly staff and no hint of pretentiousness.

The resort's architecture, furnishings and decor draw on traditional Cham culture – an ancient civilization once dominant in this region. The beachside accommodation block (separate from the main wing) faces the sea, with all 63 guest rooms offering spectacular sea views from generous balconies and open-plan, glass-fronted bathrooms. Rooms are quiet and spacious, with minimalist decor using natural materials such as granite, dark woods and white cotton – junior suites have sunken bathtubs.

The Life Wellness Spa is hidden amongst 3000 sq m of tropical hillside gardens, set back from the main resort. This all-wood, natural sanctuary incorporates three indoor treatment suites with bathtubs and Cham steam baths infused with lemongrass; outdoors, there are five bamboo treatment bungalows, tropical rain showers, rock pools and a large deck area for post-spa relaxation. Treatments are multicultural and include a Japanese-style dry sand and salt sauna and a six-hand massage. Most use locally grown ingredients.

Their Energizing, De-stress, Detox and Life Signature programmes are the first of their kind in Vietnam. During a five-day stay these inclusive packages feature specifically designed combinations of spa treatments, meals and activities – such as breathing exercises – customized according to individual needs.

Daily complimentary activities aimed at beginners range from tai chi and beach volleyball to yoga, pilates and meditation in the beachside yoga hut. Private sessions are available for those already into a practice. All-inclusive Wellness Workshops hosted by international gurus are held several times a year.

The resort has an outdoor pool and an exercise studio, and offers kayaking or boat excursions to two private islands. Senses Restaurant is perched on a clifftop with glorious sea and tropical garden views, and serves simple, fresh Vietnamese and Western cuisine with lots of fish. Fellow guests are couples and honeymooners, a few tour groups, expats and some single travellers, particularly women. From November to February the climate can be cool and rainy; the best time to stay is March to October, with mainly sunshine and little rain. There are flights to Quy Nhon airport daily from Ho Chi Minh City and thrice weekly from Hanoi, via Danang. The resort is a 45-minute drive from Quy Nhon.

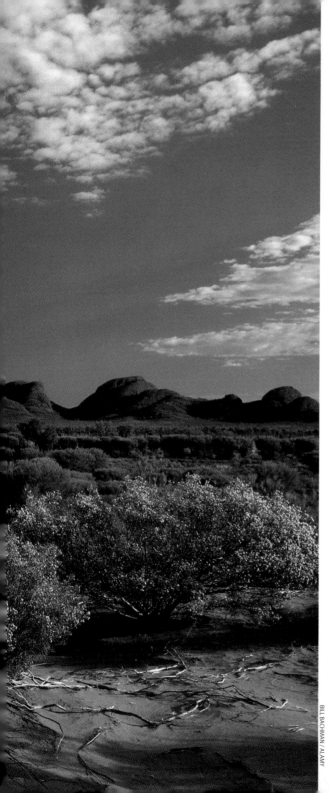

Australia, New Zealand & Pacific Islands

BILL BACHMAN / ALAMY

The wide open spaces of the Australian outback make for an unusual, off-the-beaten-track body and soul adventure.

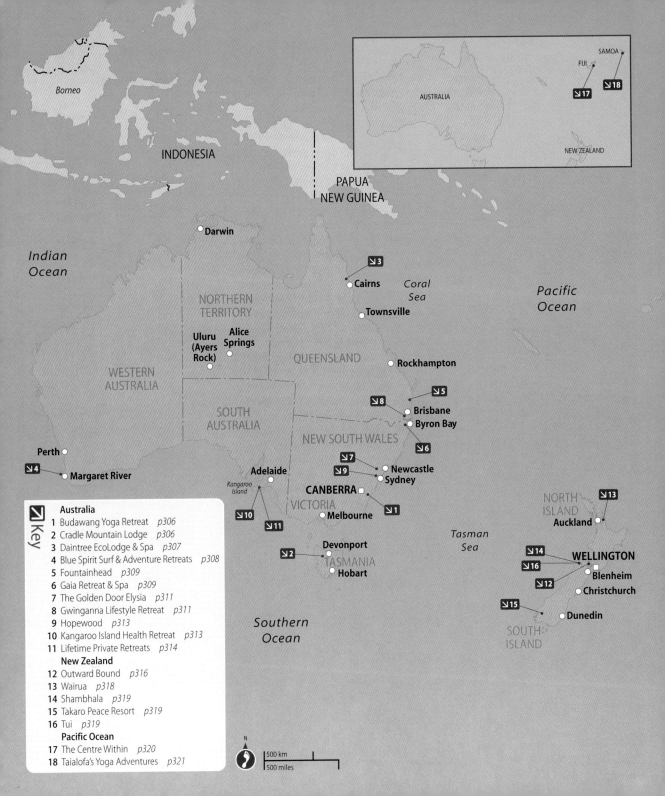

Borneo

INDONESIA

PAPUA
NEW GUINEA

AUSTRALIA

FIJI

SAMOA

↘17

↘18

NEW ZEALAND

Darwin

Indian
Ocean

↘3

Cairns

*Coral
Sea*

Townsville

NORTHERN
TERRITORY

Uluru
(Ayers
Rock)

Alice
Springs

QUEENSLAND

Rockhampton

*Pacific
Ocean*

WESTERN
AUSTRALIA

SOUTH
AUSTRALIA

↘5

↘8

Brisbane

Byron Bay

NEW SOUTH WALES

↘6

Perth

↘4

Margaret River

Adelaide

*Kangaroo
Island*

↘7

↘9

Newcastle

Sydney

↘10

CANBERRA

↘1

↘11

VICTORIA

Melbourne

NORTH
ISLAND

↘13

*Tasman
Sea*

Auckland

Devonport

↘2

TASMANIA

Hobart

WELLINGTON

↘14

↘16

Blenheim

↘12

Christchurch

*Southern
Ocean*

↘15

Dunedin

SOUTH
ISLAND

↘ Key

Australia
1 Budawang Yoga Retreat   *p306*
2 Cradle Mountain Lodge   *p306*
3 Daintree EcoLodge & Spa   *p307*
4 Blue Spirit Surf & Adventure Retreats   *p308*
5 Fountainhead   *p309*
6 Gaia Retreat & Spa   *p309*
7 The Golden Door Elysia   *p311*
8 Gwinganna Lifestyle Retreat   *p311*
9 Hopewood   *p313*
10 Kangaroo Island Health Retreat   *p313*
11 Lifetime Private Retreats   *p314*
New Zealand
12 Outward Bound   *p316*
13 Wairua   *p318*
14 Shambhala   *p319*
15 Takaro Peace Resort   *p319*
16 Tui   *p319*
Pacific Ocean
17 The Centre Within   *p320*
18 Taialofa's Yoga Adventures   *p321*

N

500 km
500 miles

Introduction

It's little surprise that many people feel like emigrating to this part of the world; it boasts inspirational landscapes, lots of space and a more balanced attitude to living. In Australia, some inventive tour operators have cooked up wellbeing trips to get you off the tourist trail and into the bush, while Blue Spirit is a successful, unpretentious combination of surfing, adventure and yoga in a gorgeous wine-growing region. The unspoilt wilderness and crisp air of Kangaroo Island will have you feeling better in no time, whether you're going to detox or to indulge. Alternatively, arrange a DIY retreat at the hippy beachside haven of Byron Bay. To be replenished in a rainforest, head to Daintree EcoLodge in Queensland, one of the world's original eco-friendly spas.

There are plenty of pampering places in the Pacific Ocean: try an inventive yoga holiday on tropical Samoa, or, if you're feeling anxious, get back to basics on a spiritual retreat in Fiji.

The verdant and beautiful Coromandel peninsula in New Zealand has attracted Buddhist communities and artists for years. Explore your creativity at the unpretentious Wairua, be nurtured in plush surroundings at the Takaro Peace Resort in New Zealand's far south, or pursue a budding interest on one of the many healing, creative and spiritual courses on offer at the well-respected Mana Retreat Centre. If you're wondering where you're going in life, New Zealand offers one of the best locations in the world for an Outward Bound course.

“ ” *We are all better than we know. If only we can come to discover this, we may never again settle for less.*
Kurt Hahn, founder of Outward Bound

Travel essentials

Australia

Getting there Principal international airports are Perth for Western Australia, Sydney for New South Wales and Brisbane or Cairns for Queensland. Tasmania has no international airport, so go via Melbourne or Sydney, both with flight and ferry connections to Tasmania. From Europe, the most competitive fares are via Asia (20-30 hours, including stopovers). No carriers fly non-stop. From New Zealand, book direct flights (three hours) with **Qantas**, **Air New Zealand** and **Freedom Air**. Qantas offers direct flights from Los Angeles, New York, San Francisco and Vancouver, with non-stop routes from Los Angeles and San Francisco (14 hours). The closest airports to Byron Bay are Balina and Coolangatta.

Best time to visit Peak season in the south is the summer holidays, from mid-December to late January, when flights from Europe and North America are most expensive. Summer can be very hot, even in the south, while in the north, the weather can be very humid with heavy downpours. In northern Australia, the busiest time is winter, with dry, warm weather. Autumn (April and May) is a good time to visit many regions. In Queensland, September and October are the best months, before it gets too hot. February and March are the wettest months. Winter in New South Wales, in June, July and August, is mild, and August and September are the driest months. February and March are the best months for walking in Tasmania.

New Zealand

Getting there International flights arrive at Auckland, Wellington and Christchurch airports. There are no non-stop flights from London; stopovers are either Amsterdam or Frankfurt, Los Angeles in the US or Asian cities such as Bangkok, Kuala Lumpur and Singapore.

Best time to visit New Zealand has a temperate climate, so weather can be unpredictable. Summer from November to March is the busiest time of year, especially at Christmas and throughout January when international flights are at their most expensive. Late spring (September and October) and early autumn (March and April) are less busy and often enjoy good weather. Winter (May to September) is the quietest period and, although it's wetter, it generally doesn't rain continuously for long periods of time.

Pacific islands

Getting there As one of the Pacific's main airport hubs, Fiji is served by many international flights from all over the world, including Los Angeles (11 hours), Auckland (two hours) and Sydney (three hours). Flights from London go via Los Angeles and take around 22 hours. Travel to Samoa is generally via Los Angeles (11 hours), San Francisco and Auckland (four hours). From Europe, fly to Los Angeles or Sydney, although there are no non-stop flights from Sydney to Samoa.

Best time to visit Both Fiji and Samoa enjoy a similar year-round tropical climate. May to October is the best time to visit, with cooler, drier weather. The rainy season runs from November to March, with a possibility of cyclones, and it can be very humid at this time. Temperatures are around 26-30°C all year.

Healthy stopovers in Sydney

Sydney's a busy place, but you can still find peace in the city if you've got a night or two there. For a gorgeous, top-of-the-range boutique hotel, try **Blue** (from US$400 per room per night, T+61 (0)2-9331 9000, www.tajhotels.com/sydney) in a surprisingly peaceful bay on the finger wharf at Woolloomooloo. The loft rooms in the old wharf building are particularly amazing and the staff are young and genuine. The hotel's **Spa Chakra** (T+61 (0)2-9368 0888, www.spachakra.com) is a luxurious medi-spa, with a focus on good health as well as five-star pampering; nearby are the Royal Botanic Gardens where you can spend an afternoon chilling out with the birds.

More affordable but equally serene is the laid-back and arty **Regents Court** (from US$214 per room per night, T+61 (0)2-9358 1533, www.regentscourt.com.au), a surprising oasis in Potts Point near Kings Cross with a resident writer programme. The roomy studios have fully stocked kitchenettes and there's a guest garden on the roof full of blooms and with amazing views.

There's nothing flash about the **Crest Hotel** (from US$140 per room per night, T+61 (0)2 9358 2755, www.thecresthotel.com.au), but the rooms have plenty of floor space and the harbour view is breathtaking. The hotel's Ginseng Bathhouse is an authentic Korean spa, and hugely popular with locals. Be prepared to wander around in the nude, lose most of your skin and be shouted at – this is how it's been in Asia for centuries and it's fantastically invigorating.

Alternatively, **Dive** (from US$128 per room per night, T+61 (0)2-9665 5538, www.divehotel.com.au) is not as its name would suggest, but a friendly, family-run boutique hotel at beautiful Coogee Beach. Take your morning yoga practice down to the rocks by the sea, then swim in Wylie's baths.

For some respite in the city, go to **Govindas** T+61 (0)2-9380 5155, www.govindas.com.au) to eat an ayurvedic meal and catch an Aussie flick, or drop in on hatha yoga classes, meditation or chanting. Or there's a great range of classes at **Samadhi Yoga** (T+61 (0)2-9517 3280, www.samadhibliss.com) in the funky suburb of Newtown.

Eat me

Australia is the land of smoothies, organic cafés and the freshest seafood, so you won't have to try hard to eat like a yoga goddess whilst you're here. Wheat-free and dairy-free are the norm and if it isn't organic, it won't get through the doors of half the restaurants. This is the country to indulge your detox dreams.

Freshly squeezed juices can be found everywhere – try different combinations such as beetroot, carrot, ginger and parsley for a shot of vitamin A and beta carotenes that help combat ageing and provide cancer-fighting antioxidants. The parsley can help maintain healthy blood vessels and acts as a diuretic. For a refreshing blast of goodness try watermelon juice with fresh mint: watermelon is high in potassium and will keep you hydrated; mint aids digestion and cleanses your system.

Barbecued seafood is the perfect healthy meal and nowhere will it taste better than 'down under'. Try grilled Balmain bugs (a bit like small lobsters) or baby octopus, which are a great source of iron, selenium and vitamin B12.

In New Zealand try the local crayfish and green-lipped mussels – the latter are rich in glycosaminoglycan (a natural anti-inflammatory). Don't miss manuka honey which has been hailed as a miracle product thanks to its strong antibacterial properties. Kiwi fruits are grown in abundance and are packed with potassium and high in folate, magnesium, vitamin E and fibre. Kumara appears on virtually every menu in the country – a sweet potato, it's a rich source of antioxidants, virtually free of fat and cholesterol, and high in fibre.

On the Pacific islands, enjoy the huge variety of salads, vegetables, fruit and seafood. Lobsters, a good source of omega-3, are considered to be some of the best in the world. Then there's the abundance of ripe, refreshing tropical fruit to enjoy, from watermelons and papayas to guavas and pineapples. Look out for cassava, a starchy root that's a good source of calcium, phosphorous and vitamin C. You'll find it steamed, boiled or pureed and served in place of potatoes. It's also delicious fried or cooked in curries.

Australia, New Zealand & Pacific Islands

TAIALOFA

LIFETIME PRIVATE RETREATS

ANAHATA

Australia offers some pristine environments in which to recharge, inventive wellbeing trips to take you off the beaten track and funky Byron Bay where it's easy to DIY.

Fact file

- **Visa:** All nationalities except New Zealanders need visas
- **IDD:** +61
- **Currency:** Australian dollar ($)
- **Time zone:** Perth GMT +8 hours; Sydney GMT +10 hours
- **Electricity:** 240v
- **Tourist board:** www.australia.com

YOGA RETREAT

Budawang Yoga Retreat

Budawang, New South Wales
T+61 (0)2-4457 3682
www.budawang.com
From US$285 per person for 2 nights

Budawang is an eco-friendly bush haven near the south coast of New South Wales. Throughout the year the family opens the house and additional rooms for weekend dru yoga retreats. Surrounded by dense green forest, the 51-acre property has almost 1 km of frontage on the environmentally protected Clyde river.

Mary-Louise Parkinson runs the retreats with her husband Mark, with children helping out. She has a string of credentials – including a pilot's licence – and each retreat is unique as she tailors the practice to her guests. The retreats are intimate, with regulars from Sydney, Canberra and increasingly, the USA and Europe. Bookings are essential.

Accommodation is homely; there are just five guest rooms, two in the main house, the others separate, with one to three people per room. If you end up sharing, privacy screens are installed. Many of the roomy beds have been handmade and the focus is on comfort, so expect plenty of bedding to snuggle into. It's the personal touches that make this retreat special: knitted socks, bath oils and robes are provided, and the guest kitchen has a ready supply of fruit, herbal teas, nuts and home-made cookies. Wholesome, delicious vegetarian meals are provided throughout the weekend.

Dru yoga practice is the focus of the retreat and Mary-Louise's style makes it accessible for all ages and levels of experience. The practice utilizes the power of the heart, with gentle, flowing movements to remove blockages in the body (see glossary). Her caring guidance ensures everyone gets the most out of the morning and evening sessions. During the day, you can go walking or swim in the river, climb Pigeon House

---

Own only what you can carry with you.

Alexander Solzhenitsyn

Mountain, enjoy a relaxing massage or find a strategically placed hammock and read a book from the guest library while you get into the swing of things.

Mary-Louise brings in special guests for workshops – this could be African drumming or belly dancing, or Aboriginal bush tucker, showing you the indigenous ways of collecting food. A Budawang retreat reminds you of the healing power of nature and leaves you feeling uplifted, nourished and revitalized.

Budawang is a 3½-hour drive from Sydney or a 2½-hour drive from Canberra. Daily buses run from central Sydney to Milton. Alternatively enjoy a picturesque train ride Sydney to Bomaderry (Nowra), where you will be met and transferred to the retreat. Retreats are run from February to November. Being close to the coast, Budawang has a temperate climate with just enough cool weather in winter to enjoy the cosy indoor fire.

FOREST RETREAT

Cradle Mountain Lodge

Cradle Mountain-Lake St Clair National Park, Tasmania
T+61 (0)2-9299 2103
www.cradlemountainlodge.com.au
From US$100 per person per night.

Voyages' Cradle Mountain Lodge sits on the edge of the Cradle Mountain-Lake St Clair National Park, part of the World

Heritage-listed Tasmanian wilderness. Built in 1973 as a base camp, it is still a destination for walkers, and a great place to come if you're into trekking but want some luxury to return to afterwards.

You sleep in one of 86 cabins dotted around the forest (the King Billy and Spa suites have wood burning stoves). Rivers and creeks intersect the property, and trout and platypuses inhabit the pond. There are 20 walking tracks of varying difficulty in the immediate vicinity, and the national park is next door. The guided walks are excellent, and leave daily in most weather conditions. After a day's walking, unwind in the Waldheim Alpine Spa, where there are plenty of treatments to soothe aching legs, feet and muscles.

The buffet breakfast is superb, but lunch at the Tavern is an uninspired menu of pub food and the walkers' picnic hamper is no more than an overpriced school lunch. The Highlands restaurant has two- or three-course fine-dining menus for dinner, though there are few healthy and vegetarian choices, and the desserts are rich, so walk hard.

Other guests are mostly couples from Australia. February and March are peaceful times to visit – avoid the summer, when the lodge has lots of groups. Fly to Melbourne, then Devonport, from where there's a transfer service to the lodge four days a week (from US$50 one way). Alternatively, fly to Hobart and drive 4½ hours to the lodge.

Cradle Mountain Lodge.

Daintree EcoLodge & Spa

Daintree, Queensland
T+61 (0)7-4098 6100
www.daintree-ecolodge.com.au
From US$375 per person per night

Renowned throughout Australia, the Daintree EcoLodge is the first and is the original and most successful ecotourism destination in the country. The luxury cabins and multi-award-winning spa attract honeymooners, couples celebrating milestones and lots of Americans and Europeans.

In the past few years there's been a shift in ideology at the lodge. Alongside the themes of indigenous experience, luxury and environmental awareness, a new slogan has appeared: 'Life is not a dress rehearsal'. Owners Terry and Cathy Maloney fell prey to cancer within 18 months of each other, and their subsequent lifestyle changes have influenced the business.

Guests can now have a personal session with a naturopath or a nutritionist, a yoga or meditation class, or shiatsu, all in the privacy of their luxurious villa. There are 15 of these perched on stilts up to 20 m high. It's worthwhile getting one of the 10 de luxe cabins each with its own jacuzzi on the mesh-enclosed balcony; late afternoon is an excellent time for a bath, when the breeze plays among the ferns and light dances through the canopy.

The lodge offers three-, five- or seven-night wellbeing packages that include a lifestyle consultation and some gentle exercise, such as walking or stretching. Alongside Aboriginal art classes, yoga (a blend of kundalini yoga and qigong) is now on the activities schedule, with classes on a deck beside the waterfall.

Not included in the wellbeing package, but a must, is a treatment at the spa. The service is sensational, from the moment you wander in to choose your products, to the fruit kebab and herbal tea in the post-treatment chill out lounge. The spa uses Li'Tya products, as well as their own range

based on the traditional healing practices of the Kuku Yalanji people, the property's original inhabitants. Treatments incorporate Aboriginal techniques.

There are fascinating signature treatments, including 'Wawu Jirakul' meaning 'your spirit cleansed', held by the waterfall. After some breathing exercises, a ritual then creates a sacred space and the guest is covered in moist ochres from the creek, then massaged as they dry soft and smooth like talcum powder. A feathering movement and a gentle massage follows, then the ochres are washed off with water from the waterfall.

Native ingredients from the property also appear on the dining table. The rainforest salad at Julaymba restaurant is a feast of vibrant colours; prices are surprisingly reasonable and the food is fresh, creative and light. At breakfast, try one of Terry's jungle juices, which he credits for his good health today.

The interpretative rainforest walk isn't much of a walk, but it's an essential part of a stay at the Daintree EcoLodge. Learn about the culture and traditions of the Kuku Yalanji people and connect with the environment around you. The Lodge also runs cancer retreats and corporate health retreats which occasionally mean that the whole lodge is booked out.

Fly to Cairns. There is one scheduled transfer service per day from Cairns airport and hotels (from US$60). Otherwise, it's a stunning 90-minute drive from Cairns and 40 minutes from Port Douglas. February and March are wet months, although some may appreciate the smaller number of tourists at this time.

Daintree Ecolodge & Spa.

Wellbeing holiday

Blue Spirit surf and adventure retreats

🪁 ⛰ 🍎 🧍 🏃 ↘4

Uplifting surfing adventure holidays with yoga at their heart, Blue Spirit retreats are set in the stunning Margaret River area on the southwest coast of Western Australia, a region well known for its wines but less widely known as an adventure playground for anyone willing to give things a go.

Where you stay You stay in a modern two-storey beach house with wide verandas, from which you can see only one other house and a couple of paddocks amid the sea of native peppermint trees, banksia and grass trees, with the Indian Ocean in the distance. The house sleeps up to 14 guests in spacious twins or triples. Evenings are the only time the group is at the house, when everyone gathers in the lounge or on the back veranda for a glass of the local wine and to catch the dramatic sunset.

What you do Each day starts with yoga, held underneath the house to a chorus of squawking birds. The practice, which is suitable for beginners, complements the surfing; stretching sore arms and working on the legs and hips for a quick 'pop up' on the wave. After a substantial breakfast everyone piles onto the bus for three hours of surfing on beautiful beaches. Learners use long foam boards and are in the water after a brief lesson on land. Everyone at Blue Spirit is a surfer, from the cook to the massage therapist, so you're in good hands.

BLUE SPIRIT

❝❞

The retreat was physically demanding, but every time I challenged myself I was rewarded with a pod of dolphins coming in close to play, or the distant spume of a whale. By the last day, I was confident enough to catch a few waves on my own and wobbled to my feet more often than not. As much as the yoga complemented the surfing, the chance to let our hair down during the wine tour balanced all that healthy activity. I went on the Blue Spirit retreat to learn to surf, but came away with far more than that. And best of all - I made some amazing friends.

Jo Hegerty

Other adventure activities on offer include abseiling a small, medium or large cliff, enjoying the crystal aquamarine waters of Geograph Bay from a sea kayak, meandering through giant Boranup Forest and swimming in rock pools at South Beach. There are also winery tours, and each guest receives a half-hour rejuvenating massage from a local therapist. Evening activities include meditation, belly dancing, and the fine art of pizza twirling.

What you eat and drink Meals are served at long tables inside or out. Sam the singing chef produces a great selection of food, from sushi to local lamb chops to perfectly poached eggs in the morning. All dietary requirements are catered for. Lunch is usually a picnic, eaten in yet another inspiring location between adventures.

Who goes People mainly in their thirties, from around the globe, who've always wanted to have a go at surfing, but find the idea of a surf retreat a little too much. With yoga and meditation in the mix, they know that they'll be with like-minded people and won't feel intimidated.

Essentials T+61 (0)8-9757 9284, www.bluespiritretreats.com.au. The five-day retreats cost from US$1700 for five nights and run from November to April. There are women's only retreats as well as mixed. Wetsuits are provided. Bring insect repellent, at least two swimsuits, walking shoes, a hat, slippers and something warm for yoga – and don't forget your camera. Margaret River is three hours' drive south of Perth – transfers from the airport are included. It's a good idea to spend a few days after the retreat exploring the area.

DETOX RETREAT

Fountainhead

○ ⋔ ◉ ⊛ ◒ ↘5

Maleny, Queensland
T+61 (0)7-5494 3494
www.fountainhead.com.au
From US$220 per person per night

In the hills behind the Sunshine Coast, Fountainhead is an organic health retreat that focuses on cleansing the body, clearing the mind and tackling emotional obstacles. The main building stands out against the relentless green, with cobalt-blue walls surrounding the kitchen, dining room and lounge; an outdoor heated pool, spa and 25-m lap pool.

People come here to detox, kick-start a healthy regime, alleviate depression or a serious illness, or just to chill out. There are plenty of places to loll around – the lounge is full of deep, comfy sofas and there are sunloungers on the deck. Watch for platypuses on the banks of the lake or hide among the citrus groves for some time out.

Six cabins are nestled among the avocado trees, each decorated in bold, bright colours for energy and inspiration. Each has a lounge area and kitchenette, and a spa bath. Larger cabins have two bedrooms. A cheaper option is a room in Platypus Lodge, the original farmhouse, with country B&B-style rooms and shared bathroom.

The juice detox starts every Monday and you should arrive a day or two before to prepare. There are four large juices a day, plus a range of herbal teas and filtered water. A stretch class and a walk are on offer every day, and the hosts recommend two sessions in the steam room, a spa and twice-daily body brushing. Book therapies for the days of the detox as it makes it that much easier to stick it out. These take place at your cabin and are either body treatments or personal development sessions, such as life coaching.

When you do eat, the food is fantastic, colourful and creative, utilizing veggies from the garden and fruits from the trees, plus nuts, fish and shellfish. Fellow guests could be anywhere from 17 to 80, probably women from the cities of Australia, although an increasing number of men attend the depression retreats. Throughout the year there's a programme of 10-day cancer retreats and depression retreats as well as a boot camp, which focuses on fitness – there are no detox programmes during these retreats.

Fly to Brisbane. Fountainhead will organize transfers to the tacky Aussie World with Sun Air buses, then pick you up from there. Domestic travellers fly to the Sunshine Coast, to be picked up from Maroochydore airport.

HILLSIDE RETREAT

Gaia Retreat & Spa

⊕ ⊙ ⬟ ○ ⋔ ◉ ◉ ○ ◆ ↘6

Byron Bay hinterland, New South Wales
T+61 (0)2-6687 1216
www.gaiaretreat.com.au
From US$1000 per person for 3 nights full board

High in the hills behind Byron Bay, Gaia Retreat & Spa is a real haven for those looking to relax and unwind. This sophisticated hideaway, which has room for 36 guests, opened at the beginning of 2005 and is the brainchild of Olivia Newton John who occasionally checks in for some relaxation. Warm greys and billowing saffron curtains complement the earthy wood and cane furnishings in Kukura House, the main lounge and guest area. Guests can choose from the library of books and games, and head out to the covered deck, or tuck themselves away in a cushioned alcove.

Half of the Samoan-style longhouse is dedicated to dining and there are individual tables so guests can choose to eat alone or with others. Apart from the daily buffet breakfast, a personal menu is arranged for each guest to achieve individual goals. People come to Gaia for many reasons and whether they're there to de-stress, lose some weight or pamper themselves, an appropriate menu is devised.

Meals at Gaia use local produce, often from their own garden, organic if possible, and vegetable-based (but include fish and poultry). That's not to say red meat isn't available – a stay at Gaia isn't punishment

Left: Lap pool at Fountainhead. **Right:** Gaia.

Australia, New Zealand & Pacific Islands Australia

Unusual adventures in Oz

Inventive tour operators have cooked up some brilliant trips to get you off the tourist trail and into the bush. **Willis's Walkabouts Bushwalking Holidays** (T+61 (0)8-8985 2134, www.bushwalkingholidays.com.au) runs a bushwalking health retreat to Kakadu twice a year, combining daily yoga and meditation with healthy food, visits to ancient Aboriginal art sites and swimming in crystal-clear waters. You'll be walking in some of Kakadu's most beautiful and remote areas high up on the escarpment above Twin Falls, led by experienced bushwalking guide, Cassie Newnes, and yoga and dance teacher, Jenny Devlin. This is untracked wild land with rejuvenating fresh air and some rarely seen art sites – and you won't meet other tourists as you need permits for the area. Jenny will tailor her sessions to accommodate all levels. Both guides have experience of working with indigenous communities, and Cassie is also a trained massage therapist who will help ease your knots along the way. You fly to Darwin, from where transfers are included. The trip takes up to 10 people and costs from US$1000.

Alternatively, get close to the earth on an Aboriginal Tour with **Desert Tracks** (T+61 (0)2-6232 4080, www.deserttracks.com.au), a company owned and operated by the indigenous Pitjantjatjara people of central Australia. The 'Pit Lands' in the central Australian desert is an area wholly given over to the country's indigenous people. Desert Tracks leads three- and five-day tours through an area of harsh but amazing landscape: pink desert dotted with the odd cattle station and kangaroo. The trip costs from US$879 per person for three days.

With no written history, no chiefs, and no sense of property, the Aborgines have been deemed by anthropologists to be the world's only true communist society, and these trips will give you a real insight into how this community works. Led by Anangu guides, you'll learn how Aborigines track food and water using 'songlines' – invisible paths mapped out in song and passed down through generations. Each day you walk at a brisk hunter-gatherer pace, camp out in swags (a tent and a sleeping bag in one) and have the chance to visit sacred sites and see cave paintings and traditional dance displays.

Be prepared for extreme weather changes – pack layers and a high-factor sunscreen. The Cultural Icons three-day tour and the five-day Angatja Bush College have set departure dates. The five-day Ngintaka Songline Heritage Trail is the most intense experience (from US$1500 per person), but it only runs if a private group books it. Fly to Uluru (Ayers Rock) airport; trips usually start from Voyages' Ayers Rock Resort (www.ayersrockresort.com.au).

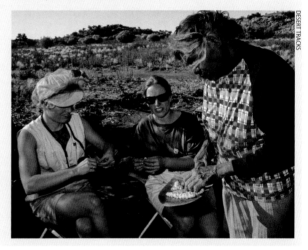

DESERT TRACKS

and if a guest really wants a steak one night, staff will order it in. Wine is served with the three-course dinner and coffee is available, but only on request.

The rooms are all beautifully turned out, continuing the colour theme from Kukura House, and are nestled among subtropical gardens. Whether you go for a Layana room, Sura terrace or Acala suite will depend on how much private space you require.

Gaia is not a health retreat, but there are plenty of opportunities to get back on track. There's yoga or tai chi every morning in the small studio by the spa, a tennis court and heated pool, plus plenty of walking. As well as the ongoing schedule of activities, including art classes and meditation, guests can draw on the wealth of practitioners at Byron Bay for other therapies and treatments, such as kinesiology and pilates; just let Gaia's staff know what you're after and they'll source the best practitioner to come to you.

As well as hosting guest yoga retreats from the likes of Jessie Chapman (www.radiance retreats.com), Gaia runs four-night retreats with in-house teacher Flo Fenton and her fusion of iyengar, ashtanga and satyananda (www.intouchyogabyronbay.com). There are also fitness retreats, workshops for women, cooking and nutrition retreats and sculpture workshops.

Byron Bay is only a 25-minute drive away, but most people won't want to leave Gaia during their stay here. Instead, devote any spare time to the Amala Spa, where treatments draw on Aboriginal and Asian healing techniques and products (from US$100 for a 90-minute massage).

Fellow guests are likely to be Australian and female, half on their own, half in pairs. Most people will be there to tackle stress and lifestyle-related health issues, but others come to recuperate from serious illness. Fly to Ballina or Coolangatta airports, from where Gaia offers complimentary transfers.

The Golden Door Elysia

🌐 🌿 🔆 ☀ ⏲ 🔥 🌀 ⊕ 🌟 ◐ ↘7

Hunter Valley, New South Wales
T+61 (0)2-4993 8500
www.goldendoor.com.au
From US$1400 per person for 5 days

The Golden Door Elysia is a luxury purpose-built health retreat in the heart of the Hunter Valley wine region. Guests can stay independently and devise their own programme, or go on a five- to seven-day Golden Door Programme. It's totally unrelated to The Golden Door in the US.

You stay in one of 74 villas set in a circle around the periphery, each with a balcony overlooking the valley. Villas have one, two or three bedrooms and are everything you'd expect from a five-star hotel: fluffy white towels, robes and slippers, king-size bed, TV, DVD player, deep bath, and a great view. The main building is warm, contemporary and luxurious, including a lounge and balcony for communal relaxation and a dining area with a long balcony overlooking the valley.

Facilities include pools, a gym, basketball and tennis courts and yoga rooms, although these are uninspiring and a little dark.

Each day starts with tai chi on beautiful Meditation Hill, followed by the choice of a walk or deep-water running. A gorgeous breakfast is followed by a stretch class, after which the timetable varies, with choices including pilates, yoga, fitball, mountain biking, volleyball, circuit training and meditation classes. The day ends with the option of another walk, and then stretching. Classes are of a varying standard, so experiment with different teachers. Dinner is at 1830 and on some evenings (if you can keep your eyes open) there is a seminar or workshop to follow, though these are held in a conference-like room far too reminiscent of the corporate world.

The wellness centre offers naturopathy, counselling, hypnotherapy, dietary and medical advice. The pranic healing, watsu and samvahan vibrational massage treatments are the strongest and most effective treatments on offer. The Golden Door Programme includes two Swedish massages, a facial and a visit to the dietician or naturopath. You're likely to opt for more treatments, so allow some extra budget.

There is strictly no caffeine, alcohol or smoking; all food is organic, and salt- and sugar-free. On the Golden Door programme you'll have vegetarian set meals with some fish. If you're here independently, there's the option of meat and dessert. Fellow guests are of all ages. Some have personal issues to deal with such as illness, or the breakdown of a relationship, or big decisions to make, while others come with partner, daughter or mother as a treat.

The Golden Door has another property in Queensland, but there's no opportunity for independent stays and the experience is less polished. Elysia is a two-hour drive from Sydney; or 45 minutes from Newcastle Airport. There is a mini-bus service available from Central train station in Sydney for US$45 return.

Gwinganna Lifestyle Retreat

🌐 🌿 🔆 ☀ ⏲ 🔥 🌀 ⊕ 🌟 ↘8

Tallebudgera, Queensland
T+61 (0)7-5589 5000
www.gwinganna.com
From US$650 for 2 nights, based on 2 sharing

Set in 160 ha with views across the valley and out to the Pacific Ocean and the Brisbane skyline, Gwinganna offers a number of interesting lifestyle and health programmes which run throughout the year, including organic cookery and nutrition workshops, yoga and hiking breaks, adventure weekends, detox weeks and the popular five-day Optimum Wellness programme.

The retreat mixes colonial-style buildings

GOLDEN DOOR

GWINGANNA

Left: Golden Door Elysia. **Above**: Gwinganna.

Do-it-yourself retreat: Byron Bay

Just south of the Queensland border in New South Wales, Byron Bay is a small town with a big reputation. For many years it's been seen as the place for alternative lifestyles and, while there are more surf shops than organic food stores these days, Byron has everything you need to create a tailor-made wellbeing holiday.

Where you stay Inspiring accommodation for all budgets is in plentiful supply. **Arts Factory Lodge** (T+61 (0)2-6685 7709, www.artsfactory.com.au, from US$30 per person per night) is the original commune-cum-hostel, with tipis, tents and wagons as dorms and rooms. There's always plenty going on: learn fire-juggling or drumming, make your own didgeridoo; or head up to the studio in the Buddha Bar for the daily programme of yoga, dance and hula-hoop classes. People come from all over the world to stay at the lodge – some never leave.

The lodge has expanded to become the Arts Factory Village (contact details above, click on 'luxury abodes'), with self-contained accommodation for all budgets. The Garden Burees (from US$200 per night) are stunning, intimate two-storey huts in Balinese style, with basic kitchen and a spa bath downstairs, and double bed upstairs. The villas (from US$380 per night) are top of the range. There's a private heated spa and plunge pool outdoors and a fully stocked kitchen. Modern, stylish and in a much higher price bracket than the original, the villas still have that unmistakable Arts Factory touch: step through carved wooden doors into the composting toilet or spend some time in the yoga/meditation room.

Byron also does guesthouses and B&Bs extremely well. Pick of the bunch are **Byron Bay Guesthouse** (T+61 (0)4-2100 8886, www.byronbayguesthouse.com, from US$115 per room per night) for Balinese-inspired space and serenity, and **Burns at Byron** (T+61 (0)4-2117 4056, from US$90 per room per night) an intimate B&B with an outdoor bath and shower for stargazing.

Hire a car and get out into the Byron hinterland for a total escape. The creativity and style of Byron continues into the subtropical forest. A 15-minute drive up into the hills, the **Green Mango Hideaway** (T+61 (0)2-6684 7171, www.greenmango. com.au, from US$125 per room per night) is an idyllic B&B run by an English couple. Guests have the run of the house and there's an huge garden for morning yoga. The Garden King or King Suite would be ideal for a private retreat and there's plenty of walking.

What you do The options for yoga are many and varied. Local paper *The Echo* has class timetables for the Main Beach Yoga and Massage Studio above the Main Beach surf lifesaving club at the top of town, Byron Yoga Centre at Belongil, and Byron Iyengar Yoga out near the arts and industry estate. Most classes are about US$12 each.

Private tuition is a great way to develop your practice. **Flo Fenton** (T+61 (0)2-6685 9910, www.intouchyogabyronbay.com) is a fabulous teacher (see also below), focusing on trouble spots and developing a personalized programme for you to follow. She teaches flowing, dynamic yoga and her lovely, gentle nature is truly nurturing (from US$50 per 90-minute session).

It's well worth taking a trip up to the lovely Bangalow studio to have a class with yogalates creator, **Louise Solomon** (T+61 (0)2-6687 2031; www.yogalates.com.au). It may seem like a gentle workout, but you'll feel it the next day (US$14 per class). Yogalates classes are also held in Byron at **Ambaji Wellness Centre** (T+61 (0)2-6685 6620, www.ambaji.com.au), where Flo Fenton teaches as well. The centre is open every day for free lunchtime meditation and many of Byron's best healers and therapists are represented here: with everything from reiki to psychic and tarot readings, this old beach house has it all.

Every second person you meet in Byron is a massage therapist, so choose carefully. For the best kahuna massage in town, go to **Bien-Etre** (T+61 (0)2-6680 7405, www.bienetre.com.au; from US$60 for one hour). Create a personal bodywork and pampering programme at **Cocoon** (T+61 (0)2-6685 5711, www.cocoonbyron.com.au) and **Quintessence** (T+61 (0)2-6685 5533, www.quintessencebyron.com.au). Owner of both, Annette Batchelor, will help devise a series of treatments, beginning with a consultation, to suit your needs. Massage and iridology are available at Quintessence; Cocoon next door takes care of inner health and beauty with body treatments and naturopathic consultations based on a variety of philosophies, including homeopathic (see glossary).

The **Ayurveda College** (T+61 (0)2-6632 2244, www.ayurveda house.com.au) has a clinic in town, Byron Ayurveda Centre, where you can have treatments, including shirodara, or health and lifestyle consultations. And if you want to get your health back on track, Michael Reynolds at the **Naturopath Bodyworks Clinic** (T+61 (0)2-6685 7550) can develop a detox or cleansing programme, while wife Jeanne takes care of deep tissue and other massages.

with furnishings imported from Thailand to create an Old World village atmosphere. Accommodation is in comfortable rooms and houses, all in a relaxed rural setting. The superb facilities include an exercise studio with sprung timber floor, an outdoor yoga deck with ocean and valley views, a state-of-the-art gym, two swimming pools, and sun loungers on a deck overlooking the ocean. There's even a heritage church, used for yoga and the amazing Sound Garden experience, a sort of acoustic relaxation.

Most programmes feature the inventive 'dreamtime' (adopted from the Aborigine word), which are afternoons of 'strategic relaxation' where the hardest decision you'll have to make is how to spend time between your spa treatments. These use the organic Phyt's skincare range from France – try 'Heavenessence and Beyond' – a two-hour treatment combining the ancient Hawaiian tradition of Ka Huna, healing hot stones, a natural oil and mineral salt scrub, followed by an Australian Bush Essence bath.

The creative chefs make colourful, delicious dishes. Fellow guests are mostly women aged 35-55 or couples. Fly to Gold Coast airport, from where courtesy transfers are provided at set times on arrival day (and included in the package). January, April and September are the most popular times to visit, so avoid them if you want some peace and quiet.

Hopewood

🌐 🕐 🕑 👥 🔬 ⚙️ ✳️ ⭕ ↘9

Wallacia, New South Wales
T+61 (0)2-4773 8401
www.hopewood.com.au
From US$1000 all-inclusive per person per night

Hopewood was Australia's first health retreat, built in the 1960s by visionary and philanthropist LO Bailey. It's situated in what is now the western extremity of Sydney's suburbs, and has all the charm of a nursing home when taken at face value. The reception, dining hall and guest lounge have the air of a

1950s motel, and the budget rooms within the main building are small and bare with single beds. If detoxing, guests are better off staying in one of the separate balcony units, which, although in desperate need of updating, have high ceilings, a daybed and private balcony looking out into the bush.

Despite its aesthetic shortcomings, Hopewood has a long list of regulars who come time and time again to get back on track. Interestingly, many have tried the more glamorous health retreats, yet still return to Hopewood. The reason is the unparalleled care and attention given to everyone who signs up to a programme. Hopewood is not the place to come for some pampering and a bit of light detoxing; people come here to change, or even save, their lives. The Optimal Health and Wellbeing seven-night package is the most popular. The food is fantastic: creative and cleansing, it is vegetarian and oil-free with no added salt.

Hopewood is an hour's drive along the M4 from Sydney, or take the train to Penrith then either catch a taxi or the No 795 Warragamba bus to Hopewood. Summer months are very hot and school holidays are busy.

Kangaroo Island Health Retreat

🌐 ⚕️ 🕐 🔬 ⚙️ ⭕ ↘10

Emu Bay, Kangaroo Island, South Australia
T+61 (0)8-8553 5374
www.kihealthretreat.com
From US$1685 for 5 days

Kangaroo Island is one of the most pristine and untouched environments in Australia, a perfect place for a detox from the inside out. And that's what you'll get here, in the safe hands of the retreat's founder and facilitator, Sue McCarthy, the epitome of good health and with 25 years' experience in the detox business. You stay for five days and have the choice of a moderate or dynamic detox programme.

Custom-built by Sue and her husband, Austin, the lodge houses up to six people in a fresh, clean and cosy setting surrounded by stunning views of Emu Bay. Within an hour of arrival, your cleanse is under way and you begin the daunting task of drinking at least eight litres of water a day. Each morning begins at 0630 with a litre of water and a

Kangaroo Island Health Retreat.

🍽 Soul food

A stay at **Gunya Titjikala** (T+61 (0)2-9211 2322, www.gunya.com.au) in Australia's Northern Territory provides a unique insight into indigenous culture with great benefits for the local community. Staying in de luxe safari tents in the desert 120 km south of Alice Springs, guests can experience first-hand the way of life of the Titjikala desert people. From US$1000 per tent per night, the experience doesn't come cheap, but 50% of the profits go to fund health and education for the community and help preserve this ancient culture – the example set to other communities in Australia is invaluable. Although Gunya Tourism offers a luxury product, it is philanthropically funded and channels profits into other indigenous tourism opportunities.

3-km walk. The rest of your day is filled with nutrition workshops, sessions in yoga and pilates, a spa, sauna and plunge-pool ritual, more walking, a swim in the ocean, afternoon naps, numerous trips to the toilet and more water. On the moderate programme you eat three meals a day and drink only water in between meals. On the dynamic programme you drink water with a little fruit and vegetable juice for the first three days before easing back into food for the final two days. When you do eat, it's organic wholefood that is easy to digest, such as fruit, brown rice, soup, yoghurt and salads. Most of the food is sourced directly from Sue's garden.

Australians from the east coast make up the majority of the visitors, but you will find a great mixture of ages, personalities and levels of health and fitness, including many repeat guests. Plan ahead as only 30 programmes for six people are offered each year. Go when the weather is mild and warm, from September to early December, or March to

May. Fly to Adelaide, from where it's a 20-minute flight to Kingscote airport on Kangaroo Island – the retreat is a 20-minute bus ride. See glossary for more on detox.

ISLAND RETREAT
Lifetime Private Retreats

🌐 ⛺ ☀ 🏔 ♻ 🏃 **✈11**

Kangaroo Island
T+61 (0)8-8354 2368
www.life-time.com.au
From US$500 per person per night

Three secluded and beautiful homes in a remote 40 ha on Kangaroo Island, Lifetime is a wonderful sanctuary where you can come to chill out and enjoy nature, or receive tailor-made attention. Run by brother and sister team, Nick and Rachel Hannaford, the property has been in the family since their grandfather bought the land in 1945, and has a well-cared for, relaxed ambience.

A chef who has cooked for the likes of Mick Jagger and the Dalai Lama, Rachel is also a vinyasa flow yoga and meditation teacher, who trained with Baron Baptiste

(www.baronbaptiste.com) in the USA. There are optional yoga and meditation classes at 0800 every morning, and specialized yoga and meditation retreats throughout the year, as well as general health retreats which include photography, natural health, gourmet cooking and painting workshops as well as yoga and meditation.

Go swimming in the sea, walk the island, fly a kite or spot wildlife – there are fur seals, endemic kangaroos, wallabies, and koalas, as well as a mass of bird life. Each house is secluded from the others and luxuriously turned out, with king-size beds, deep-pile bathrobes, flatscreen TVs and DVD players, powerful telescopes, and various hidden treats. You'll also have your own yoga mats, art materials, boogie boards, snorkel and goggles, beach balls, kites and croquet sets.

There's a minimum stay of two nights – but extend to at least three to make the most of it. Fly to Adelaide airport, from where it's a 20-minute flight to Kingscote airport on the island, or take a ferry from Cape Jervis to Penneshaw, 1½ hours' away. Transfers are included in the package – pay extra for a helicopter flight and tour.

LIFETIME PRIVATE RETREATS

Lifetime Private Retreats.

Breathe deep: where to meditate in Australia

Well-run meditation retreats take place all year round in some of Australia's most beautiful landscapes, including islands, rainforest and mountains. Open to beginners and experienced practitioners alike, they're a wonderful way to replenish your spirit.

Director of the **Well-Aware-Ness** centre in Sydney (T+61 (0)2-9460 4131, www.zululines.com), John Carter was a Buddhist monk for 11 years before studying to become a psychologist. Today he practises 'mindfulness therapy', fusing Western theory with Buddhist wisdom, and three times a year he takes time out to lead a meditation retreat (from US$1300 per person all inclusive for five days. The location for the mid-year retreat couldn't be more inspiring – Lord Howe island is just 11 km long and you stay at **Arajilla** (www.arajilla.com.au), a haven nestled among the banyan trees and kentia palms. Meditation and yoga take place in the yurt, a light, airy space based on the nomadic Mongols' traditional homes. These retreats aren't intensive; guests are free to wander the beaches, go bushwalking or do some more private reflection during the day, and Arajilla serves alcohol and decadent desserts. The New Year eight-day retreat takes place in Byron Bay, staying at **Sangsurya** (www.sangsurya.com.au).

Alternatively, head to **Prema Shanti** (T+61 (0)7-4098 9006, www.premashanti.com) a relaxed, B&B-style meditation retreat in Daintree Rainforest in Queensland (from US$45 per person per night). It's like being at a friend's place here, and you join in co-owner Mara's yoga practice, which is a hybrid of iyengar and ashtanga and whatever she feels you need on the day. The morning and evening meditation is generally unguided, with yoga nidra some evenings, all taking place at the Temple, an open room with wooden floors and surrounded by deep balconies. Discussion on meditation is welcomed; just mention that you'd like some tips. Guests are expected to help with the washing up, and to do one hour of selfless service daily. Noble silence is observed from 2130.

For a more structured retreat, the **Blue Mountains Insight Meditation Centre** (T+61 (0)2-4788 1024, www.meditation.asn.au) is in a peaceful setting in the small town of Medlow Bath, two hours by train from Sydney. It runs regular retreats in vipassana or insight meditation, in the tradition of the late venerable Mahasi Sayadaw of Burma. Programmes range from a beginners' weekend to a 40-day spiritual retreat, and you can also stay on a private retreat (payment by donation). The **Vipassana Meditation Centre** (T+61 (0)2-4787 7436, www.bhumi.damma.org) at Blackheath is also in the Blue Mountains and offers more taxing 10-day silent meditation retreats in the tradition of SN Goenka. The oldest vipassana centre in Australia, it is situated on 15 ha of beautiful bushland covered with flowering heath and eucalyptus trees. Accommodation is basic but comfortable and rooms are heated in winter. Payment is by donation. See page 282 for what to expect on a silent meditation retreat.

For a gentler route to serenity, the **Satyananda Residential Yoga Retreat Centre** (T+61 (0)2-4377 1171, www.satyananda.net) at Mangrove Creek is 1½ hours' drive from Sydney. This ashram sits on a bend in the slow-flowing creek, its neat and simple wooden buildings withdrawn beneath glorious sandstone cliffs and towering gum trees (from US$45 per person per night). Come here to experience satyananda yoga, the style from the Bihar School of Yoga in India (see page 223), which combines gentle stretching asanas with practices such as yoga nidra, kirtan, mouna and karma yoga (see glossary). About 40 residents live here in a community all year round. The gentle ambience they create and the exquisite setting make this a very nourishing place to be, and as well as daily meditation and yoga, bushwalking, kayaking, volleyball and swimming are on offer.

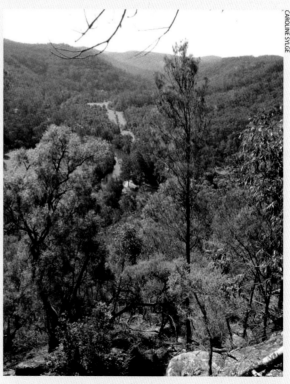

CAROLINE SYLGE

Australia, New Zealand & Pacific Islands Australia

Be creative, get alternative, go back to nature or change your life in some of the world's most inspiring landscapes.

Fact file

- **Visa:** Not required for citizens of Australia, Canada, the US and most EU countries including the UK
- **IDD:** +64
- **Currency:** New Zealand dollar ($)
- **Time zone:** GMT +12 hours
- **Electricity:** 230v
- **Tourist board:** www.newzealand.com

PERSONAL DEVELOPMENT HOLIDAY

Outward Bound

Anakiwa
T +64 (0)4-472 3440
www.outwardbound.co.nz
From US$1600 for 8 days

Outward bound.

Based on the waterside in the stunning Marlborough Sounds at the top of the South Island, Outward Bound's adventurous and challenging personal development courses are designed to instill the knowledge and belief that there is always more inside you than you think.

A charitable trust founded by educator Kurt Hahn in Wales in 1941 (www.kurthahn.org), Outward Bound courses use experiential learning – learning through doing – to help you find out more about yourself and others. The New Zealand branch is one of 47 international schools in 42 countries. A range of courses of varying length is on offer for different age groups – the eight-day Discovery course for those aged 27 and over is one of the most popular.

During the Discovery course, you will be given various daily activities designed to take you out of your comfort zone and help you discover your potential, conquer your fears, boost your motivation and understand what's needed to form effective relationships. Activities involve running, swimming, sailing, rock climbing, hiking, canoeing and camping, both in groups and alone. Instructors are kind, highly skilled and ensure a safe and supportive environment.

You are often not told what you will do until the moment you start an activity. Many activities are group-based, and finishing tasks alone is actively discouraged. That said, the heart of the course is being left alone in the bush for 36 hours to 'think about things'; during this time you're given a few tasks to complete, one of which is writing a letter to yourself which is then posted to you six months after the end of the course. Every day you sit as a group and are encouraged to open up about what you have learnt; these group sessions get more open as the week goes on.

Everything is designed to be practical – do not expect any luxuries. When you are not camping, accommodation is in no-frills twin bunk-bedded rooms, sharing four hot

Outward Bound New Zealand pushed me right out of my comfort zone. We were a very mixed group, yet we all clicked, which was vital, and I realized how much more effective we were as an organized group rather than as a collection of individuals. I found not being told what we were doing next a little irritating, and being left out in the bush alone with minimal rations and a few ground sheets was not my cup of tea – but this is how we all learnt. There were full group sessions when we all talked about how we felt, which wasn't my thing at all, but as the week went on and everyone got to know each other, this experience changed and deepened a lot. On the last day after a 14-hour hike and a particularly intense one-hour session, some of the group came out with some very serious decisions to be made. Since then we have been in a lot of contact – I genuinely think that's 13 friends I've made for life. I quit smoking during the week too – and, a year on, I haven't touched one cigarette.

Bill Foley

Alternative retreats in New Zealand

New Zealand has some well-run and very affordable places to stay offering alternative workshops, yoga and meditation, or just the chance to relax. The **Mana Retreat Centre** (T+64 (0)7-866 8972, www.manaretreat.com), 20 minutes south of Coromandel town, is one of the best, set up high in the bush-covered hills of the Coromandel Ranges on a 120-ha property overlooking the expanse of Manaia harbour. An excellent selection of stimulating and eclectic courses run all year round, including voice and movement exploration, bodywork, meditation, yoga, gourmet vegetarian cooking, sweat lodge workshops, gospel singing and osteopathic studies. Many of the teachers have been coming here for years and are personally endorsed by the trustees of Mana, who are also healers and therapists.

The main teaching space, the Octagon, has superb acoustics and picture windows with incredible views over the beautifully maintained gardens to the harbour in the distance. In the bush there's a wooden sauna, and lovely places to sit. The showpiece is the Tara Sanctuary at the foot of Mount Pukewhakataratara, accessed through an uphill bush trail. Come up here alone and try out the acoustics: however self-conscious you might feel you will be amazed at how good you sound. The nearest airport is Auckland. From US$160 for a weekend.

Alternatively, **Aio Wira** (T+64 (0)9-810 9396, www.aiowira.org.nz) is a peaceful, simple place on 4 ha of mature native bush in the Waitakere Ranges, west of Auckland. Come alone for your own personal retreat, to attend an alternative group workshop or, in the spring and summer, undertake a five-day fast. Aio Wira (meaning 'peace wheel' in the Maori language) was set up by a group of yoga students in 1970, and much of the decor hasn't changed much since, but it's a warm and intimate space with a sauna, outdoor spa pool and the Sanctuary, a wooden-framed building earmarked specifically for meditation and quiet reflection. Pay from US$35 per person per day. There are circular bush trails, regular yoga and meditation weekends take place, and shiatsu, hellerwork, lymphatic drainage, naturopathic consultations, massage, wraps and facials are available at an additional cost.

For an utterly amazing location, the **Anahata Yoga Retreat** (T+64 (0)3-525 9887, www.anahata-retreat.org.nz), at Takaka, lies 600 m above sea level with expansive views over Golden Bay and Farewell Spit. It's run along ashram lines by the inspiring, warm and dedicated Swami Muktidharma, originally from Colombia, who spent 16 years in India with his guru and yoga master, Paramahamsa Satyananda. His delightful wife, Swami Karma Karuna, specializes in yoga for women. Swami Muktidharma has the ability to demystify any teaching and deliver practical advice on how to live with awareness not only in the ashram setting but back in the wider world too. Come here to experience ashram life for as long as you want, or to take part in the six-day Explore Yourself interactive programme. Rooms are small and simple; the Chakra House is well worth the extra (from US$70 per night) – a round, straw bale house with its own kitchenette, inspiring art on the walls and stunning bay views. A night at Anahata costs from US$40 per person.

Pujjis Wellness Retreat (T+64 (0)3-546 9551, www.pujjis.com), is a place to come to if you're exhausted and need to be nurtured . This family home is beside a river and enclosed in a pine-clad valley, you'll find more dramatic scenery elsewhere in New Zealand – the focus here is on the inside, and you're encouraged to do very little, though massage, yoga therapy and counselling are offered. From US$90 per person per night.

Yoga on the beach near Anahata.

showers. Food is simple and plentiful, with sandwiches, flapjacks, cheese and tinned fish out in the bush, and lots of fruit and vegetables, meat-based dishes and hot pies back at base – vegetarians, vegans and gluten-free diets can be catered for. No drinking or smoking is allowed, you are up at 0600 every day, and one 14-hour hike has you up at 0300.

Outward Bound takes a maximum of 14 people, and attracts anyone who wants to take time out to think about their next step, or who wants a challenge. The courses are run predominantly for New Zealanders, but take a number of people from overseas. Courses all start at the Picton ferry terminal – fly from any airport in New Zealand to Blenheim, catch the ferry from Wellington or the train from Christchurch. Pack layers and some good trainers. Be prepared for a challenging and exciting week, and come alone.

Creative retreat

Wairua  13

The Coromandel Peninsula is a narrow spine of steep, verdant mountains tumbling onto pretty beaches and clean seas. A beautiful place with great energy, it has attracted Buddhist communities and artists for years, and, in Wairua, two professional artists have built an unpretentious yet profound retreat, where you can rekindle your creativity.

Where you stay Set in a remote and magical valley, accessible only by ford or drawbridge, there's a wooden lodge with star-shaped roof and wrap-around veranda – rocking chair, wisteria and all. It presides over gardens flowing out into native forest and two rivers below. You stay in one of just four generous en suite rooms with original paintings and floor-to-ceiling glass doors that open onto the lawns. The only sounds are rivers and birds. There's a fully equipped art studio and inspiring art reference library. Pièce de résistance is a fabulous outdoor bathhouse, where you soak and bubble, in utter privacy, amongst the trees.

What you do You are led step by step from sketching to carving, often out in the elements, by owner Louise McRae. After letting you sleep as long as you can, she takes you to meditate in special spots in the woods, then into the creative process. You might start by studying rocks in the riverbed, with Louise skilfully nudging you from stiff, edited drawings to expressive marks. Next, you might head into the studio, where, glass of wine in hand, you're encouraged to become yet freer – flicking, dripping, scribbling with coloured paint. The spirit of playful exploration is infectious. Self-consciousness slips away.

After some guided visualizations of your passions, values and iconic moments, you start drawing symbols which help you create from within. Depending on your workshop, you could, for example, be taught to use power tools and given huge pillars of fragrant wood to carve, sand and etch into totems. In this or any other medium, you spend happy hours shaping an expression of your life, loves and hopes – a liberating, wordless meditation.

Wielding new tools and getting through little creative crises leads to a satisfied tiredness of mind and body. Unseen dips in the rivers and bewitching soaks in the outdoor bathhouse restore and calm as you reflect on your day's creation in total natural peace.

What you eat and drink Louise and husband Hamish are passionate about their cooking. They spoil you with modern Pacific dishes which they present like works of art. In the studio, you're served beautiful local cheeses and little pots of home-made chutney to keep you fuelled. There are risottos full of garden herbs, gingery brochettes with dips, and Provençal lamb stews, all served outdoors. It's clean, imaginative cooking, willingly tailored to your food preferences, and made with such care that you feel truly pampered, although there's no pretension in this retreat.

Who goes Kiwi mothers treating themselves to a change of scene, independent travellers with imagination, people who find themselves thinking over-rationally. It's a good place to come alone, for you eat comfortably together and share experiences in the studio, or bring a friend. Stay two to five days.

Essentials Whitianga, Coromandel Peninsula, T0800-924782, www.wairuaretreat.co.nz. From US$430 per room per day. Arrive on the Auckland to Coromandel ferry, a stunning 1½ hours (ferries don't run daily; check www.360discovery.co.nz for details), rather than a three-hour drive, some of which is on winding unsealed roads. The New Zealand winter (May-October) is rainy but it's a creative and homely time to come. Sunniest months are December to February.

> 66 99
>
> Though I'm normally frustrated by my disobedient left hand, Waiura had me drawing with my wrong hand and 'letting life's experiences come out in the marks'. I became immersed in the flow. Stimulated, pampered, rested and well fed, I left feeling fresh, alive and excited by my possibilities again.
>
> *Rosie Walford*

ROSIE WALFORD

COASTAL RETREAT

Shambhala

🌀 ⛱ 🏵 ☑14

Takaka, Golden Bay
T+64 (0)3-525 8463
www.homepages.paradise.net.nz/shambhala
From US$15 per person per night

Shambhala is a lovingly created self-catering lodge perched on a hill with sweeping views of the magnificent Golden Bay. It's a wonderfully peaceful place to come to chill out or to do your own meditation or yoga practice, from November to May. During the winter, various yoga and meditation retreats are on offer.

There's a special ambience here. The yoga and meditation space is spectacular, with floor-to-ceiling windows and views across the bay. Iyengar yoga and guided meditation sessions take place twice a week during the summer, and you are welcome to use the space for your own practice any other time.

Lovingly designed by the Buddhist owner, every pathway and gatepost at Shambhala has been decorated with mosaics of shells and stones. There are spacious gardens and a large veranda for lounging on, a comfortable indoor sitting room with books, board games and a piano, and the beach on your doorstep.

Three rooms are in the main house, two sleeping four and one double, and another four doubles are in a separate building higher up the hill. Rooms are simple and comfortable, and there's a well-designed communal kitchen that is a joy to use. Loos are composted, most energy is generated by solar power and there is a rainwater collection system for the water supply.

Beach near Shambhala.

Your fellow guests are likely to be self-aware travellers looking for peace and quiet. Shambhala is 16 km from Takaka – if you're not driving, you can get a bus from Nelson to Mussel Inn, from where they'll pick you up.

VALLEY RETREAT

Takaro Peace Resort

⛱ ⛰ ◉ ❋ ❋ ❋ ◯ ☑15

Te Anau
T+64 (0)3-249 1166
www.takarolodge.com
From US$400 per room per night

Takaro is an organic lifestyle retreat and rejuvenation centre tucked away in a remote valley in the far south of New Zealand.

The main lodge, chalets and spa are set on a gently elevated plateau, overlooking an expanse of meadow which slopes down to a river. You'll hear a loud morning chorus of tuis and bellbirds on the way to breakfast, and there's access to rejuvenating private or guided river and forest walks – sometimes accompanied by the resort dog.

You stay in one of 10 extremely comfortable turf-roofed chalets with wide verandas decked out according to one of the five elements and laid out according to feng shui principles: think underfloor heating, Pierre Cardin robes, handmade soaps, and – despite it being a 'peace resort' – wide screen TVs and DVD players. Takaro also has six large traditional chalets which are much older and plainer yet solid and spacious. The public spaces are clean and fresh, all pastel colours and abstract art.

There's a whirlpool, steam room, sauna and (slightly dated) pool area to relax in. Takaro's signature rejuvenation treatment takes place with others in a special room and uses deep tissue massage, music, meditation, organic face packs and an expert touch 'to clean out blockages and rekindle lost enthusiasm' – it's sublimely relaxing, and not to be missed. You can also have energy healing sessions, qigong, relaxation and vocal exercise classes, and a session with a professional I Ching expert to help you make

decisions about health, relationships or career. Staff are delightful, attentive and extremely hard working.

The food is simple, creative and utterly delicious, taking full advantage of the seasonal organic produce and herbs in the gardens: think blue cod soup with coconut, locally caught salmon with baby spinach and wasabi yoghurt, and boysenberry tart. There is a licensed bar, as well as organic juices and subtle teas brewed with home-grown herbs.

Fellow guests are wealthy and well-travelled professionals, from all four corners of the globe, though most are from America, Germany and the UK. Children are welcome. The busiest times are from December to February, Takaro never feels crowded. Fly to Queenstown, from where it's possible to hire a car, charter a light plane or helicopter, or take a shuttle minivan to Te Anau, from where it's a 30-minute drive – transfers can be arranged.

RURAL RETREAT

Tui

☀ ◯ ☑16

T+64 (0)3-535 8399
www.tuitrust.org.nz
From US$130 per person

One of the best ways to rejuvenate body and soul in New Zealand is to get outdoors. For a taste of the outdoor life which brings you right up close to nature, Tui is a long-established permaculture community living on the edge of the Abel Tasman Park on a particularly lovely bay. This spiritual and educational trust runs various retreats and workshops all year round. The Earth Spirit workshop will have you identifying a salad of weeds in the wild, reading energy spots and water lines on the land, and communing with plants. The community has a strong knowledge of Maori wisdom and runs survival courses in the wild especially for boys and their fathers. You sleep out in one of two canvas domes or a tipi – or bring your own tent to be more private. Prices are for a four-night retreat and are all inclusive.

ROSIE WALFORD

Pacific Islands

Explore yourself or just relax on tropical isles.

Fact file

- Fiji: None required for citizens of most EU countries (including the UK), US, Canada, Australia and New Zealand. Samoa: Issued on arrival for all nationalities
- **IDD:** Fiji +679; Samoa +685
- **Currency:** Fiji dollar ($); Samoan tala (WS$)
- **Time zone:** : Fiji GMT+12 hours; Samoa GMT -11 hours
- **Electricity:** Fiji 240v, Samoa 230v
- **Tourist board:** www.bulafiji.com; www.visitsamoa.ws

ISLAND RETREAT

The Centre Within

Koro Island, Fiji
T+679 992 7204
www.thecenterwithin.com
From US$1150 per person per week

Set on a remote rainforest island surrounded by coral reefs, The Centre Within is run by healer Thom Cronkhite, and creativity and writing consultant Caroline Cottom, international spiritual teachers who have over 30 years' experience helping people to learn how to live from a place of deep peace. They are joint authors of *The Isle of Is: A Guide to Awakening*, a clearly written practical book about how to be in the present moment and access your potential from within.

Three- and five-day retreats run all year round to help you find out more about who you are and where you need to be. This isn't a typical meditation retreat – you'll focus on such things as presence, energy and gratitude as well as meditation, and explore concepts based in truths found in all major religions – though you don't have to be religious or even spiritual to attend. Expect

🌀 Soul food

Not-for-profit organization **Green Force** (T+44 (0)20-7470 8888, www.greenforce.org) runs 10-week conservation expeditions to Fiji (costing from US$4800) in partnership with the Wildlife Conservation Society, to help create a UNESCO Seascape reserve. Research takes place on the Nasonisoni reef, one of Fiji's premier dive locations, where, after proper PADI training, you'll carry out surveys into fish populations and help locate ecologically important marine zones. You'll be based in a camp under palm trees, and also be involved in a local schools conservation project.

---

the highest level of integrity in teaching and presentation; everyone is welcome, and the retreats attract a wide range of ages and nationalities, people alone or travelling with friends or family.

Your base is the rustic and tranquil Koro Beach resort, where you stay in beachfront *bures* (bungalows) and dine under a spreading mango tree. Food is naturally organic fruit, vegetables and fish sourced locally, and alcohol and smoking are discouraged. There are good coastal and rainforest walks, treks to nearby waterfalls and natural pools for swimming, and you can kayak to nearby Sand Island to go snorkelling.

Travel to Koro is by plane or overnight ferry, accessible from the two largest islands, Viti Levu and Vanua Levu. Transfers from the wharf or airport to the resort are included. It's hot and rainy from January to April – but retreats run all year round. Cronkhite and Cottom also lead workshops in the US and New Zealand.

Above: The Centre Within. **Right:** Taialofa.

YOGA HOLIDAY

Taialofa's yoga adventures

🌐 🛖 🎣 ⊿18

Samoa
T+685 (0)7-96400
www.rawshakti.com
From US$1400 per person per week

The postcard-perfect islands of the Pacific Ocean are peaceful and beautiful places to recharge. For something very special, head to tropical Samoa in the South Pacific, where Robert Louis Stevenson found his paradise isle on Western Samoa and chose to live out his days. You can visit his house and get into the Samoan culture on a yoga adventure with Taialofa, an American who was born on the island of Upolu and has been practising yoga since she was 13 years old. Her mother is a yoga teacher, and she grew up living and breathing the lifestyle.

A trained sivananda yoga teacher, Taialofa has studied practically every form there is and her classes are a blend of all her knowledge, but centred on vinyasa flow. She is now based full time in Samoa with husband Kevin, also a certified yoga teacher, whom she met when he was working as a Peace Corps volunteer.

Come for a week or two, and join a group or arrange a private itinerary. You'll have daily yoga and guided meditation on beaches, beside waterfalls and in village *fales* (houses). Visits are made to islands such as Namua, where there's no electricity and you sleep in open beach *fales* next to a lagoon. Your trip will have you dining with villagers, learning

The body is a house of many windows: there we all sit, showing ourselves and crying on the passers-by to come and love us.

Robert Louis Stevenson

the local language, swimming and snorkelling in clean, cool waters, visiting local cultural sites and caves. A couple of nights will be spent at the laid-back and lovely **Coconuts Beach Club** (www.coconuts beachclub.com).

Food is vegetarian and locally sourced; you'll be introduced to local plants and herbs, and get to try the Samoan *koko* (organic hot chocolate). Taialofa's holidays attract everyone from yoga devotees to urban professionals looking to de-stress. She also runs yoga and life coaching retreats in Samoa with American life coach, Helaine Iris (www.pathofpurpose.com), and is building her own yoga spa on 4 ha of land with banyan trees and ocean views. Fly to LA, from where flights go to Apia on Samoa once a week. The London to New Zealand flight with Air New Zealand goes via LA and Samoa.

Pampered in the Pacific

If it's a luxurious wellbeing escape you're after, **Namale** (from US$500 per room per night, T+679 885 0435, www.namalefiji.com) in Fiji's untouristy north has just 16 *bures* (rooms) and two villas set in 130 ha. Set on a volcanic cliff overlooking the Koro Sea with rainforest at its back, it has the island's best spa – try the 'Spirit of Fiji', a traditional Fijian bobo massage which uses Swedish strokes, spiralling movements and percussion to invigorate body and spirit.

Navutu Stars (from US$385 per room per night, T+679 644 0553, www.navutustarsfiji.com), in the Yasawa archipelago, is a more low-key, barefoot kind of place, whose Italian owners serve fantastic Italian-inspired food with a tropical twist. It has nine rooms nestled on three bays and a small spa offering massages, facials and scrubs using local ingredients – stay in the Grand Bure if you're looking for pure tranquillity. Alternatively, head across the ocean to the spectacular Bora Bora in French Polynesia, where at the **Bora Bora Lagoon Resort & Spa** (from US$600 per room per night, T+689 604000, www.orient-express.com) you can have treatments using local plants, flowers and fruits in treetop rooms – try the hair and scalp massage with monoi oil, or soothe sun-kissed skin with a ritualized application of tamanu balm.

Australia, New Zealand & Pacific Islands Pacific Islands

TAIALOFA

TAIALOFA

NAVUTU STARS

SIMON HEYES

The Americas

Chilling out on Suasi Island, Lake Titicaca, Peru.

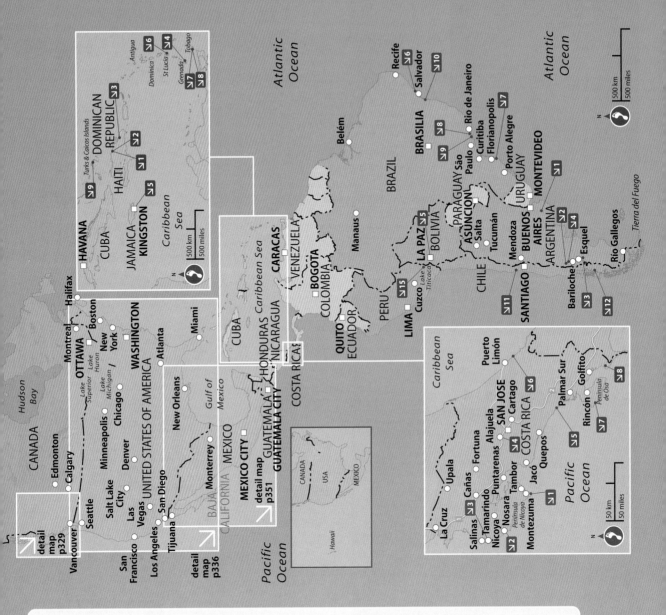

◪ Key

Costa Rica

Introduction

If you've a hunch that there must be more to life, the Americas are worth exploring in your search for what that might be: surf and get into yoga in Costa Rica, dance or indulge in the Caribbean, lose yourself trekking in some of Canada's most remote spots, or have a detoxifying adventure on Brazil's Costa Verde. This area of the world boasts some of the loveliest places to hole up for a DIY retreat – do it by the sweet, clear waters of Bacalar lagoon in southern Mexico, in a boutique hotel in California's Desert Hot Springs, or at a Chilean natural spa. For those in need of one-to-one attention or safe solitude in an inspiring environment, two family-run estancias in Argentina may be just the ticket – La Corona and Peuma Hue are both run by women dedicated to the art of healing.

If you've always fancied a stay at a health and fitness retreat, the USA has the space, the climate and the know-how to offer the best in the world. Try the gruelling schedule at The Ashram, or save up and head for the most privileged of spaces at Cal-a-Vie or The Golden Door. Alternatively, get back in touch with the healing techniques of the past by sampling shamanism on a trip through the Andes, or sweat it all out in an authentic Mexican *temazcal*. All-round wellbeing holidays aimed at anyone feeling generally stressed can be found across the region – try a bikini boot camp or a warrior week at the sassy Amansala, on Mexico's Yucatán peninsula, or organize a bespoke break with nearby Paradise Retreats.

❝ ❞ *There must be more to life than having everything.*
Maurice Sendak

Travel essentials

Canada

Getting there Montreal, Toronto and Vancouver are Canada's main international airports. From the UK, carriers such as **Zoom Airlines** (www.flyxzoom.com) and **Canadian Affair** (www.canadianaffair.com) operate direct flights from London Gatwick to Halifax for Nova Scotia. If travelling from the US, direct flights link many cities across the border, or take a **Greyhound** bus (www.greyhound.com), which has a network extending into Canada. By train, a twice-daily service links New York to Montreal and Toronto and, on the west coast, a daily train connects Seattle and Vancouver. See www.seat61.com for more details. From Australia and New Zealand, flights go via LA or Hawaii.

Best time to visit Winters in Canada can be severe; from November to March it is very cold with snowfalls throughout the country, except on the west coast. British Columbia enjoys the mildest weather, while Ontario has a continental climate with cold winters and hot summers.

USA

Getting there For visits to California, fly to LA, San Diego or San Francisco. For east coast states, fly to Boston or New York and take an onward flight, train or bus. For Colorado, Denver is the main hub, while Utah is served by Salt Lake City. Arizona is served by Tucson, but there are no direct flights from Europe. Hawaii's Kona and Hilo international airports are served mainly by flights from Honolulu, which is reached direct from Auckland and Sydney (www.qantas.com, www.airzealand.com) and major US cities (for connections to Canada and European destinations).

Best time to visit California enjoys one of the sunniest climates in the US, especially in the desert region of Palm Springs. The best time to visit is October to December and April to May, avoiding the hottest months of July and August, although San Francisco has cooler summers. The likeliest months for rain are January to March and winters are generally mild. Desert areas in Utah and Arizona are mostly dry with year-round high temperatures. New England states such as Vermont have a changeable climate, with snowfalls in winter and mild summers. Colorado experiences cold but dry winters and hot summers. Hawaii has a tropical climate, with August recording the highest temperatures and the coldest months being February and March. Hawaii's peak tourist season is December to April.

Mexico

Getting there Mexico City is the country's main international airport, but most centres are in the Yucatán and the Pacific coast, within easy reach of Cancún and Puerto Vallarta respectively. European scheduled and charter airlines fly to Cancún. Puerto Vallarta is well connected to major US cities with some flights to Toronto, but travellers from Europe must go via a US airport. For Baja California, fly to San Diego

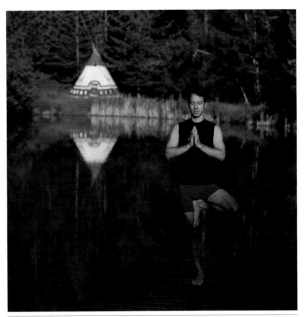

Feathered Pipe Ranch, USA.

and then travel overland. Mexico has an efficient domestic air and bus network for onward travel from Mexico City.

Best time to visit Generally the best time to visit is October to April, although there are significant regional variations. June to October is the rainy season for many areas, although in the Yucatán – affected by the Caribbean hurricane season – this runs from October to January and April to July. Don't be deterred by the rainy season, as in many areas, this may mean showers for just a few hours a day. Except for the drier Baja California region, coastal areas can be humid all year round. To avoid the crowds, don't visit the Yucatán in December.

Costa Rica

Getting there San José is the main international airport. Direct scheduled flights from the US arrive daily from Atlanta, Dallas Fort Worth, Houston, New York, Miami and Philadelphia. Flying from other US cities involves a stop in Mexico City, Cancún or Guatemala. Scheduled flights from Toronto and Montreal in Canada go via Havana and San Salvador. Charter airlines flying from North America include **Air Transat** (www.airtransat.com) and **North West** (www.nwa.com). There are no direct flights from the UK; fly via a US city, Madrid (www.iberia.com), Düsseldorf (www.itu.com) or Amsterdam (www.martinair.com). From Australia and New Zealand, fly to LA and take an onward flight from there.

Best time to visit Costa Rica has a tropical climate. On the Pacific coast and in the central highlands, December to April is the dry season and May to November the rainy season, peaking in the wettest months of September and October. Rainfall usually occurs for only a

Eat me

Think hot chillies, zingy limes and luscious fruits bursting with ripeness and you're part way to conjuring up the detox-friendly foods to be found in this part of the world. Don't miss out the traditional dish of ceviche in Latin America; this dish of thinly sliced raw white fish is 'cooked' in lime juice and contains virtually no fat. It's typically served with sweet limes, raw onion rings and tomatoes so you'll be filling your system with Omega-3, vitamin C and antioxidants with hardly any calories. Also keep your eyes peeled for the appearance of quinoa (pronounced keenwah) on the menu. This small round grain, which is grown widely in Bolivia and Peru, looks similar to millet and has a mild, nutty flavour. It's exceptionally rich in protein and contains plenty of calcium, iron and B vitamins. It's served in place of rice and is the staple ingredient in many dishes across South America. One food not to be missed is chia. Considered by many to be a genuine 'superfood', it was once used by Aztec

warriors as an energy supplement. Chia is gluten free, high in fibre, protein, antioxidants and minerals, and believed to make your hair and skin glow. The tiny seeds are often soaked in water so they take on a gel-like consistency before being used as a low-fat substitute in baking. Grinding chia produces a fine meal which can be made into delicious porridge, bread or cakes. Added to fruit juice it's known in Mexico as chia fresca. You'll also find the sprouts of the chia plant in salads or alongside main dishes.

If you're in North America or Canada, then look out for cranberries. Those grown here are bigger and juicier than elsewhere in the world and are oozing vitamin C and antioxidants. Eating a handful a day, or drinking their juice, can help prevent urinary tract infections, cancer and heart disease. Americans are also big on pomegranate juice, which is rich in polyphenols, some of the most powerful of all antioxidants.

few hours a day, however, and there are less tourists at this time of year. In the Caribbean, rain falls more regularly all year. The drier months are February to June, September and October.

Caribbean

Getting there   Many scheduled and charter flights serve the Caribbean islands from Europe and North America. No direct flights operate between Australia and New Zealand and the Caribbean; fly via a US city such as New York or Miami for the best deals. Santo Domingo, Santiago and Puerto Plata international airports serve the Dominican Republic. Jamaica has two international airports, Kingston and Montego Bay, with direct flights to Canada, the US and Europe. **Excel Airways** (www.goldencaribbean.com) offers non-stop flights from the UK to Grenada and Tobago. **Virgin Atlantic** and **British Airways** (www.ba.com) have non-stop flights from London to St Lucia. BA flies from London to Tobago via Antigua, and **Caribbean Airlines** (www.caribbean-airlines.com) flies from London to Trinidad.

Best time to visit   The Caribbean has a tropical climate, with more rainfall on mountainous, forested islands such as St Lucia than low-lying coral islands. December to April are the coolest and driest months, with occasional showers. The wettest weather is during the hurricane season from June to November, with most hurricanes occurring in August and September. Located just south of the hurricane belt, Tobago rarely gets hit, but still has tropical storms during this period.

South America

Getting there   Most international flights to **Brazil** arrive at Rio de

Janeiro and São Paulo. Many scheduled airlines operate non-stop flights to these two cities from major European airports, with a few carriers offering direct flights to Salvador from Lisbon (www.flytap.com) and Frankfurt (www.varig.com.br). From North America, direct flights link the main US cities and Toronto to Rio and São Paulo. Travel from Australia and New Zealand involves at least one stop, typically via another South American city. Alternatively, fly via the US. Buenos Aires is the gateway for **Argentina**, with onward flights to Bariloche in the Lake District. **British Airways** flies non-stop to Buenos Aires and **Aerolíneas Argentinas** (www.aerolineas.com.ar) go via Madrid. AA also fly from several US cities, while **Air Canada** (www.aircanada.com) and **Avianca** (www.avianca.com) fly from Toronto and Montreal via Colombia or Chile. From Australia and New Zealand, **Aerolíneas Argentinas**, **Air New Zealand** (www.airnewzealand.com) and **Qantas** (www.qantas.com.au) fly from Sydney via Auckland.

Best time to visit   The best time to visit **Brazil** is April to June and August to October. In Rio, the winter is from May to September with weather similar to a north European summer. Further south around São Paulo, the climate is more like a north European autumn. The main rainfall for Rio and São Paulo is from November to March, while in the north around Salvador, rain falls from April to August. Along the coast, it is comparatively humid. The busiest periods are during the main holiday seasons of mid-December to mid-January, around Carnaval, and from mid-June to mid-August. The best time to visit the Argentine Lake District is March and early April, when days are still clear and resorts are quieter. Although cool, October and November are also good months to visit.

Canada

Canada

Clayoquot Wilderness Resort

Tofino, BC
T+1 (1)250-726 8235
www.wildretreat.com
From US$4132 per person for 3 nights

A 30-minute boat ride from the town of Tofino is Clayoquot's Bedwell River Outpost, an ultra-elegant eco-safari-style resort and a great place for a DIY retreat. Nestled in a nine-mile-long fjord and surrounded by mountains, it is set in the fragile biosphere of Clayoquot Sound, a UNESCO-designated reserve. Accommodation consists of 20 large tents boasting one or two Adirondack-style queen beds with down duvets. All are furnished with gorgeous antiques, opulent rugs, oil lamps and heirloom accessories. Chef Tim May's critically acclaimed modern natural cuisine features fresh local products. Rates include all meals, resort activities, one massage treatment and return plane transfers from Tofino.

Coastal Trek

Forbidden Plateau, Courtenay, BC
T+1 (1)250-897 8735
www.coastaltrekresort.com
From US$3150 per person per week

Coastal Trek is based at a remote lodge nestled against the side of Mount Beecher on Vancouver Island, in an area covered in hiking trails. Guides Andrea and Shayne Stuchbery love the outdoor lifestyle and their enthusiasm is infectious. Your stay is a blend of fresh air and exercise, fitness training, morning stretching, and food preparation classes, supported by like-minded people, relaxing therapies, and meals designed to satisfy and educate.

Andrea is intuitive about balancing guests' wishes and needs, and is generous with her time. Hikes start small and increase in length during your stay, passing ancient forests, alpine meadows dotted with flowers, waterfalls, lakes and streams, and zigzagging across mountain passes. Experienced guides accommodate differences in walking pace.

Canada offers inspiring landscapes for trekking and chilling out in the sun or winter retreating.

Fact file

- **Visa:** Not required for citizens of the US, Australia, New Zealand and EU countries
- **IDD:** +1
- **Currency:** Candian dollar ($)
- **Time zone:** British Columbia GMT-8 hours; Ontario GMT-5 hours; Nova Scotia GMT-4 hours
- **Electricity:** 120v
- **Tourist board:** www.travelcanada.ca

Coastal Trek.

The lodge boasts massive windows spanning the lower and upper floors, and 12 en suite guest rooms are in a quiet wing to one side, complete with heated floors, luxurious linen and queen-sized beds. West coast seasonal produce is featured on the menu; their signature dish is wild salmon baked on a cedar plank. There are loads of veggies, dessert every other day, and no alcohol. Packed lunches are filling, healthy and plentiful. Allergies and special diets can be catered for.

The retreat attracts people in their 30s and 40s whose busy lifestyles have limited the amount of time they have for physical exercise or for playing a sport they once enjoyed. Bring citronella insect repellent, comfortable hiking boots and sunscreen. Expect to be relaxed, tired and rejuvenated, and to take home a plan of action to keep you on track. Stay at least a week – two-to-three-week stays are common.

From Vancouver International Airport catch a commuter plane to Comox airport (www.pacific-coastal.com) or an Airporter shuttle (www.yvrairporter.com) to the Greyhound station (www.greyhound.ca) and take the bus to Courtenay, from where pickups can be arranged.

We hiked out to Cruikshank Canyon. I was hot and getting tired, when the trail ended on a wide, flat ledge. A cool breeze lifted my mood and swept my mind clear. We were standing atop a 1500-ft sheer cliff face stretching as far as the eye could see. In a few minutes we were watching a bald eagle slowly spiralling upwards on the currents. A hush settled over me, and the hike back took on a meditative quality.

Elain Evans

ISLAND RETREAT

Hollyhock

Cortes Island, BC
T+1 (1)250-935 6576
www.hollyhock.ca
From US$127 per room per night

This vibrant, non-profit making retreat centre buzzes with energy, running two or three different workshops each week in wellbeing, arts and culture, leadership and global change. More than 70 topics are on offer from May to October, and the place attracts creative, friendly people from all walks of life.

You stay in weathered guesthouses nestling on a shrub-covered hill which rises gently from a beach embedded with oysters. There are also tents and dormitory rooms. Circular workshop spaces bring the outdoors inside by using rough-hewn wood walls, log pole ceilings and skylights. The Sanctuary, the meditation space, is a cob house.

You can also stay here and not attend a workshop – there's morning meditation, a yoga class, use of two hot tubs, a holistic library, forest walks, beach trips, rowing boats, and astrology talks.

The heart of Hollyhock is an organic flower and vegetable garden. The produce and herbs are used in the kitchen, where Moreka creates simple fresh meals inspired by locally grown regional foods. The Hollyhock yeast dressing is a must.

Be brave and the gods will be with you.

Rainer Maria Rilke

The Americas Canada

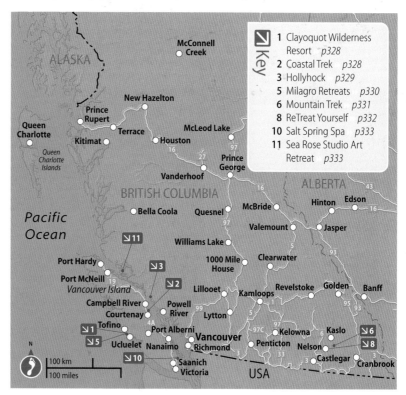

Key

1 Clayoquot Wilderness Resort   *p328*
2 Coastal Trek   *p328*
3 Hollyhock   *p329*
5 Milagro Retreats   *p330*
6 Mountain Trek   *p331*
8 ReTreat Yourself   *p332*
10 Salt Spring Spa   *p333*
11 Sea Rose Studio Art Retreat   *p333*

GREG OSOBA

Fly to Vancouver, then to Campbell River on Pacific Coastal (www.pacific-coastal.com), or take two buses (www.yvrairporter.com will get you to the bus depot and www.greyhound.ca will take you the rest of the way). From Campbell River, you can take two ferry trips and a ride on the Cortes Connection (US$24, www.cortesconnection.com) or a water taxi (from US$152, T+1 (1)250-287 7577) to Manson's Landing, from where a pickup by Hollyhock's van can be arranged. There is no taxi service on the island, and Manson's Landing is a 30-minute walk from Hollyhock.

FOREST RETREAT

Kejimkujik National Park camping

⊛ ⊘ ◿4

Nova Scotia
T+1 (1)902-682 2772
www.pc.gc.ca
From US$20 per camp per night

To escape into the wilderness, hire a canoe with a friend or family in Kejimkujik National Park in the west of Nova Scotia, first inhabited by the Mi'kmaq Indians over 4000 years ago. This is one of the least-visited parts of Canada and offers true respite, where you can wake to the sound of chipmunks and cook your own meals on an open fire.

Kejimkujik National Park hires out canoes (from US$28 per day) and various camping pitches with picnic tables, firewood and long-drop toilets, which you book in

advance. Once booked, these are yours exclusively, so you'll be completely alone and at peace (and responsible for your own safety). You can hike, take a dip in rivers and lakes, meditate, or just be. You'll see loons, turtles, even black bears, and there are easily accessible hiking trails through the cathedral-high pine trees, though some of the best stretches of forest are only accessible by boat or on foot. At certain points the river will run dry, and you'll need to carry your canoe and gear to the next stretch.

Bring all your own camping gear, layers of clothing, a detailed map and a compass, plus plenty of supplies. The Canada Parks Agency will offer you comprehensive advice. Kejimkujik National Park is a two-hour drive from Halifax, the nearest transport hub.

YOGA & ACTIVITY HOLIDAY

Milagro Retreats

⊕ ◬ ◍ ⊛ ◿5

Vancouver Island, BC
T+1 (1)800-565 0992
www.milagroretreats.com
From US$350 per person per week

Milagro Retreats, a mix of yoga, surfing, body treatments and chilling out, are led by Shani Cranston, a holistic therapist and vegetarian

chef in her mid-thirties with a passion for nurturing others. In Canada the base is Tofino, on the beautiful west coast of Vancouver Island's Pacific Rim Park.

You stay a remote corner of Bella Pacifica campground (www.bellapacifica.com) on MacKenzie Beach, where guests are encouraged to camp and reconnect with nature, or for an additional US$35 per night you can stay at the Tofino Botanical Gardens (www.tofinobotanicalgardens.com), a 10-minute walk or three-minute bike ride away. The camping experience is far from roughing it - bring one dollar coins for a hot shower.

Mornings start with an invigorating yoga session quite often led by visiting instructors from across North America, and usually hatha-based. Beginners and experienced practitioners are welcome, and classes are held on the beach (weather permitting).

In the afternoons you go surfing with the **Surf Sister Surf School** (www.surfsister.com) in Tofino, which provides everything you need. Instructors are professional, and the challenge of this workout creates good group camaraderie. In the likely event that you dive headlong off your board, the sand is soft and free from rocks.

After lunch you can enjoy relaxing bodywork treatments at the **Reflections Spa** (www.reflectionsholisticretreat.com). A

KEJIMKUJIK

hot-stone therapy session is the perfect way to warm up and relax surfed-out muscles. Clay wraps, salt glows and shiatsu are also on offer. Evenings allow time for walks along the beach, a tarot card reading from Shani or quiet reflection. Bedtime comes early, allowing plenty of time to rejuvenate for another transformational day.

Shani cooks all the meals, using ingredients grown in her own organic garden, and she is quick to share her recipes. Lunches are not provided but the nearby Sobo snack stop provides organic food, from shrimp cakes to fish tacos. Guests are allowed to bring wine to accompany meals though over-indulgence is discouraged .

The surfing component of the retreat attracts an age mix from 19- to 50-year-olds – some retreats are for women only. Milagro also runs retreats outside Canada, including Baja California. Craig's Air (www.craigair.com) provides a twice-daily service to Tofino from Vancouver's south terminal. From there it's a stunning bus or taxi ride to Tofino. Group cars can also be arranged: liaise with Milagro.

HEALTH & FITNESS RETREAT

Mountain Trek

🌐 ⭕ 🏃 ⊕ ⊗ ↘6

British Columbia
T+1 (1)250-229 5636
www.hiking.com
From US$3158 per a week

Set amongst the fjord-like valleys and mountain peaks of British Columbia, Mountain Trek holidays combine hiking, biking or kayaking around the rolling hills and

Far left: Hollyhock Sanctuary. **Below left:** Kejimkujik National Park camping. **Above left:** Milagro Retreats. **Above and right:** Mountain Trek holidays take you into the magnificent mountains and fjord-like valleys of British Columbia.

picturesque Kootenay Lake with yoga and treatments.

The Mountain Trek lodge is a beautifully designed, timber-framed building surrounded by 34 acres of private forest. The 12 en suite bedrooms are modest and cosy, featuring locally made furniture, handmade quilts and very comfortable beds. For more space, book one of the larger rooms upstairs. As you walk into the spacious, welcoming lobby, you notice aromatherapy fragrances in the air, and the blazing fire in the spacious lounge creates a friendly atmosphere.

Hiking is at the core of the Mountain Trek programme and the numerous scenic trails cater for all levels of fitness. The guides are ex-park rangers with years of experience and a good knowledge of the local flora and fauna. After a hard day out on the mountains or in the gym, an outdoor jacuzzi and sauna will soothe tired muscles, or you can take a dip in the local hot springs. Swedish massage is included in the package with additional treatments such as reiki and reflexology at an extra cost. These are the relaxing highlights of a busy day that begins

with a 0600 wake-up call, followed by yoga – a combination of vinyasa and hatha – as you watch the sun rise.

Mountain Trek is also known for its rigorous FitPlan Plus programme. It introduces those who are serious about losing weight to a common-sense food and fitness regime based on organic, healthy eating and exercise rather than food deprivation. Although you follow a reduced-calorie menu, a day's meals may consist of cereal, a protein shake and frittata for breakfast, a turkey cob salad at lunchtime and broccoli leekie soup and poached herbed halibut with green beans for dinner. You don't feel like you're missing out too much.

Guests are male and female, mostly aged from 35 to 60, from the USA, or city types from Canada and Europe and, with no single supplement to pay, mostly travelling alone. A two-week stay is best, but don't over-pack: they provide tracksuits, T-shirts and bathrobes as well as a daily complimentary laundry service – and the dress code is always casual. The nearest airport is Castlegar, just over an hour away. There is a Mountain Trek shuttle every Friday afternoon.

FOREST RETREAT

Northern Edge Algonquin nature retreat

Algonquin Provincial Park, Ontario
T+1 (1)705-386 1595
www.algonquincanada.com
From US$475 for 3 nights

Located at the edge of picturesque Algonquin Provincial Park, Northern Edge offers a uniquely Canadian experience, combining outdoor recreation, yoga and creative expression in a wonderful natural environment.

This extraordinary place was founded by Todd and Martha Lucier, who lead a lot of the retreats. Todd has taught outdoor recreation for almost 20 years and lectures on ecotourism, while Martha has practised shamanism for 10 years and counsels groups

and individuals. Trips are tailored around the seasons, such as the four-day Yoga and the Zen of Sea Kayaking in spring and summer, and Yoga and the Zen of Winter, which includes snowshoeing, sledding and ice-skating. Other retreats have an artistic focus – the Tom Thomson Experience enables you to explore the landscapes of the renowned Group of Seven artists, and there are brilliant photography weekends.

Food is gourmet vegetarian, featuring organically grown and fairtrade foods, prepared in an on-site kitchen or by guides while on trips. Accommodation, for up to 24 guests, includes rooms in the original solar-powered cedar cabin, cabins with wood stoves in the balsam fir forest, and canvas cabins in the maple forest.

Guests are primarily North Americans of all ages, and range from seasoned adventurers to people just dipping their toe into a new experience. The ratio of guests to guides is four to one, ensuring lots of individual attention. Northern Edge is about 2½ hours from Toronto and is accessible by bus and train to South River, at which point a shuttle service to the retreat is available.

Take some time before or after the retreat to explore Algonquin Park, 7500 sq km of rivers, maple forest, spruce bogs, beaver ponds, campgrounds, lakes and cliffs, with a

diverse mix of plant and animal life. For canoeing and trekking options visit www.algonquinpark.ca.

YOGA & ACTIVITY HOLIDAY

ReTreat Yourself

British Columbia
www.retreatyourself.net
From US$2500 for 4 days

ReTreat Yourself runs annual yoga and snowboarding retreats for women already into the sport. Led by professional rider, Barrett Christy, these indulgent breaks of four days are a wonderful way of improving your technique. The venues change, but trips run regularly to **Baldface** (T+1 (1)250-352 0006, www.baldface.net), a skiing and snowboarding lodge in remote British Columbia where you'll enjoy untouched powder runs and afternoon yoga sessions to help your body recover.

Accommodation is in luxurious chalets, with gourmet food and wine tastings included, and there are luxurious massages and beauty treatments to be enjoyed. The trip attracts mainly professional women and takes a maximum of 36. The price includes safety equipment, food, accommodation,

Above: Algonquin Provincial Park. **Right:** British Columbia boasts some of the world's top snowboarding resorts. **Top right:** Sea Rose Studio Art Retreat.

board rentals, daily yoga classes, wine tasting, demos of the latest Gnu boards designed by Christy, a mountain top toast and goodie bags. Fly to Nelson, from where it's a five-minute helicopter ride (also included in the price).

HEALTH & FITNESS RETREAT

Ste Anne's

Grafton, Ontario
T+1 (1)905-349 2493
www.haldimandhills.com
From US$460 per person per night

A serene retreat with a warm and easy-going ambience, Ste Anne's is part of the Canadian Haldimand Hills chain, set on gently rolling slopes overlooking Lake Ontario. It's built around a gracious 1850 fieldstone farmhouse in 570 acres of farmland with a natural underground spring.

You stay in the main building, in the original farmhouse or in one of two Hudson's Bay Company Heritage Suites with fireplaces and whirlpool bathtubs. Play tennis, hike across the estate or chill out on tree-shaded lounge chairs. There are two pools, including an outdoor one filled with the property's spring water, a plunge pool, hot tub and eucalyptus sauna.

Aveda body and skincare treatments are on offer, or try the signature treatments, which use locally available and organic foods and herbs in a variety of seasonally based treats: these include 'Apple Peel and Sweet Honey Facial' in the autumn, 'Warm Chocolate Swedish Massage' in winter and the 'Maple Showers' body treatment in the spring. Lifestyle counselling, nutrition sessions and fitness classes are also on offer.

Executive chef, Christopher Ennew, prepares simple, creative and flavourful dishes using seasonal vegetables and herbs grown in their own gardens. You can go on a Specific Carbohydrate Diet, which has been used to alleviate, and even reverse, intestinal disorders such as colitis.

The retreat is a 1½-hour drive from Toronto. Pack light, and expect to wear white bathrobes and slippers most of the time. If you drive, explore the quaint historic towns of Cobourg and Port Hope en route.

NATURAL SPA RETREAT

Salt Spring Spa

Salt Spring Island, BC
T+1 (1)800-665 0039
www.saltspringspa.com
From US$175 per room per night

Located on the northeast side of Salt Spring Island overlooking the Trincomali Channel, this spa is the site of a natural salt spring which contains 41 different minerals and a 10% salt solution, great for cleansing and relaxing. It's self-catering here, but a great place to kick back and relax. You stay in one of 12 spacious chalets, which boast high ceilings, wood stoves and a private mineral water tub each – ask for a chalet on the lawn for more privacy and a better view. Each chalet has its own kitchen and an outdoor deck.

Decent ayurvedic massages and *shirodara* treatments are available, as well as optional hatha yoga and meditation classes, and two-week panchakarma courses can be arranged in advance (see page 210 for more on ayurveda). Take out a boat early in the morning, when the water is usually flat calm, or play badminton on the grass court.

Stock up on organic produce at the market in Centennial Park, open every Saturday from April to October, and there are other shops and restaurants nearby. Fly to Vancouver, and take the bus (www.translink.bc.ca) to Tsawwassen Ferry Terminal, from where there are two ferries that go directly to Salt Spring (see www.bcferries.com).

CREATIVE RETREAT

Sea Rose Studio Art Retreat

Echo Bay, Simoon Sound, BC
T+1 (1)20-974 8134
www.zoombuy.net/searose
From US$240 per person per day

Tap into your artistic self-expression in a remote and beautiful location at Echo Bay, in the Broughton Archipelago off northern Vancouver Island. Professional artist and teacher, Yvonne Maximchuk, leads personalized artist retreats here for instruction in watercolours, acrylics, drawing and pottery.

You'll have three hours of artistic tuition each day, and times are dictated by your own personal muse and what's going on around you – pods of killer whales passing by in the summer, for example, wild flowers in the spring and salmon spawning runs in the autumn. Aromatherapy and lomi lomi massages can be arranged in advance.

You stay in comfortable private rooms with en suite bathrooms. Fresh west coast seafood is the mainstay of the menu, and guests are even invited to try their hand at catching the salmon for dinner (for which a fishing licence is required) or pulling the crab trap. Vegetables come from the garden. Wine is served with dinner and guests can bring their own. Buy anything you need beforehand, as there isn't a shop in sight.

If you've ventured this far, consider asking Yvonne to arrange a whale-watching trip out of Telegraph Cove, or grizzly bear viewing in Knight Inlet. The retreat attracts artistic types, from beginners to professionals, mostly women aged 40-60, but all are welcome. Bring your own art supplies; Yvonne can advise on necessary materials and create starter kits for beginners with advance notice.

Fly on Pacific Coastal Airlines (www.pacific-coastal.com) or Eagle Air (www.flyeagleair.com) from Vancouver to Port Hardy (from US$200, for just over an hour's flight), then take a connector shuttle to Port McNeill. There is also a bus service (www.greyhound.ca) to Port McNeill from Vancouver (US$125 for a nine-hour trip). Yvonne will pick up retreat guests in her boat from Port McNeill for the 25 nautical miles to Echo Bay. Guests can also catch a floatplane on the thrice-weekly mail run for US$129 with Pacific Eagle Aviations (eagleair@island.net).

Above: Tanglefoot Lodge. **Below right:** Back to Earth yoga backpacking. **Bottom right:** Cal-a-Vie.

RURAL RETREAT

Tanglefoot Lodge

🌍 🐸 ♨ ☀ ⭕ 🏃 🎧 🌍 🚴 🌱 💡 ↘12

Lakefield, Ontario
T+1 (1)705-877 8564
www.tanglefootlodge.com
From US$175 per person for 2 nights

This rustic cedarwood building surrounded by forest is a healing retreat set in the Kawartha region of Ontario, which boasts navigable streams, rivers and lakes. Owners Nicky and Russ Hazard embrace an eco-friendly, yogic philosophy here – try drum workshops, a juice fast, some hydrotherapy, the sweat lodge or a visit to local aboriginal healing sites.

There are just five simple double rooms with shared bathrooms – you can also camp. Russ is a therapist who has studied shamanism and yoga for more than 20 years, and he runs many of the workshops. The Renewal Weekend is the most popular retreat, combining yoga, meditation and detoxification with individual naturopath consultations. Six to eight musical retreats are offered each year, including drum-making and an exploration of aboriginal instruments such as the djembe and didgeridoo. A two-week yoga retreat is available, and month-long stays were introduced in 2007.

Nicky prepares vegetarian fare which is so popular with guests that a cookbook has been produced at their request. Visitors are primarily North American and European, some of whom are particularly drawn to work with renowned musicians in the studio on the premises. Guests are a mix of both sexes, while women-only retreats are also offered. There is a strict limit of 10 guests.

From Toronto, take the bus to Peterborough, from where it's a 25-minute drive, and pickups are free. Group cars are arranged for guests when possible.

Salt Spring Spa.

YOGA & ACTIVITY HOLIDAY

Back to Earth yoga backpacking

Yosemite National Park, California
T+1 (1)510-652 2000
www.backtoearth.com
From US$400 per person for 3-5 days

California-based Back to Earth runs three- to five-day yoga and trekking trips through Yosemite National Park, with inspirational vistas of the Yosemite Valley and Half Dome, delicious vanilla-scented pine forests, and refreshing rivers in which to swim. You'll be expertly guided by one of Back to Earth's founders, Eric Fenster or Ari Derfel.

You walk about six miles into the park and set up a remote base camp on a spectacular site away from the traffic. You then practise yoga in the morning and afternoon, in a wonderfully inspiring outdoor 'studio' with mountain views, and go for day hikes. You eat three delicious organic meals a day and, in the evenings, enjoy an outdoor fire under the stars accompanied by music and storytelling.

The price includes guides, meals, group gear, permits and camping. Fly to San Francisco, from where you could rent a car or join a carpool with the group. The trip attracts

TYLER BLANKS

CAL-A-VIE

people of all ages and backgrounds. You need to be in good physical shape so you can carry up to 20 kg of gear in your backpack.

HEALTH & FITNESS RETREAT

Cal-a-Vie

Vista, California
T+1 (1)760- 945 2055
www.cal-a-vie.com
From US$3440 for 3-night programme

This secluded, seductive destination health and fitness retreat for privileged people is like a Provençal village, complete with a meditation chapel that was originally constructed in Dijon in 1603 and transplanted to southern California. You'll smell roses, lavender and rosemary everywhere, hear the sound of softly cascading water and enjoy vistas of the neighbouring California foothills.

Pale-pink stucco buildings, many furnished with original 18th-century French antiques, are surrounded by a hilly 60 ha etched with hiking trails. For those not into hillwalking, there are gentler walks along the paths of a nearby golf course plus treadmills galore. The service and attention here – as you'd expect – are second to none. Only 40 can be accommodated at any one time, with a staff of 100.

Guests are inspired to make positive changes with personal daily programmes for stress reduction, relaxation, weight control and personal fitness. Classes, from cardio kickboxing to power yoga, take place in a state-of-the-art 1500 sq m pavilion where French windows open onto to terraces and patios and overlook the Olympic-size pool. The spectacular fitness centre includes studios for yoga, pilates and dance, weight room, kick-boxing and fitness assessment area, treadmills, spinning bikes and free weights in a 200 sq m studio.

The group interacts or withdraws at will and receives varied daily beauty treatments that are an integral part of their programme. For many, Chef Steve Pernetti's Friday-night cooking demonstration is a highlight of the

The US has the space and know-how for the world's best health and fitness retreats, whatever your budget.

Fact file

- **Visa:** Not required for citizens with machine-readable passports of Canada, Australia, New Zealand and most EU countries including the UK

- **IDD:** +1

- **Currency:** US dollar ($)

- **Time zone:** East coast GMT -5 hours; west coast GMT -8 hours

- **Electricity:** 120v

- **Tourist board:** Each state has its own; see www.towd.com

DUNTON HOT SPRINGS

Dunton Hot Springs.

NATURAL SPA RETREAT

Dunton Hot Springs

Dunton, near Dolores, Colorado
T+1 (1)970-882 4800
www.duntonhotsprings.com
From US$250 per person per night

Dunton Hot Springs is a renovated ghost town in Colorado's Rocky Mountains offering solitude, an Old West ambience and spectacular mountain scenery. There are plenty of soaking locations for the mineral-rich hot springs: a pool in the bathhouse, one inside a cabin, and several natural pools scattered throughout the resort. You sleep in one of 15 log cabins, some of which have fireplaces and private hot springs. If you're feeling adventurous, try the beautifully appointed tipi. There's spectacular hiking, horse riding, whitewater rafting and heli-skiing in the area, and yoga retreats sometimes take place – teachers include UK-based Liz Lark (www.lizlark.com), who also runs retreats to Costa Rica and Kenya (see page 177). Spa treatments include Swedish massage, craniosacral therapy and reflexology.

Food is sourced from Dunton's own farm and vineyard, purchased through local farmers' markets, or gathered from the nearby mountains and forests. Regional airports include Durango, Telluride, Cortez and Montrose. Prices are all inclusive.

week. His beautifully presented meals are pure, fresh spa cuisine.

Fly to San Diego, from where it's a 40-minute drive. Alternatively, it's a 15-minute drive from the Amtrak station in Oceanside and two hours south of Los Angeles airport.

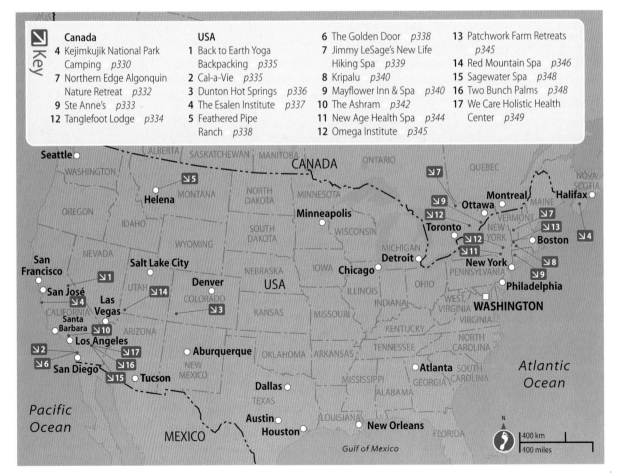

Key

Canada
4 Kejimkujik National Park Camping   *p330*
7 Northern Edge Algonquin Nature Retreat   *p332*
9 Ste Anne's   *p333*
12 Tanglefoot Lodge   *p334*

USA
1 Back to Earth Yoga Backpacking   *p335*
2 Cal-a-Vie   *p335*
3 Dunton Hot Springs   *p336*
4 The Esalen Institute   *p337*
5 Feathered Pipe Ranch   *p338*

6 The Golden Door   *p338*
7 Jimmy LeSage's New Life Hiking Spa   *p339*
8 Kripalu   *p340*
9 Mayflower Inn & Spa   *p340*
10 The Ashram   *p342*
11 New Age Health Spa   *p344*
12 Omega Institute   *p345*

13 Patchwork Farm Retreats   *p345*
14 Red Mountain Spa   *p346*
15 Sagewater Spa   *p348*
16 Two Bunch Palms   *p348*
17 We Care Holistic Health Center   *p349*

Coastal retreat

The Esalen Institute

Founded in 1962, Esalen is an educational institute dedicated to the exploration of human potential, situated on the California coast at Big Sur. It hosts over 400 alternative education and personal growth workshops a year, addressing all aspects of mind, body and spirit. With breathtaking views of Big Sur and a backdrop of mountains, natural hot springs and numerous walks through the 11-ha estate, the beautiful location itself has a transformative effect.

Where you stay Esalen offers three categories of simple accommodation: standard rooms for two or three, with some shared bathrooms; single-sex bunk-bed rooms accommodating three or more; and 'sleeping bag space' in some of the meeting rooms. A single supplement costs US$100 a day. The facilities are inspiring, including a wooden arts centre surrounded by mosaics, sculptures, stained glass and exotic flowers, and a tranquil wooden meditation house, open 24 hours a day.

What you do Esalen pioneered the experiential workshop in the sixties so to teach here is a genuine badge of honour, and the facilitators and speakers are experts in their field. To help you decide on the areas that really interest you, try an Experiencing Esalen workshop which provides an introduction to a number of different subjects.

With so many weekend and five-day workshops on offer, you can create the retreat you need, whether that includes photography, poetry or watercolours, or more emotionally driven self-expression with Writing from the Heart or Art, Dreams and Problem Solving. Music, rhythm and movement are given space in the Dance Dome where yoga and martial arts take their turn with Finding Your Long-lost Musician and Dancing with the Spirits. The Body and Movement programme also includes massage, in particular the signature Esalen massage technique, and LaStone therapy.

Relationship and psychology workshops allow for more in-depth self-exploration, alongside spiritual journeys that embrace Taoism, shamanism and Zen. Guidance on achieving success at work, learning more about sustainability or cookery and nutrition creates a more outwards-facing experience.

Make sure you also take time to absorb the beauty of your surroundings. Natural mineral springs flow from the ground at 48°C and the individual and group hot tubs built into the cliff allow for serious relaxation. Created by award-winning architect Mickey Muennig, the baths, showers and massage rooms were designed to optimize the views of the ocean. At the right time of year, you can watch migratory whales and their young pass by.

What you eat and drink The three meals a day are lovingly prepared with produce from Esalen's own organic farm and garden. Meat, dairy, vegetarian, vegan and raw foods are served at every meal along with a selection of teas, coffee and fruit. Alcohol is available from a cash-only bar, along with sweets and chocolate.

Who goes Esalen draws visitors of all ages from all over the world, although most are American. The men and women who come here share a desire to discover and explore, and are often from an intellectual background. A large number of people are on a return visit.

Essentials A weekend at Esalen (T+1 (1)831-667 3005, www.esalen.org) costs from US$465. The institute is dedicated to supporting workshops, so personal retreats without workshop attendance are not always possible. If you're a first time visitor, orientation groups on Fridays and Sundays will help you acclimatize. There is no mobile phone reception, although there is some limited internet access and phone cards are available from the bookshop. There is no ATM or banking facilities so make sure you bring enough cash for your stay. Fly to Monterey airport. A pickup and drop-off service operates on Fridays and Sundays at a cost of US$60 each way.

I have never found another place in the world as beautiful and spiritual as Esalen. The classes have given me many friends and taught me many lessons – the wilderness, the setting on the Big Sur and the temperate climate make it a magical place.   *Mo Macris*

Feathered Pipe Ranch

Helena, Montana
T+1 (1)406-442 8196
www.featheredpipe.com
From US$1395 per person per retreat

Montana is one of the USA's least populous states. Nestled in the Rocky Mountains at the edge of the Helena National Forest, the Feathered Pipe Ranch is a beautiful retreat that runs five- or seven-day rolling programmes in an intimate setting.

Situated on the banks of a tranquil alpine lake, the ranch offers shared and private rooms in a yurt, tipi or cabin beside a stream or tucked into tiny mountain meadows. Each offers a back-to-nature experience but with comfortable beds and cosy bedding – you share a cedar bathhouse, which also has a massage room, a sauna and a spring-fed hot tub.

Retreats on offer include hatha, vinyasa flow and iyengar yoga, martial arts, mysticism and meditation. The line-up of visiting teachers includes Erich Schiffman (www.movingintostillness.com), and Seane Corn (www.seanecorn.com). Also on offer is Swedish massage, hot-stone therapy, acupuncture and naturopathic and chiropractic consultations.

Native grasses and mountain flowers –

many with medicinal uses – grow prolifically here and you can learn some botany during an early morning guided hike through the forests and lush alpine meadows. An organic garden – a fine spot for meditation – sits at the edge of the lake. End your day of yoga with a sauna or a soak in the hot tub followed by a bracing skinny-dip.

Food is organic, sourced from the kitchen garden or from local and regional producers, including the occasional free-range chicken or grass-fed beef or lamb. Suppers range from polenta with a fresh tomato-basil sauce to lavish Indian meals complete with home-made chutneys.

Guests come from all over the United States and some from the UK and Europe. Ages and backgrounds are diverse, from hip New York yoga instructors to active retirees and even the occasional celebrity. The number of guests ranges from 10 to 50.

Workshops run from late-May to early-September, but whatever the season, be prepared for unpredictable weather, and bring layers. Helena Regional Airport (www.helenaairport.com) has connections to

major hubs, including Salt Lake City, Minneapolis and Seattle. The Ranch offers an airport shuttle service for US$50 return.

During the winter months, the Feathered Pipe sponsors yoga instruction and tours in Mexico, Cambodia and India. Its sister institution, the 3300-ha Blacktail Ranch in Wolf Creek, Montana, also offers courses but with a traditional Western twist.

The Golden Door

Escondido, California
T+1 (1)760-744 5777
www.goldendoor.com
From US$7500 per person per week

The Golden Door is one of the world's most desirable spa destinations. You do actually enter through a golden door, giving you the distinct impression that you are leaving the real world behind.

The complex's design is influenced by the ancient Honjin inns of Japan, with a series of

Above: Feathered Pipe Ranch.
Right: Sunrise over the koi pond at The Golden Door.

Breathe deep: where to meditate in the USA

There are hundreds of well-run meditation retreats in inspiring locations across the US catering for beginners as well as experienced practitioners. For vipassana, or insight meditation, one of the best is **Spirit Rock Meditation Center**, at Woodacre, California (T+1 (1)415-488 0164, www.spiritrock.org), set in 160 ha of forest, meadow and grassland. The land was originally sacred Native American, and it feels incredibly peaceful and private here. Residential retreats run from three days to two months and can host up to 100 participants. A four-day course costs US$300. You stay in either single or shared rooms in the simple halls of residence. Bring your own sheets, pillowcase and towel, and lots of layers, as temperatures vary; bathrooms are shared. Meals are vegetarian and mostly organic. Woodacre is a 20-minute drive from the San Rafael exit on highway 101, and an hour from San Francisco airport.

The **Shambhala Mountain Center** (www.shambhalamountain.org), set in 240 ha in a high mountain valley at Red Feather Lakes, near Fort Collins, Colorado, offers regular retreats and courses in Tibetan Buddhism as well as hosting courses on other traditions and related subjects such as Jewish meditation, death and dying, yoga and tai chi. Retreats last from three days to six months. Founded in 1971 by the Tibetan Buddhist monk, Chogyam Trungpa, the centre is home to the Great Stupa of Dharmakaya, the largest and most elaborate in North America.

Accommodation costs from US$69 per room per night and the centre is a three-hour drive from Denver International Airport.

To experience Zen Buddhist meditation in the US, the **Deer Park Monastery** in California (www.deerparkmonastery.org), and the **Green Mountain Dharma Centre** in Vermont (www.greenmountaincenter.org) are sister retreats to Plum Village in France (see page 97). They all teach Zen Buddhism according to Thich Nhat Hanh, the Vietnamese Zen master, poet and peace activist. See Essentials for more on meditation retreats.

SPIRIT ROCK

---

one-storey buildings set around Japanese raked-sand gardens. The whole effect is one of simple beauty, from the wooden stairs up the hillside to the stone lanterns and koi-filled ponds. Oriental paintings and antiques, bamboo floors and shoji screens decorate minimalist rooms (with Western beds), which open on to private patios or terraces, always with a serene view. Outside, there are orange-scented paths and a herb-scented labyrinth.

The overall efficiency and professionalism here is impressive. Each of the maximum 42 guests has a housekeeper who delivers the daily 'fan' (activity schedule) with her breakfast tray, and takes and returns laundry daily; a masseur or masseuse for a daily massage and an aesthetician for a daily hour of beauty (deep cleansing facial, salt glow exfoliation, aromatherapy and pedicure). A

personal trainer prepares a take-home fitness programme.

Guests come to shed a few pounds (the food is mostly organic and grown on site), tighten abs doing pilates, trim thighs on morning hikes and stretch limbs in yoga sessions. Those who enjoy camaraderie find it here, while those seeking solitude and spirituality will also be satisfied.

Golden Door provides fitness clothing and kimonos. The final treatment is a manicure and hairstyling, so guests leave looking as good as they feel. Most weeks are dedicated to female guests, though four weeks are for men only and four weeks are mixed. Guests range in age from 20 up to 70-plus. Programmes run from Sunday to Sunday, and the rate is all-inclusive.

Shuttle transfers are available from San Diego airport, about 40 miles south, and from

Amtrak Oceanside rail station (reached from Union Station in Los Angeles).

Jimmy LeSage's New Life Hiking Spa

Killington, Vermont
T+1 (1)802-422 4302
www.newlifehikingspa.com
From US$219 per room per night

Jimmy LeSage's New Life Hiking Spa is an affordable, down-to-earth fitness holiday that takes place for four months of the year (from mid-May to end-September) at the Inn at Six Mountains, in central Vermont.

Jimmy LeSage founded New Life nearly

30 years ago and he has been directing its programmes ever since. An all-round fitness instructor and trained counsellor who pays an impressive attention to detail and group awareness, his common-sense approach to fitness involves fresh air, healthy food, lots of exercise and enough choice to please everybody.

Accommodation is nothing special: decor is modern farmhouse and en suite bathrooms are cramped and dated, but the best rooms have vaulted ceilings and balconies with expansive views.

The Inn (which functions as a ski lodge for the rest of the year) is minutes away from numerous lush trails up the Green Mountains. Hikes range from simple 'nature walks' through field, dell, and farmland, to the 'advanced' 370-m quasi-mountain climb. The guest-to-instructor ratio is intentionally low, sometimes falling to an impressive 1:1.

For non-hikers, there are plenty of other exercise options. Days start with qigong and stretching. In the afternoons there are treatments, fitness classes, and also excursions. Evening activities tend toward the educational: cooking, nutrition, sound therapy and local geology. The more boisterous may prefer line dancing, or unwinding at the bar.

All meals are low calorie, low fat and low salt; breakfast and lunch can be skimpy. Tender meat dishes and rainbow salads at dinner help compensate, but if you want more food, let Jimmy know. The retreat attracts mainly American professionals in their late thirties to fifties who want to get fit. Some guests come solely for the hiking, others for the yoga; men come mainly to de-stress, and there are women on the pound-a-day-weight-loss plan (www.newlifediet.com). Cameraderie is strong, though the trip does take up to 40 guests.

Fly to Boston, then on to Rutland with Rutland Air, from where it's a 20-minute taxi ride to Killington. Bring swim, rain, and exercise gear, layers of clothing, insect repellent and comfortable walking boots.

Right: Jimmy LeSage. **Far right:** Kripalu.

YOGA RETREAT

Kripalu

🌐 🔹 🔺 ☀ ⭕ 🔘 ◉ ✪ ✪ ✪ ⭕ ⊠8

Lenox, Massachusetts
T+1 (1)866-200 5203
www.kripalu.org
From US$168 per person per day

Located in the Berkshires of western Massachusetts, Kripalu is a yoga and health centre with the feel of a small college campus. Despite basic accommodation, it's a playful and carefree place in a lovely rural location, offering an impressive menu of over 700 spiritual and educational programmes per year and drawing big names in the American yoga scene such as Deepak Chopra, Shiva Rea and Rodney Yee. It is dedicated to self enquiry through yoga in the fullest sense of the word, and draws inspiration from spiritual, religious, secular and scientific worlds.

Founded by Amrit Desai, Kripalu yoga focuses on the potential for transformation and fulfilment through deep asana practices that emphasise inward focus, meditation and breathwork. The centre runs a world famous yoga teacher training programme, and there are hundreds of Kripalu trained instructors teaching all over the world.

Originally built in the 1950s as a seminary school, there's one main building housing up to 450 people. Bedrooms are bare and free from distractions, with singles, doubles and a dormitory room sleeping from six to 22. The Sun Room, with a big window and spectacular views, is a great place to curl up

with a book. Buffet-style organic vegetarian meals, with some poultry and fish, are served in the large dining room. Breakfast is often eaten in silence.

The programmes attract people from across the globe of all ages and life stages, and cover a wide range of health, spiritual and fitness retreats, from an Organic Juice Purification Retreat to Painting and Yoga in the Berkshires. You can also come for an R&R (retreat and renewal) break and create your own schedule. Kripalu offers classes and evening events that are open to all – try DansKinetics, a free-form dance class.

Stay for as little as three days, or up to three months on a volunteer programme. Kripalu is 2½ hours from New York City and two hours from Boston. Albany is the closest regional airport.

HOTEL & SPA

Mayflower Inn and Spa

🌐 🔹 🔺 ⭕ 🔘 ◉ ✪ ✪ ✪ ⭕ ◐ ⊠9

Washington, Connecticut
T+1 (1)860-868 9466
www.mayflowerinn.com
From US$4200 per person for 3 nights

There isn't a window at the Mayflower that doesn't offer a spectacular view of the landscaped grounds. Inside, rooms are luxuriously furnished with antique four-poster beds, fireplaces and great swathes of romantic drapes. The spa is 2000 sq m of gorgeousness: come for three- to five-night packages.

There are soundproofed walls, a glimmering

Delve into the desert

With sage-studded deserts and stark, steep mountains, Arizona has a mystical quality which, today, draws artists and others from across the globe to enjoy the winter sun and some of the best wellbeing resorts the US has to offer.

Tucson is in the south of Arizona and home to two of the state's most famous health and fitness retreats. **Miraval** (T+1 (1)520-825 4000, www.miravalresort.com), near Catalina, is set in 55 ha with palm trees. Its 102 rooms are decorated in southwest style, with adobe exteriors, beamed ceilings and comfy furnishings. Set at the foot of the Santa Catalina Mountains, it offers mountain biking, horse riding and climbing, as well as meditation, yoga and treatments from ayurveda to craniosacral bodywork. You can drink alcohol, but the spa serves healthy cuisine and encourages mindfulness and healthy choices. Expect to pay from US$585 per person per night.

Located in the northwest foothills of Tucson, in 28 ha of lush, cactus-filled landscape, **Canyon Ranch** (T+1 (1)800-742 9000, www.canyonranch.com) is at the cutting edge of the health and fitness world. Enjoy colourful sunsets, and an exemplary expert staff of doctors and therapists who specialize in nutrition, exercise, medical health and spirituality. Individual *casitas* clustered around the property sleep about 250 guests for a minimum of four nights. The spacious and immaculate rooms have a southwestern feel and blend in perfectly with the

ARIZONA TOURIST BOARD

The Americas USA

landscape – splash out on a Casa Grande. The list of activities and classes is endless: from cooking, pottery, music, hiking and golf to stress management, qigong and do yoga. The Life Enhancement Programme, a wellness retreat for 39 guests, is especially popular. Canyon Ranch costs from US$ 3280 for four nights, and has a sister ranch at Lenox, Massachusetts, where packages start at three nights.

Sedona (visitsedona.com) is packed with sacred Native American sites and is known as a New Age place for spirituality and healing. Children of the sixties still live and thrive here; some are involved as healers, intuitives, tour guides or as therapists at healing centres offering everything from astrology to reiki. There's also brilliant hiking to be had in Sedona's Boynton Canyon (at 1400 m) with magical views of Red Rock mountains and the buttes, canyons and cliffs in the Secret Mountain Wilderness. Sedona's best-regarded wellness retreat is **Mii Amo** (T+1 (1)928-203 8500, www.miiamo.com), an intimate destination spa built in the style of the Native North American cliff dwellers. Its 16 earth-coloured adobe *casitas* are clustered together to one side of the spa building on an expansive 28-ha propery. Meditate in The Crystal Grotto, practise yoga, take part in one of the 'talking circles' or take yourself off for a hike. Rooms cost from US$1090 per night.

CANYON RANCH

swimming pool with iridescent blue tiles, and a steam room with a pale violet glowing dome. The Garden Room is the star attraction, a large sitting area in which almost everything is white – the paintings, the orchids, the sofas, the crystals on the coffee table, even the spines of the art books lining the walls.

There's a wide range of activities and treatments, from standard spa fare to more unorthodox offerings such as archery, fly fishing, memoir writing and even knitting. Fitness classes cater to all levels, and there are some great signature treatments – try the 90-minute red flower ritual, which includes a ginger grass scrub and a shiatsu massage.

You can eat regular meals or opt for more calorie-conscious 'spa cuisine' – dishes include roast vegetable frittata, lobster and tomato

Health and fitness retreat

The Ashram 🤸 🍎 🧘 🏃 ↘10

Nestled in the Santa Monica Mountains at Calabasas, The Ashram's demanding programme cleanses the body and soul through rigorous hikes, restorative yoga and healthy eating. Just 10 miles inland from coastal Malibu, yet a world away in spirit, it's been full to capacity every week since its inception over 30 years ago, yet no money has ever been spent on marketing. While the programme is brutally tough, a non-competitive and loving atmosphere permeates, and guests leave with a transformed feeling that is nothing short of euphoric.

Where you stay Guests stay in a two-storey 1970s house in a tranquil canyon adjacent to rolling countryside dotted with horse studs, and scenic mountains. It is a small, intimate setting: bedrooms are in earth tones with a few hand-painted designs on the walls and, though they are no frills, bed linen is soft cotton and there are simple touches which make it feel homely. There are five doubles, three singles and four shared bathrooms for 13 guests. One of the shared bedrooms is semi-outdoors, referred to as 'the porch', and will appeal to those who like to fall asleep under the moonlight. Guests congregate in a cosy living room where the focal point is a stone fireplace. Outdoor space includes a patio area with a generous hot tub and a small pool. The yoga dome is a groovy structure, a short climb from the house.

What you do There's an exhausting – and compulsory – detox and fitness programme. Guests surrender themselves to the curriculum, which means you don't have to make a single decision during your stay. The omnipresent Catharina, a jovial Swedish woman, runs the place. She conducts one-on-one interviews upon arrival to understand why each guest has come.

The week-long programme begins on a Sunday afternoon and ends on a Saturday morning. Monday to Friday are the strenuous days. Each morning one of the leaders wakes you at 0600 and the day begins with yoga, followed by breakfast at 0730. At 0900, the group and three leaders head out for the five-hour hike, which is the main activity of each day, after which you have lunch. In the afternoon you have a massage, take part in a pool class with water volleyball and a weight class. Each guest gets one massage per day, a necessity after the tough hikes. Evening yoga begins at 1800, then dinner is served at 1930, after which most guests crawl to their beds and collapse.

The hikes vary each day, getting progressively harder as the week unfolds: they start at three miles on the first day, building to 14 miles then reducing back to three. The terrain is superb and covers all that southern California is known for – mountains, valleys, waterfalls and beaches. A snack of chopped fruit and vegetables is served at the mid-point on the hike each day. While the Ashram is not for the faint-hearted, a nurturing environment full of laughter exists. The leaders want your trip to be a success.

What you eat and drink Guests are requested to give up caffeine and any other stimulants two weeks prior to coming to avoid headaches and withdrawals. Organic vegetarian food is served three times per day. The Ashram does not reveal the calorie count, but it's around 1000-1200 per day. These lean meals are definitely part of the challenge but the food is nevertheless flavoursome and delicious.

THE ASHRAM

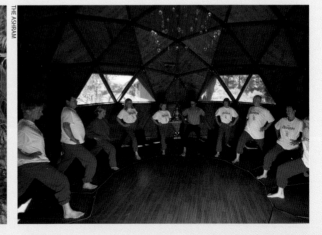

Many guests are eager to recreate the menu at home so a recipe book is handed out at the end of the week. The menu varies each day: breakfast may be a seven-grain hot cereal with orange and grapefruit slices, lunch soya protein tacos with Mexican garnishes, and dinner a quinoa salad with beets. You drink either water or herbal tea. There is an optional weigh-in upon arrival and departure.

Who goes The Ashram takes 13 people per week. Ages vary from 18-65, though most are in their thirties and forties, and predominantly from the US: 60% women and 40% men. Most people are here as a respite from stressful lives, or to lose weight, reinvigorate and detoxify. It's also very popular with Hollywood celebrities. It's best to come alone, so you can focus on yourself, although couples and friends do sometimes attend. Whatever your fitness level, a strong desire to prevail is mandatory. You need to be eager to take on the challenge because it's your own inner strength to get you through the week.

Essentials The week-long programme costs US$4000, which is all-inclusive, including scheduled transfers to and from LA. If you miss the van shuttle or fly into any of the other surrounding airports, The Ashram will arrange a car service which you pay directly. You need to book six months in advance, but there's also a waiting list, worth going on if you can jump at the last minute if there's a cancellation. Laundry is done daily so pack extremely light. The two vital items to bring are a well broken-in pair of walking/hiking shoes and a camelpak for hydrating. Don't bring new boots or shoes. The Ashram provides sweatshirts/pants, T-shirts and bathrobes. Best months are October-December, April and May. July and August are the hottest there's a chance of rain from January to March. Mobile phones are not permitted during hikes or classes, but can be used during downtime away from other guests. Singles rooms are difficult to secure and are given on a first-come-first-served basis. The Ashram occasionally runs trips to Mallorca. To contact them: T+1 (1)818-222 6900, www.theashram.com.

66 99

On my last day at The Ashram I put on the jeans I arrived in and they were so loose I could roll the waist over three times. While the weight loss was gratifying, I realized I had achieved so much more at this special hideaway. We were all boiled down to our most raw state, physically and emotionally, and it was the perfect sanctuary to do some deep thinking. Don't be put off by the seemingly ordinary rooms when you arrive - the experience here is absolutely extraordinary.

Eleanor Seaman

Healthy stopovers in New York

New York City rightly earns its reputation as the fastest city in the world, but there are still plenty of spots to escape the chaos. If money is no issue, the stunning views of the city from the **Mandarin Oriental** (from US$600 per room per night, T+1 (1)212-805 8800, www.mandarinoriental.com) will leave you peacefully floating above it all. It has New York's fanciest five-star spa on the 35th floor, complete with a swimming pool with floor-to-ceiling windows and body wraps with flavours to match the season. Coming back down to earth is not difficult, especially as the hotel sits perched on the corner of Central Park.

More affordable is the plush **Dream Hotel** (from US$250 per room per night, T+1 (1)212-247 2000, www.dreamny.com), in Manhattan's midtown, with all sorts of amenities, restaurants and bars. Author and mind-body physician, Deepak Chopra, opened the Chopra Center and Spa here in 2006, where you'll find massage, yoga, and Eastern healing arts such as sound meditation, in a bohemian-chic atmosphere. It's the sister property to the main Chopra Center at La Costa Resort & Spa in San Diego (see www.chopra.com).

While there's nothing opulent about **Pickwick Arms** (T+1 (1)212-355 0300, www.pickwickarms.com), at around US$100 per person per night, it could be a creative answer to those on a stricter budget in one of the world's most expensive cities. The rooms are small, but they're clean, modern and central. Just around the corner is **Bliss** (T+1 (1)212-401 2001, www.blissworld.com), the well-known spa at the W Hotel, which specializes in facials and skin treatments.

Regain your breathing space in downtown Manhattan at the **Open Center Meditation Room** (83 Spring Street, SoHo, www.opencenter.org), a non-profit holistic centre offering courses, yoga, massage and a meditation room intended to "nourish the soul". Otherwise, there's **Bikram Yoga NYC** (T+1 (1)212-288 9642, www.bikramyoganyc.com) which uses a low-wattage heating system, non-toxic paint and bamboo flooring.

If you feel like getting out of town entirely, head to the mountains around the Hudson Valley. Less than two hours north of the city by bus is the **Atmananda Retreat Centre** (T+1 (1)212-625 1511, www.atmananda.com/retreat.html), a yoga centre with a sweat lodge and B&B nestled in a popular hiking area, costing from US$50 per person per night. Or go for a weekend to the **Sivananda Ashram Yoga Ranch** (T+1 (1)845-436 6492, www.sivananda.org/ranch/) set in 30 ha in New York's Catskill Mountains and surrounded by forest and wild flowers. The centre is 100 miles from New York City – a group van leaves every Friday at 1800 from New York Sivananda Yoga Vedanta Centre and returns every Sunday evening. Prices depend on workshops.

---

gazpacho and salade niçoise with ahi tuna. Fellow guests will be drifting around wearing cashmere blankets and blissful expressions.

The nearest major airports are those in New York (two hours away); Boston's Logan airport is three hours away. From there you can rent a car or arrange a pickup by the hotel.

New Age Health Spa

Neversink, New York
T+1 (1)800-682 4348
www.newagehealthspa.com
From US$204 per person per night based on double occupancy

The New Age Health Spa is a quiet, affordable retreat in the Catskill Mountains, 2½ hours' drive from New York City. An unpretentious place, it attracts down-to-earth guests who want understatement rather than luxury.

Fitness programmes include cardiovascular classes, African healing dance, aerobics and hiking. Meditation, yoga, tai chi and water tai chi are on offer, as well as a juice fast and detox, and classes in cooking and growing organic food. Don't miss the Alpine Tower, a five-storey jungle gym, which provides a good chance to break the ice with fellow guests. There's a nearby American bald-eagle watch, and a Native American sweat lodge runs monthly between May and November.

In the spa, the 'Native Sun Purification', a Native American method of cleansing the hair and scalp, is recommended along with 'Paradise Mountain Rain', a Dead Sea salt exfoliation followed by a mud bath. Massages, body wraps, facials, beauty treatments, and colonics are available.

Treatments start from US$85; book in advance to ensure a place.

The interior decor is rather dated, though clean and fresh, and reminiscent of a traditional American home with floral fabrics and painted wicker furniture. Rooms vary, but all are en suite, and some have whirlpool

NEW AGE HEALTH SPA

tubs. None have TVs or phones.

There is a daily 1500-calorie plan, consisting of mainly vegetarian food. However, you can eat as much or little as you please: this is not a place to feel guilty. Breakfast is buffet style and lunch and dinner both offer a salad buffet with organic dark leafy greens grown on-site. No caffeine or alcohol is permitted; choose from a variety of delicious herbal teas.

Clientele are mostly American women, aged 30 to 60, but the number of men is increasing. There is a two-night minimum stay and prices include accommodation, meals and most classes. July and August are peak months, but the area is stunning in the snow. Fly to JFK, La Guardia or Newark. The spa offers a car service to meet you at your hotel or airport. Transfers from New York City cost US$130 (or US$80 each for two).

Omega Institute

🌿 🍵 ♨ ☀ ○ ⚘ ◉ ✿ ✺ ◐ ⛰12

Rhinebeck, New York
T+1 (1)800-944 1001
www.eomega.org
From US$135 per person per day

Omega is a holistic centre, just two hours north of New York City in the Hudson River Valley, and the kind of place where you'll feel like a pioneer in the wilderness.

Accommodation is rustic, spartan and quiet: choose from cottages with private or shared bathrooms, dorm rooms, tented cabins or tents. While the buildings are close and connected by walking paths, there's a real feeling of space and tranquillity. Most people do an R&R (rejuvenation and rest) programme, or select from hundreds of interesting workshops on offer: try the enticing Juicy Pens & Thirsty Paper or the Calming Heart & Clear Mind. Daily classes such as yoga, meditation, tai chi, and evening programmes such as concerts, movies, dances, lectures and readings are open to all.

The lake is an idyllic spot to unwind. Guests can be found painting, practising tai

chi and canoeing, or simply relaxing in a hammock and reading. The Japanese meditation garden offers a peaceful place to sit. The sanctuary, a cedar building surrounded by water with lily pads and beautiful flowers, is another peaceful site for meditation, while the wellness centre has a sauna and offers a variety of holistic therapies.

Food is primarily vegetarian, with local produce and fresh-baked breads. Most people come for two to five days, and some stay as long as a month. The place attracts a bohemian crowd, mostly Americans in their thirties and forties. It's open from April to October. Drive, or take the train or charter bus from New York City. Bring insect repellent (mosquitoes can be a problem), and decent walking shoes.

Omega also runs week-long retreats in the Caribbean and Costa Rica.

Patchwork Farm Retreats

🌿 ♨ ☀ ⚘ ◉ ✺ ◐ ⛰13

West Hawley, Massachusetts
T+1 (1)413-527 5819
www.writingretreats.org
From US$525 per person for 3 nights

Every September, the roving Patchwork Farm Retreats runs a creative four-day writing and yoga retreat at **Stump Sprouts** (www.stumpsprouts.com), a lovely 180-ha farmstead in West Hawley, Massachusetts. Patchwork's retreats attract anyone

Far left: New Age Health Spa.
Left above and below: Omega Institute.
Below: Patchwork Farm Retreats.

RED MOUNTAIN SPA

RED MOUNTAIN SPA

The appropriately named Red Mountain Spa blends in well with the rugged red sandstone landscapes of the Mojave Desert in Utah.

interested in yoga or writing, often looking for some kind of life change.

Patricia Lee Lewis, poet and senior partner at Amherst Writers & Artists (www.awa.org), and founder of Patchwork Farm Retreats, together with yoga and meditation teacher Charles MacInerney (www.yogateacher.com) of Expanding Paradigms, have created a safe, but liberating environment in which to retreat. Writing circles encourage mainly memoir writing. At times, participants may be reading work aloud, only to find themselves in tears. If this happens, peers wait patiently – and without comment – for the reading to resume. Afterward, the AWA method used by Patricia informs the group response, concentrating on what worked, not what didn't, and certainly not why an author might have cried.

There are two or three daily yoga and meditation circles before or after writing, which take the edge off. Connection to self, others, and the local environment is a critical component of Patchwork, and students can feel this. The retreats attract a lot of repeat guests, and those who come alone, or for the first time, are quickly integrated.

You stay in simple, camp-like bedrooms, and share bathrooms. Charming wood burning stoves heat the lodge, the barn (where 'circles' assemble) and the sauna hut. Treatments are available from local practitioners and include shiatsu, Swedish and deep tissue massage, reiki and craniosacral therapy. The closest airport is about two hours away, in Albany, New York. Patchwork holds other retreats around the globe including at Villa Sumaya in Guatemala (see page 356) and Los Naranjos in Mexico (see page 355).

(see page 356) (see page 355)

HEALTH & FITNESS RETREAT

Red Mountain Spa

Irvins, New St George, Utah
T+1 (1)435-673 4905
www.redmountainspa.com
From US$295 per person per night

In a gorgeous location in the Mojave Desert, with views of dramatic red sandstone cliffs, Red Mountain offers an impressive range of workshops inspired by the Native North American community, as well as treatments using local plants and herbs.

Dotted around the landscape are 82 guest rooms in two-storey buildings, all decorated in earth tones with natural materials, and bathrooms with slate floors and granite surfaces. There are also 12 luxury villas with one- or two-bedroom suites.

The Sagestone Spa and Salon boasts floor-to-ceiling windows overlooking the red rocks, 14 treatment rooms – including two wet rooms and a couples room – and 40 treatments, many using indigenous products such as lavender and sage (try the 'Adobe Lavender Hydrating Cocoon' or the 'Canyon Sage Warm Stone Massage'). Acupuncture is also available.

There are studios for over 50 active classes, from aerobics to salsa, an indoor pool and an outdoor pool where guests can lounge on chaises, adjacent to a quiet haven with a Japanese sand garden, an impressive lava bed garden and a sacred spiral arch.

It's easy to go hiking in the nearby Zion National Park and Grand Canyon, two of the most striking attractions in the USA. Hearty healthy meals are available, as well as a special detox menu, and cooking classes.

Red Mountain attracts outdoor people of all ages as well as those looking to detox and lose weight. Irvins is near St George and an

Where to retreat in Hawaii

If you're looking for a body and soul escape on Hawaii's Big Island, head away from the western side, where all of the larger resorts are situated. In spacious and well-tended grounds packed with tropical flowers and Asian sculptures, **Ramashala** (T+1 (1)808-965 0068, www.ramashala.com) is in the Puna district, a colourful enclave of artists, writers and farmers, with coconut palms, papaya, mango and avocado trees, orchids and the most delicious macadamia nuts around. It's managed by Rebecca Andrist, co-founder of Ananda Health and Yoga, which runs health and detox retreats in Europe and India (see page 200). Come here for a week's group yoga retreat, alone or with a friend or partner, and enjoy daily yoga, tai chi, meditation, nutrition classes, Swedish and Thai massage, reflexology, watsu and 100% natural and organic wraps and tropical body scrubs. There's a jacuzzi and warm mineral ponds, and you can also undertake a bespoke detox, juice fast or holistic weight-loss programme as well as attend creative vegetarian and raw food cookery classes. There is a wonderful black-sand beach a five-minute walk away, where you can spot sea turtles, dolphins and whales, or hike in the rainforests and lava fields, and to the nearby active volcano, where you can observe lava flowing into the ocean, an amazing sight. Rooms cost US$100-150 per night.

Alternatively, head to **Serenity in Hawaii** (T+1 (1)808-775 1614, www.serenityinhawaii.com), a secluded, homely escape to the north of Big Island at Honokaa. Run by the very hospitable Bob and Anita Cawley, who used to run The Yoga Studio in Santa Barbara, California, it sleeps just two in a smart white wooden house set on a hillside. The guest apartment is painted in neutral colours, with large windows and a Japanese-style bed complete with Tempurpedic mattress and organic bedding. One-to-one yoga classes, meditation and qigong are available, and Anita is trained in reiki and aromatherapy. Acupuncture, beauty treatments and massage therapies can be arranged in reputable neighbouring spas. Vegetables are organic and home-grown wherever possible, and you can eat as much fresh fruit as you like, all straight from the tree. Anita can also devise a detox menu for you. Visit Kalopa National Forest, hike through the valley, sunbathe on the beach or photograph picturesque waterfalls. Serentiy costs from US$135 per room per night.

For something different, Judith Seelig's two-week annual **Yoga and Sound Hawaii** retreat (T+44 (0)20-8815 0912, www.yogaandsound.com) is an opportunity to swim with wild dolphins and watch whales off the coast, as well as enjoy classes in Judith's distinctive blend of yoga and sound. Encountering these magnificent creatures is an exhilarating experience and scientifically proven to help you feel happy by increasing the release of endorphins. During January and February, whales and dolphins arrive in Hawaiian waters to conceive or give birth, some having travelled 3000 miles to do so. Males and females sing resonantly to one another; the boat Judith uses has a hydrophone, so it is almost guaranteed you will hear these underwater songs. Judith's studies on vibration add healing value to the experience, as she is able to help interpret your emotional reactions to them.

The two-week retreat costs from US$2875 per person, excluding flights and accommodation. Judith also runs retreats to Morocco (see page 171) and to the Earth Spirit Centre in the UK (see page 32).

Left: Whale-watching with Yoga and Sound Hawaii. **Above**: Ramashala.

incredibly scenic two-hour drive from Las Vegas. Shuttles transfer guests from the airport. It's an hour's flight from Salt Lake City (or a four-hour drive).

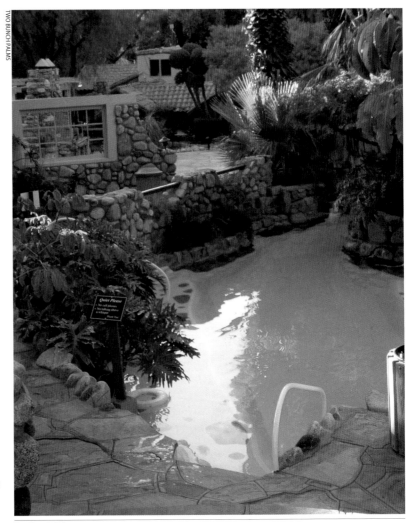

TWO BUNCH PALMS

Two Bunch Palms.

NATURAL SPA RETREAT

Sagewater Spa

🌐 🏊 🎧 ⚙️ ✴️ 🎵 ⏳15

Desert Hot Springs, California
T+1 (1)760-251 1668
www.sagewaterspa.com
From US$205 per night

Situated among the mountains, cacti and wild desert flowers of Palm Springs, Sagewater is a stylish minimalist boutique hotel created from a remodelled 1950s building and renowned for its on-site mineral water that bubbles from a well at 74°C (165°F). Against the sharp white retro architecture and crisp white linen, red chairs offer a splash of colour, and the white walls and aquamarine pool contrast wonderfully with azure skies and the 360° vista of snow-topped mountains.

Spa body and beauty treatments incorporate a variety of therapies. Aveda and high-grade aromatherapy oils are used alongside some herbal products for facials and massages – craniosacral, deep tissue, lymphatic, scalp-reflex, lomi lomi and hot-stone – body wraps and scrubs. Thai massage and shiatsu are also offered as well as their invigorating 'water shiatsu', which is taken in the watsu tub. Some of the more unusual treatments are the 'bindi', an exfoliating treatment that combines ayurvedic herbs with hot-oil massage, and 'raindrop' which promotes vitality through the reflexes using a centuries-old Tibetan technique. Private yoga classes are also on offer.

There are only seven spacious and simple rooms, so there's a personal feel with individual attention. Guests are mainly people in the creative and visual arts, from the US, Europe and Australia, and aged from 25 to 60. Minimum stay is two nights, three during holidays. It's a 15-minute drive from Palm Springs, or two hours from LA.

DESERT RETREAT

Two Bunch Palms

🌐 🏊 🎧 ⚙️ ✴️ 🎵 ⏳16

Desert Hot Springs, California
T+1 (1)760-329 8791
www.twobunchpalms.com
From US$195 per person per night

Rumour has it that the first permanent buildings at Two Bunch Palms sprang up in the 1920s as a remote hideaway for Al Capone. Today, this private 100-ha resort is a green oasis in California's Mojave Desert, and a pristine sanctuary. The natural mineral springs, once enjoyed by Mafia bosses and movie stars, now flow into a tranquil stone grotto and therapy pools, the warm waters central to a luxurious diversity of body treatments.

Shaded by palms and giant tamarisk trees and surrounded by immaculate landscaped gardens, the large en suite guestrooms, suites and villas are situated near the grotto area or overlooking the lakes. Crisp white bedlinen, tiled floors and ample armchairs and sofas in

SAGEWATER SPA

Sagewater Spa.

desert walks. The Indian Canyons are close by, as well as world-class shopping in Palm Springs and Cabazon's 150 outlet stores.

Two Bunch Palms is remote enough to draw in A-list guests, but most are stressed-out city types, some staying for a long weekend, others a week or longer. Desert Hot Springs has an incredible 330-plus days of sunshine a year. June to September is off season when air temperatures can reach 49°C. Fly to Palm Springs; the spa is a 10-minute drive away.

DETOX RETREAT

We Care Holistic Health Center

Desert Hot Springs, California
T+1 (1)760-251 2261
www.wecarespa.com
From US$944 per person for 3 days

In the serene mountain setting of California's Desert Hot Springs, We Care offers detox retreats in an intimate and homely atmosphere. Its 17 comfortable air-conditioned rooms complement the desert landscape, with rich earth tones, sky-blue walls and mosaics and tiled floors, while fine-quality bed linen, fireplaces and oversized sunken baths add touches of luxury.

There are daily colonics, and lymphatic massage, body scrubs, reflexology, acupressure and sacred-stone massage encourage cleansing and rejuvenation from the outside. Combined with yoga, meditation, movement classes and desert walks, you soon feel genuinely centred. The liquid fasting programme incorporates organic raw vegetable juices, soups, herbal teas and products such as spirulina, wheatgrass and acidophilus, as well as supplements.

We Care is a popular destination for professionals from the US, as well as models, musicians and actors. Desert temperatures can reach nearly 50°C in summer, so winter is the best time to stay. Fly to Palm Springs, a 15-minute drive away. See Essentials for what to expect from a detox.

---

soft biscuit shades lend a calming, homely feel, but there are also touches of extravagance in the art deco furnishings and stained glass.

This is one of the few places on earth with hot natural mineral springs that don't carry any sulphurous odour. The waters, drawn up through artesian wells, average 64°C and are cooled by a state-of-the-art delivery system for the grotto, swimming pools, watsu and aqua reflexology treatment pools.

The staff are extremely experienced with a broad range of healing knowledge and this is reflected in the range of treatments. As well as water-based therapies, mud wraps using local clay, scrubs and traditional treatments such as Thai, lymphatic, aromatherapy and ayurvedic massages, there is a selection of esoteric signature treatments such as 'Native American Renewal', a calming, meditative therapy with burning incense, energy clearing, blessings and a sand and aloe scrub followed by a herbal oil massage. You can also do tai chi, and yoga with a teacher trained at the Kripalu Centre (see page 340).

In the cosy old-world restaurant, the Ritz-Carlton-trained chef serves up the freshest ingredients, relying almost exclusively on local growers, ranchers and fishermen. There is a focus on low-fat,

66 99

So many gods, so many creeds, so many paths that wind and wind, while just the art of being kind is all the sad world needs.

Ella Wheeler Wilcox

low-sodium ingredients with plenty of salads, fish and shellfish on the menu. You also have a choice of indulgent desserts and a generous wine list.

If you want to explore the area, day trips include the Joshua Tree National Park and

Mexico

Mexico is a heart-warming place for worn-out bodies and stressed-out souls; stay at a chic coastal retreat or head for a holistic haven on the clean, sweet waters of Bacalar lagoon.

Fact file

- **Visa:** Not required for citizens of EU countries, the US, Canada, Australia and New Zealand
- **IDD:** + 52
- **Currency:** Mexican peso (MXN)
- **Time zone:** GMT -6 hours
- **Electricity:** 127v
- **Tourist board:** www.visitmexico.com

WATERSIDE RETREAT

Akal Ki

Bacalar lagoon
T+52 (01)983-835 8795
www.akalki.com
From US$150 per room per night

At the southern tip of Bacalar lagoon in one of the few areas on the Yucatán Peninsula coast unspoilt by tourism, Akal Ki is a marvellously peaceful retreat with *palapas* (huts) built right over the water. Akal Ki means 'sweet lagoon' in Maya and, though surrounded by jungle, this strip of the lagoon – known as the Lagoon of Seven Colours after its many different shades of blue – has few rocks and little vegetation, making it crystal clear and ideal for swimming.

The creation of two friends, cinematographer Luis Antunez and businessman Arturo Arroyo, Akal Ki comprises 20 ha of jungle, most of which is undeveloped. As well as being used by yoga and meditation groups, it's open to individuals who want to retreat somewhere peaceful and natural for a minimum stay of three days. A long driveway from the main road to the lagoon ensures you'll hear no noise other than the lapping of the water and intermittent breezes.

You sleep in two-person *palapas* made of wood and stone with simple decor, most with decking and steps right into the lagoon. There is a *temazcal* (sweat lodge), and a meditation and yoga pavilion – classes on offer vary according to guest teachers. Thai and Mexican dishes use home-grown organic vegetables and local fish, and are served in a spacious restaurant overlooking the lagoon.

The various treatments on offer take their inspiration from the four elements: meditation (air), the *temazcal* (fire), yoga (earth), and water treatments such as 'jenzu', a fantastic seawater massage, and aqua yoga, which is especially good for those with a lot of bodily pain.

Ritual is very much a part of the experience here – you can renew your spiritual vows as a couple or take part in a special ceremony to say goodbye to someone you didn't see before they died. You are required to give thanks to the environment on entering the resort, and to give something back to it before you leave, be it planting a seed or painting a picture. Fellow guests are from all over the world, usually in their thirties and forties. Fly to Belize or Cancún, or take an internal flight from Mexico City to Chetumal. Pickups can be arranged.

CAROLINE SYLGE

Above: Bacalar lagoon. **Top right:** The Centre of the Concious Dream.

DANIEL STONE

The Centre of the Conscious Dream

♨ ☀ ⚲ ◯ ↘2

San Luis Potosí
T+52 (01)488-881 8126
www.12consciousdreamers.com
From US$435 per person per week

The Centre of the Conscious Dream is run by respected English healer Daniel Stone and his Mexican wife Arbolita Pashak, also a healer and teacher. They supervise desert retreats to teach the art of 'conscious dreaming', a term Daniel uses to describe energies in all our states: waking, sleeping, life and death. He believes these energies are intricately connected to the natural world around us, and that we can learn to channel them in order to transcend time and heal ourselves.

The Americas Mexico

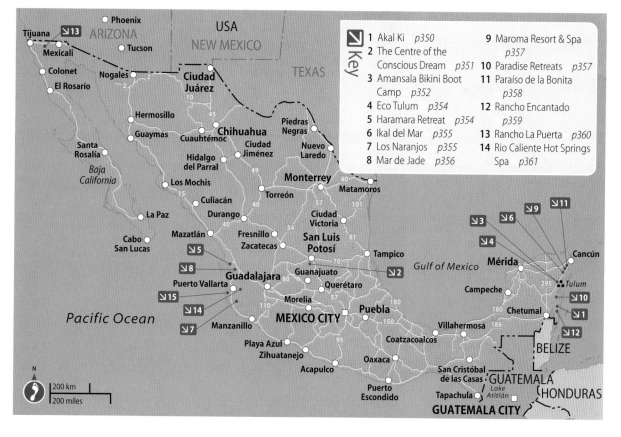

Wellbeing holiday

Amansala Bikini Boot Camp

Amansala is a sassy, well-designed resort on a clean and beautiful stretch of beach at Tulum. Its Bikini Boot Camps are perfect if you want to de-stress, eat healthily and exercise but enjoy a touch of pampering too. Despite its name, the approach is laid-back and the onus is on you to make it as hard or as easy as you want it to be; this isn't the place to come if you're looking to be held by the hand through a serious fitness regime. It's the creation of feisty globetrotter, Melissa Perlman, who built it having fallen in love with Tulum years before.

Where you stay You'll be in one of 16 en suite *cabanas* built from wood and stone with thatched *palapa* roofs. Each *cabana* has whitewashed walls, lovely high ceilings and decorated stone floors. Lilac, lemon yellow and white linens cover the comfortable beds, and mosquito nets are provided. There are thoughtful design details throughout, such as locally made punpkin lampshades, and coloured bottles built into the walls to catch the sunlight.

Cabana 16 is one of the best, set back a little from the beach and away from the full roar of the waves. It has a lovely big bed made from a slab of stone, an indoor sitting area in which to sprawl, and its own veranda. Most rooms have an outside area with a hammock, and there are plenty of loungers, hammocks and swinging daybeds in the main beach area. Brilliant pink and orange are the dominant colours

❝❞

My boyfriend and I slept soundly every night and came away tanned, energized and happy – the morning walks by the roaring sea were particularly effective. We were lucky to have Bridget Shields (www.bridgetshields.com) from New York as our guest yoga teacher. She took a breath-based class to a randomly mixed CD of Indian chants and Jack Johnson lyrics – a surprisingly effective way to get us to focus on the movements instead of our minds. Learning to belly dance with Bridget was also a highlight. We were in a small group of just 10, which included a lieutenant from the NYPD, a production editor for a German fashion magazine, a renal nurse from Florida and two Irish friends now living in New York. Everyone got on well and had a relaxed approach to each other and the week. My boyfriend was the only man but he loved it. We'd both go back for sure.

Caroline

throughout the resort, picked out in the towels, hammocks, yoga mats, plastic flowered plates, drinking cups and cushions.

Five minutes' walk away is Amansala's second property, Casa Magna, once the home of Columbian drugs baron Pablo Escobar but now a designer haven which New York celebrities think nothing of renting for US$35,000 a week. This is used to accommodate the overflow on busy Bikini Boot Camp weeks, and for couples on their own tailor-made visits who may be in need of reconnecting with each other as well as themselves.

What you do Every day starts with an hour-long power walk at the civilized time of 0800, the first half hour of which is done in silence. There is then a changing schedule of classes which, as well as yoga, meditation and circuit training, includes a range of dance sessions. Teachers tend to be from the US, and are a mix of guest and resident. Classes take place in a stone pavilion with lots of light and protection from mosquitoes.

Morning or afternoon trips are built into the programme, including a 5-km bike ride to the local Maya ruins and a swim at a local *cenote*, or sinkhole. After dinner, you'll get to paint, brush up on your Spanish or try out African drumming. There's plenty of beach time built into the programme, and two (very good) massages a week are included, though you can have as many more as you want for US$65 a pop. You'll also get to experience the cleansing effects of the local clay, used as an all-round beautifier and medicine. The ever-present waves are guaranteed to blow all those mental cobwebs away, whether you're playing in them or just listening to them crashing on the shore.

BRIDGET SHIELDS

What you eat and drink Food is high fibre, high protein, low fat and delicious. Breakfast is a simple choice of fresh fruits, yoghurt, muesli and scrambled eggs with vegetables. Lunch and dinner feature locally caught white fish such as mero and boccinetta, or tender organic chicken, usually grilled whole or as kebabs and cooked with a Mexican twist using salsas, chilli, avocado and jicama. Beer, wine and spirits are served – including some delicious fresh fruit margaritas. Meals are eaten looking out to sea in a shaded shelter, where there's also a high wooden bar.

Who goes The boot camp attracts lots of accomplished, educated and busy women in need of some 'me' time, a sprinkling of men and a few couples. Warrior Weeks are also on offer, often alongside the Bikini Boot Camps, aimed mainly at men who want more of an adventure week, and include sea-kayaking, mountain biking andspearfishing, as well as cardio training, power yoga and beach workouts. Most guests are from the US, though there are an increasing number of Europeans. There could be guests staying here who are not part of the Boot Camp programme, or visiting yoga groups wanting to keep to themselves.

Essentials The six-night package costs from US$1842 and includes all meals, classes and activities, two massages and a Maya clay treatment. The Boot Camp runs from September to April – March and April are particularly good times to visit when it's warm but not too hot and still windy enough to keep mosquitoes at bay. The average number of guests is between 15 and 20, never more than 25. It can feel crowded at full capacity, so ask Amansala in advance to advise on particularly popular weeks. Fly to Cancún, from where a private taxi costs a staggering US$120 for the 1½-hour drive. Alternatively, take a Green Line shuttle bus for US$35 per person, or a public bus from just US$8 direct to Tulum or via Playa del Carmen. From Tulum bus station it's a US$10 taxi ride to Amansala. Amansala (www.amansala.com) is a resort and open at other times.

Daniel translated his dreams into music, theatre and creative writing before discovering shamanism. After a decade of travelling and studying with indigenous teachers, he established the Shamanic School of Dreaming in 1995. He now runs courses in Europe, including at the Brightlife centre on the Isle of Man (see page 27).

The retreat is tailored to the individual, and starts with a private consultation to address your needs. Daniel uses shamanic healing to refresh and heal the body: through sound vibration, music, crystals and massage, he helps you rebalance and rid the body of redundant energy. In further private consultations, Daniel looks for your spirit guide and interprets your night dreams. Retreats can also focus on Maya teachings, astrology and culture, and Arbolita can provide a personal Maya calendar reading. *Temazcal* sessions are held regularly.

The Centre is in the Senora Desert, at the end of a 300-km pilgrimage route taken by the indigenous Huricuta. According to Huichol legend the sun rose from the mountain over the Centre, which Daniel now calls an 'inter-dimensional doorway'. There is a simple temple and studio for meditation and workshops. You can either stay in your own tent in the grounds, in a dorm, or in a private room in their Round House. The bathroom is shared. Food is freshly prepared and is included in the price.

Courses are run in English and Spanish and attract a variety of open-minded individuals of all ages, from Europe, Canada and Mexico. Minimum stay is one week. The nearest town is Matehuala. Fly to Mexico City, from where transport will be arranged – liaise with Daniel.

COASTAL RETREAT

Eco Tulum

Tulum
T+1 (1)800-514 3066
www.ecotulum.com
From US$95 per room per night

Eco Tulum offers three unpretentious, beachside resorts in Tulum – Cabañas Copal, Azulik and Zahra. Azulik is the quietest, most spacious and most private place to stay – its 15 wooden villas have bathtubs made of carved tree trunks, great sea views, and hanging beds on private decks. Each resort shares the rustic **Maya Spa** (www.maya-spa.com), based at Cabañas Copal, which specializes in affordable local Maya treatments including an exfoliating Maya bath in a wooden tub, or the deeply cleansing Maya clay massage. There are daily yoga sessions in the yoga shala, and *temazcal* ceremonies three times a week, but the best thing on offer is the local holistic massage – look out for Chandree, who owns The Healing House (see Paradise Retreats, page 357).

COASTAL RETREAT

Haramara Retreat

Sayulita, Jalisco
T+52 (01)329-291 3028
www.haramararetreat.com
US$85-160 per person per night, full board

This pristine, 12-acre virgin forest property, home to many creatures and birds, runs downhill to its own lovely beach. The owner,

CAROLINE SYLGE

◗ Body language

Sweating it out

The *temazcal* is a ritual ceremony that has been practised by the indigenous people of Mexico for hundreds of years. The Mexican version of the sweat lodge, it is a thanksgiving to the four elements, and a healing for the spirit as well as the body. You enter the womb of mother earth when you enter the *temazcal*, and when you exit you are born a new being. Traditionally, it took place in a square- or dome-shaped building constructed from branches and then covered with blankets, and was preceded by a day of fasting. There are *temazcal* sessions open to newcomers all over Mexico. Done properly, the experience can be very intense, even magical.

Red-hot rocks are placed in the centre of the construction, and a group sits around them. The door is closed, and a medicine man leads the group in prayer and songs, all designed to connect the insiders to each of the four elements. During the ceremony, the door is opened four times, to let out people who want to leave (there is no returning), and to bring in more hot rocks. Different emotions and thoughts come up for different people, and everyone is encouraged to contribute something from their own traditions if they feel the need. After each contribution, herbal water is poured over the rocks to create more healing steam. This continues until everyone is in agreement to open the fourth and final door. Everyone then leaves, rinses off (hopefully in the sea or lagoon if you're near the coast), then shares soup and tea to break their fast.

The Americas Mexico

Sajeela, is a yogini who studied in India for 13 years and is dedicated both to the land and the evolution of the human spirit. She owned and operated Osho Oasis, in Tulum, before Hurricane Roxanne struck in 1995.

You can stay here alone or with a friend or partner, or join a yoga retreat. Various types of yoga are offered by a rota of visiting teachers; many of these are open to individuals, including those run by the Feathered Pipe Ranch in the US (see page 338). Things slow down in the rainy season, around August and September, but the centre is open all year. Haramara employs excellent bodyworkers offering various types of massage as well as reiki.

Beautiful open-air, thick-walled cabins are named after gems like amethyst and rose quartz, and gems they are. Each has cut-out windows entirely open to the sun, moon and stars. A few have a resident iguana or other adopted 'pets', but guests are encouraged not to keep food in the rooms as the curious and greedy coatimundi will come looking for it. Each bungalow is slightly different but all have open-air showers, thatch roofs, comfortable beds (though sheets are rough) with mosquito netting, several hammocks, and lovely jungle and sea views.

The *palapa* roof of the large open-air

⬤ Soul food

Meaningful travel provider **i-to-i** (T0870-333 2332, www.i-to-i.com) offers a range of community-based travel projects throughout Mexico, such as work with special-needs children, teaching English in rural villages and helping to collect and distribute food to some of Mexico's poorest families. The company also offers travel with altruistic work on its Meaningful Tour: The Yucatán Peninsula Experience – a two-week trip where you live alongside and help support the local Maya communities, as well as take in the local sights.

dining room is made of 60,000 palms in the traditional manner; floors are polished matt-finish cement, and the space is beautifully lit by lanterns at night. Delightful, nutritious and beautifully presented food is prepared by Argentine chef, Mariano Garcés. Think fresh, light-green gazpacho of nopal cactus, green tomatillo, and spinach followed by a simply prepared local fish with polenta, and for dessert, a carrot-yoghurt parfait.

Most guests take a taxi from the Puerto Vallarta airport direct to Sayulita, or public transport from Puerto Vallarta and then a short taxi ride to the retreat.

HOTEL & SPA

Ikal del Mar

◉ ◉ ◉ ◉ ◉ ⬛6

Riviera Maya
T+52 (01)984-877 3000
www.ikaldelmar.com
From US$585 per room per night

Set up by a group of Mexican friends, this boutique hotel boasts 30 well-designed villas in a jungle garden, and unpretentious service. A pool, tiny yoga room, *temazcal* and massage beds overlook a good stretch of beach. Huge blue, black and lime green butterflies dance everywhere, and tropical plants abound. The beach here is rocky, but they have built decking out to the sea so you can swim away from the rocks.

Each villa is very private, with jungle trees and shrubs surrounding your own small plunge pool, hammock and daybed. Decor is minimalist and beds have fantastically soft linens. Locally home-made soap is brought to the door on your arrival, and notebooks and poems are strewn on your bed at night. It's a shame there's a rather noisy air-conditioning system, which you'll sometimes hear from neighbouring villas.

The spa is a lovely relaxing space, its design based around circles, with single sex jacuzzis and steam rooms. You'll get 'seeds of abundance' on your arrival, which allows you US$30 off a treatment if it rains. There's a refreshing range of signature treatments on

Ikal del Mar massage beds.

offer: try the 'hammock massage', where after a classic rub with avocado oil you lie clothed in a hammock, while the therapist uses her feet to apply gentle pressure to your back and legs; or the 'Awakening of the Senses', guaranteed to refresh the most jaded of office-bound souls. Have your treatment in one of the outdoor spaces, not in the air-conditioned treatment rooms.

There are lots of light and nutritious things on the gourmet menu; they're especially good at grills and a range of tasty ceviches.

The place attracts couples – you'll feel left out if you're here alone. Fly to Cancún, from where it's a 60-km drive, or pickups can be arranged (US$100 round trip).

JUNGLE RETREAT

Los Naranjos

◉ ◉ ☀ ◉ ◉ ◉ ⬛7

Yelapa, Jalisco
T+52 (01)322-209 5179
www.ranchoyelapa.com
From US$35 per person per night

Half an hour away from Puerto Vallarta, but only accessible by boat, this jungle retreat offers as many or as few activities as guests desire. Totally surrounded by vegetation, it is cool even during the hottest part of the day. Red hibiscus and stands of willowy bamboo, goldfish ponds and a wet-season waterfall enhance the rustic property.

There's a homely feel to this beautiful place. Hang out in the large, open dining/living room – with two lovable whippets who have the run of the place – or take advantage of one of the locally arranged

LOS NARANJOS

Above: Los Naranjos. **Right:** Paradise Retreats.

trips: there's whale- and dolphin-watching, snorkelling, diving, and paragliding. The (mainly vegetarian) food is popular – chef April Jones has produced a vegetarian cookbook by demand – and meat and fish are also available on request.

There's a sensory-isolation room or dugout-canoe hammock for meditation; Swedish and deep tissue massage are on offer, and, if you're into music, you can jam with the owner, Jarrett, who plays the clarinet, saxophone and flute. There's good walking in the surrounding area, including an invigorating hike up to Cathedrall Falls. Patchwork Farm runs yoga and creative-writing retreats here (see page 345), and **Expanding Paradigms** (www.yogateacher.com) runs yoga and meditation retreats.

Surrounding the three main guest cabins are copa de oro bushes with their substantial blooms, along with lime, orange, and passion fruit trees, and the owner's bronze statues dot the garden. In the rustic cabins, mosquito nets surround hanging beds of wood, and the cement floors are covered in *petates*, locally woven mats. In the bathrooms, modern standard-issue sinks and toilets are juxtaposed with half-stone walls and *palapa*-thatch roofs.

Although it's technically open (and the grounds are lush and beautiful) during the rainy season (July-October), there are few classes at that time and sometimes only a friendly caretaker on the site. The bay-side town of Yelapa is accessible by boat only. Transport from Puerto Vallarta or Boca de Tomatlan, 30 minutes south of Puerto Vallarta on the bay of Banderas, is arranged when you book.

COASTAL RETREAT

Mar de Jade

Playa de Chacala
T+1 (1)800-257 0532
www.mardejade.com
US$110 per person per night

A friendly Mexican retreat with few frills, based on a beautiful beach an hour north of Puerto Vallarta, Mar de Jade hosts a range of interesting courses from November to April, or you can stay as an individual the rest of the year.

There are lots of good vibes here, and the owner, Laura del Valle, is heavily involved in helping the disenfranchized indigenous and mestizo people of the area. You can volunteer at the community development centre and primary-care clinic for migrant workers for a spot of karma yoga.

Group retreats include Sufi dancing, Zen meditation and yoga holidays led by popular American teachers such as Beverley Murphy (www.yogapath.com). Nothing takes place during the two weeks at Easter, when revellers shatter the place's yoga-like calm.

During the rest of the year there are various yoga, meditation, cooking and Spanish classes on offer, as well as beauty treatments and massage in the spa – the masseuse who does the deep tissue massage is especially recommended. There's a communal steam room and outdoor plunge pool, beach views from the second-floor treatment rooms, and the large, wood-floored yoga and meditation room faces the Mar de Jade, or Jade Sea.

Rooms are clean if basic, with foam mattresses, tiled bathrooms and ceiling fans. A buffet caters to vegan and macrobiotic diets, but also serves great fish – try the paella or fish grilled over coals. Note that the beach is rocky in the rainy season (June-October) but the sand returns each November.

Sacred lake

Lake Atitlán in Guatemala has long been a hang-out for alternatively minded Westerners. On its shores is **Villa Sumaya Guest House and Retreat Centre** (T+502 5617 1209, www.villasumaya.com, from US$50 per room per night).

Accessible only by boat, with awe-inspiring views of three volcanoes and surrounding mountains, this idyllic spot offers an impressive range of yoga and personal development retreats led by visiting teachers, mainly from America. Subjects include Tibetan Buddhism, emotional intelligence, various types of yoga, photography and Thai massage. **Patchwork Farm** runs yoga and creative-writing retreats (see page 345), and **Expanding Paradigms** runs yoga and meditation retreats (www.yogateacher.com).

As well as yoga, guests can hike up the volcanoes or through the mountains to nearby Maya villages, swim in the lake, sunbathe, or enjoy a sauna or hot tub. A range of healing treatments is available, including Swedish and Thai massage, acupuncture, and intuitive energy work. Appointments should be scheduled in advance as the therapists have active private practices.

Villa Sumaya can arrange the 2½-hour shuttle ride from Guatemala City airport for US$100. Arrive in Panajachel and head for the Tzanjuyu dock. Pay US$10-25 for a private boat (*lancha*) to get there any time, or US$3 for a seat on the public *lancha* – the last one leaves at 1700. The rainy season is between July and November, although it's still beautifully sunny in the mornings. The hurricane season is in October. Avoid late March and April, when a fog obscures the view of the volcanoes.

Walk or take a boat trip to nearby beaches such as the pristine Playa de las Cuevas, where the crystalline water and gentle surf make it great for swimming. Boats from Chacala beach can be hired for whale-watching from December to April. Mar de Jade is 9 km from highway 200 and best accessed from Puerto Vallarta's airport by advance arrangement; it's about US$80 for up to three passengers and US$140 for more than nine passengers. The cheapest option is to get a bus to Las Varas (US$8) and a taxi from there (US$10).

HOTEL & SPA

Maroma Resort & Spa

Riviera Maya
T+52 (01)998-872 8200
www.maromahotel.com
From US$480 per room per night

If you're looking for high-end luxury and a yoga holiday, Maroma is set right on the beach in a 200-ha former coconut plantation. US yoga teacher, Cyndi Lee, founder of **Om Yoga Centre** in New York (www.omyoga.com), leads three five-night yoga holidays a year. Cyndi also practises Tibetan Buddhism and will lead a meditation session each morning at a leisurely 0830, followed by an invigorating two-hour yoga

class. The late-afternoon class will be more relaxing, with hip opening stretches and restorative poses. In the afternoons you can enjoy beach or spa time.

The rest of the year, yoga classes are offered by in-house Mexican yoga instructor and personal trainer, Mary Carmen Guerra, a warm and friendly teacher who weaves tai chi, pilates and dance into her yoga sessions, which take place in a small but lovely rooftop yoga pavilion with 360° views.

Maroma was created as a private beach hideaway by architect José Luis Moreno, who used sacred Maya geometry to align each building to the stars in order to help negative energy flow out, and positive energy flow in. The expansion of the hotel has since diluted the vision, but Maroma still offers barefoot glamour, with a good beach, friendly service, and spacious rooms with ocean or garden views. Expect margaritas on arrival, and little white golf buggies zipping round the pathways.

The Kinan Spa offers indulgent (and expensive) treatments – therapists for the 'God & Goddess' rituals (US$320) were trained by local expert Mallina, from Rancho Encantado (see next spread). Yoga retreats cost from US$2820 per person for five nights. Maroma is 20 miles south of Cancún airport. The entrance to the estate is at Km 51 of the highway, south of Puerto Morelos; or pickups can be arranged.

WELLBEING HOLIDAY

Paradise Retreats

Riviera Maya
T+44 (0)1277-355812
www.paradise-retreats.com
From US$1600 per person per week

Paradise Retreats runs group and bespoke getaways on the beautiful cost of the Maya Riviera. A weekly rolling programme of pilates, yoga and nourishing treatments runs from late January to late April, and bespoke retreats for friends or partners can be arranged at any time throughout the year to focus on their needs in private, be it to recover from an illness, consider a life change or de-stress.

An English pilates teacher and member of the Pilates Foundation, Elizabeth White set up Paradise Retreats in 2002 to offer personalized attention to her clients, and she now runs retreats with her Canadian partner, Brett, a masseur and Tibetan Buddhist meditation teacher. Elizabeth integrates pilates with her experience of kundalini yoga, skinner releasing (www.skinner releasing.com) and her dance training at Laban (www.laban.org), and also offers sessions on nutrition.

Group trips take a maximum of 12 and are open to beginners as well as those who are advanced in pilates or yoga. Having lived in the area Elizabeth has built up a network of local contacts and can arrange anything from a colonic to traditional acupunture with local Maya therapists. For bespoke retreats, Elizabeth will tailor accommodation according to your tastes and budget, all of it offering privacy and exclusivity away from the tourist crowd, including chef and driver.

The group retreats take place at Boca Paila Camps, a selection of tent-cabins raised on stilts and reached by sandy lanes winding through the palm forest inside the Sian Ka'an nature reserve. Daily classes are in the tipi-style studio overlooking the beach, and treatments take place throughout the day at the treatment room or your own bungalow.

For the more intensive workshops there is a boat trip across the lagoon to The Healing House, a basic, large and airy stone house in the middle of the jungle at José Ma Pino Suárez, at the edge of Sian Ka'an. It's the creation of local Italian therapist Chandree, who gives energizing holistic massages and offers reiki master courses, together with her Mexican-Sicilian partner, Cuauhtemoc, also a reiki master.

The Healing House offers a karma yoga-style kitchen where everyone mucks in. At Boca Paila Camps, there's a large brunch after morning class, an evening meal and plenty of fresh fruits and snacks available from the restaurant throughout the day. All retreats discourage dairy, wheat and red meat: tell them if you want to detox.

Group retreats cost from US$1600 per person per week, based on two sharing, and include two daily classes, two Maya treatments, accommodation, food, transfers and a *temazcal*. Bespoke retreats start at US$2520. The Healing House is available all year round for stays of three days or more for those who want to be close to nature and away from the world (from US$50 per person per night) – book through Paradise Retreats.

HOTEL & SPA
Paraíso de la Bonita

Riviera Maya
T+52 (01)998-872 8300
www.paraisodelabonita.com
From US$920 per night

A privately owned five-star hotel on the Riviera Maya, Paraíso de la Bonita is a curious mix of the funky, over-grand and kitsch: rooms are themed around different countries, there are caged birds, and there is just a little too much concrete everywhere. That said, it boasts the first officially registered thalassotherapy centre in North America. The Mexican owners, Elisa and Carlos Gosselin, have French ancestry and love thalassotherapy.

The therapists here are excellent, and there's an impressive outdoor hydrotherapy pool filled with clean salt water, set just back from a pristine beach and with a stunning view out to sea. Various face and body treatments use the Thalgo range of products from France, but the janzu, or 'peaceful river therapy', is one of the best treatments on offer (see box below for a first person account).

Come off-season, when the holiday-makers have gone, and indulge yourself in a package of treatments. There's also a lovely over-water pavilion for yoga. See box on page 101 for more information on thalassotherapy.

66 99

I am in my swimsuit, I'm boiling hot and a little uptight. The first janzu I've ever had is going to be conducted by a Mexican guy called Manuel Machuca, who has kind eyes and greets me in a wetsuit. He gives me a clip to put on my nose, and I step into a large pool filled with clean salt water. I have no idea what to expect. I'm a little fearful and check the nose clip more than I need to.

Manuel then puts one arm under my legs, one under my head, and I lie back. He begins slowly swirling me in the water, getting my body to gently twist, slowly to the left, then to the right. I close my eyes. I enjoy the flow of my limbs through the water, but am holding up my head, trying not to allow the salt water into my eyes, and still feel tense.

Manuel proceeds with his moves, and I slowly begin to relax. My legs, arms and back are gently manipulated as the salt water keeps me buoyant. He is at my feet, waving my body like a sheet; then he's at my head, shaking me from side to side. Gradually, I stop trying to hold my head up and just let go.

My forehead and eyes submerge but I have my eyes closed, and they don't sting. I begin to enjoy the play of light over my eyelids, and the feel of the warm salt water on my face. I listen, and the whirl of the water sounds muffled and comforting, as if I am in the womb.

When Manuel completely submerges me I am taken by surprise. I close my mouth, and wait. But with each new movement, I gain confidence. The feel of the warm water and the infused light from the sun above the surface is enthralling. I now completely trust Manuel. My back arches and I feel free, like a dancer. I am curled up, and I feel trusting, like a baby. I am stretched out, feet crossed, and twirled around, and I feel like a sea snake, rolling and playing.

I am unaware of how much time has passed. My eyes have been closed for the whole time, and I am floating in my head. I am taken to areas of the pool where there are jets of water and held there in a foetal position. I hear increasingly loud underwater sounds, which play over my ears and face, waking up my senses. Gradually the sounds fade, my head is lifted and I am put on a stone seat in the shallows. Manuel thanks me. I feel as if I have let go of something I didn't need, and want to have a janzu every day for at least a week. For the rest of the day I feel calm, light and intensely happy.

Caroline

Rancho Encantado

🌐 ♨ 🏔 🎧 ♻ ✳ ❄ ⚡ N12

Bacalar lagoon
T+52 (01)983-101 3358
www.encantado.com
From US$160 per room per night

Rancho Encantado is a holistic resort with a gentle, calm atmosphere set beside the clear blue waters of Bacalar lagoon. Filled with clean, sweet water and fed by subterranean streams, the lagoon is deliciously fresh and light to swim in and makes the setting very special indeed.

There are 12 *palapas* (huts), each with a porch or garden area featuring two brightly coloured hammocks. Though they are spacious and comfortable enough, their decor is slightly old fashioned and in need of sprucing up. It's worth paying extra for one of the five by the lakeside, not least because you'll be further away from the road noise, which you can hear at night. There is also one air-conditioned suite with its own decking and steps down to the water.

The main reason to come here is to experience a treatment from Mallina, doctor of Oriental medicine, Aztec ceremonial dancer, long-term bodyworker, and also resort manager. Her speciality is Hawaiian Temple bodywork, or lomi lomi, an extraordinarily powerful massage guaranteed to release bodily and emotional tensions. Go for the whole 'God' or 'Goddess' treatment (US$100) – see box above right for a full description.

Encantado also features a short promenade to some shaded over-water decking where you can swing in a hammock and watch the bird-life; a pretty, green-tiled outdoor jacuzzi, and a traditional *temazcal* where full-moon ceremonies are conducted every month by Mallina's partner, Atzin, a medicine man from Mexico City. The resort can also arrange trips to newly excavated and little-known Maya archaeological sites.

Mallina teaches qigong and meditation in the 'cathedral', a thatched pavilion with a

Mallina has expert hands and a huge heart. In a rustic palapa on the edge of the lagoon, her and a helper indulged me in a 'Goddess' treatment. Wrapped up in very hot sheets soaked with detoxifying herbs, I begin to sweat, while my face is pampered and cleansed with freshly picked fruit, flowers and honey. The sheets are removed, and my whole body is vigorously scrubbed with a delicious concoction of rock salt and honey. I wash it off by slipping naked into the clean, sweet water of the lagoon, a step away. No one is about, and I feel as if I am losing months of negative energy as well as bodily grime as I swim gently through the water. I emerge, smiling, and sit on the wooden steps of the deck to be doused with bucketfuls of warm camomile tea. The change in temperature is the most nourishing feeling, and I feel looked after and cherished. Nothing, however, prepares me for the pinnacle of this treatment, the lomi lomi massage, in which Mallina is an expert.

Otherwise known as Hawaiian Temple Bodywork, this four-handed massage is more like a tabletop dance, in which my body is eased and rubbed, cradled and moved in whatever direction Mallina and her fellow therapist feel it needs to be. It is far more than a physical release, and as I breathe deeply with each new movement, I feel a great welling up inside me, as if all my deepest fears have been unleashed. Mallina is totally in tune and tells me to keep breathing as I try to hold my breath, encouraging me to use my voice to express and release. I make a sound, which is both surprisingly difficult, and liberating. The massage gets more vigorous, and more emotional, till eventually I have tears streaming down my face. I keep breathing, and making strange noises, until I feel an inner calm; the kind you feel when you've been crying for hours. Finally at peace, my body is laid out and covered, and I slip into a restful sleep. When I wake, Mallina sits beside me. We exchange smiles, nothing more, and she leaves me in peace.

Caroline

The Americas Mexico

RANCHO LA PUERTA

high ceiling, or you can use the space to do your own practice. Hatha yoga classes are sometimes available with a local teacher, and occasional yoga and other personal development retreats led by visiting teachers are held throughout the year.

Food is Mexican-style fish or chicken dishes, with vegetarian options. Beer, wine and huge glasses of home-made energy fruit drinks are also on offer. Your fellow guests are likely to be alternative types in their thirties, forties and fifties, and from the US and Europe. A lot of groups use Encantado for their own retreats, so check in advance if you'd prefer to be here alone, when Mallina can organize bespoke spa weeks. Fly to Belize or Cancún, or take an internal flight from Mexico City to Chetumal - pickups can be arranged. At the time of going to press, Rancho Encantado was up for sale, though Mallina had no intention of leaving.

HEALTH & FITNESS RETREAT

Rancho La Puerta

🌐 🍴 🅰 ☀ ⭕ 🐎 ⭐ ⚙ ⚙ ⚙ ⭕ ☑13

Tecate, Baja California
T+52 (01)858-764 5500
www.rancholapuerta.com
From US$2535 per person per week

Rancho La Puerta, founded by Edmond and Deborah Szekely in 1940, is the original

destination fitness resort and spa, and welcomes 125 guests each week to its 1200 ha of gardens, mountains and meadows.

Its 87 rooms are remarkably spacious and private with a distinctive collection of Mexican folk art. The facilities are impressive and include a charming art studio, heated swimming pools, various gyms (including three set in the vineyard), tennis courts, a theatre, three health centres, and a labyrinth set in the ranch's ancient oak groves for meditation.

A typical day could start early with a trail, mountain or breakfast hike. After which you can pick from a variety of fitness classes including yoga, pilates, tai chi, and African dance. Afternoons are for spa pampering – try the 'Happy Hands & Feet' (a combination of reflexology and paraffin) or the Thai Massage, which is popular. There are terrific outdoor whirlpools with clothing-optional sunbathing decks.

La Cocina que Canta (The Kitchen that Sings), which opened in spring 2007, is a cooking school comprising a hands-on classroom/kitchen, cookbook library, and culinary gift shop, all set in the heart of Tres Estrellas, the Ranch's 2½-ha organic farm, where you can learn how to combine fresh, organic ingredients in inspiring ways.

For meals, chef Jesús Gonzales prepares delightful semi-vegetarian cuisine featuring organic fruits and vegetables (many grown

on the ranch), and fresh seafood driven in daily from the port of Ensenada.

The ranch attracts mostly Americans from New York and California, especially girlfriends and mothers with their daughters. Plan your visit around weekly themes that interest you – the African dance week might also feature photography classes and a full guest lecture series, for example. Weeks run from Saturday to Saturday. Free pickups are provided to and from San Diego airport.

NATURAL SPA RETREAT

Rio Caliente Hot Springs Spa

🌐 ⭕ ⭐ ⚙ ⚙ ⚙ ⚙ ☑14

Primavera State Forest, Guadalajara
T+1 (1)800-200 2927
www.riocaliente.com
From US$152 per person per night

Nestled on the slopes of an ancient volcano in the heart of Mexico's beautiful Primavera Forest, Rio Caliente is an unpretentious and very affordable restorative retreat. Its four swimming pools and steam room are fed by mineral-rich thermal waters from a volcanic lake deep underground, and towering palm trees give the place a tropical, almost primordial feel.

You stay in comfortable en suite bungalow-style casitas, each with its own fireplace, some with private terraces. The two

> **❝❞**
>
> Resolve to be yourself –
> he who finds himself,
> loses his misery.
>
> *Matthew Arnold*

main thermal pools are refilled in rotation every week; one is always exquisitely hot, the other refreshingly tepid. There are male and female plunge pools, and a naturally heated Aztec-style steam room, kept fragrant with fresh bunches of eucalyptus and sage.

The waters here are alkaline and rich in salts, minerals, and lithium, famed for its antidepressant properties. Visit the steam room to detox, then bathe to soak up the benefits through your skin. Drink as much of the spa's water as possible – it's said to restore your body's pH balance and combat the acidity of modern life. It tastes peculiar, but you can feel it doing you good.

Spa treatments include massages, reflexology, facials, manicures and pedicures, micro-dermabrasion, cellulite treatments, mud footbaths and clay mud wraps. Bio-resonance therapy is also available (see glossary). There are guided hikes with breathtaking mountain views, including a steamy waterfall and a blissfully hot natural jacuzzi. There is a daily yoga class, a water exercise class, and an evening programme of lectures and activities such as self-hypnosis or transcendental meditation. For US$28 an hour you can ride the spa's own horses.

Dining is sociable, with fantastic views of the surrounding scenery. Exotic birds flock to feed from a bird table just outside. You eat generous organic vegetarian buffet-style meals, served with freshly squeezed juices.

The spa's delicious recipes are available to take away in a book entitled *The Whole Enchilada*. There is a daily stall selling indigenous arts and crafts on the patio, and day trips to nearby destinations such as the market town of Tonalá, the brewery in Tequila, or the recently archaeological discovery at Teuchitlán.

Guests are mainly American professionals, who come alone or with a friend, partner or family member. It's an unpretentious place where most people will feel instantly at home. Bring hiking boots, a torch, and insect repellent. Rio Caliente is a 45-minute drive from Guadalajara airport – a taxi costs US$45. The rainy season is from July to September, but even then it's mostly sunny and doesn't rain for long.

COASTAL RETREAT

Verana

🌐 ⛰ 🌐 ❄ ◐ ↘15

Jalisco
T+52 (01)322-200 5107
www.verana.com
From US$380 per room per night

Californian set decorator, Heinz Legler, built this secluded hideaway with his French wife Veronique Lièvre, an interior designer. Their collective creativity is instantly striking; the eight houses have individual designs and combine modern architecture with traditional Mexican features.

Yoga practice includes hatha and a mix of vinyasa, ashtanga and iyengar. Classes are taken overlooking the ocean and mountainside. Spa treatments include invigorating coconut sugar scrubs and banana detox. Also try watsu or a healing aromatherapy bath in their sunken stone pool: it can be hired at night for romantic starlit soaking. The infinity pool is also stunning, overlooking the bay of Banderas.

Accommodation varies – the Palapa House has no walls but steep thatched roofs over the bed and light white drapes, whereas the huge double bed in the Tea House is completely exposed and overlooks the ocean – but the feeling is fresh throughout. There are lots of natural elements such as twisted wooden furniture and stone bowls. The elongated stone verandas, where you can recline under the bougainvillea, feel very luxurious. Meals are cooked with local ingredients; book a session in the kitchen and take home the recipes. Whale-watching trips, walks to waterfalls, birdwatching and kayaking are all available.

Verana appeals to stressed professionals and a younger, more fashionable crowd. Book in advance. Fly to Puerto Vallarta and take a taxi to Boca de Tomatlan harbour, where a boat picks you up. There is a short walk along a dirt track but a donkey carries your bags.

Left: Rancho La Puerta. **Above and right**: Verana.

Costa Rica

A lush place to rejuvenate, Costa Rica offers pampering palaces, yoga in the jungle or spa time with surfing on some of the world's greatest waves.

Fact file

- **Visa:** Not required for citizens of EU countries, the US, Canada, Australia and New Zealand
- **IDD:** +506
- **Currency:** Costa Rican colon (CRC)
- **Time zone:** GMT -6 hours
- **Electricity:** 110v
- **Tourist board:** www.visitcostarica.com

COASTAL RETREAT

Estudio Los Almendros

☀ ⊛ ↘1

Between Cabuya and Montezuma, Nicoya Peninsula
T+506 642 0378
www.somaritmoscostarica.com
From US$30 per room per night

A rustic retreat in gardens between the jungle and the ocean, Estudio Los Almendros is set at the tip of the Nicoya Peninsula in the environs of Cabo Blanco National Park. Venezuelan owner, Ninoska Gómez, is an inspiring, experienced somatic movement specialist who has dedicated her studio to therapy – for adults and children – and Latin American dance. The centre is small and there are no regular on-site staff, so book in advance.

Ninoska combines somatic movement (see glossary) with the use of giant gym balls, creating stretches and positions that feel both relieving and invigorating. Classes take place in the studio or by the beach. Don't miss the opportunity to learn some salsa and merengue; Ninoska is a fabulous dancer and offers classes on an ad hoc basis.

● **Soul food**

Rainforest Concern (T+44 (0)20-7229 2093, www.rainforestconcern.org) runs volunteer trips to the Pacuare Rainforest Reserve in Costa Rica from March to August, when you can help protect the giant leatherback turtle from poachers. Staying in a lovely back-to-nature beach location, you'll monitor the laying and hatching of these sea turtles, as well as protecting them. The Pacuare Reserve lies on the Caribbean coast between Puerto Limón and Tortuguero National Park, and contains 800 ha of lowland tropical rainforest and a 6-km beach, which is the turtles' nesting ground.

Accommodation is basic, spread around the tropical garden that sprawls from the forested hillside down to the sea. The colourfully painted wooden Rancho Redondo has a kitchenette and room for four and there are two *ranchitos* (little ranchos) that sleep two in single beds. There's a natural pool where you are free to swim naked between December and May. Nature trails, snorkelling trips and the bars and cafés of the picturesque village of Montezuma are all close at hand.

Fly to Tambor from San José. Taxis meet flights, and buses can be picked up from the main road just outside the airport.

YOGA RETREAT

Nosara Yoga Institute

⬤ ↘2

Nosara
T+1 (1)866-439 4704
www.nosarayoga.com
From US$968 per course (7-8 days)

Leading kripalu teacher, Don Stapleton, and his wife Amba founded the Nosara Yoga Institute in 2000. It is now a renowned yoga teachers' training centre, but also runs regular workshops and retreats, drop-in classes, and a popular Surf Yoga programme twice a year aimed at those who know yoga and who want to learn to surf (Nosara is a major surf spot).

Retreats vary each year but are taken by influential yoga masters, mainly from the US, such as Shiva Rea (www.shivarea.com), who has developed Surf Yoga, and Christy DeBurton (www.christydeburton.com), who offers a seven-day all-inclusive retreat where you can practise yoga, learn to surf, snorkel, and take a jungle canopy tour. Yoga is done in the Rancho Pavilion, with an imposing thatched roof and open sides to let in both light and colours from the garden. There's also a smaller studio, Tree Tops, positioned high on a hill overlooking the sea.

There is no accommodation at Nosara Yoga Institute but the Stapletons will recommend a handful of neighbouring hotels to suit your budget. The most popular option is the lively **Café de Paris** (from US$69, www.cafedeparis.net), which offers both private and dormitory rooms and a good restaurant. For a luxury option, try **Harbor Reef Hotel** (from US$89, www.harbor reef.com), which is also very close to the institute.

Fly to Nosara from San José. Alternatively, a bus leaves the Empresario Alfaro bus terminal in San José (Avenida 5 and Calle 14) at 0600 daily and takes around six hours.

and views of the mountains). There are meditation gardens, a walking labyrinth and a small drumming circle. At night there's a fantasy backdrop of stars over the mountains and a midnight swim is recommended.

Panacea mostly attracts single female travellers and couples. They can arrange transfers from San José, Liberia or Tamarindo airports. Tamarindo is a 45-minute drive from Liberia.

66 99

The more selfish you are the more agitated you will be.

Janki Chopra

YOGA RETREAT
Panacea

🌐 ⛺ ☀ 👥 👤 ⚙ ❄ 🌀 ☯ ↘3

Tamarindo
T+506 653 8515
www.panaceacr.com
From US$715 per person for 7 nights

The Panacea philosophy is total detachment from your everyday life, and its secluded mountain setting overlooking the Pacific Ocean makes this instantly achievable. Yoga classes are held daily in a palm-thatched rancho with polished teak floors. Gentle moves (mainly iyengar) involve plenty of breathwork and change according to individual requirements. Water aerobics classes in an infinity pool on the side of the mountain are an invigorating complement to

yoga. Try the aromatherapy tub, where water circulates while diffusing aromatherapy oils into the air. Life coaching is also on offer.

In order to maintain a personal feel, there are just six rustic terracotta-tiled *cabinas* (bungalows), at staggered levels on the mountainside. They each have a very simple but comfy bedroom and en suite, and are painted in muted earthy tones with attractive wooden beamed ceilings. Each has a small private veranda with a hammock, and stunning views.

Food is vegetarian (with some fresh seafood) using locally sourced ingredients, served in their simple, three-walled dining room (the missing wall opens out to the pool

RURAL RETREAT
Pura Vida

🌐 ⛺ 👥 👤 ⚙ ❄ 🌀 ↘4

Alajuela
T+1 (1)770-483 0238
www.puravidaspa.com
From US$1070 per person for 7 nights

American couple, Pauline and Michael Clegg (owners of Maya Tulum in Mexico, and Pura Vida USA), founded holistic retreat Pura Vida in 2000, after several years of living in Costa Rica. The couple have taught yoga since the seventies and, since Pura Vida's inception, have attracted a diverse range of internationally renowned practitioners such as yoga teachers Doug Swenson and Shiva Rea, Eckhart Tolle, author of *The Power of Now*, and Rachel Brice, a top belly dance teacher.

Below left: Panacea. Below right: Pura Vida.

The Americas Costa Rica

PANACEA

PURA VIDA

Surf and yoga holidays

Costa Rica offers some of the world's greatest waves, which attract surfers from all over the globe. A number of surf retreats now cater exclusively for women, combining surfing with spa treatments for alittle side pampering, and yoga to help keep limbs stretched and supple and shorten recovery time after minor injuries. Retreats are especially good if you are on your own. Most women attending are beginners or intermediate, but every level is accommodated.

For the ultimate feel-good experience, try the eco-conscious **VOEC** (pronounced 'voice') surf and yoga camp (T+506 653 0852, www.voecretreats.com), located on the beach in the vibrant party town of Tamarindo. A six-night package includes accommodation, meals, daily surf and yoga lessons, one private surf lesson, two spa treatments at Coco Spa, a surf excursion to remote waves, and use of surf equipment. VOEC yoga teachers have trained with a variety of masters and you will find their stretches are the perfect complement to getting up on a board. The 2005 women's longboard champion, Kristy Murphy, helps even the novice feel safe in the water. Meals are included and taken in a different Tamarindo restaurant each night, so you can sample a great selection of local cuisine and social ambience. To refresh tired limbs after surfing, Coco Spa offers pampering such as hot-stone massages and beauty treatments. Try their Costa

Rican chocolate facials, coffee body scrubs and lime coconut salt scrubs and take the treatment on the beach. Even more fun are their workshops where you can make volcanic clay masks or aromatherapy oils to take home. VOEC costs from US$2095 per person for a week.

Alternatively, **Kelea Surf Spa** (T+1 (1)949-492 7263, www.keleasurfspa.com) is based at Malpaís, one of Costa Rica's hippest up-and-coming locations. Kelea includes local hiking and a canopy tour as well as six mornings of surf instruction and three afternoons of yoga or pilates. You surf at Playa Carmen, a seemingly endless beach break with no coral and virtually empty waves. The water temperature is around 26°C all year round so you can surf in your bikini. If you want a break, the forested hills behind the hotel are full of tropical wildlife and exotic birds, and views from the top are spectacular. You'll find the locally sourced organic home-made spa treatments rewardingly indulgent. Try pineapple or papaya body wraps and coconut massage or an Aveda facial. One massage is included in the price; all other treatments are extra. Practise your meditation (vital to help improve focus and balance during surfing) on the beach just after 1800, while the sky turns orange and pink as the sun sinks into the Pacific. Kelea costs from US$1575 per person for a seven-night package.

Perched at 1800 m amidst coffee plantations, there is an instantly fresh feel to this place. Explore the landscaped gardens which are full of vibrant red ginger lilies and delicate peach-coloured hibiscus flowers. There is also a pagoda offering views of San José and the central valley, a swimming pool,

hot tub and hammocks.

Yoga is practised twice daily by a changing rota of teachers. Staff usually offer hatha-based yoga, while visiting teachers take classes once a week, offering opportunities for different yoga practices. There are five yoga halls: three are almost

always in use by various groups; the smaller ones are less busy and available for private practice or meditation.

Open to any individual, the week-long Mind, Body, Spirit programme includes one massage, 10 yoga sessions, three meals a day and excursions such as whitewater rafting and a trip to Poas, an active volcano with stunning views. Other treatments at Pura Vida's wellness centre cost extra – try the aroma spa treatments or a watsu session.

Food is predominately vegetarian, with some chicken and fish. There is a huge emphasis on fruit and vegetables. All of the dishes are mouth-watering and dining is communal. Wine and beer are available, organic where possible.

Two rooms at Pura Vida have private jacuzzis but, other than that, accommodation is deliberately simple, with neutral colours and almost-bare walls (and no TVs or phones). Most rooms have private balconies and panoramic views of the valley. There are also fully furnished 'tentalows' in the garden, a good budget option.

Pura Vida mainly attracts single women, groups of girlfriends, mother/daughter breaks and some couples. Children are welcome and there is a babysitting service available. All Pura Vida packages include transfers from San José airport.

Similar Mind, Body, Spirit programmes and yoga retreats are also available at Pura Vida's sister properties at **Maya Tulum** in Mexico (www.mayatulum.com), and **Pura Vida USA** in the foothills of the Blue Ridge Mountains (www.puravidausa.com).

Rancho Pacífico

🌐 👤 ⚕ ⚙ ⚡ ↘5

Uvita
T+506 825 8370
www.ranchopacifico.com
From US$1325 per person for 7 nights

American owner, Garrison, and his Costa Rican wife, Silvia Jiminez-Krause, have created a boutique-style retreat that combines mountain, jungle and ocean. This is a luxurious, restorative escape with lots of opportunities to indulge in less health-conscious pleasures – guests are even invited to sip champagne during spa treatments.

There are two daily morning hatha-based yoga classes that include some energetic moves, and the yoga studio is always open to guests. Each villa has its own spa garden and soaking tub, so treatments can be taken in complete privacy, though the secluded treatment decks perched amid the jungle are recommended, as is the rooftop spa, which has breathtaking views of the rainforest and Pacific. There's also a sweat cave, infinity pool, and an outdoor stone jacuzzi.

Treatment products are made from local natural resources, such as coffee, chocolate, coconut, volcanic lavender, ginger, rainforest flowers and mud. Massages range from lymph drainage, trigger point therapy to hot stone and four hands. Silvia was Costa Rica's first female ear, nose and throat surgeon, and now carries out and oversees botox and minor cosmetic surgery at Rancho Pacífico.

Food is sumptuous Caribbean fusion with grilled meats and fish – almost every ingredient has been produced organically within a 20-mile radius of the hotel. There are five suites and three villas and no plans to extend. To eliminate the need for air conditioning, the windows are screened instead of glazed and, in the villas, two entire walls are made solely from screen material so you can keep cool while you enjoy the spectacular views.

Rancho mainly attracts single women, couples and honeymooners. Don't miss Marino Ballena National Park, where you can see whales pass between February and April. Rancho Pacífico can arrange transfers by car from hotels in San José, from the airport, or from Palma Sur airport.

Samasati Nature Retreat.

Samasati Nature Retreat

🌐 ♨ 🏔 ⚙ ⚡ ↘6

Puerto Limón
T+506 756 8015
www.samasati.com
From US$125 per person per night

Samasati nestles in lush green jungle on Costa Rica's little-visited Caribbean coastline. In 1995, the owners bought 110 ha of thick jungle to guarantee privacy from neighbouring development and, today, the area remains relatively untouched.

Samasati gained its reputation from its visiting alternative health specialists who use it for their workshops and retreats. Yoga, yoga philosophy and teacher training workshops are run annually; other retreats include meditation, shamanic dance, and wellbeing weeks, or you can stay here simply as a guest.

Bungalows, restaurants and yoga studios are hidden amongst the foliage, and the smell of the jungle is energizing. The wooden yoga platforms are protected by mosquito nets but open to the forest and the sounds of warbling birds, monkey howls and the hum of a million insects. Vinyasa flow and iyengar yoga is practised twice daily, though you need to pay extra for it.

A full meditation session follows every yoga class, or you are free to relax in the jacuzzi. Spa treatments include deep tissue and Swedish massage, chakra balancing, reflexology, fruit scrubs, aromatherapy and Bach flower treatments. Most of the products are hand-made and water is from an on-site spring.

Ten en suite bungalows and two fully equipped cottages with open verandas are beautifully constructed from reforested wood. Choose an elevated one that allows exquisite ocean views. There are five more basic rooms for those on a lower budget, with shared bathroom.

For evening meals enjoy a vegetarian buffet, with fish by request, cooked by locals from a menu rich in soya, tofu, beans, eggs, cheese, fruits and vegetables. Beer and wine

The Americas Costa Rica

FAMILY YOGA

THE YOGA FARM

Above left: World Family Yoga. **Above**: Yoga Farm.

are available, and special diets are catered for. Guests are likely to be women and couples; families and children of all ages are welcome.

The laid-back Caribbean region is reflected in the food and music, though note that Puerto Limón is a working port with little in the way of tourist interest. The people, though, are chilled and friendly and won't hassle you to spend your money. Samasati can arrange transfers from San José airport or your hotel, or book a taxi to take you from the airport to Gran Terminal Caribe (bus station) where buses run until 1530 to Puerto Limón.

YOGA & ACTIVITY HOLIDAY
World Family Yoga

🎏 ✳ ⬂7

Osa Peninsula
T+1 (1)707-826 0239
www.worldfamilyyoga.com
US$1250/700 per adult/child per week

World Family Yoga is a not-for-profit organization that donates a percentage of its income to support local children. It runs a regular yoga trip for families to the remote and pristine Osa Peninsula, accessible only by boat.

You stay at Guaria de Osa in private bungalows, and wake up to screeching howler monkeys, scarlet macaws flying overhead, and the sweet smell of ylang-ylang

trees. Yoga is taught by World Family Yoga founders, Christine McArdle-Oquendo and Peggy Profant, experienced anusara-inspired yoga teachers who focus on alignment in transformative, heart-centered sessions. Classes are offered twice daily for both children and adults separately.

Families can choose to go dolphin-watching, horse riding, snorkelling and hiking through Corcovado, Costa Rica's premier rainforest reserve. Surfing and boogie-boarding can be enjoyed nearby, or just curl up in a hammock with a book before your evening class.

RAINFOREST RETREAT
The Yoga Farm

🎏 👤 🌙 ✳ 🌿 ⬂8

Punta Banco
www.yogafarmcostarica.org
From US$30 per person per night

The Yoga Farm in Punta Banco is a laid-back retreat with the spirituality of a yogic lifestyle at its heart. Set on a mountainside surrounded by primary rainforest and near the beach, it's a great place to get back to nature.

There are guided horse riding trips and hikes through the rainforest; you can swim in the ocean or nearby waterfall, and massage and reiki sessions can be arranged. You can

also explore the customs and culture of the local Guaymi on a homestay with an indigenous family, giving you the chance to learn native crafts, natural remedies and traditional building techniques.

The beautiful open-air yoga studio is an inspiring venue for daily practice overlooking the canopy of trees and the Pacific Ocean; classes are taught by a number of different teachers. Accommodation is in basic but clean timber-framed rooms with good firm beds and panoramic views across the rainforest. Rooms are offered on a first come, first served basis, so you may be in a private room or a shared dorm.

The Yoga Farm is committed to an environmentally friendly lifestyle (recycling, farming organically and using modern composting toilets and solar power). Guests are requested to bring biodegradable personal care products, and the goal is for the farm to become completely self-sufficient.

Three meals a day are provided, using the home-grown tropical organic fruits and vegetables. There's always a vegan option and freshly picked fruit. Meat, dairy and eggs are on offer a few times a week, or go to one of the cafés at the nearby beach.

The rate includes accommodation, food and yoga. Stay at least five nights to make the most of it. Fly to Golfito and take a taxi for about US$50 one way.

Dominican Republic

Blue Moon Retreat

🌐 ⛱ ☀ ⊗ ⊘ ↘1

Los Brazos, Cabarete
T+1-809 (1)757 0614
www.bluemoonretreat.net
From US$40-60 per night for 2 sharing;
US$500 a month.

In the foothills of the Cordillera Septentrional, the mountain range which runs along the north coast of the Dominican Republic, Blue Moon Retreat sits in 15 ha of gardens and enjoys 360° views of the surrounding countryside. Sublimely peaceful, the lush rolling hills are dotted with royal palms and fruit trees with the sea in the distance.

Accommodation is in four simple bungalows containing six suites and two family suites, each with their own colourful and distinctive decor. Each cabaña is covered in artwork, and murals flow over the roof and down the walls. Guests are encouraged to participate in this living art and if you have a good idea for a theme which could be used to decorate a bungalow, you can stay for free and all materials will be provided so that you can develop your artistic expression.

You can hire the whole place if there's a group of you, and Eneyda and Gideon will organize yoga and meditation classes on demand. Long-term renters who may be living in the country for a few months also use it as a comfortable bolt-hole away from the holiday atmosphere of the coast. The restaurant serves authentic Indian food in the evenings; you sit on floor cushions and eat with your right hand off banana leaves instead of plates. Ingredients are all sourced locally from farmers, butchers, fishermen and bakers in the area.

Blue Moon is 40 minutes' drive inland from the international airport and 20 minutes from Cabarete for beach activities.

Right: Natura Cabañas.

Natura Cabañas

🌐 ☀ ⊕ ⊗ ⊙ ⊘ ↘2

Perla Marina, Cabarete
T1-809 (1)571 1507
www.naturacabana.com
US$160 per night for 2 sharing

This little family-owned and operated hotel is just along the north coast of the Dominican Republic from Cabarete, one of the greatest locations in the world for windsurfing and kiteboarding. Natura Cabañas is secluded and private, on a wild bit of seashore, tucked away from anything remotely busy but within easy reach of the action if you want it.

The rustic little thatched cabañas are scattered between palm trees and blend in with the landscape. The tiny spa offers steam baths, mud wraps, massages, peeling and wrapping with Dead Sea salt, and facials. Hatha yoga classes are held three times a week and occasionally there are weekend yoga retreats. African dance classes are held twice a week after sunset and accompanied by very atmospheric live drum music. The Chilean chef prepares lots of fresh seafood as well as Dominican specialities.

Dance, dream and indulge your fantasies on one of these happy and happening isles.

Fact file

- **Visa:** Not required for citizens of Canada, Australia, New Zealand and EU countries

- **IDD:** Dominican Republic +809; Grenada +473; Jamaica +876; St Lucia +758; Tobago +868

- **Currency:** Dominican Republic, Dominican peso (RD$); Jamaica, Jamaican dollar ($); Grenada and St Lucia, East Caribbean dollar (EC$); Tobago, Trinidad dollar (TT$)

- **Time zone:** Dominican Republic, Grenada, St Lucia, Tobago GMT -4 hours; Jamaica GMT -5 hours

- **Electricity:** 110v in Dominican Republic and Jamaica; Grenada 220v; St Lucia 240v; Tobago 115v

- **Tourist board:** www.godominican republic.com, www.grenada grenadines.com, www.visitjamaica.com, www.stlucia.org, www.visittnt.com

Go green on Dominica

Lying between the islands of Guadeloupe and Martinique, Dominica (www.dominica.dm) is the first country in the world to be officially benchmarked by Green Globe 21 as an ecotourist destination. This little-known former British colony is a nature lover's paradise.

Stay here at the **Jungle Bay Resort** at Delices (from US$179 per night, per person sharing, T+1-767 (1)446 1789, www.junglebaydominica.com), a tropical 23-ha rainforest hideaway in the foothills of Morne Trois Pitons National Park. There are 35 spacious tropical hardwood chalets perched on wooden stilts on a remote rainforest hillside, near the roaring Atlantic. Yoga is done in two huge studios, one on an open-sided veranda, with a full view of the sea. Classes are usually taken by Glenda, who has years of experience, teaches a mix of styles and exudes an enviable calm.

Daytime adventures include trekking through the rainforest, visits to mineral hot springs, bathing below hidden waterfalls or sea kayaking. Diving, tai chi, qigong and meditation are also

on offer, as well as retreats from visiting teachers. The Spa du Soleil is a treehouse with five treatment rooms enjoying the soothing sound of the sea. Delicious mangoes and papaya, great juices, spring water and home-baked bread are all on offer.

The **3 Rivers Eco Lodge** at Rosalie (from US$20 per person per night, T+1-767 (1)446 1886, www.3riversdominica.com) is a small, award-winning ecolodge in 2½ ha of a lush rainforest valley surrounded by rivers. It's a relaxed, friendly place where guests mix with locals and each other. You're near an Atlantic black-sand beach, and there are four lovely natural pools to swim in or meditate beside. British-born owner Jem funds green technology in the community.

Accommodation is basic, mostly in green-roofed wooden chalets with hammocks on the balcony, set in a garden planted with fruit trees, vegetables and flowers. Jem can arrange visits to a herb farm and a village in the indigenous Carib territory, as well as artists workshops and sustainable living workshops.

VILLAGE RETREAT

Villa Serena

Las Galeras, Samaná
T+1-809 (1)538 0000
www.villaserena.com
From US$160 per night for a double room

The village of Las Galeras, at the very tip of the Samaná Peninsula, feels like the end of the world. With its deserted beach of shimmering sand overlooking the empty expanse of the Atlantic Ocean, it's as far from a teeming Caribbean resort as you can get. Villa Serena, set in lush gardens just outside the village, is a serene Victorian colonial-style house with verandas, surrounded by palm trees and with its own small private beach. There are yoga classes every morning in the tropical gardens, and tai chi classes as the sun sets.

The hotel has 21 spacious rooms individually decorated in soft, cool colours, each with its own terrace or balcony. Borrow a kayak, bike to explore the miles of tracks that lead from the village to Samaná's deserted beaches, or take a hike into the

surrounding hills. A masseur is on hand after the day's exertions. From mid-January to mid-March each year over 10,000 humpback whales come to breed in the Bay of Samaná,

and the hotel can arrange a boat excursion to see this amazing spectacle. From Samaná International Airport it's a one hour journey to Las Galeras. Price includes breakfast.

GAIL SIMMONS

Villa Serena.

Grenada

CREATIVE RETREAT

Maca Bana

⊘ ☀ ○ ⋔ ◉ ⊕ ⊘ ⊿4

Point Salines
T+1-473 (1)439 5355
www.macabana.com
US$265-595 per night

Maca Bana is a charming low-key collection of villas set on a hilltop to catch the breeze, but with a restaurant and bar down on the beach. The spectacular view stretches all the way from the southern tip of the island along the bays and beaches of the southwest coast and up to the capital, St George's.

Art classes are a highlight, conducted by owner Rebecca Thompson, who describes art as 'food for the soul'. Lessons are either out in the field or in the studio, or both. Studio sessions are used to develop and finish off your artwork after a few hours sitting on a riverbank gazing at the green forest, or under a palm tree on a beach. After nourishing your soul, the enthusiastic chefs from the Aquarium restaurant on the beach (owned by Rebecca's husband, Uri) can give you a cooking lesson in your villa.

You can have a massage (full body, incorporating Swedish, Indian and shiatsu techniques, or Thai yoga) from local masseuse, Tash Mitch, on your deck overlooking the sea with the breeze fanning your body. Other treatments include reflexology, ayurvedic facial, aromatherapy, and chakra balancing. Couples can be taught to massage each other.

There are five individually decorated two-bed and two one-bed villas in pretty gardens, with fully-fitted kitchens, satellite TV and Wi-Fi access, decks, sun beds and a hot tub for a bit of private hydrotherapy, and an infinity pool. The elegant but rustic open-air Aquarium restaurant is tucked under a cliff with water trickling down it. Food is international with a Caribbean twist.

Jamaica

HOTEL & SPA

Strawberry Hill

⊘ ⚫ ⋔ ◉ ⊕ ⊛ ⊘ ⊿5

Irish Town, Kingston
T+1-876 (1)944 8400
www.islandoutpost.com
US$590-990 per night for 2 sharing

Only a short drive from the capital, Kingston, yet worlds away in terms of tranquillity, Strawberry Hill was a coffee and fruit plantation house until it was blown away by Hurricane Gilbert in 1988. It was the home of Chris Blackwell, founder of Island Records (Bob Marley was brought here to recuperate after being shot in 1976). Now beautifully converted into one of the loveliest spa hotels in the Caribbean, the 12 plantation-style cottages are perched on the hillside with stunning views of Kingston bay.

Part of Chris Blackwell's Island Outpost group of very desirable retreats, the spa offers one- to seven-night 'living' packages during which you can enjoy a variety of therapies.

Spa facilities include a hydrotherapy room, dry sauna, plunge pool, yoga shala and fitness equipment. Guided walks, mountain bikes, birdwatching and other excursions into the Blue Mountains are also organized. Yoga is available daily, while yoga and meditation retreats are offered from time to time. Food is gourmet fusion Jamaican cuisine based on local ingredients, and can be designed to fit with your elemental spa package.

The cottages are light, bright and elegant, with hardwood floors and traditional mahogany furniture made on site. They vary in size from studio suites to one-bedroom villas, but all have a fabulous outlook over the forest down to the city and the sea. The curved infinity pool also has a view to die for, as does the veranda, one of the places where you can dine.

Staying here is not cheap – though prices include all meals, drinks, taxes and service charges, plus some treatments – and you can expect your fellow guests to be well-heeled American or European couples, in the 30 to 60 age group. If you want to combine Strawberry Hill with a spa by the sea, head for its sister hotel **The Caves**, a small establishment with charming cottages perched on cliffs above the waves in Negril at the western tip of Jamaica.

The Americas Jamaica

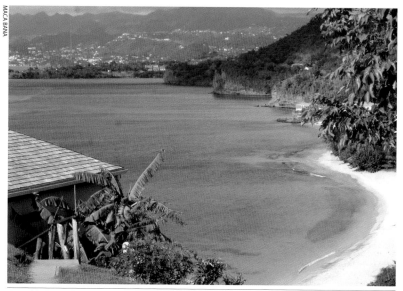

MACA BANA

View of the beach from Maca Bana.

Thinking outside the hammock

The Caribbean isn't just for chilling out by the beach and being pampered – it's also the base for some well-run active and wellbeing holidays which will uplift both body and soul.

First up is a focus on dance, highly appropriate for the Caribbean, where Latin American and Afro-Caribbean music and dances such as salsa and merengue reflect everyone's love of life and enjoyment of their bodies. Holistic holiday experts **Skyros** (T+44 (0)20-7267 4424, www.skyros.co.uk) runs salsa and yoga trips to Havana in Cuba twice a year (from US$1370 per person). There's daily expert salsa tuition, and each person is assigned a local Cuban dance partner. Classes take place in a dance studio close to your base, the four-star Habana Libre hotel. You can also enjoy morning yoga sessions, beach time, the city and its vibrant culture. Other workshops on offer depend on the trip leader and may include voice work, writing and life coaching.

Caledonia Languages Abroad (T+44 (0)131-621 7721, www.caledonialanguages.co.uk) organizes dance classes to complement its Spanish language groups in Cuba and the Dominican Republic, and its French language groups in Guadeloupe. In Santiago de Cuba you can take daily dance classes followed by party nights in the salsa clubs practising what you have learned. The teachers are from Cutumba, one of the two top dance and music companies in Cuba, and students have their own professional dance partner.

For a spot of luxury, UK-based wellbeing company **Yogoloji** (T+44 (0)20-7730 7473, www.yogoloji.co.uk) runs 10-day retreats based at Jamoon, a seven-bedroom Etruscan-style private villa on the estate of the luxurious Sandy Lane golf and spa resort in Barbados, in January, March, May, October and November. Enjoy yoga and pilates on a coral stone terrace, holistic treatments and massage in the villa's own therapy room, a private beach area and swimming pool, and all the adventure activities that the island has to offer, including surfing, kitesurfing, diving, windsurfing and sea kayaking as well as pottery and ceramic workshops, golf and tennis. It costs US$4140 per person.

For pilates in a tropical setting, American-born Lynne Gentle runs bespoke pilates holidays on Antigua in January, February, March and November. For **Pilates Caribe!** you stay at Belle Vue House, a marvellous four-bedroom villa with a pool and jacuzzi set high on Cherry Hill, 10 minutes from the harbour, bars and restaurants. The breaks are open to beginners as well as those already into pilates – regular weeks for singles or couples are planned. Lynne is a member of the Pilates Foundation UK and a qualified Gyrotonic teacher. You get two pilates mat-work

classes a day, and the rest of the time is yours to relax, swim, sail and explore the area. Massage and other body treatments are also available (from US$1530 per person per week). Lynne also runs Pilates en Provence in France (see page 93).

Finally **The Body Holiday** at Le Sport (T+44 (0)870-389 1929, www.thebodyholiday.com) on Cariblue Beach at the northern end of St Lucia offers the chance to get into a whole host of activities including sailing, waterskiing, water polo, archery, tennis and golf as well as tai chi, yoga, pilates and salsa dancing. The decor and set up are a little Butlins-meets-Dallas, but the vibe is friendly and the opportunities for action impressive – stress management classes are also on offer, as well as excellent pampering and holistic treatments. From US$285 per person per night.

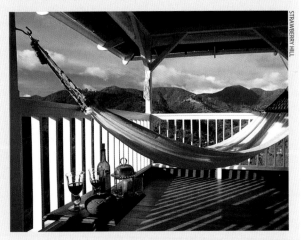

St Lucia

ISLAND RETREAT

Anse Chastanet

Soufrière
T+1-758 (1)459 7000
www.ansechastanet.com
From US$265 per room per night

Anse Chastanet is one of those special places whose beauty immediately soothes you after a long journey. The hotel's grounds stretch from a volcanic dark-sand beach up and over a promontory, giving picturesque views of the magnificent Gros Piton and Petit Piton.

It is owned by architect Nick Troubeztkoy, who has built it sympathetically in harmony with the landscape. Rooms and suites are all open and airy with views over the rainforest and the sea. Jade Mountain (from US$795 per night) is a hotel within a hotel on the top of Morne Anse Chastanet – each suite is open to the elements on one side, where instead of a wall there is an infinity pool looking out

🍴 Soul food

For a chance to live and learn in a Caribbean community, **Community Service Alliance** (T1-809 (1)363 0961, www.communityservicealliancedr.org) offers short-term volunteer placements in the Dominican Republic for a minimum of three weeks. Placements are tailored to your interests and abilities as well as local need, and could include helping out in local schools, summer camps and orphanages, working with disabled children and adults or teaching English. You can combine them with Spanish language learning at CSA's centre, based at Santo Domingo, which also runs intensive Spanish immersion courses.

SARAH CAMERON

Kariwak Village.

across the bay to the Pitons.

There are no phones, radios, TVs or internet connection – just peace and quiet and the luxury of being totally removed from the rest of the world. Offshore is a marine park, and the whole area is now a UNESCO World Heritage site. Diving, hiking and mountain biking are popular, while tour boats visit for snorkelling and swimming off the beach.

The Kai Belté Spa is at sea level between the scuba centre and the beach restaurant. Another spa, Kai Mer, is up on top of the hill, where you can have Swedish or deep tissue massage, aromatherapy, shiatsu, reflexology or Thai foot massage. Beauty treatments are also on offer. Where possible they use fresh tropical flowers, fruits and vegetables such as avocado, bananas, papaya, aloe, lime, coconut and honey for natural treatments.

There are two excellent restaurants using local produce, and herbs and vegetables from the hotel's organic garden. The Trou au Diable restaurant on the beach has an Indian chef and tandoori ovens and serves Indian/Caribbean food, while the Piton restaurant further up the hill offers a more traditional international cuisine. Most guests are European or North and South American couples looking for romance and relaxation.

Tobago

HOTEL & SPA

Kariwak Village

Crown Point
T+1-868 (1)639 8442
www.kariwak.com
US$90-125 per room per night

The Kariwak was established in the 1970s and has a long-running programme of yoga and retreats. It's a little oasis in the middle of the main tourist area of Tobago, eight minutes from Store Bay beach, but completely different in atmosphere from the other hotels in the area.

Oleander, allamanda, torch ginger and jasmine are interspersed with avocado, lime, passion fruit and sugar cane in the garden, while a neat and tidy kitchen garden supplies the restaurant with aromatic and flavoursome herbs. Hummingbirds and tanagers flit about, cocricos shout from the rooftops and some 20 species of birds and many butterflies can be seen from your strategically-placed hammock near the large jacuzzi.

There are 18 rooms in thatched cabañas clustered round the main pool and shielded by dense foliage. Six more rooms are set back in the gardens, where you will get less noise from the pool and restaurant.

A complimentary early morning class of stretching, yoga or tai chi is held five days a week in high season in the *ajoupa*, a large, thatched, open-sided building with a polished wooden floor (popular with small lizards). You can also take part in weekly iyengar yoga and Buddhist meditation classes. Yoga, qigong and feng shui retreats led by visiting teachers are held occasionally.

The holistic health centre offers a wide variety of treatments, including ayurvedic and Indian head massage, reflexology and reiki. You can also have a bath in a swirling

The Americas Tobago

pool of ozonated water heated to a temperature of 37° C, which improves blood circulation and is great for your skin.

Fresh, seasonal and tasty food is on offer, with lots of vegetarian options, served in the open air under a thatched roof, where paintings and sculptures by local artists are on display (and for sale). Kariwak attracts an eclectic mix of guests, around 60% of whom are repeat visitors.

YOGA RETREAT

Moonlight Mountain Retreat

🌀 ⛲ ☀ 👪 🐾 🔧 ↘8

Scarborough
T1-868 (1)639 4346
www.moonlightmountainretreat.com
US$30 per person per night

Perched up in the hills, in a village above Tobago's capital, Scarborough, with views to both the Caribbean and Atlantic sides of the island, this tranquil retreat is surrounded by the abundant tropical flora and fauna typical of Tobago's rainforest. Traditional in style with balconies and wooden fretwork, it was built using feng shui principles in its design and furnishings. Come here for yoga retreats of a week or two, or to stay as an individual on a B&B basis.

Moonlight Mountain is owned by Brit Ginny Plumpton, and her Tobagonian husband, Kelly. Ginny holds the British Wheel of Yoga Diploma and has been teaching for over 25 years, offering both hatha and ashtanga yoga at all levels. Other courses led by visiting teachers in yoga, art and a variety of therapies run throughout the year.

There are four bedrooms upstairs, three of which face the Atlantic and share two bathrooms, while the fourth is en suite and looks out to Plymouth on the Caribbean coast. Most rooms open out on to the veranda, where you can practise yoga, relax with a book in a hammock, take a dip in the plunge pool and enjoy the view and the breeze. There's also a self-catering apartment.

As well as daily meditation and yoga, you can explore the rainforest, go birdwatching, snorkelling and diving, or just laze on the beach. Massage and reflexology are available by the pool. There are also classes in silk painting or life drawing, and Ginny and Kelly can help you master the intricacies of reggae and soca rhythms before you head for the local nightlife.

Kelly usually cooks breakfast and the meat or fish dishes; Penny, the reflexologist, specializes in vegetarian food for yoga enthusiasts, while Ginny whips up a storm with her delicious cheesecakes and ice cream. Try delicious smoothies with fruit picked from the garden, and the local ginger beer, mauby, or sorrel and fresh lemonade to quench your thirst.

For treatments on the beach, **Boboshanti's Herbal Steam Bath and Massage** is a small wooden shack at Castara, offering excellent massages and beauty treatments using fresh avocado, ripe bananas and cornmeal – or try the brown-sugar body scrub. There's also a steam room which uses 13 local herbs, many of them grown in the sand around the hut. Treatments cost from US$25.

A one-week residential workshop costs US$450, including all meals, yoga tuition, one massage, and airport transfers.

Turks & Caicos

ISLAND RETREAT

Como Shambhala Retreat

🌀 👪 🌐 ✪ ⚽ 🔧 ↘9

Parrot Cay
T1-649 (1)946 7788
www.parrotcay.como.bz
From US$450 per room per night

A private 400-ha island with nothing on it except the hotel, beach, bush and swamp, Parrot Cay boasts the gorgeous Como Shambhala Retreat offering Asian-inspired holistic therapies and regular yoga retreats by American expert teachers such as Eric Schiffman and Rodney Yee. Reached by launch from Providenciales, the nearest island with an international airport, its privacy makes it a favourite with film stars and celebrities. Accommodation varies from hotel rooms to beach houses or large three-bedroom beach villas with butler service, all furnished with dark hardwoods, white drapes and wooden floors in a fresh, minimalist style. Parrot Cay is part of the Como hotel group (see also page 259).

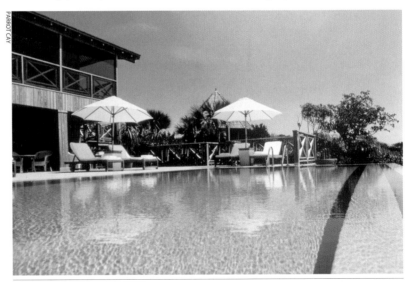

PARROT CAY

Como Shambhala Retreat at Parrot Cay.

The Americas Tobago

Argentina

RURAL RETREAT

Estancia La Corona Sanctuary

Carlos Casares, Provincia de Buenos Aires
T+44 (0)1364-642261
www.lacoronasanctuary.com
From US$945 per person per week

An extraordinarily peaceful and nourishing spot surrounded by wide open spaces, this working farm, a family estancia (ranch), is available from November to March. You'll be looked after by Serena Fraser, who was born here and whose brother, Alastair, runs the farm. A mother of six who founded a theatre school for the unemployed and taught there for 25 years, Serena excels at giving individual attention and is dedicated to making your stay a nourishing one.

Part of the land has been left as virgin territory, ideal for horse rides in the cool early morning or late afternoon. Serena can teach beginners and there are 12 horses to suit every ability. You'll see wild horses grazing, and all over the estate spoonbills, flamingos, egrets, and many kinds of duck, storks and blackneck swans abound.

The retreat sleeps six people in luxurious colonial-style rooms, cooled by old-fashioned fans. There are three en suite bedrooms, one with its own sitting room. The house is an elegant and comfortable space – the sumptuous furnishings of the main sitting room change according to season.

Do whatever you need or want to do, and be as private or as sociable as you like. Meditate in the dappled light of 'The Dome', a circle of incredible-shaped trees, enjoy sunrise or sunset from one of the benches dotting the landscape, walk and take photographs, lie in a hammock and read, write or do nothing. There's a swing chair on the veranda, a small library full of mind, body spirit books, a pool table and an untreated swimming pool, its water flowing to the fig trees.

Sitting and walking meditation, hot- or cold-stone massage and reiki treatments are available from local therapist, Adriana Malone. Visiting yoga teachers take daily classes – these include sivananda teacher and holistic therapist, Debs Stanley, who runs the small retreat company Awakening Touch in the UK (www.awakeningtouch.co.uk).

A breakfast of fruits, yoghurts, breads and scrambled egg is eaten on the veranda, lunch of light salads and local dishes is taken in a pergola by the pool, and there's optional tea at 1700. Dinner is served at around 2130. All

Above and top: Estancia La Corona.

Experience shamanism or nourish yourself on an estancia in some of the most remote spots on earth.

Fact file

- **Visa:** Not required for citizens of Canada, Australia, New Zealand and EU countries

- **IDD:** Argentian +54; Bolivia +591; Brazil +55; Chile +56; Peru +51

- **Currency:** Argentina, peso ($); Bolivia, boliviano (Bs); Brazil, real ($); Chile, peso ($); Peru, new sol (s/)

- **Time zone:** Argentina, Brazil GMT -3 hours; Bolivia, Chile GMT -4 hours (-3 in summer); Peru -5 hours

- **Electricity:** Argentina, Chile, Peru 220v; Bolivia 110/220v; Brazil 110/220v

- **Tourist board:** www.turismo.gov.ar; www.turismobolivia.bo; www.turismo.gov.br; www.sernatur.cl;www.peru.org.pe

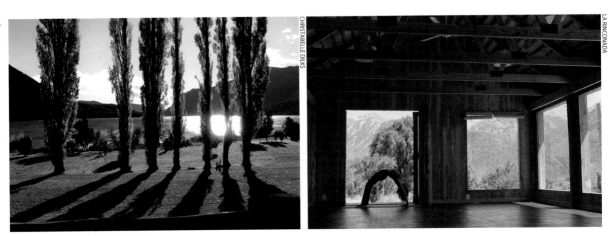

tastes are catered for. Everything is produced on the farm, from seasonal fruits to veggies and free-range meat.

La Corona attracts anyone looking to recharge. Stay for a minimum of three nights, but more like 10 to make the most of it. There's a single supplement of US$54 per day, but it's an ideal place for the single traveller.

The hottest time is from mid-December to the end of February; November and March are cooler but still warm enough to swim. Fly to Buenos Aires or Ezeiza airport; from either it's a three- to four-hour drive – transfers can be arranged (US$118 each way).

WATERSIDE RETREAT

Estancia Peuma Hue

Bariloche
T+54 (0)9294-450 1030
www.peuma-hue.com
From US$121 per person per day

Evelyn Hoter's mission was to create a place of healing through contact with nature, and she's chosen the right place. Estancia Peuma Hue ('place of dreams' in Mapuche) sits right on the shore of navy-blue Lago Gutiérrez, in 200 ha of its own beautiful land, surrounded by mighty jagged peaks, thickly forested with ancient virgin beech woods and filled with wildlife.

You can visit Peuma Hue as part of an organized retreat (yoga, tai chi, bodywork, or life coaching), but the beauty of this place is that you can also come independently at any time and benefit from the healing atmosphere. Evelyn Hoter is an experienced therapist and life coach who creates a very special relationship with her guests.

Ride horses deep into the forest with the resident horse whisperer, climb up to pristine waterfalls, take a kayak out onto the calm waters of the lake, practise yoga or meditate. Your experience of nature here will most definitely transform you. There's also guided trekking, rock climbing and abseiling, and tango lessons can be arranged on request.

Lots of therapies are on offer, including deep tissue massage, reflexology, shiatsu and reiki. The main therapist, Zule, specializes in chi nei tsang, or try *pases mágicos*, which is an ancient bodywork technique used by the Toltecs, based on seven patterns, or sequences of positions and movements, to redistribute energy in the body.

Accommodation is in ample double bedrooms with private bathrooms, in four buildings spread out along the shore. There are two luxurious main houses and two very comfortable log cabins, one of which is some way up the mountain with incredible views. The master suite has a jacuzzi with views of the stars, and in all houses there are roaring log fires when it's cold enough, and decks to sit out on when it's warm.

There are little nooks where you can sit quietly, but it's best to make the most of your proximity to forest, mountain and water by meditating outdoors. There's also the 'temple' on the hillside, with a wonderfully healing atmosphere, which is ideal for meditation or reflection.

Peuma Hue attracts interesting and questioning people, either alone or with friends or family. Guests eat together in the evenings, and the food is excellent – plentiful, organic and locally sourced. There are traditional Argentine barbecues for those who want them, but vegetarians are catered for with creativity and flair.

All activities and meals are included in the price. Peuma Hue is just 30 minutes on a good road from Bariloche, in the heart of the Lake District, which is a two-hour flight from Buenos Aires. The weather is unpredictable, so bring hiking boots and waterproofs, and warm clothing for the evenings. Stay at least three days, preferably more.

YOGA RETREAT

La Rinconada Ranch

Near Los Alerces National Park
T+54 (0)29441-560 1061
www.larinconadaranch.com
From US$150 per room per night

La Rinconada is a typical Patagonian ranch house, converted to a retreat centre by the energetic Kyle and Adam Canepa, who hail from Santa Fe, New Mexico. The 325-ha ranch is set in stunningly beautiful surroundings on the edge of Los Alerces National Park, in the Rivadavia valley.

In the gardens there's a light and airy yoga studio with floor-to-ceiling windows, and an organic vegetable plot, supplying the ranch with good wholesome food. It's the perfect place for one of their regular yoga weeks (from US$1825 per person) led by visiting teachers, or for a family yoga holiday led by Kyle Canepa herself.

The day usually starts with a meditation session, followed by breakfast and three hours of yoga – inspired by views of lake and mountain. After lunch, there's plenty of time to walk, ride horses, or explore the national park by boat or on foot. A restorative yoga practice in the afternoon relaxes you for an evening of good food and conversation over a delicious dinner served with fine wines.

Family retreats include imaginative, child-friendly activities led by English-speaking play leaders, and horse riding trips to interesting places nearby, or to enjoy a traditional tea in a nearby Welsh colony.

Far left: Estancia Peuma Hue. Left: La Rinconada Ranch. Above: Las Balsas.

Accommodation is in simple and very comfortable rooms, painted white with bold checked bed covers, and modern luxurious bathrooms. The living room is homely and there are plenty of places in the grounds from which to admire the view.

To reach La Rinconada, fly from Buenos Aires to Esquel or Bariloche, where you could also hire a car, enabling you to explore this beautiful region.

HOTEL & SPA

Las Balsas

Villa La Angostura, Lake District
T+54 (0)2944-494308
www.lasbalsas.com
From US$300 per room per night

An intimate boutique hotel hidden away on its own private beach in Argentina's Lake District, this Relais & Chateaux property is a lovely place to feel utterly pampered in stunning surroundings. The lakeside spa is a harmonious stone complex of pools, jacuzzi and massage rooms, where an impressive range of treatments is offered in a blissfully calm atmosphere. There's also nearby trekking and horse riding, and skiing in winter.

The hotel is exquisitely furnished yet homely, with a calm, elegant main sitting room, and lots of little places for relaxing or just lapping up the view. Accommodation is in twelve individually designed rooms with private bathrooms, all cosy and comfortable, with floor-to-ceiling windows filled with your own private view of Lago Nahuel Huapi.

The grand suites are favoured by visiting royalty and celebrities (service here is utterly discreet), but there's nothing formal or stuffy about the atmosphere. The restaurant is one of Argentina's finest, where chef Pablo Campoy makes exquisite creations from delicious local produce.

Marisa is the resident masseuse, and her treatments – especially her altus massage – are designed to reach you spiritually and emotionally as well as physically. She's an very perceptive woman, applying ancient techniques as you lie on the huge circular massage bed in the high-ceilinged tower.

Once you're cleansed emotionally, Marisa sends you out to swim in the warm pool, elevated above the lake so that you're surrounded by mountains – a very special experience. Watsu and hot-stone, ayurvedic, Thai and shiatsu massage, reiki and reflexology are all available, as well as facial treatments, seaweed or mud wraps, and lymph drainage.

Las Balsas is 50 miles from Bariloche airport, with daily two-hour flights from Buenos Aires. Hire a car and drive here, since the landscapes all around are stunning, with three national parks on your doorstep.

Soul food

UK-based cultural and educational travel company, **Experiment in International Living** (www.eiluk.org), has volunteer programmes available in Argentina, with intensive Spanish language training and homestays with local families as part of the experience. Three-month projects include teaching English, working in a children's hospital, helping local organisations teach women about health & disease prevention, assisting staff at schools in rural areas, painting schools and public buildings, and serving at soup kitchens. In addition to the projects listed, it also has a nine-month teaching project in Sante Fe (from March to November).

The Americas Argentina

CHRISTABELLE DILKS

Bolivia

Bolivia Mística

Near La Paz
T+591 (0XX)2-279 1742
www.boliviamistica.com
From US$20 per person per night

Bolivia Mística is made up of two mountain retreats. Its main establishment, the **Allkamari High Mountain Eco resort & Retreat Center**, is a 40-minute drive from Bolivia's capital, La Paz. It's in an area held sacred by local Aymara people, and a visit here offers a rare insight into Andean culture.

A variety of programmes provide a fascinating history of the region. You can also learn about shamanic therapies and rituals with Don Miguel Kavlin, take a trip to the Inca

🍴 Soul food

Volunteering agency, **i-to-i** (T0870-333 2332, www.i-to-i.com) offers travellers the chance to get involved in a whole host of rewarding conservation efforts in Argentina, Bolivia, Peru, Brazil, Honduras, Costa Rica and Guatemala, ranging from animal rescue and rehabilitation of turtles, iguanas and big cats, to conservation work in the rainforests and coastal regions. Cloud forest conservation projects are available in Ecuador, for example, or head to the Gálapagos islands, where volunteers assist with planting new crops, or with light building activities, or help maintain the trails around the island together with hiking to nearby lagoons, forests, beaches and villages to explore the ecological and human dynamics of the Galápagos.

Island Of The Sun on Lake Titicaca, relax in hot thermal waters at Sajama National Park, or visit the Aymara village of Camiraya.

Yoga teachers Nam Nidham and Carmen Castañeda Kavlin take classes in the crisp open air and are both inspiring and patient. All programmes can include as much yoga, pilates and tai chi as you wish – ashtanga, hatha, iyengar and kundalini are all on offer. You can indulge in some shiatsu, reflexology or hot-stone massage, or try an Andean, Amazonian or native North American healing ritual to relax and clear your mind.

Cosy private and dormitory rooms are available in adobe-built cabins, and solar heating is used throughout. There are also family rooms with kitchen facilities and private suites with a solarium and breathtaking views of the Andes.

The second site, **Wizard's Mountain Jungle Resort & Retreat Center**, is in the Bolivian Amazon, perched on the mountainside with beautiful forest views. The centre is a 50-minute flight from La Paz, and is close to Madidi National Park, one of the world's richest biodiversity reserves.

The centre has family, double and dormitory cabins, constructed from wood and bamboo with thatched roofs. All have shared bathrooms with hot water. The same tours, yoga and spa treatments are available here, but you can also book a trip on Bolivia's longest zip-line canopy tour, which runs for 1200 m, some 40 m above the ground.

For more wildlife, staff can take you swimming with pink river dolphins on the flooded pampas. Wizard's Mountain also offers a variety of trekking options through verdant forests and cascading jungle waterfalls; you can even take an inflatable kayak on the rivers. For an unusual retreat, guests can trek to a sacred indigenous site on Wizard's Mountain. There is a basic refuge there for an overnight stay.

You can visit year round but it rains from December to March. Fly to La Paz; at 3800 m, you must allow a couple of days to adjust to the altitude.

Brazil

Convento do Carmo

Salvador
T+55 (0XX)71-3327 8400
www.pousadas.pt
From US$415 per room per night

This Carmelite convent dates from 1586 and was reopened in 2005 as part of the Pousadas de Portugal chain, which specializes in hotels set in renovated historic buildings. Located on the outskirts of the old Pelhourinho district of Salvador, the hotel is an oasis of calm in the city.

The spa offers regular treatments (from US$45) such as deep tissue and hot-stone massage, as well as massage with tropical herbs; or try the 'Convento Atmosphere', a treatment used to reduce stress that dates from the 17th century. There's a gym and an attractive outdoor swimming pool.

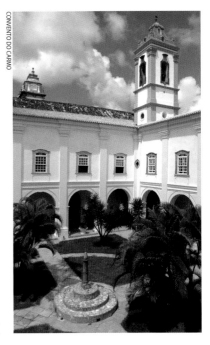

CONVENTO DO CARMO

Convento do Carmo.

You can stay in a double or a suite; rooms with the warmest feel are those wit h imposing wooden ceilings. The master suite has butler service. Junior Suite 235 is rumoured to be the quietest place to stay.

Gourmet meals are served in the dining room, which retains much of the original artwork. In addition, whilst 'pousar-ing' (chilling out) you are offered fresh-baked vanilla cream pastries and coconut water from green (unripe) coconuts, which is refreshing and delicious.

It is worth looking at the church and museum here, which are fabulous examples of Brazilian colonial architecture. Salvador da Bahia is designated a UNESCO World Heritage site so check out the sights: 365 churches, antique markets and beaches. Rates include breakfast. Fly to Salvador.

YOGA RETREAT
Enchanted Mountain Center

Garopaba
www.enchantedmountainbrazil.com
From US$795 per person per week

Enchanted Mountain Center runs yoga retreats and teacher training courses in an area that possesses nine of Brazil's best beaches. It was set up by yoga teachers Joseph and Lilian Le Page, who teach nearly all of the yoga classes themselves, with other retreats led by visiting teachers, mainly from the US.

Joseph is the founder of Integrative Yoga Therapy and has trained thousands of yoga teachers and therapists in the United States and around the world. There is a minimum of two yoga classes a day, in one of three separate yoga spaces – the main practice area is an octagonal room with breathtaking mountain and ocean views. Yoga philosophy, mudra practice and chanting are optional and included in the price.

Although just 15 minutes away from the fishing village of Garopaba, and with room to accommodate 100 guests, the centre remains peaceful, offering attractive, spacious chalets

for two to four people, which are spread across the 100-acre rainforest property. Each unit has a private bath and is decorated with Brazilian handicrafts.

Daily transport to the beach and eco-adventure tours are part of any retreat. Hike through the rainforest, or take day trips to the 20-m Zanella Falls and Itaimbe Canyon, one of the largest in the Americas. Massage and bodywork sessions are available, or try surfing or rafting.

Healthy stopovers in Rio

If you need somewhere to stay in Rio, the **Ipanema Plaza** (from US$120 per room per night, T+55 (0XX)21-3687 2000, www.ipanemaplaza.com.br) offers quiet and comfortable rooms and a pool at a reasonable price. For a clifftop setting, ocean views, two pools, a massage deck, and just seven spacious suites with balconies, **La Suite** (from US$390 per room per night, T+55

(0XX)21-2484 1962, www.lamaison ario.com) is an immaculate, French-owned boutique hotel in the affluent Joatinga area, near a surfing beach. Alternatively, drape yourself somewhere private in the supremely elegant 1920s **Copacabana Palace** (from US$445 per room per night, T+55 (0XX)21-2548 7070, www.copacabanapalace.com.br) set right on the beach.

The food is locally grown and organic. Fresh tropical fruits are the highlight of the breakfast buffet and, although most of the meals are vegetarian, freshly-caught fish often makes an appearance at dinner. The centre attracts an international crowd in their thirties to fifties, singles and couples, most of whom practise yoga, but are not necessarily experts. Not all programmes are run by English speakers, so check when you book. Fly to Florianopolis; a taxi from here will cost US$75.

◐ Body language
Dancing for life

Throughout Brazil, and at retreats such as **Body and Soul Adventures** (page 378) or **Sukhavati** (page 380), you'll be able to try capoeira, a dance-like Afro-Brazilian martial art, first practised in Brazil by African slaves in the 16th century, during Portuguese colonial rule. It is believed to have been initially an African tribal dance, which the slaves developed into a martial art as a form of self-defence. Others say that it was a martial art first, which the Africans disguised as a dance when the slave owners forbade them to practise – they were vastly outnumbered by the slaves, and feared for their lives. Either way, participants form a *roda* (circle) and take turns playing instruments, singing, and sparring in pairs in the centre of the circle with acrobatic play, sweeps, kicks and head butts. More rewarding to watch, but lots of fun to try, capoeira is challenging, as the combination of strength, flexibility and agility is hard to master. Three styles are practised: capoeira Angola (very slow, almost ritual movements), makulele (performed with sticks imitating the canefield tools which were formerly used as weapons) and capoeira regional, which was developed in the 20th century and is a very fast and powerful version of the original.

Wellbeing holiday

Body & Soul Adventures

This superbly-run fitness, adventure and detox retreat is based at the secluded and serene Paraty-Mirím, close to the entrance of Mamangua, a region of tropical rainforest, majestic green mountains and pristine vanilla-coloured beaches. The week can be as serious or relaxed as you need – some come to detox, to lose weight, give up smoking or drinking and kick-start a healthy lifestyle, others to escape a stressful job, relax and rejuvenate.

Where you stay BSA bases itself at two lodges, backed by mountains and overlooking a tranquil bay. Casa Grande, the main hilltop lodge, is built with massive wood columns and over 1000 small windows. There's a sauna with windows, so you can soak and watch the ocean, and an indoor yoga area – morning yoga is done on a grass lawn in the sunshine.

Casa Grande has three guest rooms, one double, one triple and an upstairs room, which sleeps up to three, with its own jacuzzi overlooking the ocean and two private veranda areas. The four most luxurious rooms are a short walk away in a second lodge called Casa do Mar – each has a balcony over the sea. There's also a huge veranda and a lovely large living room at the second lodge, where some evening activities take place.

Little details everywhere give a tropical feel: local bamboo lamps, hand-painted mats, and vases of flowers plucked from the forest.

What you do Expect a challenging sequence of yoga, hiking, sea kayaking, swimming, surfing and capoeira, all expertly run by co-founder Michael Mitchell, manager and yoga teacher Kirtan. All the staff are efficient yet warm and relaxed, and very accommodating.

Mornings begin with a vinyasa flow yoga class at 0730, tailored to

66 99

This was a near-perfect mix of action and relaxation, where I sweated myself into a rejuvenated state in an inspirational location. It was great to try sexy stuff like surfing and capoeira as well as the (very beautiful) forest hikes and coastal kayaking. The staff are supportive, efficient and kind – Kirtan especially is an exceptional teacher who manages to keep experienced yogis challenged while not ignoring beginners. Time seemed to go too quickly – next time I'd save up to stay longer than a week, and bring far fewer clothes.

Caroline

each individual. Kirtan trained with one of Brazil´s most prominent yoga teachers, Regina-Shakti, and teaches hatha vinyasa yoga. Occasionally, other hand-picked yoga teachers will also take classes. A mix of eucalyptus and peppermint oils is available for guests to breathe in before class as a natural energizer. In the evenings expect a more restorative yoga session, with deep stretches to ease you after the day's activities. If you're a beginner, you're encouraged to attend a term of yoga classes before you come on the trip.

Most of the day is taken up by challenging rainforest hikes, or kayaking along the coast. You're advised to prepare in advance by cutting out coffee, drinking more water and herbal teas, and upping your cardio workout with more walking, cycling or gym work. You usually hike or kayak around five to six hours a day (14 to 21 km). The level of difficulty rises as the week progresses and, by the end of the week, you'll have walked and kayaked around 100 km. Each activity is accompanied by patient and supportive guides-cum-trainers, so guests can find their rhythm, be it fast or slow.

Surfing usually takes place once or twice during the week at nearby beaches, depending on conditions. The staff have their own longboards, and can give private lessons to interested guests. Capoeira lessons are offered once a week, as well as a traditional performance one evening. There is also a weekly arts and crafts workshop, and optional meditation sessions on a small man-made beach by the dock.

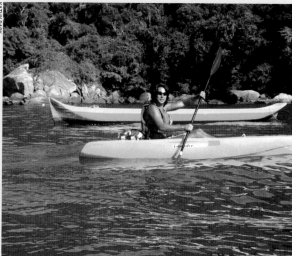

KATHY PARK

of fruit is served for dessert. On the last night, you'll have a *luau*, or Hawaiian barbecue, to celebrate your week, with live Brazilian music. Guests are encouraged to dress in white, a Brazilian tradition to symbolize a fresh start.

Who goes Fellow guests are aware, fun people who want to challenge themselves physically as well as nurture body and soul. Most are aged between 30 and 50, and likely to come from New York, California or the UK (mainly from London). The majority come alone, though couples are welcome. About 70% of guests are women. Repeat visits are common, and many people extend their week – the staff are expert at getting in touch with airlines on the Friday afternoon to rearrange flights.

Essentials Body & Soul Adventures (T+44 (0)20-3002 0936, www.bodysouladventures.com) runs from Sunday to Saturday, February to December. It costs from US$2000 per person per week for a triple occupancy room, US$2500 for a double occupancy room and US$3500 for a single room. The luxury suite with hot tub is US$8000, split between three people. Ten-day programmes, yoga intensives and other special weeks are also available, and you can extend your stay for two or three weeks or more. The price includes all meals and snacks, accommodation for six nights, 12 yoga sessions, 45 hours of supervised hiking, kayaking and other activities, five full-body massages, cultural entertainment and transfers.

Fly to Rio de Janeiro, from where it's a 3¾-hour road transfer. Factor in some time before or after your trip to visit Paraty, a lovely colonial port town with art galleries, museums and chuches to explore, as well as nearby biking, sailing, surfing and horse riding.

After each day of physical activity, guests are treated to a one-hour sports therapy massage in cabanas at the water's edge. Depending on the time of year, ayurvedic massage, reiki and rolfing are also available. A blend of lavender and tea tree oil is available for cuts or scrapes, arnica for aching muscles, and fresh aloe vera for soothing and rehydrating the skin.

What you eat and drink All meals are eaten together, and you dine at the main lodge on a veranda overlooking the ocean with a built-in barbecue where supper is sometimes prepared. Expect low-calorie/high-fibre organic fare at every meal made from fresh local ingredients. There's strictly no coffee or alcohol allowed. As well as lots of water, teas such as apple-cinnamom, ginger, green, fennel and camomile are served throughout the day, and snacks include fresh fruit, homemade guacamole with celery and the energy-packed Brazilian açaí smoothie, made with banana, mango, honey and the Amazonian wonder-berry, açaí, which is full of antioxidants.

Breakfast is hearty home-made oatmeal, or granola with home-made yogurt, raisins and Brazil nuts, and a choice of herbal teas; lunch is a healthy takeaway eaten on the hike. Two suppers during the week are freshly caught fish, grilled, with steamed vegetables; otherwise food is vegetarian – BBQ tofu kebabs with peppers and pineapple, or aubergine stuffed with ricotta and spinach. A small piece

BODY SOUL ADVENTURES

Pousada Picinguaba

Picinguaba, Costa Verde
T+55 (0XX)12-3836 9105
www.picinguaba.com
From US$898 per person for a 4-night
package

This colonial Portuguese-style mansion overlooking a sumptuous protected bay on Brazil's stunning Costa Verde is a wonderful place to restore a stressed-out soul. Set close to a small fishing village in the heart of a nature park, it boasts organic food, unpretentious service, and lots of good vibes.

People come here to disconnect from everyday life and reconnect with themselves, individually, as a couple or as a family. There's no TV, no air-conditioning, no telephones in the room, no internet access and no mobile phone signal. Fellow guests include lots of mid-thirties professionals from London, Paris and New York, but the place attracts a diverse mix of individuals and family groups of all ages and nationalities.

You stay in one of just ten simple, comfortable rooms decorated with Brazilian naive art and looking out onto the lush subtropical gardens. There's a large deck overlooking the ocean, where people gather to chat over early evening drinks. Excellent do-in massages (US$70 per hour) are available in-room with physiotherapist and masseuse, Simone, as well as acupuncture. Yoga is sometimes on offer, or just do your own.

This UNESCO World Heritage site is a natural playground of spectacular landscapes – stand under jungle waterfalls, kayak across the bay to Praia Fazenda, then run along the deserted 3-km beach. More serious guided treks can be arranged, as well as surf classes, fishing, horse riding, diving, sea kayaking and boat trips to deserted islands. The historic colonial port town of Paraty is just 25 minutes away by car.

The Pousada's chef prepares simple but tasty organic dishes – think shrimp risotto, ceviche (raw fish marinated with fruits and

Pousada Picinguaba.

spices), or a *picanha churascos* (Brazilian BBQ). There are lots of fresh vegetables and wonderful Brazilian fruit. Everything is flexible: eat breakfast late, or ask for dinner in a different setting.

Most people stay for six to eight nights. The low season, from May/June to September, is actually a great time to come, when it's very sunny but not too hot. Peak season from December to February is busier. A four-night package includes private

Soul food

The **Task Brasil Trust** (T+44 (0)20-7735 5545, www.taskbrasil.org.uk) is a small UK-based charity set up to help abandoned street children in Brazil. It runs various projects to improve the lives of children and pregnant teenage girls, especially those living on the streets of Rio de Janeiro. You can get involved as a volunteer in Brazil, to help the children with sports, reading and writing, music, art and computer skills. Volunteer at the UK or US offices, or make a donation.

transfers from Rio or São Paulo (about 3½ hours), breakfast, dinner and taxes. You can also take the bus from both airports to Paraty, a cheaper option. Avoid renting a car, unless you feel confident driving in big cities.

Sukhavati

Itacaré
T+55 (0XX)73-3086 1778
www.sukhavati.net
From US$120 per room per night

On the fringes of a rainforest, the Sukhavati retreat in Itacaré overlooks a sweeping bay of white sand – a tranquil panorama to complement the Buddhist meditation, yoga and soothing massages on offer. There's also the opportunity for capoeira and eco-adventure packages, including rafting and jungle walks, so the pace doesn't have to be slow all the time.

You'll be staying in one of six Polynesian-style bungalows, tucked between the palm trees. Some have been built 3 m above the ground, which makes you feel like you're in a tree house. The modest exteriors hide naturally elegant, polished-wood

SIMON HEYES

The Americas Brazil

Be brave. Take risks.
Nothing can substitute
experience.

Paulo Coelho

interiors, complete with draped beds, couches and colourful rugs. You'll also have your own deck with hammocks and deckchairs as well as room service and a minibar. For extra peace and quiet, stunning views and a more luxurious feel, book into the beachfront de luxe bungalow.

Meditation is at the spiritual heart of this retreat. Classes are taken by owner Eckhart, one of the few westerners fully qualified as a lama and meditation teacher in the Karma Kagyu Buddhist tradition. Eckart invites guests to explore the Diamond Way of Tibetan Buddhism, often described as the crown jewel of Buddha's teaching.

Ayurvedic massage is available, or try capoeira (see glossary), taught by teachers from the Serra Grande Capoeira association. There are also beginners' classes in ashtanga yoga, with more advanced courses available on request. Canoeing, mountain biking, rafting, hang-gliding and walks through the rainforest provide a chance to experience the inspiring landscape and get the blood pumping. All activities are available on request rather than provided on a daily basis.

Only breakfast is included in the price. The on-site restaurant offers typical Bahian and Asian dishes, plus vegetarian options. Romantics can dine under the stars on the beach or surrounded by rainforest. Fly to Ilheus, 38 km north of Sukhavati – transfers are provided. Car rental is also available at the airport. UK-based wellbeing company **Yogoloji** runs annual retreats here (see www.yogoloji.com, or page 49).

Chile

YOGA RETREAT

Canal Om

🌐 ⛰ ⓦ ❁ 🅿 ⓝ11

Ensenada, near Los Vilos
T+56 (0)2-233 1524
www.canalom.com
From US$75 per room per night

Two hours from Santiago, at Ensenada, Canal Om emerges from cliffs overlooking the Pacific Ocean. This yoga retreat, workshop venue and teacher training centre, which opened in 2007, is a peaceful sanctuary that blends in harmoniously with its surrounding countryside. The owner, Gustavo Ponce, also runs Yoga Shala, one of the largest yoga schools in Latin America.

The architecture has a Japanese influence, which enhances the serenity of the environment. If you have the choice, go for the rooms with a view: Ahimsa, Sattva and Tao are spacious doubles and overlook the ocean. There are 20 rooms in total, all simply furnished, clean, fresh and spanning a range of budgets, some with shared bathrooms, some en suite. Each is painted a different colour and showcases artwork by students.

The grounds are carefully tended, with paths leading to quiet, secluded spots for reflection and contemplation, although you may come across a resident llama, ostrich or peacock. Facilities include a meditation hall, a sauna for 15 with views of the ocean, three seawater pools, a freshwater infinity pool, a jacuzzi on the cliff edge, tennis courts and an area for archery. Horse riding, surfing lessons and boat trips can also be arranged.

Yoga courses and workshops are held in the large, fully equipped practice hall and are led by many well-respected teachers. These include owner Gustavo, a former diplomat who has studied with world-renowned teachers such as BKS Iyengar, Sri K Pattabhi Jois and TKV Desikachar, and who has himself created three new hatha yoga methods –

dynamic yoga, prana shakti yoga and sattva yoga. Teacher training course are also available. For more details, visit www.yogashala.cl/english/training /sattva_english.htm.

Meals are vegetarian and the focus is on fresh, organic produce and dishes with real nutritional value. Your fellow guests are likely to be from the USA and Europe, but students from around the world also gather at the long wooden tables.

Canal Om is open full time during the summer – mid-December to February – and for the rest of the year at weekends or when a group hosts its own yoga retreat. The UK-based wellbeing company **Yogoloji** runs annual 10-day retreats which include include yoga practice twice a day, one-to-one sessions, yoga therapy and ayurvedic massage (see also page 210).

Ensenada is between Pichidangui and Los Vilos. Fly to Santiago airport, from where you can hire a car or be picked up. If there is a group of 10 or more, you'll be collected in a minivan.

NATURAL SPA RETREAT

Puyuhuapi Lodge and Spa

🌐 ⛰ ♨ ❁ ⓦ ❁ ⓝ12

Puyuhuapi, Chilean Patagonia
T+56 (0)6-732 5117
www.patagonia-connection.com
From US$1200 per person for 5 days

The journey to Puyuhuapi is an adventure in itself, down the rocky Carretera Austral, through the remoter reaches of Chilean Patagonia, amidst steep mountains and dramatic fjords. When your boat draws up at Puyuhuapi's jetty, you'll know you've reached a rare kind of place, where everything has been created to facilitate a peaceful retreat from modern life.

The modern wooden building stands amidst virgin forest, utterly isolated from civilization on the shore of the glassy Bahía Dorita. It's a light and spacious place, simple enough not to detract from the splendour of its natural setting, but warm enough to feel cosy at nights. The 33 minimalist bedrooms

The Americas Chile

PUYUHUAPI LODGE & SPA

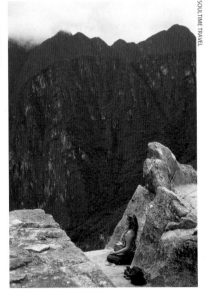

SOULTIME TRAVEL

Above: Puyuhuapi Lodge and Spa. **Right**: Soultime Travel.

are all airy and calm, with modern design in local wood, and stunning views through the huge windows.

There are two outdoor thermal pools of different temperatures, in a natural setting with spectacular views over the fjord below. Once you've steeped yourself under a vast Patagonian sky, a swim in the clear waters of the fjord is a delicious experience. Smart treatment rooms are arranged around an indoor thermal pool, with great views of the fjord and mountains through an immense wall of glass. There are jacuzzis and whirlpools, a sauna and hammam.

Particularly recommended are the 'Thaloform' treatments, combining thermal waters with sea algae and hydro-massage, to balance the nervous system and alleviate muscle pain. There are yoga classes,or go trekking and cycling through virgin forest.

Fine organic food is served, much of it grown in the lodge's kitchen garden. A wide range of people come here, from families to couples of all ages searching for a luxurious break. The five-day package includes use of the spa, all meals, wine and transfers, and a boat trip to the San Rafael lagoon. Fly to Balmaceda airport and drive or take a taxi to the the village of Puyuhuapi (five hours), where you'll be collected by boat. Bring warm clothing, hiking boots and waterproofs, and a swimming costume.

Peru

SPIRITUAL HOLIDAY
Ecotribal Tours & Expeditions

◐ ◉ ✪ ◯ ↘13

T+44 (0)1974-241638
www.ecotribal.com
From US$2300 for 15 days

Ecotribal was created to support Peru's indigenous communities and help them achieve sustainability, through trading and organized expeditions. During their two- or three-week Healing Tour you are given a sense of how these traditional cultures have lived for centuries, on a journey that takes you through deserts, mountains and rainforest. You will have the chance to visit the sacred sites of the Incas, explore the ancient towns and experience a traditional healing ceremony. With good food and overnight stays in comfortable mid-range hotels, inns and lodges, you don't need to be a hardened traveller or extremely fit to enjoy this trip.

The itinerary is fairly relaxed – the morning begins with an optional tai chi class led by a teacher from the UK-based Taiji Qigong Foundation (www.uktqf.co.uk). The idea is that, even though you're on the move, you'll have

the time to relax and let the experiences of your journey touch somewhere spiritually deeper than the average tourist trek through Peru.

As well as visits to Machu Picchu, the historic Inca capital, Cuzco, pre-Inca pyramids in the northern deserts, and thermal baths, museums and markets, your trip will also include horse riding through the largest dry forest in the Americas. The three-week option includes five days of rainforest exploration. There are also talks on Peruvian healing traditions and shamanic techniques, their history and contemporary practice.

You will also have the option to participate in healing sessions with a coastal and jungle shaman, a ritual that has evolved over millennia to create a three-way connection between you, the shaman and the universe or spirit. This ceremony involves drinking shamanic medicine, a herbal brew, which may include the San Pedro cactus, which contains mescaline, a hallucinogenic substance intended to expand consciousness. This can have unpredictable and possibly unpleasant side effects if used insensitively and without understanding of the healing process. The decision on what 'medicine' each person takes is worked out with the shaman in advance. If he feels attendees are not ready, the medicine will contain cleansing, healing herbs and nothing stronger, but everything is optional.

For some, it is this experience of shamanism that brings them on the Healing Tour, for others it is an interest in wilderness, ancient cultures or wildlife. Ecotribal also runs other adventure-based expeditions. Your travelling companions will be of all ages, couples and singles, and mainly from Europe and the US. The group of 10 to 14 people meet in Lima, your destination airport.

UK-based Shamanism company **Eagle's Wing** (see page 31) and US-based **Shamanic Journeys** (see www.shamanic journeys.com) also run trips to Peru.

Suasi Island, in Lake Titicaca.

SIMON HEYES

YOGA & ACTIVITY HOLIDAY

Soultime Travel

🌐 ⛰ ☀ ❄ ↘14

Southern Peru
T+54 (0) 11-4541 1743
www.soultime-travel.com
From US$2100 per person for 24 days

Argentina-based company, Soultime Travel, runs a 24-day tour of southern Peru, combined with regular classes in hatha yoga, dance and the healing arts. The trip is aimed at anyone interested in exploring Peru more spiritually, and who has an interest in yoga or dance, including beginners.

You'll be looked after by a Latin American travel guide who has expertise in the healing arts and sound meditation, together with hatha yoga and dance teacher, Sandra Morrel, who is based at Ibiza Moving Arts in Spain (see page 115).

The trip includes off-the-beaten-track hikes in the Colca Canyon, the islands of Lake Titicaca, and the Sacred Valley of the Incas, near Cuzco, as well as an optional trek along the Inca Trail. You stay in locally run hotels and eat in local restaurants. The company uses local operators, thus ensuring that money is ploughed back into the community. Fly to Lima, where you will be picked up. The price includes accommodation, some meals, transfers, guides and excursions. Trips are run

once a year – bespoke group trips can also be arranged at other times with at least six months advance notice, as well as similar trips through the Bolivian Andes, the Atacama Desert and northwest Argentina.

ISLAND RETREAT

Suasi Island

🏃 ✈ ⚡ ↘15

Lake Titicaca
T+51 (0)1-213 9725
www.casa-andina.com/suasi
From US$461 per person for 2 nights

Situated in the remote northeast of Lake Titicaca, Suasi is a private 43-ha island, lodge and eco-reserve, part of the Casa Andina Private Collection, and a real haven in the beautiful but harsh altiplano (high Andean plateau).

Choose from 24 comfortable rooms, most with balconies and all with views over the lake, and skylights through which you can see the stars at night. The whole lodge runs on solar energy. There is no heating in the rooms, but goose down duvets and hot-water bottles keep you warm at night. For a special occasion, or more privacy, the

lakeshore Andean Cottage has two rooms and offers 24-hour butler service via a walkie-talkie. There are fireplaces in the communal areas, an Andean sauna and good massages on offer from local therapists. Superb food blends local staples and specialities – think smoked trout tartare with *limo chile* and dill, or quinoa tabouleh salad.

This is a great place to learn about Lake Titicaca and the altiplano; and the island has an Andean cultural interpretation centre and library. Walk along island trails or the beach, visit protected areas to check out the flowers and wildlife, or see Andean farming plots with aromatic and medicinal herbs. The more active can also kayak around the island, or hike up Mulluni Hill for views of the Cordillera Real. At nearly 4000 m above sea level, don't try to do too much – walk slowly, eat and drink lightly at first, and take care in the sun.

The island is open all year. Stay at least two nights, and book in advance. A three-day package includes all meals and activities on the island and transfers by 4WD on land. The nearest airport is Juliaca, the nearest port Puno. You can arrive by road (two hours, then a short boat ride) or by lake (four hours from Puno).

Directory

SPA SHOW™

TRAVEL · WELLBEING · BEAUTY
24th-25th NOVEMBER 2007 OLYMPIA, LONDON

IN ASSOCIATION WITH
The Sunday Telegraph

www.spashow.co.uk

*The Spa Show is the ultimate
exhibition showcasing the very best
boutique spas and hotels, day spas,
retreats, spa products and treatments.*

*Including: Spa & Golf * Spa & Honeymoon
Spa & Dive * Free Spa treatments * Yoga & pilaties*

Index

Index

Credits

Footprint credits

Editor: Alan Murphy
Map editor: Sarah Sorensen
Layout and production: Patrick Dawson, Sophie Blacksell
Proof reader: Sarah Sorensen

Publisher: Patrick Dawson
Editorial: Felicity Laughton, Nicola Jones, Jo Williams
Cartography: Robert Lunn, Kevin Feeney, John Higgins
Cover design: Robert Lunn
Design: Mytton Williams
Sales and marketing: Andy Riddle
Advertising: Debbie Wylde, Zoë Jackson
Finance and administration: Elizabeth Taylor

Photography credits

Title page: Caroline Sylge
Front cover: The Pilion Centre, Caroline Sylge, Barberyn Beach
Back cover: Molino del Rey, Nicki Grihault, Ayurveda Pavilions, tourismebretagnephotos.com, Caroline Sylge

Print

Manufactured in India by Replika Press Pvt Ltd
Pulp from sustainable forests

The colour maps are not intended to have any political significance.

Every effort has been made to ensure that the facts in this guidebook are accurate. However, travellers should note that places change, owners move on and properties close or are sold. Travellers should also obtain advice from consulates, airlines etc about travel and visa requirements before travelling. The authors and publishers cannot accept responsibility for any loss, injury or inconvenience however caused.

Publishing information

Body & Soul escapes
1st edition
© Footprint Handbooks Ltd
April 2007

ISBN 978-1-904777-91-5
CIP DATA: A catalogue record for this book is available from the British Library

® Footprint Handbooks and the Footprint mark are a registered trademark of Footprint Handbooks Ltd

Published by Footprint

6 Riverside Court
Lower Bristol Road
Bath BA2 3DZ, UK
T +44 (0)1225 469141
F +44 (0)1225 469461
discover@footprintbooks.com
www.footprintbooks.com

Footprint feedback

We try as hard as we can to make each Footprint guide as up to date as possible but, of course, things always change. If you want to let us know about your experiences – good, bad or ugly – then don't delay, go to www.footprintbooks.com and send in your comments.